AF179046

# Mitsubishi Magna & Verada Automotive Repair Manual

## by Jeff Killingsworth and John H Haynes

Member of the Guild of Motoring Writers

**Models covered:**

Mitsubishi Magna and Verada

    Magna TE, TF, TH, TJ, TL & TW Series
    Verada KE, KF, KH, KJ KL & KW Series

1996 – 2005

*Does not include four-cylinder or All Wheel Drive models*

**Haynes Australia Pty Limited**
haynes.com

68757-10R5

## Acknowledgments

We are grateful to the Chrysler Corporation for providing technical information and certain illustrations. Wiring diagrams provided exclusively for Haynes North America, Inc. by Valley Forge Technical Communications. Technical writers who contributed to this project include Tim Imhoff and Larry Warren.

## © Haynes Australia Pty Limited. 2001, 2003, 2011

ABN 59 618 618 992

With permission from J.H. Haynes & Co. Ltd.

## A book in the Haynes Automotive Repair Manual Series

**ISBN-10: 1-56392-938-4**

**ISBN-13: 978-1-56392-938-0**

While every attempt is made to ensure that the information in this manual is correct, no liability can be accepted by the authors or publishers for loss, damage or injury caused by any errors in, or omissions from, the information given.

# Contents

Mitsubishi TH Series Magna Advance

Mitsubishi TJ Series ll Magna

# About this manual

## Its purpose

The purpose of this manual is to help you get the best value from your vehicle. It can do so in several ways. It can help you decide what work must be done, even if you choose to have it done by a dealer service department or a repair shop; it provides information and procedures for routine maintenance and servicing; and it offers diagnostic and repair procedures to follow when trouble occurs.

We hope you use the manual to tackle the work yourself. For many simpler jobs, doing it yourself may be quicker than arranging an appointment to get the vehicle into a shop and making the trips to leave it and pick it up. More importantly, a lot of money can be saved by avoiding the expense the shop must pass on to you to cover its labor and overhead costs. An added benefit is the sense of satisfaction and accomplishment that you feel after doing the job yourself.

## Using the manual

The manual is divided into Chapters. Each Chapter is divided into numbered Sections, which are headed in bold type between horizontal lines. Each Section consists of consecutively numbered paragraphs.

At the beginning of each numbered Section you will be referred to any illustrations which apply to the procedures in that Section. The reference numbers used in illustration captions pinpoint the pertinent Section and the Step within that Section. That is, illustration 3.2 means the illustration refers to Section 3 and Step (or paragraph) 2 within that Section.

Procedures, once described in the text, are not normally repeated. When it's necessary to refer to another Chapter, the reference will be given as Chapter and Section number. Cross references given without use of the word "Chapter" apply to Sections and/or paragraphs in the same Chapter. For example, "see Section 8" means in the same Chapter.

References to the left or right side of the vehicle assume you are sitting in the driver's seat, facing forward.

Even though we have prepared this manual with extreme care, neither the publisher nor the author can accept responsibility for any errors in, or omissions from, the information given.

### NOTE

A **Note** provides information necessary to properly complete a procedure or information which will make the procedure easier to understand.

### CAUTION

A **Caution** provides a special procedure or special steps which must be taken while completing the procedure where the Caution is found. Not heeding a Caution can result in damage to the assembly being worked on.

### WARNING

A **Warning** provides a special procedure or special steps which must be taken while completing the procedure where the Warning is found. Not heeding a Warning can result in personal injury.

# Introduction to the Mitsubishi Magna/Verada

The Mitsubishi Magna/Verada is available in four-door sedan and station wagon body styles. The model features an all steel uni-body construction.

The Magna and Verada both share the same 3.0 and 3.5-litre V6 DOHC 24 valve engine with multi-port fuel injection. The engine transmits power to the front wheels through either a five-speed manual transaxle or a four-speed or five-speed automatic transaxle via independent driveaxles.

The independent front suspension consists of a MacPherson strut/coil spring suspension system with a stabiliser bar. The rear suspension differs between sedan and wagon models. The sedan uses a independent suspension, featuring coil spring/shock absorber units. The wagon used a beam axle, coil springs mounted on lower control arms, upper control arms and shock absorbers.

The rack and pinion steering unit is mounted behind the engine with power-assist available as optional equipment. All models are equipped with power assisted front and rear disc brakes with an antilock braking system available as optional equipment.

# Vehicle identification numbers

Modifications are a continuing and unpublicised process in vehicle manufacturing. Since spare parts manuals and lists are compiled on a numerical basis, the individual vehicle numbers are essential to correctly identify the component required.

## Vehicle Identification Number (VIN)

This very important identification number is stamped on the firewall adjacent to the Compliance Plate **(see illustration)**. The VIN also appears on the Vehicle Certificate of Title and Registration. It contains information such as where and when the vehicle was manufactured, the model year and the body style and should be referred to when ordering renewal parts **(see illustration)**.

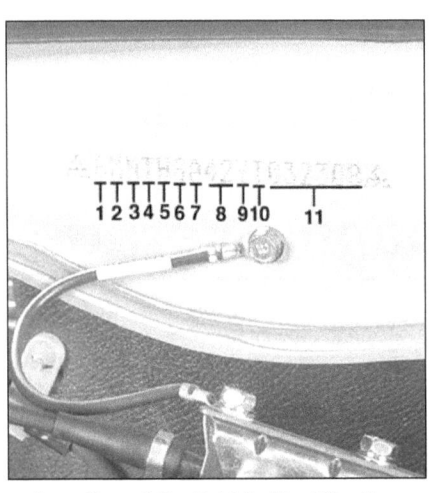

**Location of the Vehicle Identification Number (VIN) (arrow)**

| Number | Items | Contents |
|---|---|---|
| 1 | Geographic Area | 6 - Australia |
| 2 | Country within Geographic area | M - Australia |
| 3 | Manufacture | M - Mitsubishi Motors |
| 4 | Car line | T - Magna; K - Verada |
| 5 | Series | E, F, H, J, L, W |
| 6 | Engine/transmission combinations | 3 - 3.0 litre MPI, Leaded fuel (Man) <br> 4 - 3.0 litre MPI, Leaded fuel (Auto) <br> 5 - 3.0 litre MPI, Unleaded fuel (Man) <br> 6 - 3.0 litre MPI, Unleaded fuel (Auto) <br> 7 - 3.5 litre MPI, Unleaded fuel (Man) <br> 8 - 3.5 litre MPI, Unleaded fuel (4 speed Auto) <br> 9 - 3.5 litre MPI, Unleaded fuel (5 speed Auto) |
| 7 | Price class | A - V6 Advance, LS <br> D - Executive, ES <br> K - V6 Altera LS <br> U - Altera <br> S - Sports <br> H - 3.5 Ei <br> X - 3.5 Xi |
| 8 | Body type | 42 - Sedan; 46 - Wagon |
| 9 | Year | S - 1995; T - 1996; U - 1997; W - 1998; <br> X - 1999; Y - 2000; 1 - 2001; 2-2002; <br> 3-2003; 4-2004; 5-2005 |
| 10 | Assembly plant | T - Tonsley Park |
| 11 | Body number | 000001 to 999999 |

**Vehicle Identification Number chart**

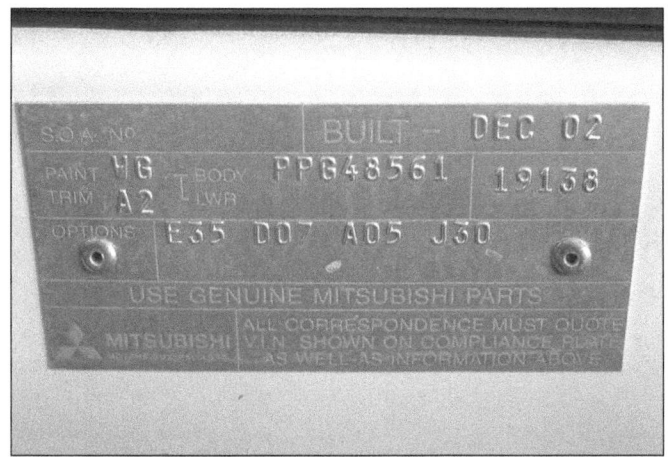

Location of the Data Plate

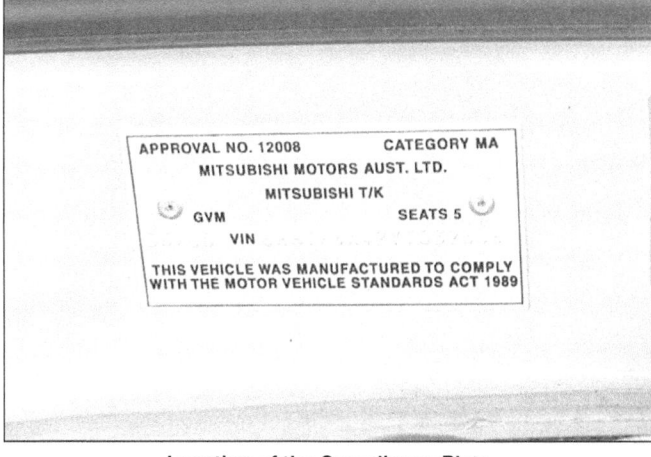

Location of the Compliance Plate

## Compliance Plate

The Compliance Plate is located on the firewall in the engine compartment **(see illustration)**. The Compliance Plate certifies the vehicle has met the specific safety, environmental and consumer protection requirements required by the Australian Design Rules (ADR). The Compliance Plate also contains the VIN and must never be removed from the vehicle.

## Data Plate

The manufacturer's Data Plate is attached to the firewall in the engine compartment adjacent to the Compliance Plate **(see illustration)**. The Data Plate contains such information as the name of the manufacturer, the month and year of production, the trim and paint codes and the option codes. The trim, paint and option codes should be referred to when ordering renewal parts.

## Engine identification numbers

The engine identification number is stamped on a pad adjacent to the transaxle bellhousing on V6 engines **(see illustration)**.

## Transaxle identification numbers

The manual transaxle identification number is stamped on top of the clutch housing. The automatic transaxle identification number is stamped on the top of the transaxle case.

Location of the engine identification number - V6 engine

# Buying parts

Spare parts are available from many sources, which generally fall into one of two categories - authorised dealer parts departments and independent retail auto parts stores. Our advice concerning these parts is as follows:

*Retail auto parts stores:* Good auto parts stores will stock frequently needed components which wear out relatively fast, such as clutch components, exhaust systems, brake parts, tune-up parts, etc. These stores often supply new or reconditioned parts on an exchange basis, which can save a considerable amount of money. Discount auto parts stores are often very good places to buy materials and parts needed for general vehicle maintenance such as oil, grease, filters, spark plugs, belts, touch-up paint, bulbs, etc. They also usually sell tools and general accessories, have convenient hours, charge lower prices and can often be found not far from home.

*Authorised dealer parts department:* This is the best source for parts which are unique to the vehicle and not generally available elsewhere (such as major engine parts, transmission parts, trim pieces, etc.).

*Warranty information:* If the vehicle is still covered under warranty, be sure that any spare parts purchased - regardless of the source - do not invalidate the warranty!

To be sure of obtaining the correct parts, have engine and chassis numbers available and, if possible, take the old parts along for positive identification.

# Maintenance techniques, tools and working facilities

## *Maintenance techniques*

There are a number of techniques involved in maintenance and repair that will be referred to throughout this manual. Application of these techniques will enable the home mechanic to be more efficient, better organised and capable of performing the various tasks properly, which will ensure that the repair job is thorough and complete.

### Fasteners

Fasteners are nuts, bolts, studs and screws used to hold two or more parts together. There are a few things to keep in mind when working with fasteners. Almost all of them use a locking device of some type, either a lockwasher, locknut, locking tab or thread adhesive. All threaded fasteners should be clean and straight, with undamaged threads and undamaged corners on the hex head where the wrench fits. Develop the habit of renewing all damaged nuts and bolts with new ones. Special locknuts with nylon or fibre inserts can only be used once. If they are removed, they lose their locking ability and must be renewed.

Rusted nuts and bolts should be treated with a penetrating fluid to ease removal and prevent breakage. Some mechanics use turpentine in a spout-type oil can, which works quite well. After applying the rust penetrant, let it work for a few minutes before trying to loosen the nut or bolt. Badly rusted fasteners may have to be chiselled or sawed off or removed with a special nut breaker, available at tool stores.

If a bolt or stud breaks off in an assembly, it can be drilled and removed with a special tool commonly available for this purpose. Most automotive machine shops can perform this task, as well as other repair procedures, such as the repair of threaded holes that have been stripped out.

Flat washers and lockwashers, when removed from an assembly, should always be replaced exactly as removed. Renew any damaged washers with new ones. Never use a lockwasher on any soft metal surface (such as aluminium), thin sheet metal or plastic.

### Fastener sizes

For a number of reasons, automobile manufacturers are making wider and wider use of metric fasteners. Therefore, it is important to be able to tell the difference between standard (sometimes called U.S. or SAE) and metric hardware, since they cannot be interchanged.

All bolts, whether standard or metric, are sized according to diameter, thread pitch and length. For example, a standard M12 - 1.75 x 25 metric bolt is 12 mm in diameter, has a thread pitch of 1.75 mm (the distance between threads) and is 25 mm long. The two bolts are nearly identical, and easily confused, but they are not interchangeable.

In addition to the differences in diameter, thread pitch and length, metric and standard bolts can also be distinguished by examining the bolt heads. To begin with, the distance across the flats on a standard bolt head is measured in inches, while the same dimension on a metric bolt is sized in millimetres (the same is true for nuts). As a result, a standard spanner should not be used on a metric bolt and a metric spanner should not be used on a standard bolt. Also, most standard bolts have slashes radiating out from the centre of the head to denote the grade or strength of the bolt, which is an indication of the amount of torque that can be applied to it. The greater the number of slashes, the greater the strength of the bolt. Grades 0 through 5 are commonly used on automobiles. Metric bolts have a property class (grade) number, rather than a slash, moulded into their heads to indicate bolt strength. In this case, the higher the number, the stronger the bolt. Property class numbers 8.8, 9.8 and 10.9 are commonly used on automobiles.

Strength markings can also be used to distinguish standard hex nuts from metric hex nuts. Many standard nuts have dots stamped into one side, while metric nuts are marked with a number. The greater the number of dots, or the higher the number, the greater the strength of the nut.

Metric studs are also marked on their ends according to property class (grade). Larger studs are numbered (the same as metric bolts), while smaller studs carry a geometric code to denote grade.

It should be noted that many fasteners, especially Grades 0 through 2, have no distinguishing marks on them. When such is the case, the only way to determine whether it is standard or metric is to measure the thread pitch or compare it to a known fastener of the same size.

Standard fasteners are often referred to as SAE, as opposed to metric. However, it should be noted that SAE technically refers to a non-metric fine thread fastener only. Coarse thread non-metric fasteners are referred to as USS sizes.

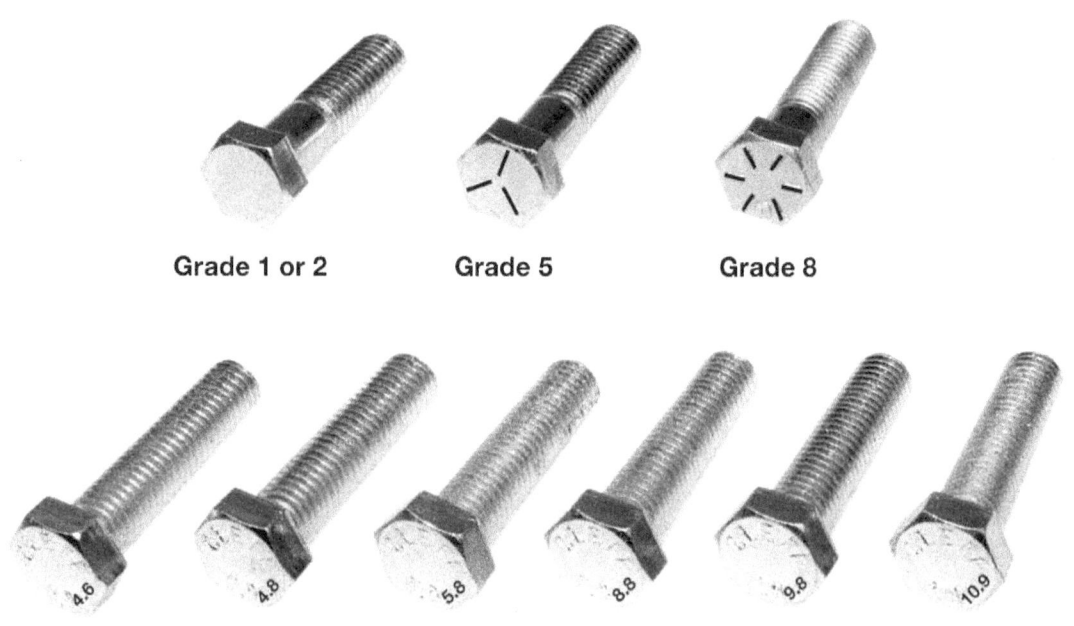

Grade 1 or 2          Grade 5          Grade 8

Bolt strength marking (standard/SAE/USS; bottom - metric)

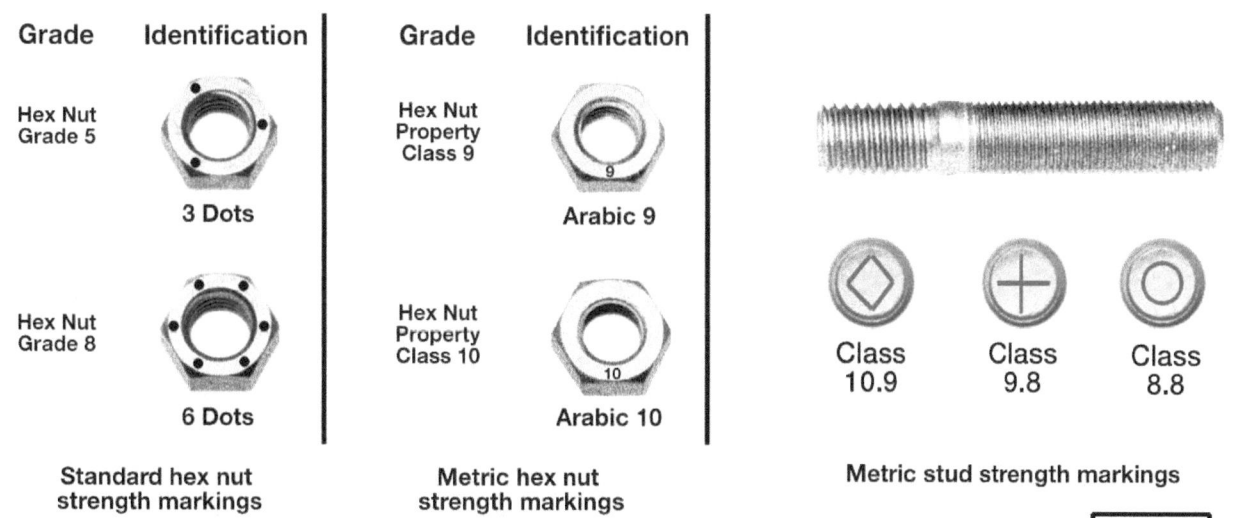

| Grade | Identification | Grade | Identification |
|---|---|---|---|
| Hex Nut Grade 5 | 3 Dots | Hex Nut Property Class 9 | Arabic 9 |
| Hex Nut Grade 8 | 6 Dots | Hex Nut Property Class 10 | Arabic 10 |

Class 10.9     Class 9.8     Class 8.8

Standard hex nut strength markings

Metric hex nut strength markings

Metric stud strength markings

Since fasteners of the same size (both standard and metric) may have different strength ratings, be sure to reinstall any bolts, studs or nuts removed from your vehicle in their original locations. Also, when renewing a fastener, make sure that the new one has a strength rating equal to or greater than the original.

### Tightening sequences and procedures

Most threaded fasteners should be tightened to a specific torque value (torque is the twisting force applied to a threaded component such as a nut or bolt). Overtight-ening the fastener can weaken it and cause it to break, while undertightening can cause it to eventually come loose. Bolts, screws and studs, depending on the material they are made of and their thread diameters, have specific torque values, many of which are noted in the Specifications at the beginning of each Chapter. Be sure to follow the torque recommendations closely. For fasteners not assigned a specific torque, a general torque value chart is presented here as a guide. These torque values are for dry (unlubricated) fasteners threaded into steel or cast iron (not aluminium). As was previously mentioned, the size and grade of a fastener determine the amount of torque that can safely be applied to it. The figures listed here are approximate for Grade 2 and Grade 3 fasteners. Higher grades can tolerate higher torque values.

Fasteners laid out in a pattern, such as cylinder head bolts, sump bolts, differential cover bolts, etc., must be loosened or tightened in sequence to avoid warping the component. This sequence will normally be shown in the appropriate Chapter. If a specific pattern is not given, the following procedures can be used to prevent warping.

Initially, the bolts or nuts should be assembled finger-tight only. Next, they should be tightened one full turn each, in a

| Metric thread sizes | Nm | Ft-lbs |
|---|---|---|
| M-6 | 9 to 12 | 6 to 9 |
| M-8 | 19 to 28 | 14 to 21 |
| M-10 | 38 to 54 | 28 to 40 |
| M-12 | 68 to 96 | 50 to 71 |
| M-14 | 109 to 154 | 80 to 140 |

| Pipe thread sizes | | |
|---|---|---|
| 1/8 | 7 to 10 | 5 to 8 |
| 1/4 | 17 to 24 | 12 to 18 |
| 3/8 | 30 to 44 | 22 to 33 |
| 1/2 | 34 to 47 | 25 to 35 |

| U.S. thread sizes | | |
|---|---|---|
| 1/4 - 20 | 9 to 12 | 6 to 9 |
| 5/16 - 18 | 17 to 24 | 12 to 18 |
| 5/16 - 24 | 19 to 27 | 14 to 20 |
| 3/8 - 16 | 30 to 43 | 22 to 32 |
| 3/8 - 24 | 37 to 51 | 27 to 38 |
| 7/16 - 14 | 55 to 74 | 40 to 55 |
| 7/16 - 20 | 55 to 81 | 40 to 60 |
| 1/2 - 13 | 75 to 108 | 55 to 80 |

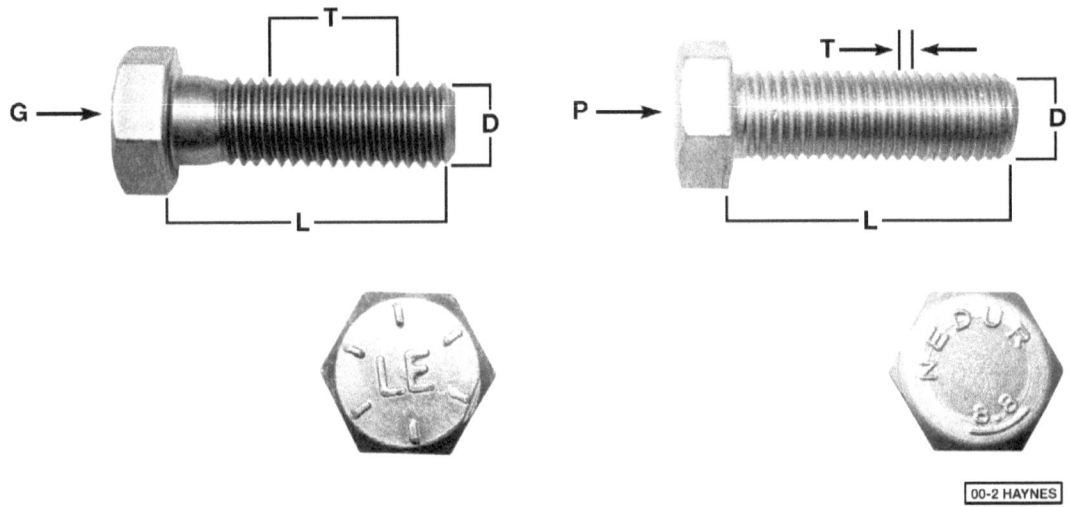

00-2 HAYNES

**Standard (SAE and USS) bolt dimensions/grade marks**

- G  Grade marks (bolt strength)
- L  Length (in inches)
- T  Thread pitch (number of threads per inch)
- D  Nominal diameter (in inches)

**Metric bolt dimensions/grade marks**

- P  Property class (bolt strength)
- L  Length (in millimetres)
- T  Thread pitch (distance between threads in millimetres)
- D  Diameter

criss-cross or diagonal pattern. After each one has been tightened one full turn, return to the first one and tighten them all one-half turn, following the same pattern. Finally, tighten each of them one-quarter turn at a time until each fastener has been tightened to the proper torque. To loosen and remove the fasteners, the procedure would be reversed.

### Component disassembly

Component disassembly should be done with care and purpose to help ensure that the parts go back together properly. Always keep track of the sequence in which parts are removed. Make note of special characteristics or marks on parts that can be refitted more than one way, such as a grooved thrust washer on a shaft. It is a good idea to lay the disassembled parts out on a clean surface in the order that they were removed. It may also be helpful to make sketches or take instant photos of components before removal.

When removing fasteners from a component, keep track of their locations. Sometimes threading a bolt back in a part, or putting the washers and nut back on a stud, can prevent mix-ups later. If nuts and bolts cannot be returned to their original locations, they should be kept in a compartmented box or a series of small boxes. A cupcake or muffin tin is ideal for this purpose, since each cavity can hold the bolts and nuts from a particular area (ie. sump bolts, valve cover bolts, engine mount bolts, etc.). A pan of this type is especially helpful when working on assemblies with very small parts, such as the carburettor, alternator, valve train or interior dash and trim pieces. The cavities can be marked with paint or tape to identify the contents.

Whenever wiring looms, harnesses or connectors are separated, it is a good idea to identify the two halves with numbered pieces of masking tape so they can be easily reconnected.

### Gasket sealing surfaces

Throughout any vehicle, gaskets are used to seal the mating surfaces between two parts and keep lubricants, fluids, vacuum or pressure contained in an assembly.

Many times these gaskets are coated with a liquid or paste-type gasket sealing compound before assembly. Age, heat and pressure can sometimes cause the two parts to stick together so tightly that they are very difficult to separate. Often, the assembly can be loosened by striking it with a soft-face hammer near the mating surfaces. A regular hammer can be used if a block of wood is placed between the hammer and the part. Do not hammer on cast parts or parts that could be easily damaged. With any particularly stubborn part, always recheck to make sure that every fastener has been removed.

Avoid using a screwdriver or bar to prise apart an assembly, as they can easily mar the gasket sealing surfaces of the parts, which must remain smooth. If levering is absolutely necessary, use an old broom handle, but keep in mind that extra clean up will be necessary if the wood splinters.

After the parts are separated, the old gasket must be carefully scraped off and the gasket surfaces cleaned. Stubborn gasket material can be soaked with rust penetrant or treated with a special chemical to soften it so it can be easily scraped off. A scraper can be fashioned from a piece of copper tubing by flattening and sharpening one end. Copper is recommended because it is usually softer than the surfaces to be scraped, which reduces the chance of gouging the part. Some gaskets can be removed with a wire brush, but regardless of the method used, the mating surfaces must be left clean and smooth. If for some reason the gasket surface is gouged, then a gasket sealer thick enough to fill scratches will have to be used during reassembly of the components. For most applications, a non-drying (or semi-drying) gasket sealer should be used.

### Hose removal tips

**Warning:** *If the vehicle is equipped with air conditioning, do not disconnect any of the A/C hoses without first having the system depressurised by a dealer service department or a service station.*

Hose removal precautions closely parallel gasket removal precautions. Avoid scratching or gouging the surface that the hose mates against or the connection may leak. This is especially true for radiator hoses. Because of various chemical reactions, the rubber in hoses can bond itself to the metal spigot that the hose fits over. To remove a hose, first loosen the hose clamps that secure it to the spigot. Then, with slip-joint pliers, grab the hose at the clamp and rotate it around the spigot. Work it back and forth until it is completely free, then pull it off. Silicone or other lubricants will ease removal if they can be applied between the hose and the outside of the spigot. Apply the same lubricant to the inside of the hose and the outside of the spigot to simplify refitting.

As a last resort (and if the hose is to be renewed anyway), the rubber can be slit with a knife and the hose peeled from the spigot. If this must be done, be careful that the metal connection is not damaged.

If a hose clamp is broken or damaged, do not reuse it. Wire-type clamps usually weaken with age, so it is a good idea to renew them with screw-type clamps whenever a hose is removed.

## Tools

A selection of good tools is a basic requirement for anyone who plans to maintain and repair his or her own vehicle. For the owner who has few tools, the initial investment might seem high, but when compared to the spiralling costs of professional auto maintenance and repair, it is a wise one.

To help the owner decide which tools are needed to perform the tasks detailed in this manual, the following tool lists are offered: *Maintenance and minor repair, Repair/overhaul* and *Special.*

The newcomer to practical mechanics should start off with the *maintenance and minor repair* tool kit, which is adequate for the simpler jobs performed on a vehicle. Then, as confidence and experience grow, the owner can tackle more difficult tasks, buying additional tools as they are needed.

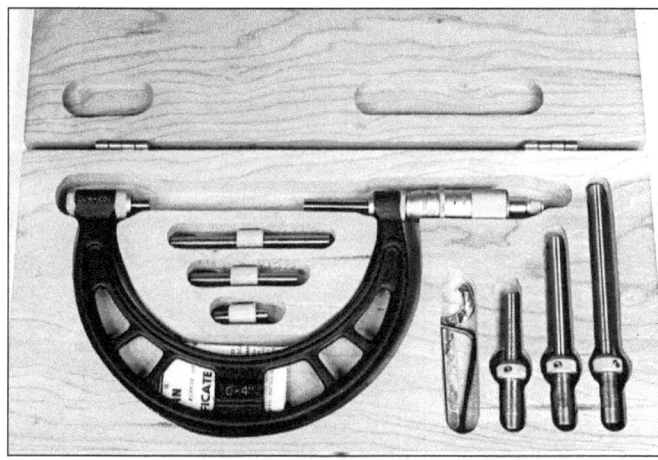

**Micrometer set**

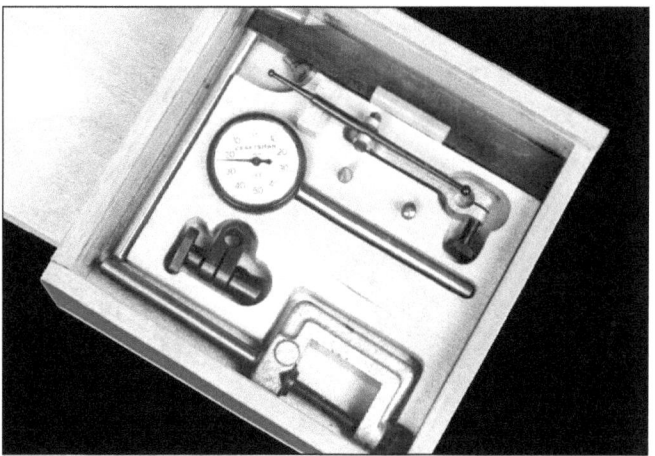

**Dial indicator set**

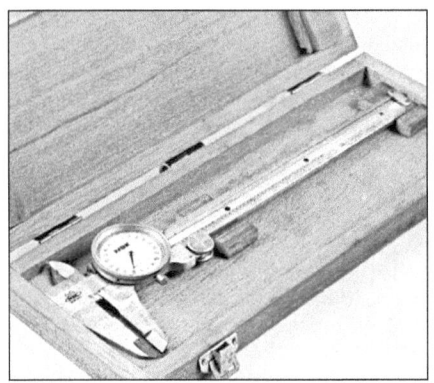

Dial caliper

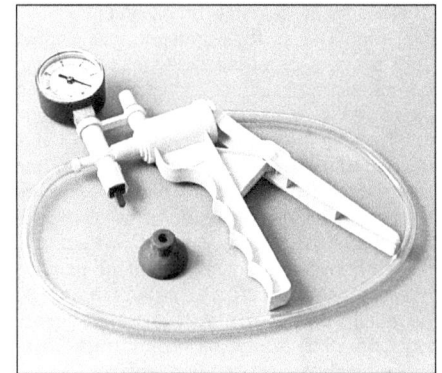

Hand-operated vacuum pump

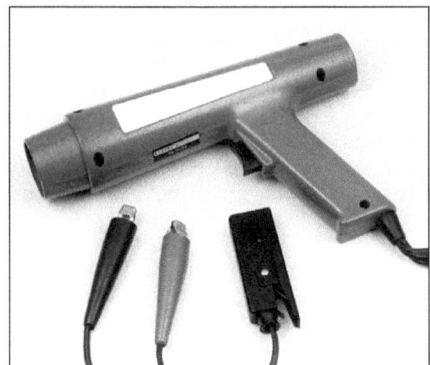

Timing light

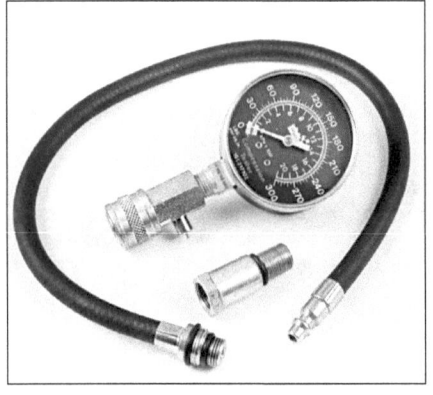

Compression gauge with spark plug
hole adaptor

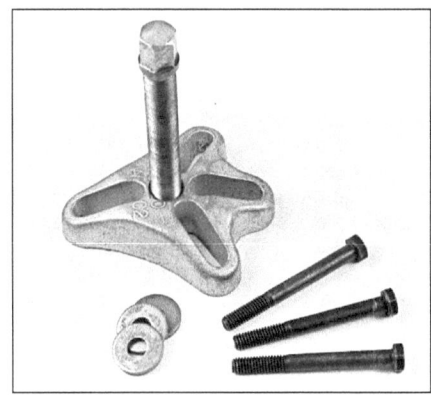

Damper/steering wheel puller

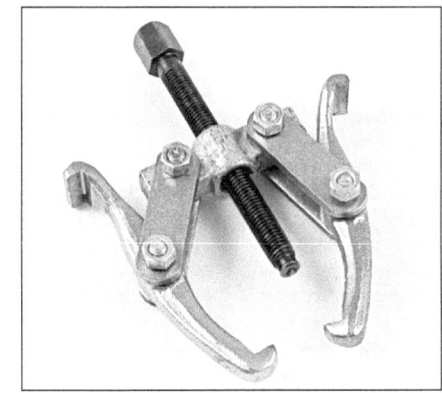

General purpose puller

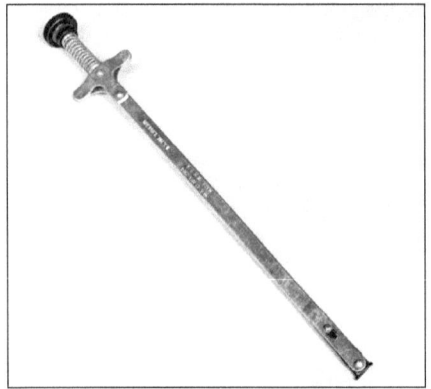

Hydraulic lifter removal tool

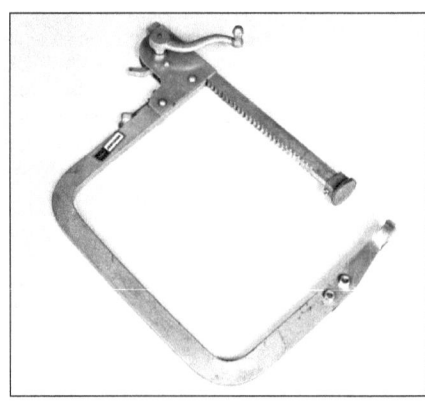

Valve spring compressor

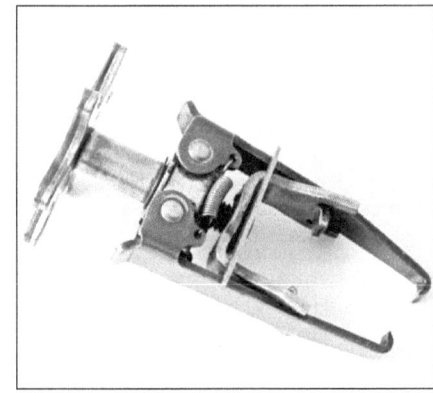

Valve spring compressor

Ridge reamer

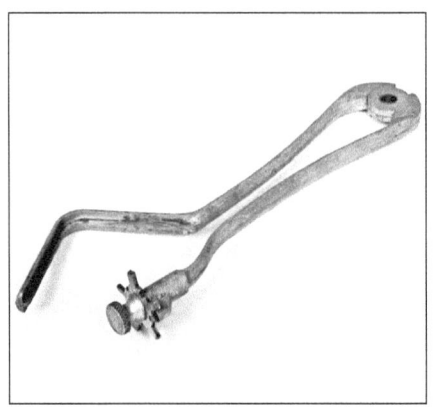

Piston ring groove cleaning tool

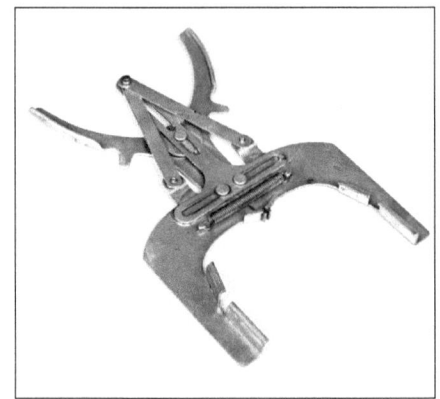

Ring removal/installation tool

Ring compressor

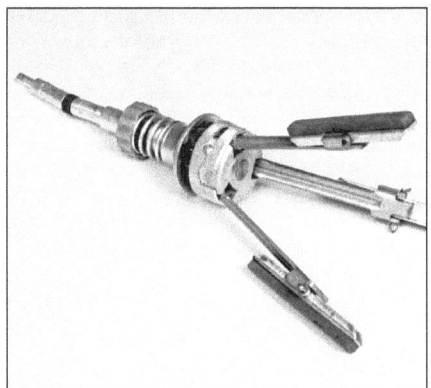

Cylinder hone

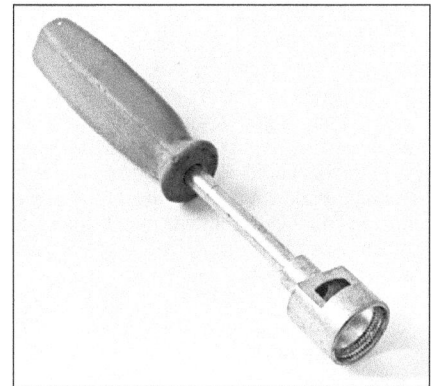

Brake hold-down spring tool

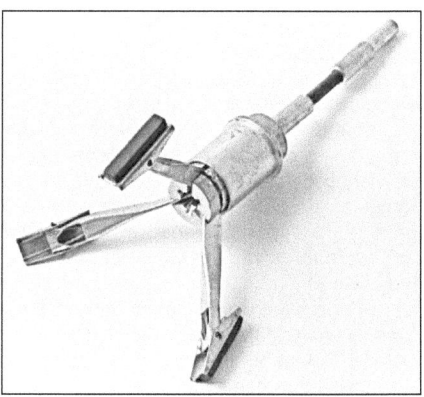

Brake cylinder hone

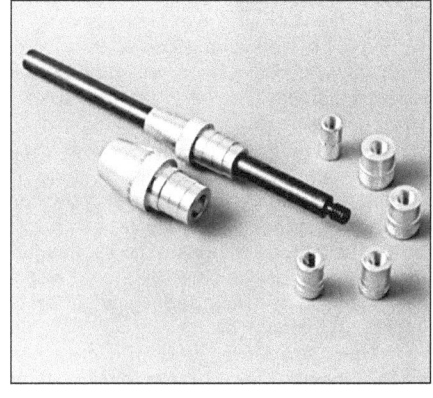

Clutch plate alignment tool

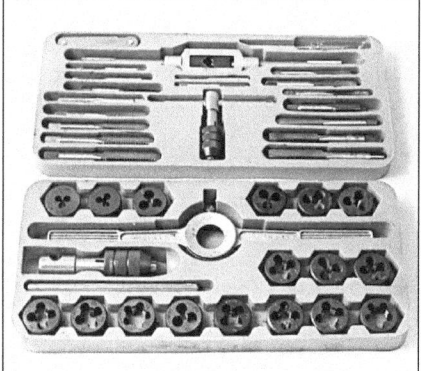

Tap and die set

Eventually the basic kit will be expanded into the *repair and overhaul* tool set. Over a period of time, the experienced do-it-yourselfer will assemble a tool set complete enough for most repair and overhaul procedures and will add tools from the special category when it is felt that the expense is justified by the frequency of use.

## Maintenance and minor repair tool kit

The tools in this list should be considered the minimum required for performance of routine maintenance, servicing and minor repair work. We recommend the purchase of combination spanner (box-end and open-end combined in one spanner). While more expensive than open end spanners, they offer the advantages of both types of spanners.

> *Combination spanner set (6 mm to 19 mm)*
> *Adjustable spanner*
> *Spark plug wrench with rubber insert*
> *Spark plug gap adjusting tool*
> *Feeler gauge set*
> *Brake bleeder wrench*
> *Standard screwdriver*
> *Phillips screwdriver*
> *Combination pliers*
> *Hacksaw and assortment of blades*
> *Tyre pressure gauge*
> *Grease gun*
> *Oil can*

> *Fine emery cloth*
> *Wire brush*
> *Battery post and cable cleaning tool*
> *Oil filter wrench*
> *Funnel (medium size)*
> *Safety goggles*
> *Jackstands (2)*
> *Drain pan*

**Note:** *If basic tune-ups are going to be part of routine maintenance, it will be necessary to purchase a good quality stroboscopic timing light and combination tachometer/dwell meter. Although they are included in the list of special tools, it is mentioned here because they are absolutely necessary for tuning most vehicles properly.*

## Repair and overhaul tool set

These tools are essential for anyone who plans to perform major repairs and are in addition to those in the maintenance and minor repair tool kit. Included is a comprehensive set of sockets which, though expensive, are invaluable because of their versatility, especially when various extensions and drives are available. We recommend the 1/2-inch drive over the 3/8-inch drive. Although the larger drive is bulky and more expensive, it has the capacity of accepting a very wide range of large sockets. Ideally, however, the mechanic should have a 3/8-inch drive set and a 1/2-inch drive set.

> *Socket set(s)*
> *Reversible ratchet*
> *Extension*
> *Universal joint*
> *Torque wrench (same size drive as sockets)*
> *Ball peen hammer*
> *Soft-face hammer (plastic/rubber)*
> *Standard screwdriver*
> *Standard screwdriver (stubby)*
> *Phillips screwdriver*
> *Phillips screwdriver (stubby - No. 2)*
> *Pliers - vise grip*
> *Pliers - lineman's*
> *Pliers - needle nose*
> *Pliers - snap-ring (internal and external)*
> *Cold chisel*
> *Scribe*
> *Scraper (made from flattened copper tubing)*
> *Countrepunch*
> *Pin punches*
> *Steel rule/straightedge*
> *Allen wrench set (4 mm to 10 mm)*
> *A selection of files*
> *Wire brush (large)*
> *Jackstands (second set)*
> *Jack (scissor or hydraulic type)*

**Note:** *Another tool which is often useful is an electric drill with a chuck capacity of 10 mm and a set of good quality drill bits.*

## Special tools

The tools in this list include those which are not used regularly, are expensive to buy, or which need to be used in accordance with their manufacturer's instructions. Unless these tools will be used frequently, it is not very economical to purchase many of them. A consideration would be to split the cost and use between yourself and a friend or friends. In addition, most of these tools can be obtained from a tool rental shop on a temporary basis.

This list primarily contains only those tools and instruments widely available to the public, and not those special tools produced by the vehicle manufacturer for distribution to dealer service departments. Occasionally, references to the manufacturer's special tools are included in the text of this manual. Generally, an alternative method of doing the job without the special tool is offered. However, sometimes there is no alternative to their use. Where this is the case, and the tool cannot be purchased or borrowed, the work should be turned over to the dealer service department or an automotive repair shop.

*Valve spring compressor*
*Piston ring groove cleaning tool*
*Piston ring compressor*
*Piston ring installation tool*
*Cylinder compression gauge*
*Cylinder ridge reamer*
*Cylinder surfacing hone*
*Cylinder bore gauge*
*Micrometers and/or dial calipers*
*Hydraulic lifter removal tool*
*Balljoint separator*
*Universal-type puller*
*Impact screwdriver*
*Dial indicator set*
*Stroboscopic timing light (inductive pick-up)*
*Hand operated vacuum/pressure pump*
*Tachometer/dwell meter*
*Universal electrical multimeter*
*Cable hoist*
*Brake spring removal and installation tools*
*Floor jack*

## Buying tools

For the do-it-yourselfer who is just starting to get involved in vehicle maintenance and repair, there are a number of options available when purchasing tools. If maintenance and minor repair is the extent of the work to be done, the purchase of individual tools is satisfactory. If, on the other hand, extensive work is planned, it would be a good idea to purchase a modest tool set from one of the large retail chain stores. A set can usually be bought at a substantial savings over the individual tool prices, and they often come with a tool box. As additional tools are needed, add-on sets, individual tools and a larger tool box can be purchased to expand the tool selection. Building a tool set gradu-

ally allows the cost of the tools to be spread over a longer period of time and gives the mechanic the freedom to choose only those tools that will actually be used.

Tool stores will often be the only source of some of the special tools that are needed, but regardless of where tools are bought, try to avoid cheap ones, especially when buying screwdrivers and sockets, because they won't last very long. The expense involved in replacing cheap tools will eventually be greater than the initial cost of quality tools.

## Care and maintenance of tools

Good tools are expensive, so it makes sense to treat them with respect. Keep them clean and in useable condition and store them properly when not in use. Always wipe off any dirt, grease or metal chips before putting them away. Never leave tools lying around in the work area. Upon completion of a job, always check closely under the bonnet for tools that may have been left there so they won't get lost during a test drive.

Some tools, such as screwdrivers, pliers, spanners and sockets, can be hung on a panel mounted on the garage or workshop wall, while others should be kept in a tool box or tray. Measuring instruments, gauges, meters, etc. must be carefully stored where they cannot be damaged by weather or impact from other tools.

When tools are used with care and stored properly, they will last a very long time. Even with the best of care, though, tools will wear out if used frequently. When a tool is damaged or worn out, renew it. Subsequent jobs will be safer and more enjoyable if you do.

## *How to repair damaged threads*

Sometimes, the internal threads of a nut or bolt hole can become stripped, usually from overtightening. Stripping threads is an all-too-common occurrence, especially when working with aluminium parts, because aluminium is so soft that it easily strips out.

Usually, external or internal threads are only partially stripped. After they've been cleaned up with a tap or die, they'll still work. Sometimes, however, threads are badly damaged. When this happens, you've got three choices:

1) *Drill and tap the hole to the next suitable oversize and refit a larger diameter bolt, screw or stud.*
2) *Drill and tap the hole to accept a threaded plug, then drill and tap the plug to the original screw size. You can also buy a plug already threaded to the original size. Then you simply drill a hole to the specified size, then run the threaded plug into the hole with a bolt and jam nut. Once the plug is fully seated, remove the jam nut and bolt.*

3) *The third method uses a patented thread repair kit like Heli-Coil or Slimsert. These easy-to-use kits are designed to repair damaged threads in straight-through holes and blind holes. Both are available as kits which can handle a variety of sizes and thread patterns. Drill the hole, then tap it with the special included tap. Refit the Heli-Coil and the hole is back to its original diameter and thread pitch.*

Regardless of which method you use, be sure to proceed calmly and carefully. A little impatience or carelessness during one of these relatively simple procedures can ruin your whole day's work and cost you a bundle if you wreck an expensive part.

## *Working facilities*

Not to be overlooked when discussing tools is the workshop. If anything more than routine maintenance is to be carried out, some sort of suitable work area is essential.

It is understood, and appreciated, that many home mechanics do not have a good workshop or garage available, and end up removing an engine or doing major repairs outside. It is recommended, however, that the overhaul or repair be completed under the cover of a roof.

A clean, flat workbench or table of comfortable working height is an absolute necessity. The workbench should be equipped with a vise that has a jaw opening of at least 10 cm.

As mentioned previously, some clean, dry storage space is also required for tools, as well as the lubricants, fluids, cleaning solvents, etc. which soon become necessary.

Sometimes waste oil and fluids, drained from the engine or cooling system during normal maintenance or repairs, present a disposal problem. To avoid pouring them on the ground or into a sewage system, pour the used fluids into large containers, seal them with caps and take them to an authorised disposal site or recycling centre. Plastic jugs, such as old antifreeze containers, are ideal for this purpose.

Always keep a supply of old newspapers and clean rags available. Old towels are excellent for mopping up spills. Many mechanics use rolls of paper towels for most work because they are readily available and disposable. To help keep the area under the vehicle clean, a large cardboard box can be cut open and flattened to protect the garage or shop floor.

Whenever working over a painted surface, such as when leaning over a fender to service something under the bonnet, always cover it with an old blanket or bedspread to protect the finish. Vinyl covered pads, made especially for this purpose, are available at auto parts stores.

# Jacking and towing

## Jacking

**Warning:** *The jack supplied with the vehicle should only be used for changing a tyre or placing jackstands under the frame. Never work under the vehicle or start the engine while this jack is being used as the only means of support.*

The vehicle should be on level ground. Place the shift lever in Park, if you have an automatic, or Reverse if you have a manual transaxle. Block the wheel diagonally opposite the wheel being changed. Set the parking brake.

Remove the spare tyre and jack from stowage. Remove the wheel cover and trim ring (if so equipped) with the tapered end of the lug nut wrench by inserting and twisting the handle and then prising against the back of the wheel cover. Loosen the wheel lug nuts about 1/4-to-1/2 turn each.

Place the scissors-type jack under the side of the vehicle and adjust the jack height until it fits in the notch in the vertical rocker panel flange nearest the wheel to be changed. There is a front and rear jacking point on each side of the vehicle (see your owners manual).

Turn the jack handle clockwise until the tyre clears the ground. Remove the lug nuts and pull the wheel off. Renew it with the spare.

Refit the lug nuts with the beveled edges facing in. Tighten them snugly. Don't attempt to tighten them completely until the vehicle is lowered or it could slip off the jack. Turn the jack handle counterclockwise to lower the vehicle. Remove the jack and tighten the lug nuts in a diagonal pattern.

Refit the cover (and trim ring, if used) and be sure it's snapped into place all the way around.

Stow the tyre, jack and spanner. Unblock the wheels.

## Towing

As a general rule, the vehicle should be towed with the front (drive) wheels off the ground. If a professional tow vehicle is not available, place the front wheels on an approved towing dolly. **Caution:** *Never tow a vehicle with an automatic transaxle from the rear with the front wheels on the ground.*

Vehicles can be towed from the front only with all four wheels on the ground, provided that speeds don't exceed 45 kph and the distance is not over 30 kilometres. Before towing a vehicle equipped with an automatic transaxle, check the transmission fluid level (see Chapter 1). If the level is below the HOT line on the dipstick, add fluid or use a towing dolly. When towing a vehicle equipped with a manual transaxle with all four wheels on the ground, be sure to place the shift lever in neutral and release the parking brake. The ignition key must be in the Off (not Lock) position, since the steering lock mechanism isn't strong enough to hold the front wheels straight while towing.

Equipment specifically designed for towing should be used. It should be attached to the main structural members of the vehicle, not the bumpers or brackets.

Safety is a major consideration when towing and all applicable laws must be obeyed. A safety chain system must be used at all times.

# Booster battery (jump) starting

Observe these precautions when using a booster battery to start a vehicle:

a) *Before connecting the booster battery, make sure the ignition switch is in the Off position.*
b) *Turn off the lights, heater and other electrical loads.*
c) *Your eyes should be shielded. Safety goggles are a good idea.*
d) *Make sure the booster battery is the same voltage as the dead one in the vehicle.*
e) *The two vehicles MUST NOT TOUCH each other!*
f) *Make sure the transaxle is in Neutral (manual) or Park (automatic).*
g) *If the booster battery is not a maintenance-free type, remove the vent caps and lay a cloth over the vent holes.*

Connect the red jumper cable to the positive (+) terminals of each battery **(see illustration)**.

Connect one end of the black jumper cable to the negative (-) terminal of the booster battery. The other end of this cable should be connected to a good earth on the vehicle to be started, such as a bolt or bracket on the body.

Start the engine using the booster battery, then, with the engine running at idle speed, disconnect the jumper cables in the reverse order of connection.

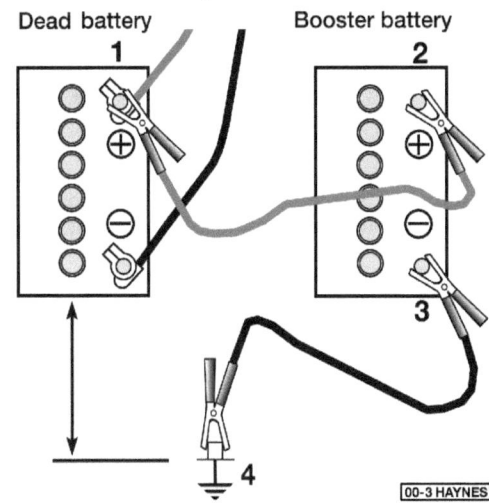

Make the booster battery cable connections in the numerical order shown (note that the negative cable of the booster battery is NOT attached to the negative terminal of the dead battery)

# Automotive chemicals and lubricants

A number of automotive chemicals and lubricants are available for use during vehicle maintenance and repair. They include a wide variety of products ranging from cleaning solvents and degreasers to lubricants and protective sprays for rubber, plastic and vinyl.

## Cleaners

**Carburettor cleaner and choke cleaner** is a strong solvent for gum, varnish and carbon. Most carburettor cleaners leave a dry-type lubricant film which will not harden or gum up. Because of this film it is not recommended for use on electrical components.

**Brake system cleaner** is used to remove grease and brake fluid from the brake system, where clean surfaces are absolutely necessary. It leaves no residue and often eliminates brake squeal caused by contaminants.

**Electrical cleaner** removes oxidation, corrosion and carbon deposits from electrical contacts, restoring full current flow. It can also be used to clean spark plugs, carburettor jets, voltage regulators and other parts where an oil-free surface is desired.

**Demoisturants** remove water and moisture from electrical components such as alternators, voltage regulators, electrical connectors and fuse blocks. They are non-conductive, non-corrosive and non-flammable.

**Degreasers** are heavy-duty solvents used to remove grease from the outside of the engine and from chassis components. They can be sprayed or brushed on and, depending on the type, are rinsed off either with water or solvent.

## Lubricants

**Motor oil** is the lubricant formulated for use in engines. It normally contains a wide variety of additives to prevent corrosion and reduce foaming and wear. Motor oil comes in various weights (viscosity ratings) from 5 to 80. The recommended weight of the oil depends on the season, temperature and the demands on the engine. Light oil is used in cold climates and under light load conditions. Heavy oil is used in hot climates and where high loads are encountered. Multi-viscosity oils are designed to have characteristics of both light and heavy oils and are available in a number of weights from 5W-20 to 20W-50.

**Gear oil** is designed to be used in differentials, manual transmissions and other areas where high-temperature lubrication is required.

**Chassis and wheel bearing grease** is a heavy grease used where increased loads and friction are encountered, such as for wheel bearings, balljoints, tie-rod ends and universal joints.

**High-temperature wheel bearing grease** is designed to withstand the extreme temperatures encountered by wheel bearings in disc brake equipped vehicles. It usually contains molybdenum disulfide (moly), which is a dry-type lubricant.

**White grease** is a heavy grease for metal-to-metal applications where water is a problem. White grease stays soft under both low and high temperatures (usually from -56 to +106-degrees C), and will not wash off or dilute in the presence of water.

**Assembly lube** is a special extreme pressure lubricant, usually containing moly, used to lubricate high-load parts (such as main and rod bearings and cam lobes) for initial start-up of a new engine. The assembly lube lubricates the parts without being squeezed out or washed away until the engine oiling system begins to function.

**Silicone lubricants** are used to protect rubber, plastic, vinyl and nylon parts.

**Graphite lubricants** are used where oils cannot be used due to contamination problems, such as in locks. The dry graphite will lubricate metal parts while remaining uncontaminated by dirt, water, oil or acids. It is electrically conductive and will not foul electrical contacts in locks such as the ignition switch.

**Moly penetrants** loosen and lubricate seized, rusted and corroded fasteners and prevent future rusting or freezing.

**Heat-sink grease** is a special electrically non-conductive grease that is used for mounting electronic ignition modules where it is essential that heat is transferred away from the module.

## Sealants

**RTV sealant** is one of the most widely used gasket compounds. Made from silicone, RTV is air curing, it seals, bonds, waterproofs, fills surface irregularities, remains flexible, doesn't shrink, is relatively easy to remove, and is used as a supplementary sealer with almost all low and medium temperature gaskets.

**Anaerobic sealant** is much like RTV in that it can be used either to seal gaskets or to form gaskets by itself. It remains flexible, is solvent resistant and fills surface imperfections. The difference between an anaerobic sealant and an RTV-type sealant is in the curing. RTV cures when exposed to air, while an anaerobic sealant cures only in the absence of air. This means that an anaerobic sealant cures only after the assembly of parts, sealing them together.

**Thread and pipe sealant** is used for sealing hydraulic and pneumatic fittings and vacuum lines. It is usually made from a Teflon compound, and comes in a spray, a paint-on liquid and as a wrap-around tape.

## Chemicals

**Anti-seize compound** prevents seizing, galling, cold welding, rust and corrosion in fasteners. High-temperature ant-seize, usually made with copper and graphite lubricants, is used for exhaust system and exhaust manifold bolts.

**Anaerobic locking compounds** are used to keep fasteners from vibrating or working loose and cure only after refitting, in the absence of air. Medium strength locking compound is used for small nuts, bolts and screws that may be removed later. High-strength locking compound is for large nuts, bolts and studs which aren't removed on a regular basis.

**Oil additives** range from viscosity index improvers to chemical treatments that claim to reduce internal engine friction. It should be noted that most oil manufacturers caution against using additives with their oils.

**Petrol additives** perform several functions, depending on their chemical make-up. They usually contain solvents that help dissolve gum and varnish that build up on carburettor, fuel injection and inlet parts. They also serve to break down carbon deposits that form on the inside surfaces of the combustion chambers. Some additives contain upper cylinder lubricants for valves and piston rings, and others contain chemicals to remove condensation from the fuel tank.

## Miscellaneous

**Brake fluid** is specially formulated hydraulic fluid that can withstand the heat and pressure encountered in brake systems. Care must be taken so this fluid does not come in contact with painted surfaces or plastics. An opened container should always be resealed to prevent contamination by water or dirt.

**Weatherstrip adhesive** is used to bond weatherstripping around doors, windows and luggage compartment lids. It is sometimes used to attach trim pieces.

**Undercoating** is a petroleum-based, tar-like substance that is designed to protect metal surfaces on the underside of the vehicle from corrosion. It also acts as a sound-deadening agent by insulating the bottom of the vehicle.

**Waxes and polishes** are used to help protect painted and plated surfaces from the weather. Different types of paint may require the use of different types of wax and polish. Some polishes utilise a chemical or abrasive cleaner to help remove the top layer of oxidised (dull) paint on older vehicles. In recent years many non-wax polishes that contain a wide variety of chemicals such as polymers and silicones have been introduced. These non-wax polishes are usually easier to apply and last longer than conventional waxes and polishes.

# Conversion factors

**Length (distance)**

| | | | | | |
|---|---|---|---|---|---|
| Inches (in) | X 25.4 | = Millimetres (mm) | X 0.0394 | = Inches (in) |
| Feet (ft) | X 0.305 | = Metres (m) | X 3.281 | = Feet (ft) |
| Miles | X 1.609 | = Kilometres (km) | X 0.621 | = Miles |

**Volume (capacity)**

| | | | | | |
|---|---|---|---|---|---|
| Cubic inches (cu in; in$^3$) | X 16.387 | = Cubic centimetres (cc; cm$^3$) | X 0.061 | = Cubic inches (cu in; in$^3$) |
| Imperial pints (Imp pt) | X 0.568 | = Litres (l) | X 1.76 | = Imperial pints (Imp pt) |
| Imperial quarts (Imp qt) | X 1.137 | = Litres (l) | X 0.88 | = Imperial quarts (Imp qt) |
| Imperial quarts (Imp qt) | X 1.201 | = US quarts (US qt) | X 0.833 | = Imperial quarts (Imp qt) |
| US quarts (US qt) | X 0.946 | = Litres (l) | X 1.057 | = US quarts (US qt) |
| Imperial gallons (Imp gal) | X 4.546 | = Litres (l) | X 0.22 | = Imperial gallons (Imp gal) |
| Imperial gallons (Imp gal) | X 1.201 | = US gallons (US gal) | X 0.833 | = Imperial gallons (Imp gal) |
| US gallons (US gal) | X 3.785 | = Litres (l) | X 0.264 | = US gallons (US gal) |

**Mass (weight)**

| | | | | | |
|---|---|---|---|---|---|
| Ounces (oz) | X 28.35 | = Grams (g) | X 0.035 | = Ounces (oz) |
| Pounds (lb) | X 0.454 | = Kilograms (kg) | X 2.205 | = Pounds (lb) |

**Force**

| | | | | | |
|---|---|---|---|---|---|
| Ounces-force (ozf; oz) | X 0.278 | = Newtons (N) | X 3.6 | = Ounces-force (ozf; oz) |
| Pounds-force (lbf; lb) | X 4.448 | = Newtons (N) | X 0.225 | = Pounds-force (lbf; lb) |
| Newtons (N) | X 0.1 | = Kilograms-force (kgf; kg) | X 9.81 | = Newtons (N) |

**Pressure**

| | | | | | |
|---|---|---|---|---|---|
| Pounds-force per square inch (psi; lbf/in$^2$; lb/in$^2$) | X 0.070 | = Kilograms-force per square centimetre (kgf/cm$^2$; kg/cm$^2$) | X 14.223 | = Pounds-force per square inch (psi; lbf/in$^2$; lb/in$^2$) |
| Pounds-force per square inch (psi; lbf/in$^2$; lb/in$^2$) | X 0.068 | = Atmospheres (atm) | X 14.696 | = Pounds-force per square inch (psi; lbf/in$^2$; lb/in$^2$) |
| Pounds-force per square inch (psi; lbf/in$^2$; lb/in$^2$) | X 0.069 | = Bars | X 14.5 | = Pounds-force per square inch (psi; lbf/in$^2$; lb/in$^2$) |
| Pounds-force per square inch (psi; lbf/in$^2$; lb/in$^2$) | X 6.895 | = Kilopascals (kPa) | X 0.145 | = Pounds-force per square inch (psi; lbf/in$^2$; lb/in$^2$) |
| Kilopascals (kPa) | X 0.01 | = Kilograms-force per square centimetre (kgf/cm$^2$; kg/cm$^2$) | X 98.1 | = Kilopascals (kPa) |

**Torque (moment of force)**

| | | | | | |
|---|---|---|---|---|---|
| Pounds-force inches (lbf in; lb in) | X 1.152 | = Kilograms-force centimetre (kgf cm; kg cm) | X 0.868 | = Pounds-force inches (lbf in; lb in) |
| Pounds-force inches (lbf in; lb in) | X 0.113 | = Newton metres (Nm) | X 8.85 | = Pounds-force inches (lbf in; lb in) |
| Pounds-force inches (lbf in; lb in) | X 0.083 | = Pounds-force feet (lbf ft; lb ft) | X 12 | = Pounds-force inches (lbf in; lb in) |
| Pounds-force feet (lbf ft; lb ft) | X 0.138 | = Kilograms-force metres (kgf m; kg m) | X 7.233 | = Pounds-force feet (lbf ft; lb ft) |
| Pounds-force feet (lbf ft; lb ft) | X 1.356 | = Newton metres (Nm) | X 0.738 | = Pounds-force feet (lbf ft; lb ft) |
| Newton metres (Nm) | X 0.102 | = Kilograms-force metres (kgf m; kg m) | X 9.804 | = Newton metres (Nm) |

**Vacuum**

| | | | | | |
|---|---|---|---|---|---|
| Inches mercury (in. Hg) | X 3.377 | = Kilopascals (kPa) | X 0.2961 | = Inches mercury |
| Inches mercury (in. Hg) | X 25.4 | = Millimetres mercury (mm Hg) | X 0.0394 | = Inches mercury |

**Power**

| | | | | | |
|---|---|---|---|---|---|
| Horsepower (hp) | X 745.7 | = Watts (W) | X 0.0013 | = Horsepower (hp) |

**Velocity (speed)**

| | | | | | |
|---|---|---|---|---|---|
| Miles per hour (miles/hr; mph) | X 1.609 | = Kilometres per hour (km/hr; kph) | X 0.621 | = Miles per hour (miles/hr; mph) |

**Fuel consumption***

| | | | | | |
|---|---|---|---|---|---|
| Miles per gallon, Imperial (mpg) | X 0.354 | = Kilometres per litre (km/l) | X 2.825 | = Miles per gallon, Imperial (mpg) |
| Miles per gallon, US (mpg) | X 0.425 | = Kilometres per litre (km/l) | X 2.352 | = Miles per gallon, US (mpg) |

**Temperature**

Degrees Fahrenheit = (°C x 1.8) + 32

Degrees Celsius (Degrees Centigrade; °C) = (°F - 32) x 0.56

*It is common practice to convert from miles per gallon (mpg) to litres/100 kilometres (l/100km), where mpg (Imperial) x l/100 km = 282 and mpg (US) x l/100 km = 235*

# Fraction/Decimal/Millimetre Equivalents

## DECIMALS TO MILLIMETRES

| Decimal | mm | Decimal | mm |
|---|---|---|---|
| 0.001 | 0.0254 | 0.500 | 12.7000 |
| 0.002 | 0.0508 | 0.510 | 12.9540 |
| 0.003 | 0.0762 | 0.520 | 13.2080 |
| 0.004 | 0.1016 | 0.530 | 13.4620 |
| 0.005 | 0.1270 | 0.540 | 13.7160 |
| 0.006 | 0.1524 | 0.550 | 13.9700 |
| 0.007 | 0.1778 | 0.560 | 14.2240 |
| 0.008 | 0.2032 | 0.570 | 14.4780 |
| 0.009 | 0.2286 | 0.580 | 14.7320 |
| | | 0.590 | 14.9860 |
| 0.010 | 0.2540 | | |
| 0.020 | 0.5080 | | |
| 0.030 | 0.7620 | | |
| 0.040 | 1.0160 | 0.600 | 15.2400 |
| 0.050 | 1.2700 | 0.610 | 15.4940 |
| 0.060 | 1.5240 | 0.620 | 15.7480 |
| 0.070 | 1.7780 | 0.630 | 16.0020 |
| 0.080 | 2.0320 | 0.640 | 16.2560 |
| 0.090 | 2.2860 | 0.650 | 16.5100 |
| | | 0.660 | 16.7640 |
| 0.100 | 2.5400 | 0.670 | 17.0180 |
| 0.110 | 2.7940 | 0.680 | 17.2720 |
| 0.120 | 3.0480 | 0.690 | 17.5260 |
| 0.130 | 3.3020 | | |
| 0.140 | 3.5560 | | |
| 0.150 | 3.8100 | | |
| 0.160 | 4.0640 | 0.700 | 17.7800 |
| 0.170 | 4.3180 | 0.710 | 18.0340 |
| 0.180 | 4.5720 | 0.720 | 18.2880 |
| 0.190 | 4.8260 | 0.730 | 18.5420 |
| | | 0.740 | 18.7960 |
| 0.200 | 5.0800 | 0.750 | 19.0500 |
| 0.210 | 5.3340 | 0.760 | 19.3040 |
| 0.220 | 5.5880 | 0.770 | 19.5580 |
| 0.230 | 5.8420 | 0.780 | 19.8120 |
| 0.240 | 6.0960 | 0.790 | 20.0660 |
| 0.250 | 6.3500 | | |
| 0.260 | 6.6040 | | |
| 0.270 | 6.8580 | 0.800 | 20.3200 |
| 0.280 | 7.1120 | 0.810 | 20.5740 |
| 0.290 | 7.3660 | 0.820 | 21.8280 |
| | | 0.830 | 21.0820 |
| 0.300 | 7.6200 | 0.840 | 21.3360 |
| 0.310 | 7.8740 | 0.850 | 21.5900 |
| 0.320 | 8.1280 | 0.860 | 21.8440 |
| 0.330 | 8.3820 | 0.870 | 22.0980 |
| 0.340 | 8.6360 | 0.880 | 22.3520 |
| 0.350 | 8.8900 | 0.890 | 22.6060 |
| 0.360 | 9.1440 | | |
| 0.370 | 9.3980 | | |
| 0.380 | 9.6520 | | |
| 0.390 | 9.9060 | 0.900 | 22.8600 |
| 0.400 | 10.1600 | 0.910 | 23.1140 |
| 0.410 | 10.4140 | 0.920 | 23.3680 |
| 0.420 | 10.6680 | 0.930 | 23.6220 |
| 0.430 | 10.9220 | 0.940 | 23.8760 |
| 0.440 | 11.1760 | 0.950 | 24.1300 |
| 0.450 | 11.4300 | 0.960 | 24.3840 |
| 0.460 | 11.6840 | 0.970 | 24.6380 |
| 0.470 | 11.9380 | 0.980 | 24.8920 |
| 0.480 | 12.1920 | 0.990 | 25.1460 |
| 0.490 | 12.4460 | 1.000 | 25.4000 |

## FRACTIONS TO DECIMALS TO MILLIMETRES

| Fraction | Decimal | mm | Fraction | Decimal | mm |
|---|---|---|---|---|---|
| 1/64 | 0.0156 | 0.3969 | 33/64 | 0.5156 | 13.0969 |
| 1/32 | 0.0312 | 0.7938 | 17/32 | 0.5312 | 13.4938 |
| 3/64 | 0.0469 | 1.1906 | 35/64 | 0.5469 | 13.8906 |
| 1/16 | 0.0625 | 1.5875 | 9/16 | 0.5625 | 14.2875 |
| 5/64 | 0.0781 | 1.9844 | 37/64 | 0.5781 | 14.6844 |
| 3/32 | 0.0938 | 2.3812 | 19/32 | 0.5938 | 15.0812 |
| 7/64 | 0.1094 | 2.7781 | 39/64 | 0.6094 | 15.4781 |
| 1/8 | 0.1250 | 3.1750 | 5/8 | 0.6250 | 15.8750 |
| 9/64 | 0.1406 | 3.5719 | 41/64 | 0.6406 | 16.2719 |
| 5/32 | 0.1562 | 3.9688 | 21/32 | 0.6562 | 16.6688 |
| 11/64 | 0.1719 | 4.3656 | 43/64 | 0.6719 | 17.0656 |
| 3/16 | 0.1875 | 4.7625 | 11/16 | 0.6875 | 17.4625 |
| 13/64 | 0.2031 | 5.1594 | 45/64 | 0.7031 | 17.8594 |
| 7/32 | 0.2188 | 5.5562 | 23/32 | 0.7188 | 18.2562 |
| 15/64 | 0.2344 | 5.9531 | 47/64 | 0.7344 | 18.6531 |
| 1/4 | 0.2500 | 6.3500 | 3/4 | 0.7500 | 19.0500 |
| 17/64 | 0.2656 | 6.7469 | 49/64 | 0.7656 | 19.4469 |
| 9/32 | 0.2812 | 7.1438 | 25/32 | 0.7812 | 19.8438 |
| 19/64 | 0.2969 | 7.5406 | 51/64 | 0.7969 | 20.2406 |
| 5/16 | 0.3125 | 7.9375 | 13/16 | 0.8125 | 20.6375 |
| 21/64 | 0.3281 | 8.3344 | 53/64 | 0.8281 | 21.0344 |
| 11/32 | 0.3438 | 8.7312 | 27/32 | 0.8438 | 21.4312 |
| 23/64 | 0.3594 | 9.1281 | 55/64 | 0.8594 | 21.8281 |
| 3/8 | 0.3750 | 9.5250 | 7/8 | 0.8750 | 22.2250 |
| 25/64 | 0.3906 | 9.9219 | 57/64 | 0.8906 | 22.6219 |
| 13/32 | 0.4062 | 10.3188 | 29/32 | 0.9062 | 23.0188 |
| 27/64 | 0.4219 | 10.7156 | 59/64 | 0.9219 | 23.4156 |
| 7/16 | 0.4375 | 11.1125 | 15/16 | 0.9375 | 23.8125 |
| 29/64 | 0.4531 | 11.5094 | 61/64 | 0.9531 | 24.2094 |
| 15/32 | 0.4688 | 11.9062 | 31/32 | 0.9688 | 24.6062 |
| 31/64 | 0.4844 | 12.3031 | 63/64 | 0.9844 | 25.0031 |
| 1/2 | 0.5000 | 12.7000 | 1 | 1.0000 | 25.4000 |

# Safety first!

Regardless of how enthusiastic you may be about getting on with the job at hand, take the time to ensure that your safety is not jeopardised. A moment's lack of attention can result in an accident, as can failure to observe certain simple safety precautions. The possibility of an accident will always exist, and the following points should not be considered a comprehensive list of all dangers. Rather, they are intended to make you aware of the risks and to encourage a safety conscious approach to all work you carry out on your vehicle.

## Essential DOs and DON'Ts

**DON'T** rely on a jack when working under the vehicle. Always use approved jackstands to support the weight of the vehicle and place them under the recommended lift or support points.

**DON'T** attempt to loosen extremely tight fasteners (ie. wheel lug nuts) while the vehicle is on a jack - it may fall.

**DON'T** start the engine without first making sure that the transmission is in Neutral (or Park where applicable) and the parking brake is set.

**DON'T** remove the radiator cap from a hot cooling system - let it cool or cover it with a cloth and release the pressure gradually.

**DON'T** attempt to drain the engine oil until you are sure it has cooled to the point that it will not burn you.

**DON'T** touch any part of the engine or exhaust system until it has cooled sufficiently to avoid burns.

**DON'T** siphon toxic liquids such as petrol, antifreeze and brake fluid by mouth, or allow them to remain on your skin.

**DON'T** inhale brake lining dust - it is potentially hazardous (see *Asbestos* below).

**DON'T** allow spilled oil or grease to remain on the floor - wipe it up before someone slips on it.

**DON'T** use loose fitting wrenches or other tools which may slip and cause injury.

**DON'T** push on wrenches when loosening or tightening nuts or bolts. Always try to pull the wrench toward you. If the situation calls for pushing the wrench away, push with an open hand to avoid scraped knuckles if the wrench should slip.

**DON'T** attempt to lift a heavy component alone - get someone to help you.

**DON'T** rush or take unsafe shortcuts to finish a job.

**DON'T** allow children or animals in or around the vehicle while you are working on it.

**DO** wear eye protection when using power tools such as a drill, sander, bench grinder, etc. and when working under a vehicle.

**DO** keep loose clothing and long hair well out of the way of moving parts.

**DO** make sure that any hoist used has a safe working load rating adequate for the job.

**DO** get someone to check on you periodically when working alone on a vehicle.

**DO** carry out work in a logical sequence and make sure that everything is correctly assembled and tightened.

**DO** keep chemicals and fluids tightly capped and out of the reach of children and pets.

**DO** remember that your vehicle's safety affects that of yourself and others. If in doubt on any point, get professional advice.

## Asbestos

Certain friction, insulating, sealing, and other products - such as brake linings, brake bands, clutch linings, torque converters, gaskets, etc. - may contain asbestos. Extreme care must be taken to avoid inhalation of dust from such products, since it is hazardous to health. If in doubt, assume that they do contain asbestos.

## Fire

Remember at all times that petrol is highly flammable. Never smoke or have any kind of open flame around when working on a vehicle. But the risk does not end there. A spark caused by an electrical short circuit, by two metal surfaces contacting each other, or even by static electricity built up in your body under certain conditions, can ignite petrol vapours, which in a confined space are highly explosive. Do not, under any circumstances, use petrol for cleaning parts. Use an approved safety solvent.

Always disconnect the battery earth (-) cable at the battery before working on any part of the fuel system or electrical system. Never risk spilling fuel on a hot engine or exhaust component. It is strongly recommended that a fire extinguisher suitable for use on fuel and electrical fires be kept handy in the garage or workshop at all times. Never try to extinguish a fuel or electrical fire with water.

## Fumes

Certain fumes are highly toxic and can quickly cause unconsciousness and even death if inhaled to any extent. Petrol vapour falls into this category, as do the vapours from some cleaning solvents. Any draining or pouring of such volatile fluids should be done in a well ventilated area.

When using cleaning fluids and sol-vents, read the instructions on the container carefully. Never use materials from unmarked containers.

Never run the engine in an enclosed space, such as a garage. Exhaust fumes contain carbon monoxide, which is extremely poisonous. If you need to run the engine, always do so in the open air, or at least have the rear of the vehicle outside the work area.

If you are fortunate enough to have the use of an inspection pit, never drain or pour petrol and never run the engine while the vehicle is over the pit. The fumes, being heavier than air, will concentrate in the pit with possibly lethal results.

## The battery

Never create a spark or allow a bare light bulb near a battery. They normally give off a certain amount of hydrogen gas, which is highly explosive.

Always disconnect the battery earth (-) cable at the battery before working on the fuel or electrical systems.

If possible, loosen the filler caps or cover when charging the battery from an external source (this does not apply to sealed or maintenance-free batteries). Do not charge at an excessive rate or the battery may burst.

Take care when adding water to a non maintenance-free battery and when carrying a battery. The electrolyte, even when diluted, is very corrosive and should not be allowed to contact clothing or skin.

Always wear eye protection when cleaning the battery to prevent the caustic deposits from entering your eyes.

## Household current

When using an electric power tool, inspection light, etc., which operates on household current, always make sure that the tool is correctly connected to its plug and that, where necessary, it is properly earthed. Do not use such items in damp conditions and, again, do not create a spark or apply excessive heat in the vicinity of fuel or fuel vapour.

## Secondary ignition system voltage

A severe electric shock can result from touching certain parts of the ignition system (such as the spark plug wires) when the engine is running or being cranked, particularly if components are damp or the insulation is defective. In the case of an electronic ignition system, the secondary system voltage is much higher and could prove fatal.

# Troubleshooting

## Contents

This section provides an easy reference guide to the more common problems which may occur during the operation of your vehicle. These problems and their possible causes are grouped under headings denoting various components or systems, such as Engine, Cooling system, etc. They also refer you to the chapter and/or section which deals with the problem.

Remember that successful troubleshooting is not an art practiced only by professional mechanics. It is simply the result of the right knowledge combined with an intelligent, systematic approach to the problem. Always work by a process of elimination, starting with the simplest solution and working through to the most complex - and never overlook the obvious. Anyone can run the fuel tank dry or leave the lights on overnight, so don't assume that you are exempt from such oversights.

Finally, always establish a clear idea of why a problem has occurred and take steps to ensure that it doesn't happen again. If the electrical system fails because of a poor connection, check the other connections in the system to make sure that they don't fail as well. If a particular fuse continues to blow, find out why - don't just install one fuse after another. Remember, failure of a small component can often be indicative of potential failure or incorrect functioning of a more important component or system.

## Engine

### 1 Engine will not rotate when attempting to start

1 Battery terminal connections loose or corroded (Chapter 1).
2 Battery discharged or faulty (Chapter 1).
3 Automatic transaxle not completely engaged in Park (Chapter 7).
4 Broken, loose or disconnected wiring in the starting circuit (Chapters 5 and 12).
5 Starter motor pinion jammed in flywheel ring gear (Chapter 5).
6 Starter solenoid faulty (Chapter 5).
7 Starter motor faulty (Chapter 5).
8 Ignition switch faulty (Chapter 12).
9 Starter pinion or flywheel teeth worn or broken (Chapter 5).
10 Defective main fusible link (see Chapter 12).
11 Engine locked-up (Chapter 2).

### 2 Engine rotates but will not start

1 Fuel tank empty.
2 Battery discharged, terminal connections loose or corroded (engine rotates slowly) (Chapter 5).
3 Fault in the carburettor or fuel injection system (Chapter 4).

4 Faulty fuel pump (Chapter 4).
5 Broken or stripped timing chain or belt (Chapter 2).
6 Ignition components damp or damaged (Chapter 5).
7 Worn, faulty or incorrectly gapped spark plugs (Chapter 1).
8 Defective ignition coil (Chapter 5).
9 Loose distributor is changing ignition timing (Chapter 5).
10 Broken, loose or disconnected wires at the ignition coil (Chapter 5).

### 3 Engine hard to start when cold

1 Battery discharged or low (Chapter 1).
2 Faulty fuel system (Chapter 4).
3 Fault in engine control system (Chapter 6).
4 Faulty ignition system (Chapter 5).
5 Faulty or incorrectly gapped spark plugs (Chapter 1).

### 4 Engine hard to start when hot

1 Air filter clogged (Chapter 1).
2 Faulty fuel system (Chapter 4).
3 Fault in engine control system (Chapter 6).
4 Faulty ignition system (Chapter 5).
5 Corroded battery connections, especially ground (Chapter 1).

### 5 Starter motor noisy or excessively rough in engagement

1 Pinion or flywheel gear teeth worn or broken (Chapter 5).
2 Starter motor mounting bolts loose or missing (Chapter 5).

### 6 Engine starts but stops immediately

1 Loose or faulty electrical connections at distributor, coil or alternator (Chapter 5).
2 Insufficient fuel reaching the fuel injector(s) (Chapters 1 and 4).
3 Fault in the fuel injection system (Chapter 4).
4 Fault in the ignition system (Chapter 5).
5 Vacuum leak at the PCV, inlet manifold or fuel injection system (Chapters 1 and 4).
6 Idle speed incorrect (Chapter 1).
7 Faulty EGR valve (Chapter 6).
8 Uneven or low cylinder compression (Chapter 2).

### 7 Oil puddle under engine

1 Sump gasket and/or sump drain bolt washer leaking (Chapter 2).

2 Oil pressure sending unit leaking (Chapter 2).
3 Valve cover leaking (Chapter 2).
4 Engine oil seals leaking (Chapter 2).
5 Oil pump housing leaking (Chapter 2).
6 Oil filter leaking (Chapter 1).

### 8 Engine lopes while idling or idles erratically

1 Vacuum leak (Chapters 2 and 4).
2 Leaking EGR valve (Chapter 6).
3 Air filter clogged (Chapter 1).
4 Fuel pump not delivering sufficient fuel to the fuel injection system (Chapter 4).
5 Leaking head gasket (Chapter 2).
6 Timing belt and/or sprockets worn (Chapter 2).
7 Camshaft lobes worn (Chapter 2).
8 Fault in the fuel injection system (Chapter 4).

### 9 Engine misses at idle speed

1 Spark plugs worn or not gapped properly (Chapter 1).
2 Faulty spark plug wires (Chapter 1).
3 Vacuum leak (Chapters 2 and 4).
4 Incorrect ignition timing (Chapter 1).
5 Uneven or low cylinder compression (Chapter 2).
6 Fault in the fuel injection system (Chapter 4).

### 10 Engine misses throughout driving speed range

1 Fuel filter clogged and/or impurities in the fuel system (Chapter 1).
2 Fault in the fuel injection system (Chapter 4).
3 Faulty or incorrectly gapped spark plugs (Chapter 1).
4 Incorrect ignition timing (Chapter 1).
5 Cracked distributor cap, disconnected distributor wires or damaged distributor components (Chapters 1 and 5).
6 Defective spark plug wires (Chapters 1 or 5).
7 Faulty emission system components (Chapter 6).
8 Low or uneven cylinder compression pressures (Chapter 2).
9 Weak or faulty ignition system (Chapter 5).
10 Vacuum leak (Chapter 4).

### 11 Engine stumbles on acceleration

1 Spark plugs fouled (Chapter 1).
2 Problem with fuel injection system (Chapter 4).
3 Fuel filter clogged (Chapters 1 and 4).
4 Incorrect ignition timing (Chapter 1).

5    Inlet manifold air leak (Chapters 2 and 4).
6    EGR system malfunction (Chapter 6).

## 12   Engine surges while holding accelerator steady

1    Intake air leak (Chapter 4).
2    Fuel pump or fuel pressure regulator faulty (Chapter 4).
3    Problem with fuel injection system (Chapter 4).
4    Problem with the emissions control system (Chapter 6).

## 13   Engine stalls

1    Idle speed incorrect (Chapter 1).
2    Fuel filter clogged and/or water and impurities in the fuel system (Chapters 1 and 4).
3    Distributor components damp or damaged (Chapter 5).
4    Faulty emissions system components (Chapter 6).
5    Faulty or incorrectly gapped spark plugs (Chapter 1).
6    Faulty spark plug wires (Chapter 1).
7    Vacuum leak (Chapters 2 and 4).
8    Problem with the fuel injection system (Chapter 4).

## 14   Engine lacks power

1    Incorrect ignition timing (Chapter 5).
2    Excessive play in distributor shaft (Chapter 5).
3    Worn rotor, distributor cap, spark plug wires or faulty coil (Chapters 1 and 5).
4    Faulty or incorrectly gapped spark plugs (Chapter 1).
5    Problem with the fuel injection system (Chapter 4).
6    Plugged air filter (Chapter 1).
7    Brakes binding (Chapter 9).
8    Automatic transaxle fluid level incorrect (Chapter 1).
9    Clutch slipping (Chapter 8).
10   Fuel filter clogged and/or impurities in the fuel system (Chapters 1 and 4).
11   Emission control system not functioning properly (Chapter 6).
12   Low or uneven cylinder compression pressures (Chapter 2).
13   Obstructed exhaust system (Chapters 2 and 4).

## 15   Engine backfires

1    Emission control system not functioning properly (Chapter 6).
2    Ignition timing incorrect (Chapter 1).
3    Faulty secondary ignition system (cracked spark plug insulator, faulty plug wires, distributor cap and/or rotor) (Chapters 1 and 5).
4    Problem with the fuel injection system (Chapter 4).
5    Vacuum leak (Chapters 2 and 4).
6    Valves sticking (Chapter 2).

## 16   Pinging or knocking engine sounds during acceleration or uphill

1    Incorrect grade of fuel.
2    Ignition timing incorrect (Chapter 1).
3    Fuel injection system faulty (Chapter 4).
4    Improper or damaged spark plugs or wires (Chapter 1).
5    Worn or damaged distributor components (Chapter 5).
6    EGR valve not functioning (Chapter 6).
7    Vacuum leak (Chapters 2 and 4).

## 17   Engine runs with oil pressure light on

1    Low oil level (Chapter 1).
2    Idle rpm below specification (Chapter 1).
3    Short in wiring circuit (Chapter 12).
4    Faulty oil pressure sender (Chapter 2).
5    Worn engine bearings and/or oil pump (Chapter 2).

## 18   Engine diesels (continues to run) after switching off

1    Idle speed too high (Chapter 1).
2    Excessive engine operating temperature (Chapter 3).
3    Ignition timing in need of adjustment (Chapter 5).
4    Excessive carbon deposits on valves and pistons (see Chapter 2).

## Engine electrical system

## 19   Battery will not hold a charge

1    Alternator drivebelt defective or not adjusted properly (Chapter 1).
2    Battery electrolyte level low (Chapter 1).
3    Battery terminals loose or corroded (Chapter 1).
4    Alternator not charging properly (Chapter 5).
5    Loose, broken or faulty wiring in the charging circuit (Chapter 5).
6    Short in vehicle wiring (Chapter 12).
7    Internally defective battery (Chapters 1 and 5).

## 20   Alternator light fails to go out

1    Faulty alternator or charging circuit (Chapter 5).
2    Alternator drivebelt defective or out of adjustment (Chapter 1).
3    Alternator voltage regulator inoperative (Chapter 5).

## 21   Alternator light fails to come on when key is turned on

1    Warning light bulb defective (Chapter 12).
2    Fault in the printed circuit, dash wiring or bulb holder (Chapter 12).

## Fuel system

## 22   Excessive fuel consumption

1    Dirty or clogged air filter element (Chapter 1).
2    Incorrectly set ignition timing (Chapter 1).
3    Emissions system not functioning properly (Chapter 6).
4    Fuel injection system not functioning properly (Chapter 4).
5    Low tyre pressure or incorrect tyre size (Chapter 1).
6    Uneven or low cylinder compression (Chapter 2).

## 23   Fuel leakage and/or fuel odor

1    Leaking fuel feed or return line (Chapters 1 and 4).
2    Tank overfilled.
3    Evaporative canister filter clogged (Chapters 1 and 6).
4    Problem with fuel injection system (Chapter 4).

## Cooling system

## 24   Overheating

1    Insufficient coolant in system (Chapter 1).
2    Water pump drivebelt defective or out of adjustment (Chapter 1).
3    Radiator core blocked or grille restricted (Chapter 3).
4    Thermostat faulty (Chapter 3).
5    Electric coolant fan inoperative or blades broken (Chapter 3).
6    Radiator cap not maintaining proper pressure (Chapter 3).
7    Ignition timing incorrect (Chapter 1).

## 25 Overcooling

1    Faulty thermostat (Chapter 3).
2    Inaccurate temperature gauge sending unit (Chapter 3).

## 26 External coolant leakage

1    Deteriorated/damaged hoses; loose clamps (Chapters 1 and 3).
2    Water pump defective (Chapter 3).
3    Leakage from radiator core or coolant reservoir bottle (Chapter 3).
4    Engine drain or water jacket core plugs leaking (Chapter 2).

## 27 Internal coolant leakage

1    Leaking cylinder head gasket (Chapter 2).
2    Cracked cylinder bore or cylinder head (Chapter 2).

## 28 Coolant loss

1    Too much coolant in system (Chapter 1).
2    Coolant boiling away because of overheating (Chapter 3).
3    Internal or external leakage (Chapter 3).
4    Faulty radiator cap (Chapter 3).

## 29 Poor coolant circulation

1    Inoperative water pump (Chapter 3).
2    Restriction in cooling system (Chapters 1 and 3).
3    Water pump drivebelt defective/out of adjustment (Chapter 1).
4    Thermostat sticking (Chapter 3).

## Clutch

## 30 Pedal travels to floor - no pressure or very little resistance

1    Hydraulic release system leaking or air in the system (Chapter 8).
2    Broken release bearing or fork (Chapter 8).

## 31 Unable to select gears

1    Faulty transaxle (Chapter 7).
2    Faulty clutch disc or pressure plate (Chapter 8).

3    Faulty release lever or release bearing (Chapter 8).
4    Faulty shift lever assembly or rods (Chapter 8).

## 32 Clutch slips (engine speed increases with no increase in vehicle speed)

1    Clutch plate worn (Chapter 8).
2    Clutch plate is oil soaked by leaking rear main seal (Chapter 8).
3    Clutch plate not seated (Chapter 8).
4    Warped pressure plate or flywheel (Chapter 8).
5    Weak diaphragm springs (Chapter 8).
6    Clutch plate overheated. Allow to cool.
7    Piston stuck in bore of clutch release cylinder, preventing clutch from fully engaging (Chapter 8).

## 33 Grabbing (chattering) as clutch is engaged

1    Oil on clutch plate lining, burned or glazed facings (Chapter 8).
2    Worn or loose engine or transaxle mounts (Chapters 2 and 7).
3    Worn splines on clutch plate hub (Chapter 8).
4    Warped pressure plate or flywheel (Chapter 8).
5    Burned or smeared resin on flywheel or pressure plate (Chapter 8).

## 34 Transaxle rattling (clicking)

1    Release fork loose (Chapter 8).
2    Low engine idle speed (Chapter 1).

## 35 Noise in clutch area

Faulty bearing (Chapter 8).

## 36 Clutch pedal stays on floor

1    Broken release bearing or fork (Chapter 8).
2    Hydraulic release system leaking or air in the system (Chapter 8).

## 37 High pedal effort

1    Piston binding in bore of release cylinder (Chapter 8).
2    Pressure plate faulty (Chapter 8).
3    Incorrect size master or release cylinder (Chapter 8).

## Manual transaxle

## 38 Knocking noise at low speeds

1    Worn driveaxle constant velocity (CV) joints (Chapter 8).
2    Worn side gear shaft counterbore in differential case (Chapter 7A).*

## 39 Noise most pronounced when turning

Differential gear noise (Chapter 7A).*

## 40 Clunk on acceleration or deceleration

1    Loose engine or transaxle mounts (Chapters 2 and 7A).
2    Worn differential pinion shaft in case.*
3    Worn side gear shaft counterbore in differential case (Chapter 7A).*
4    Worn or damaged driveaxle inboard CV joints (Chapter 8).

## 41 Clicking noise in turns

Worn or damaged outboard CV joint (Chapter 8).

## 42 Vibration

1    Rough wheel bearing (Chapters 1 and 10).
2    Damaged driveaxle (Chapter 8).
3    Out of round tyres (Chapter 1).
4    Tyre out of balance (Chapters 1 and 10).
5    Worn CV joint (Chapter 8).

## 43 Noisy in neutral with engine running

1    Damaged input gear bearing (Chapter 7A).*
2    Damaged clutch release bearing (Chapter 8).

## 44 Noisy in one particular gear

1    Damaged or worn constant mesh gears (Chapter 7A).*
2    Damaged or worn synchronisers (Chapter 7A).*
3    Bent reverse fork (Chapter 7A).*
4    Damaged fourth speed gear or output gear (Chapter 7A).*
5    Worn or damaged reverse idler gear or idler bush (Chapter 7A).*

## 45 Noisy in all gears

1 Insufficient lubricant (Chapter 7A).
2 Damaged or worn bearings (Chapter 7A).*
3 Worn or damaged input gear shaft and/or output gear shaft (Chapter 7A).*

## 46 Slips out of gear

1 Worn or improperly adjusted linkage (Chapter 7A).
2 Transaxle loose on engine (Chapter 7A).
3 Shift linkage does not work freely, binds (Chapter 7A).
4 Input gear bearing retainer broken or loose (Chapter 7A).*
5 Dirt between clutch cover and engine housing (Chapter 7A).
6 Worn shift fork (Chapter 7A).*

## 47 Leaks lubricant

1 Side gear shaft seals worn (Chapter 7A).
2 Excessive amount of lubricant in transaxle (Chapters 1 and 7A).
3 Loose or broken input gear shaft bearing retainer (Chapter 7A).*
4 Input gear bearing retainer O-ring and/or lip seal damaged (Chapter 7A).*
5 Striking rod seal leaking (Chapter 7A).
6 Vehicle speed sensor O-ring leaking (Chapter 7A).

## 48 Hard to shift

Shift linkage loose or worn (Chapter 7A).

*Although the corrective action necessary to remedy the symptoms described is beyond the scope of this manual, the above information should be helpful in isolating the cause of the condition so that the owner can communicate clearly with a professional mechanic.*

## Automatic transaxle

**Note:** *Due to the complexity of the automatic transaxle, it is difficult for the home mechanic to properly diagnose and service this component. For problems other than the following, the vehicle should be taken to a dealer or transaxle shop.*

## 49 Fluid leakage

1 Automatic transaxle fluid is a deep red colour. Fluid leaks should not be confused with engine oil, which can easily be blown onto the transaxle by air flow.
2 To pinpoint a leak, first remove all built-up dirt and grime from the transaxle housing

with degreasing agents and/or steam cleaning. Then drive the vehicle at low speeds so air flow will not blow the leak far from its source. Raise the vehicle and determine where the leak is coming from. Common areas of leakage are:
a) *Pan* (Chapters 1 and 7).
b) *Dipstick tube* (Chapters 1 and 7).
c) *Transaxle oil lines* (Chapter 7).
d) *Speedometer adapter* (Chapter 7).
e) *Driveaxle oil seals* (Chapter 7).

## 50 Transaxle fluid brown or has a burned smell

Transaxle fluid overheated (Chapter 1).

## 51 General shift mechanism problems

1 Chapter 7, Part B, deals with checking and adjusting the shift linkage on automatic transaxles. Common problems which may be attributed to poorly adjusted linkage are:
a) *Engine starting in gears other than Park or Neutral.*
b) *Indicator on shifter pointing to a gear other than the one actually being used.*
c) *Vehicle moves when in Park.*
2 Refer to Chapter 7B for the shift linkage adjustment procedure.

## 52 Transaxle will not shift properly

The transaxle is electronically controlled. This type of problem - which is caused by a malfunction in the control unit, a sensor or solenoid, or the circuit itself - is beyond the scope of this manual. Take the vehicle to a dealer service department or a competent automatic transmission shop.

## 53 Engine will start in gears other than Park or Neutral

Neutral start switch out of adjustment or malfunctioning (Chapter 7B).

## 54 Transaxle slips, shifts roughly, is noisy or has no drive in forward or reverse gears

There are many probable causes for the above problems, most of them are internal transaxle problems. Before taking the vehicle to a repair shop, check the level and condition of the fluid as described in Chapter 1. Correct the fluid level as necessary or change the fluid and filter if needed. If the problem persists, have a professional diagnose the cause.

## Driveaxles

## 55 Clicking noise in turns

Worn or damaged outboard CV joint (Chapter 8).

## 56 Shudder or vibration during acceleration

1 Excessive toe-in (Chapter 10).
2 Incorrect spring heights (Chapter 10).
3 Worn or damaged inboard or outboard CV joints (Chapter 8).
4 Sticking inboard CV joint assembly (Chapter 8).

## 57 Vibration at highway speeds

1 Out of balance front wheels and/or tyres (Chapters 1 and 10).
2 Out of round front tyres (Chapters 1 and 10).
3 Worn CV joint(s) (Chapter 8).

## Brakes

**Note:** *Before assuming that a brake problem exists, make sure that:*
a) *The tyres are in good condition and properly inflated* (Chapter 1).
b) *The front end alignment is correct* (Chapter 10).
c) *The vehicle is not loaded with weight in an unequal manner.*

## 58 Vehicle pulls to one side during braking

1 Incorrect tyre pressures (Chapter 1).
2 Front end out of alignment (have the front end aligned).
3 Front, or rear, tyre sizes not matched to one another.
4 Restricted brake lines or hoses (Chapter 9).
5 Malfunctioning caliper assembly (Chapter 9).
6 Loose suspension parts (Chapter 10).
7 Loose calipers (Chapter 9).
8 Excessive wear of brake pad material or disc on one side.

## 59 Noise (high-pitched squeal when the brakes are applied)

Front and/or rear disc brake pads worn out. The noise comes from the wear sensor rubbing against the disc (does not apply to all vehicles). Renew pads with new ones immediately (Chapter 9).

## 60 Brake roughness or chatter (pedal pulsates)

1    Excessive lateral runout (Chapter 9).
2    Uneven pad wear (Chapter 9).
3    Defective disc (Chapter 9).

## 61 Excessive brake pedal effort required to stop vehicle

1    Malfunctioning power brake booster (Chapter 9).
2    Partial system failure (Chapter 9).
3    Excessively worn brake pads (Chapter 9).
4    Piston in caliper stuck or sluggish (Chapter 9).
5    Brake pads contaminated with oil or grease (Chapter 9).
6    Brake disc grooved and/or glazed (Chapter 1).
7    New pads fitted and not yet seated. It will take a while for the new material to seat against the disc.

## 62 Excessive brake pedal travel

1    Partial brake system failure (Chapter 9).
2    Insufficient fluid in master cylinder (Chapters 1 and 9).
3    Air trapped in system (Chapters 1 and 9).

## 63 Dragging brakes

1    Incorrect adjustment of brake light switch (Chapter 9).
2    Master cylinder pistons not returning correctly (Chapter 9).
3    Restricted brakes lines or hoses (Chapters 1 and 9).
4    Incorrect parking brake adjustment (Chapter 9).

## 64 Grabbing or uneven braking action

1    Malfunction of proportioning valve (Chapter 9).
2    Malfunction of power brake booster unit (Chapter 9).
3    Binding brake pedal mechanism (Chapter 9).

## 65 Brake pedal feels spongy when depressed

1    Air in hydraulic lines (Chapter 9).
2    Master cylinder mounting bolts loose (Chapter 9).
3    Master cylinder defective (Chapter 9).

## 66 Brake pedal travels to the floor with little resistance

1    Little or no fluid in the master cylinder reservoir caused by leaking caliper piston(s) (Chapter 9).
2    Loose, damaged or disconnected brake lines (Chapter 9).

## 67 Parking brake does not hold

Parking brake linkage improperly adjusted (Chapters 1 and 9).

## Suspension and steering systems

**Note:** *Before attempting to diagnose the suspension and steering systems, perform the following preliminary checks:*
a)  *Tyres for wrong pressure and uneven wear.*
b)  *Steering universal joints from the column to the rack and pinion for loose connectors or wear.*
c)  *Front and rear suspension and the rack and pinion assembly for loose or damaged parts.*
d)  *Out-of-round or out-of-balance tyres, bent rims and loose and/or rough wheel bearings.*

## 68 Vehicle pulls to one side

1    Mismatched or uneven tyres (Chapter 10).
2    Broken or sagging springs (Chapter 10).
3    Wheel alignment out-of-specifications (Chapter 10).
4    Front brake dragging (Chapter 9).

## 69 Abnormal or excessive tyre wear

1    Wheel alignment out-of-specifications (Chapter 10).
2    Sagging or broken springs (Chapter 10).
3    Tyre out-of-balance (Chapter 10).
4    Worn strut damper (Chapter 10).
5    Overloaded vehicle.
6    Tyres not rotated regularly.

## 70 Wheel makes a thumping noise

1    Blister or bump on tyre (Chapter 10).
2    Improper strut damper action (Chapter 10).

## 71 Shimmy, shake or vibration

1    Tyre or wheel out-of-balance or out-of-round (Chapter 10).
2    Loose or worn wheel bearings (Chapters 1, 8 and 10).
3    Worn tie-rod ends (Chapter 10).
4    Worn lower balljoints (Chapters 1 and 10).
5    Excessive wheel runout (Chapter 10).
6    Blister or bump on tyre (Chapter 10).

## 72 Hard steering

1    Lack of lubrication at balljoints, tie-rod ends and rack and pinion assembly (Chapter 10).
2    Front wheel alignment out-of-specifications (Chapter 10).
3    Low tyre pressure(s) (Chapters 1 and 10).

## 73 Poor returnability of steering to centre

1    Lack of lubrication at balljoints and tie-rod ends (Chapter 10).
2    Binding in balljoints (Chapter 10).
3    Binding in steering column (Chapter 10).
4    Lack of lubricant in steering gear assembly (Chapter 10).
5    Front wheel alignment out-of-specifications (Chapter 10).

## 74 Abnormal noise at the front end

1    Lack of lubrication at balljoints and tie-rod ends (Chapters 1 and 10).
2    Damaged strut mounting (Chapter 10).
3    Worn control arm bushes or tie-rod ends (Chapter 10).
4    Loose stabiliser bar (Chapter 10).
5    Loose wheel nuts (Chapters 1 and 10).
6    Loose suspension bolts (Chapter 10).

## 75 Wander or poor steering stability

1    Mismatched or uneven tyres (Chapter 10).
2    Lack of lubrication at balljoints and tie-rod ends (Chapters 1 and 10).
3    Worn strut assemblies (Chapter 10).
4    Loose stabiliser bar (Chapter 10).
5    Broken or sagging springs (Chapter 10).
6    Wheels out of alignment (Chapter 10).

## 76 Erratic steering when braking

1    Wheel bearings worn (Chapter 10).
2    Broken or sagging springs (Chapter 10).
3    Leaking brake caliper (Chapter 10).
4    Warped brake disc (Chapter 10).

## 77  Excessive pitching and/or rolling around corners or during braking

1    Loose stabiliser bar (Chapter 10).
2    Worn strut dampers or mountings (Chapter 10).
3    Broken or sagging springs (Chapter 10).
4    Overloaded vehicle.

## 78  Suspension bottoms

1    Overloaded vehicle.
2    Worn strut dampers (Chapter 10).
3    Incorrect, broken or sagging springs (Chapter 10).

## 79  Cupped tyres

1    Front wheel or rear wheel alignment out-of-specifications (Chapter 10).
2    Worn strut dampers (Chapter 10).
3    Wheel bearings worn (Chapter 10).

4    Excessive tyre or wheel runout (Chapter 10).
5    Worn balljoints (Chapter 10).

## 80  Excessive tyre wear on outside edge

1    Inflation pressures incorrect (Chapter 1).
2    Excessive speed in turns.
3    Front end alignment incorrect (excessive toe-in). Have professionally aligned.
4    Suspension arm bent or twisted (Chapter 10).

## 81  Excessive tyre wear on inside edge

1    Inflation pressures incorrect (Chapter 1).
2    Front end alignment incorrect (toe-out). Have professionally aligned.
3    Loose or damaged steering components (Chapter 10).

## 82  Tyre tread worn in one place

1    Tyres out-of-balance.
2    Damaged or buckled wheel. Inspect and renew if necessary.
3    Defective tyre (Chapter 1).

## 83  Excessive play or looseness in steering system

1    Wheel bearing(s) worn (Chapter 10).
2    Tie-rod end loose (Chapter 10).
3    Steering gear loose (Chapter 10).
4    Worn or loose steering intermediate shaft (Chapter 10).

## 84  Rattling or clicking noise in steering gear

1    Steering gear loose (Chapter 10).
2    Steering gear defective.

# Chapter 1
# Tune-up and routine maintenance

## Contents

## Specifications

### Recommended lubricants and fluids

**Note:** *Listed here are manufacturer recommendations at the time this manual was written. Manufacturers occasionally upgrade their fluid and lubricant specifications, so check with your local auto parts store for current recommendations.*

| | |
|---|---|
| Engine oil | |
| TE/TF/TH and KE/KF/KH models | API grade SH |
| TJ/TL/TW and KJ/KL/KW models | API grade SJ |
| Viscosity | See accompanying chart |
| Automatic transaxle fluid* | |
| TE/TF/TH and KE/KF/KH models 4-speed | Mitsubishi ELC4-SP II automatic transmission fluid |
| TJ/TL/TW and KJ/KL/KW models 4 or 5-speed | Mitsubishi ELC4-SP III automatic transmission fluid |
| Manual transaxle lubricant | SAE 75/85W API GL-5 gear oil |
| Engine coolant | |
| TE/TF/TH/TJ and KE/KF/KH/KJ models | 50/50 mixture of ethylene-glycol-based and demineralised water |
| TL/TW and KL/KW models | 30/50 mixture of Mitsubishi genuine coolant and demineralised water |

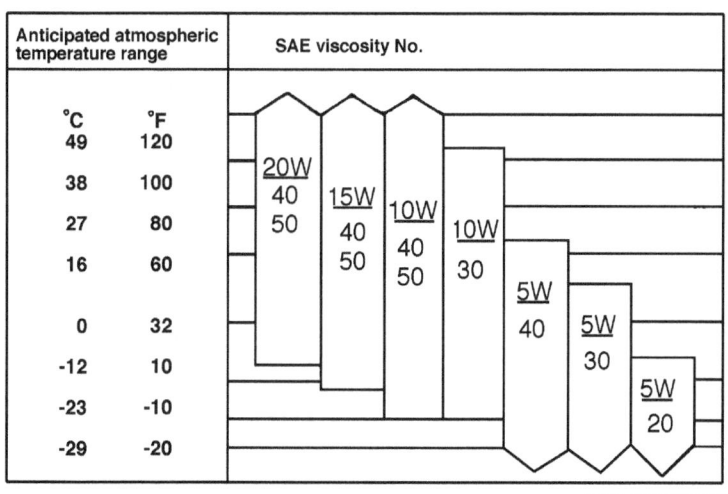

Engine oil viscosity chart - for best fuel economy and cold starting, select the lowest SAE viscosity number for the expected temperature range

68755 CH1 HAYNES

## Recommended lubricants and fluids

| | |
|---|---|
| Brake fluid ............................................................................... | DOT 4 brake fluid |
| Power steering system | |
| TE/TF/TH/TJ and KE/KF/KH/KJ models........................................... | ES-X64022 Type 3 Mitsubishi power steering fluid |
| TL/TW and KL/KW models ............................................................. | Dexron II automatic transmission fluid |
| Rear wheel bearing grease.............................................................. | Multi-purpose, non-melt No. 2 wheel bearing grease |

## Capacities*

| | |
|---|---|
| Engine oil (with filter) | |
| 3.0 litre ............................................................................. | 4.3 litres |
| 3.5 litre ............................................................................. | 4.7 litres |
| Automatic transaxle fluid | |
| Dry refill .......................................................................... | 8.5 litres |
| Service refill..................................................................... | 5.5 litres ** |
| Manual transaxle lubricant ................................................... | 2.8 litres |
| Coolant ................................................................................ | 9.5 litres |

*All capacities approximate. Add as necessary to bring to appropriate level.

** When servicing the transaxle, a further 5.5 litres of fluid is required for flushing.

## Ignition system

| | |
|---|---|
| Spark plug type and gap | |
| 1998 and earlier | |
| NGK | |
| Front bank ................................................................ | BKR6E-11 or equivalent @ 1.0 to 1.1 mm (pre-gapped) |
| Rear bank ................................................................. | PFR6G-11 or equivalent @ 1.0 to 1.1 mm (pre-gapped) |
| Nippon Denso | |
| Front bank ................................................................ | K20P-U11 or equivalent @ 1.0 to 1.1 mm (pre-gapped) |
| Rear bank ................................................................. | PK20PR-11 or equivalent @ 1.0 to 1.1 mm (pre-gapped) |
| 1999 and later | |
| NGK | |
| Front bank ................................................................ | BKR5E-11 or equivalent @ 1.0 to 1.1 mm (pre-gapped) |
| Rear bank ................................................................. | PFR5J-11 or equivalent @ 1.0 to 1.1 mm (pre-gapped) |
| Champion | |
| Front bank ................................................................ | RC10YCC4 or equivalent @ 1.0 to 1.1 mm (pre-gapped) |
| Rear bank ................................................................. | RC10PYP4 or equivalent @ 1.0 to 1.1 mm (pre-gapped) |
| Idle speed | |
| @ 5 degrees BTDC............................................................. | 700 ± 100 rpm |
| @ 15 degrees BTDC........................................................... | 705 rpm |
| A/C idle up ...................................................................... | 900 rpm |
| Ignition timing | |
| 1998 and earlier | |
| Electronic spark timing cut....................................... | 5 degrees + 2 degrees BTDC @ idle |
| With electronic spark timing ..................................... | 15 degrees + 2 degrees BTDC @ idle |
| 1999 and later (Non adjustable) | |
| 3.0 litre ..................................................................... | 15 degrees + 3 degrees BTDC @ idle |
| 3.5 litre ..................................................................... | 10 degrees + 3 degrees BTDC @ idle |
| Firing order ........................................................................ | 1-2-3-4-5-6 |

## Cooling system

| | |
|---|---|
| Thermostat rating | |
| Starts to open .................................................................. | 82 degrees C |
| Fully open......................................................................... | 95 degrees C |

## Drivebelt deflection

| | |
|---|---|
| Alternator and air conditioning | |
| New ................................................................................. | 6.0 to 7.2 mm |
| Used................................................................................. | 8.2 to 9.3 mm |
| Power steering and oil pump | |
| New ................................................................................. | 8.4 to 9.3 mm |
| Used | |
| TE/TF/TH/TJ and KE/KF/KH/KJ models ..................................... | 11.0 to 14.2 mm |
| TL/TW and KL/KW models ........................................................ | 11.7 to 13.4 mm |

68755-1-specs HAYNES

**Cylinder location and distributor rotation**

The blackened terminal shown on the distributor cap indicates the number one spark plug wire position

## Clutch

| | |
|---|---|
| Pedal freeplay at clevis pin.............................................. | 1 to 3 mm |
| Pedal free travel (includes freeplay) ................................... | 6 to 13 mm |

## Brakes

| | |
|---|---|
| Disc brake pad lining thickness (minimum, front and rear) .................... | 1.0 mm |
| Brake pedal freeplay ............................................................. | 3 to 8 mm |

## Steering

| | |
|---|---|
| Steering wheel freeplay limit (engine running)........................................ | 30 mm |

## Torque specifications

| | Nm |
|---|---|
| Alternator | |
|     Fixing bolt ......................................................... | 20 to 25 |
|     Fixing nut .......................................................... | 21 to 30 |
| Automatic transaxle | |
|     Valve body cover bolts.............................................. | 10 to 12 |
|     Drain plug.......................................................... | 30 to 35 |
| Brake caliper guide bolt | |
|     Front ............................................................... | 30 to 40 |
|     Rear................................................................ | 49 to 59 |
| Engine sump drain plug ................................................. | 39 |
| Engine valve cover bolts ............................................... | 3.4 |
| Manual transaxle drain and filler plugs................................ | 32 |
| Spark plugs ........................................................... | 20 to 28 |
| Wheel lug nuts........................................................ | 90 to 110 |

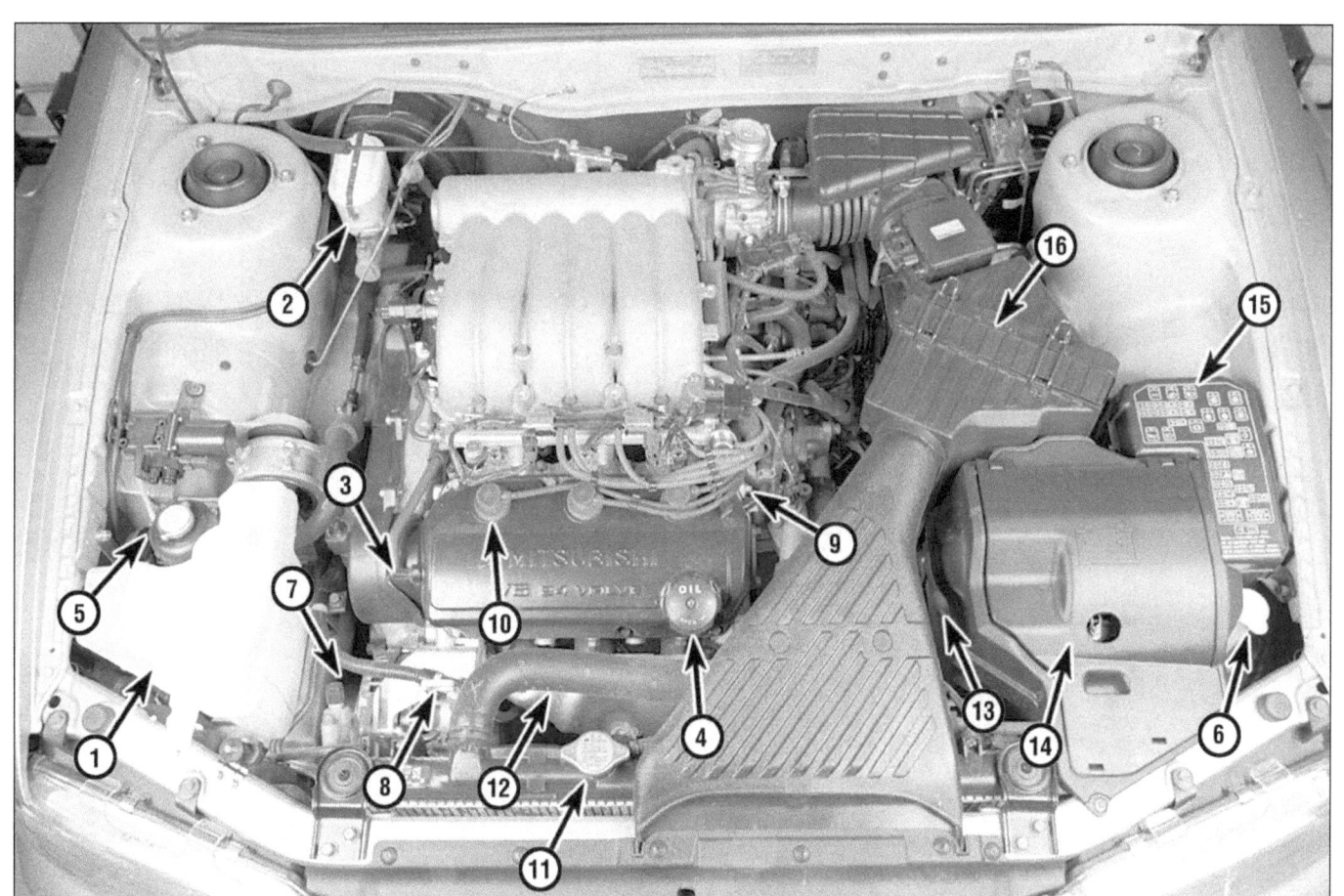

**Typical engine compartment checking points**

| | | | | | |
|---|---|---|---|---|---|
| 1 | Windscreen washer fluid reservoir | 7 | Engine drivebelt | 12 | Radiator hose |
| 2 | Brake master cylinder fluid reservoir | 8 | Engine oil dipstick | 13 | Automatic transaxle fluid dipstick |
| 3 | PCV valve | 9 | Spark plug wire | 14 | Battery |
| 4 | Engine oil filler cap | 10 | Spark plug | 15 | Fuse block |
| 5 | Power steering fluid reservoir | 11 | Radiator cap | 16 | Air cleaner |
| 6 | Coolant reservoir | | | | |

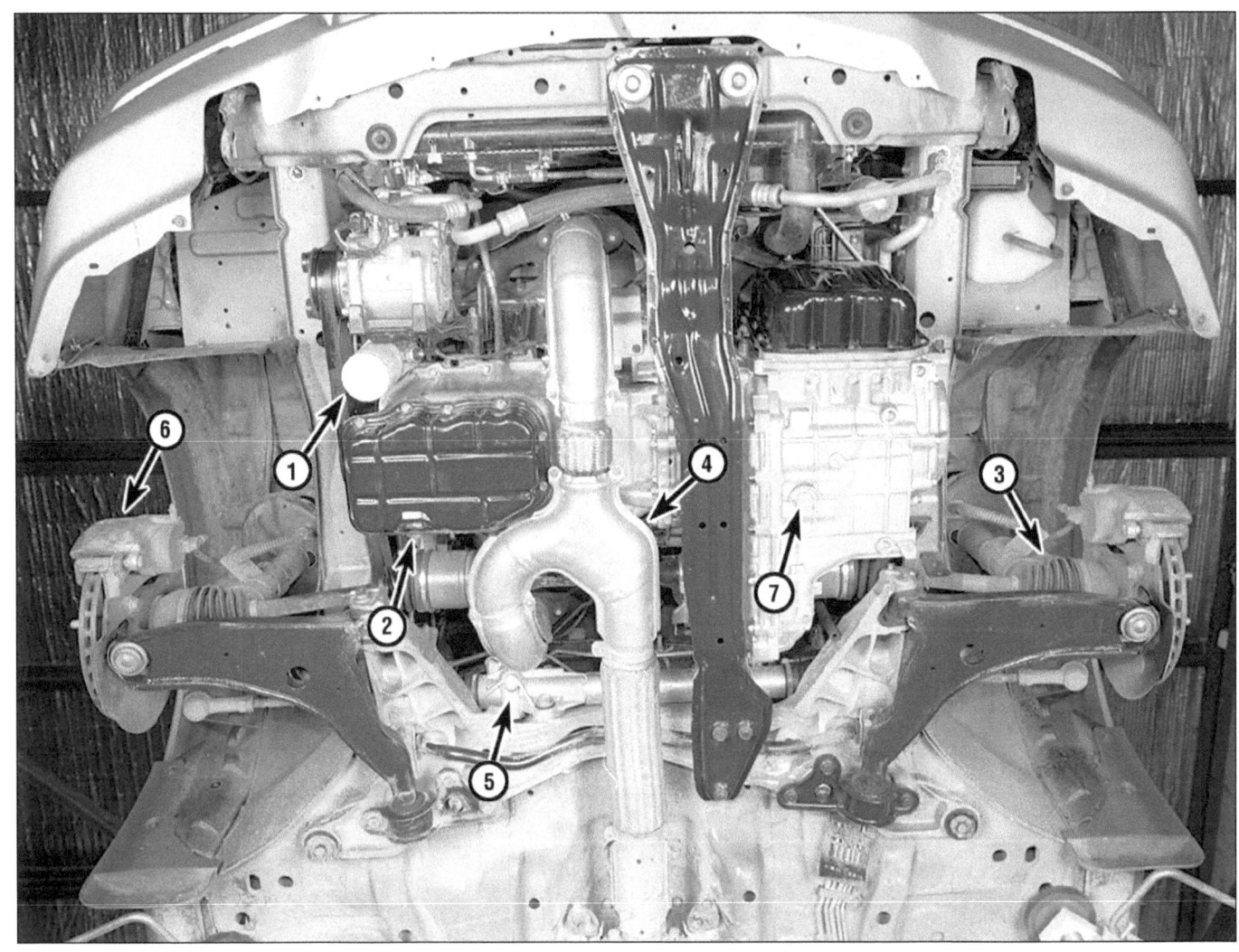

**Typical engine compartment underside checking points**

| | | | | | |
|---|---|---|---|---|---|
| 1 | Engine oil filter | 4 | Exhaust system | 6 | Disc brake caliper |
| 2 | Engine sump drain plug | 5 | Steering gear | 7 | Automatic transaxle drain plug |
| 3 | Driveaxle CV joint boot | | | | |

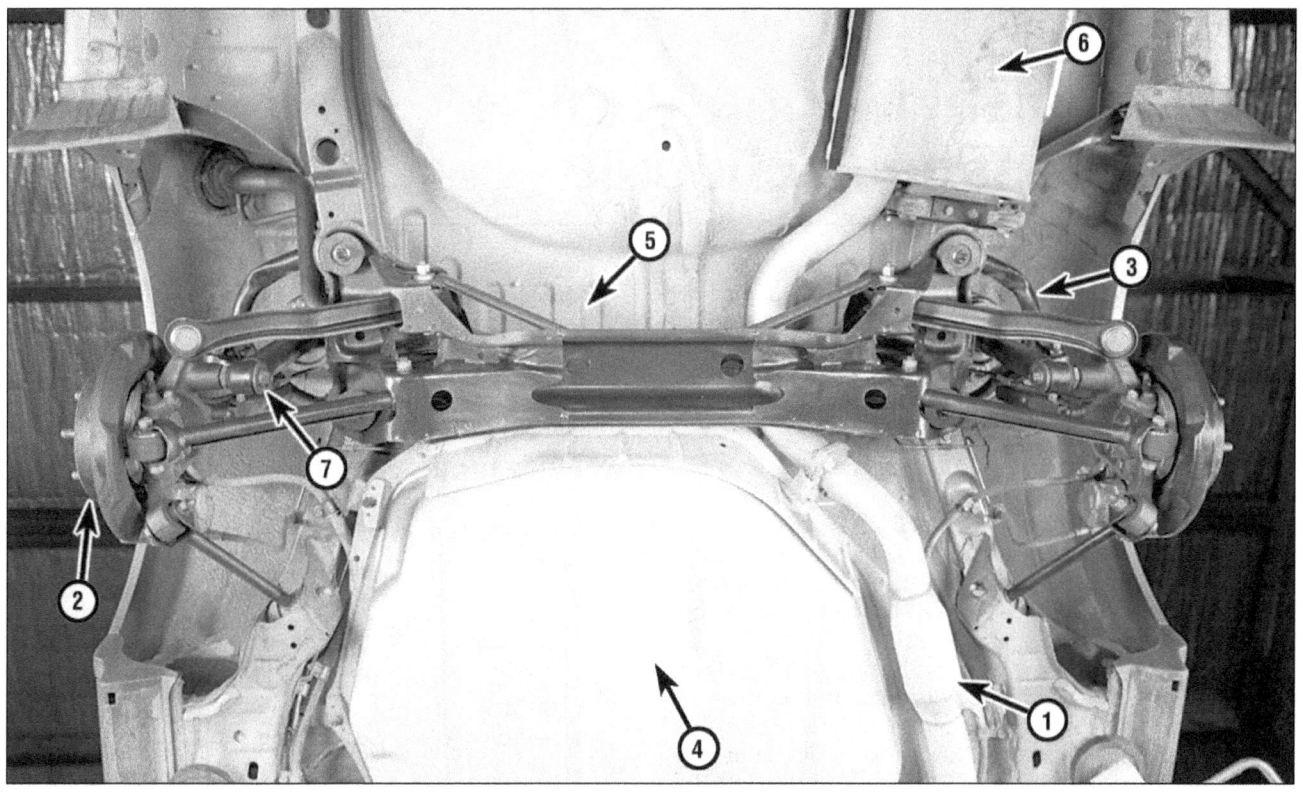

**Typical rear underside components (sedan model)**

| | | | | | | | |
|---|---|---|---|---|---|---|---|
| 1 | Exhaust pipe | 3 | Strut | 5 | Rear axle assembly | 7 | Knuckle assembly |
| 2 | Disc brake | 4 | Fuel tank | 6 | Muffler | | |

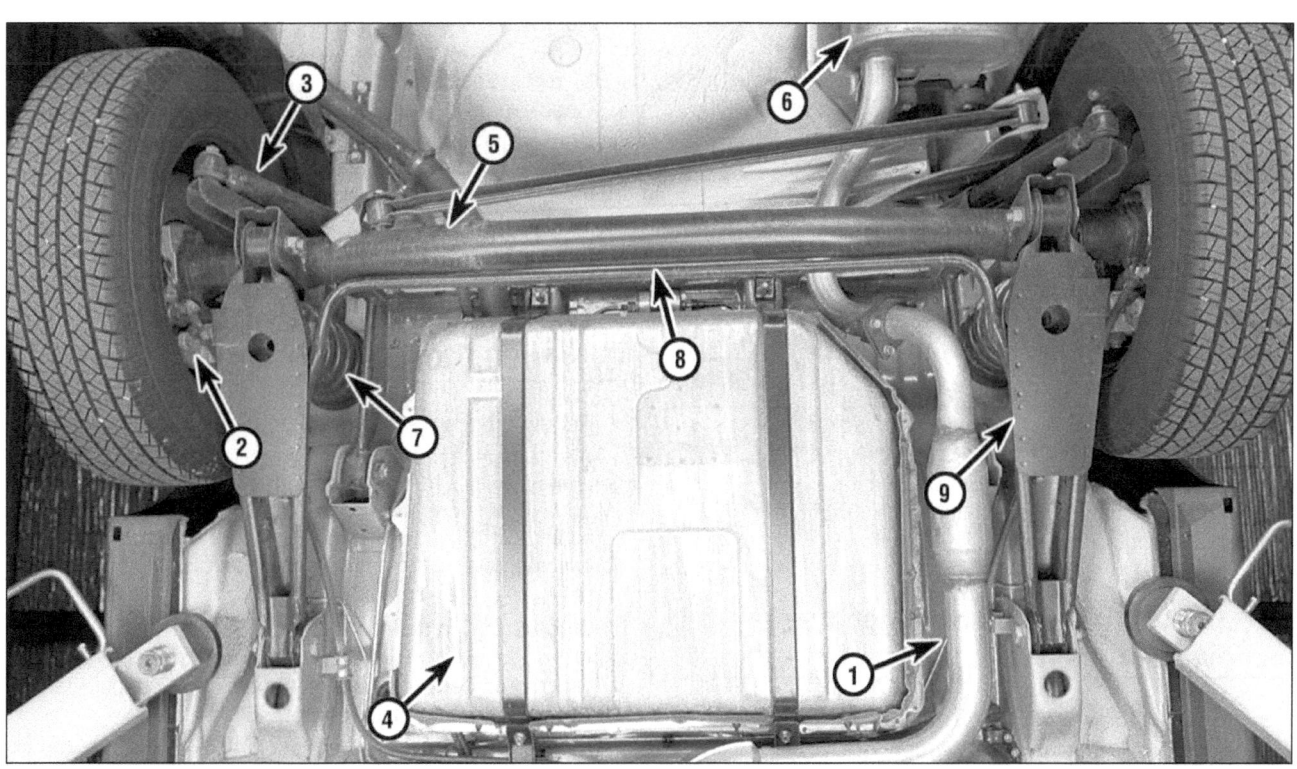

**Typical rear underside components (station wagon model)**

| | | | | | | | |
|---|---|---|---|---|---|---|---|
| 1 | Exhaust pipe | 4 | Fuel tank | 7 | Rear spring |
| 2 | Disc brake | 5 | Rear axle assembly | 8 | Fuel filter |
| 3 | Shock absorber | 6 | Muffler | 9 | Lower control arm |

# 1 Mitsubishi Magna/Verada Maintenance schedule

The following maintenance intervals are based on the assumption that the vehicle owner will be doing the maintenance or service work, as opposed to having a dealer service department do the work. Although the time/distance intervals are loosely based on factory recommendations, most have been shortened to ensure, for example, that such items as filters, lubricants and fluids are checked/changed at intervals that promote maximum engine/driveline service life. Also, subject to the preference of the individual owner interested in keeping his or her vehicle in peak condition at all times, and with the vehicle's ultimate resale in mind, many of the maintenance procedures may be performed more often than recommended in the following schedule. We encourage such owner initiative.

When the vehicle is new it should be serviced initially by a factory authorised dealer service department to protect the factory warranty. In many cases the initial maintenance check is done at no cost to the owner (check with your dealer service department for more information).

## Every 500 kilometres or weekly, whichever comes first

Check the engine oil level (Section 4)
Check the engine coolant level (Section 4)
Check the windscreen washer fluid level (Section 4)
Check the water (electrolyte) in the battery (Section 4)
Check the brake fluid level (Section 4)
Check the clutch fluid level - manual transaxle models (Section 4)
Check the tyres and tyre pressures (Section 5)

## Every 5000 kilometres or 3 months, whichever comes first

*All items listed above plus . . .*
Check the power steering fluid level (Section 6)
Check the automatic transaxle fluid level (Section 7)
Change the engine oil and oil filter (Section 8)

## Every 10,000 kilometres or 6 months, whichever comes first

Inspect/renew the windscreen wiper blades (Section 9)
Check and service the battery (Section 10)
Check/adjust and renew the drivebelts (Section 11)
Inspect/renew all underbonnet hoses (Section 12)
Check the cooling system (Section 13)
Check manual transaxle lubricant level (Section 14)
Rotate the tyres (Section 15)

Inspect the brakes (Section 16)
Inspect steering and suspension components (Section 17)
Inspect the exhaust system (Section 18)
Inspect fuel system components (Section 19)

## Every 20,000 kilometres or 12 months, whichever comes first

*All items listed above plus . . .*
Check/renew the air filter (Section 20)*
Check/adjust the engine idle speed (Section 21)
Check/renew Positive Crankcase Ventilation (PCV) valve (Section 22)
Inspect evaporative emissions control system components (Section 23)
Inspect driveaxle boots (Section 24)*

## Every 40,000 kilometres or 24 months, whichever comes first

Renew the fuel filter (Section 25)
Inspect/renew the spark plug wires, distributor cap and rotor (Section 26)
Check/renew the spark plugs (Section 27)
Check ignition timing (Section 28)
Drain, flush and refill the cooling system (Section 29)
If the vehicle is equipped with an automatic transaxle, change the fluid and filter (Section 30)*
If the vehicle is equipped with a manual transaxle, drain and refill it with new lubricant (Section 31)

## Every 100,000 kilometres

Renew the timing belt (see Chapter 2)

* This item is affected by "severe" operating conditions as described below. If the vehicle in question is operated under "severe" conditions, perform all maintenance indicated with an asterisk (*) at 10,000 kilometres/6 month intervals. Consider the conditions "severe" if most driving is done . . .

In dusty areas
When towing a trailer
At low speeds or with extended periods of engine idling
When outside temperatures remain below freezing and most trips are less than four kilometres

** If most driving is done under one or more of the following conditions, change the automatic transaxle fluid every 20,000 kilometres:

In heavy city traffic where the outside temperature regularly reaches 32-degrees C or higher.

In hilly or mountainous terrain
Frequent trailer pulling

## 2  Introduction

This Chapter is designed to help the home mechanic maintain the Mitsubishi Magna/Verada series front-wheel drive models with the goals of maximum performance, economy, safety and reliability in mind.

Included is a master maintenance schedule, followed by procedures dealing specifically with each item on the schedule. Visual checks, adjustments, component renewal and other helpful items are included. Refer to the accompanying illustrations of the engine compartment and the underside of the vehicle for the locations of various components.

Adhering to the distance/time maintenance schedule and following the step-by-step procedures, which is simply a preventive maintenance program, will result in maximum reliability and vehicle service life. Keep in mind that it is a comprehensive program - maintaining some items but not others at the specified intervals will not produce the same results.

As you service the vehicle, you will discover that many of the procedures can - and should - be grouped together because of the nature of the particular procedure you're performing or because of the close proximity of two otherwise unrelated components to one another.

For example, if the vehicle is raised for chassis lubrication, you should inspect the exhaust, suspension, steering and fuel systems while you're under the vehicle. When you're rotating the tyres, it makes good sense to check the brakes, since the wheels are already removed. Finally, let's suppose you have to borrow or rent a torque wrench. Even if you only need it to tighten the spark plugs, you might as well check the torque of as many critical fasteners as time allows.

The first step in this maintenance program is to prepare yourself before the actual work begins. Read through all the procedures you're planning to do, then gather up all the parts and tools needed. If it looks like you might run into problems during a particular job, seek advice from a mechanic or an experienced do-it-yourselfer.

## 3  Tune-up general information

The term tune-up is used in this manual to represent a combination of individual operations rather than one specific procedure.

If, from the time the vehicle is new, the routine maintenance schedule is followed closely and frequent checks are made of fluid levels and high wear items, as suggested throughout this manual, the engine will be kept in relatively good running condition and the need for additional work will be minimised.

More likely than not, however, there will be times when the engine is running poorly

due to lack of regular maintenance. This is even more likely if a used vehicle, which has not received regular and frequent maintenance checks, is purchased. In such cases, an engine tune-up will be needed outside of the regular routine maintenance intervals.

The first step in any tune-up or diagnostic procedure to help correct a poor running engine is a cylinder compression check (see Chapter 2). This check will help determine the condition of internal engine components and should be used as a guide for tune-up and repair procedures. For instance, if a compression check indicates serious internal engine wear, a conventional tune-up will not improve the performance of the engine and would be a waste of time and money. Because of its importance, the compression check should be done by someone with the right equipment and the knowledge to use it properly.

The following procedures are those most often needed to bring a generally poor running engine back into a proper state of tune.

### *Minor tune-up*

Clean, inspect and test the battery (Section 10)
Check all engine related fluids (Section 4)
Check and adjust the drivebelts (Section 11)
Renew the spark plugs (Section 27)
Inspect the distributor cap and rotor (Section 26)
Inspect the spark plug and coil wires (Section 26)
Inspect the fuel system (Section 19)
Check and adjust the idle speed (Section 21)
Check the ignition timing (Section 28)
Check the PCV valve (Section 22)
Check the air filter (Section 20)
Check the cooling system (Section 13)
Check all underbonnet hoses (Section 12)

### *Major tune-up*

All items listed under Minor tune-up, plus . . .

Check the EGR system (see Chapter 6)
Check the ignition system (see Chapter 5)
Check the charging system (see Chapter 5)

Check the fuel system (see Chapter 4)
Check the evaporative emissions control system (Section 23)
Renew the air filter (Section 20)
Renew the fuel filter (Section 19)
Renew the distributor cap and rotor (Section 26)
Renew the spark plug wires (Section 26)

## 4  Fluid level checks (500 kilometres or weekly)

**Note:** *The following fluid level checks should be done on a 500 kilometre or weekly basis. Additional fluid level checks can be found in specific maintenance procedures which follow. Regardless of intervals, be alert for fluid leaks under the vehicle which would indicate a leak to be fixed immediately.*
**Warning:** *The electric cooling fan can activate at any time, even when the ignition is in the Off position. Disconnect the fan motor or negative battery cable when working in the vicinity of the fan.*
1    Fluids are an essential part of the lubrication, cooling, brake and windscreen washer systems. Because the fluids gradually become depleted and/or contaminated during normal operation of the vehicle, they must be periodically replenished. See Recommended lubricants and fluids at the beginning of this Chapter before adding fluid to any of the following components. **Note:** *The vehicle must be on level ground when fluid levels are checked.*

### *Engine oil*

*Refer to illustrations 4.2, 4.4 and 4.6*
2    The engine oil level is checked with a dipstick located on the side of the engine at the front of the car **(see illustration)**. It extends through a tube and into the sump at the bottom of the engine.
3    The oil level should be checked before the vehicle has been driven, or about 15 minutes after the engine has been shut off. If the oil is checked immediately after driving the vehicle, some of the oil will remain in the upper engine components, resulting in an inaccurate reading on the dipstick.

**4.2 Engine oil dipstick location (arrow)**

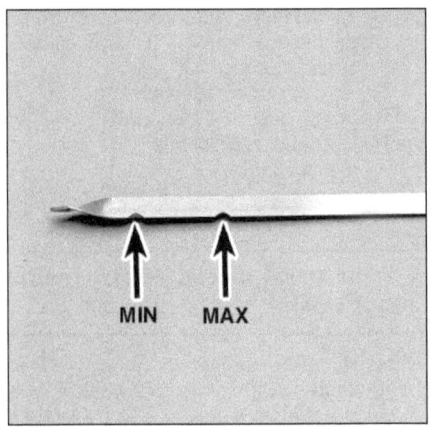

**4.4  The oil level should be between the MIN and MAX marks - if it isn't, add enough oil to bring the level to or near the MAX mark (it takes one full liter to raise the level from the MIN to the MAX)**

**4.6  Rotate the oil filler cap anticlockwise to remove it - always make sure the area around the opening is clean before removing the cap; this prevents dirt from contaminating the engine**

**4.9a  Do not remove the radiator cap when the engine is warm**

4     Pull the dipstick out and wipe all the oil off the end with a clean rag or paper towel. Insert the clean dipstick all the way back into the tube, then pull it out again. Note the oil at the end of the dipstick. Add oil as necessary to keep the level between the MIN mark and the MAX mark on the dipstick **(see illustration)**.
5     Don't overfill the engine by adding too much oil, since it may result in oil fouled spark plugs, oil leaks or oil seal failures.
6     Oil is added to the engine after removing the cap from the valve cover **(see illustration)**. An oil can spout or funnel may help to reduce spills.
7     Checking the oil level is an important preventive maintenance step. A consistently low oil level indicates oil leakage through damaged seals, defective gaskets or past worn rings or valve guides. If the oil looks milky in colour or has water droplets in it, the cylinder head gasket may be blown or the head or block may be cracked. The engine should be checked immediately. The condition of the oil should also be noted. Whenever you check the oil level, slide your thumb and index finger up the dipstick before wiping off the oil. If you see small dirt or metal particles clinging to the dipstick, the oil should be changed (Section 8).

### Engine coolant

*Refer to illustrations 4.9a and 4.9b*
**Warning:** *Do not allow antifreeze to come in contact with your skin or painted surfaces of the vehicle. Flush contaminated areas immediately with plenty of water. Don't store new coolant or leave old coolant lying around where it's accessible to children or pets - they're attracted by its sweet taste. Ingestion of even a small amount of coolant can be fatal! Wipe up garage floor and drip pan coolant spills immediately. Keep antifreeze containers covered and repair leaks in your cooling system as soon as they are noted.*
8     All vehicles covered by this manual are

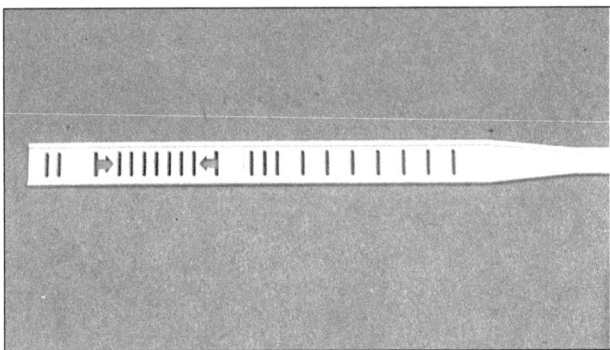

**4.9b  Make sure the coolant level in the reservoir is between the upper and lower marks on the dipstick - if it's below the lower mark, add the prescribed mixture of antifreeze and water until the level is correct**

equipped with a pressurised coolant recovery system. A white plastic coolant reservoir located in the engine compartment is connected by a hose to the radiator filler neck. If the engine overheats, coolant escapes through a valve in the radiator cap and travels through the hose into the reservoir. As the engine cools, the coolant is automatically drawn back into the cooling system to maintain the correct level.
9     The coolant level in the reservoir should be checked regularly. **Warning:** *Do not remove the radiator cap to check the coolant level when the engine is warm* **(see illustration)**. The level in the reservoir varies with the temperature of the engine. When the engine is cold, the coolant level should be at or slightly above the L mark on the reservoir dip stick **(see illustration)**. Once the engine has warmed up, the level should be at or near the F mark. If it isn't, allow the engine to cool, then remove the cap from the reservoir and add a 50/50 mixture of ethylene glycol-based antifreeze and water.
10     Drive the vehicle and recheck the coolant level. If only a small amount of coolant is required to bring the system up to the proper level, water can be used. However, repeated additions of water will dilute the antifreeze and water solution. In order to maintain the proper ratio of antifreeze and water, always top up the coolant level with the correct mixture. An empty plastic bottle makes an excel-

lent container for mixing coolant. Do not use additional rust inhibitors or additives, they are already in the antifreeze.
11     If the coolant level drops consistently, there may be a leak in the system. Inspect the radiator, hoses, filler cap, drain plugs and water pump (see Section 13). If no leaks are noted, have the radiator cap pressure tested by a service station.
12     If you have to remove the radiator cap **(see illustration 4.9a)**, wait until the engine has cooled, then wrap a thick cloth around the cap and turn it to the first stop. If coolant or steam escapes, let the engine cool down longer, then remove the cap.
13     Check the condition of the coolant as well. It should be relatively clear. If it's brown or rust coloured, the system should be drained, flushed and refilled. Even if the coolant appears to be normal, the corrosion inhibitors wear out, so it must be renewed at the specified intervals.

### Windscreen washer fluid

*Refer to illustration 4.14*
14     Fluid for the windscreen washer system is located in a plastic reservoir in the engine compartment **(see illustration)**. On station wagon models the rear wiper washer is supplied from the same tank.
15     In milder climates, plain water can be used in the reservoir, but it should be kept no more than 2/3 full to allow for expansion if the

**4.14 The windscreen washer fluid reservoir is located on the drivers side fender - open the cap and fill the reservoir to the full mark**

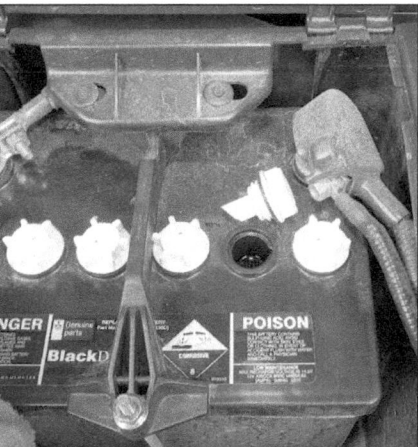

**4.19 Remove the cell caps to check the electrolyte (water) level in the battery - if the level is low, add distilled water only**

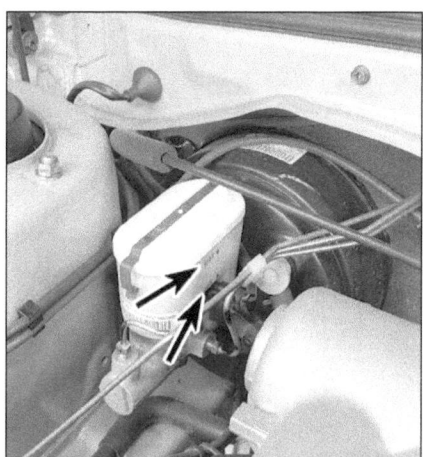

**4.21 The brake master cylinder is mounted on the front of the power booster - the brake fluid level should be between the MIN and MAX marks (don't let it drop below MIN)**

water freezes. In colder climates, use windscreen washer system antifreeze, available at any auto parts store, to lower the freezing point of the fluid. Mix the antifreeze with water in accordance with the manufacturer's directions on the container. **Caution:** *Don't use cooling system antifreeze - it will damage the vehicle's paint.*

16    To help prevent icing in cold weather, warm the windscreen with the defroster before using the washer.

### Battery electrolyte

*Refer to illustration 4.19*

**Warning:** *Certain precautions must be followed when checking or servicing a battery. Hydrogen gas, which is highly flammable, is produced in the cells, so keep lighted tobacco, open flames, bare light bulbs and sparks away from the battery. The electrolyte inside the battery is dilute sulfuric acid, which can burn skin and cause serious injury if splashed in your eyes (wear safety glasses). It'll also ruin clothes and painted surfaces. Remove all metal jewelry which could contact the positive battery terminal and a grounded metal source, causing a direct short.*

17    Vehicles equipped with a maintenance-free battery require no maintenance - the battery case is sealed and has no removable caps for adding water.

18    If a maintenance-type battery is refitted, the caps on top of the battery should be removed periodically to check for a low electrolyte level. This check is more critical during warm summer months.

19    Remove each of the caps and add distilled water to bring the level in each cell to the split ring in the filler opening **(see illustration)**.

20    At the same time, the battery water level is checked, the overall condition of the battery and related components should be noted. See Section 10 for the complete battery check and maintenance procedures.

### Brake and clutch fluid

*Refer to illustration 4.21*

21    The brake master cylinder is mounted on the front of the power booster unit in the engine compartment **(see illustration)**. The clutch master cylinder (used on manual transaxle-equipped models) is located next to the power booster unit. Clutch fluid level is checked in the same manner as brake fluid.

22    The fluid inside is readily visible. The level should be between the MIN and MAX marks on the reservoir. If a low level is indicated, be sure to wipe the top of the reservoir cover with a clean rag to prevent contamination of the brake system before removing the cover.

23    When adding fluid, pour it carefully into the reservoir to avoid spilling it onto surrounding painted surfaces. Be sure the specified fluid is used, since mixing different types of brake fluid can cause damage to the system. See Recommended lubricants and fluids at the front of this Chapter or your owner's manual. **Warning:** B*rake fluid can harm your eyes and damage painted surfaces, so use extreme caution when handling or pouring it. Do not use brake fluid that has been standing open or is more than one year old. Brake fluid absorbs moisture from the air. Excess moisture can cause a dangerous loss of braking effectiveness.*

24    At this time the fluid and master cylinder can be inspected for contamination. The system should be drained and refilled if deposits, dirt particles or water droplets are seen in the fluid (see Section 4).

25    After filling the reservoir to the proper level, make sure the cover is on tight to prevent fluid leakage.

26    The brake fluid level in the master cylinder will drop slightly as the pads and the brake shoes at each wheel wear down during normal operation. If the master cylinder requires repeated additions to keep it at the proper level, it's an indication of leakage in the brake system, which should be corrected immediately. Check all brake lines and con-

nections (see Section 16 for more information).

27    If, upon checking the master cylinder fluid level, you discover the reservoir empty or nearly empty, the brake system should be bled (see Chapter 9).

---

**5    Tyre and tyre pressure checks (500 kilometres or weekly)**

---

*Refer to illustrations 5.2, 5.3, 5.4a, 5.4b and 5.8*

1    Periodic inspection of the tyres may spare you the inconvenience of being stranded with a flat tyre. It can also provide you with vital information regarding possible problems in the steering and suspension systems before major damage occurs.

2    The original tyres on this vehicle are equipped with 12.7 mm side bands that will

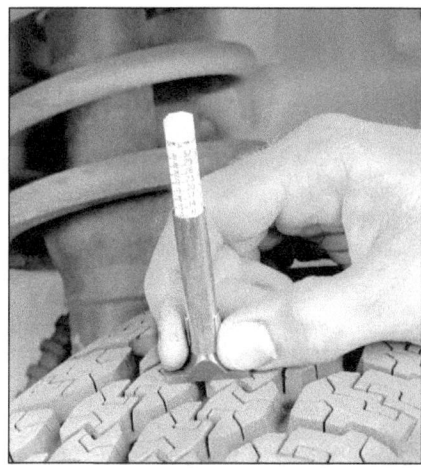

**5.2 Use a tyre tread depth indicator to monitor tyre wear - they are available at auto parts stores and service stations and cost very little**

UNDERINFLATION

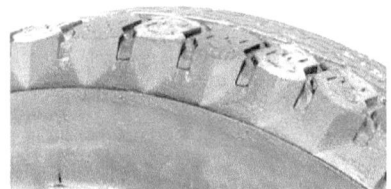

CUPPING

Cupping may be caused by:
- Underinflation and/or mechanical irregularities such as out-of-balance condition of wheel and/or tyre, and bent or damaged wheel.
- Loose or worn steering tie-rod or steering idler arm.
- Loose, damaged or worn front suspension parts.

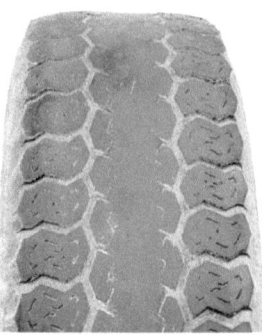

OVERINFLATION

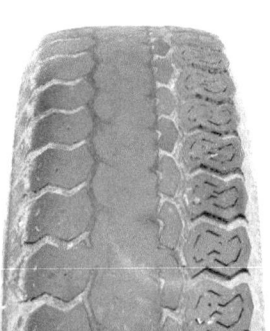

INCORRECT TOE-IN
OR EXTREME CAMBER

FEATHERING DUE
TO MISALIGNMENT

**5.3  This chart will help you determine the condition of the tyres, the probable cause(s) of abnormal wear and the corrective action necessary**

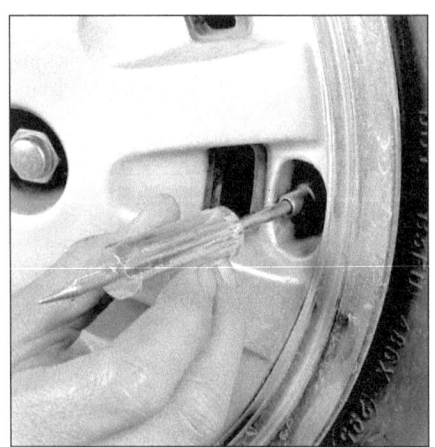

**5.4a  If a tyre loses air on a steady basis, check the valve core first to make sure it's snug (special inexpensive tools are commonly available at auto parts stores)**

**5.4b  If the valve core is tight, raise the corner of the vehicle with the low tyre and spray a soapy water solution onto the tread as the tyre is turned slowly - leaks will cause small bubbles to appear**

appear when tread depth reaches 1.6 mm, but they don't appear until the tyres are worn out. Tread wear can be monitored with a simple, inexpensive device known as a tread depth indicator **(see illustration)**.

3    Note any abnormal tread wear **(see illustration)**. Tread pattern irregularities such as cupping, flat spots and more wear on one side than the other are indications of front end alignment and/or balance problems. If any of these conditions are noted, take the

vehicle to a tyre shop or service station to correct the problem.

4    Look closely for cuts, punctures and embedded nails or tacks. Sometimes a tyre will hold air pressure for a short time or leak down very slowly after a nail has embedded itself in the tread. If a slow leak persists, check the valve stem core to make sure it's tight **(see illustration)**. Examine the tread for an object that may have embedded itself in

the tyre or for a "plug" that may have begun to leak (radial tyre punctures are repaired with a plug that's refitted in a puncture). If a puncture is suspected, it can be easily verified by spraying a solution of soapy water onto the suspected area **(see illustration)**. The soapy solution will bubble if there's a leak. Unless the puncture is unusually large, a tyre shop or service station can usually repair the tyre.

5    Carefully inspect the inner sidewall of each tyre for evidence of brake fluid. If you see any, inspect the brakes immediately.

6    Correct air pressure increases the lifespan of the tyres, improves fuel economy and enhances overall ride quality. Tyre pressure cannot be accurately estimated by looking at a tyre, especially if it's a radial. A tyre pressure gauge is essential. Keep an accurate gauge in the vehicle. The pressure gauges attached to the nozzles of air hoses at petrol stations are often inaccurate.

7    Always check tyre pressure when the tyres are cold. Cold, in this case, means the vehicle has not been driven over a kilometre in the three hours preceding a tyre pressure check. A pressure rise of 27.5 to 55 kPa is not uncommon once the tyres are warm.

8    Unthread the valve cap protruding from the wheel or hubcap and push the gauge firmly onto the valve stem **(see illustration)**. Note the reading on the gauge and compare

**5.8 To extend the life of the tyres, check the air pressure at least once a week with an accurate gauge (don't forget the spare!)**

the figure to the recommended tyre pressure shown on the label attached to the inside of the glove compartment door. Be sure to refit the valve cap to keep dirt and moisture out of the valve stem mechanism. Check all four tyres and, if necessary, add enough air to bring them up to the recommended pressure.

9    Don't forget to keep the spare tyre inflated to the specified pressure (refer to your owner's manual or the tyre sidewall).

## 6    Power steering fluid level check (every 5000 kilometres or 3 months)

*Refer to illustrations 6.2 and 6.6*
**Warning:** *The electric cooling fan can activate at any time, even when the ignition is in the Off position. Disconnect the fan motor or negative battery cable when working in the vicinity of the fan.*

1    Unlike manual steering, the power steering system relies on fluid which may, over a period of time, require replenishing.
2    The fluid reservoir for the power steering pump is located on the drivers side inner fender panel next to the windscreen washer fluid tank. **(see illustration)**.
3    For the check, the front wheels should be pointed straight ahead and the engine should be off.
4    Use a clean rag to wipe off the reservoir cap and the area around the cap. This will help prevent any foreign matter from entering the reservoir during the check.
5    Remove the cap and note the dipstick attached to it.
6    Wipe off the fluid with a clean rag, reinsert the dipstick, then withdraw it and read the fluid level. The level should be between the MIN and MAX marks **(see illustration)**. Never allow the fluid level to drop below the MIN mark.
7    If additional fluid is required, pour the specified type directly into the reservoir,

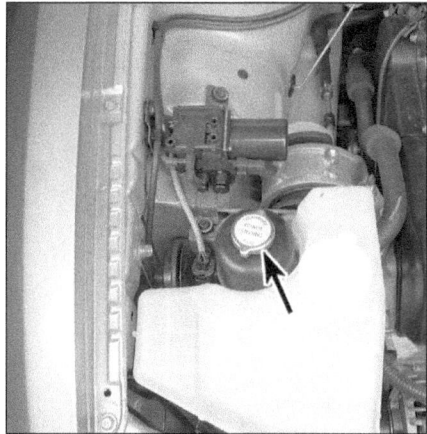

**6.2 The power steering fluid filler cap/ dipstick is located on the drivers side inner fender panel next to the windscreen washer fluid tank (arrow) - unthread the cap to check the dipstick and/or add fluid**

using a funnel to prevent spills.
8    If the reservoir requires frequent fluid additions, all power steering hoses, hose connections and the power steering pump should be carefully checked for leaks.

## 7    Automatic transaxle fluid level check (every 5000 kilometres or 3 months)

*Refer to illustrations 7.4 and 7.6*
**Warning:** *The electric cooling fan can activate at any time, even when the ignition is in the Off position. Disconnect the fan motor or negative battery cable when working in the vicinity of the fan.*

1    The level of the automatic transaxle fluid should be carefully maintained. Low fluid level can lead to slipping or loss of drive, while overfilling can cause foaming, loss of fluid and transaxle damage.
2    The transaxle fluid level should only be checked when the engine is at normal oper-

**7.4 The automatic transaxle fluid dipstick (arrow) is located under the air inlet**

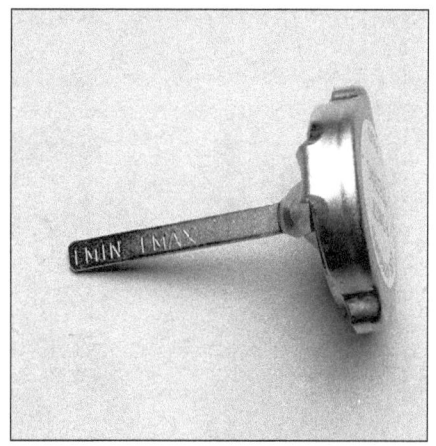

**6.6 The power steering fluid level should be kept between the MIN and MAX lines on the dipstick**

ating temperature. **Caution:** *If the vehicle has just been driven for a long time at high speed or in city traffic in hot weather, or if it has been pulling a trailer, an accurate fluid level reading cannot be obtained. Allow the fluid to cool down for about 30 minutes.*
3    Park on level ground, apply the parking brake and start the engine. While the engine is idling, depress the brake pedal and move the selector lever through all the gear ranges, beginning and ending in Neutral.
4    With the engine still idling, remove the dipstick **(see illustration)**.
5    Wipe the fluid off the dipstick with a clean rag and reinsert it until the cap seats.
6    Pull the dipstick out again. The fluid level should be in the HOT range **(see illustration)**. If the level is at the low side of the range, add the specified automatic transmission fluid through the dipstick tube with a funnel.
7    Add the fluid a little at a time and keep checking the level until it's correct.
8    The condition of the fluid should also be checked along with the level. If the fluid at the end of the dipstick is black or a dark reddish-brown colour, or if it smells burned, the fluid

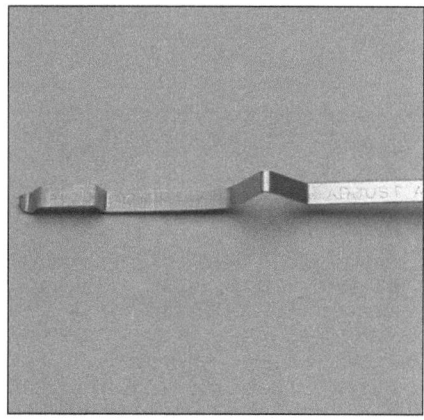

**7.6 Check the fluid with the transaxle at normal operating temperature - the level should be kept in the HOT range (between the two lines)**

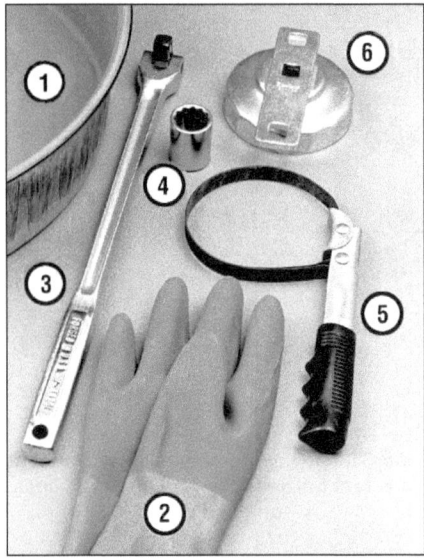

**8.3 These tools are required when changing the engine oil and filter**

1   *Drain pan* - It should be fairly shallow in depth, but wide to prevent spills
2   *Rubber gloves* - When removing the drain plug and filter, you will get oil on your hands (the gloves will prevent burns)
3   *Breaker bar* - Sometimes the oil drain plug is tight and a long breaker bar is needed to loosen it
4   *Socket* - To be used with the breaker bar or a ratchet (must be the correct size to fit the drain plug - six-point preferred)
5   *Filter wrench* - This is a metal band-type wrench, which requires clearance around the filter to be effective
6   *Filter wrench* - This type fits on the bottom of the filter and can be turned with a ratchet or breaker bar (different size spanners are available for different types of filters)

should be changed (Section 31). If you're in doubt about the condition of the fluid, purchase some new fluid and compare the two for colour and odor.

---

**8   Engine oil and filter change (every 5000 kilometres or 3 months)**

---

*Refer to illustrations 8.3, 8.9, 8.14 and 8.18*
1   Frequent oil changes are the most important preventive maintenance procedures that can be done by the home mechanic. As engine oil ages, it becomes diluted and contaminated, which leads to premature engine wear.
2   Although some sources recommend oil filter changes every other oil change, a new filter should be refitted every time the oil is changed.
3   Gather together all necessary tools and

**8.9 Use the proper size box-end spanner or six-point socket to remove the oil drain plug to avoid rounding it off**

materials before beginning this procedure **(see illustration)**.
4   You should have plenty of clean rags and newspapers handy to mop up any spills. Access to the underside of the vehicle is greatly improved if the vehicle can be lifted on a hoist, driven onto ramps or supported by jackstands. **Warning:** *Do not work under a vehicle which is supported only by a bumper, hydraulic or scissors-type jack.*
5   If this is your first oil change, get under the vehicle and familiarise yourself with the locations of the oil drain plug and the oil filter. The engine and exhaust components will be warm during the actual work, so note how they are situated to avoid touching them when working under the vehicle.
6   Warm the engine to normal operating temperature. If the new oil or any tools are needed, use this warm-up time to gather everything necessary for the job. Refer to Recommended lubricants and fluids at the beginning of this Chapter for the type of oil required.
7   With the engine oil warm (warm engine oil will drain better and more built-up sludge will be removed with it), raise and support the vehicle. Make sure it's safely supported!
8   Move all necessary tools, rags and newspapers under the vehicle. Set the drain pan under the drain plug. Keep in mind that the oil will initially flow from the pan with some force; position the pan accordingly.
9   Being careful not to touch any of the hot exhaust components, use a spanner to remove the drain plug near the bottom of the sump **(see illustration)**. Depending on how hot the oil is, you may want to wear gloves while unthreading the plug the final few turns.
10   Allow the old oil to drain into the pan. It may be necessary to move the pan as the oil flow slows to a trickle.
11   After all the oil has drained, wipe off the drain plug with a clean rag. Small metal particles may cling to the plug and would immediately contaminate the new oil.
12   Clean the area around the drain plug opening and refit the plug. Tighten it securely

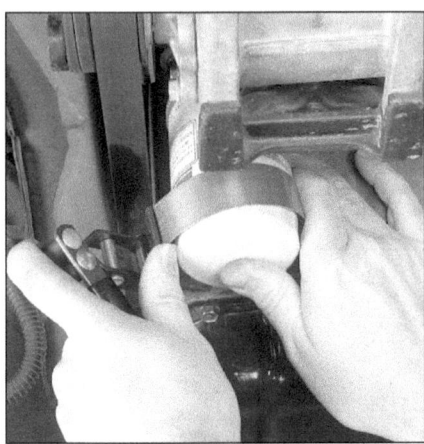

**8.14 The oil filter is usually on very tight and will require a special spanner for removal - DO NOT use the spanner to tighten the new filter**

with the spanner. If a torque wrench is available, use it to tighten the plug.
13   Move the drain pan into position under the oil filter.
14   Use the filter wrench to loosen the oil filter **(see illustration)**. Chain or metal band filter wrenches may distort the filter canister, but it doesn't matter since the filter will be discarded anyway.
15   Completely unthread the old filter. Be careful; it's full of oil. Empty the oil inside the filter into the drain pan.
16   Compare the old filter with the new one to make sure they're the same type.
17   Use a clean rag to remove all oil, dirt and sludge from the area where the oil filter mounts to the engine.
18   Apply a light coat of clean oil to the rubber gasket on the new oil filter **(see illustration)**.
19   Attach the new filter to the engine, following the tightening directions printed on the filter canister or packing box. Most filter manufacturers recommend against using a spanner due to the possibility of over-tightening the filter and damaging the seal.

**8.18 Lubricate the oil filter gasket with clean engine oil before refitting the filter on the engine**

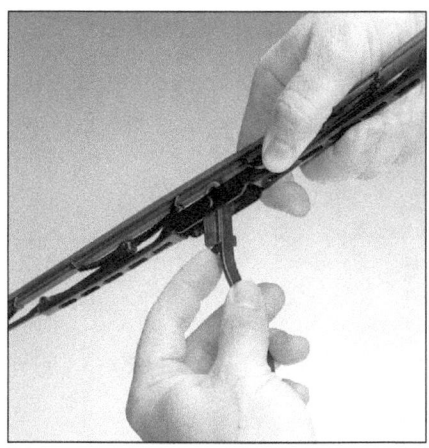

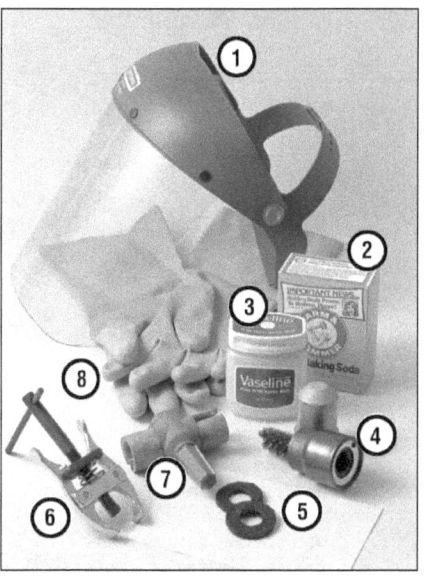

**9.5  Rotate the wiper blade away from the windscreen and depress the locking tab then slide the blade down and away from the arm**

**9.6  Use small screwdriver to prise the blade retaining clip from the end of the wiper arm, then slide the insert out of the wiper arm**

**10.1  Tools and materials required for battery maintenance**

20   Remove all tools, rags, etc. from under the vehicle, being careful not to spill the oil in the drain pan, then lower the vehicle.
21   Move to the engine compartment and locate the oil filler cap.
22   Pour the fresh oil through the filler opening into the engine. A funnel should be used to prevent spills.
23   Pour four litres of fresh oil into the engine. Wait a few minutes to allow the oil to drain into the pan, then check the level on the oil dipstick (see Section 4 if necessary). If the oil level is above the MIN mark, start the engine and allow the new oil to circulate.
24   Run the engine for only about a minute and then shut it off. Immediately look under the vehicle and check for leaks at the sump drain plug and around the oil filter. If either is leaking, tighten with a bit more force.
25   With the new oil circulated and the filter now completely full, recheck the level on the dipstick and add more oil as necessary.
26   During the first few trips after an oil change, make it a point to check frequently for leaks and proper oil level.
27   The old oil drained from the engine cannot be reused in its present state and should be disposed of. Oil reclamation centres, auto repair shops and petrol stations will normally accept the oil, which can be refined and used again. After the oil has cooled it can be drained into a container (capped plastic jugs, topped bottles, milk cartons, etc.) for transport to a disposal site.

---

**9    Windscreen wiper blade inspection and renewal (every 10,000 kilometres or 6 months)**

*Refer to illustrations 9.5 and 9.6*
1    The windscreen wiper and blade assembly should be inspected periodically for damage, loose components and cracked or worn blade elements.
2    Road film can build up on the wiper

blades and affect their efficiency, so they should be washed regularly with a mild detergent solution.
3    The action of the wiping mechanism can loosen bolts, nuts and fasteners, so they should be checked and tightened, as necessary, at the same time the wiper blades are checked.
4    If the wiper blade elements are cracked, worn or warped, or no longer clean adequately, they should be renewed with new ones.
5    Lift the arm assembly away from the glass for clearance and detach the blade assembly from the arm **(see illustration)**.
6    Remove the lock tabs on the end of the wiper and slide the insert out **(see illustration)**.
7    Slide the new insert into place until the locking tab can be snapped over the end of the insert.

---

**10   Battery check, maintenance and charging (every 10,000 kilometres or 6 months)**

*Refer to illustrations 10.1, 10.5, 10.6a, 10.6b, 10.6c and 10.7*
**Warning:** *Certain precautions must be followed when checking and servicing the battery. Hydrogen gas, which is highly flammable, is always present in the battery cells, so keep lighted tobacco and all other open flames and sparks away from the battery. The electrolyte inside the battery is actually dilute sulfuric acid, which will cause injury if splashed on your skin or in your eyes. It will also ruin clothes and painted surfaces. When removing the battery cables, always detach the negative cable first and hook it up last!*

*Check and maintenance*
1    Battery maintenance is an important procedure which will help ensure that you aren't stranded because of a dead battery.

1    *Face shield/safety goggles* - When removing corrosion with a brush, the acidic particles can easily fly up into your eyes
2    *Baking soda -* A solution of baking soda and water can be used to neutralise corrosion
3    *Petroleum jelly* - A layer of this on the battery posts will help prevent corrosion
4    *Battery post/cable cleaner -* This wire brush cleaning tool will remove all traces of corrosion from the battery posts and cable clamps
5    *Treated felt washers* - Placing one of these on each post, directly under the cable clamps, will help prevent corrosion
6    *Puller -* Sometimes the cable clamps are very difficult to pull off the posts, even after the nut/bolt has been completely loosened. This tool pulls the clamp straight up and off the post without damage.
7    *Battery post/cable cleaner -* Here is another cleaning tool which is a slightly different version of number 4 above, but it does the same thing
8    *Rubber gloves* - Another safety item to consider when servicing the battery; remember that's acid inside the battery!

Several tools are required for this procedure **(see illustration)**.
2    When checking/servicing the battery, always turn the engine and all accessories off.
3    Remove the caps and check the electrolyte (water) level in each of the battery cells (see Section 4). It must be above the plates. There's usually a split-ring indicator in each cell to indicate the correct level. If the level is low, add distilled water only, then refit the cell caps. **Caution:** *Overfilling the cells may cause electrolyte to spill over during periods*

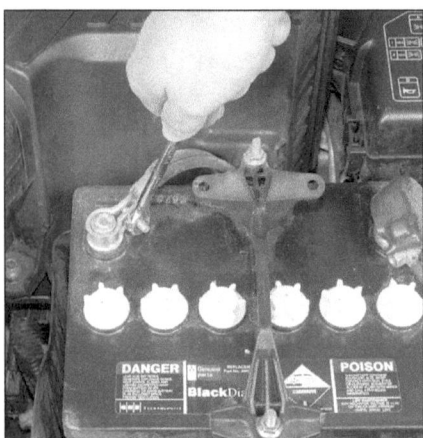

**10.5  Use a spanner to check the tightness of the battery cable bolts; when removing corroded bolts, it may be necessary to use special battery pliers**

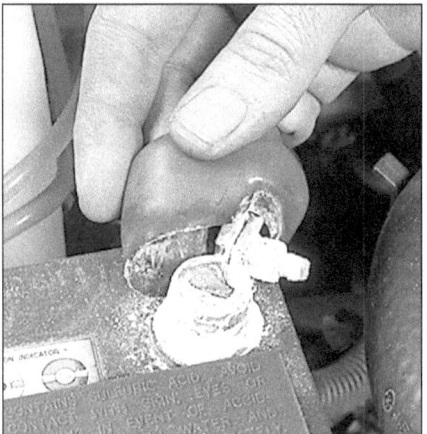

**10.6a  Battery terminal corrosion**

**10.6b  When cleaning the cable clamps, all corrosion must be removed (the inside of the clamp is tapered to match the taper on the post, so don't remove too much material)**

**10.6c  Regardless of the type of tool used on the battery posts, a clean, shiny surface should be the result**

**10.7  Make sure the battery hold-down nuts (arrows) are tight**

of heavy charging, causing corrosion and damage to nearby components.

4    The external condition of the battery should be checked periodically. Look for damage such as a cracked case.

5    Check the tightness of the battery cable bolts **(see illustration)** to ensure good electrical connections. Inspect the entire length of each cable, looking for cracked or abraded insulation and frayed conductors.

6    If corrosion (visible as white, fluffy deposits) **(see illustration)** is evident, remove the cables from the terminals, clean them with a battery brush and refit them **(see illustrations)**. Corrosion can be kept to a minimum by applying a layer of petroleum jelly or grease to the terminals.

7    Make sure the battery carrier is in good condition and the hold-down clamp is tight **(see illustration)**. If the battery is removed (see Chapter 5 for the removal and refitting procedure), make sure that no parts remain in the bottom of the carrier when it's refitted. When refitting the hold-down clamp, don't over-tighten the nuts.

8    Corrosion on the carrier, battery case and surrounding areas can be removed with a solution of water and baking soda. Apply the mixture with a small brush, let it work, then rinse it off with plenty of clean water.

9    Any metal parts of the vehicle damaged by corrosion should be coated with a zinc-based primer, then painted.

### Charging

10    Remove all of the cell caps (if equipped) and cover the holes with a clean cloth to prevent spattering electrolyte. Disconnect the negative battery cable and hook the battery charger leads to the battery posts (positive to positive, negative to negative), then plug in the charger. Make sure it is set at 12 volts if it has a selector switch.

11    If you're using a charger with a rate higher than two amps, check the battery regularly during charging to make sure it doesn't overheat. If you're using a trickle charger, you

can safely let the battery charge overnight after you've checked it regularly for the first couple of hours.

12    Remove the cell caps and measure the specific gravity with a hydrometer every hour during the last few hours of the charging cycle. Hydrometers are available inexpensively from auto parts stores - follow the instructions that come with the hydrometer. Consider the battery charged when there's no change in the specific gravity reading for two hours and the electrolyte in the cells is gassing (bubbling) freely. The specific gravity reading from each cell should be very close to the others. If not, the battery probably has a bad cell(s).

13    A sealed (sometimes called maintenance-free) battery may have been refitted. The cell caps on this type of battery cannot be removed. No electrolyte checks are required and water cannot be added to the cells.

14    Some batteries with sealed tops have built-in hydrometers on the top that indicate the state of charge by the colour displayed in the hydrometer window. Normally, a bright-coloured hydrometer indicates a full charge and a dark hydrometer indicates the battery still needs charging. Check the battery manu-

facturer's instructions to be sure you know what the colours mean.

15    If the battery has a sealed top and no built-in hydrometer, you can hook up a voltmeter across the battery terminals to check the charge. A fully charged battery should read 12.6 volts or higher.

---

### 11   Drivebelt check, adjustment and renewal (every 10,000 kilometres or 6 months)

---

*Refer to illustrations 11.3a, 11.3b, 11.4, 11.6a and 11.6b*

### Check

1    The drivebelts are either V-belts or V-ribbed belts. The alternator, power steering (if equipped) and air conditioner (if equipped) drivebelts are located at the front of the engine. The good condition and proper adjustment of the belts is critical to the operation of the engine. Because of their composition and the high stresses to which they are

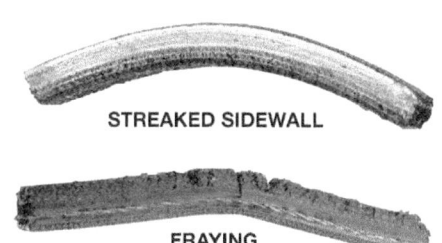

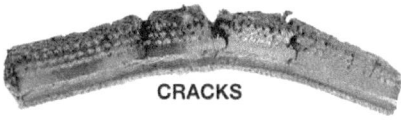

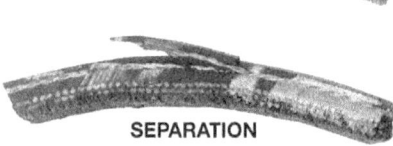

STREAKED SIDEWALL

FRAYING

CRACKS

SEPARATION

GLAZING

OIL SOAKED

TENSILE BREAK

**11.3a Here are some of the more common problems associated with drivebelts (check the belts very carefully to prevent an untimely breakdown)**

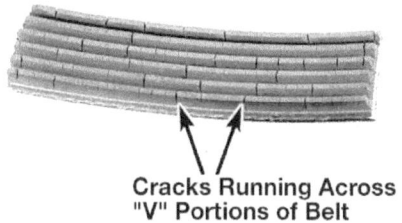

**ACCEPTABLE**

Cracks Running Across "V" Portions of Belt

**UNACCEPTABLE**

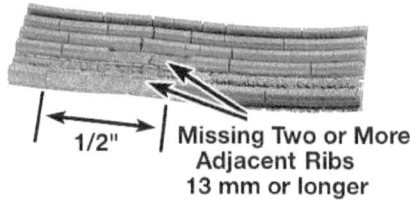

1/2"    Missing Two or More Adjacent Ribs 13 mm or longer

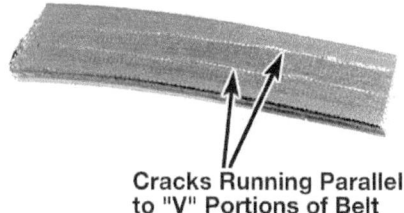

Cracks Running Parallel to "V" Portions of Belt

**11.3b Check V-ribbed belts for signs of wear like these - if the belt looks worn, renew it**

**11.4 Measuring drivebelt deflection with a straightedge and ruler**

**11.6a Alternator/air conditioning drivebelt adjustment details**

A    Lock nut
B    Adjustment bolt

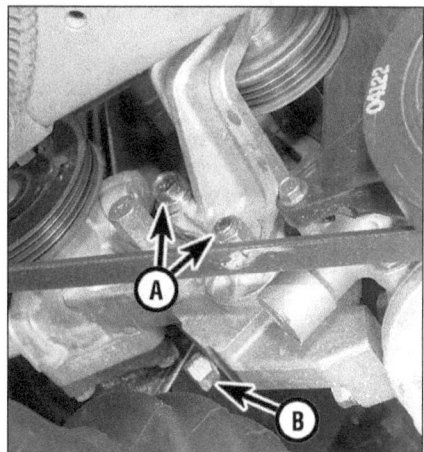

**11.6b Power steering drivebelt adjustment details**

A    Lock bolts
B    Adjustment bolt

subjected, drivebelts stretch and deteriorate as they get older. They must therefore be periodically inspected.

2    The number of belts used on a particular vehicle depends on the accessories refitted. One belt transmits power from the crankshaft to the alternator and air conditioning compressor. The power steering pump is driven by another belt off the crankshaft.

3    With the engine off, open the bonnet and locate the drivebelts. With a flashlight, check each belt: On V-belts, check for cracks and separation of the belt plies **(see illustration)**. On V-ribbed belts, check for separation of the adhesive rubber on both sides of the core, core separation from the belt side and a severed core. Also on V-ribbed belts, check for separation of the ribs from the adhesive rubber, cracking or separation of the ribs, and torn or worn ribs or cracks in the inner ridges of the ribs **(see illustration)**. On both belt types, check for fraying and glazing, which gives the belt a shiny appearance. Both sides of the belt should be inspected, which means you will have to twist the belt to check the underside. Use your fingers to feel the belt where you can't see it. If any of the above conditions are evident, renew the belt (go to Step 7).

4    The tightness of each belt is checked by pushing on it at a distance halfway between the pulleys **(see illustration)**. Apply about 44.5 Newtons of force with your thumb and see how much the belt moves down (deflects). Refer to the Specifications listed in this Chapter for the amount of deflection allowed in each belt.

## Adjustment

5    If adjustment is necessary, it is done by moving the tension pulley on the bracket.

6    Loosen the tension pulley lock bolt and

nut (if equipped) **(see illustrations)**. Turn the adjusting bolt to tension the belt, then retighten the lock bolts **(see illustration)**.

## Renewal

7    To refit a belt, follow the above proce-

dures for drivebelt adjustment, but slip the belt off the pulleys and remove it. To renew some belts, you'll have to remove other belts to get at the one you're renewing because of the way the belts are arranged on the crankshaft pulley. Because of this and because belts tend to wear out more or less together, it is a good idea to renew all belts at the same time. Mark each belt and its appropriate pulley groove so the renewal belts can be refitted in their proper positions.

8     Take the old belts to the parts store in order to make a direct comparison for length, width and design.

9     After renewing a V-ribbed drivebelt, make sure it fits properly in the ribbed grooves in the pulleys. It is essential that the belt be properly centered.

10   Adjust the belt(s) in accordance with the procedure outlined above.

## 12   Underbonnet hose check and renewal (every 10,000 kilometres or 6 months)

**Caution:** *Renewal of air conditioning hoses must be left to a dealer service department or air conditioning shop that has the equipment to depressurise the system safely. Never remove air conditioning components or hoses until the system has been depressurised.*

### *General*

1     High temperatures in the engine compartment can cause the deterioration of the rubber and plastic hoses used for engine, accessory and emission systems operation. Periodic inspection should be made for cracks, loose clamps, material hardening and leaks.

2     Information specific to the cooling system hoses can be found in Section 13.

3     Some, but not all, hoses are secured to the fittings with clamps. Where clamps are used, check to be sure they haven't lost their tension, allowing the hose to leak. If clamps aren't used, make sure the hose has not expanded and/or hardened where it slips over the fitting, allowing it to leak.

### *Vacuum hoses*

4     It's quite common for vacuum hoses, especially those in the emissions system, to be colour coded or identified by coloured stripes molded into them. Various systems require hoses with different wall thickness, collapse resistance and temperature resistance. When renewing hoses, be sure the new ones are made of the same material.

5     Often the only effective way to check a hose is to remove it completely from the vehicle. If more than one hose is removed, be sure to label the hoses and fittings to ensure correct refitting.

6     When checking vacuum hoses, be sure to include any plastic T-fittings in the check. Inspect the fittings for cracks and the hose where it fits over the fitting for distortion,

which could cause leakage.

7     A small piece of vacuum hose (6.35 mm inside diameter) can be used as a stethoscope to detect vacuum leaks. Hold one end of the hose to your ear and probe around vacuum hoses and fittings, listening for the "hissing" sound characteristic of a vacuum leak. **Warning:** *When probing with the vacuum hose stethoscope, be very careful not to come into contact with moving engine components such as the drivebelts, cooling fan, etc.*

### *Fuel hose*

**Warning:** *There are certain precautions which must be taken when inspecting or servicing fuel system components. Work in a well ventilated area and do not allow open flames (cigarettes, appliance pilot lights, etc.) or bare light bulbs near the work area. Mop up any spills immediately and do not store fuel soaked rags where they could ignite.* **Caution:** *Relieve the fuel system pressure before disconnecting any fuel lines (see Chapter 4).*

8     Check all rubber fuel lines for deterioration and chafing. Check especially for cracks in areas where the hose bends and just before fittings, such as where a hose attaches to the fuel filter.

9     High quality fuel line should be used for fuel line renewal. Never, under any circumstances, use unreinforced vacuum line, clear plastic tubing or water hose for fuel lines. On fuel-injected models, special high-pressure fuel hoses are used. Be sure to obtain an exact renewal.

10   Spring-type clamps are commonly used on fuel lines. These clamps often lose their tension over a period of time, and can be damaged during removal. Renew all spring-type clamps with screw clamps whenever a hose is renewed.

### *Metal lines*

11   Sections of metal line are often used for fuel line between the fuel pump and fuel injection system. Check carefully to be sure the line has not been bent or crimped and cracks have not started in the line.

12   If a section of metal fuel line must be renewed, only seamless steel tubing should be used, since copper and aluminum tubing don't have the strength necessary to withstand normal engine vibration.

13   Check the metal brake lines where they enter the master cylinder and brake proportioning unit (if used) for cracks in the lines or loose fittings. Any sign of brake fluid leakage calls for an immediate thorough inspection of the brake system.

## 13   Cooling system check (every 10,000 kilometres or 6 months)

*Refer to illustration 13.4*

1     Many major engine failures can be attributed to a faulty cooling system. If the vehicle is equipped with an automatic trans-

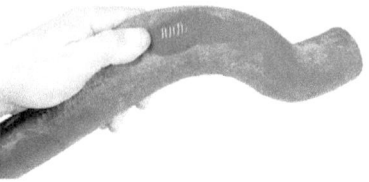

Check for a chafed area that could fail prematurely.

Check for a soft area indicating the hose has deteriorated inside.

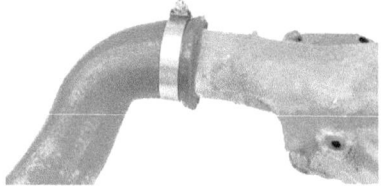

Overtightening the clamp on a hardened hose will damage the hose and cause a leak.

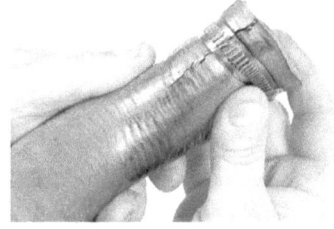

Check each hose for swelling and oil-soaked ends. Cracks and breaks can be located by squeezing the hose.

**13.4 Hoses, like drivebelts, have a habit of failing at the worst possible time - to prevent the inconvenience of a blown radiator or heater hose, inspect them carefully as shown here**

axle, the cooling system also cools the transaxle fluid and thus plays an important role in prolonging transaxle life.

2     The cooling system should be checked with the engine cold. Do this before the vehicle is driven for the day or after the engine has been shut off for at least three hours.

3     Remove the radiator cap by turning it to the left until it reaches a stop. If you hear a hissing sound (indicating there is still pressure in the system), wait until it stops. Now press down on the cap with the palm of your hand and continue turning to the left until the cap can be removed. Thoroughly clean the cap, inside and out, with clean water. Also clean the filler neck on the radiator. All traces of corrosion should be removed. The coolant inside the radiator should be relatively transparent. If it's rust coloured, the system

should be drained and refilled (Section 13). If the coolant level isn't up to the top, add additional antifreeze/coolant mixture (see Section 4).

4    Carefully check the large upper and lower radiator hoses along with the smaller diameter heater hoses which run from the engine to the firewall. Inspect each hose along its entire length, renewing any hose which is cracked, swollen or shows signs of deterioration. Cracks may become more apparent if the hose is squeezed **(see illustration)**. Regardless of condition, it's a good idea to renew hoses with new ones every two years.

5    Make sure that all hose connections are tight. A leak in the cooling system will usually show up as white or rust coloured deposits on the areas adjoining the leak. If wire-type clamps are used at the ends of the hoses, it may be a good idea to renew them with more secure screw-type clamps.

6    Use compressed air or a soft brush to remove bugs, leaves, etc. from the front of the radiator or air conditioning condenser. Be careful not to damage the delicate cooling fins or cut yourself on them.

7    Every other inspection, or at the first indication of cooling system problems, have the cap and system pressure tested. If you don't have a pressure tester, most petrol stations and repair shops will do this for a minimal charge.

## 14    Manual transaxle lubricant level check (every 10,000 kilometres or 6 months)

1    The manual transaxle does not have a dipstick. To check the lubricant level, raise the vehicle and support it securely on jackstands. On the lower rear side of the transaxle housing, you will see a plug. Remove it. If the lubricant level is correct, it should be up to the lower edge of the hole.

2    If the transaxle needs more lubricant (if the level is not up to the hole), use a syringe to add more. Stop filling the transaxle when the lubricant begins to run out the hole.

3    Refit the plug and tighten it securely. Drive the vehicle a short distance, then check for leaks.

## 15    Tyre rotation (every 10,000 kilometres or 6 months)

*Refer to illustration 15.2*

1    The tyres should be rotated at the specified intervals and whenever uneven wear is noticed. Since the vehicle will be raised and the tyres removed anyway, check the brakes (Section 16) at this time.

2    Radial tyres must be rotated in a specific pattern **(see illustration)**.

3    Refer to the information in Jacking and towing at the front of this manual for the

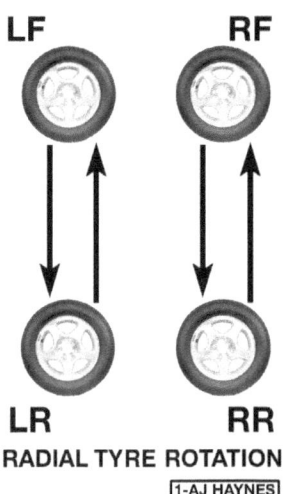

**15.2  The recommended tyre rotation pattern for these vehicles**

proper procedures to follow when raising the vehicle and changing a tyre. If the brakes are to be checked, do not apply the parking brake as stated. Make sure the tyres are blocked to prevent the vehicle from rolling.

4    Preferably, the entire vehicle should be raised at the same time. This can be done on a hoist or by jacking up each corner and then lowering the vehicle onto jackstands placed under the frame rails. Always use four jackstands and make sure the vehicle is firmly supported.

5    After rotation, check and adjust the tyre pressures as necessary and be sure to check the lug nut tightness.

6    For further information on the wheels and tyres, refer to Chapter 10.

## 16    Brake check (every 10,000 kilometres or 6 months)

### Disc brakes

*Refer to illustration 16.5*
**Note:** *For detailed photographs of the brake system, refer to Chapter 9.*

1    In addition to the specified intervals, the brakes should be inspected every time the wheels are removed or whenever a defect is suspected. Any of the following symptoms could indicate a potential brake system defect: The vehicle pulls to one side when the brake pedal is depressed; the brakes make squealing or dragging noises when applied; brake travel is excessive; the pedal pulsates; brake fluid leaks, usually onto the inside of the tyre or wheel.

2    Loosen the wheel lug nuts.

3    Raise the vehicle and place it securely on jackstands.

4    Remove the wheels (see Jacking and towing at the front of this book, or your owner's manual, if necessary).

**16.5  You will find an inspection hole like this in each caliper - placing a steel ruler across the hole should enable you to determine the thickness of the remaining pad material for both inner and outer pads**

5    There are two pads, an outer and an inner, in each caliper. The pads are visible through small inspection holes in each caliper **(see illustration)**.

6    Check the pad thickness by looking at each end of the caliper and through the inspection hole in the caliper body. If the lining material is less than the specified thickness, renew the pads. **Note:** *Keep in mind that the lining material is riveted or bonded to a metal backing plate and the metal portion is not included in this measurement.*

7    If it is difficult to determine the exact thickness of the remaining pad material by the above method, or if you are concerned about the condition of the pads, remove the caliper(s), then remove the pads from the calipers for further inspection (refer to Chapter 9).

8    Once the pads are removed from the calipers, clean them with brake cleaner and remeasure them with a small steel pocket ruler or a vernier caliper.

9    Check the brake disc. Look for score marks, deep scratches and burned spots. If these conditions exist, the hub/disc assembly will have to be removed (see Chapter 9).

10    Before refitting the wheels, check all brake lines and hoses for damage, wear, deformation, cracks, corrosion, leakage, bends and twists, particularly in the vicinity of the rubber hoses at the calipers. Check the clamps for tightness and the connections for leakage. Make sure that all hoses and lines are clear of sharp edges, moving parts and the exhaust system. If any of the above conditions are noted, repair, reroute or renew the lines and/or fittings as necessary (refer to Chapter 9).

11    Refit the wheels and tighten the wheel lug nuts finger tight.

12    Remove the jackstands and lower the vehicle.

13    Tighten the wheel lug nuts to the torque listed in this Chapter's Specifications.

## Parking brake

14   A simple method of checking the parking brake is to park the vehicle on a steep hill with the parking brake set and the transmission in Neutral. If the parking brake cannot prevent the vehicle from rolling, it is in need of adjustment (see Chapter 9).

## 17   Steering and suspension check (every 10,000 kilometres or 6 months)

*Refer to illustration 17.6*

**Note:** *For detailed illustrations of the steering and suspension components, refer to Chapter 10.*

### With the wheels on the ground

1   With the vehicle stopped and the front wheels pointed straight ahead, rock the steering wheel gently back and forth. If free-play is excessive, a front wheel bearing, main shaft yoke, intermediate shaft yoke, lower arm balljoint or steering system joint is worn or the steering gear is out of adjustment or broken. Refer to Chapter 10 for the appropriate repair procedure.

2   Other symptoms, such as excessive vehicle body movement over rough roads, swaying (leaning) around corners and binding as the steering wheel is turned, may indicate faulty steering and/or suspension components.

3   Check the shock absorbers by pushing down and releasing the vehicle several times at each corner. If the vehicle does not come back to a level position within one or two bounces, the shocks/struts are worn and must be renewed. When bouncing the vehicle up and down, listen for squeaks and noises from the suspension components. Additional information on suspension components can be found in Chapter 10.

### With the vehicle raised

4   Raise the vehicle and support it securely on jackstands. See Jacking and towing at the front of this book for the proper jacking points.

5   Check the tyres for irregular wear patterns (see Section 5) and proper inflation. See Section 5 in this Chapter for information regarding tyre wear and Section 17 or Chapter 10 for the wheel bearing renewal procedures.

6   Inspect the universal joint between the steering shaft and the steering gear housing. Check the steering gear housing for grease leakage or oozing. Make sure that the dust seals and boots are not damaged and that the boot clamps are not loose **(see illustration)**. Check the steering linkage for looseness or damage. Check the tie-rod ends for excessive play. Look for loose bolts, broken or disconnected parts and deteriorated rubber bushes on all suspension and steering components. While an assistant turns the

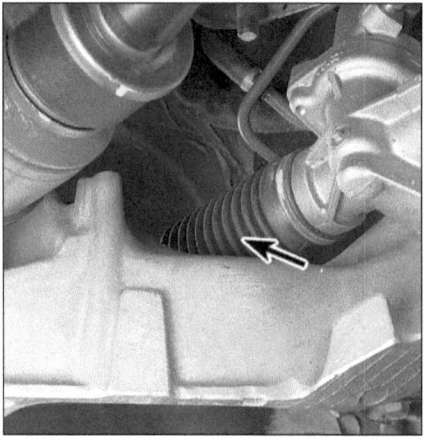

**17.6  Push on the steering gear boot (arrow) to check for cracks and lubricant leaks**

steering wheel from side to side, check the steering components for free movement, chafing and binding. If the steering components do not seem to be reacting with the movement of the steering wheel, try to determine where the slack is located.

7   Inspect the balljoint boots for damage and leaking grease. Renew the boots with new ones if they are damaged (see Chapter 10).

## 18   Exhaust system check (every 10,000 kilometres or 6 months)

*Refer to illustration 18.2*

1   With the engine cold (at least three hours after the vehicle has been driven), check the complete exhaust system from its starting point at the engine to the end of the tailpipe. This should be done on a hoist where unrestricted access is available.

2   Check the pipes and connections for evidence of leaks, severe corrosion or damage. Make sure that all brackets and hangers are in good condition and tight **(see illustration)**.

3   At the same time, inspect the underside of the body for holes, corrosion, open seams, etc. which may allow exhaust gases to enter the passenger compartment. Seal all body openings with silicone or body putty.

4   Rattles and other noises can often be traced to the exhaust system, especially the mounts and hangers. Try to move the pipes, muffler and catalytic converter. If the components can come in contact with the body or suspension parts, secure the exhaust system with new mounts.

5   Check the running condition of the engine by inspecting inside the end of the tailpipe. The exhaust deposits here are an indication of engine state-of-tune. If the pipe is black and sooty or coated with white deposits, the engine is in need of a tune-up, including a thorough fuel system inspection and adjustment.

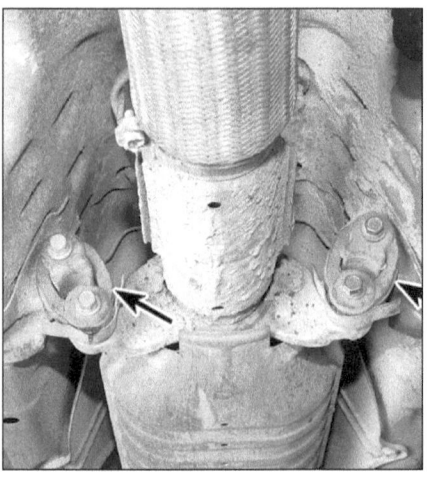

**18.2  Check the rubber exhaust system hangers (arrows) for cracks and deterioration - renew any that are in poor condition**

## 19   Fuel system check (every 20,000 kilometres or 12 months)

**Warning:** *Petrol is extremely flammable, so take extra precautions when you work on any part of the fuel system. Don't smoke or allow open flames or bare light bulbs near the work area, and don't work in a garage where a natural gas-type appliance (such as a water heater or clothes dryer) with a pilot light is present. If you spill any fuel on your skin, rinse it off immediately with soap and water. When you perform any kind of work on the fuel tank, wear safety glasses and have a Class B type fire extinguisher on hand.*

**Caution:** *Do not disconnect any fuel lines until you relieve the fuel system pressure (see Chapter 4).*

1   If you smell petrol while driving or after the vehicle has been sitting in the sun, inspect the fuel system immediately.

2   Remove the petrol filler cap and inspect if for damage and corrosion. The gasket should have an unbroken sealing imprint. If the gasket is damaged or corroded, renew the cap.

3   Inspect the fuel feed and return lines for cracks. Check the metal fuel line connections to make sure they are tight.

4   Since some components of the fuel system - the fuel tank and part of the fuel feed and return lines, for example - are underneath the vehicle, they can be inspected more easily with the vehicle raised on a hoist. If that's not possible, raise the vehicle and secure it on jackstands.

5   With the vehicle raised and safely supported, inspect the fuel tank and filler neck for punctures, cracks and other damage. The connection between the filler neck and the tank is particularly critical. Sometimes a rubber filler neck will leak because of loose clamps or deteriorated rubber. These are problems a home mechanic can usually rectify. **Warning:** *Do not, under any cir-*

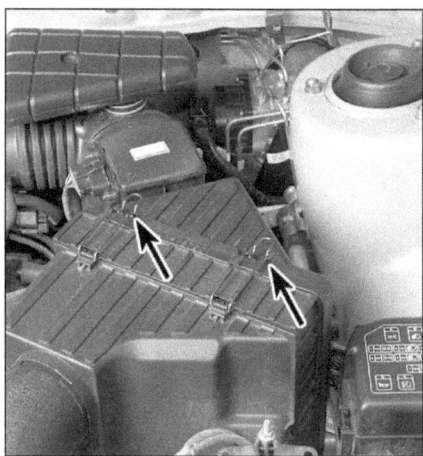

**20.1  Release the spring clips securing the cover to the air cleaner housing**

**20.2  Pull the cover back and remove the air filter element**

**21.3  Engine tachometer connector location (arrow) and terminal identification**

cumstances, try to repair a fuel tank (except rubber components). A welding torch or any open flame can easily cause fuel vapors inside the tank to explode.

6    Carefully check all rubber hoses and metal lines leading away from the fuel tank. Check for loose connections, deteriorated hoses, crimped lines and other damage. Carefully inspect the lines from the tank to the injection system. Repair or renew damaged sections as necessary.

## 20    Air filter renewal (every 20,000 kilometres or 12 months)

**Warning:** The electric cooling fan can activate at any time, even when the ignition is in the Off position. Disconnect the fan motor or negative battery cable when working in the vicinity of the fan.

*Refer to illustrations 20.1 and 20.2*

1    Detach the spring clips retaining the cover to the air cleaner housing **(see illustration)**.

2    Pull the cover back and remove the air filter element **(see illustration)**.
3    Renew the air filter element, making sure the outer edge is properly seated in the housing.
4    Refit the filter in between the cover and air cleaner body then secure the spring clips.

## 21    Engine idle speed check and adjustment (every 20,000 kilometres or 12 months)

### Engine idle speed

*Refer to illustrations 21.3, 21.4 and 21.5*
**Note:** *Idle speed screw is preset at the factory and is not considered a routine maintenance adjustment. Before any adjustment is made check that the fuel system, spark plugs and idle speed servo are working properly also check for any possible engine vacuum leaks.*
1    Engine idle speed is the speed at which the engine operates when no accelerator

pedal pressure is applied, as when stopped at a traffic light. This speed is critical to the performance of the engine itself, as well as many engine subsystems.
2    Firmly set the parking brake and block the wheels to prevent the vehicle from rolling. Put the transaxle in Neutral.
3    Hook up a hand-held tachometer according to the manufacturers instructions to the engine tachometer connector terminal number three **(see illustration)**.
4    Using the diagnostic connector located inside of the car on the driver side knee bolster next to the centre console **(see illustration)**. Insert a jumper wire from terminals 1 and 4. **Note:** *On TH-KH and later models a factory MUT-II diagnosis tool must be used to set the idle speed.* Start the engine and allow it to reach normal operating temperature.
5    With the air conditioner and the vehicle lights off check the idle speed. If the idle speed is incorrect adjust the idle speed **(see illustration)**.
6    Remove the jumper wire and run for a few minutes. Idle should be to specifications.

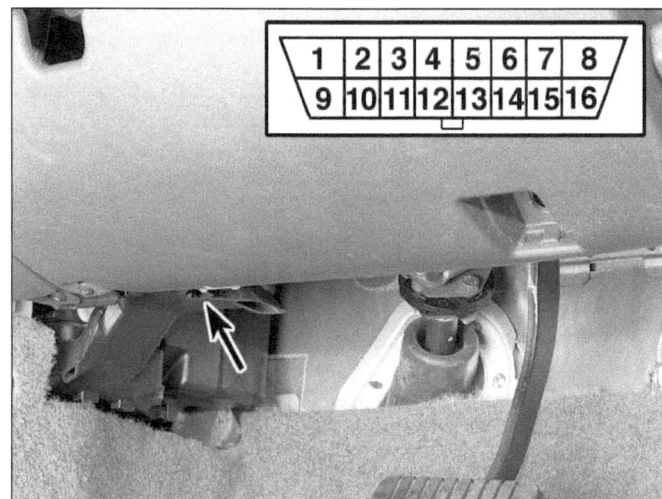

**21.4  Diagnostic connector location and terminal identification**

**21.5  Adjust speed adjustment screw location**

**22.1  PCV valve location (arrow)**

## 22  Positive Crankcase Ventilation (PCV) valve check and renewal (every 40,000 kilometres or 24 months)

*Refer to illustrations 22.1 and 22.3*

1    The PCV valve is located in the front of the valve cover, **(see illustration)** above the timing belt cover.

2    To test the PCV valve, remove the valve from the valve cover without disconnecting the hose.

3    With the engine idling, place your finger over the valve opening. If there's no vacuum felt at the valve, remove the valve from the hose and check for vacuum at the hose **(see illustration)**. If the hose is p[lugged, renew the hose.

4    If the hose is good, use a short section of wire to check the plunger inside the valve for freedom of movement. If the valve is plugged, renew the valve.

5    When purchasing a new PCV valve, make sure it's for your particular vehicle and engine size. Compare the old valve with the new one to make sure they're the same.

## 23  Evaporative emissions control system check (every 40,000 kilometres or 24 months)

*Refer to illustration 23.2*

1    The function of the evaporative emissions control system is to draw fuel vapors from the fuel tank and fuel system, store them in a charcoal canister and route them to the inlet manifold, through a purge control valve, during normal engine operation.

2    The most common symptom of a fault in the evaporative emissions system is a strong fuel odor in the engine compartment. If a fuel odor is detected, inspect the charcoal canister, located in the engine compartment **(see illustration)**. Check the canister, purge control valve and all hoses for damage and deterioration.

3    The evaporative emissions control system is explained in more detail in Chapter 6.

**22.3  Using a small blade screw driver carefully separate the PCV valve from the hose**

**24.2  Flex the driveaxle boots by hand to check for cracks or leaking grease**

## 24  Driveaxle boot check (every 40,000 kilometres or 24 months)

*Refer to illustration 24.2*

1    The driveaxle boots are very important because they prevent dirt, water and foreign material from entering and damaging the constant velocity (CV) joints. Oil and grease can cause the boot material to deteriorate prematurely, so it's a good idea to wash the

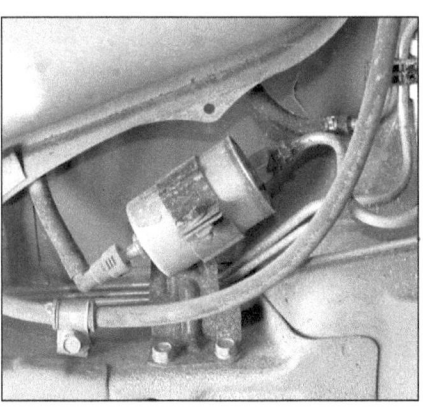

**25.2a  Typical fuel filter location (sedan)**

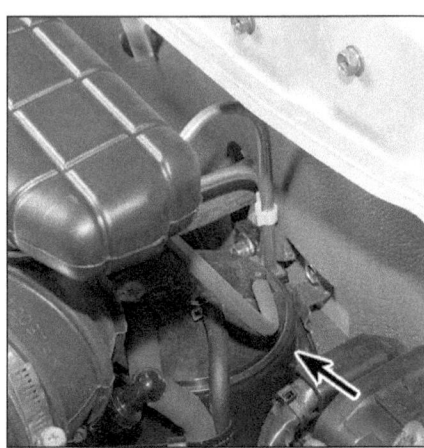

**23.2  The evaporative emissions system charcoal canister is mounted on the firewall (arrow) behind the upper inlet manifold and next to the ABS brake unit (if equipped)**

boots with soap and water.

2    Inspect the boots for tears and cracks as well as loose clamps **(see illustration)**. If there is any evidence of cracks or leaking lubricant, they must be renewed as described in Chapter 8.

## 25  Fuel filter renewal (every 40,000 kilometres or 24 months)

*Refer to illustrations 25.2a, 25.2b, 25.4 and 25.5*

**Warning:** *Petrol is extremely flammable, so take extra precautions when you work on any part of the fuel system. Don't smoke or allow open flames or bare light bulbs near the work area, and don't work in a garage where a natural gas-type appliance (such as a water heater or clothes dryer) with a pilot light is present. If you spill any fuel on your skin, rinse it off immediately with soap and water. When you perform any kind of work on the fuel tank, wear safety glasses and have a Class B type fire extinguisher on hand.*

1    Relieve the fuel system pressure (see Chapter 4).

2    Place a container or rags under the filter.

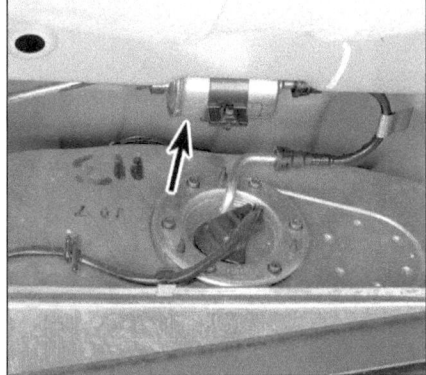

**25.2b  Typical fuel filter location (wagon)**

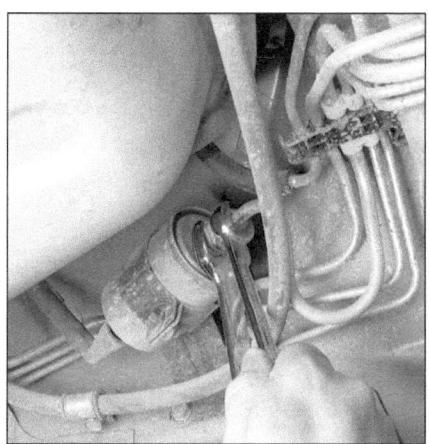

**25.4 Remove the filter outlet line using a spanner to hold the filter and a line spanner to break the fuel line fitting free**

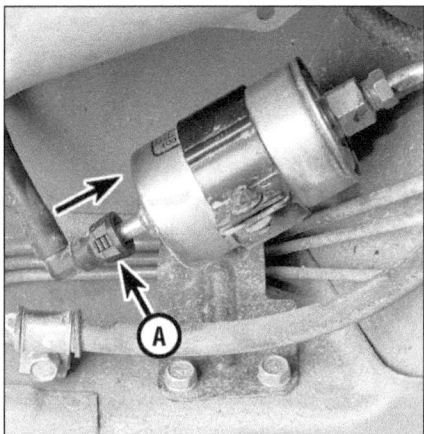

**25.5 Disconnect the fuel filter inlet line by pushing the line towards the filter (arrow) and squeezing the tabs (A) then pull the line away from the filter**

It is secured under the car near the fuel tank **(see illustrations)**.

3   Inspect both ends of the filter to see if they're clean. If more than a light coat of dust is present, clean the fittings before proceeding.

4   Starting from the outlet side, using a backup spanner on the filter and a line spanner on the fuel line fitting **(see illustration)**.

5   Remove the inlet line side by pushing the line towards the filter and depressing the connector tabs **(see illustration)** then pull the line away from the filter. Remove the filter from the retaining bracket and remove the filter.

6   Drain the fuel from the filter and then test it by blowing through it from the inlet end. If it is plugged, the fuel tank may need to be cleaned.

7   Fit the new filter into the bracket and refit the inlet line by pushing it onto the filter nipple until the two locking tabs click. Check the line connection by pulling the line away from the filter. If the line doesn't pull apart the connection is correct.

8   Refit the outlet side line being careful

not to cross thread the line which could ruin the filter or possibly the line. Tighten the filter retainer strap and outlet line using a spanner and backup spanner.

9   Start the engine and check for fuel leaks at the filter.

---

## 26   Spark plug wire, distributor cap and rotor check and renewal (every 40,000 kilometres or 24 months)

---

*Refer to illustrations 26.4, 26.11a, 26.11b and 26.12*

1   The spark plug wires should be checked whenever new spark plugs are fitted.

2   Begin this procedure by making a visual check of the spark plug wires while the engine is running. In a darkened garage (make sure there is ventilation) start the engine and observe each plug wire. Be careful not to come into contact with any moving engine parts. If there is a break in the

wire, you will see arcing or a small spark at the damaged area. If arcing is noticed, make a note to obtain new wires, then stop the engine and allow to cool and check the distributor cap and rotor.

3   The spark plug wires should be inspected one at a time to prevent mixing up the order, which is essential for proper engine operation. Each original plug wire should be numbered to help identify its location. If the number is illegible, a piece of tape can be marked with the correct number and wrapped around the plug wire.

4   With the engine off and cool, disconnect the plug wire from the spark plug. Twist and pull only on the rubber boot **(see illustration)**.

5   Check inside the boot for corrosion, which will look like a white crusty powder.

6   Push the wire and boot back onto the end of the spark plug and into the spark plug tube. It should fit tightly onto the end of the plug. If it doesn't, remove the wire and use pliers to carefully crimp the metal connector inside the wire boot until the fit is snug.

7   Using a clean rag, wipe the entire length of the wire to remove built-up dirt and grease. Once the wire is clean, check for burns, cracks and other damage. Do not bend the wire sharply, because the conductor within the wire might break.

8   Disconnect the wire from the distributor cap. Again, pull only on the rubber boot. Check for corrosion and a tight fit. Press the wire back into the distributor cap.

9   Inspect the remaining spark plug wires, making sure that each one is securely fastened at the distributor and spark plug when the check is complete.

10   If new spark plug wires are required, purchase a set for your specific engine model. Pre-cut wire sets with the boots already refitted are available. Remove and renew the wires one at a time to avoid mix-ups in the firing order.

11   Detach the distributor cap by loosening the retaining screws **(see illustration)**. Look inside it for cracks, carbon tracks and worn,

**26.4 When removing the spark plug wires, pull only on the boot and use a twisting/pulling motion**

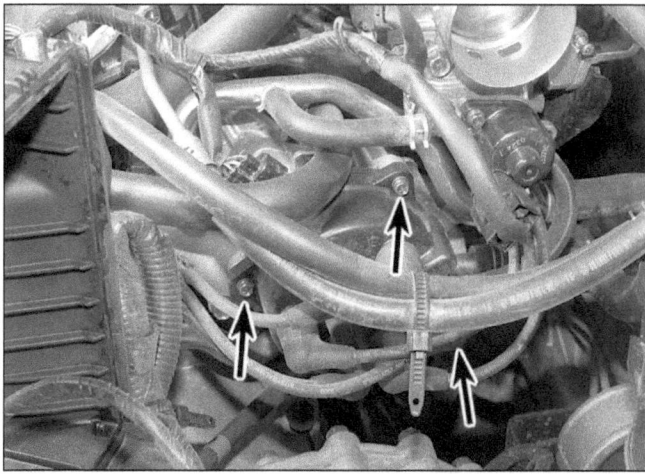

**26.11a Use a small screwdriver to loosen the distributor cap retaining screws (arrows)**

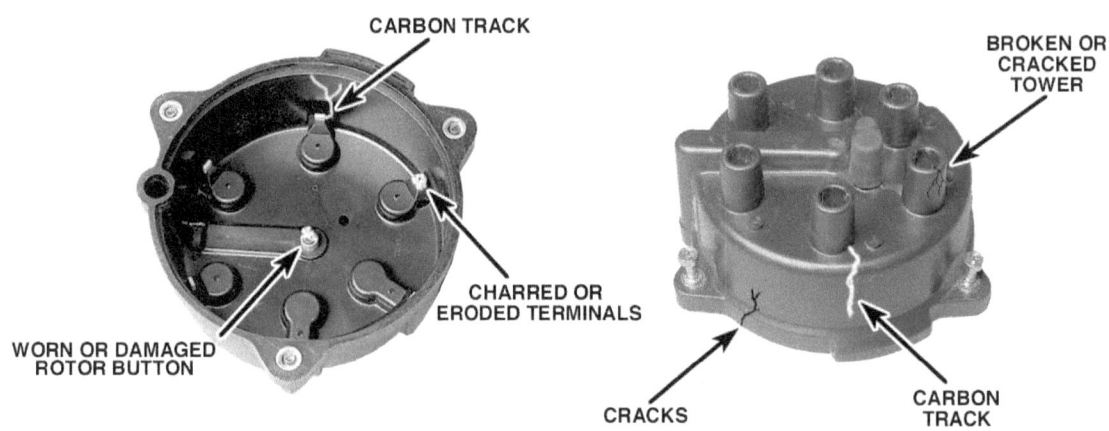

CARBON TRACK

BROKEN OR CRACKED TOWER

CHARRED OR ERODED TERMINALS

WORN OR DAMAGED ROTOR BUTTON

CRACKS

CARBON TRACK

**26.11b  Shown here are some of the common defects to look for when inspecting the distributor cap (if in doubt about its condition, fit a new one)**

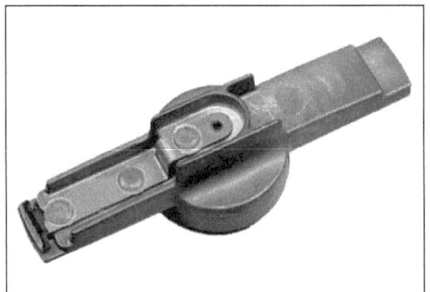

**26.12  The ignition rotor should be checked for wear and corrosion (if in doubt about its condition, buy a new one)**

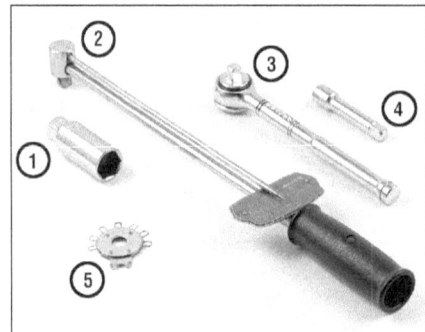

**27.1  Tools required for changing spark plugs**

1   **Spark plug socket -** This will have special padding inside to protect the spark plug's porcelain insulator
2   **Torque wrench -** Although not mandatory, using this tool is the best way to ensure the plugs are tightened properly
3   **Ratchet -** Standard hand tool to fit the spark plug socket
4   **Extension -** Depending on model and accessories, you may need special extensions and universal joints to reach one or more of the plugs
5   **Spark plug gap gauge -** This gauge for checking the gap comes in a variety of·styles. Make sure the gap for your engine is included.

**27.4a  Spark plug manufacturers recommend using a wire type gauge when checking the gap - if the wire does not slide between the electrodes with a slight drag, adjustment is required**

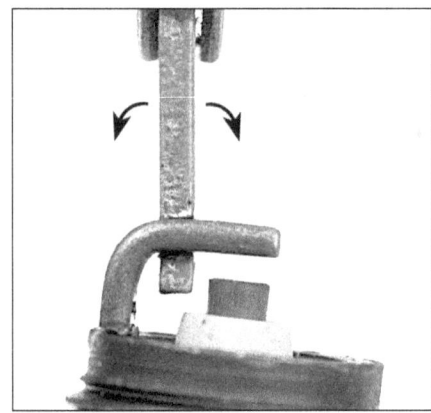

**27.4b  To change the gap, bend the *side* electrode only, as indicated by the arrows, and be very careful not to crack or chip the porcelain insulator surrounding the center electrode**

burned or loose contacts **(see illustration).**
12   Pull the rotor off the distributor shaft and examine it for cracks and carbon tracks **(see illustration).** Renew the cap and rotor if any damage or defects are noted.
13   It is common practice to fit a new cap and rotor whenever new spark plug wires are refitted, but if you wish to continue using the old cap, clean the terminals first.
14   When fitting a new cap, remove the wires from the old cap one at a time and attach them to the new cap in the exact same location - do not simultaneously remove all the wires from the old cap or firing order mix-ups may occur.

---

**27   Spark plug check and renewal (every 40,000 kilometres or 24 months)**

---

*Refer to illustrations 27.1, 27.4a, 27.4b, 27.8 and 27.10*
1   Spark plug renewal requires a spark plug socket which fits onto a ratchet. This socket is lined with a rubber grommet to protect the porcelain insulator of the spark plug and to hold the plug while you insert it into the spark plug hole. You will also need a wire-type feeler gauge to check and adjust the spark plug gap and a torque wrench to

tighten the new plugs to the torque listed in this Chapter's specifications **(see illustration).**
2   When renewing the plugs, purchase the new plugs in advance, adjust them to the proper gap and then renew each plug one at a time. **Note:** *When buying new spark plugs, it's essential that you obtain the correct plugs for your specific vehicle. This information can be found in this Chapter's Specifications.*
3   Inspect each of the new plugs for defects. If there are any signs of cracks in the porcelain insulator of a plug, don't use it.
4   Check the electrode gaps of the new plugs. Check the gap by inserting the wire

gauge of the proper thickness between the electrodes at the tip of the plug **(see illustration).** The gap between the electrodes should be identical to that listed in this Chapter's

**27.8  Use a socket and extension to unthread the spark plug**

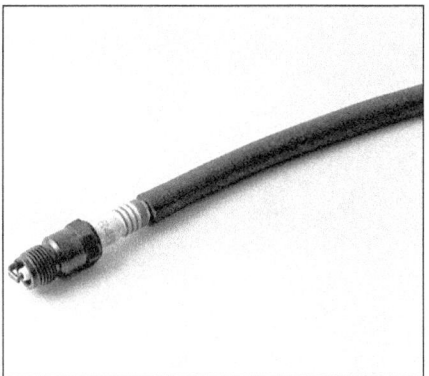

**27.10  A length of snug fitting rubber hose will save time and prevent damaged threads when refitting the spark plugs**

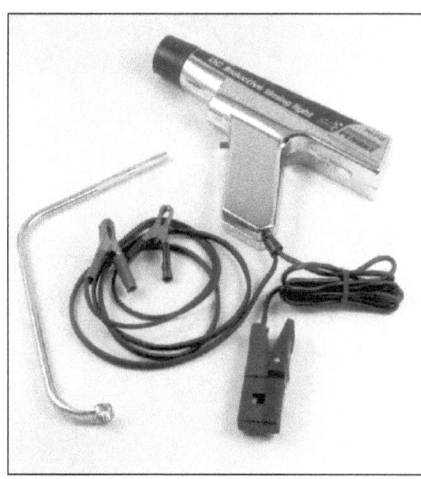

**28.1  An Inductive pick-up timing light which flashes a bright concentrated beam of light when the number one spark plug fires. Connect the leads according to the instructions supplied with the light to check the ignition timing.**

Specifications or as specified in the owner's manual. If the gap is incorrect, use the notched adjuster on the feeler gauge body to bend the curved side electrode slightly **(see illustration)**.

5    If the side electrode is not exactly over the centre electrode, use the notched adjuster to align them. **Caution:** If the gap of a new plug must be adjusted, bend only the base of the ground electrode; do not touch the tip.

### Removal

6    To prevent the possibility of mixing up spark plug wires, work on one spark plug at a time. Remove the wire and boot from one spark plug. Grasp the boot - not the cable - as shown, give it a half twisting motion and pull it off **(see illustration 26.4)**.

7    If compressed air is available, blow any dirt or foreign material away from the spark plug area before proceeding (a common bicycle pump will also work).

8    Remove the spark plug **(see illustration)**.

9    Compare each old spark plug with those shown in the photos located in the inside rear cover of this manual to determine the overall running condition of the engine.

### Refitting

10   It's often difficult to insert spark plugs into their holes without cross-threading them. To avoid this possibility, fit a short piece of snug fitting rubber hose over the end of the spark plug **(see illustration)**. The flexible hose acts as a universal joint to help align the plug with the plug hole. Should the plug begin to cross-thread, the hose will slip on the spark plug, preventing thread damage. Tighten the plug securely.

11   Attach the plug wire to the new spark plug, again using a twisting motion on the boot until it is firmly seated on the end of the spark plug.

12   Follow the above procedure for the remaining spark plugs, refitting them one at a time to prevent mixing up the spark plug wires.

---

## 28   Ignition timing check (every 40,000 kilometres or 24 months)

*Refer to illustrations 28.1 and 28.3*

**Note:** *This ignition timing procedure only checks the base timing setting specified by the factory. Timing cannot be adjusted, therefore the purpose of this check is to verify that the computer is controlling the ignition timing and that the base setting is correct. In most cases, the ignition system can be checked (see Chapter 5) but if the base setting remains incorrect, the ECU (computer) is defective. Take the vehicle to the dealer service department to verify and repair the ignition system problem(s).*

1    Some special tools are required for this procedure **(see illustration)**. The engine must be at normal operating temperature. Make sure the idle speed is correct (see Section 21).

2    Apply the parking brake and block the wheels to prevent movement of the vehicle. The transmission must be in Park (automatic) or Neutral (manual).

3    Locate the timing marks at the front of the engine (they should be visible from above after the bonnet is opened) **(see illustration)**. The crankshaft pulley has a notch in it and the timing belt cover has a protrusion with raised numbers. Clean the cover with solvent so the numbers are visible.

4    Use chalk or white paint to mark the notch in the crankshaft pulley.

5    Highlight the point on the cover that corresponds to the ignition timing specification listed in this Chapter's Specifications.

6    Hook up the timing light by following the manufacturer's instructions (an inductive pick-up timing light is preferred). Generally, the power leads are attached to the battery terminals and the pick-up lead is attached to the number one spark plug wire. The number one spark plug is the one closest to the front of the engine. **Caution:** *If an inductive pick-up timing light isn't available, don't puncture the spark plug wire to attach the timing light pick-up lead. Instead, use an adapter between the spark plug and plug wire. If the insulation on*

**28.3  The timing marks are located at the front of the engine - highlight the notch in the crankshaft pulley and the appropriate mark on the timing belt cover**

*the plug wire is damaged, the secondary voltage will jump to ground at the damaged point and the engine will misfire.*

7    Make sure the timing light wires are routed away from the drivebelts and fan, then start the engine.

8    Allow the idle speed to stabilise, then point the flashing timing light at the timing marks - be very careful of moving engine components!

9    The mark on the crankshaft pulley will appear stationary. If it's aligned with the specified point on the timing cover, the ignition timing is correct.

10   If the timing is incorrect, have the ECU (computer) checked by a dealer service department or other qualified repair facility.

11   Turn off the engine and remove the timing light.

**29.4  Remove the splash shield retaining screws (arrows)**

**29.5  Typical radiator drain plug location (arrow)**

## 29   Cooling system servicing (draining, flushing and refilling) (every 40,000 kilometres or 24 months)

**Warning:** *Antifreeze is a corrosive and poisonous solution, so be careful not to spill any of the coolant mixture on the vehicle's paint or your skin. If this happens, rinse immediately with plenty of clean water. Consult local authorities regarding proper disposal procedures for antifreeze before draining the cooling system. In many areas, reclamation centres have been established to collect used oil and coolant mixtures. The electric cooling fan can activate at any time, even when the ignition is in the Off position. Disconnect the fan motor or negative battery cable when working in the vicinity of the fan.*

1    Periodically, the cooling system should be drained, flushed and refilled to replenish the antifreeze mixture and prevent formation of rust and corrosion, which can impair the performance of the cooling system and cause engine damage. When the cooling system is serviced, all hoses and the radiator cap should be checked and renewed if necessary.

### Draining

*Refer to illustrations 29.4, 29.5, 29.6a and 29.6b*

2    Apply the parking brake and block the wheels. If the vehicle has just been driven, wait several hours to allow the engine to cool down before beginning this procedure.
3    Once the engine is completely cool, remove the radiator cap.
4    Remove the splash cover located beneath the radiator **(see illustration)**. Then move a large container under the radiator drain plug.
5    Loosen the drain plug **(see illustration)** and allow the coolant to drain into the large container.
6    After the coolant stops flowing out of the radiator tighten the drain plug. Move the

**29.6a  Typical front block drain location**

container under the engine block drain plugs **(see illustrations)**. Remove the plug(s) and allow the coolant in the block to drain.
7    While the coolant is draining, check the condition of the radiator hoses, heater hoses and clamps (refer to Section 13 if necessary).
8    Renew any damaged clamps or hoses (refer to Chapter 3 for detailed renewal procedures).

### Flushing

9    Once the system is completely drained, flush the radiator with fresh water from a garden hose until water runs clear at the drain. The flushing action of the water will remove sediments from the radiator but will not remove rust and scale from the engine and cooling tube surfaces.
10    These deposits can be removed by the chemical action of a cleaner. Follow the procedure outlined in the manufacturer's instructions. If the radiator is severely corroded, damaged or leaking, it should be removed (see Chapter 3) and taken to a radiator repair shop.
11    Remove the overflow hose from the coolant recovery reservoir. Drain the reservoir

**29.6b  Typical rear block drain location**

and flush it with clean water, then reconnect the hose.

### Refilling

12    Refit and tighten the block drain plug(s).
14    Place the heater temperature control in the maximum heat position.
15    Slowly add new coolant (a 50/50 mixture of water and antifreeze) to the radiator until it's full. Add coolant to the reservoir up to the lower mark.
16    Leave the radiator cap off and run the engine in a well-ventilated area until the thermostat opens (coolant will begin flowing through the radiator and the upper radiator hose will become hot).
17    Turn the engine off and let it cool. Add more coolant mixture to bring the level back up to the lip on the radiator filler neck. **Note:** *The system will not work properly if there is any air left in the system.*
18    Squeeze the upper radiator hose to expel air, then add more coolant mixture if necessary. Refit the radiator cap.
19    Start the engine, allow it to reach normal operating temperature and check for leaks.

**30.11 Use a box-end spanner to remove the automatic transaxle drain plug**

## 30   Automatic transaxle fluid and filter change (every 40,000 kilometres or 24 months)

*Refer to illustration 30.8*

1    At the specified time intervals, the automatic transaxle fluid should be drained and renewed.

2    Before beginning work, purchase the specified transmission fluid (see Recommended lubricants and fluids at the front of this Chapter).

3    Other tools necessary for this job include jackstands to support the vehicle in a raised position, a drain pan capable of holding at least six litres, newspapers and clean rags.

4    The fluid should be drained immediately after the vehicle has been driven. Hot fluid is more effective than cold fluid at removing built-up sediment. **Warning:** *Fluid temperature can exceed 175-degrees C in a hot transaxle. Wear protective gloves.*

5    If this is your first transaxle fluid change, get under the vehicle and familiarise yourself with the locations of the transaxle drain plug and the filter. The engine and exhaust components will be warm during the actual work, so note how they are situated to avoid touching them when working under the vehicle.

6    After the vehicle has been driven to warm up the fluid, raise it and place it on jackstands for access to the transaxle drain plug.

7    Remove the front and passenger side splash guards from under the vehicle, being careful not to touch any of the hot exhaust components.

8.    Release the clip retaining the right hand side oil cooler hose and disconnect the hose from the radiator cooler pipe.

9    Connect a suitable length of hose over the radiator cooler pipe and place the end of the hose into a drain pan capable of holding about 6 litres of hot transaxle fluid. **Warning:** *Use care to avoid scalding as the fluid may be very hot..*

10    Place the transaxle in Neutral, start the engine and allow it to idle for no longer than 1 minute. Stop the engine when the fluid stops discharging.

11    Set the drain pan under the drain plug, and being careful not to touch any of the hot exhaust components, use a spanner to remove the drain plug near the bottom **(see illustration)**. Depending on how hot the fluid is, you may want to wear gloves while unthreading the plug the final few turns.

12    Allow the old fluid to drain into the pan. It may be necessary to move the pan as the fluid flow slows to a trickle.

13    After all the fluid has drained, wipe off the drain plug with a clean rag. Small metal particles may cling to the plug and would immediately contaminate the new fluid.

14    Clean the area around the drain plug opening and refit the plug. Tighten it securely with the spanner.

### TE/TF/TH/TJ and KE/KF/KH/KJ models

15    Move the drain pan into position under the fluid filter (if equipped).

16    Using a filter wrench loosen the external filter located on top of the transaxle. Chain or metal band filter wrenches may distort the filter canister, but it doesn't matter since the filter will be discarded anyway.

17    Completely unthread the old filter. Be careful; it's full of transaxle fluid. Empty the fluid inside the filter into the drain pan.

18    Compare the old filter with the new one to make sure they're the same type.

19    Use a clean rag to remove all fluid, dirt and sludge from the area where the filter mounts to the transaxle.

20    Apply a light coat of clean transaxle fluid to the rubber gasket on the new filter.

21    Attach the new filter to the transaxle, following the tightening directions printed on the filter canister or packing box. Most filter manufacturers recommend against using a spanner due to the possibility of over-tightening the filter and damaging the seal.

### All models

**Note:** *If the transaxle fluid is contaminated with metal or friction material particles, consult an automatic transmission specialist or an authorised dealer. If badly contaminated, the manufacturer recommends to overhaul the transaxle, renew the oil filter (where applicable) and flush the transaxle and cooler, using clean automatic transaxle fluid.*

22    Add the recommended new fluid through the transaxle dipstick tube until the level reaches halfway between the bottom edge of the dipstick and the Hot mark.

23    Repeat from step 8 again to flush the system. Where applicable, the oil filter does not require changing again.

24    When satisfied that the fluid has drained again and it is clean, install the drain plug with a new sealing washer and tighten to the specified torque.

25    Remove all tools, rags, etc. from under the vehicle, being careful not to spill the oil in the drain pan, then lower the vehicle.

26    With the engine off, add new fluid to the transaxle through the dipstick tube (see Recommended lubricants and fluids for the recommended fluid type and capacity). Use a funnel to prevent spills. It is best to add a little fluid at a time, continually checking the level with the dipstick (Section 7). Allow the fluid time to drain into the pan.

27    Start the engine and shift the selector into all positions from Park through Low, then shift into Park and apply the parking brake.

28    With the engine idling, check the fluid level. Allow the engine and transaxle to reach operating temperature and add fluid up to the HOT level on the dipstick.

## 31   Manual transaxle lubricant change (every 40,000 kilometres or 24 months)

1    Place a drain pan under the transaxle and remove the drain plug.

2    When the fluid has completely drained, refit the drain plug. Tighten it to the torque listed in this Chapter's Specifications.

3    Remove the filler plug and add new lubricant until it begins to run out of the filler hole (Section 14). See Recommended lubricants and fluids for the specified lubricant type. Refit the filler plug.

# Notes

# Chapter 2 Part A
# V6 engine

## Contents

## Specifications

### General

Displacement

| | |
|---|---|
| 6G72 | 3.0 litres |
| 6G74 | 3.5 litres |
| Firing order | 1-2-3-4-5-6 |

Cylinder numbers (drivebelt end-to-transaxle end)

| | |
|---|---|
| Front (radiator side) | 2-4-6 |
| Rear (firewall side) | 1-3-5 |

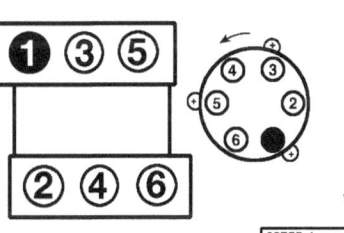

**Cylinder location and distributor rotation**

*The blackened terminal shown on the distributor cap indicates the number one spark plug wire position*

### Camshafts

| | |
|---|---|
| Runout | 0.10 mm |
| Endplay | |
| Standard | 0.10 to 0.20 mm |
| Service limit (minimum) | 0.04 mm |
| Journal diameter | 44.93 to 44.94 mm |
| Bearing journal oil clearance | 0.06 to 0.10 mm |
| Lobe height | |
| Inlet | 37.58 mm |
| Exhaust | 36.95 mm |
| Lobe wear limit | 0.50 mm |

### Cylinder head

| | |
|---|---|
| Warpage limit | 0.20 mm |
| Maximum allowable machining | 0.20 mm |

### Inlet manifolds

| | |
|---|---|
| Warpage limit | 0.20 mm |

### Oil pump

| | |
|---|---|
| Tip clearance | 0.06 to 0.18 mm |
| Rotor end clearance | 0.4 to 0.10 mm |
| Body clearance | 0.025 to 0.070 mm |

## Torque specifications

| | Nm |
|---|---|
| Rocker arm shaft bolts | 31 |
| Lower inlet manifold nuts | 21 |
| Upper inlet manifold nuts/bolts | 17 |
| EGR tube-to-upper inlet manifold bolts | 18 |
| Distributor nut | 23 |
| Engine mounts | |
|    Front engine mount | |
|       Through bolt | 98 to 118 |
|       Through bolt bracket nuts | 98 to 118 |
|       Dynamic damper bolts | 12 |
|    Front roll insulator | |
|       Through bolt and nut | 69 |
|       Mount-to-frame bolts | 44 |
|       Front centre member bolts | 88 |
|    Rear roll insulator | |
|       Through bolt | 69 to 78 |
|       Mount-to-frame bolts | 44 |
|       Rear centre member bolts | 52 |
|    Transmission mount | |
|       Through bolt and nut | 78 |
|       Mount-to-transmission studs | 81 |
| Exhaust manifold nuts | 29 |
| Exhaust manifold heat shield bolts | 13 |
| Exhaust pipe-to-manifold nuts | 49 |
| Crankshaft pulley-to-crankshaft bolt | 181 |
| Camshaft sprocket bolt | 88 |
| Camshaft thrust case bolts | 12 |
| Timing belt cover | |
|    M8 bolts | 11 |
|    M10 bolts | 13 |
| Auto tensioner bolts | 23 |
| Tensioner pulley bolt | 48 |
| Tensioner arm bolt | 44 |
| Cylinder head bolts | 108 |
| Flywheel mounting bolts | 98 |
| Driveplate mounting bolts* | 74 |
| Oil pressure switch | 10 |
| Oil sump | |
|    Lower bolts | 11 |
|    Upper bolts | 6 |
| Oil pump assembly mounting bolts | 13 |
| Oil pump relief plug | 44 |
| Oil pick-up tube-to-pump bolts | 18 |
| Oil pump cover bolts | 10 |
| Thrust case bolts | 12 |
| Valve cover bolts | 3.5 |

* Apply a thread locking compound to the threads prior to refitting.

## 1 General information

This Part of Chapter 2 is devoted to in-vehicle repair procedures for the 3.0 and 3.5L V6 engines. All information concerning engine removal and refitting and engine block and cylinder head overhaul can be found in Chapter 2, Part B.

The following repair procedures are based on the assumption that the engine is in the vehicle. If the engine has been removed from the vehicle and mounted on a stand, many of the steps outlined in this Part of Chapter 2 will not apply.

The Specifications included in this Part of Chapter 2 apply only to the procedures contained in this Part. Part B of Chapter 2 contains the Specifications necessary for cyl-inder head and engine block rebuilding.

The 60-degree 24 valve V6 has a cast iron block and aluminum cylinder heads with a camshaft in each cylinder head. The engine block has thin-walled sections for light weight. A "cradle frame" main bearing casting - the main bearing caps are cast as a unit, with a bridge, or truss, connecting them - supports the cast ductile iron crankshaft.

Both camshafts are driven off the crankshaft by a cog belt. A spring loaded tensioner, adjusted by an eccentric type locknut, maintains belt tension. Each camshaft actuates two valves per cylinder through hydraulic lash adjusters and shaft-mounted forged aluminum rocker arms.

Each cast aluminum three-ring piston has two compression rings and a three-piece oil control ring. The piston pins are pressed into forged steel connecting rods. The flat-topped pistons produce a 9.0:1 compression ratio.

The distributor, which is mounted on the transaxle end of the rear cylinder head, is driven by a helical gear on the camshaft. The water pump, which is bolted to the timing belt end of the engine block, is driven off the crankshaft by the timing belt. The gear type oil pump is mounted in the oil pump case and attached to the timing belt cover. It is driven by the crankshaft.

From the oil pump, oil travels through the filter to the main oil gallery, from which it is routed either directly to the main bearings, crankshaft, connecting rod bearings and pistons and cylinder walls or to the cylinder heads.

**3.6 Valve cover mounting bolts (arrows)**

## 2  Repair operations possible with the engine in the vehicle

Many major repair operations can be accomplished without removing the engine from the vehicle.

Clean the engine compartment and the exterior of the engine with some type of degreaser before any work is done. It will make the job easier and help keep dirt out of the internal areas of the engine.

Depending on the components involved, it may be helpful to remove the bonnet to improve access to the engine as repairs are performed (refer to Chapter 11 if necessary). Cover the fenders to prevent damage to the paint. Special pads are available, but an old bedspread or blanket will also work.

If vacuum, exhaust, oil or coolant leaks develop, indicating a need for gasket or seal renewal, the repairs can generally be made with the engine in the vehicle. The inlet and exhaust manifold gaskets, sump gasket, camshaft and crankshaft oil seals and cylinder head gaskets are all accessible with the engine in place.

Exterior engine components, such as the inlet and exhaust manifolds, the sump (and the oil pump), the water pump, the starter motor, the alternator, the distributor and the fuel system components can be

removed for repair with the engine in place.

Since the cylinder heads can be removed without pulling the engine, camshaft and valve component servicing can also be accomplished with the engine in the vehicle. Renewal of the timing belt and sprockets is also possible with the engine in the vehicle.

In extreme cases caused by a lack of necessary equipment, repair or renewal of piston rings, pistons, connecting rods and rod bearings is possible with the engine in the vehicle. However, this practice is not recommended because of the cleaning and preparation work that must be done to the components involved.

## 3  Valve cover - removal and refitting

### Removal

*Refer to illustrations 3.6 and 3.7*

1   Disconnect the negative battery cable.

2   Remove the air cleaner assembly (see Chapter 4).

3   If removing the rear valve cover (near the firewall), remove the upper inlet manifold (see Section 4).

4   Clearly label then remove the spark plug wires from the valve cover (see Chapter 1 if necessary).

5   Clearly label and then disconnect any emission hoses and electrical cables which connect to or cross over the valve cover.

6   Remove the valve cover bolts and lift off the cover **(see illustration)**. If the cover sticks to the cylinder head, tap on it with a soft-face hammer or place a wood block against the cover and tap on the wood with a hammer. **Caution:** *If you have to prise between the valve cover and the cylinder head, be extremely careful not to gouge or nick the gasket surfaces of either part. A leak could develop after reassembly.*

7   Remove the spark plug tube seals. Even if they look OK, they should be renewed **(see illustration)**.

8   Thoroughly clean the valve cover and remove all traces of old gasket material. Gasket removal solvents are available from auto parts stores and may prove helpful. After cleaning the surfaces, degrease them with a rag soaked in lacquer thinner or acetone.

### Refitting

9   Refit the new spark plug seals onto the tubes.

10   Refit a new gasket on the cover, using RTV sealant to hold it in place.

11   Tighten the valve cover bolts in 3 steps to the torque listed in this Chapter's Specifications using a criss-cross pattern starting in the middle of the cover and working outwards.

12   The remaining refitting steps are the reverse of removal. When complete, run the engine and check for oil leaks.

### Spark plug tube renewal

13   Remove the applicable valve cover (see above).

14   Grasp spark plug tube with locking pliers, carefully twist back and forth and remove the tube from cylinder head.

15   Clean the locking agent from the tube and the recess in cylinder head with solvent, and dry thoroughly.

16   Apply a small amount of Loctite No. 271, or equivalent, around the lower end of the tube and refit the tube into the cylinder head. Carefully tap the tube into the recess with a wood block and mallet until it is fully seated in the cylinder head.

## 4  Inlet manifold - removal and refitting

### Upper inlet manifold

**Removal**

*Refer to illustrations 4.3a, 4.3b, 4.5, 4.6 and 4.7*

1   Disconnect the negative battery cable (see Chapter 5, Section 1).

2   Remove the air filter inlet duct from the throttle body (see Chapter 4).

3   Clearly label and disconnect all hoses, wires, brackets and emission lines which attach to the inlet manifold **(see illustrations)**.

**3.7 Remove and renew the seal from each spark plug tube**

**4.3a Disconnect the throttle position sensor connector (arrow)**

**4.3b  Disconnect the vacuum hoses from the throttle body fitting (arrows)**

4    Disconnect the accelerator cable and cruise control cable (if applicable) from the throttle body (see Chapter 4 if necessary).
5    Remove the bolts securing the upper inlet manifold to the right and left side support brackets **(see illustration)**.
6    Remove the EGR tube **(see illustration)**.
7    Loosen the upper inlet manifold bolts 1/4 turn at a time until they can be removed by hand. Remove the upper inlet manifold from the engine **(see illustration)**. If it sticks, tap the manifold with a soft-face hammer or

carefully prise it from the lower inlet manifold. **Caution:** *Do not prise between gasket sealing surfaces.*
8    To minimize the chance of gasket debris or other contamination from getting into the engine, place clean rags into the lower inlet manifold passages.
9    Remove all traces of gasket material from both the upper and lower inlet manifold by carefully scraping them using a suitable gasket scraper. **Caution:** *The inlet manifold components are made of aluminium and are easily nicked or gouged. Do not damage the gasket surfaces or a leak may result after the work is complete. Gasket removal solvents are available from auto parts stores and may prove helpful.*
10    Using a precision straightedge and feeler gauge, check the upper and lower inlet manifold mating surfaces for warpage **(see illustration 4.22)**. If the warpage on any surface exceeds the limits listed in this Chapter's Specifications, the discrepant inlet manifold must be renewed.

### Refitting

11    Remove the rags from the lower inlet manifold. Use a shop vacuum to remove any contamination that may be present.
12    Refit the upper inlet manifold, using a new gasket. Tighten the bolts in 3 stages, working from the centre out, to the torque listed in this Chapter's Specifications.

13    Refit the EGR tube using new gaskets. Tighten the bolts to the torque listed in this Chapter's Specifications.
14    The remaining refitting steps are the reverse of removal.

## *Lower inlet manifold*

### Removal

*Refer to illustration 4.22*
15    Perform the fuel pressure relief procedure (see Chapter 4).
16    Remove the upper inlet manifold (see above).
17    Remove the fuel rail and injector assembly (see Chapter 4).
18    Loosen the inlet manifold nuts in the *reverse* order of the tightening sequence **(see illustration 4.24)**, 1/4 turn at a time until they can be removed by hand. Remove the washers.
19    Remove the lower inlet manifold from the engine. If it sticks, tap the manifold with a soft-face hammer or carefully prise it from the heads. **Caution:** *Do not prise between gasket sealing surfaces.*
20    To minimize the chance of gasket debris or other contamination from getting into the engine, place clean rags into the cylinder head inlet passages.
21    Remove all traces of gasket material from the upper and lower inlet manifold and cylinder heads by carefully scraping them

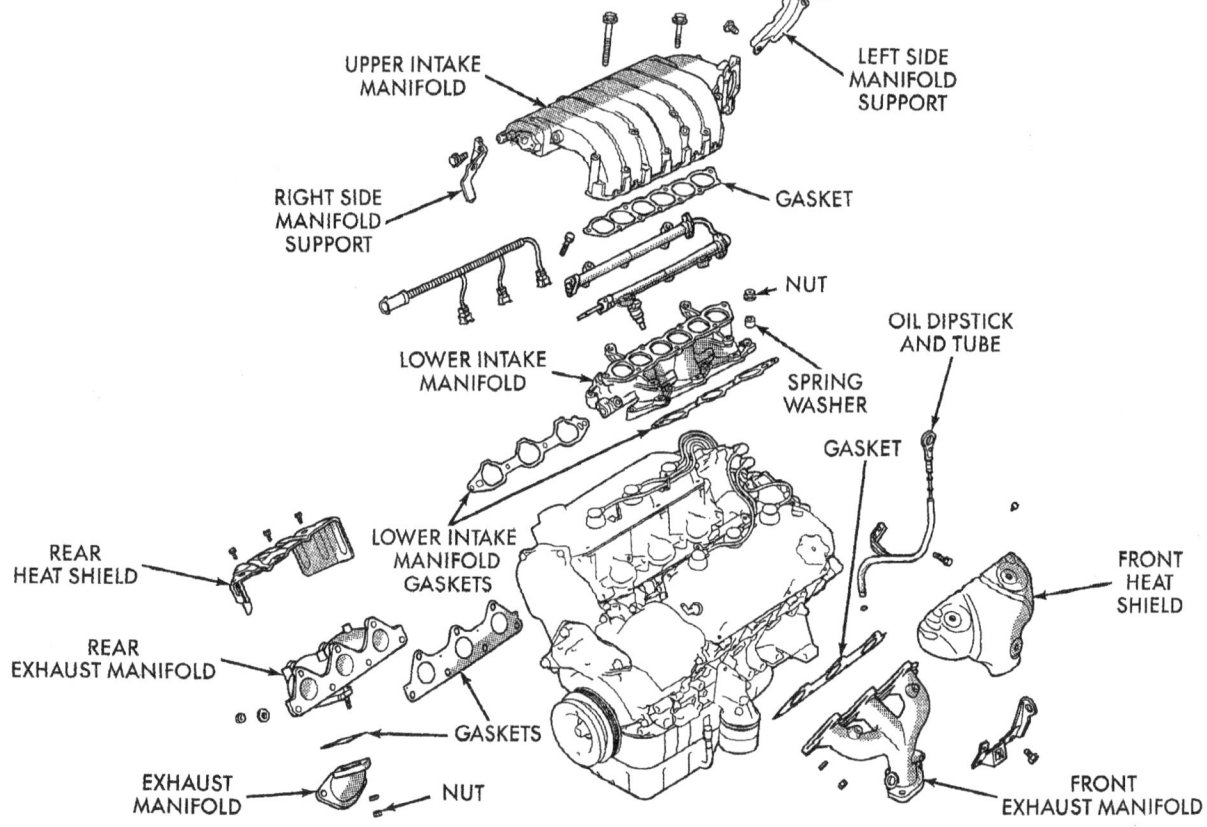

**4.5  Exploded view of V6 engine inlet and exhaust system components**

**4.6 From the rear of the upper inlet manifold, remove the EGR mounting bolts (arrows)**

using a suitable gasket scraper. **Caution:** *The inlet manifold components and cylinder heads are made of aluminum and are easily nicked or gouged. Do not damage the gasket surfaces or a leak may result after the work is complete. Gasket removal solvents are available from auto parts stores and may prove helpful.*

22 Using a precision straightedge and feeler gauge, check the upper and lower inlet manifold gasket surfaces for warpage **(see illustration)**. Check the gasket surface on the cylinder head also. If the warpage on any surface exceeds the limits listed in this Chapter's Specifications, the discrepant component must be renewed.

### Refitting

*Refer to illustration 4.24*

23 Remove the rags from the cylinder head inlet passages. Use a shop vacuum to remove any contamination that may be present.

24 Refit the lower inlet manifold, using a new gaskets. Tighten the nuts in three stages, in the sequence shown **(see illustration)** to the torque listed in this Chapter's Specifications.

25 Refit the fuel rail (see Chapter 4).

26 Refit the upper inlet manifold, using a new gasket. Tighten the bolts in three stages, working from the centre out, to the torque listed in this Chapter's Specifications.

27 Refit the EGR tube using new gaskets. Tighten the bolts to the torque listed in this Chapter's Specifications.

28 The remaining refitting steps are the reverse of removal.

## 5 Exhaust manifold - removal and refitting

**Warning:** *Allow the engine to cool completely before beginning this procedure.*
**Note:** *This procedure can be used to remove one or both of the exhaust manifolds as required.*

### *Removal*

*Refer to illustrations 5.3, 5.8 and 5.9*

1 Disconnect the negative battery cable.

2 Raise the vehicle and support it securely on jackstands.

3 Remove the exhaust manifold heat shield(s) **(see illustration)**. Before attempting to remove the rear manifold heat shield, disconnect the oxygen sensor wiring harness at the connector. In order to remove the front manifold heat shield, the alternator upper bracket must be removed.

4 To make removal easier, apply penetrating oil to the exhaust manifold and manifold-to-pipe fasteners.

5 Working under the vehicle, remove the exhaust manifold cross-over pipe.

6 Disconnect the oxygen sensor wiring harness at the connector.

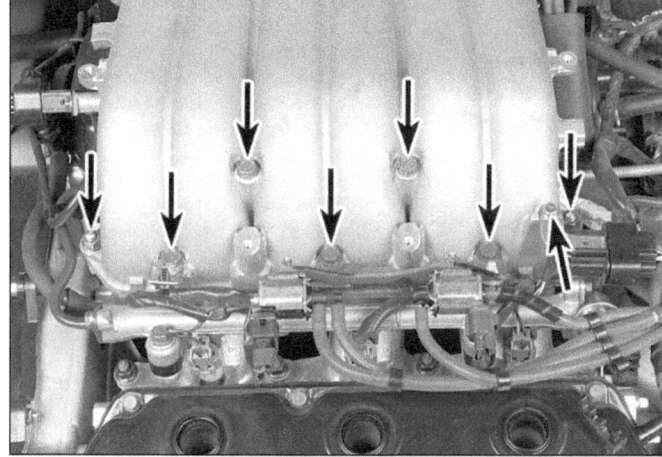

**4.7 Starting from the ends and working inward, remove the upper inlet manifold mounting bolts**

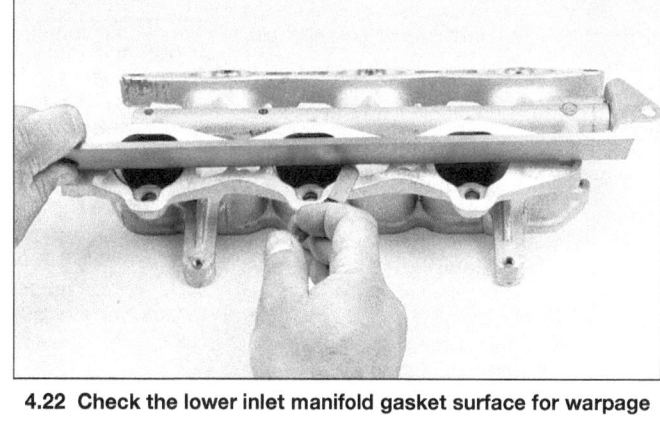

**4.22 Check the lower inlet manifold gasket surface for warpage**

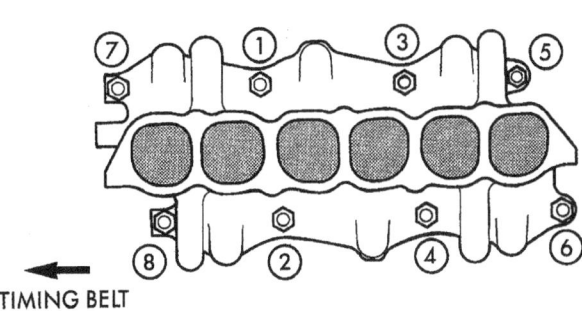

**4.24 Lower inlet manifold nut tightening sequence**

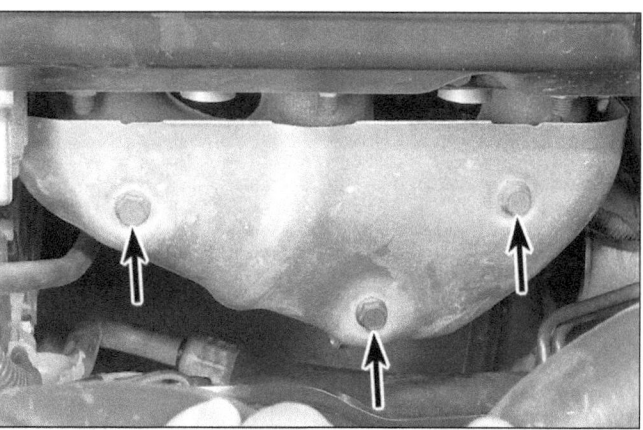

**5.3 Exhaust manifold heat shield bolts (arrows) (front exhaust manifold shown) - the upper alternator bracket must be removed to extract the upper left heat shield bolt**

**5.8 Exhaust manifold-to-exhaust system joint (arrows)**

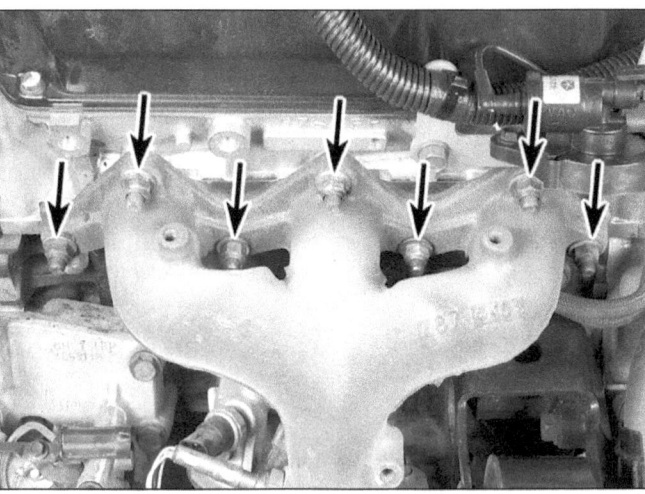

**5.9 Exhaust manifold mounting nuts (arrows) (front manifold shown, heat shield removed)**

7    If you are removing the rear exhaust manifold (near the firewall), remove the power steering pump bracket (see Chapter 10).

8    If you are removing the rear exhaust manifold (near the firewall), detach the exhaust system from the manifold **(see illustration)**. **Note:** *It may be necessary to remove, or partially remove, the exhaust system to facilitate rear manifold removal (see Chapter 4 if necessary).*

9    Unscrew the mounting nuts, remove the exhaust manifold and gasket **(see illustration)**.

10    Using a wire brush, clean the exhaust manifold studs, replacing any that show thread damage.

11    Using a scraper, remove all traces of gasket material from the exhaust manifold, cylinder head, and exhaust pipe mating surfaces and inspect them for wear and cracks. **Caution:** *When removing gasket material from any surface, especially aluminum, be very careful not to scratch or gouge the gasket surface. Any damage to the surface may a leak after reassembly. Gasket removal solvents are available from auto parts stores and may prove helpful.*

12    Using a precision straightedge and feeler gauge, check the exhaust manifold gasket surfaces for warpage. Check the surface on the cylinder head also. If the warpage on any surface exceeds the limits listed in this Chapter's Specifications, the exhaust manifold and/or cylinder head must be renewed or resurfaced by an automotive machine shop.

## Refitting

13    Refit the new exhaust gasket(s) onto the cylinder head.

14    Apply Loctite No. 271 to the exhaust manifold mounting stud threads.

15    Refit the manifold, washers and nuts. Tighten the nuts in three stages, working from the centre out, to the torque listed in this Chapter's Specifications.

16    The remaining refitting steps are the

reverse of removal. Refit a new gasket(s) between the exhaust manifold and exhaust pipe(s). Tighten the nuts to the torque listed in this Chapter's Specifications.

17    Run the engine and check for exhaust leaks.

---

## 6    Timing belt - removal, inspection and refitting

---

**Caution:** *If the timing belt failed with the engine operating, damage to the valves may have occurred. Perform an engine compression check after belt renewal to determine if any valve damage is present.*

### *Removal*

*Refer to illustrations 6.4a, 6.4b, 6.6, 6.7, 6.9, 6.11a, 6.11b, 6.12 and 6.13*

**Caution:** *Do not turn the crankshaft or camshafts after the timing belt has been removed, as this will damage the valves from contact*

with the pistons. *Do not try to turn the crankshaft with the camshaft sprocket bolt(s) and do not rotate the crankshaft counterclockwise as viewed from the timing belt end of the engine.*

**Note:** *In order to perform this procedure, a special tool is required to properly tension the timing belt. The manufacturers tool number is "EMD 998767" and may be available from a dealership parts department.*

1    Position the number one piston to the top of the cylinder.

2    Disconnect the negative battery cable.

3    Remove the drivebelts (see Chapter 1).

4    Loosen the large bolt in the centre of the crankshaft damper/pulley. It might be very tight, to break it loose insert a large screwdriver or bar through the opening in the pulley to keep the crankshaft stationary, then loosen the bolt with a socket and breaker bar. Remove the bolt, washer and dam-per/pulley from the crankshaft **(see illustrations)**.

5    After removing the crankshaft pulley,

**6.4a To keep the crankshaft from turning, insert a large screwdriver or bar through the opening in the damper/pulley and wedge it against the engine block, then loosen the bolt with a socket and breaker bar**

**6.4b Remove the damper/pulley from the crankshaft**

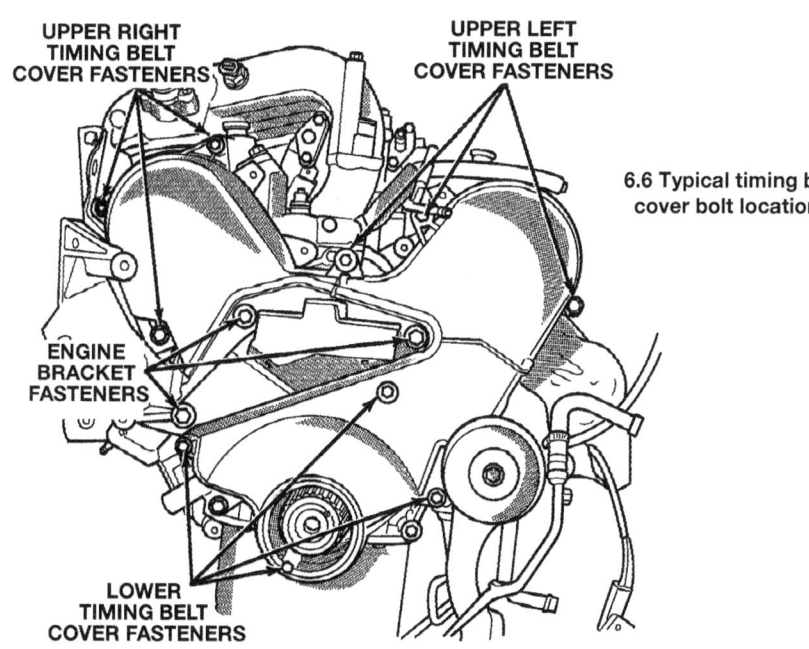

6.6 Typical timing belt cover bolt locations

UPPER RIGHT TIMING BELT COVER FASTENERS

UPPER LEFT TIMING BELT COVER FASTENERS

ENGINE BRACKET FASTENERS

LOWER TIMING BELT COVER FASTENERS

reinstall the crankshaft bolt using an appropriate spacer (this will enable you to turn the crankshaft later).

6  Remove the upper-left timing belt cover **(see illustration)**.

7  Remove the lower timing belt cover **(see illustration)**.

8  Detach the power steering pump bracket from the engine (see Chapter 10 if necessary).

9  Remove the upper-right timing belt cover **(see illustration)**.

10  Remove the right (passenger side) engine mount and the mounting bracket from the engine (see Section 17). **Note:** *Make sure the engine is supported with a floor jack placed under the oil pan. Place a wood block on the jack head to prevent the floor jack from denting or damaging the oil pan.*

11  Make sure the timing marks on the crankshaft sprocket and camshaft sprockets align with their respective marks before removing the timing belt **(see illustrations)**.

12  If you plan to reuse the timing belt, paint an arrow on it to indicate the direction of rotation (clockwise) **(see illustration)**.

6.7  Remove the bolts (arrows) that attach the timing belt lower cover to the engine

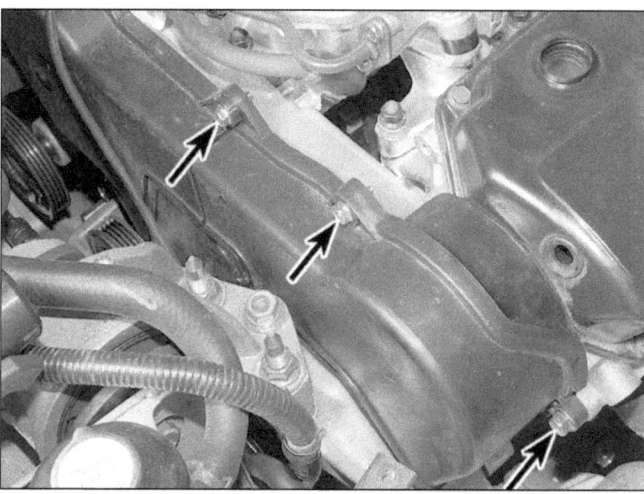

6.9 Typical right side timing belt cover bolt locations

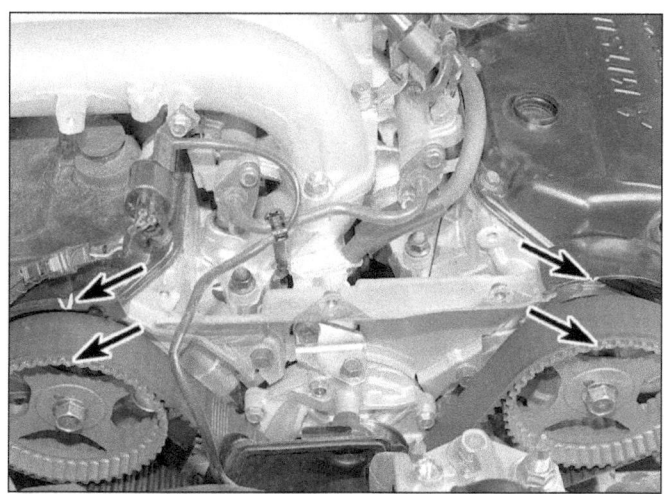

6.11a  Verify that the camshaft sprocket timing marks are aligned with their respective marks on the rear timing belt covers

6.11b  Crankshaft timing belt sprocket and oil pump housing timing marks (arrows)

**6.12  Paint an arrow on the timing belt in the direction of rotation (clockwise) so it may be reinstalled in the same direction**

**6.13  Timing belt tensioner mounting bolts (arrows)**

**6.18  Carefully inspect the timing belt for damage or wear - bending it backwards will often make defects more apparent**

13    Loosen the timing belt tensioner mounting bolts and then remove the tensioner **(see illustration)**. **Note:** *The tensioner piston will extend when the assembly is removed.*

14    Carefully slip the timing belt off the sprockets and set it aside. If you plan to reuse the timing belt, place it in a plastic bag - do not allow the belt to come in contact with any type of oil or water as this will greatly shorten belt life.

## Inspection

*Refer to illustration 6.18*

15    With the timing belt covers removed, now is a good time to inspect the front crankshaft and camshaft seals for leakage. If leakage is evident, renew them (see Section 7 and 8, respectively).

16    Inspect the water pump for evidence of leakage (usually indicated by a trail of wet or dried coolant). Check the pulley for excessive radial play and bearing roughness. Replace if necessary (see Chapter 3).

17    Rotate the tensioner pulley and idler pulley by hand and move them side-to-side to detect bearing roughness and/or excessive play. Visually inspect all timing belt sprockets

for any signs of damage or wear. Replace as necessary.

18    Inspect the timing belt for cracks, separation, wear, missing teeth and oil contamination **(see illustration)**. Replace the belt if it's in questionable condition or the engine mileage is close to that referenced in the *Maintenance Schedule* (see Chapter 1).

19    Check the timing belt tensioner unit for leaks or any other obvious damage, renew if necessary.

## Refitting

*Refer to illustrations 6.22, 6.24, 6.25 and 6.27*

20    Confirm that the timing marks on both camshaft sprockets are aligned with their respective marks on the rear timing belt covers **(see illustration 6.11a)**. Reposition the camshafts if required. **Caution:** *If it is necessary to rotate the camshafts to align the timing marks, first rotate the crankshaft slightly counterclockwise (three notches on the sprocket) to ensure the valves do not contact the pistons.*

21    Position the crankshaft sprocket with the timing marks aligned **(see illustration 6.11b)**.

22    Refit the timing belt as follows; first place the belt onto the right camshaft sprocket (the one towards the rear of the vehicle) and clamp it to the sprocket, while maintaining tension on the belt, wrap it under the water pump pulley and place it onto the left sprocket camshaft sprocket. Secure the timing belt to the left camshaft sprocket **(see illustration)**. Continue to wrap the timing belt over the idler pulley, around the crankshaft sprocket and finishing with the tensioner pulley. Remove the clamps from the camshaft sprockets.

23    Make sure the timing belt is tight between the left camshaft sprocket and the crankshaft sprocket, all the slack is at the tensioner pulley and all the timing marks are aligned.

24    Before refitting, the timing belt tensioner piston must be compressed into the tensioner housing. Place the tensioner in a vise so the surface with the pin hole is facing up. Slowly compress the tensioner using the vise, then refit an appropriate size Allen wrench or drill bit through the body and into the piston to retain the piston in this position **(see illustration)**. Remove the tensioner from the vise.

**6.22 Binder clips (arrows) can be used to retain the timing belt in position on the camshaft sprockets during refitting**

**6.24 Using a vise (lined with soft-jaws), compress the timing belt tensioner piston until the holes in the housing and piston align. Then place a small Allen wrench (arrow) or drill bit, through the holes to keep the piston in position for refitting**

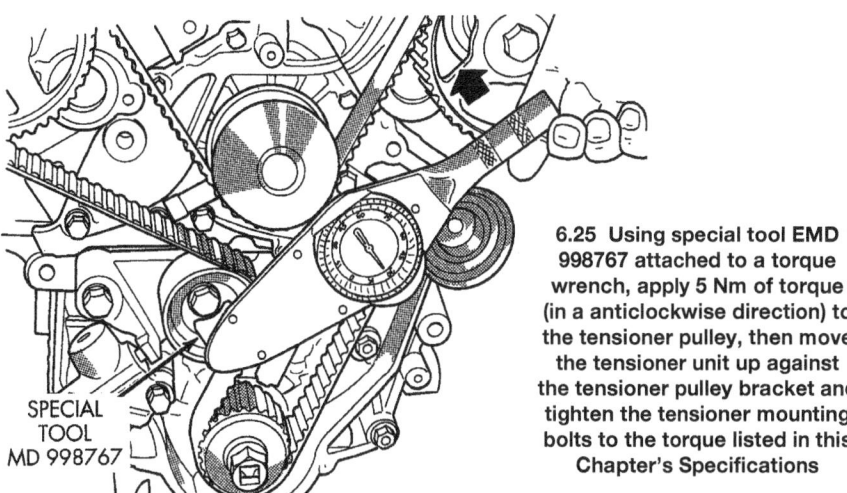

**6.25  Using special tool EMD 998767 attached to a torque wrench, apply 5 Nm of torque (in a anticlockwise direction) to the tensioner pulley, then move the tensioner unit up against the tensioner pulley bracket and tighten the tensioner mounting bolts to the torque listed in this Chapter's Specifications**

25    Using the special tool "EMD 998767" engaged in the tensioner pulley, have an assistant apply 5 Nm of tension in a anticlockwise direction **(see illustration)**.

26    With the torque applied to the tensioner

**6.27  If the timing belt tension is set correctly, the tensioner piston retaining pin (arrow) (an Allen wrench in this case) can be removed and refitted easily**

pulley, refit the tensioner assembly. Move the tensioner up against the tensioner pulley bracket and tighten the mounting bolts to the torque listed in this Chapter's Specifications. Remove the torque wrench and special tool from the tensioner pulley.

27    Remove the Allen wrench or drill bit retaining the piston from the tensioner. The timing belt tension is correct when the tensioner piston retaining pin (Allen wrench or drill bit) can be withdrawn and reinserted easily **(see illustration)**. Verify that the timing marks on the camshaft sprockets and crankshaft sprocket are still aligned with their respective timing marks **(see illustrations 6.11a and 6.11b)**.

28    Using the bolt in the centre of the crankshaft sprocket, slowly turn the crankshaft clockwise two complete revolutions. **Caution:** *If you feel strong resistance while turning the crankshaft - STOP, the valves may be hitting the pistons from incorrect valve timing. Stop and re-check the valve timing.* **Note:** *The camshafts and crankshaft sprocket marks will align every two revolutions of the crankshaft.* Recheck the alignment of the timing marks **(see illustrations 6.11a and 6.11b)**.

If the marks do not align properly, remove the timing belt tensioner, slip the belt off the camshaft sprockets, realign the marks, reinstall the belt and tensioner, then check the alignment again.

29    After crankshaft rotation, recheck the timing belt tension by inserting the tensioner piston retaining pin (Allen wrench or drill bit) back into the tensioner. If the retaining pin cannot be inserted and withdrawn freely, readjust the timing belt tension and repeat Steps 24 through 29.

30    The remaining refitting steps are the reverse of removal. Tighten the crankshaft damper/pulley bolt to the torque listed in this Chapter's Specifications.

## 7   Crankshaft front oil seal - renewal

*Refer to illustrations 7.2, 7.3 and 7.5*
**Caution:** *Do not rotate the camshafts or crankshaft when the timing belt is removed or damage to the engine may occur.*

1    Remove the timing belt (see Section 6).

2    Remove the crankshaft timing belt sprocket using a gear puller. Remove the Woodruff key from the crankshaft keyway **(see illustration)**.

3    Wrap the tip of a small screwdriver with vinyl tape. Carefully use the screwdriver to prise the seal out of its bore **(see illustration)**. Take care to prevent damaging the oil pump assembly, the crankshaft and the seal bore.

4    Thoroughly clean and inspect the seal bore and sealing surface on the crankshaft. Minor imperfections can be removed with fine emery cloth. If there is a groove worn in the crankshaft sealing surface (from contact with the seal), installing a new seal will probably not stop the leak.

5    Lubricate the new seal with engine oil and using a hammer and the appropriate size socket, drive the seal into the bore until it's flush with the oil pump housing **(see illustration)**.

**7.2  After removing the timing belt sprocket, remove the Woodruff key (arrow) from the crankshaft**

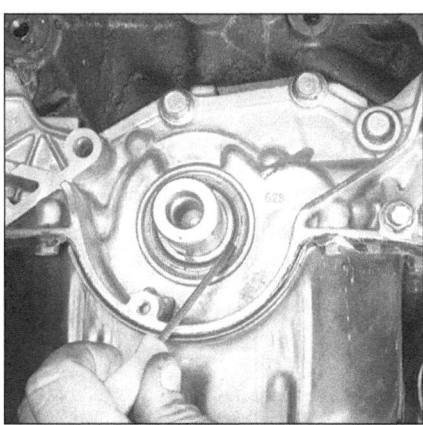

**7.3  Using a hooked tool or screwdriver, carefully prise the crankshaft front seal out of its bore - DO NOT nick or scratch the crankshaft or seal bore**

**7.5  Lubricate the new seal with clean engine oil and drive it into place using a hammer and socket**

**8.3 To hold the camshaft while removing the sprocket bolt, use an old piece of timing belt wrapped around the sprocket and a chain wrench as shown**

**8.4 Using a hooked tool or screwdriver, carefully prise the camshaft seal out of the bore - DO NOT nick or scratch the camshaft or seal bore**

**8.6a Using a hammer and the appropriate size socket, drive the camshaft seal into the bore until it is flush with the cylinder head**

6    Refit the Woodruff key into the slot in the crankshaft. Place the crankshaft timing belt sprocket onto the crankshaft with the timing belt retaining lip facing inward (toward the engine).

7    The remaining refitting steps are the reverse of removal. Tighten the crankshaft pulley bolt to the torque listed in this Chapter's Specifications.

8    Start the engine and check for oil leaks.

## 8    Camshaft oil seal - renewal

*Refer to illustrations 8.3, 8.4, 8.6a and 8.6b*
**Caution:** *Do not rotate the camshafts or crankshaft when the timing belt is removed or damage to the engine may occur.*

1    Remove the timing belt (see Section 6).

2    Rotate the crankshaft counterclockwise until the crankshaft sprocket is three notches BTDC. This will prevent engine damage if the camshaft sprocket is inadvertently rotated during removal.

3    While keeping the camshaft from rotat-

ing, remove the camshaft sprocket bolt. Then using two large screwdrivers, lever the sprocket off the camshaft. **Note:** *A strap-type damper/pulley holder tool is available at most auto parts stores and is recommended for this procedure, however, if you are not going to reuse the old timing belt, you can wrap a piece of it around the sprocket and use a chain wrench to hold the sprocket in place as shown* **(see illustration)**.

4    Carefully prise out the camshaft oil seal using a small hooked tool or screwdriver **(see illustration)**. Don't scratch the bore or damage the camshaft in the process (if the camshaft is damaged, the new seal will end up leaking).

5    Clean the bore and coat the outer edge of the new seal with engine oil or multi-purpose grease. Also lubricate the seal lip.

6    Using a socket with an outside diameter slightly smaller than the outside diameter of the seal and a hammer **(see illustration)**, carefully drive the new seal into the cylinder head until it's flush with the face of the cylinder head. If a socket isn't available,

a short section of pipe will also work. **Note:** *If engine location makes it difficult to use a hammer to refit the camshaft seal, fabricate a seal refitting tool from a piece of pipe cut to the appropriate length, a bolt and a large washer* **(see illustration)**. *Place the section of pipe over the seal and thread the bolt into the camshaft. The seal can now be pressed into the bore by tightening the bolt.*

7    Refit the camshaft sprocket, aligning the pin in the camshaft with the hole in the sprocket. Using an appropriate tool to hold the camshaft sprocket, tighten the camshaft sprocket bolt to the torque listed in this Chapter's Specifications.

8    Refit the timing belt (see Section 6).

9    Run the engine and check for oil leaks.

## 9    Rocker arm and hydraulic valve lash adjuster assembly - removal, inspection and refitting

### *Removal*

1    Disconnect the negative battery cable.

2    Position the number one piston to the top of the cylinder.

3    Remove the valve cover(s) as required (see Section 3).

4    Prior to removing the rocker arm shafts, identify each rocker arm and shaft as to its proper location (cylinder number and inlet or exhaust). **Caution:** *Do not interchange the rocker arms onto a different shaft or shaft assemblies onto a different location as this could lead to premature wear.*

5    Loosen the rocker arm shaft bolts 1/4-turn at a time, until they can be loosened by hand, in the *reverse* order of the tightening sequence **(see illustration 9.17)**. Completely loosen the bolts, but do not remove them, leaving them in place will prevent the assembly from falling apart when it is lifted off the cylinder head.

6    Lift the rocker arms and shaft assemblies from the cylinder head and set them on the workbench. **Note:** *The hydraulic*

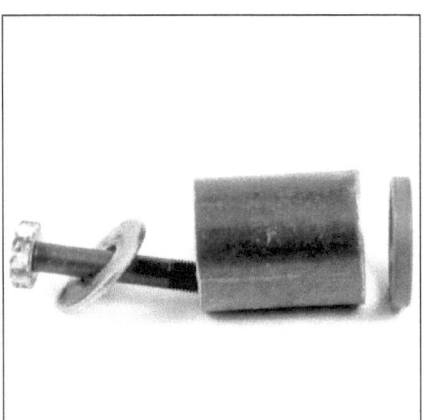

**8.6b If the space is too confined to use a hammer to drive the seal in place, fabricate a tool using a bolt, washer and section of pipe. Place the section of pipe over the seal and thread the bolt into the camshaft to press the seal into the bore**

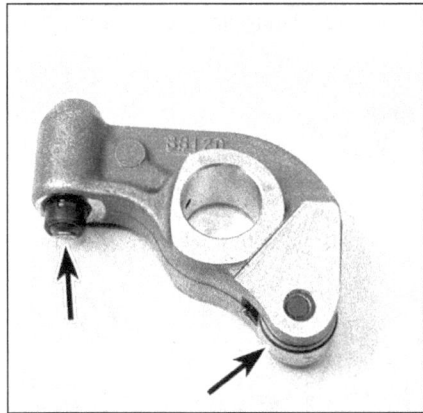

**9.8 Visually inspect the hydraulic lash adjuster and roller (arrows) for damage and excessive play - check the rocker arm shaft bore for score marks or excessive wear**

**9.14  The inlet rocker arm shaft springs (arrows) must be refitted as shown**

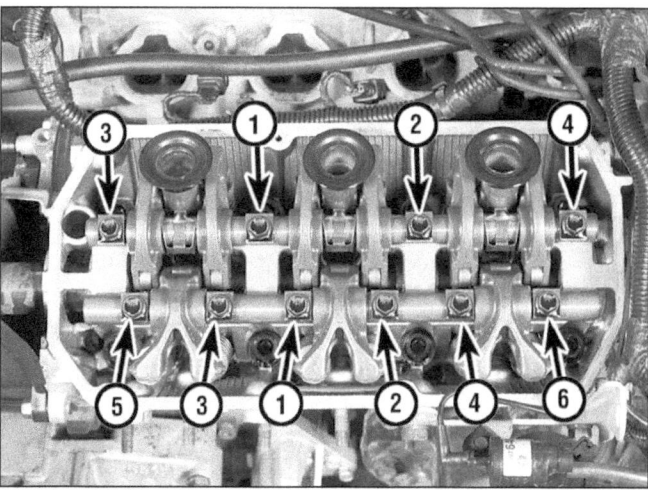

**9.17  Rocker arm shaft bolt TIGHTENING sequence**

*valve lash adjusters may become dislodged from the rocker arms during shaft removal. If required, secure the adjusters in place with vinyl tape.*

7    Disassemble the rocker arm shaft components paying close attention to their positions. **Note:** *To keep the rocker arms and related parts in order, it's a good idea to remove them and put them onto two lengths of wire (such as unbent coat hangers) in the same order as they're removed, marking each wire (which simulates the rocker shaft) as to which end would be the front of the engine.*

## Inspection

*Refer to illustration 9.8*

**Note:** *The valve lash adjuster is an integral part of each rocker arm and cannot be renewed separately. If defective, both must be renewed.*

8    Visually check the rocker arms for excessive wear or damage **(see illustration)**. Replace them if evidence of wear or damage is found.

9    Inspect each lash adjuster carefully for signs of wear and damage, particularly on the surface that contacts the valve tip. Use a small diameter wire to check the oil holes for restrictions.

10    Since the lash adjusters frequently become clogged, we recommend replacing the rocker arm/lash adjuster assembly if you're concerned about their condition or if the engine is exhibiting valve "tapping" noises.

11    Inspect all rocker arm shaft components. Look for cracks, worn or scored surfaces or other damage. Replace any parts found to be damaged or worn excessively.

## Refitting

*Refer to illustrations 9.14 and 9.17*

12    Prior to refitting, the lash adjusters must be partially full of engine oil - indicated by little or no plunger action when the adjuster is depressed. If there's excessive plunger travel, place the rocker arm assembly into

clean engine oil and pump the plunger until the plunger travel is eliminated. **Note:** *If the plunger still travels within the rocker arm when full of oil it's defective and the rocker arm assembly must be renewed.*

13    Refit the rocker arms (and springs - inlet shafts only) onto the shafts, making sure they are reinstalled in their original locations.

14    On the inlet rocker arm shafts, make sure that the springs are refitted on the shaft in the correct locations **(see illustration)**.

15    On the right (rear) cylinder head, refit the rocker arm assemblies with the flat at the end of each rocker arm shaft located at the timing belt end of the engine and positioned toward their respective valves.

16    On the left (front) cylinder head, refit the rocker arm assemblies with the flat at the end of each rocker arm shaft located at the transaxle end of the engine and positioned toward their respective valves.

17    Tighten the rocker arm shaft bolts in sequence shown **(see illustration)** in three steps to the torque listed in this Chapter's Specifications.

18    The remaining refitting steps are the reverse of removal. Run the engine and

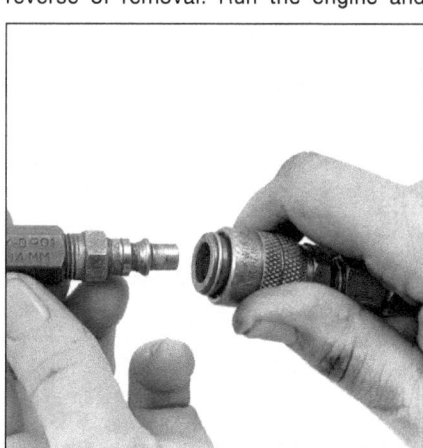

**10.5  On the left (front) cylinder head, remove the thrust cover and carefully withdraw the camshaft**

check for oil leaks and proper operation.

19    When re-starting the engine after replacing the rocker arm/lash adjusters, the adjusters will normally make "tapping" noises due to air in the lubrication system. To bleed air from the lash adjusters, start the engine and allow it to reach operating temperature, slowly raise the speed of the engine from idle to 3,000 rpm and back to idle over a one minute period. If, after several attempts, the adjuster(s) do not become silent, renew the defective rocker arm/lash adjuster assembly.

## 10  Camshafts - removal, inspection and refitting

**Note:** *The camshaft(s) cannot be removed with the cylinder head(s) fitted on the engine.*

## Removal

*Refer to illustration 10.5*

1    Remove the rocker arm shaft assemblies (see Section 9).

2    If you are removing the camshaft in the right (rear) cylinder head, remove the distributor (see Chapter 5).

3    Remove the cylinder head (see Section 12).

4    On the right cylinder head, carefully withdraw the camshaft from the distributor opening in the rear of the cylinder head. **Caution:** *Do not damage the camshaft lobes or bearing journals during removal.* **Note:** *If you are removing both camshafts, identify each one as it is removed from the cylinder head so that it may be refitted back in it's original location.*

5    On the left (front) cylinder head, remove the thrust case from the rear of the cylinder head and withdraw the camshaft **(see illustration)**. **Caution:** *Do not damage the camshaft lobes or bearing journals during removal.*

6    Remove the camshaft seal(s) from the cylinder head(s) (see Section 8 if necessary).

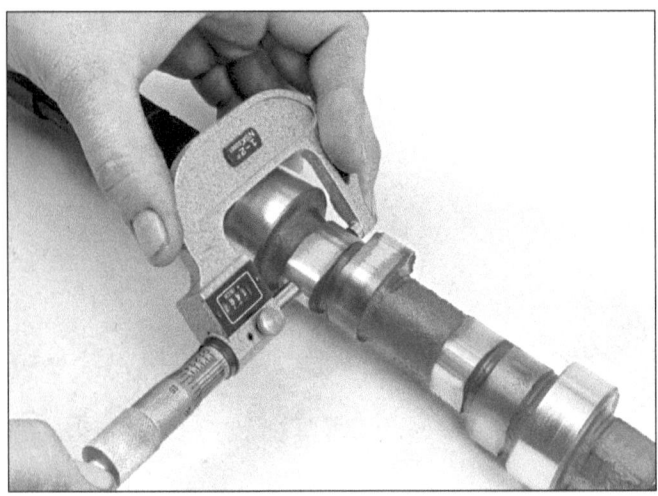

**10.10 Check the camshaft lobes for wear with a micrometer**

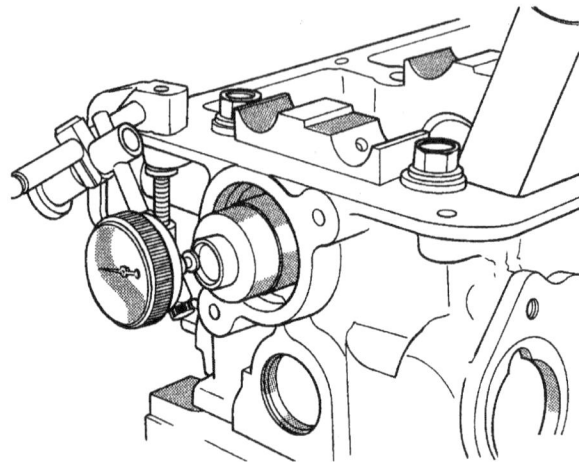

**10.13 Measure the camshaft endplay with a dial indicator positioned on the sprocket end of the camshaft as shown**

## Inspection

*Refer to illustration 10.10*

7    Using a suitable scraper, remove all traces of gasket material from all gasket surfaces. **Caution:** *When removing gasket material from any surface, especially aluminum, be very careful not to scratch or gouge the gasket surface. Any damage to the surface may a leak after reassembly. Gasket removal solvents are available from auto parts stores and may prove helpful.*

8    Thoroughly clean the camshaft(s) with a rag soaked in lacquer thinner or acetone. Visually inspect the camshaft(s) for wear and/or damage to the lobe surfaces, bearing journals and seal contact surfaces. Visually inspect the camshaft bearing surfaces in the cylinder head(s) for scoring and other damage. Cylinder head renewal may be necessary if the camshaft bearing surfaces in the head are damaged or excessively worn.

9    Replace any component that fails the above inspections.

10    Using a micrometer, check the camshaft lobes for excessive wear by measuring the centre of the lobe (the area the rocker arm roller rides on) and comparing it with the edges of the lobes (the area the rocker arm roller does not ride on) **(see illustration)**. If any wear is indicated, check the corresponding rocker arm, renew the camshaft and rocker arms if necessary.

### Camshaft endplay measurement

*Refer to illustration 10.13*

11    Lubricate the camshaft(s) and cylinder head bearing journals with clean engine oil.

12    Carefully insert the camshaft into the cylinder head and refit the thrust case or distributor as applicable. Tighten the bolts to the torque listed in this Chapter's Specifications.

13    Fit a dial indicator set up on the cylinder head and place the indicator tip on the camshaft at the sprocket end **(see illustration)**.

14    Using a screwdriver, carefully prise the camshaft to the rear of the cylinder head until

it stops. Zero the dial indicator and prise the camshaft forward. The amount of indicator travel is the camshaft endplay. Compare the endplay measurement with the tolerance listed in this Chapter's Specifications. If the endplay is excessive, check the camshaft and cylinder head thrust bearing surfaces for wear and renew components as necessary.

## Refitting

*Refer to illustration 10.15*

15    Very carefully clean the camshaft and bearing journals. Liberally coat the bearing journals, lobes and thrust bearing surfaces of the camshaft with engine assembly lube or engine oil **(see illustration)**.

16    Carefully insert the camshaft into the cylinder head. On the left side cylinder head, refit the thrust case, using a new O-ring, and tighten the bolts to the torque listed in this Chapter's Specifications.

17    Refit a new camshaft oil seal in the cylinder head (see Section 8).

18    Inspect the cylinder head bolts and refit the cylinder head(s) (see Section 12). Torque the cylinder head bolts as described in Section 12.

19    If removed, refit the distributor using a new O-ring (see Chapter 5). Tighten the mounting nuts to the torque listed in the Chapter 5 Specifications.

20    The remaining refitting steps are the reverse of removal. Start the engine and check for leaks and proper operation.

---

## 11  Valve springs, retainers and seals - renewal

---

*Refer to illustrations 11.5, 11.7, 11.8, 11.13 and 11.15*

**Note:** *Broken valve springs and defective valve stem seals can be renewed without removing the cylinder heads. Two special tools and a compressed air source are normally required to perform this operation, so*

*read through this Section carefully and rent or buy the tools before beginning the job.*

1    Remove the appropriate valve cover (see Section 3).

2    Remove the rocker arm assemblies (see Section 9).

3    Remove the spark plugs from the cylinder head (see Chapter 1 if necessary).

4    Turn the crankshaft until the piston in the affected cylinder is at the top of the cylinder on the compression stroke. If you're replacing all of the valve stem seals, begin with cylinder number one and work on the valves for one cylinder at a time. Move from cylinder-to-cylinder following the firing order sequence (see this Chapter's Specifications).

5    Thread an adapter into the spark plug hole **(see illustration)** and connect an air hose from a compressed air source to it. Most auto parts stores can supply the air hose adapter. **Note:** *Many cylinder compression gauges utilize a screw-in fitting that may work with your air hose quick-disconnect fitting.*

6    Apply compressed air to the cylinder. **Warning:** *The piston may be forced down by compressed air, causing the crankshaft to*

**10.15 Prior to installing the camshaft, lubricate the bearing journals, thrust surfaces and lobes with engine assembly lube or clean engine oil**

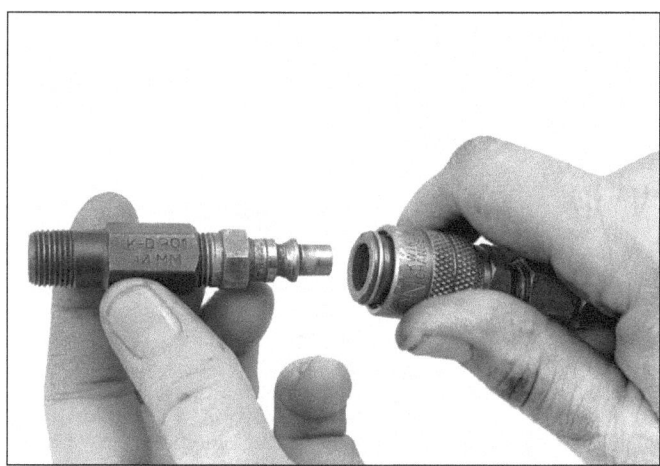

**11.5 This is what the air hose adapter that threads into the spark plug hole looks like - they're readily available from auto parts stores**

**11.7 Use a small magnet (shown) or needle-nose pliers to remove the valve spring keepers - be careful not to drop them down into the engine!**

*turn suddenly. If the wrench used when positioning the number one piston at TDC is still attached to the crankshaft pulley bolt, it could cause damage or injury when the crankshaft moves.*

7   Stuff clean shop rags into the cylinder head holes above and below the valves to prevent parts and tools from falling into the engine, then use a valve spring compressor tool to compress the spring. Remove the keepers with small needle-nose pliers or a magnet **(see illustration)**.

8   Remove the spring retainer and valve spring. Next, using pliers remove the valve guide seal and then lift off spring seat **(see illustration)**. **Caution:** *If air pressure fails to hold the valve in the closed position during this operation, the valve face and/or seat is probably damaged. If so, the cylinder head will have to be removed for additional repair operations.*

9   Wrap a rubber band or tape around the top of the valve stem so the valve won't fall into the combustion chamber, then release the air pressure.

10   Inspect the valve stem for damage.

Rotate the valve in the guide and check the end for eccentric movement, which would indicate that the valve is bent.

11   Move the valve up-and-down in the guide and make sure it doesn't bind. If the valve stem binds, either the valve is bent or the guide is damaged. In either case, the head will have to be removed for repair.

12   Pull up on the valve stem to close the valve, reapply air pressure to the cylinder to retain the valve in the closed position, then remove the tape or rubber band from the valve stem.

13   Refit the valve spring seat. Lubricate the valve stem with clean engine oil and place the new valve guide seal. Tap it into place with deep socket **(see illustration)**.

14   Refit the spring in position over the valve.

15   Refit the valve spring retainer. Compress the valve spring and carefully position the keepers in the groove. Apply a small dab of grease to the inside of each keeper to hold it in place if necessary **(see illustration)**.

16   Remove the pressure from the spring tool and make sure the keepers are seated.

17   Disconnect the air hose and remove the adapter from the spark plug hole. Repeat the procedure for any other defective valves.

18   Refit the rocker arm assemblies (see Section 9).

19   Refit the spark plug and connect the wire(s).

20   Refit the valve cover (see Section 3).

21   Start and run the engine, then check for oil leaks and unusual sounds coming from the valve cover area.

### 12   Cylinder head - removal and refitting

**Caution:** *Allow the engine to cool completely before beginning this procedure.*

### *Removal*

*Refer to illustrations 12.11, 12.18, 12.19a and 12.19b*

1   Disconnect the negative battery cable.

2   Position the number one piston to the top of the cylinder.

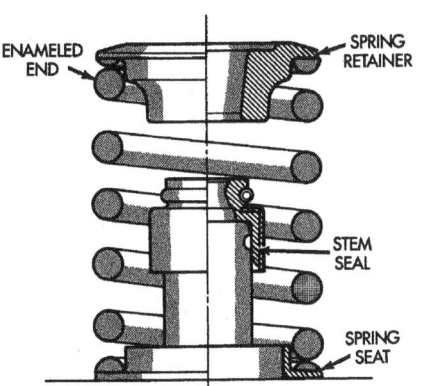

**11.8 Cut-away view of the valve seal and spring components**

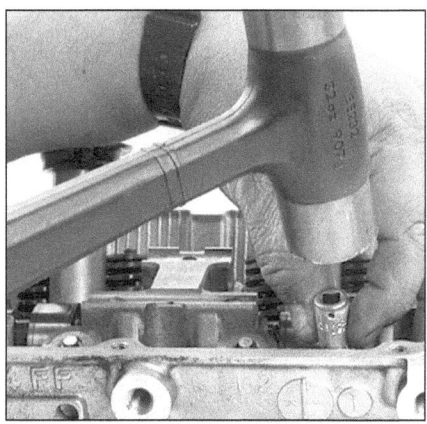

**11.13 Gently tap the new seal onto the valve guide with a hammer and deep socket**

**11.15 Apply a small dab of grease to each keeper before refitting to hold it in place on the valve stem until the spring is released**

**12.11  Remove the EGR valve and engine lifting bracket (arrows)**

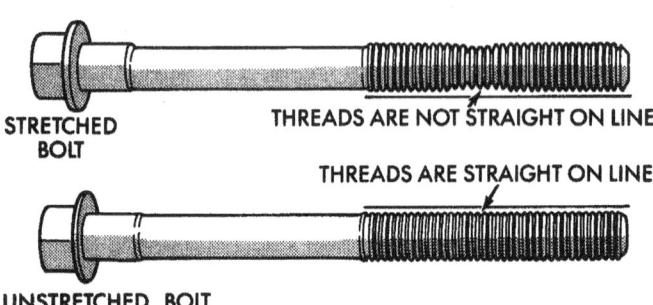

**12.18  Place a precision straightedge along the cylinder head bolt thread profile as shown, if any part of the bolt threads are not on the straightedge, the bolt is stretched and must be renewed**

3    Remove the upper and lower inlet manifolds (see Section 4).

4    Drain the cooling system, remove the spark plugs and spark plug wires (see Chapter 1). **Note:** *Leave the plug wires attached to the distributor cap.*

5    If you are removing the right (rear) cylinder head, remove the distributor (see Chapter 5).

6    Remove the thermostat housing from the rear of the cylinder heads (see Chapter 3).

7    Remove rocker arm shaft assemblies (see Section 9).

8    If you are removing the right (rear) cylinder head, remove the bolts securing the power steering reservoir and hoses to the cylinder head and position them out of the way (see Chapter 10).

9    Disconnect the power steering pump bracket from the engine (see Chapter 10).

10   Remove the exhaust manifold(s) (see Section 5).

11   If you are removing the right (rear) cylinder head, remove the EGR valve from the rear of the cylinder head **(see illustration)**.

12   Remove the timing belt (see Section 6).

13   Remove camshaft sprocket(s) (see Section 8).

14   Clearly label and disconnect any hoses, lines, brackets or electrical connections that may interfere with cylinder head removal.

15   Loosen the cylinder head bolts, 1/4-turn at a time, in the *reverse* order of the tightening sequence **(see illustration 12.24)** until they can be removed by hand.

16   Carefully lift the cylinder head straight up and place it on wood blocks to prevent damage to the sealing surfaces. If the head sticks to the engine block, dislodge it by placing a wood block against the head casting and tapping the wood with a hammer or by prying the head with a prybar placed carefully on a casting protrusion. **Note:** *If further disassembly of the cylinder head is required, refer to Part B of this Chapter.*

17   Remove all traces of old gasket material from the block and head. Special gasket removal solvents that soften gaskets and make removal much easier are available at auto parts stores. **Caution:** *The cylinder head is aluminum, be very careful not to gouge the sealing surfaces.* When working

on the block, place clean shop rags into the cylinders to help keep out debris. Use a vacuum to remove any contamination from the engine. Use a tap of the correct size to chase the threads in the engine block. Clean and inspect all threaded fasteners for damage.

18   Inspect the cylinder head bolt threads for "necking," where the diameter of threads narrow due to bolt stretching **(see illustration)**. If any cylinder head bolt exhibits damage or necking, it must be renewed.

19   Using a precision straightedge and feeler gauge, check all gasket surfaces for warpage **(see illustrations)**. If the warpage on any surface exceeds the limits listed in this Chapter's Specifications, the discrepant component must be renewed or resurfaced by an automotive machine shop.

20   Refer to Part C of this Chapter for cleaning and inspection of the cylinder head.

### *Refitting*

*Refer to illustrations 12.22, 12.23 and 12.24*

21   Refit the camshaft(s) if removed (see Section 10).

**12.19a  Checking the cylinder head-to-engine block gasket surface for warpage**

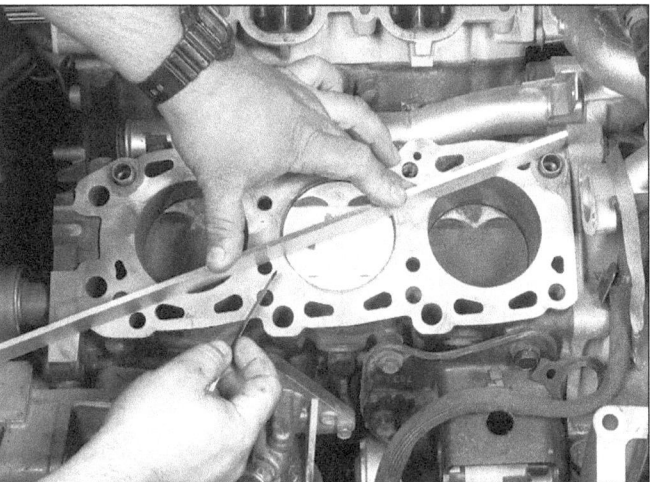

**12.19b  Checking the engine block head gasket surface for warpage**

**12.22  When installing the head gasket onto the block, make sure all passages in the block align with the holes in the gasket**

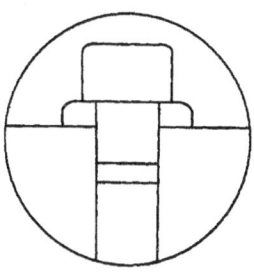

**12.23  Refit the head bolt washers as shown**

**12.24  Cylinder head bolt TIGHTENING sequence**

22    Place a new gasket on the engine block **(see illustration)**. Use no sealer unless indicated by the gasket manufacturer. Note any directions printed on the gasket such as "Front" or "This side up." Place the cylinder head(s) in position on the engine block.
23    Refit the washers onto the cylinder head bolts as shown **(see illustration)**. Apply clean engine oil to the cylinder head bolt threads and refit them into the cylinder head.
24    Tighten the cylinder head bolts in the sequence shown **(see illustration)** progressing in three stages to the torque listed in this

Chapter's Specifications using a 10 mm Allen Hex.
25    The remaining refitting steps are the reverse of removal.
26    Refill the cooling system and check all fluid levels (see Chapter 1 if necessary).
27    Start the engine and let it run until normal operating temperature is reached. Check for leaks and proper operation.

## 13  Oil sump - removal and refitting

### *Removal*

*Refer to illustrations 13.5, 13.10, 13.12, 13.14a and 13.14b*
1    Disconnect the negative battery cable.
2    Raise the vehicle and support it securely on jackstands.
3    Remove the accessory drivebelt splash shield (see Chapter 1).
4    Drain the engine oil (see Chapter 1).
5    Remove the dipstick tube **(see illustration)**.
6    Remove the starter motor (see Chapter 5).
7    Remove the engine-to-transmission support brackets.
8    Remove the exhaust manifold crossover pipe (see Section 5).
9    Remove the transaxle inspection cover.
10    Remove the lower oil sump mounting bolts and remove the sump **(see illustration)**.
11    Remove the oil pump pickup tube and screen assembly.
12    Remove the mounting bolts and separate the oil pan from the engine block enough to facilitate oil pump pickup tube removal. If the pan is stuck, tap it with a soft-face hammer **(see illustration)** or place a wood block against the pan and tap the wood block with a hammer. **Caution:** *If you're wedging something between the oil pan and the engine block to separate them, be extremely careful not to gouge or nick the gasket surface of either part; an oil leak could result.*
13    Remove the oil pan from the vehicle.

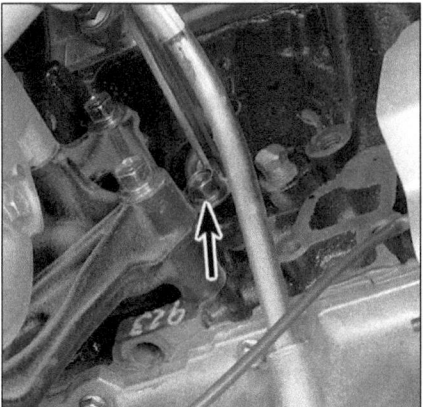

**13.5  Engine oil dipstick tube mounting bolt (arrow)**

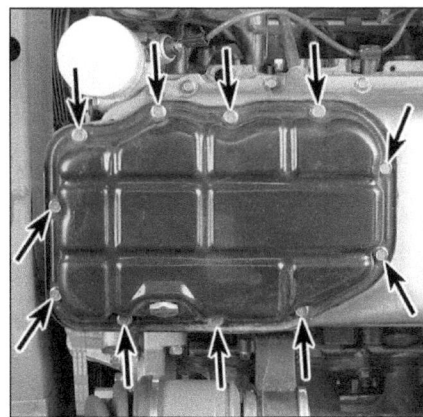

**13.10  Lower sump mounting bolts (arrows)**

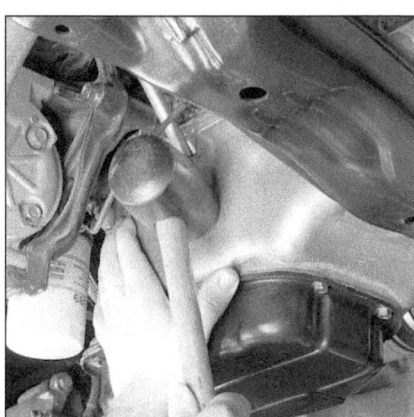

**13.12  If the pan is stuck, tap it with a soft-face hammer or place a wood block against the pan and tap the wood block with a hammer to jar it loose**

**13.14a Thoroughly clean the oil pan and engine block gasket surfaces with a scraper to remove all traces of old gasket material**

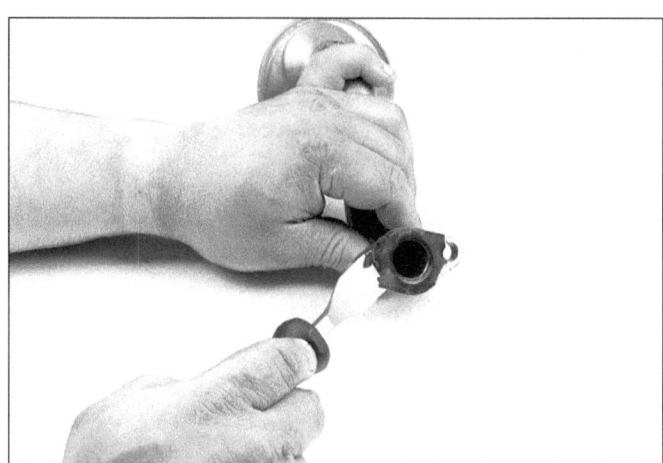

**13.14b Remove the old gasket from the oil pump pick up tube**

14   Thoroughly clean all gasket sealing surfaces. Use a scraper to remove all traces of old gasket material **(see illustrations)**. Gasket removal solvents are available at auto parts stores and may prove helpful. Check the oil pan sealing surface for distortion. Straighten or renew as necessary. After cleaning and straightening (if necessary), wipe the gasket surfaces of the pan and block clean with a rag soaked in lacquer thinner or acetone.

### Refitting

15   Apply a 3 mm bead of RTV sealant to the upper sump. Also apply a light coating of RTV sealant to the underside of the oil pan bolt heads.
16   Place the oil sump into position under the engine block and refit the oil pump pick-up tube. Tighten the bolts to the torque listed in this Chapter's Specifications.
17   Place the oil sump against the engine block and refit the bolts. Working from the centre and proceeding outward in a criss-cross pattern, tighten the sump bolts to the torque listed in this Chapter's Specifications.

18   Apply a 3 mm bead of RTV sealant to the lower sump and refit the lower sump to the upper sump. Working from the centre and proceeding outward in a criss-cross pattern, tighten the sump bolts to the torque listed in this Chapter's Specifications.
19   The remaining refitting steps are the reverse of removal.
20   Lower the vehicle and fill the crankcase with the proper quantity and grade of engine oil (see *Recommended lubricants and fluids* at the beginning of Chapter 1) and run the engine, checking for leaks. Road test the vehicle and check for leaks again.

---

## 14   Oil pump - removal, inspection and refitting

### Removal

*Refer to illustrations 14.7, 14.8, 14.9 and 14.10*
1   Disconnect the negative battery cable.
2   Raise the vehicle and support it securely on jackstands.

3   Remove the drivebelts (see Chapter 1).
4   Remove the timing belt (see Section 6) and crankshaft sprocket and Woodruff key (see Section 7).
5   Remove the oil sump (see Section 13).
6   If equipped, remove the air conditioning compressor bracket from the engine and position it out of the way.
7   Remove the bolts and detach the oil pump assembly from the engine **(see illustration)**. **Caution:** *If the pump doesn't come off by hand, tap it gently with a soft-faced hammer or prise on a casting boss.*
8   Remove the oil filter passage O-ring seals and discard them. They may stick to the engine block as shown **(see illustration)** or remain in the oil pump housing.
9   Remove the oil pump rotor cover **(see illustration)**.
10   New rotors are manufactured with arrows on them which are aligned at refitting. If both arrows are not clearly visible **(see illustration)**, use a permanent marker to match-mark the rotors so they can be refitted back in their original position. Remove the inner and outer rotor from the body. **Caution:**

**14.7 Remove the oil pump assembly mounting bolts (arrows) and detach it from the engine - bolt (A) also secures the air conditioning compressor bracket (if equipped)**

**14.8 The oil filter passage O-ring seals (arrows) may remained attached to the engine block**

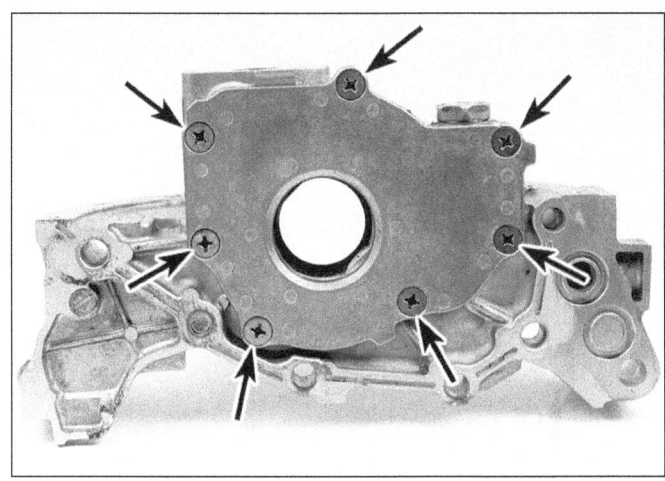

14.9 Remove the rotor cover mounting screws (arrows)

14.10 The alignment mark has worn off the inner rotor on this oil pump; in this case we'll use a permanent marker to match-mark the rotors for reinstallation - oil pressure relief cap bolt (A)

*Be very careful with these components. Close tolerances are critical in creating the correct oil pressure. Any nicks or other damage will require renewal of the complete pump assembly.*

11    Using a hammer and drift, carefully and evenly drive the crankshaft front seal from the oil pump housing and discard it.

12    Disassemble the oil pressure relief valve assembly, taking note of the way the relief valve piston is refitted. Unscrew the cap bolt and remove the bolt, washer, spring and relief valve **(see illustration 14.10)**.

13    Thoroughly clean all gasket sealing surfaces. Use a scraper to remove all traces of old gasket material. Gasket removal solvents are available at auto parts stores and may prove helpful. Check the oil pan sealing surface for distortion. Straighten or renew as necessary. After removing the residual gasket material, wipe the gasket surfaces of the oil pan and block clean with a rag soaked in lacquer thinner or acetone.

### Inspection

*Refer to illustrations 14.16a, 14.16b, 14.16c, and 14.16d*

14    Clean all oil pump components with solvent and inspect them for excessive wear and/or damage. Replace as required. **Note:** *If either rotor is damaged, they must be renewed as a set.*

15    Inspect the oil pressure relief valve piston sliding surface and valve spring for damage. **Note:** *If either the spring or the valve is damaged, they must be renewed as a set.*

16    Refit the rotors into the pump housing with the match-marks aligned **(see illustration)**. Check the oil pump rotor clearances using a precision straightedge and feeler gauges **(see illustrations)**. Compare the results to the tolerances listed in this Chapter's Specifications. Replace both rotors if any clearance is out of tolerance.

ALIGNMENT MARKS

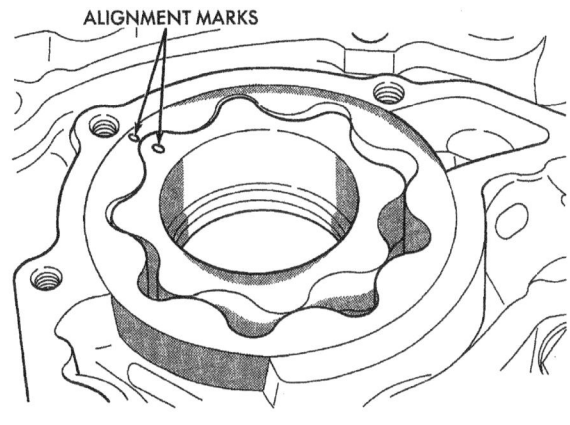

14.16a Refit the rotors into the oil pump body with the match marks aligned

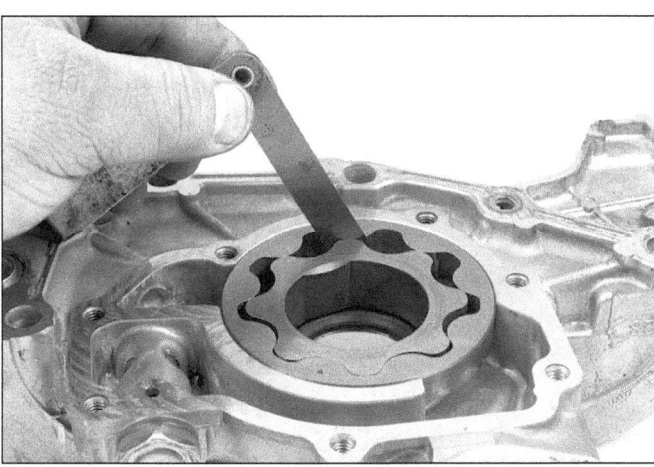

14.16b Use a feeler gauge to measure the inner rotor-to-outer rotor lobe clearance

14.16c Measuring the outer rotor-to-pump body clearance

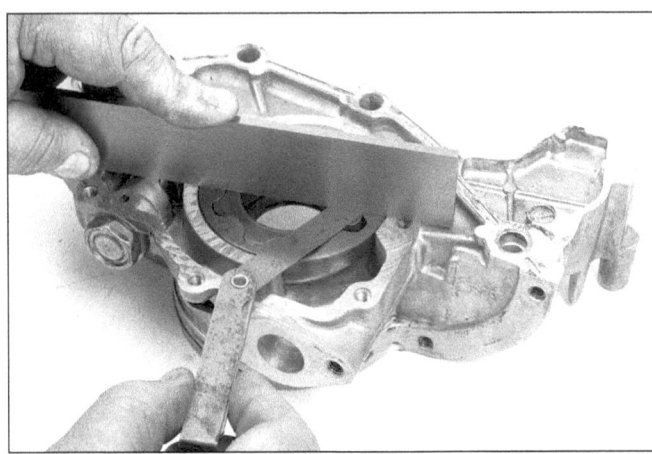

**14.16d  Place a precision straightedge over the rotors and measure the clearance between the rotors and the straightedge to determine the rotor-to-cover clearance**

**14.19  Refit new O-ring seals on the oil filter passages (arrows)**

## Refitting

*Refer to illustration 14.19*

17    Lubricate the relief valve piston, piston bore and spring with clean engine oil. Refit the relief valve piston into the bore maintaining original orientation followed by the spring and cap bolt. Tighten the cap bolt to the torque listed in this Chapter's Specifications. **Note:** *If the relief valve piston is refitted incorrectly, serious engine damage could occur.*

18    Lubricate the oil pump rotor recess in the housing and the inner and outer rotors with clean engine oil. Refit the rotors into the pump housing with the match-marks aligned **(see illustration 14.16a)**. Next, fill the rotor cavity with clean engine oil and refit the cover. Tighten the cover screws to the torque listed in this Chapter's Specifications.

19    Refit new O-ring seals in the oil pump passages located on the pump body **(see illustration)**. If necessary, apply a light coating of grease on the O-rings to hold them in place.

20    Refit the new crankshaft front seal into the oil pump housing (see Section 7).

21    Apply a 3 mm bead of anaerobic sealant to the oil pump body sealing surface, and position the pump assembly on the block aligning the inner rotor and crankshaft drive flats. Refit the mounting bolts.

22    If equipped, refit the air conditioning bracket onto the engine (one bolt secures both the air conditioning bracket and the oil pump housing).

23    Tighten the oil pump attaching bolts **(see illustration 14.7)** to the torque listed in this Chapter's Specifications.

24    Refit the Woodruff key, crankshaft timing belt sprocket (see Section 7) and timing belt (see Section 6).

25    Refit the oil sump (see Section 13).

26    If applicable, fit a new oil filter (see Chapter 1).

27    The remaining refitting steps are the reverse of removal.

28    Lower the vehicle and fill the crankcase with the proper quantity and grade of oil (see *Recommended lubricants and fluids* Section

in Chapter 1).

29    Connect the negative battery cable to the earth stud.

30    After the sealant has cured per the manufacturer's directions, start the engine and check for leaks.

---

## 15   Flywheel/driveplate - removal and refitting

---

### Removal

*Refer to illustration 15.5*

1    Raise the vehicle and support it securely on jackstands.

2    Remove the transaxle assembly (see Chapter 7). If equipped with a manual transaxle, remove the clutch assembly (see Chapter 8).

3    To ensure correct alignment during reinstallation, match-mark the backing plate and flywheel/driveplate to the crankshaft before removal.

4    Remove the bolts securing the flywheel/driveplate to the crankshaft. A tool is available a most auto parts stores to hold the flywheel/driveplate while loosening the bolts, if the tool is not available, wedge a screwdriver

in the ring gear teeth to jam the flywheel/driveplate.

5    Remove the flywheel/driveplate from the crank-shaft **(see illustration)**.

6    Clean the flywheel/driveplate to remove any grease and oil. Inspect it for cracks, distortion and missing or excessively worn ring gear teeth. Replace if necessary.

7    Clean and inspect the mating surfaces of the flywheel/driveplate and the crankshaft. Check the crankshaft rear main seal for leakage; if leakage is evident renew it before reinstalling the flywheel/driveplate (see Section 16).

### Refitting

8    Position the flywheel/driveplate and backing plate against the crankshaft. Align the previously applied match marks. Before installing the bolts, apply thread locking compound to the threads.

9    Hold the flywheel/driveplate with the special holding tool, or wedge a screwdriver in the ring gear teeth to keep the fly-wheel/driveplate from turning as you tighten the bolts to the torque listed in this Chapter's Specifications.

10    The remaining refitting steps are the reverse of removal.

**15.5  Remove the flywheel/driveplate from the crankshaft**

**16.3 Carefully prise the crankshaft seal out of the bore - DO NOT nick or scratch the crankshaft or seal bore**

**16.6 With the seal retainer supported on wood blocks, use a hammer and drift to drive the seal out of the retainer**

## 16 Rear main oil seal - renewal

*Refer to illustrations 16.3, 16.6 and 16.12*

1 The crankshaft rear main oil seal is pressed into a retainer and bolted to the rear of the engine block.

2 Remove the flywheel/driveplate (see Section 15).

3 The crankshaft rear main oil seal can be renewed without removing the oil pan or seal retainer. However, this method is NOT recommended because the lip of the seal is quite stiff and it's possible to cock the seal in the retainer bore or damage it during refitting. If you want to take the chance, carefully and evenly prise out the old seal using a 3/16 flat blade screwdriver - do not to damage the crankshaft sealing surface **(see illustration)**. Apply a light coating of clean engine oil to the crankshaft seal journal and the lip of the new seal then carefully tap the new seal into place using a hammer and socket. The seal lip is stiff, so carefully work it onto the seal journal of the crankshaft with a smooth object like the rounded end of a socket extension as you tap the seal into place **(see illustration 16.12)**. Don't force it or you may damage the seal.

4 The following method is recommended and requires removal of the oil sump (see Section 13).

5 Remove the mounting bolts from the crankshaft rear seal retainer and separate the retainer from the engine block.

6 Using a hammer and drift, carefully drive the old seal out of the retainer and discard it **(see illustration)**.

7 Thoroughly clean all gasket sealing surfaces. Use a scraper to remove all traces of old gasket material. Gasket removal solvents are available at auto parts stores and may prove helpful. Check the oil pan sealing surface for distortion. Straighten or renew as necessary. After removing the residual gasket material, wipe the gasket surfaces clean using a rag soaked in lacquer thinner or acetone.

8 Thoroughly clean and inspect the seal bore and sealing surface on the crankshaft. Minor imperfections can be removed with fine emery cloth. If there is a groove worn in the crankshaft sealing surface (from contact with the seal), installing a new seal will probably not stop the leak.

9 Fit the new seal into the retainer using a socket (or block of wood) and a hammer.

Drive it in until it's flush with the retainer.

10 Apply a 3 mm bead of RTV sealant to the retainer gasket sealing surface.

11 Lubricate the lip of the new seal and the crankshaft sealing surface with a light coat of clean engine oil.

12 Place the seal retainer in position on the engine block and refit the mounting bolts. The seal lip is stiff, so carefully work it onto the seal journal of the crankshaft with a smooth object like the rounded end of a socket extension as you tap the seal into place **(see illustration)**. Don't force it or you may damage the seal. Tighten the bolts to the torque listed in this Chapter's Specifications.

13 Refit the oil sump (see Section 13).

14 The remaining refitting steps are the reverse of removal.

## 17 Engine mounts - check and renewal

1 Engine mounts seldom require attention, but broken or deteriorated mounts should be renewed immediately or the added strain placed on the driveline components may cause damage or wear.

### *Check*

2 During the check, the engine must be raised slightly to relieve the weight from the mounts.

3 Raise the vehicle and support it securely on jackstands, then position a jack under the engine oil sump. Place a large wood block between the jack head and the oil sump to prevent oil sump damage, then carefully raise the engine just enough to take the weight off the mounts. **Warning:** *DO NOT place any part of your body under the engine when it's supported only by a jack!*

4 Inspect the mounts to see if the rubber is cracked, hardened or separated from the metal backing. Sometimes the rubber will split right down the centre.

**16.12 Using a rounded object like a socket extension, carefully work the seal onto the crankshaft**

17.9a Front engine mount mounting bolts and nuts (arrows)

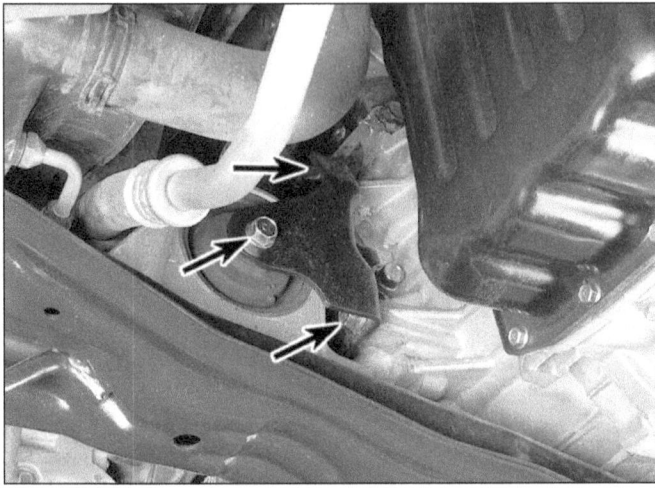

17.9b Front roll stopper mounting bolts (arrows)

17.9c Engine centre member support mounting bolts (arrows)

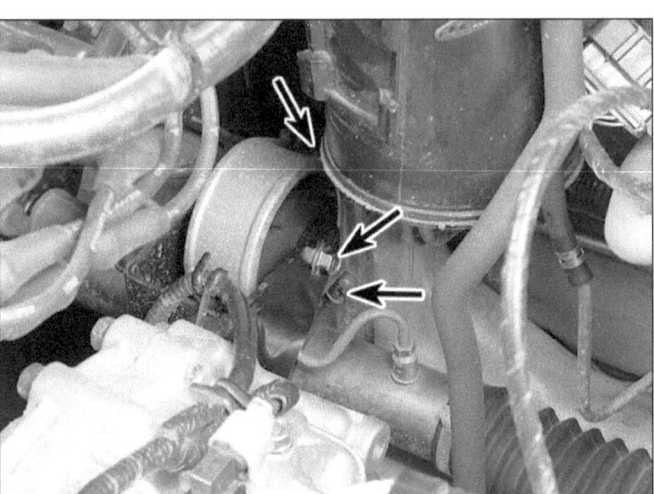

17.9d Rear roll stopper mounting bolts (arrows)

5    Check for relative movement between the mount plates and the engine or frame (use a large screwdriver or prise bar to attempt to move the mounts). If movement is noted, lower the engine and tighten the mount fasteners.

6    Rubber preservative may be applied to the mounts to slow deterioration.

### Renewal

*Refer to illustrations 17.9a, 17.9b, 17.9c 17.9d and 17.9e*

7    Disconnect the negative battery cable. Raise the vehicle and support it securely on jackstands.

8    Place a floor jack under the engine (with a wood block between the jack head and oil sump) and raise the engine slightly to relieve the weight from the mount to be renewed.

9    Remove the fasteners and detach the mount from the frame and engine **(see illus-**

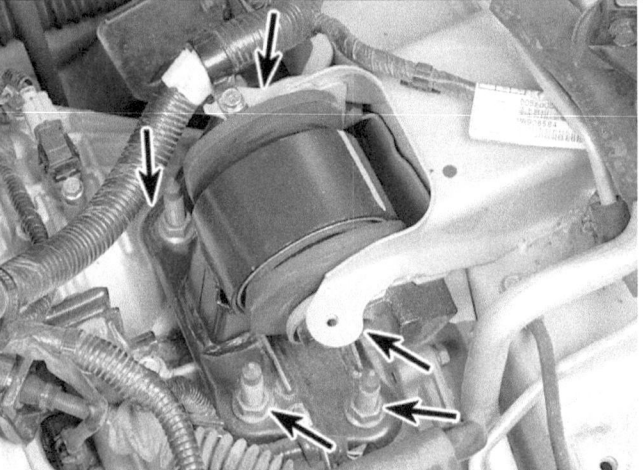

17.9e Transmission mount and bracket mounting nuts and bolts (arrows) - battery tray removed for clarity

**trations)**. **Caution:** *Do not disconnect more than one mount at a time, except during engine/transaxle removal.*

10    Refitting is the reverse of removal. Use thread locking compound on the mount bolts and be sure to tighten them securely.

# Chapter 2  Part B
# General engine overhaul procedures

## Contents

## Specifications

### General

Engine designations
| | |
|---|---|
| 6G72 | 3.0L |
| 6G74 | 3.5L |

Displacement
| | |
|---|---|
| 3.0L | 2972 cc |
| 3.5L | 3497 cc |

Bore and stroke
| | |
|---|---|
| 3.0L | 91.1 X 76.0 mm |
| 3.5L | 93.0 X 85.8 mm |
| Cylinder compression pressure | 900 to 1200 kPa |
| Oil pressure (at idle) | 80 kPa or more |

### Engine block

Bore diameter
| | |
|---|---|
| 3.0L | 91.1 mm |
| 3.5L | 93.0 mm |
| Cylinder ovality | 0.01 mm |

## Pistons and rings

| | |
|---|---|
| Piston diameter | |
|     3.0L | 91.1 mm |
|     3.5L | 93.0 mm |
| Piston-to-bore clearance | 0.02 to 0.04 mm |
| Piston ring side clearance | |
|     Top compression ring | |
|         Standard | 0.03 to 0.07 mm |
|         Service limit | 0.10 mm |
|     Second compression ring | |
|         Standard | 0.02 to 0.06 mm |
|         Service limit | 0.1 mm |
| Piston ring end gap | |
|     Top compression ring | |
|         Standard | 0.30 to 0.45 mm |
|         Service limit | 0.80 mm |
|     Second compression ring | |
|         Standard | 0.45 to 0.60 mm |
|         Service limit | 0.80 mm |
|     Oil ring | |
|         Standard | |
|             3.0L | 0.20 to 0.60 mm |
|             3.5L | 0.10 to 0.35 mm |
|         Service limit | 1.00 mm |

## Crankshaft and connecting rods

| | |
|---|---|
| Crankshaft endplay | |
|     Standard | 0.05 to 0.25 mm |
|     Limit | 0.30 mm |
| Main bearing journal | |
|     Diameter | 60.0 mm |
|     Taper limit | 0.005 mm |
|     Ovality limit | 0.03 mm |
| Connecting rod journal | |
|     Diameter | 50.0 mm |
|     Taper limit | 0.005 mm |
|     Out-of-round limit | 0.03 mm |
| Main bearing oil clearance | 0.02 to 0.04 mm |
| Connecting rod bearing oil clearance | 0.02 to 0.05 mm |
| Connecting rod endplay (side clearance) | 0.10 to 0.25 mm |

## Cylinder head and valves

| | |
|---|---|
| Head warpage limit | 0.20 mm |
| Valve seat angle | 44-degrees |
| Valve face angle | 45 to 45.5-degrees |
| Valve length | |
|     Inlet | 112.30 mm |
|     Exhaust | 114.10 mm |
| Valve stem diameter | 6.0 mm |
| Valve guide inside diameter | 6.0 mm |
| Valve stem-to-guide clearance | |
|     Inlet | 0.02 to 0.05 mm |
|     Exhaust | 0.04 to 0.07 mm |
| Valve head margin width | |
|     Inlet | 1.0 mm |
|     Exhaust | 1.2 mm |
| Valve spring free length | 51.0 mm |
| Valve spring fitted height | 44.2 mm |
| Valve spring out of square | 4-degrees |

## Torque specifications*

| | Nm |
|---|---|
| Connecting rod bearing cap nuts | 51 |
| Main bearing cap bolts | |
|     3.0 litre | 93 |
|     3.5 litre | 70-80 |

* **Note:** *Refer to Part B for additional torque specifications.*

# 1  General information

Included in this portion of Chapter 2 are the general overhaul procedures for the cylinder head(s) and internal engine components.

The information ranges from advice concerning preparation for an overhaul and the purchase of renewal parts to detailed, step-by-step procedures covering removal and refitting of internal engine components and the inspection of parts.

The following Sections have been written based on the assumption the engine has been removed from the vehicle. For information concerning in-vehicle engine repair, as well as removal and refitting of the external components necessary for the overhaul, see Chapter 2, Part A.

The Specifications included in this Part are only those necessary for the inspection and overhaul procedures which follow. Refer to Part A for additional Specifications.

# 2  Engine overhaul - general information

*Refer to illustration 2.4*

It's not always easy to determine when, or if, an engine should be completely overhauled, as a number of factors must be considered.

The number of kilometers driven is not always an indication that an overhaul is needed. Frequency of servicing is probably the most important consideration. An engine that's had regular and frequent oil and filter changes, as well as other required maintenance, will most likely give many thousands of kilometers of reliable service. Conversely, a neglected engine may require an overhaul very early in its life.

Excessive oil consumption is an indication that piston rings, valve seals and/or valve guides are in need of attention. Make sure oil leaks aren't responsible before deciding the rings and/or guides are bad. Perform a cylinder compression check to determine the extent of the work required (see Section 3).

Remove the oil pressure sending unit and check the oil pressure with a gauge refitted in its place **(see illustration)**. Compare the results to this Chapter's Specifications. As a general rule, engines should have approximately 69 kPa of oil pressure for every 1,000 rpm. If the pressure is extremely low, the bearings and/or oil pump are probably worn out.

Loss of power, rough running, knocking or metallic engine noises, excessive valve train noise and high fuel consumption rates may also point to the need for an overhaul, especially if they're all present at the same time. If a complete tune-up doesn't remedy the situation, major mechanical work is the only solution.

An engine overhaul involves restoring the internal parts to the specifications of a

**2.4  Oil pressure switch location - V6 engine**

new engine. During an overhaul, the piston rings are renewed and the cylinder walls are reconditioned (rebored and/or honed). If a rebore is done by an automotive machine shop, new oversize pistons will also be refitted. The main bearings, connecting rod bearings and camshaft bearings are generally renewed with new ones and, if necessary, the crankshaft may be reground to restore the journals. Generally, the valves are serviced as well, since they're usually in less-than-perfect condition at this point. While the engine is being overhauled, other components, such as the starter and alternator, can be rebuilt as well. The end result should be a like new engine that will give many trouble free kilometers. **Note:** *Critical cooling system components such as the hoses, drivebelts, thermostat and water pump MUST be renewed with new parts when an engine is overhauled. The radiator should be checked carefully to ensure it isn't clogged or leaking* (see Chapter 3). *Also, we don't recommend overhauling the oil pump - always fit a new one when an engine is rebuilt.*

Before beginning the engine overhaul, read through the entire procedure to familiarise yourself with the scope and requirements of the job. Overhauling an engine isn't particularly difficult, if you follow all of the instructions carefully, have the necessary tools and equipment and pay close attention to all specifications; however, it can be time consuming. Plan on the vehicle being tied up for a minimum of two weeks, especially if parts must be taken to an automotive machine shop for repair or reconditioning. Check on availability of parts and make sure any necessary special tools and equipment are obtained in advance. Most work can be done with typical hand tools, although a number of precision measuring tools are required for inspecting parts to determine if they must be renewed. Often an automotive machine shop will handle the inspection of parts and offer advice concerning reconditioning and renewal. **Note:** *Always wait until the engine has been completely disassembled and all components, especially the engine block, have been inspected before deciding what*

**3.6  A compression gauge with a threaded fitting for the spark plug hole is preferred over the type that requires hand pressure to maintain the seal**

*service and repair operations must be performed by an automotive machine shop. Since the block's condition will be the major factor to consider when determining whether to overhaul the original engine or buy a rebuilt one, never purchase parts or have machine work done on other components until the block has been thoroughly inspected. As a general rule, time is the primary cost of an overhaul, so it doesn't pay to refit worn or substandard parts.*

As a final note, to ensure maximum life and minimum trouble from a rebuilt engine, everything must be assembled with care in a spotlessly clean environment.

# 3  Cylinder compression check

*Refer to illustration 3.6*

1    A compression check will tell you what mechanical condition the upper end (pistons, rings, valves, head gaskets) of the engine is in. Specifically, it can tell you if the compression is down due to leakage caused by worn piston rings, defective valves and seats or a blown head gasket. **Note:** *The engine must be at normal operating temperature and the battery must be fully charged for this check.*

2    Begin by cleaning the area around the spark plugs before you remove them. Compressed air should be used, if available, otherwise a small brush or even a bicycle tire pump will work. The idea is to prevent dirt from getting into the cylinders as the compression check is being done.

3    Remove all of the spark plugs from the engine (see Chapter 1).

4    Block the throttle wide open.

5    Disable the ignition system by disconnecting the primary wires from the coil (see Chapter 5). Also, disable the fuel injection system, by unplugging the electrical connector to the fuel pump (see *Fuel pressure relief procedure* in Chapter 4).

6    Refit the compression gauge in the number one spark plug hole **(see illustration)**.

7    Crank the engine over at least seven compression strokes and watch the gauge. The compression should build up quickly in a healthy engine. Low compression on the first stroke, followed by gradually increasing pressure on successive strokes, indicates worn piston rings. A low compression reading on the first stroke, which doesn't build up during successive strokes, indicates leaking valves or a blown head gasket (a cracked head could also be the cause). Deposits on the undersides of the valve heads can also cause low compression. Record the highest gauge reading obtained.

8    Repeat the procedure for the remaining cylinders and compare the results to this Chapter's Specifications.

9    If the readings are below normal, add some engine oil (about three squirts from a plunger-type oil can) to each cylinder, through the spark plug hole, and repeat the test.

10   If the compression increases after the oil is added, the piston rings are definitely worn. If the compression doesn't increase significantly, the leakage is occurring at the valves or head gasket. Leakage past the valves may be caused by burned valve seats and/or faces or warped, cracked or bent valves.

11   If two adjacent cylinders have equally low compression, there's a strong possibility the head gasket between them is blown. The appearance of coolant in the combustion chambers or the crankcase would verify this condition.

12   If one cylinder is about 20-percent lower than the others, and the engine has a slightly rough idle, a worn exhaust lobe on the camshaft could be the cause.

13   If the compression is unusually high, the combustion chambers are probably coated with carbon deposits. If that's the case, the cylinder head(s) should be removed and decarbonised.

14   If compression is way down or varies greatly between cylinders, it would be a good idea to have a leak-down test performed by an automotive repair shop. This test will pinpoint exactly where the leakage is occurring and how severe it is.

## 4   Vacuum gauge diagnostic checks

*Refer to illustration 4.4*

A vacuum gauge provides valuable information about what is going on in the engine at a low-cost. You can check for worn rings or cylinder walls, leaking cylinder head or inlet manifold gaskets, restricted exhaust, stuck or burned valves, weak valve springs, improper ignition or valve timing and ignition problems.

Unfortunately, vacuum gauge readings are easy to misinterpret, so they should be used in conjunction with other tests to confirm the diagnosis.

Both the absolute readings and the rate of needle movement are important for accurate interpretation. Most gauges measure vacuum in kilo-Pascals (kPa). As a point of reference, normal atmospheric pressure at sea level is 101.325 kPa. As vacuum increases (or atmospheric pressure decreases), the reading will decrease. Also, for every 300 meters increase in elevation above sea level; the gauge readings will decrease about 3.4 kPa.

Connect the vacuum gauge directly to inlet manifold vacuum, not to ported vacuum **(see illustration)**. Be sure no hoses are left disconnected during the test or false readings will result.

Before you begin the test, allow the engine to warm up completely. Block the wheels and set the parking brake. With the transmission in Park (automatic) or Neutral (manual), start the engine and allow it to run at normal idle speed. **Warning:** *Carefully inspect the fan blades for cracks or damage before starting the engine. Keep your hands and the vacuum tester clear of the fan and do not stand in front of the vehicle or in line with the fan when the engine is running.*

Read the vacuum gauge; an average, healthy engine should normally produce between 57 and 72 kPa of vacuum with a fairly steady needle.

Refer to the following vacuum gauge readings and what they indicate about the engines condition:

1    A low steady reading usually indicates a leaking gasket between the inlet manifold and throttle body, a leaky vacuum hose, late ignition timing or incorrect camshaft timing. Check ignition timing with a timing light and eliminate all other possible causes, utilizing the tests provided in this Chapter before you remove the timing belt cover to check the timing marks.

2    If the reading is 10 to 27 kPa below normal and it fluctuates at that low reading, suspect an inlet manifold gasket leak at an inlet port or a faulty injector.

3    If the needle has regular drops of about 6 to 14 kPa at a steady rate the valves are probably leaking. Perform a compression or leak-down test to confirm this.

4    An irregular drop or down-flick of the needle can be caused by a sticking valve or an ignition misfire. Perform a compression or leak-down test and read the spark plugs.

5    A rapid vibration of about 14 kPa vibration at idle combined with exhaust smoke indicates worn valve guides. Perform a leak-down test to confirm this. If the rapid vibration occurs with an increase in engine speed, check for a leaking inlet manifold gasket or cylinder head gasket, weak valve springs, burned valves or ignition misfire.

6    A slight fluctuation of 3 to 4 kPa up and down, may mean ignition problems. Check all the usual tune-up items and, if necessary, run the engine on an ignition analyzer.

7    If there is a large fluctuation, perform a compression or leak-down test to look for a weak or dead cylinder or a blown cylinder head gasket.

**4.4 Use a vacuum gauge connected to manifold vacuum to test an engine's condition**

8    If the needle moves slowly through a wide range, check for a clogged PCV system, incorrect idle fuel mixture, throttle body or inlet manifold gasket leaks.

9    Check for a slow return after revving the engine by quickly snapping the throttle open until the engine reaches about 2,500 rpm and let it shut. Normally the reading should drop to near zero, rise above normal idle reading (about 17 kPa over) and then return to the previous idle reading. If the vacuum returns slowly and doesn't peak when the throttle is snapped shut, the rings may be worn. If there is a long delay, look for a restricted exhaust system (often the muffler or catalytic converter). An easy way to check this is to temporarily disconnect the exhaust ahead of the suspected part and perform the test again.

## 5   Engine removal - methods and precautions

If you've decided the engine must be removed for overhaul or major repair work, several preliminary steps should be taken.

Locating a suitable place to work is extremely important. Adequate work space, along with storage space for the vehicle, will be needed. If a shop or garage isn't available, at the very least a flat, level, clean work surface made of concrete or asphalt is required.

Cleaning the engine compartment and engine before beginning the removal procedure will help keep tools clean and organised.

An engine hoist or A-frame will also be necessary. Make sure the equipment is rated in excess of the combined weight of the engine and transaxle. Safety is of primary importance, considering the potential hazards involved in lifting the engine out of the vehicle.

If the engine is being removed by a novice, a helper should be available.

Advice and aid from someone more experienced would also be helpful. There are many instances when one person cannot

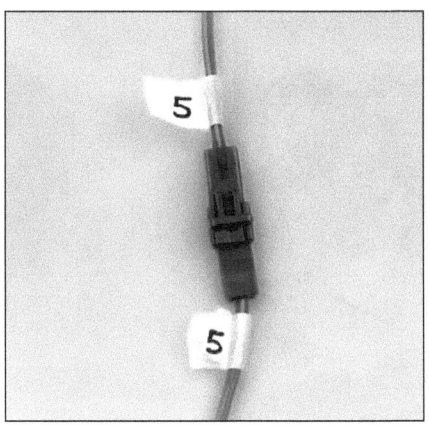

**6.4 Label each wire before unplugging the connector**

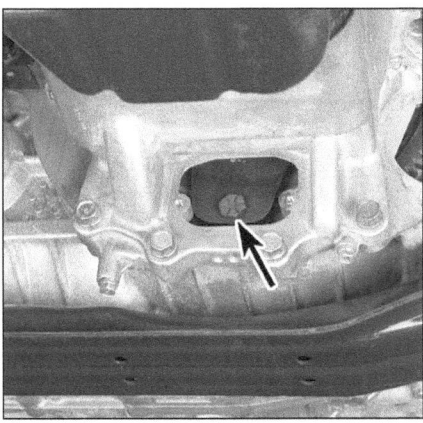

**6.17 Use a box-end spanner to remove the torque converter bolts**

simultaneously perform all of the operations required when lifting the engine out of the vehicle.

Plan the operation ahead of time. Arrange for or obtain all of the tools and equipment you'll need prior to beginning the job. Some of the equipment necessary to perform engine removal and refitting safely and with relative ease are (in addition to an engine hoist) a heavy duty floor jack, complete sets of spanners and sockets as described in the front of this manual, wooden blocks and plenty of rags and cleaning solvent for mopping up spilled oil, coolant and petrol. If the hoist must be rented, be sure to arrange for it in advance and perform all of the operations possible without it beforehand. This will save you money and time.

Plan for the vehicle to be out of use for quite a while. A machine shop will be required to perform some of the work which the do-it-yourselfer can't accomplish without special equipment. These shops often have a busy schedule, so it would be a good idea to consult them before removing the engine in order to accurately estimate the amount of time required to rebuild or repair components that may need work.

Always be extremely careful when removing and refitting the engine. Serious injury can result from careless actions. Plan ahead, take your time and a job of this nature, although major, can be accomplished successfully.

---

**6 Engine - removal and refitting**

*Refer to illustrations 6.4 and 6.17*
**Warning:** *Petrol is extremely flammable, so take extra precautions when disconnecting any part of the fuel system. Don't smoke or allow open flames or bare light bulbs in or near the work area and don't work in a garage where a natural gas appliance (such as a clothes dryer or water heater) is refitted. If you spill petrol on your skin, rinse it off immediately. Have a fire extinguisher rated for petrol fires handy and know how to use it! Also, the air conditioning system is under high pres-*

sure - have a dealer service department or service station discharge the system before disconnecting any of the hoses or fittings. **Note:** *Read through the following steps carefully and familiarise yourself with the procedure before beginning work.*

## Removal

**Note:** *The engine may be removed with the transaxle remaining in the vehicle on automatic transaxle models only. If equipped with a manual transaxle, the manufacturer recommends removing the engine and transaxle as a unit.*

1    Refer to Chapter 4 and relieve the fuel system pressure, then disconnect the negative cable from the battery.
2    Cover the fenders and cowl and remove the bonnet (see Chapter 11). Place pads or blankets over the fenders to protect the paint.
3    Remove the air cleaner assembly (see Chapter 4).
4    Label the vacuum lines, emissions system hoses, wiring connectors, ground straps and fuel lines to ensure correct refitting, then detach them. Pieces of masking tape with numbers or letters written on them work well **(see illustration)**. If there's any possibility of confusion, make a sketch of the engine compartment and clearly label the lines, hoses and wires.
5    Raise the vehicle and support it securely on jackstands. Drain the cooling system (see Chapter 1).
6    Remove the splash shields from under the vehicle.
7    Label and detach all coolant hoses from the engine.
8    Remove the coolant reservoir, cooling fan, shroud and radiator (see Chapter 3).
9    Remove the drivebelt(s) and idler, if equipped (see Chapter 1).
10    Disconnect the fuel lines running from the engine to the chassis (see Chapter 4). Plug or cap all open fittings/lines.
11    Disconnect the accelerator linkage from the engine (see Chapters).
12    Unbolt the power steering pump and set it aside (see Chapter 10). Leave the lines/ hoses attached and make sure the pump is

kept in an upright position in the engine compartment.
13    Unbolt the air conditioning compressor (see Chapter 3) and set it aside. Do not disconnect the hoses. **Caution:** *The air conditioning hoses are under high pressure. Do not disconnect the air conditioning hoses unless the system has been discharged by an automotive air conditioning technician.*
14    Drain the engine oil and remove the filter (see Chapter 1).
15    Remove the starter and the alternator (see Chapter 5).
16    Disconnect the exhaust system from the engine (see Chapter 4).
17    On automatic transaxle models, proceed as follows:

   a) *Remove the torque converter access cover, mark the relationship of the torque converter to the driveplate, then remove the torque converter bolts* **(see illustration)**. *Push the torque converter in, towards the transaxle*
   b) *Remove the bolts retaining the driveaxle centre bearing to the engine block and support the driveaxle.*
   c) *Support the transaxle with a jack. Position a block of wood on the jack head to prevent damage to the transaxle.*
   d) *Remove the transaxle-to-engine bolts.*

18    On manual transaxle models, proceed as follows:

   a) *Disconnect the hydraulic line from the clutch release cylinder, cap the open line.*
   b) *Disconnect the shift control cables from the transaxle.*
   c) *Disconnect the back-up light switch electrical connector, the ground cable and the speedometer cable from the transaxle.*
   d) *Drain the fluid from the transaxle*
   e) *Disconnect the driveaxles from the transaxle (see Chapter 8). Support the driveaxles to prevent damaging the CV joints.*

19    Attach lifting brackets to the engine. Attach an engine sling or a length of chain to the lifting brackets on the engine.
20    Roll the hoist into position and connect the sling to it. Take up the slack in the sling or chain and lift the engine only enough to remove the weight from the mounts. **Warning:** *DO NOT place any part of your body under the engine when it's supported only by a hoist or other lifting device.*
21    Remove the through bolts from the front and rear roll insulators (see Chapter 2A). Remove the torque damper, if equipped.
22    Remove the front engine mount from the engine mount bracket.
23    On manual transaxle models, remove the transaxle mount through bolt.
24    On manual transaxle models, remove the right front wheel/tire and remove the transaxle mount bracket bolts from the frame. Be careful not to drop the bolts into the frame. Remove the transaxle mount bracket from the engine compartment.

25   Recheck to be sure nothing is still connecting the engine to the vehicle (or transaxle, where applicable). Disconnect anything still remaining.

26   Raise the engine (or engine/transaxle assembly) slightly to disengage the mounts. Slowly raise the engine out of the vehicle. Check carefully to make sure nothing is hanging up as the hoist is raised. On automatic transaxle models, be sure the torque converter stays with the transaxle. On manual transaxle models, carefully push the transaxle down while lifting the unit up to clear any obstructions **(see illustration)**.

27   Once the engine/transaxle assembly is out of the vehicle, lower it to the ground and support it on wood blocks. On manual transaxle models, remove the transaxle-to-engine block bolts and carefully separate the transaxle from the engine.

28   Remove the clutch and flywheel or driveplate and mount the engine on an engine stand.

## Refitting

29   Check the engine and transaxle mounts. If they're worn or damaged, renew them.

30   If you're working on a manual transaxle equipped vehicle, refit the clutch and pressure plate (see Chapter 7). Now is a good time to fit a new clutch. Apply a dab of high-temperature grease to the input shaft.

31   Refit the manual transaxle to the engine. **Caution:** DO NOT use the transaxle-to-engine bolts to force the transaxle and engine together.

32   Attach the hoist to the engine and carefully lower the engine or engine/transaxle unit into the engine compartment. Make sure the mounts are correctly aligned and refit the mount bracket and through bolts. Refit the remaining components in the reverse order of removal. Double-check to make sure everything is connected correctly and the fasteners are tightened securely.

33   Add coolant, oil, power steering and transmission fluid as needed.

34   Run the engine and check for leaks and proper operation of all accessories, then refit the bonnet and test drive the vehicle.

35   If the air conditioning system was discharged, have it evacuated, recharged and leak tested by the shop that discharged it.

## 7   Engine rebuilding alternatives

The home mechanic is faced with a number of options when performing an engine overhaul. The decision to renew the engine block, piston/connecting rod assemblies and crankshaft depends on a number of factors, with the number one consideration being the condition of the block. Other considerations are cost, access to machine shop facilities, parts availability, time required to complete the project and the extent of prior mechanical experience.

Some of the rebuilding alternatives include:

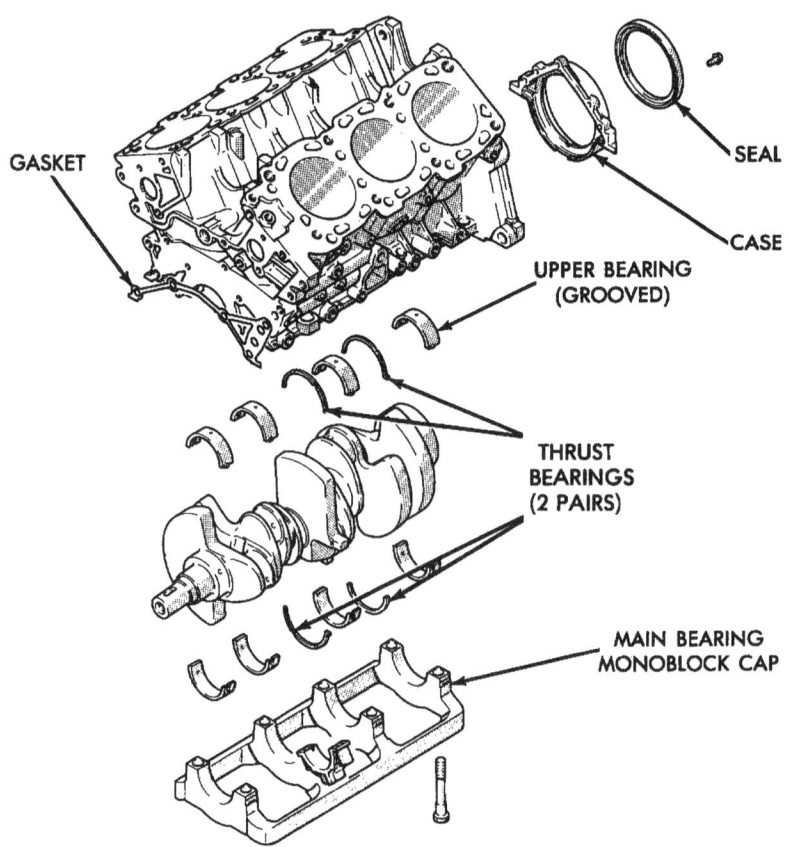

**8.5b  Exploded view of the engine block and related components - 3.0L V6 engine shown (3.5L engine similar)**

**Individual parts** - If the inspection procedures reveal the engine block and most engine components are in reusable condition, purchasing individual parts may be the most economical alternative. The block, crankshaft and piston/connecting rod assemblies should all be inspected carefully. Even if the block shows little wear, the cylinder bores should be surface honed.

**Short block** - A short block consists of an engine block with a crankshaft and piston/connecting rod assemblies already refitted. All new bearings are incorporated and all clearances will be correct. The existing camshaft, valve train components, cylinder head(s) and external parts can be bolted to the short block with little or no machine shop work necessary.

**Long block** - A long block consists of a short block plus an oil pump, sump, cylinder head(s), valve cover(s), camshaft and valve train components, timing sprockets and chain and timing belt cover. All components are fitted with new bearings, seals and gaskets incorporated throughout. The refitting of manifolds and external parts is all that's necessary.

Give careful thought to which alternative is best for you and discuss the situation with local automotive machine shops, auto parts dealers and experienced rebuilders before ordering or purchasing renewal parts.

## 8   Engine overhaul - disassembly sequence

*Refer to illustration 8.5*

1   It's much easier to disassemble and work on the engine if it's mounted on a portable engine stand. A stand can often be rented quite cheaply from an equipment rental yard. Before it's mounted on a stand, the flywheel/driveplate should be removed from the engine.

2   If a stand isn't available, it's possible to disassemble the engine with it blocked up on the floor. Be extra careful not to tip or drop the engine when working without a stand.

3   If you're going to obtain a rebuilt engine, all external components must come off first, to be transferred to the renewal engine, just as they will if you're doing a complete engine overhaul yourself. These include:

*Alternator and brackets*
*Emissions control components*
*Ignition coil, distributor, spark plug wires and spark plugs*
*Thermostat and housing cover*
*Water pump*
*EFI components*
*Inlet/exhaust manifolds*
*Oil filter*
*Engine mounts*
*Clutch and flywheel/driveplate*

**9.2 A small plastic bag, with appropriate label, can be used to store the valve train components so they can be kept together and refitted in the original location**

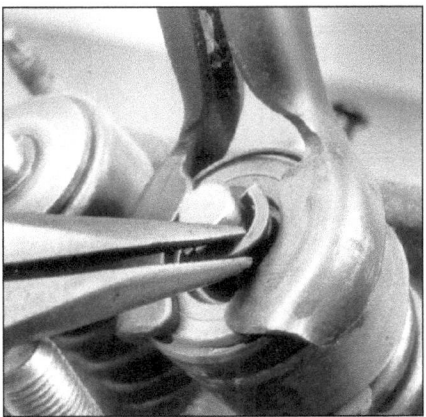

**9.3 Use a valve spring compressor to compress the spring, then remove the collets from the valve stems**

**9.4 If the valve won't pull through the guide, deburr the edge of the stem end and the area around the top of the collet groove with a file or whetstone**

**Note:** *When removing the external components from the engine, pay close attention to details that may be helpful or important during refitting. Note the refitted position of gaskets, seals, spacers, pins, brackets, washers, bolts and other small items.*

4    If you're obtaining a short block, which consists of the engine block, crankshaft, pistons and connecting rods all assembled, then the cylinder head(s), sump and oil pump will have to be removed as well. See *Engine rebuilding alternatives* for additional information regarding the different possibilities to be considered.

5    If you're planning a complete overhaul, the engine must be disassembled and the internal components removed in the following general order **(see illustration)**:

*Valve covers*
*Exhaust manifolds*
*Inlet manifold*
*Timing belt cover*
*Timing belt and sprockets*
*Rocker arm assemblies*
*Camshafts*
*Cylinder heads*
*Sump*
*Oil pump*
*Piston/connecting rod assemblies*
*Rear main oil seal housing*
*Crankshaft and main bearings*

6    Before beginning the disassembly and overhaul procedures, make sure the following items are available. Also, refer to Engine overhaul - reassembly sequence for a list of tools and materials needed for engine reassembly.

*Common hand tools*
*Small cardboard boxes or plastic bags*
*  for storing parts*
*Gasket scraper*
*Ridge reamer*
*Vibration damper puller*
*Micrometers*
*Telescoping gauges*
*Dial indicator set*
*Valve spring compressor*
*Cylinder surfacing hone*

*Piston ring groove cleaning tool*
*Electric drill motor*
*Tap and die set*
*Wire brushes*
*Oil gallery brushes*
*Cleaning solvent*

## 9  Cylinder head - disassembly

*Refer to illustrations 9.2, 9.3 and 9.4*

**Note:** *New and rebuilt cylinder heads are commonly available for most engines at dealerships and auto parts stores. Due to the fact that some specialised tools are necessary for the disassembly and inspection procedures, and renewal parts aren't always readily available, it may be more practical and economical for the home mechanic to purchase renewal head(s) rather than taking the time to disassemble, inspect and recondition the original(s).*

1    Cylinder head disassembly involves removal of the inlet and exhaust valves and related components. The rocker arm assembly and camshaft must be removed before beginning the cylinder head disassembly procedure (see Part A of this Chapter). Label the parts or store them separately so they can be refitted in their original locations.

2    Before the valves are removed, arrange to label and store them, along with their related components, so they can be kept separate and refitted in their original locations **(see illustration)**.

3    Compress the springs on the first valve with a spring compressor and remove the collets **(see illustration)**. Carefully release the valve spring compressor and remove the retainer, the spring and the spring seat (if used).

4    Pull the valve out of the head, then remove the oil seal from the guide. If the valve binds in the guide (won't pull through), push it back into the head and deburr the area around the collet groove with a fine file or whetstone **(see illustration)**.

5    Repeat the procedure for the remaining

valves. Remember to keep all the parts for each valve together so they can be refitted in the same locations.

6    Once the valves and related components have been removed and stored in an organised manner, the head should be thoroughly cleaned and inspected. If a complete engine overhaul is being done, finish the engine disassembly procedures before beginning the cylinder head cleaning and inspection process.

## 10  Cylinder head - cleaning and inspection

1    Thorough cleaning of the cylinder head(s) and related valve train components, followed by a detailed inspection, will enable you to decide how much valve service work must be done during the engine overhaul. **Note:** *If the engine was severely overheated, the cylinder head is probably warped.*

2    Scrape all traces of old gasket material and sealant off the head gasket, inlet manifold and exhaust manifold mating surfaces. Be very careful not to gouge the cylinder head. Special gasket removal solvents that soften gaskets and make removal much easier are available at auto parts stores.

3    Remove all built up scale from the coolant passages.

4    Run a stiff wire brush through the various holes to remove deposits that may have formed in them.

5    Run an appropriate size tap into each of the threaded holes to remove corrosion and thread sealant that may be present. If compressed air is available, use it to clear the holes of debris produced by this operation. **Warning:** *Wear eye protection when using compressed air!*

6    Clean the rocker arm bolt threads with a wire brush.

7    Clean the cylinder head with solvent and dry it thoroughly. Compressed air will speed the drying process and ensure that all holes and recessed areas are clean. **Note:**

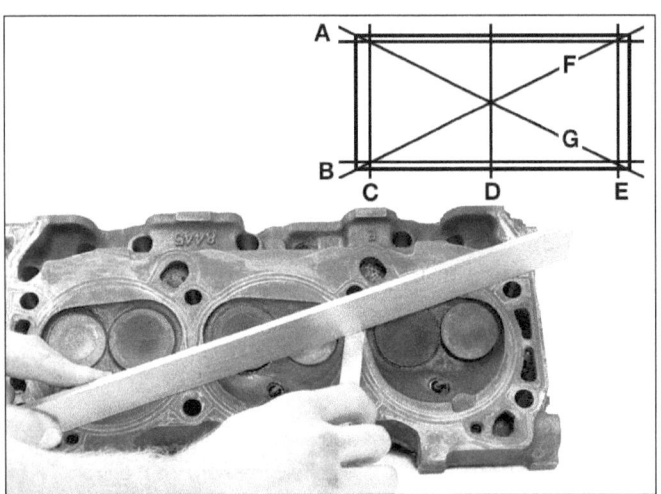

**10.12 Check the cylinder head gasket surface for warpage by trying to slip a feeler gauge under the straightedge (see this Chapter's Specifications for the maximum warpage allowed and use a feeler gauge of that thickness)**

**10.14 A dial indicator can be used to determine the valve stem-to-guide clearance (move the valve stem as indicated by the arrows)**

*Decarbonising chemicals are available and may prove very useful when cleaning cylinder heads and valve train components. They're very caustic and should be used with caution. Be sure to follow the instructions on the container.*

8    Clean the rocker arm components with solvent and dry them thoroughly (don't mix them up during the cleaning process). Compressed air will speed the drying process and can be used to clean out the oil passages.

9    Clean all the valve springs, spring seats, collets and retainers with solvent and dry them thoroughly. Do the components from one valve at a time to avoid mixing up the parts.

10 Scrape off any heavy deposits that may have formed on the valves, then use a motorised wire brush to remove deposits from the valve heads and stems. Again, make sure the valves don't get mixed up.

## Inspection

*Refer to illustrations 10.12, 10.14, 10.15, 10.16, 10.17 and 10.18*

**Note:** *Be sure to perform all of the following inspection procedures before concluding machine shop work is required. Make a list of the items that need attention.*

### Cylinder head

11   Inspect the head very carefully for cracks, evidence of coolant leakage and other damage. If cracks are found, check with an automotive machine shop concerning repair. If repair isn't possible, a new cylinder head should be obtained.

12   Using a straightedge and feeler gauge, check the head gasket mating surface for warpage **(see illustration)**. If the warpage exceeds the limit in this Chapter's Specifications, it can be resurfaced at an automotive machine shop.

13   Examine the valve seats in each of the combustion chambers. If they're pitted,

cracked or burned, the head will require valve service that's beyond the scope of the home mechanic.

14   Check the valve stem-to-guide clearance by measuring the lateral movement of the valve stem with a dial indicator attached securely to the head **(see illustration)**. The valve must be in the guide and approximately 1.5 mm off the seat. The total valve stem movement indicated by the gauge needle must be divided by two to obtain the actual clearance. After this is done, if there's still some doubt regarding the condition of the valve guides, they should be checked by an automotive machine shop (the cost should be minimal).

### Valves

15   Carefully inspect each valve face for uneven wear, deformation, cracks, pits and burned areas. Check the valve stem for scuffing and galling and the neck for cracks. Rotate the valve and check for any obvious indication that it's bent. Look for pits and excessive wear on the end of the stem. The presence of any of these conditions **(see**

illustration) indicates the need for valve service by an automotive machine shop.

16   Measure the margin width on each valve **(see illustration)**. Any valve with a margin narrower than specified in this Chapter will have to be renewed with a new one.

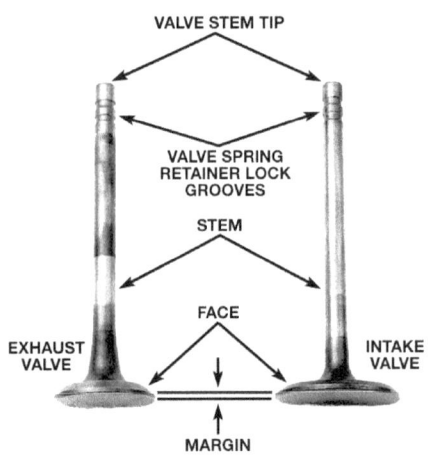

**10.15 Check for valve wear at the points shown here**

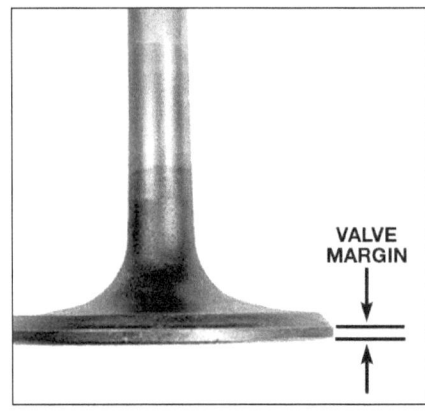

**10.16 The margin width on each valve must be as specified (if no margin exists, the valve cannot be reused)**

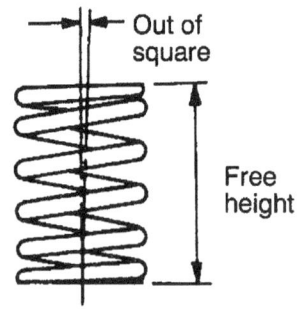

**10.17 Measure the free length of each valve spring with a dial or vernier caliper**

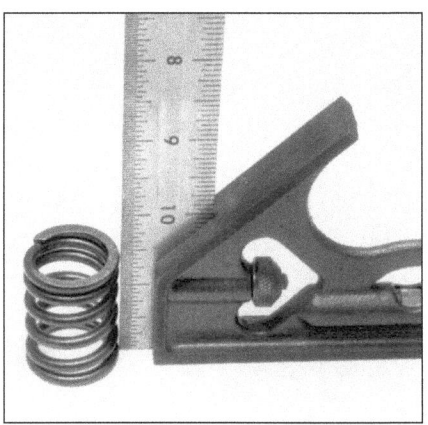

10.18  Check each valve spring for squareness

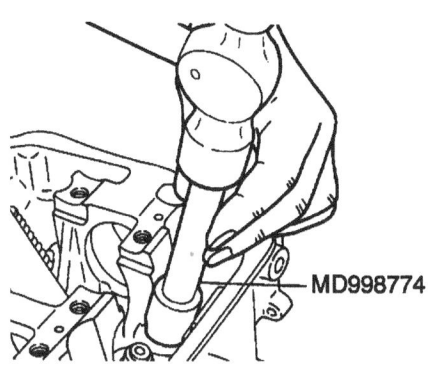

MD998774

12.4  Tap the seal onto the valve guide with a seal driver or deep socket - make sure the seals are refitted evenly and carefully to avoid damage

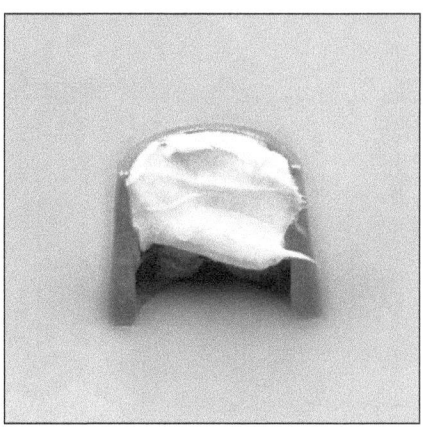

12.6  Apply a small dab of grease to each collet as shown here before refitting - it'll hold them in place on the valve stem as the spring is released

## Valve components

17   Check each valve spring for wear (on the ends) and pits. Measure the free length and compare it to this Chapter's Specifications (see illustration). Any springs that are shorter than specified have sagged and shouldn't be reused. The tension of all springs should be checked with a special fixture before deciding they're suitable for use in a rebuilt engine (take the springs to an automotive machine shop for this check).
18   Stand each spring on a flat surface and check it for squareness (see illustration). If any of the springs are distorted or sagged, renew all of them with new parts.
19   Check the spring retainers and collets for obvious wear and cracks. Any questionable parts should be renewed with new ones, as extensive damage will occur if they fail during engine operation.
20   If the inspection process indicates the valve components are in generally poor condition and worn beyond the limits specified, which is usually the case in an engine that's being overhauled, reassemble the valves in the cylinder head and refer to Section 11 for valve servicing recommendations.

## 11   Valves - servicing

1   Because of the complex nature of the job and the special tools and equipment needed, servicing of the valves, the valve seats and the valve guides, commonly known as a valve job, should be done by a professional.
2   The home mechanic can remove and disassemble the head, do the initial cleaning and inspection, then reassemble and deliver it to a dealer service department or an automotive machine shop for the actual service work. Doing the inspection will enable you to see what condition the head and valvetrain components are in and will ensure that you know what work and new parts are required when dealing with an automotive machine shop.
3   The dealer service department, or automotive machine shop, will remove the valves

and springs, recondition or renew the valves and valve seats, recondition the valve guides, check and renew the valve springs, rotators, spring retainers and collets (as necessary), renew the valve seals with new ones, reassemble the valve components and make sure the refitted spring height is correct. The cylinder head gasket surface will also be resurfaced if it's warped.
4   After the valve job has been performed by a professional, the head will be in like-new condition. When the head is returned, be sure to clean it again before refitting on the engine to remove any metal particles and abrasive grit that may still be present from the valve service or head resurfacing operations. Use compressed air, if available, to blow out all the oil holes and passages.

## 12   Cylinder head - reassembly

*Refer to illustrations 12.4, 12.6 and 12.8*
1   Regardless of whether or not the head was sent to an automotive repair shop for valve servicing, make sure it's clean before beginning reassembly.
2   If the head was sent out for valve servicing, the valves and related components will already be in place. Begin the reassembly procedure with Step 8.
3   Refit the spring seats or valve rotators (if equipped) before the valve seals.
4   Fit new seals on each of the valve guides. Using a hammer and a deep socket or seal refitting tool, gently tap each seal into place until it's completely seated on the guide (see illustration). Don't twist or cock the seals during refitting or they won't seal properly on the valve stems.
5   Beginning at one end of the head, lubricate and refit the first valve. Apply moly-base grease or clean engine oil to the valve stem.
6   Position the valve springs (and shims, if used) over the valves. Compress the springs with a valve spring compressor and carefully refit the collets in the groove, then slowly release the compressor and make sure the

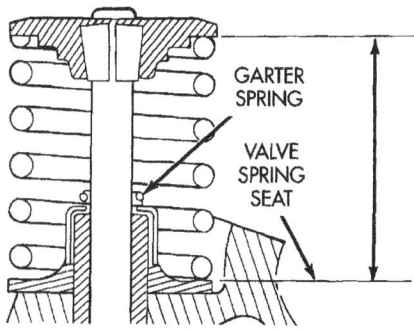

GARTER SPRING

VALVE SPRING SEAT

12.8  Check the valve spring fitted height (the distance from the spring seat to the bottom of the retainer)

collets seat properly. Apply a small dab of grease to each collet to hold it in place if necessary (see illustration).
7   Repeat the procedure for the remaining valves. Be sure to return the components to their original locations - don't mix them up!
8   Check the fitted valve spring height with a steel rule or dial caliper (see illustration). If the head was sent out for service work, the fitted height should be correct (but don't automatically assume it is). The measurement is taken from the top of each spring seat to the bottom of the retainer. If the height is greater than specified in this Chapter, shims can be added under the springs to correct it. **Caution:** *Do not, under any circumstances, shim the springs to the point where the fitted height is less than specified.*
9   Refer to Part A and refit the camshaft and rocker arm assembly onto the head.

## 13   Piston and connecting rod assembly - removal

*Refer to illustrations 13.1, 13.3, 13.4 and 13.6*
**Note:** *Prior to removing the piston/connecting rod assemblies, remove the cylinder head and the sump by referring to the appropriate Sections in Chapter 2, Part A.*

**13.1 A ridge reamer is required to remove the ridge from the top of each cylinder - do this before removing the pistons!**

**13.3 Check the connecting rod side clearance with a feeler gauge as shown**

**13.4 Mark the rod bearing caps in order from the front of the engine to the rear (one mark for the front cap, two for the second, and so on)**

1    Use your fingernail to feel if a ridge has formed at the upper limit of ring travel (approximately 6-mm from the top of each cylinder). If carbon deposits or cylinder wear have produced ridges, they must be completely removed with a special tool **(see illustration)**. Follow the manufacturer's instructions provided with the tool. Failure to remove the ridges before attempting to remove the piston/connecting rod assemblies may result in piston breakage.

2    After the cylinder ridges have been removed, turn the engine upside-down so the crankshaft is facing up.

3    Before the connecting rods are removed, check the endplay with a feeler gauge. Slide the blade between the first connecting rod and the crankshaft throw until the play is removed **(see illustration)**. The endplay is equal to the thickness of the feeler gauge. If the endplay exceeds the service limit, new connecting rods will be required. If new rods (or a new crankshaft) are refitted, the endplay may fall under the minimum specified in this Chapter (if it does, the rods will have to be machined to restore it - consult an automotive machine shop for advice if necessary). Repeat the procedure for the remaining connecting rods.

4    Check the connecting rods and caps for identification marks. If they aren't plainly marked, use a small centre-punch to make the appropriate number of indentations on each rod and cap (1, 2, 3, etc., depending on the engine type and cylinder they're associated with) **(see illustration)**.

5    Loosen each of the connecting rod cap nuts 1/2-turn at a time until they can be removed by hand. Remove the number one connecting rod cap and bearing insert. Don't drop the bearing insert out of the cap.

6    Slip a short length of plastic or rubber hose over each connecting rod cap bolt to protect the crankshaft journal and cylinder wall as the piston is removed **(see illustration)**.

7    Remove the bearing insert and push the connecting rod/piston assembly out through the top of the engine. Use a wooden or plas-

tic hammer handle to push on the upper bearing surface in the connecting rod. If resistance is felt, double-check to make sure all of the ridge was removed from the cylinder.

8    Repeat the procedure for the remaining cylinders.

9    After removal, reassemble the connecting rod caps and bearing inserts in their respective connecting rods and refit the cap nuts finger tight. Leaving the old bearing inserts in place until reassembly will help prevent the connecting rod bearing surfaces from being accidentally nicked or gouged.

10   Don't separate the pistons from the connecting rods (see Section 18 for additional information).

## 14   Crankshaft - removal

*Refer to illustrations 14.1, 14.3 and 14.4*
**Note:** *The crankshaft can be removed only after the engine has been removed from the vehicle. It's assumed the flywheel or driveplate, crankshaft pulley, timing belts, sump, oil pump, counterbalance shafts and piston/*

**13.6 To prevent damage to the crankshaft journals and cylinder walls, slip sections of rubber or plastic hose over the rod bolts before removing the pistons**

*connecting rod assemblies have already been removed. The rear main oil seal housing must be unbolted and separated from the block before proceeding with crankshaft removal.*

1    Before the crankshaft is removed, check the endplay. Mount a dial indicator with the stem in line with the crankshaft **(see illustration)**.

2    Push the crankshaft all the way to the rear and zero the dial indicator. Next, prise the crankshaft to the front as far as possible and check the reading on the dial indicator. The distance it moves is the endplay. If it's greater than the value listed in this Chapter's Specifications, check the crankshaft thrust surfaces for wear. If no wear is evident, new main bearings should correct the endplay.

3    If a dial indicator isn't available, a feeler gauge can be used. Gently prise or push the crankshaft all the way to the front of the engine. Slip feeler gauges between the crankshaft and the front face of the thrust main bearing to determine the clearance **(see illustration)**.

4    Main bearing caps have a cast-in arrow, which points to the front of the engine **(see illustration)**. Loosen the main bearing cap

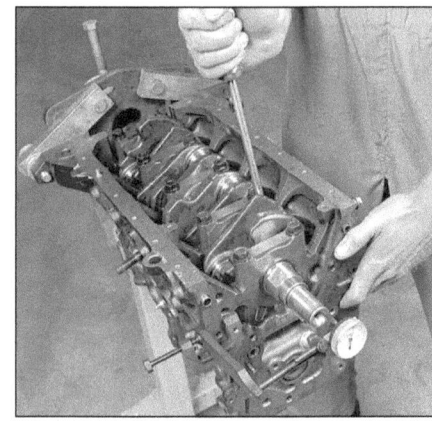

**14.1 Checking crankshaft endplay with a dial indicator**

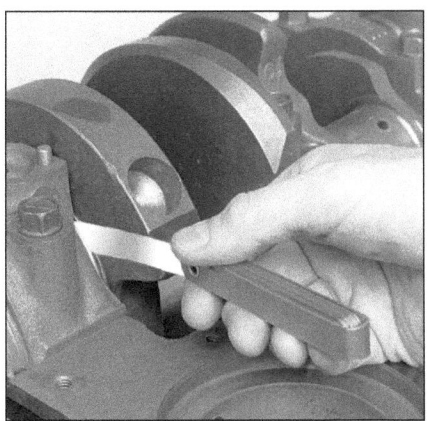

**14.3 To check crankshaft endplay with a feeler gauge, place the gauge between the thrust main bearing and the crank**

**14.4 The main bearing caps, have an arrow pointing to the front of the engine located on the first main bearing cap**

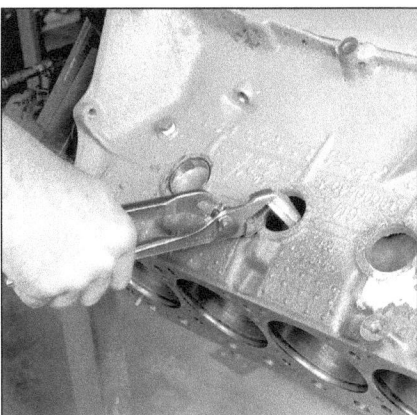

**15.4 Knock the core plugs sideways, then pull them out of the block with pliers**

bolts 1/4-turn at a time each, until they can be removed by hand. Note if any stud bolts are used and make sure they're returned to their original locations when the crankshaft is refitted.

5   Gently tap the caps with a soft-face hammer, then separate them from the engine block. If necessary, use the bolts as levers to remove the caps. Try not to drop the bearing inserts if they come out with the caps.

6   Carefully lift the crankshaft out of the engine. It may be a good idea to have an assistant available, since the crankshaft is quite heavy. With the bearing inserts in place in the engine block and main bearing caps, return the caps to their respective locations on the engine block and tighten the bolts finger tight.

## 15  Engine block - cleaning

*Refer to illustrations 15.4, 15.8 and 15.10*

1   Remove the main bearing caps and separate the bearing inserts from the caps and the engine block. Tag the bearings, indicating which cylinder they were removed from and whether they were in the cap or the block, then set them aside.

2   Using a gasket scraper, remove all traces of gasket material from the engine block. Be very careful not to nick or gouge the gasket sealing surfaces.

3   Remove all of the covers and threaded oil gallery plugs from the block. The plugs are usually very tight - they may have to be drilled out and the holes retapped. Use new plugs when the engine is reassembled.

4   Remove the core plugs from the engine block. To do this, knock one side of the plugs into the block with a hammer and punch, then grasp them with large pliers and pull them out **(see illustration)**.

5   If the engine is extremely dirty, it should be taken to an automotive machine shop to be steam cleaned or hot tanked.

6   After the block is returned, clean all oil holes and oil galleries one more time.

Brushes specifically designed for this purpose are available at most auto parts stores. Flush the passages with warm water until the water runs clear, dry the block thoroughly and wipe all machined surfaces with a light, rust preventive oil. If you have access to compressed air, use it to speed the drying process and blow out all the oil holes and galleries. **Warning:** *Wear eye protection when using compressed air!*

7   If the block isn't extremely dirty or sludged up, you can do an adequate cleaning job with hot soapy water and a stiff brush. Take plenty of time and do a thorough job. Regardless of the cleaning method used, be sure to clean all oil holes and galleries very thoroughly, dry the block completely and coat all machined surfaces with light oil.

8   The threaded holes in the block must be clean to ensure accurate torque readings during reassembly. Run the proper size tap into each of the holes to remove rust, corrosion, thread sealant or sludge and restore damaged threads **(see illustration)**. If possible, use compressed air to clear the holes of debris produced by this operation. Now is a good time to clean the threads on the head bolts and the main bearing cap bolts as well.

9   Refit the main bearing caps and tighten the bolts finger tight.

10   After coating the sealing surfaces of the new core plugs with Permatex no. 1 sealant, or equivalent, refit them in the engine block **(see illustration)**. Make sure they're driven in straight and seated properly or leakage could result. Special tools are available for this purpose, but a large socket, with an outside diameter that will just slip into the core plug, an extension and a hammer will work just as well.

11   Apply non-hardening sealant (such as Permatex no. 2 or Teflon pipe sealant) to the new oil gallery plugs and thread them into the holes in the block. Make sure they're tightened securely.

12   If the engine isn't going to be reassembled right away, cover it with a large plastic trash bag to keep it clean.

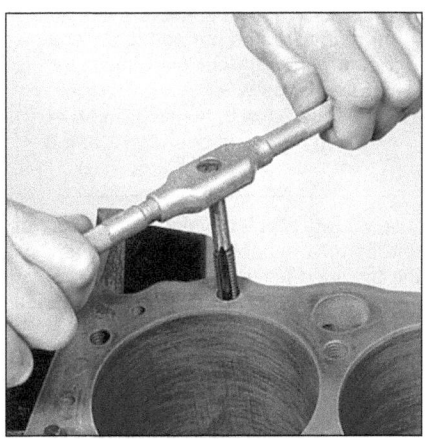

**15.8 All bolt holes in the block - particularly the main bearing cap and cylinder head bolt holes - should be cleaned and restored with a tap (be sure to remove debris from the holes after this is done)**

**15.10 A large socket on an extension can be used to drive the new core plugs into the bores**

## 16  Engine block - inspection

*Refer to illustrations 16.5a, 16.5b and 16.5c*

1   Before the block is inspected, it should be cleaned as described in Section 15.

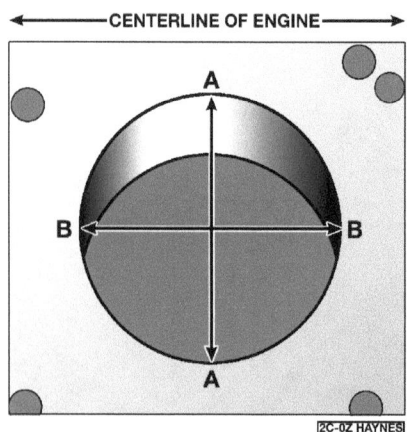

16.5a  Measure the diameter of each cylinder at a right angle to the engine centreline (A), and parallel to the engine centreline (B) - out-of-round is the difference between A and B; taper is the difference between A and B at the top of the cylinder and A and B at the bottom of the cylinder

2     Visually check the block for cracks, rust and corrosion. Look for stripped threads in the threaded holes. It's also a good idea to have the block checked for hidden cracks by an automotive machine shop that has the special equipment to do this type of work. If defects are found, have the block repaired, if possible, or renewed.
3     Check the cylinder bores for scuffing and scoring.
4     Check for cylinder taper and out-of-round conditions as follows:
5     Measure the diameter of each cylinder at the top (just under the ridge area), centre and bottom of the cylinder bore, parallel to the crankshaft axis **(see illustrations)**.
6     Next, measure each cylinder's diameter at the same three locations perpendicular to the crankshaft axis.
7     The taper of each cylinder is the difference between the bore diameter at the top of the cylinder and the diameter at the bottom.
8     The out-of-round specification is the difference between the parallel and perpendicular measurements.
9     Compare the results to this Chapter's Specifications.
10    Repeat the procedure for the remaining pistons and cylinders.
11    If the cylinder walls are badly scuffed or scored, or if they're out-of-round or tapered beyond the limits given in this Chapter's Specifications, have the engine block rebored and honed at an automotive machine shop. If a rebore is done, oversize pistons and rings will be required.
12    If the cylinders are in reasonably good condition and not worn to the outside of the limits, and if the piston-to-cylinder clearances can be maintained properly, they don't have to be rebored. Honing is all that's necessary (see Section 17).

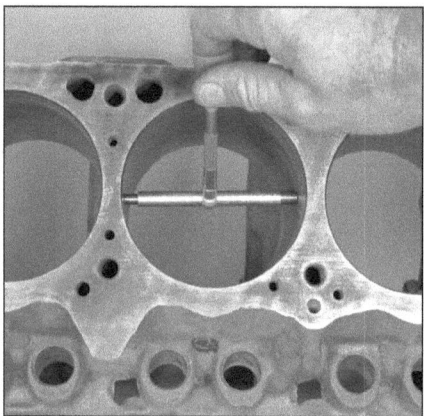

16.5b  The ability to "feel" when the telescoping gauge is at the correct point will be developed over time, so work slowly and repeat the check until you're satisfied the bore measurement is accurate

## 17   Cylinder honing

*Refer to illustrations 17.3a and 17.3b*
1     Prior to engine reassembly, the cylinder bores must be honed so the new piston rings will seat correctly and provide the best possible combustion chamber seal. **Note:** *If you don't have the tools or don't want to tackle the honing operation, most automotive machine shops will do it for a reasonable fee.*
2     Before honing the cylinders, refit the main bearing caps and tighten the bolts to the torque listed in this Chapter's Specifications.
3     Two types of cylinder hones are commonly available - the flex hone or "bottle brush" type and the more traditional surfacing hone with spring-loaded stones. Both will do the job, but for the less experienced mechanic the "bottle brush" hone will probably be easier to use. You'll also need some honing oil (kerosene will work if honing oil isn't available), rags and an electric drill motor. Proceed as follows:

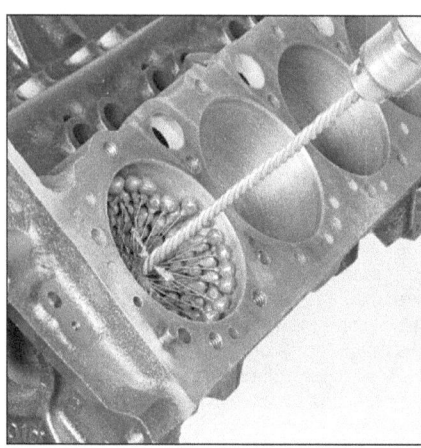

17.3a  A "bottle brush" hone will produce better results if you've never honed cylinders before

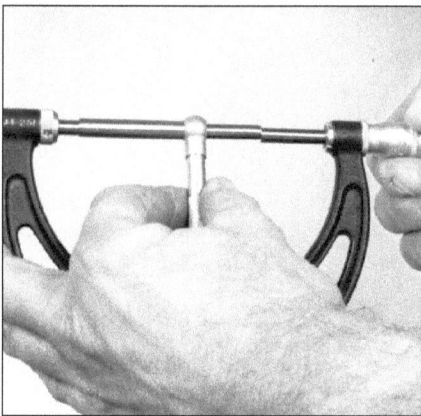

16.5c  The gauge is then measured with a micrometer to determine the bore size

a)  *Mount the hone in the drill motor, compress the stones and slip it into the first cylinder* **(see illustration)**. *Be sure to wear safety goggles or a face shield!*
b)  *Lubricate the cylinder with plenty of honing oil, turn on the drill and move the hone up-and-down in the cylinder at a pace that will produce a fine crosshatch pattern on the cylinder walls. Ideally, the crosshatch lines should intersect at approximately a 60-degree angle* **(see illustration)**. *Be sure to use plenty of lubricant and don't take off any more material than is absolutely necessary to produce the desired finish.* **Note:** *Piston ring manufacturers may specify a smaller crosshatch angle than the traditional 60-degrees - read and follow any instructions included with the new rings.*
c)  *Don't withdraw the hone from the cylinder while it's running. Instead, shut off the drill and continue moving the hone up-and-down in the cylinder until it comes to a complete stop, then compress the stones and withdraw the hone. If you're using a "bottle brush" type*

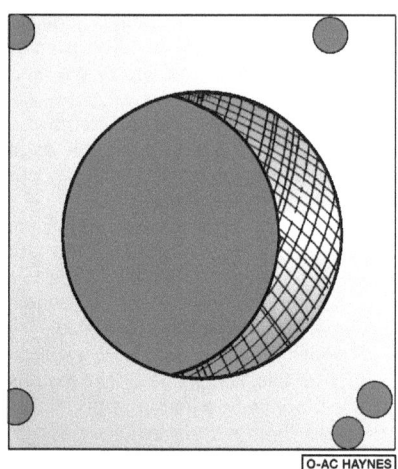

17.3b  The cylinder hone should leave a smooth, crosshatch pattern with the lines intersecting at approximately a 60-degree angle

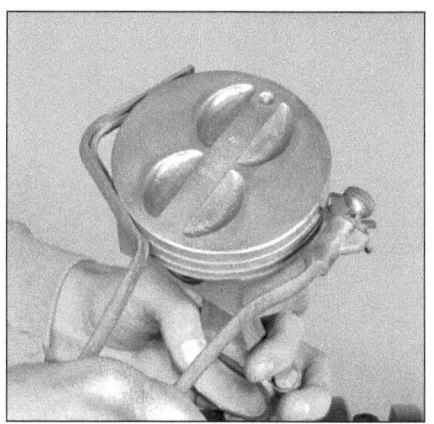

**18.4a The piston ring grooves can be cleaned with a special tool, as shown here . . .**

**18.4b . . . or a section of a broken ring**

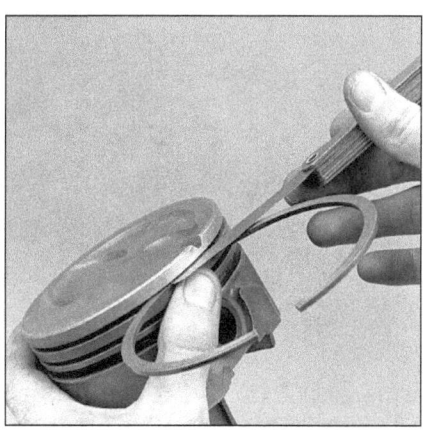

**18.10 Check the ring side clearance with a feeler gauge at several points around the groove**

*hone, stop the drill motor, then turn the chuck in the normal direction of rotation while withdrawing the hone from the cylinder.*

*d) Wipe the oil out of the cylinder and repeat the procedure for the remaining cylinders.*

4    After the honing job is complete, chamfer the top edges of the cylinder bores with a small file so the rings won't catch when the pistons are refitted. Be very careful not to nick the cylinder walls with the end of the file.

5    The entire engine block must be washed again very thoroughly with warm, soapy water to remove all traces of the abrasive grit produced during the honing operation. **Note:** *The bores can be considered clean when a lint-free white cloth - dampened with clean engine oil - used to wipe them out doesn't pick up any more honing residue, which will show up as gray areas on the cloth. Be sure to run a brush through all oil holes and galleries and flush them with running water.*

6    After rinsing, dry the block and apply a coat of light rust preventive oil to all machined surfaces. Wrap the block in a plastic trash bag to keep it clean and set it aside until reassembly.

## 18  Pistons and connecting rods - inspection

*Refer to illustrations 18.4a, 18.4b, 18.10 and 18.11*

1    Before the inspection process can be carried out, the piston/connecting rod assemblies must be cleaned and the original piston rings removed from the pistons. **Note:** *Always use new piston rings when the engine is reassembled.*

2    Using a piston ring refitting tool, carefully remove the rings from the pistons. Be careful not to nick or gouge the pistons in the process.

3    Scrape all traces of carbon from the top of the piston. A hand held wire brush or a piece of fine emery cloth can be used

once the majority of the deposits have been scraped away. Do not, under any circumstances, use a wire brush mounted in a drill motor to remove deposits from the pistons. The piston material is soft and may be eroded away by the wire brush.

4    Use a piston ring groove cleaning tool to remove carbon deposits from the ring grooves. If a tool isn't available, a piece broken off the old ring will do the job. Be very careful to remove only the carbon deposits - don't remove any metal and do not nick or scratch the sides of the ring grooves **(see illustrations)**.

5    Once the deposits have been removed, clean the piston/rod assemblies with solvent and dry them with compressed air (if available). **Warning:** *Wear eye protection. Make sure the oil return holes in the back sides of the ring grooves are clear.*

6    If the pistons and cylinder walls aren't damaged or worn excessively, and if the engine block isn't rebored, new pistons won't be necessary. Normal piston wear appears as even vertical wear on the piston thrust surfaces and slight looseness of the top ring in its groove. New piston rings, however, should always be used when an engine is rebuilt.

7    Carefully inspect each piston for cracks around the skirt, at the pin bosses and at the ring lands.

8    Look for scoring and scuffing on the thrust faces of the skirt, holes in the piston crown and burned areas at the edge of the crown. If the skirt is scored or scuffed, the engine may have been suffering from overheating and/or abnormal combustion, which caused excessively high operating temperatures. The cooling and lubrication systems should be checked thoroughly. A hole in the piston crown is an indication that abnormal combustion (preignition) was occurring. Burned areas at the edge of the piston crown are usually evidence of spark knock (detonation). If any of the above problems exist, the causes must be corrected or the damage will occur again. The causes may include inlet air leaks, incorrect fuel/air mixture, low octane fuel, ignition timing and EGR system mal-

**18.11 Measure the piston diameter at a 90-degree angle to the piston pin and 2-mm from the bottom of the skirt**

functions.

9    Corrosion of the piston, in the form of small pits, indicates coolant is leaking into the combustion chamber and/or the crankcase. Again, the cause must be corrected or the problem may persist in the rebuilt engine.

10    Measure the piston ring side clearance by laying a new piston ring in each ring groove and slipping a feeler gauge in beside it **(see illustration)**. Check the clearance at three or four locations around each groove. Be sure to use the correct ring for each groove - they are different. If the side clearance is greater than specified in this Chapter, new pistons will have to be used.

11    Check the piston-to-bore clearance by measuring the bore (see Section 16) and the piston diameter. Make sure the pistons and bores are correctly matched. Measure the piston across the skirt, at a 90-degree angle to the piston pin **(see illustration)**. The measurement must be taken 2.0 mm above the bottom of the piston skirt.

12    Subtract the piston diameter from the bore diameter to obtain the clearance. If it's greater than specified, the block will have to be rebored and new pistons and rings refitted.

**19.1 The oil holes should be chamfered so sharp edges don't gouge or scratch the new bearings**

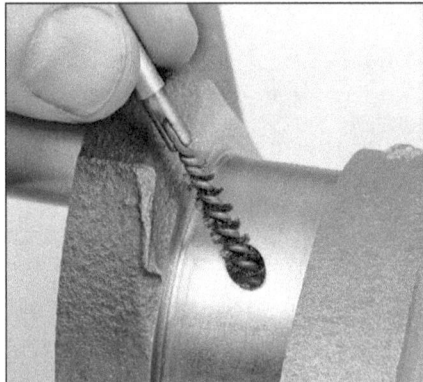

**19.2 Use a wire or stiff plastic bristle brush to clean the oil passages in the crankshaft**

**19.6 Measure the diameter of each crankshaft journal at several points to detect taper and out-of-round conditions**

13   Check the piston-to-rod clearance by twisting the piston and rod in opposite directions. Any noticeable play indicates excessive wear, which must be corrected. The piston/connecting rod assemblies should be taken to an automotive machine shop to have the pistons and rods resized and new pins fitted.

14   If the pistons must be removed from the connecting rods for any reason, they should be taken to an automotive machine shop. While they are there have the connecting rods checked for bend and twist, since automotive machine shops have special equipment for this purpose. **Note:** *Unless new pistons and/or connecting rods must be refitted, do not disassemble the pistons and connecting rods.*

15   Check the connecting rods for cracks and other damage. Temporarily remove the rod caps, lift out the old bearing inserts, wipe the rod and cap bearing surfaces clean and inspect them for nicks, gouges and scratches. After checking the rods, renew the old bearings, slip the caps into place and tighten the nuts finger tight. **Note:** *If the engine is being rebuilt because of a connecting rod knock, be sure to fit new rods.*

## 19   Crankshaft - inspection

*Refer to illustrations 19.1, 19.2, 19.6 and 19.8*

1   Remove all burrs from the crankshaft oil holes with a stone, file or scraper **(see illustration)**.

2   Clean the crankshaft with solvent and dry it with compressed air (if available). **Warning:** *Wear eye protection when using compressed air. Be sure to clean the oil holes with a stiff brush* **(see illustration)** *and flush them with solvent.*

3   Check the main and connecting rod bearing journals for uneven wear, scoring, pits and cracks.

4   Rub a piece of copper across each journal several times. If a journal picks up the copper, it's too rough and must be reground.

5   Check the rest of the crankshaft for cracks and other damage. It should be mag-

nafluxed to reveal hidden cracks - an automotive machine shop will handle the procedure.

6   Using a micrometer, measure the diameter of the main and connecting rod journals and compare the results to this Chapter's Specifications **(see illustration)**. By measuring the diameter at a number of points around each journal's circumference, you'll be able to determine whether or not the journal is out-of-round. Take the measurement at each end of the journal, near the crank throws, to determine if the journal is tapered.

7   If the crankshaft journals are damaged, tapered, out-of-round or worn beyond the limits given in the Specifications, have the crankshaft reground by an automotive machine shop. Be sure to use the correct size bearing inserts if the crankshaft is reconditioned.

8   Check the oil seal journals at each end of the crankshaft for wear and damage. If the seal has worn a groove in the journal, or if it's nicked or scratched **(see illustration)**, the new seal may leak when the engine is reassembled. In some cases, an automotive machine shop may be able to repair the journal by pressing on a thin sleeve. If repair isn't feasible, a new or different crankshaft should be refitted.

**19.8 If the seals have worn grooves in the crankshaft journals, or if the seal contact surfaces are nicked or scratched, the new seals will leak**

9   Refer to Section 20 and examine the main and rod bearing inserts.

## 20   Main and connecting rod bearings - inspection

*Refer to illustration 20.1*

1   Even though the main and connecting rod bearings should be renewed with new ones during the engine overhaul, the old bearings should be retained for close examination, as they may reveal valuable information about the condition of the engine **(see illustration)**.

2   Bearing failure occurs because of lack of lubrication, the presence of dirt or other foreign particles, overloading the engine and corrosion. Regardless of the cause of bearing failure, it must be corrected before the engine is reassembled to prevent it from happening again.

3   When examining the bearings, remove them from the engine block, the main bearing caps, the connecting rods and the rod caps and lay them out on a clean surface in the same general position as their location in the engine. This will enable you to match any bearing problems with the corresponding crankshaft journal.

4   Dirt and other foreign particles get into the engine in a variety of ways. It may be left in the engine during assembly, or it may pass through filters or the PCV system. It may get into the oil, and from there into the bearings. Metal chips from machining operations and normal engine wear are often present. Abrasives are sometimes left in engine components after reconditioning, especially when parts aren't thoroughly cleaned using the proper cleaning methods. Whatever the source, these foreign objects often end up embedded in the soft bearing material and are easily recognised. Large particles won't embed in the bearing and will score or gouge the bearing and journal. The best prevention for this cause of bearing failure is to clean all parts thoroughly and keep everything spotlessly clean during engine assembly. Frequent and regular engine oil and filter

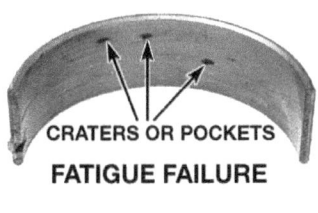

CRATERS OR POCKETS
**FATIGUE FAILURE**

BRIGHT (POLISHED) SECTIONS
**IMPROPER SEATING**

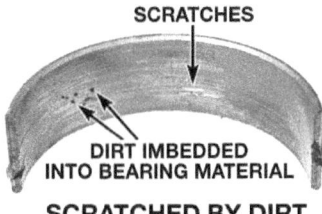

SCRATCHES

DIRT IMBEDDED INTO BEARING MATERIAL
**SCRATCHED BY DIRT**

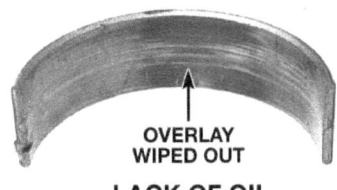

OVERLAY WIPED OUT
**LACK OF OIL**

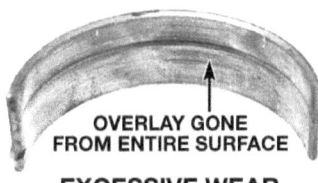

OVERLAY GONE FROM ENTIRE SURFACE
**EXCESSIVE WEAR**

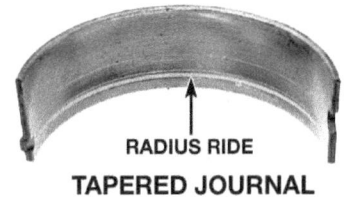

RADIUS RIDE
**TAPERED JOURNAL**

**20.1 Typical bearing failures**

changes are also recommended.

5 Lack of lubrication (or lubrication break-down) has a number of interrelated causes. Excessive heat (which thins the oil), overloading (which squeezes the oil from the bearing face) and oil leakage or throw off (from excessive bearing clearances, worn oil pump or high engine speeds) all contribute to lubrication breakdown. Blocked oil passages, which usually are the result of misaligned oil holes in a bearing shell, will also oil starve a bearing and destroy it. When lack of lubrication is the cause of bearing failure, the bearing material is wiped or extruded from the steel backing of the bearing. Temperatures may increase to the point where the steel backing turns blue from overheating.

6 Driving habits can have a definite effect on bearing life. Full throttle, low speed operation (lugging the engine) puts very high loads on bearings, which tends to squeeze out the oil film. These loads cause the bearings to flex, which produces fine cracks in the bearing face (fatigue failure). Eventually the bearing material will loosen in pieces and tear away from the steel backing. Short trip driving leads to corrosion of bearings because insufficient engine heat is produced to drive off the condensed water and corrosive gases. These products collect in the engine oil, forming acid and sludge. As the oil is carried to the engine bearings, the acid attacks and corrodes the bearing material.

7 Incorrect bearing refitting during engine assembly will lead to bearing failure as well. Tight fitting bearings leave insufficient oil clearance and will result in oil starvation. Dirt or foreign particles trapped behind a bearing insert result in high spots on the bearing which lead to failure.

## 21 Engine overhaul - reassembly sequence

1 Before beginning engine reassembly, make sure you have all the necessary new parts, gaskets and seals as well as the following items on hand:

*Common hand tools*
*Torque wrench*
*Piston ring fitting tool*
*Piston ring compressor*
*Vibration damper refitting tool*
*Short lengths of rubber or plastic hose to fit over connecting rod bolts*
*Plastigage*
*Feeler gauges*
*Fine-tooth file*
*New engine oil*
*Engine assembly lube or moly-base grease*
*Gasket sealant*
*Thread locking compound*

2 In order to save time and avoid problems, engine reassembly must be done in the following general order:

*Crankshaft and main bearings*
*Rear main oil seal housing*
*Piston/connecting rod assemblies*
*Oil pump*
*Sump*
*Cylinder heads*
*Camshafts*
*Rocker arm assemblies*
*Timing belt and sprockets*
*Timing belt cover*
*Inlet and exhaust manifolds*
*Valve covers*
*Flywheel/driveplate*

## 22 Piston ring - fitting

*Refer to illustrations 22.3, 22.4, 22.5, 22.9a, 22.9b and 22.12*

1 Before fitting the new piston rings, the ring end gaps must be checked. It's assumed the piston ring side clearance has been checked and verified correct (see Section 18).

2 Lay out the piston/connecting rod assemblies and the new ring sets so the ring sets will be matched with the same piston and cylinder during the end gap measurement and engine assembly.

3 Insert the top (number one) ring into the first cylinder and square it up with the cylinder walls by pushing it in with the top of the piston (see illustration). The ring should be near the bottom of the cylinder, at the lower limit of ring travel.

4 To measure the end gap, slip feeler gauges between the ends of the ring until a gauge equal to the gap width is found (see illustration). The feeler gauge should slide

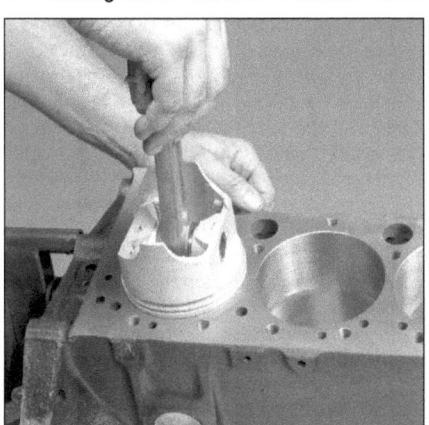

**22.3 When checking piston ring end gap, the ring must be square in the cylinder bore (this is done by pushing the ring down with the top of a piston shown)**

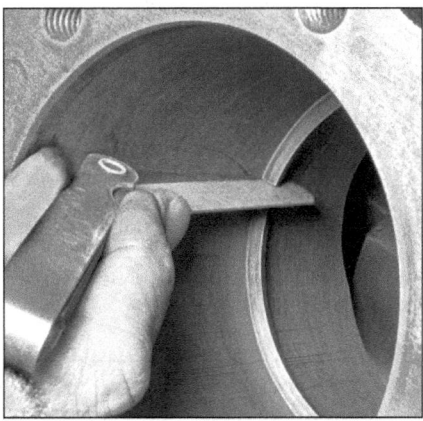

**22.4 With the ring square in the cylinder, measure the end gap with a feeler gauge**

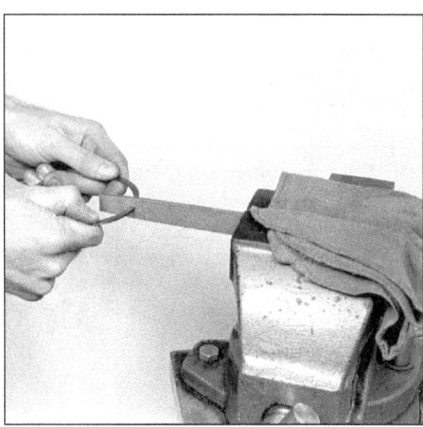

**22.5  If the end gap is too small, clamp
a file in a vise and file the ring ends
(from the outside in only) to
enlarge the gap slightly**

between the ring ends with a slight amount
of drag. Compare the measurement to this
Chapter's Specifications. If the gap is larger
or smaller than specified, double-check to
make sure you have the correct rings before
proceeding.

5    If the gap is too small, it must be
enlarged or the ring ends may come in contact with each other during engine operation,
which can cause serious engine damage. The
end gap can be increased by filing the ring
ends very carefully with a fine file. Mount the
file in a vise equipped with soft jaws, slip the
ring over the file with the ends contacting the
file teeth and slowly move the ring to remove
material from the ends. When performing this
operation, file only from the outside in **(see
illustration)**.

6    Excess end gap isn't critical unless it's
greater than 1.0 mm. Again, double-check to
make sure you have the correct rings for the
engine.

7    Repeat the procedure for each ring that
will be refitted in the first cylinder and for each
ring in the remaining cylinders. Remember to
keep rings, pistons and cylinders matched
up.

8    Once the ring end gaps have been

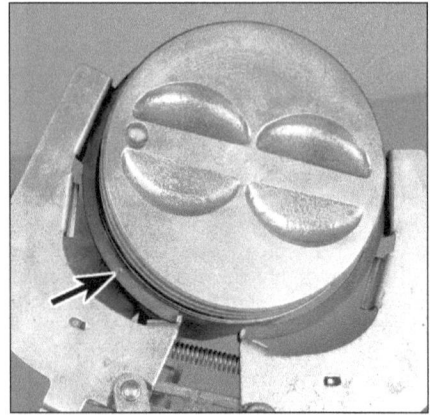

**22.12  Fitting the compression rings with
a ring expander - the mark (arrow)
must face up**

checked/corrected, the rings can be fitted on
the pistons.

9    The oil control ring (lowest one on the
piston) is usually fitted first. It's composed
of three separate components. Slip the
spacer/expander into the groove **(see illustration)**. If an anti-rotation tang is used,
make sure it's inserted into the drilled hole
in the ring groove. Next, fit the lower side
rail. Don't use a piston ring fitting tool on
the oil ring side rails, as they may be damaged. Instead, place one end of the side
rail into the groove between the spacer/
expander and the ring land, hold it firmly in
place and slide a finger around the piston
while pushing the rail into the groove **(see
illustration)**. Next, fit the upper side rail in
the same manner.

10    After the three oil ring components
have been fitted, check to make sure both
the upper and lower side rails can be turned
smoothly in the ring groove.

11    The number two (middle) ring is fitted
next. It's usually stamped with a mark, which
must face up, toward the top of the piston.
**Note:** *Always follow the instructions printed
on the ring package or box - different manufacturers may require different approaches.
Don't mix up the top and middle rings, as
they have different cross-sections.*

12    Use a piston ring fitting tool and make
sure the identification mark is facing the top
of the piston, then slip the ring into the middle
groove on the piston **(see illustration)**. Don't
expand the ring any more than necessary to
slide it over the piston.

13    Fit the number one (top) ring in the same
manner. Make sure the mark is facing up. Be
careful not to confuse the number one and
number two rings.

14    Repeat the procedure for the remaining
pistons and rings.

---

## 23  Crankshaft - refitting and main bearing oil clearance check

1    Crankshaft refitting is the first step in
engine reassembly. It's assumed at this point
that the engine block and crankshaft have

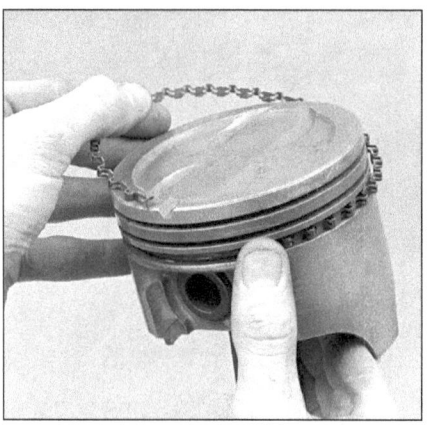

**22.9a  Refitting the spacer/expander
in the oil control ring groove**

been cleaned, inspected and repaired or
reconditioned.

2    Position the engine with the bottom facing up.

3    Remove the main bearing cap bolts and
lift out the cap assembly. Lay the cap assembly out in the same direction as removed to
ensure correct refitting.

4    If they're still in place, remove the original bearing inserts from the block and the
main bearing cap. Wipe the bearing surfaces
of the block and cap with a clean, lint-free
cloth. They must be kept spotlessly clean.

### Main bearing oil clearance check

*Refer to illustrations 23.5, 23.11, 23.13a,
23.13b, 23.15, 23.16a, 23.16b and 23.16c*
**Note:** *Don't touch the faces of the new bearing inserts with your fingers. Oil and acids
from your skin can etch the bearings.*

5    Without mixing them up, clean the back
sides of the new upper main bearing inserts
(with grooves and oil holes) and lay one in
each main bearing saddle in the block. Each
upper bearing has an oil groove and oil hole
in it. **Caution:** *The oil holes in the block must
line up with the oil holes in the upper bearing
inserts.* The thrust bearing inserts or thrust
washers must be fitted in the No. 3 bearing position **(see illustration)**. Fit the thrust
washers with the grooved side toward the
crankshaft (plain sides should be facing each
other). Fit the thrust washers so that one set
has a tab located in the block and the other
set's tab is in the main bearing cap assembly.

6    Clean the back sides of the lower main
bearing inserts (without grooves) and lay
them in the corresponding location in the
main bearing cap assembly. Make sure the
tab on the bearing insert fits into the recess
in the block or main bearing cap assembly.
**Caution:** *Do not hammer the bearing insert
into place and don't nick or gouge the bearing faces. DO NOT apply any lubrication at
this time.*

7    Clean the faces of the bearings in the
block and the crankshaft main bearing journals with a clean, lint-free cloth.

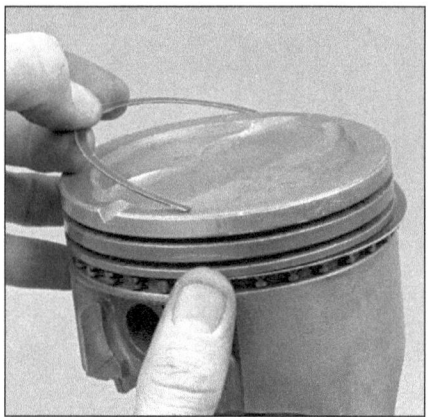

**22.9b  DO NOT use a piston ring fitting
tool when fitting the oil ring side rails**

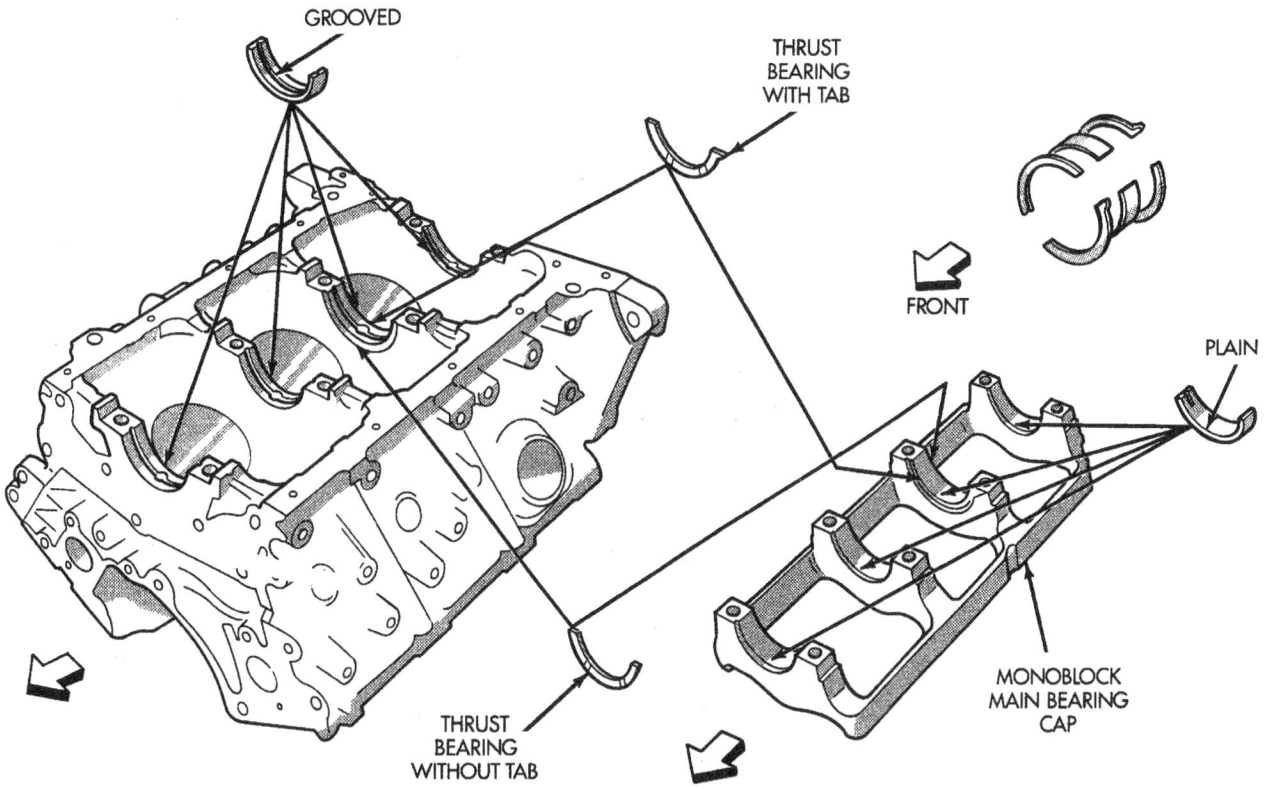

**23.5 Crankshaft main bearing and thrust washer arrangement**

8 Check or clean the oil holes in the crankshaft, as any dirt here can go only one way - straight through the new bearings.

9 Once you're certain the crankshaft is clean, carefully lay it in position in the main bearings.

10 Before the crankshaft can be permanently refitted, the main bearing oil clearance must be checked.

11 Cut several pieces of the appropriate size Plastigage (they should be slightly shorter than the width of the main bearings) and place one piece on each crankshaft main

bearing journal, parallel with the journal axis **(see illustration)**.

12 Clean the faces of the bearings in the caps and refit the cap in their original location (don't mix them up) with the arrows pointing toward the front of the engine. Don't disturb the Plastigage.

13 Don't rotate the crankshaft at any time during this operation. Starting with the centre main and working out toward the ends, tighten the main bearing cap assembly in the sequence shown **(see illustrations)** to the torque listed in this Chapter's Specification Section.

**23.11 Lay the Plastigage strips (arrow) on the main bearing journals, parallel to the crankshaft centreline**

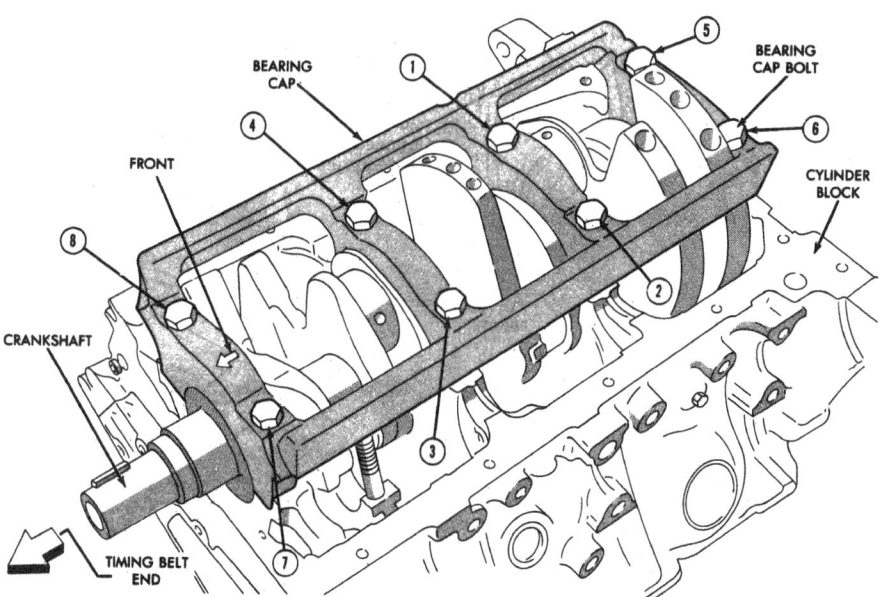

**23.13a Main bearing cap assembly tightening sequence - 3.0L V6 engine**

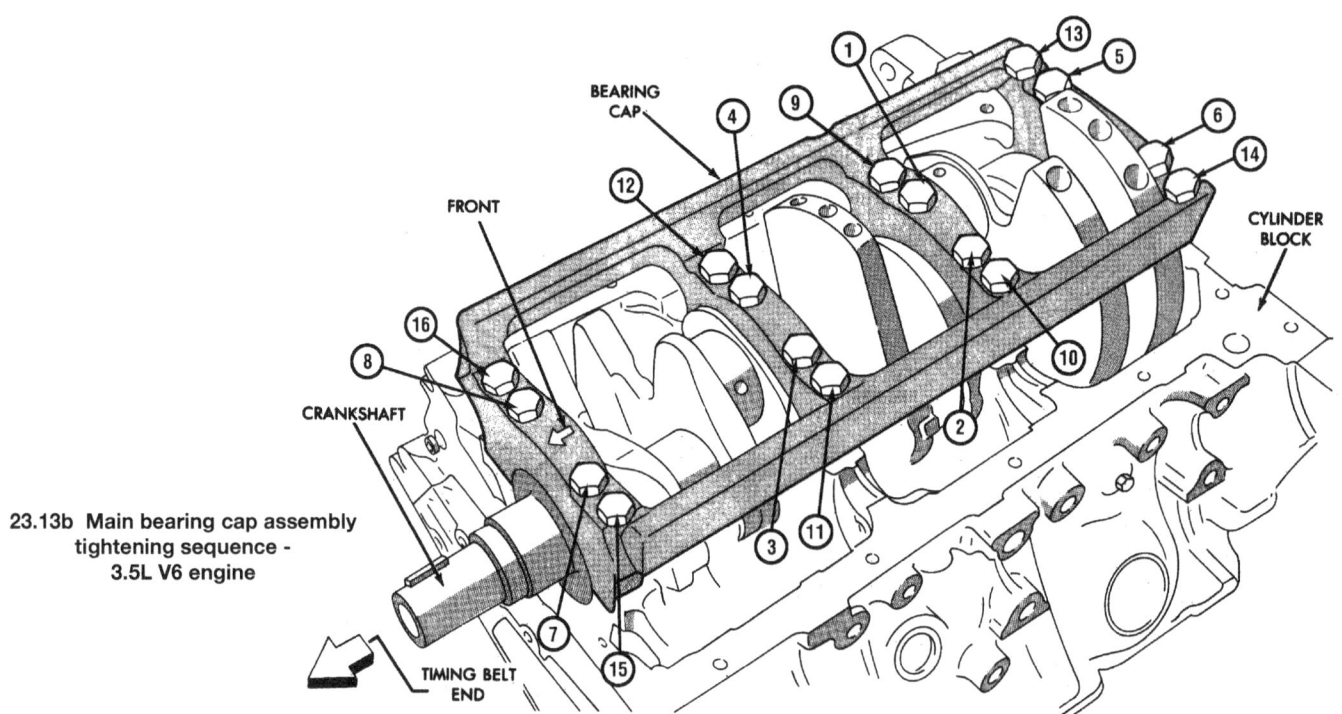

**23.13b Main bearing cap assembly tightening sequence - 3.5L V6 engine**

14   Remove the bolts and carefully lift off the main bearing cap. Don't disturb the Plastigage or rotate the crankshaft. If any of the main bearing caps are difficult to remove, tap them gently from side-to-side with a soft-face hammer to loosen them.

15   Compare the width of the crushed Plastigage on each journal to the scale printed on the Plastigage envelope to obtain the main bearing oil clearance **(see illustration)**. Check the Specifications to make sure it's correct.

16   If the clearance is not as specified, the bearing inserts may be the wrong size (which means different ones will be required. Refer to the chart to select the correct main bearing thickness noting any identifying paint marks or stampings **(see illustrations)**. Before deciding different inserts are needed, make sure no dirt or oil was between the bearing inserts and the caps or block when the clearance was measured. If the Plastigage was wider at one end than the other, the journal may be tapered (see Section 19).

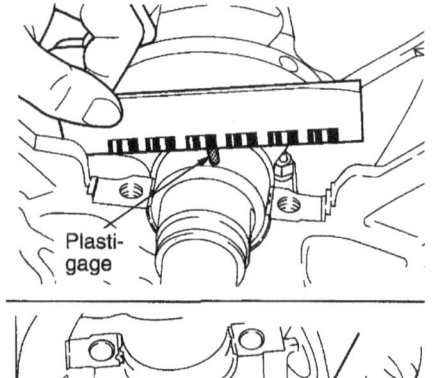

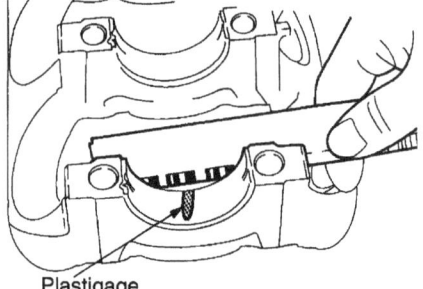

**23.15 Compare the width of the crushed Plastigage to the scale on the envelope to determine the main bearing oil clearance (always take the measurement at the widest point of the Plastigage); be sure to use the correct scale - metric and standard ones are included**

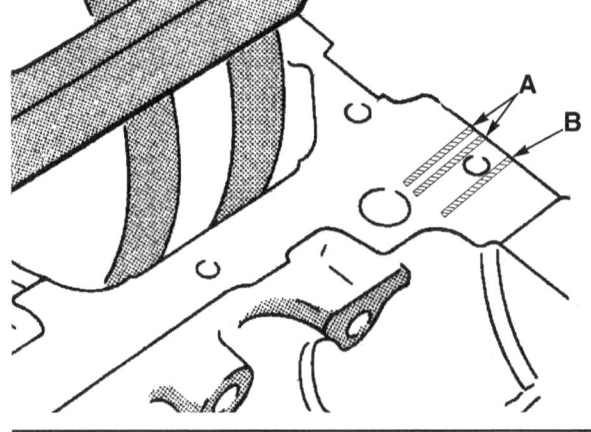

**24.16a engine block bearing bore identification mark location**

B   Cylinder bore size mark
A   Cylinder block bearing bore diameter ID mark

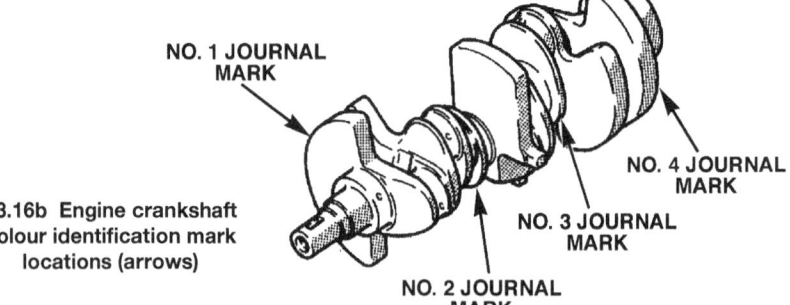

**23.16b Engine crankshaft colour identification mark locations (arrows)**

| | | Crankshaft journal | | | Cylinder block bearing bore diameter indentification mark | Baring identification colour or service part identification mark |
|---|---|---|---|---|---|---|
| Engine | Classification | Identification | | Outside diameter mm | | |
| | | Production part | Service part | | | |
| 3.0 litre | 1 | None | Yellow | 59.994 - 60.000 | I | Pink, 1 |
| 3.5 litre | | | | 63.994 - 64.000 | II | Red, 2 |
| | | | | | III | Green, 3 |
| 3.0 litre | 2 | None | None | 59.988 - 59.994 | I | Red, 2 |
| 3.5 litre | | | | 63.988 - 63.994 | II | Green, 3 |
| | | | | | III | Black, 4 |
| 3.0 litre | 3 | None | White | 59.982 - 59.988 | I | Breen, 3 |
| 3.5 litre | | | | 63.982 - 63.988 | II | Black, 4 |
| | | | | | III | Brown, 5 |

**23.16c Engine crankshaft journal and block bearing journal diameter identification chart**

17   Carefully scrape all traces of the Plastigage material off the main bearing journals and/or the bearing faces. Use your fingernail or the edge of a credit card - don't nick or scratch the bearing faces.

### Final crankshaft refitting

18   Carefully lift the crankshaft out of the engine.

19   Clean the bearing faces in the block, then apply a thin, uniform layer of moly-base grease or engine assembly lube to each of the bearing surfaces. Be sure to coat the thrust faces as well as the journal face of the thrust bearing.

20   Make sure the crankshaft journals are clean, then lay the crankshaft back in place in the block.

21   Clean the faces of the bearings in the caps, then apply lubricant to them.

22   Refit the cap to their original locations with the arrow pointing toward the front of the engine.

23   Refit the bolts.

24   Tighten the main bearing cap bolts to the torque listed in this Chapter's Specifications **(see illustrations 23.13a, 23.13b and 23.13c)**

25   Tap the ends of the crankshaft forward and backward with a lead or brass hammer to seat the crankshaft thrust surfaces.

26   Rotate the crankshaft a number of times by hand to check for any obvious binding.

27   Check the crankshaft endplay with a feeler gauge or a dial indicator as described in Section 14. The endplay should be correct if the crankshaft thrust faces aren't worn or damaged and new bearings have been refitted.

28   Refer to Section 24 and fit the new rear main oil seal.

### 24   Rear main oil seal - renewal

**Note:** *Refer to Chapter 2, Part A for the procedure and illustrations.*

The crankshaft must be refitted and the main bearing caps bolted in place before the new seal and housing assembly can be bolted to the block. **Note:** *Depending on the design of the engine stand being used, you may not be able to refit the rear seal retainer with the engine on the stand.*

### 25   Pistons and connecting rods - refitting and rod bearing oil clearance check

1   Before refitting the piston/connecting rod assemblies, the cylinder walls must be perfectly clean, the top edge of each cylinder must be chamfered, and the crankshaft must be in place.

2   Remove the cap from the end of the number one connecting rod (check the marks made during removal). Remove the original bearing inserts and wipe the bearing surfaces of the connecting rod and cap with a clean, lint-free cloth. They must be kept spotlessly clean.

### Connecting rod bearing oil clearance check

*Refer to illustrations 25.4, 25.5, 25.9, 25.11, 25.13, 25.17, 25.18a and 25.18b*

**Note:** *Don't touch the faces of the new bearing inserts with your fingers. Oil and acids from your skin can etch the bearings.*

3   Clean the back side of the new upper bearing insert, then lay it in place in the connecting rod. Make sure the tab on the bearing fits into the recess in the rod. Don't hammer the bearing insert into place and be very careful not to nick or gouge the bearing face. Don't lubricate the bearing at this time.

4   Clean the back side of the other bearing insert and refit it in the rod cap. Again, make sure the tab on the bearing fits into the recess in the cap **(see illustration)**, and don't apply any lubricant. It's critically important that the mating surfaces of the bearing and connecting rod are perfectly clean and oil free when they're assembled.

5   Position the piston ring gaps at 120-degree intervals around the piston **(see illustration)**.

6   Slip a section of plastic or rubber hose over each connecting rod cap bolt.

7   Lubricate the piston and rings with clean engine oil and attach a piston ring compressor to the piston. Leave the skirt protruding about 6-mm to guide the piston into the cylinder. The rings must be compressed until they're flush with the piston.

8   Rotate the crankshaft until the number one connecting rod journal is at BDC (Bottom Dead Centre) and apply a coat of engine oil to the cylinder walls.

9   With the mark or notch on top of the piston facing the front of the engine **(see illustration)**, gently insert the piston/connecting rod assembly into the number one cylinder bore and rest the bottom edge of the ring compressor on the engine block.

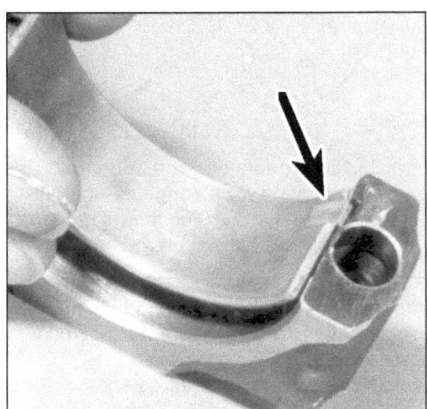

**25.4 The tab on the bearing (arrow) must fit into the recess so the bearing will seat properly**

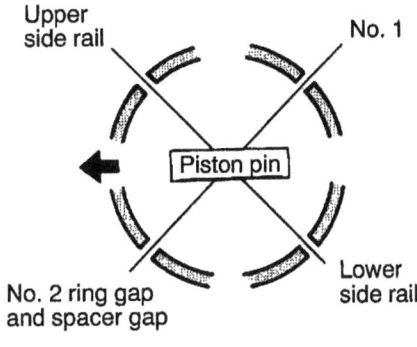

**25.5 Position the ring gaps as shown here before refitting the piston/connecting rod assemblies in the engine**

25.9  The arrow on the top of the piston must face the front of the engine

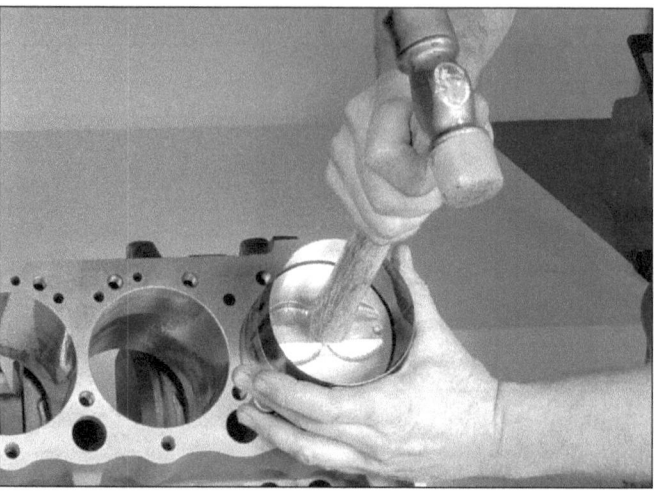

25.11  Gently drive the piston into the cylinder bore with the end of a wooden or plastic hammer handle

25.13  Lay the Plastigage strips on each rod bearing journal, parallel to the crankshaft centreline

25.17  Measure the width of the crushed Plastigage to determine the rod bearing oil clearance (be sure to use the correct scale - standard and metric ones are included)

10    Tap the top edge of the ring compressor to make sure it's contacting the block around its entire circumference.

11    Gently tap on the top of the piston with the end of a wooden or plastic hammer handle **(see illustration)** while guiding the end of the connecting rod into place on the crankshaft journal. The piston rings may try to pop out of the ring compressor just before entering the cylinder bore, so keep some pressure on the ring compressor. Work slowly, and if any resistance is felt as the piston enters the cylinder, stop immediately. Find out what's hanging up and fix it before proceeding. Do not, for any reason, force the piston into the cylinder - you might break a ring and/or the piston.

12    Once the piston/connecting rod assembly is refitted, the connecting rod bearing oil clearance must be checked before the rod cap is permanently bolted into place.

13    Cut a piece of the appropriate size Plastigage slightly shorter than the width of the connecting rod bearing and lay it in place on

the number one connecting rod journal, parallel with the journal axis **(see illustration)**.

14    Clean the connecting rod cap bearing face, remove the protective hoses from the connecting rod bolts and refit the rod cap. Make sure the mating mark on the cap is on the same side as the mark on the connecting rod.

15    Refit the nuts and tighten them to the torque listed in this Chapter's Specifications. Work up to it in three steps. **Note:** *Use a thin-wall socket to avoid erroneous torque readings that can result if the socket is wedged between the rod cap and nut. If the socket tends to wedge itself between the nut and the cap, lift up on it slightly until it no longer contacts the cap. Do not rotate the crankshaft at any time during this operation.*

16    Remove the nuts and detach the rod cap, being very careful not to disturb the Plastigage.

17    Compare the width of the crushed Plastigage to the scale printed on the Plastigage envelope to obtain the oil clearance **(see**

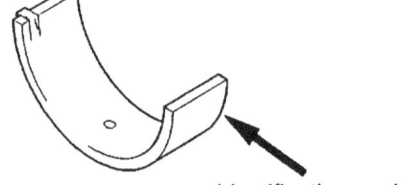

Identification mark

25.18a  Connecting rod bearing ID mark location for all engines - colour marks should match the marks on each connecting rod journal on the crankshaft

**illustration)**. Compare it to this Chapter's Specifications to make sure the clearance is correct.

18    If the clearance is not as specified, the bearing inserts may be the wrong size (which means different ones will be required). Refer to the chart to select the correct main bearing thickness noting any identifying paint marks or stampings **(see illustrations)**. Before

| Crankshaft | | | Connecting rod | | | | |
|---|---|---|---|---|---|---|---|
| Colour identification mark | | Journal outside diameter mm | Big end | | | Bearing | |
| Production part | Service part | | Identification mark | Inside diameter mm | Colour mark identification | Thickness mm | |
| None | Yellow | 54.994 - 55.000 | 0 | 58.000 - 58.006 | Pink | 1.483 - 1.486 | |
| | | | 1 | 58.006 - 58.012 | Red | 1.486 - 1.489 | |
| | | | 2 | 58.012 - 58.018 | Green | 1.489 - 1.492 | |
| None | None | 54.988 - 54.994 | 0 | 58.000 - 58.006 | Red | 1.486 - 1.489 | |
| | | | 1 | 58.006 - 58.012 | Green | 1.489 - 1.492 | |
| | | | 2 | 58.012 - 58.018 | Black | 1.492 - 1.495 | |
| None | White | 54.982 - 54.988 | 0 | 58.000 - 58.006 | Green | 1.489 - 1.492 | |
| | | | 1 | 58.006 - 58.012 | Black | 1.492 - 1.495 | |
| | | | 2 | 58.012 - 58.018 | Brown | 1.495 - 1.498 | |

25.18b  Connecting rod bearing Identification chart - 3.5L engine only

deciding different inserts are needed, make sure no dirt or oil was between the bearing inserts and the connecting rod or cap when the clearance was measured. Also, recheck the journal diameter. If the Plastigage was wider at one end than the other, the journal may be tapered (refer to Section 19).

## Final connecting rod refitting

19   Carefully scrape all traces of the Plastigage material off the rod journal and/or bearing face. Be very careful not to scratch the bearing - use your fingernail or the edge of a credit card.

20   Make sure the bearing faces are perfectly clean, then apply a uniform layer of clean moly-base grease or engine assembly lube to both of them. You'll have to push the piston into the cylinder to expose the face of the bearing insert in the connecting rod - be sure to slip the protective hoses over the rod bolts first.

21   Slide the connecting rod back into place on the journal, remove the protective hoses from the rod cap bolts, refit the rod cap and tighten the nuts to the torque listed in this Chapter's Specifications. Again, work up to the torque in three steps.

22   Repeat the entire procedure for the remaining pistons/connecting rods.

23   The important points to remember are:

a)  Keep the back sides of the bearing inserts and the insides of the connecting rods and caps perfectly clean when assembling them.

b)  Make sure you have the correct piston/ rod assembly for each cylinder.

c)  The arrow or mark on the piston must face the front (timing belt end) of the engine.

d)  Lubricate the cylinder walls with clean oil.

e)  Lubricate the bearing faces when refitting the rod caps after the oil clearance has been checked.

24   After all the piston/connecting rod assemblies have been properly refitted, rotate the crankshaft a number of times by hand to check for any obvious binding.

25   As a final step, the connecting rod endplay must be checked. Refer to Section 13 for this procedure.

26   Compare the measured endplay to this Chapter's Specifications to make sure it's correct. If it was correct before disassembly and the original crankshaft and rods were refitted, it should still be right. If new rods or a new crankshaft were refitted, the endplay may be inadequate. If so, the rods will have to be removed and taken to an automotive machine shop for resizing.

## 26  Initial start-up and break-in after overhaul

**Warning:** *Have a fire extinguisher handy when starting the engine for the first time.*

1   Once the engine has been refitted in the vehicle, double-check the engine oil and coolant levels.

2   With the spark plugs out of the engine and the ignition system disabled (see Section 3), crank the engine until oil pressure reg-

isters on the gauge or the light goes out.

3   Refit the spark plugs, hook up the plug wires and restore the ignition system functions (see Section 3).

4   Start the engine. It may take a few moments for the fuel system to build up pressure, but the engine should start without a great deal of effort. **Note:** *If backfiring occurs through the throttle body, recheck the valve timing and ignition timing.*

5   After the engine starts, it should be allowed to warm up to normal operating temperature. While the engine is warming up, make a thorough check for fuel, oil and coolant leaks.

6   Shut the engine off and recheck the engine oil and coolant levels.

7   Drive the vehicle to an area with minimum traffic, accelerate from 50 to 80 kph, then allow the vehicle to slow to 50 kph with the throttle closed. Repeat the procedure 10 or 12 times. This will load the piston rings and cause them to seat properly against the cylinder walls. Check again for oil and coolant leaks.

8   Drive the vehicle gently for the first 800 kilometres (no sustained high speeds) and keep a constant check on the oil level. It isn't unusual for an engine to use oil during the break-in period.

9   At approximately 800 to 1000 kilometres, change the oil and filter.

10   For the next few hundred kilometres, drive the vehicle normally. Don't pamper it or abuse it.

11   After 3000 kilometres, change the oil and filter again and consider the engine broken in.

# Notes

# Chapter 3
# Cooling, heating and air conditioning systems

## Contents

## Specifications

### General

| | |
|---|---|
| Cooling system capacity ....................................................................... | 9.5 litres |
| Radiator cap pressure rating................................................................. | 75 to 103 kPa |
| Thermostat rating | |
|     Opening temperature......................................................................... | 88 degrees C |
|     Fully open at ...................................................................................... | 95 degrees C |
| Coolant gauge temperature sending unit resistance ............................. | 90.5 to 117.5 at 70 degrees C |
| Refrigerant type and capacity | |
|     R-134a ............................................................................................... | 650 to 700 grams |
| Compressor oil type and capacity | |
|     SUN PAG 56 ....................................................................................... | 170 to 190 cc |

### Torque specifications

| | Nm |
|---|---|
| Air conditioning compressor mounting bolts ......................................... | 25 to 30 |
| Thermostat cover bolts .......................................................................... | 18 |
| Water pump mounting bolts | |
|     8 mm.................................................................................................. | 24 |
|     10 mm................................................................................................ | 41 |

## 1   General information

### *Engine cooling system*

All vehicles covered by this manual employ a pressurised engine cooling system with thermostatically controlled coolant circulation. An impeller-type water pump mounted on the front of the engine pumps coolant through the engine. The pump mounts directly on the engine block. The coolant flows around the combustion chambers and toward the rear of the engine. Cast-in coolant passages direct coolant near the intake ports, exhaust ports, and spark plug areas.

A wax pellet-type thermostat is located in a housing near the front of the engine. During warm-up, the closed thermostat prevents coolant from circulating through the radiator. As the engine nears normal operating temperature, the thermostat opens and allows hot coolant to travel through the radiator, where it's cooled before returning to the engine.

The cooling system is sealed by a pressure-type cap, which raises the boiling point of the coolant and increases the cooling efficiency of the system. If the system pressure exceeds the cap pressure relief value, the excess pressure in the system forces the spring-loaded valve inside the cap off its seat and allows the coolant to escape through the overflow tube into a coolant reservoir. When the system cools the excess coolant is automatically drawn from the reservoir back into the radiator.

The coolant reservoir does double duty as both the point at which fresh coolant is added to the cooling system to maintain the proper fluid level and as a holding tank for overheated coolant. This type of cooling system is known as a closed design because coolant that escapes past the pressure cap is saved and reused.

### *Heating system*

The heating system consists of a blower fan and heater core located in the heater housing, with hoses connecting the heater core to the engine cooling system. Hot engine coolant is circulated through the heater core. When the heater mode on the heater/air conditioning control panel on the instrument panel is activated, a flap door opens to expose the heater core to the passenger compartment. A fan switch on the control panel activates the blower motor, which forces air through the core, heating the air.

### *Air conditioning system*

The air conditioning system consists of a condenser mounted in front of the radiator, an evaporator mounted adjacent to the heater core, a compressor mounted on the engine, receiver/drier which contains a high pressure relief valve and the plumbing connecting all of the above components.

A blower fan forces the warmer air of the passenger compartment through the evaporator core, transferring the heat from the air to the refrigerant (sort of a "radiator in reverse"). The liquid refrigerant boils off into low pressure vapor, taking the heat with it when it leaves the evaporator.

## 2   Antifreeze - general information

**Warning:** *Do not allow antifreeze to come in contact with your skin or painted surfaces of the vehicle. Rinse off spills immediately with plenty of water. Antifreeze is highly toxic if ingested. Never leave antifreeze lying around in an open container or in puddles on the floor; children and pets are attracted by it's sweet smell and may drink it. Check with local authorities about disposing of used antifreeze. Many communities have collection centres which will see that antifreeze is disposed of safely.*

The cooling system should be filled with a water/ethylene glycol based antifreeze solution, which will prevent freezing down to at least -29-degrees C, or lower if local climate requires it. It also provides protection against corrosion and increases the coolant boiling point.

The cooling system should be drained, flushed and refilled at the specified intervals (see Chapter 1). Old or contaminated antifreeze solutions are likely to cause damage and encourage the formation of corrosion and scale in the system. Use distilled water with the antifreeze.

Before adding antifreeze, check all hose connections, because antifreeze tends to leak through very minute openings. Engines don't normally consume coolant, so if the level goes down, find the cause and correct it.

The exact mixture of antifreeze-to-water which you should use depends on the relative weather conditions. The mixture should contain 30 to 50-percent antifreeze, but should never contain more than 70-percent antifreeze. Consult the mixture ratio chart on the antifreeze container before adding coolant. Hydrometers are available at most auto parts stores to test the coolant. Use antifreeze which meets the vehicle manufacturer's specifications.

## 3   Thermostat - check and renewal

**Warning:** *Do not remove the coolant tank cap, drain the coolant or replace the thermostat until the engine has cooled completely.*

### *Check*

1    Before assuming the thermostat is to blame for a cooling system problem, check the coolant level, drivebelt tension (see Chapter 1) and temperature gauge operation.
2    If the engine seems to be taking a long time to warm up (based on heater output or temperature gauge operation), the thermostat

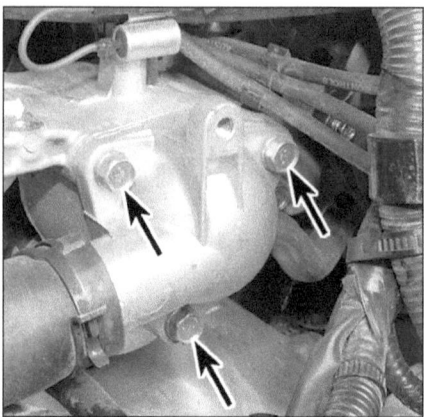

**3.10 Remove the thermostat housing cover retaining bolts (arrows)**

is probably stuck open. Replace the thermostat with a new one.
3    If the engine runs hot, use your hand to check the temperature of the upper radiator hose. If the hose isn't hot, but the engine is, the thermostat is probably stuck closed, preventing the coolant inside the engine from escaping to the radiator. Replace the thermostat. **Caution:** *Don't drive the vehicle without a thermostat. The computer may stay in open loop and emissions and fuel economy will suffer.*
4    If the upper radiator hose is hot, it means that the coolant is flowing and the thermostat is open. Consult the Troubleshooting Section at the front of this manual for cooling system diagnosis.

### *Renewal*

*Refer to illustrations 3.10 and 3.13*
5    Disconnect the negative battery cable.
6    Drain the cooling system (see Chapter 1). If the coolant is relatively new or in good condition, save it and reuse it.
7    Follow the lower radiator hose to the engine to locate the thermostat housing.
8    Loosen the hose clamp, then detach the hose from the fitting. If it's stuck, grasp it near the end with a pair of adjustable pliers and twist it to break the seal, then pull it off. If the hose is old or deteriorated, cut it off and fit a new one.
9    If the outer surface of the large fitting that mates with the hose is deteriorated (corroded, pitted, etc.) it may be damaged further by hose removal. If it is, the thermostat housing cover will have to be renewed.
10    Remove the fasteners and detach the housing cover **(see illustration)**. If the cover is stuck, tap it with a soft-face hammer to jar it loose. Be prepared for some coolant to spill as the gasket seal is broken.
11    Note how it's fitted (which end is facing up), then remove the thermostat.
12    Remove all traces of old gasket material and sealant from the housing and cover with a gasket scraper.
13    Fit a new O-ring onto the thermostat **(see illustration)**.
14    Place the thermostat into the housing,

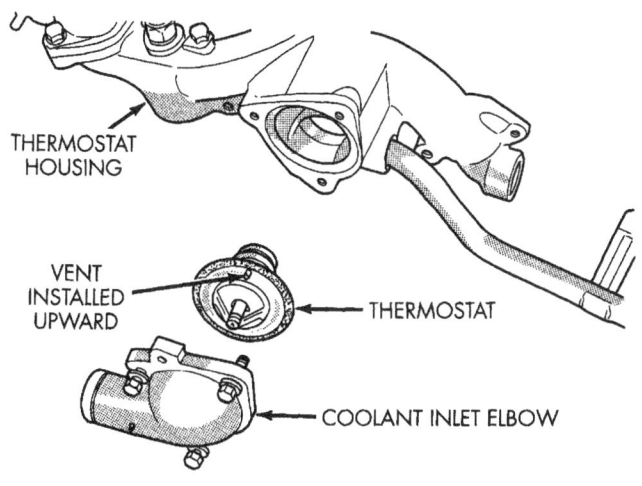

THERMOSTAT
HOUSING

VENT
INSTALLED
UPWARD

THERMOSTAT

COOLANT INLET ELBOW

**3.13 Typical thermostat refitting details**

**4.3 Disconnect the electrical connector from the engine temperature sensor (arrow)**

spring-end facing into the engine block and the vent facing up.

15   Refit the cover mounting bolts. Tighten the bolts to the torque listed in this Chapter's Specifications.

16   Reattach the hose to the fitting and tighten the hose clamp securely.

17   Refill the cooling system (see Chapter 1).

18   Start the engine and allow it to reach normal operating temperature, then check for leaks and proper thermostat operation (as described in Steps 2 through 4). See Chapter 1 for cooling system air-bleeding procedure.

---

**4   Engine cooling fans and circuit - check and component renewal**

1   The engine cooling fans are controlled by the ECU, engine temperature sensor (see Chapter 6) and four relays located in the engine compartment relay centre. When the coolant reaches a predetermined temperature, the ECU completes the fan motor relay circuit and energizes the fan(s). Depending on engine temperature the ECU will only activate the relay needed to keep the vehicle at optimum temperature. The cooling fan relay ranges are LO or HIGH (MID for 2000 and later models) for the main cooling fan and LO or HIGH for the condenser fan. If the engine overheats and the cooling fan fails to operate, perform the following tests to determine the defect.

## Check

*Refer to illustrations 4.3, 4.4 and 4.5*

2   First, check the fuses and fusible links (see wiring diagrams in Chapter 12).

3   With the engine cold start the engine and turn the air conditioning to the off position. Temporarily disconnect the engine temperature sensor **(see illustration)** located at the thermostat housing. The fans should

come on at HI speed. If the fans don't (see Chapter 6) for possible ECU problems. **Note:** *Don't leave the engine temperature sensor disconnected for too long or it will set a code and the "CHECK ENGINE" light will come on and need to be reset (see Chapter 6).*

4   If the fans did not operate with the engine temperature sensor disconnected, check the radiator and condenser fan relays for continuity **(see illustration)**.

a)   *Using an ohmmeter, check for continuity between terminals 1 and 3. There should be continuity. There should be no continuity between terminals 4 and 5.*

b)   *Using fused jumper wires, apply battery voltage and ground to terminals 1 and 3. There now should be continuity between terminals 4 and 5.*

c)   *If the relay fails to operate as described, renew the relay.*

5   If the relay's are good, test the radiator fan motors. Disconnect the electrical connector at the motor and use fused jumper wires to connect the fan directly to the battery **(see illustration)**.

a)   *Using a fused jumper wire, apply battery voltage to terminals 3 (+) and 4 (-) only for low speed.*

b)   *Using a fused jumper wire, apply battery voltage to terminals 1 (+) and 3 (+) and terminals 2 (-) and 4 (-) for high speed.*

b)   *Disconnect the electrical connector to the condensor fan motor and using a fused jumper wire, apply battery voltage to terminals 1 (+) and 2 (-) only for low speed and then terminals 3 (+) and 4 (-) only for high speed*

If the fan does not operate, renew the motor.

## Renewal

*Refer to illustrations 4.8 and 4.9*

### Main cooling fan

**Caution:** *If the stereo in your vehicle is equipped with an anti-theft system, make sure you have the correct activation code before disconnecting the battery.*

6   Disconnect the cable from the negative terminal of the battery.

7   Disconnect the cooling fan electrical connector.

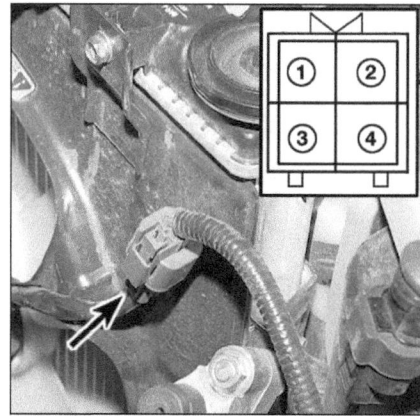

**4.4 Apply (+) battery voltage to terminal 1, (-) battery voltage to terminal 3 and check for continuity between terminals 4 and 5**

**4.5 Radiator and air conditioning condensor fan electrical terminal guide**

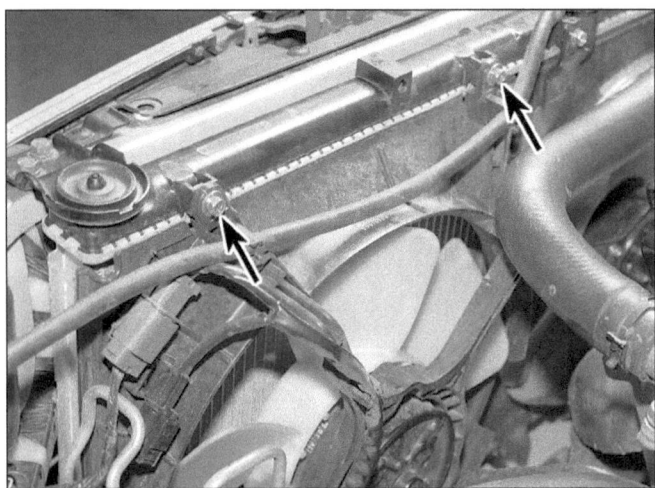

**4.8  Remove the upper bolts retaining the main cooling fan/shroud assembly to the radiator (arrows)**

**4.9  Remove the fan blade retaining nut (arrow) then remove the fan from the motor**

8    Remove the upper two radiator fan shroud bolts **(see illustration)** and loosen the bottom two retaining bolts.

9    Lift the fan assembly out of the engine compartment, being careful not to damage the radiator. To remove the motor, remove the nut from the centre of the fan **(see illustration)**, remove the fan, then remove the screws and separate the fan motor from the shroud.

10   Refitting is the reverse of removal.

### Air conditioning fan

*Refer to illustrations 4.14 and 4.15*

**Caution:** *If the stereo in your vehicle is equipped with an anti-theft system, make sure you have the correct activation code before disconnecting the battery.*

11   Air conditioned models have an additional fan located next to the main cooling fan.

12   Disconnect the negative battery cable from the battery.

13   Disconnect the fan motor electrical connector.

14   Remove the upper two retaining bolts and loosen the bottom two bolts retaining the condenser fan to the radiator **(see illustration)**. Remove the assembly, being careful not to damage the radiator.

15   To remove the motor, remove the screws and separate the fan motor from the shroud **(see illustration)**.

16   To remove the fan from the motor remove the centre nut and pull the fan blade from the motor.

17   Refitting is the reverse of the removal procedure.

---

### 5    Coolant gauge temperature sending unit - check and renewal

---

*Refer to illustrations 5.3 and 5.4*

**Warning:** *The engine must be completely cool before removing the sending unit.*

## *Check*

1    If the coolant temperature gauge is inoperative, check the fuses and fusible links

(see Chapter 12).

2    If the temperature indicator indicated excessive temperature with the engine cool, see the *Troubleshooting* in the front of the manual.

3    If the temperature gauge indicates Hot shortly after the engine is started cold, disconnect the wire at the coolant temperature sending unit **(see illustration)**. If the gauge reading drops, renew the sending unit. If the reading remains high, the wire to the gauge may be shorted to ground or the gauge is faulty.

4    If the coolant temperature gauge fails to indicate after the engine has been warmed up (approximately 10 minutes) and the fuses checked out okay, shut off the engine. Disconnect the wire at the sending unit and, using a jumper wire, connect it to a clean ground on the engine **(see illustration)**. Turn on the ignition without starting the engine. If the gauge now indicates Hot, renew the sending unit.

5    If the gauge still does not work, the circuit may be open or the gauge may be faulty.

**4.14 Remove the upper bolts retaining the air conditioning condensor fan assembly to the radiator (arrows)**

**4.15  Remove the bolts retaining the fan motor to the shroud (arrows)**

## Renewal

6   With the engine completely cool, remove the cap from the radiator to release any pressure, then refit the cap. This reduces coolant loss during sending unit renewal.

7   Disconnect the electrical connector from the sending unit.

8   Prepare the new sending unit for fitting by wrapping the threads with Teflon tape.

9   Remove the sending unit from the engine and quickly fit the new one to prevent coolant loss.

10   Tighten the sending unit securely and connect the electrical connector.

11   Check the coolant level and add, if necessary. Start the engine and check for leaks and proper gauge operation.

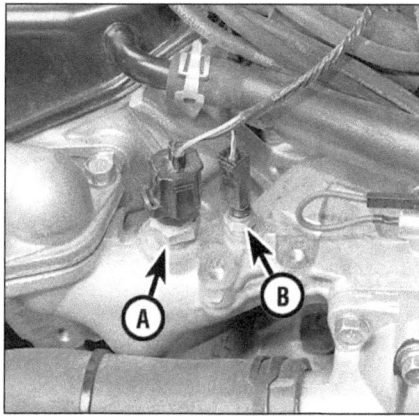

**5.3 Location of the coolant temperature sending unit**

A   *Engine temperature sensor (ECU)*
B   *Coolant gauge temperature sending unit*

**5.4 To test the temperature gauge, earth the sending unit electrical connector wire terminal - the gauge should respond**

## 6   Radiator and coolant reservoir - removal and refitting

**Warning:** *Do not start this procedure until the engine is completely cool. Do not allow antifreeze to come in contact with your skin or painted surfaces of the vehicle. Rinse off spills immediately with plenty of water. Antifreeze is highly toxic if ingested. Never leave antifreeze lying around in an open container or in puddles on the floor; children and pets are attracted by it's sweet smell and may drink it. Check with local authorities about disposing of used antifreeze. Many communities have collection centres which will see that antifreeze is disposed of safely.*

**Caution:** *If the stereo in your vehicle is equipped with an anti-theft system, make sure you have the correct activation code before disconnecting the battery.*

## Radiator

*Refer to illustrations 6.5 and 6.8*

1   Disconnect the cable from the negative terminal of the battery and remove the battery and air cleaner covers.

2   Raise the front of the vehicle and support it securely on jackstands. Remove the lower splash shields.

3   Drain the cooling system (see Chapter 1). If the coolant is relatively new or in good condition, save it and reuse it.

4   Disconnect the electrical connectors from the radiator fans.

5   If the vehicle is equipped with an automatic transaxle, disconnect the transmission fluid cooler lines **(see illustration)** and plug the lines and fittings.

6   Disconnect the coolant reservoir hose from the radiator. Loosen the upper and lower radiator hose clamps, then detach the radiator hoses from the fittings. If they're stuck, grasp each hose near the end with a pair of adjustable pliers and twist it to break the seal, then pull it off - be careful not to damage the radiator fittings! If the hoses are old or deteriorated, cut them off and fit new ones.

7   Remove the cooling fans see Section 4.

8   Remove the radiator mounting bolts **(see illustration)**.

9   Carefully lift out the radiator and fan/shroud assembly. Don't spill coolant on the vehicle or scratch the paint. Remove the bolts securing the fan/shroud assembly to the radiator.

10   With the radiator removed, it can be inspected for leaks and damage. If it needs repair, have a radiator shop or dealer service department perform the work, as special techniques are required.

11   Bugs and dirt can be removed from the radiator with a garden hose or a soft brush. Don't bend the cooling fins as this is done.

12   Refitting is the reverse of the removal procedure. Be sure the rubber cushions are seated properly at the base of the radiator.

13   After refitting, fill the cooling system with the proper mixture of antifreeze and water (see Chapter 1).

14   Start the engine and check for leaks. Allow the engine to reach normal operating temperature, indicated by the upper radiator hose becoming hot. Recheck the coolant level and add more if required.

15   If you're working on an automatic transaxle equipped vehicle, check and add fluid as needed (see Chapter 1).

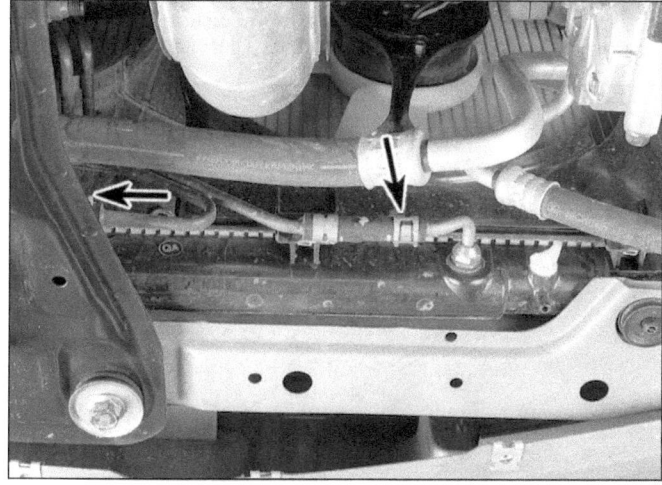

**6.5 Disconnect the transmission cooler lines from the radiator (arrows)**

**6.8 Remove the bolts (arrows) from the radiator supports**

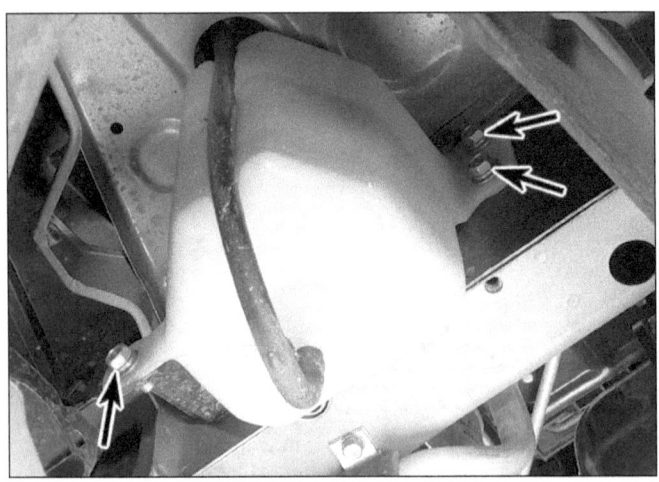

6.18 Remove the coolant reservoir mounting bolts (arrow)

8.4 Water pump mounting bolts (arrows)

## Coolant reservoir

*Refer to illustration 6.18*

16   Disconnect the hose from the radiator filler neck and inspect the hose for cracks.

17   Raise the front of the vehicle and support it securely on jackstands. Remove the left side and lower splash shields.

18   Remove the reservoir mounting bolts **(see illustration)**.

19   Lower the coolant reservoir from the body to remove it.

20   Pour the coolant into a container. Wash out and inspect the reservoir for cracks and chafing. Renew it if it's damaged.

21   Refitting is the reverse of removal.

## 7   Water pump - check

1   A failure in the water pump can cause serious engine damage due to overheating.

2   If the pump is defective, it should be renewed with a new or rebuilt unit.

3   Water pumps are equipped with weep or vent holes. If a failure occurs in the pump seal, coolant will leak from the hole. Remove the timing belt cover (see Chapter 2A) and check the water pump for leakage.

4   If the water pump shaft bearings fail, there

may be a howling sound from the water pump while the engine is running. Don't mistake drivebelt slippage, which causes a squealing sound, for water pump bearing failure.

## 8   Water pump - removal and refitting

**Warning:** *Wait until the engine is completely cool before beginning this procedure. Do not allow antifreeze to come in contact with your skin or painted surfaces of the vehicle. Rinse off spills immediately with plenty of water. Antifreeze is highly toxic if ingested. Never leave antifreeze lying around in an open container or in puddles on the floor; children and pets are attracted by it's sweet smell and may drink it. Check with local authorities about disposing of used antifreeze. Many communities have collection centres which will see that antifreeze is disposed of safely.*

## Removal

*Refer to illustration 8.4*

**Caution:** *If the stereo in your vehicle is equipped with an anti-theft system, make sure you have the correct activation code before disconnecting the battery.*

**Note:** *The water pump mounting bolts are different sizes and lengths, mark each bolt as it is removed to make sure they are refitted correctly.*

1   Disconnect the cable from the negative terminal of the battery.

2   Drain the cooling system (see Chapter 1). If the coolant is relatively new or in good condition, save it and reuse it.

3   Remove the timing belt (see Chapter 2A).

4   Remove the water pump mounting bolts **(see illustration)**. Twist and pull out on the water pump to detach it from the coolant inlet pipe and O-ring.

## Refitting

*Refer to illustrations 8.7 and 8.9*

5   Remove the gasket material from the engine block. Clean the bolt threads and the threaded holes to remove corrosion. Remove the O-ring from the inlet pipe and clean the O-ring sealing groove.

6   Compare the new pump to the old one to make sure they're identical.

7   Fit a new O-ring on the coolant inlet pipe **(see illustration)**. Lubricate the O-ring with fresh coolant - DO NOT use oil or grease to lubricate the O-ring.

8   Using a new gasket, refit the water pump. Press the water pump firmly onto the

8.7 Fit a new O-ring on the water inlet pipe (arrow)

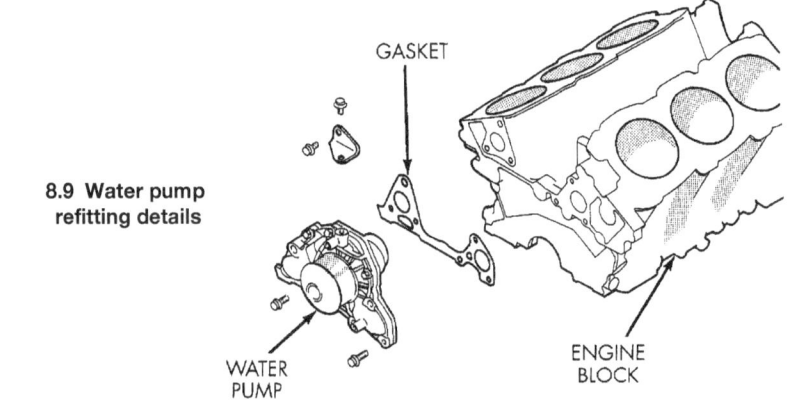

8.9 Water pump refitting details

GASKET

WATER PUMP

ENGINE BLOCK

coolant inlet pipe until the pipe seats into the housing.

9    Refit the mounting bolts and tighten them to the torque listed in this Chapter's Specifications **(see illustration)**.

10    Refit the timing belt.

11    Refill the cooling system (see Chapter 1). Run the engine and check for leaks.

---

## 9    Heater and air conditioning blower motor - circuit check

*Refer to illustrations 9.4 and 9.6*

**Note:** *This procedure applies to standard models only (with or without air conditioning). On models equipped with the optional Automatic Temperature Control, the system is controlled by an electronic control unit located on the heater/air conditioning housing. Have this system diagnosed by a dealer service department or automotive electrical specialist.*

1    Begin by switching the blower switch to each speed indicated on the switch. Listen for blower operation at the blower housing, below the glove box. If the blower motor does not operate in any speed, the blower motor, the blower switch, the blower motor relay, the wiring between the components or the fuse could be defective. Check the fuses in the fuse box and the main relay box. If the blower motor operates at one or more speeds, but not all speeds, the switch or the wiring could be defective.

2    If the blower motor does not operate, remove the trim panel under the glove box and locate the blower motor (see Section 10). Locate the blower motor electrical connector, turn the ignition On and place the blower switch in the Hi position. Using a voltmeter or test light and a suitable set of probes, backprobe the blower motor terminal corresponding to the blue wire.

a)   *If voltage is present at the terminal, backprobe the white wire terminal with a jumper wire connected to a good chas-*

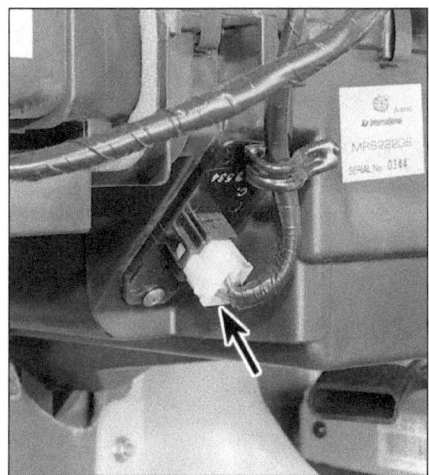

**9.6  The blower motor resistor (arrow) is located in the heater unit, behind the glove box - dash removed for clarity**

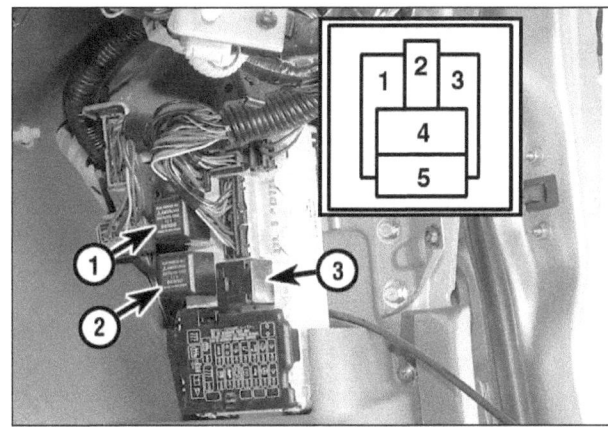

**9.4  Blower motor relay location and terminal guide**

1   *Blower relay*
2   *Defogger relay*
3   *Hazard flasher unit*

*sis ground - the blower motor should operate. If battery power is available on the blue wire, and the blower motor does not operate with the white wire connected to ground, the blower motor is faulty.*

b)   *If voltage was not present at the blue wire terminal, the blower motor relay, fuse, fusible link or related wiring is defective. Test the blower motor relay first.*

c)   *If the blower motor operates with the white wire grounded, but not under normal operation, the switch, blower resistor or wiring is defective.*

3    To test the blower switch, remove the heater/air conditioning control assembly (see Section 12). Disconnect the electrical connector from the blower motor switch and, using an ohmmeter, check for continuity between the terminals. Refer to the wiring diagrams at the end of Chapter 12 to determine the proper test points. If any of the tests indicate an open circuit where there should be continuity, renew the switch.

4    To test the blower motor relay, remove the relay from the interior compartment fuse and relay centre. Located on the drivers side kick panel. **Note:** *Some models have a HI speed blower relay located just above the blower motor.* First make sure there is voltage available at two of the terminals in the relay box (if there isn't, the fuse or the wiring is defective), then check the relay for continuity as follows **(see illustration)**:

a)   *Using an ohmmeter, check for continuity between terminals 1 and 3. There should be continuity. There should be no continuity between terminals 2 and 5.*

b)   *Using fused jumper wires, apply battery voltage and ground to terminals 1 (+) and 3 (-). There now should be continuity between terminals 2 and 5.*

5    If the relay does not operate as described, renew the relay. If the relay is good, check the ground circuit between the fuse box and the chassis.

6    To test the blower resistor, remove the glove box (see Chapter 11). Using an ohmmeter check for continuity between each of the resistor terminals **(see illustration)**. If there is an open circuit between any two terminals, renew the blower resistor.

---

## 10    Heater and air conditioning blower motor - removal and refitting

*Refer to illustration 10.5*

**Caution:** *If the stereo in your vehicle is equipped with an anti-theft system, make sure you have the correct activation code before disconnecting the battery.*

1    Disconnect the cable from the negative terminal of the battery.

2    Remove the passenger side under-dash trim panel.

3    Remove the glove compartment (see Chapter 11).

4    Disconnect the blower motor electrical connector.

5    Remove the blower motor retaining screws and lower the unit from the housing **(see illustration)**. **Note:** *On Magna models its necessary to remove the A/C belt lock controller before the blower motor can be fully removed.*

6    If you are renewing the motor, detach the fan and transfer it to the new motor. **Note:** *The HI speed blower relay is located next to the blower motor underneath the A/C belt lock controller.*

7    Refitting is the reverse of removal.

8    Run the blower and check for proper operation.

**10.5  Typical blower motor and A/C belt lock controller mounting screw locations (arrows)**

**11.3 Remove the clamps and detach the heater hoses from the firewall (arrows)**

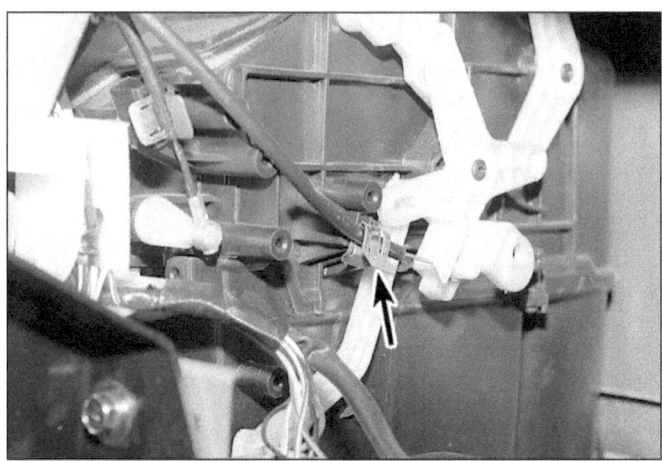

**11.6a Disconnect the mode control cable from the cable retaining clip (arrow) and slide the cable off of the lever**

## 11 Heater core - renewal

*Refer to illustrations 11.3, 11.6a, 11.6b, 11.7a and 11.7b*

**Warning 1:** *The models covered by this manual are equipped with Supplemental Restraint System (SRS), more commonly known as*

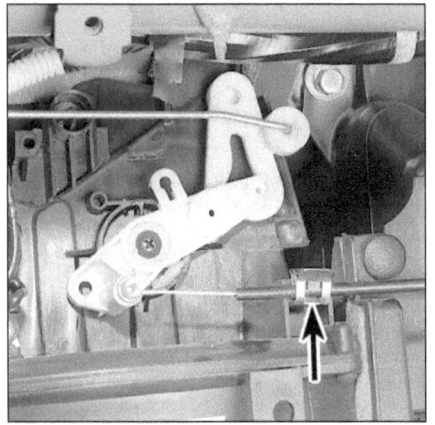

**11.6b Disconnect the air select cable (arrow) from the cable retaining clip and slide the cable off of the lever**

*airbags. Always disable the airbag system before working in the vicinity of any airbag system components to avoid the possibility of accidental deployment of the airbag(s), which could cause personal injury (see Chapter 12).*

**Warning 2:** *The air conditioning system is under high pressure. Do not loosen any fittings or remove any components until after the system has been discharged. Air conditioning refrigerant should be properly discharged into an approved container at a dealer service department or an automotive air conditioning repair facility. Always wear eye protection when disconnecting air conditioning system fittings.*

**Caution 1:** *Avoid static electricity damage to the engine ECU during removal or refitting by grounding yourself to the body of the vehicle before touching the ECU and using a special anti-static pad to store the ECU on, once it is removed.*

**Caution 2:** *If the stereo in your vehicle is equipped with an anti-theft system, make sure you have the correct activation code before disconnecting the battery.*

1    Disconnect the cable from the negative terminal of the battery.

2    Drain the cooling system (see Chapter 1). Place the temperature lever to the maximum Hot position to drain as much coolant as possible from the heater core.

3    Working in the engine compartment, disconnect the heater hoses at the firewall **(see illustration)**.

4    Remove the centre console and the instrument panel from the vehicle (see Chapter 11).

5    Remove the metal centre reinforcement structures from the dash panel. Remove the ECU (see Chapter 6).

6    Disconnect the mode control cable and air select cable from the heater unit **(see illustrations)**.

7    Remove the heater unit mounting nuts **(see illustrations)** and air ducts.

8    Remove the evaporator unit mounting nuts/bolts and have an assistant help separate the two cases without disconnecting the A/C lines. Carefully remove the heater unit from the vehicle.

9    Remove the retaining plate screws and remove the heater core from the heater unit.

10    Reassemble the heater core into heater unit. Check the operation of the air mix doors, dampers and control links, correct any problems before refitting.

11    Refit the heater unit in the reverse order of removal.

**11.7a Remove the upper heater unit mounting nuts (arrows)**

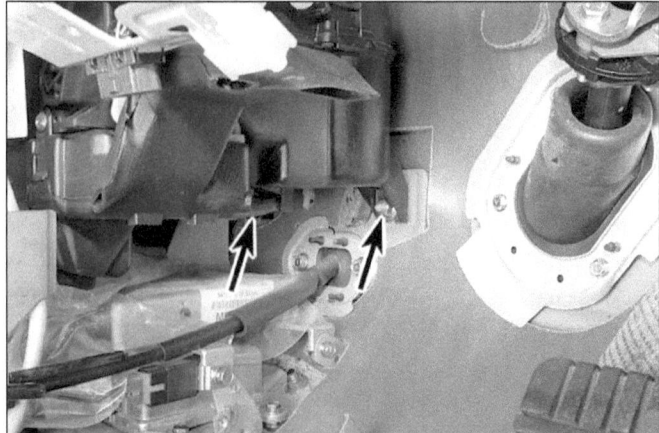

**11.7b Remove the lower heater unit mounting nuts (arrows)**

**12.4 Remove the control assembly-to-bezel retaining screws (arrows)**

12   Refit the instrument panel and centre console.
13   Refill the cooling system (see Chapter 1), reconnect the battery and start the engine. Check for leaks and proper system operation.

---

### 12   Heater and air conditioning control assembly - removal and refitting

*Refer to illustrations 12.4, 12.5 and 12.6*
**Warning:** *The models covered by this manual are equipped with Supplemental Restraint System (SRS), more commonly known as airbags. Always disable the airbag system before working in the vicinity of any airbag system components to avoid the possibility of accidental deployment of the airbag(s), which could cause personal injury (see Chapter 12).*
**Caution:** *If the stereo in your vehicle is equipped with an anti-theft system, make sure you have the correct activation code before disconnecting the battery.*

1   Disconnect the cable from the negative terminal of the battery.
2   Remove the floor centre console panel (see Chapter 11).

### *TE/TF/TH/TJ and KE/KF/ KH/ KJ models*
3   Remove the centre air outlet and the ashtray (see Chapter 11).
4   Remove the screws retaining the control unit to the trim bezel and remove the bezel **(see illustration)**.
5   Disconnect the electrical connectors from the control assembly **(see illustration)**.
6   Disconnect the control assembly cables **(see illustration)** and remove the control assembly.

### *TL/TW and KL/KW models*
7   Carefully prise the center trim panel and vent assembly out.
8   Disconnect the electrical connectors to the A/C control assembly ECU.
9   Pull the knobs and trim rings from the front of the trim panel, and remove the control assembly ECU mounting screws.
10   Separate the ECU from the trim panel.
11   Refitting is the reverse of the removal procedure.
12   Make sure all the retaining clips are securely refitted.
13   Check for proper operation of the heater and ventilation system.

---

### 13   Air conditioning and heating system - check and maintenance

### *Air conditioning system*
**Warning:** *If any component of the air conditioning system requires removal, the system must first be depressurised by a qualified technician. Because the system contains refrigerant under very high pressure, do not attempt to disconnect any part of the system yourself This could result in physical injury as well as damage to the system.*

1   The following maintenance checks should be performed on a regular basis to ensure that the air conditioner continues to operate at peak efficiency:
a) *Inspect the condition of the compressor drivebelt. If it is worn or deteriorated, renew it (see Chapter 1).*
b) *Check the drivebelt tension and, if necessary, adjust it (see Chapter 1).*
c) *Inspect the system hoses. Look for cracks, bubbles, hardening and deterioration. Inspect the hoses and all fittings for oil bubbles or seepage. If there is any evidence of wear, damage or leakage, renew the hose(s).*
d) *Inspect the condenser fins for leaves, bugs and any other foreign material that may have embedded itself in the fins. Use a "fin comb" or compressed air to remove debris from the condenser.*
e) *Make sure the system has the correct refrigerant charge.*

2   It's a good idea to operate the system for about ten minutes at least once a month. This is particularly important during the winter months because long term non-use can cause hardening, and subsequent failure, of the seals.
3   Leaks in the air conditioning system are best spotted when the system is brought up to operating temperature and pressure, by running the engine with the air conditioning ON for five minutes. Shut the engine off and inspect the air conditioning hoses and connections. Traces of oil usually indicate refrigerant leaks.
4   Because of the complexity of the air conditioning system and the special equipment required to effectively work on it, accurate troubleshooting of the system should be left to a professional technician.
5   If the air conditioning system doesn't operate at all, check the fuse panel and the air conditioning relay, located in the fuse/relay box in the engine compartment.
6   The most common cause of poor cooling is simply a low system refrigerant charge. If a noticeable drop in cool air output occurs, the following quick check will help you determine if the refrigerant level is low.

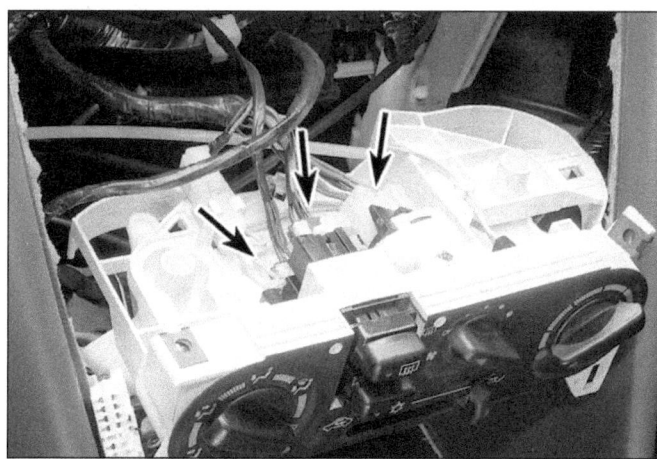

**12.5  Remove the control assembly electrical connectors (arrows)**

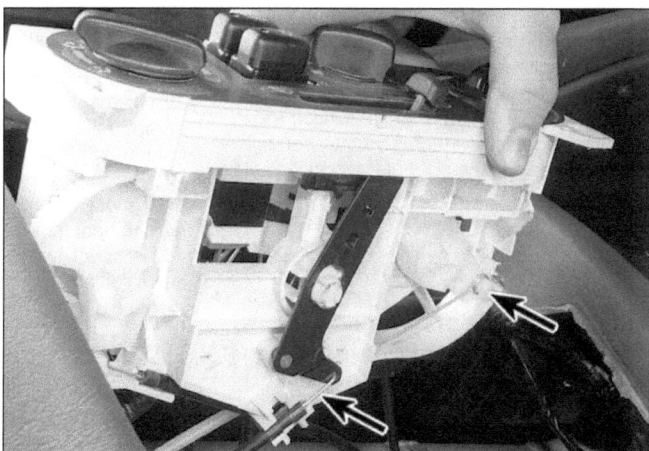

**12.6  Disconnect the control cables from the control assembly (arrows)**

14.6 Typical air conditioning compressor mounting bolts (arrows)

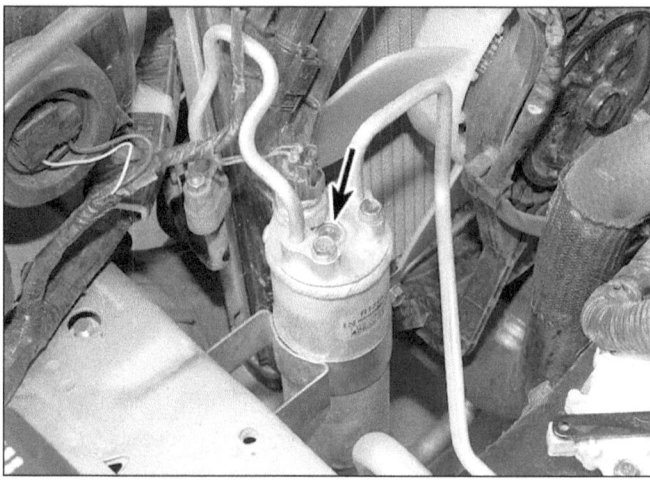

15.2 Typical receiver/drier location - note the sight glass on top (arrow)

### Checking the refrigerant charge

7 Warm the engine up to normal operating temperature.

8 Place the air conditioning temperature selector at the coldest setting and put the blower at the highest setting. Open the doors (to make sure the air conditioning system doesn't cycle off as soon as it cools the passenger compartment).

9 With the compressor engaged - the clutch will make an audible click and the centre of the clutch will rotate. After the system reaches operating temperature, feel the two pipes connected to the compressor.

10 The compressor inlet pipe should be cool, and the outlet line should be warm. If there's no perceptible difference between the two pipes, the system needs a charge. Insert a thermometer in the centre air distribution duct while operating the air conditioning system - the temperature of the output air should be considerably cooler than the ambient air temperature (an efficiently operating system will cool down to approximately 5 degrees C). If the air isn't as cold as it used to be, the system probably needs a charge. Further inspection or testing of the system is beyond the scope of the home mechanic and should be left to a professional.

11 Inspect the sight glass (located on top of the receiver/drier - see Section 15). If the refrigerant looks foamy when running, it's low. When ambient temperatures are very hot, bubbles may show in the sight glass even with the proper amount of refrigerant. With the proper amount of refrigerant, when the air conditioning is turned off, the sight glass should show refrigerant that foams, then clears.

### Heating systems

12 If the air coming out of the heater vents isn't hot, the problem could stem from any of the following causes:

a) *The thermostat is stuck open, preventing the engine coolant from warming up enough to carry heat to the heater core. Renew the thermostat (see Section 3).*

b) *A heater hose is blocked, preventing the flow of coolant through the heater core. Feel both heater hoses at the firewall. They should be hot. If one of them is cold, there is an obstruction in one of the hoses or in the heater core. Detach the hoses and back flush the heater core with a water hose. If the heater core is clear but circulation is impeded, remove the two hoses and flush them out with a water hose.*

c) *If flushing fails to remove the blockage from the heater core, the core must be renewed. (see Section 11).*

13 If the blower motor speed does not correspond to the setting selected on the blower switch, the problem could be a bad fuse, circuit, switch, blower motor resistor or motor (see Section 9).

14 If there isn't any air coming out of the vents:

a) *Turn the ignition ON and activate the fan control. Place your ear at the heating/air conditioning register (vent) and listen. Most motors are audible. Can you hear the motor running?*

b) *If you can't (and have already verified that the blower switch and the blower motor resistor are good), the blower motor itself is probably bad (see Section 9).*

15 If the carpet under the heater core is damp, or if antifreeze vapor or steam is coming through the vents, the heater core is leaking. Remove it (see Section 11) and fit a new unit (most radiator shops will not repair a leaking heater core).

16 Inspect the drain hose from the heater/air conditioning assembly, make sure it is not clogged.

---

### 14 Air conditioning compressor - removal and refitting

---

*Refer to illustration 14.6*
**Warning:** *The air conditioning system is*

under high pressure. Do not loosen any fittings or remove any components until after the system has been discharged. Air conditioning refrigerant should be properly discharged into an approved container at a dealer service department or an automotive air conditioning repair facility. Always wear eye protection when disconnecting air conditioning system fittings.

**Caution:** *If the stereo in your vehicle is equipped with an anti-theft system, make sure you have the correct activation code before disconnecting the battery.*

1 Have the refrigerant discharged at a dealer service department or an automotive air conditioning repair facility.

2 Disconnect the negative cable from the battery.

3 Disconnect the electrical connector from the compressor clutch.

4 Remove the air conditioning drivebelt (see Chapter 1).

5 Detach the refrigerant lines from the compressor. Immediately cap the open fittings to prevent the entry of dirt and moisture.

6 Remove the mounting bolts **(see illustration)** and remove the compressor from the engine compartment. **Note:** *Keep the compressor level during handling and storage. If the compressor seized or you find metal particles in the refrigerant lines, the system must be flushed out by an air conditioning technician and the receiver/drier must be renewed (see Section 15).*

7 Refit the compressor in the reverse order of removal.

8 If you are fitting a new compressor, refer to the manufacturer's instructions for adding refrigerant oil to the system. **Note:** *Drain out any oil that is present in the compressor, then add 50-ml of new refrigerant oil to the compressor - be sure to the use the correct type of oil for R-134a.*

9 Have the system evacuated, charged and leak tested by the shop that discharged it.

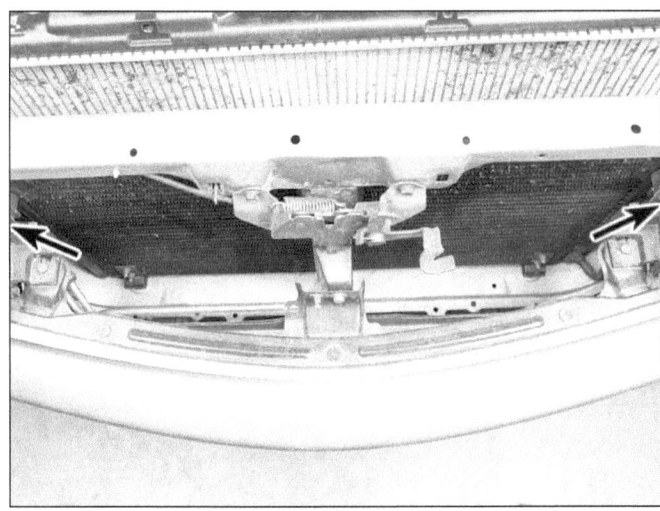

16.5  Condenser mounting bolts (arrows)

17.3  Disconnect the refrigerant lines from the evaporator inside the engine compartment (arrows)

## 15   Air conditioning receiver/drier - removal and refitting

*Refer to illustration 15.2*

**Warning:** *The air conditioning system is under high pressure. Do not loosen any fittings or remove any components until after the system has been discharged. Air conditioning refrigerant should be properly discharged into an approved container at a dealer service department or an automotive air conditioning repair facility. Always wear eye protection when disconnecting air conditioning system fittings.*

1    Have the refrigerant discharged at a dealer service department or an automotive air conditioning repair facility.
2    Detach the refrigerant lines and electrical connector from the receiver/drier. Immediately cap the open fittings to prevent the entry of dirt and moisture **(see illustration)**.
3    Remove the receiver/drier mounting bolts and detach it from the bracket.
4    Fit new O-rings on the lines and lubricate them with clean refrigerant oil.
5    If a new receiver/drier is being refitted, add 10-ml of refrigerant oil to the system - be sure to use the correct type of oil for R-134a.
6    Refitting is the reverse of removal. **Note:** *Do not remove the sealing caps from the new receiver/drier until you are ready to reconnect the lines.*
7    Have the system evacuated, charged and leak tested by the shop that discharged it.

## 16   Air conditioning condenser - removal and refitting

*Refer to illustration 16.5*

**Warning:** *The air conditioning system is under high pressure. Do not loosen any fittings or remove any components until after*

*the system has been discharged. Air conditioning refrigerant should be properly discharged into an approved container at a dealer service department or an automotive air conditioning repair facility. Always wear eye protection when disconnecting air conditioning system fittings.*

1    Have the refrigerant discharged at a dealer service department or an automotive air conditioning repair facility.
2    Remove the cooling fans and shrouds (see Section 4).
3    Remove the radiator (see Section 6).
4    Disconnect the refrigerant lines from the condenser. Immediately cap the open fittings to prevent the entry of dirt and moisture.
5    Remove the condenser mounting bolts and remove the condenser **(see illustration)**. Store the condenser upright to prevent oil loss.
6    If a new condenser is to be refitted, add 10-ml of new refrigerant oil to the system - be sure to use the correct type of oil for R-134a.
7    Refitting is the reverse of removal.
8    Have the system evacuated, charged and leak tested by the shop that discharged it.

## 17   Air conditioning evaporator - removal and refitting

*Refer to illustrations 17.3, 17.8a, 17.8b and 17.10*

**Warning 1:** *The models covered by this manual are equipped with Supplemental Restraint System (SRS), more commonly known as airbags. Always disable the airbag system before working in the vicinity of any airbag system components to avoid the possibility of accidental deployment of the airbag(s), which could cause personal injury (see Chapter 12).*
**Warning 2:** *The air conditioning system is under high pressure. Do not loosen any fittings or remove any components until after the system has been discharged. Air condi-*

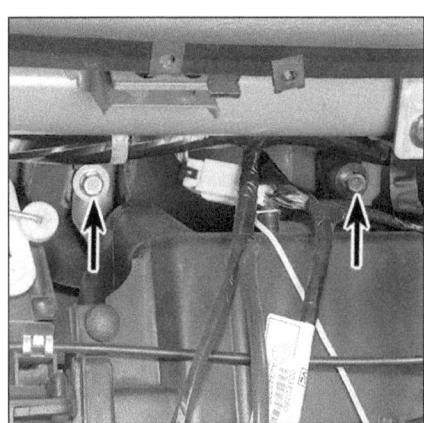

17.8a  Remove the evaporator unit upper mounting bolts . . .

*tioning refrigerant should be properly discharged into an approved container at a dealer service department or an automotive air conditioning repair facility. Always wear eye protection when disconnecting air conditioning system fittings.*
**Caution:** *If the stereo in your vehicle is equipped with an anti-theft system, make sure you have the correct activation code before disconnecting the battery.*

1    Have the refrigerant discharged at a dealer service department or an automotive air conditioning repair facility.
2    Disconnect the cable from the negative terminal of the battery.
3    Disconnect the evaporator refrigerant lines at the firewall **(see illustration)**. Immediately cap the open fittings to prevent the entry of dirt and moisture. Remove the grommet from around the tubes and remove the drain tube.
4    Remove the evaporator drain tube.
5    Remove the centre console and the instrument panel from the vehicle (see Chapter 11).
6    Remove the metal centre reinforcement

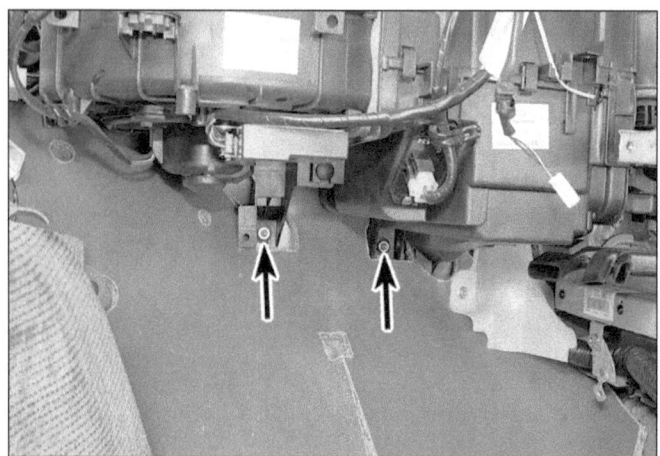

**17.8b** . . . and remove the evaporator unit lower mounting nuts, withdrawing the evaporator unit from the passenger compartment

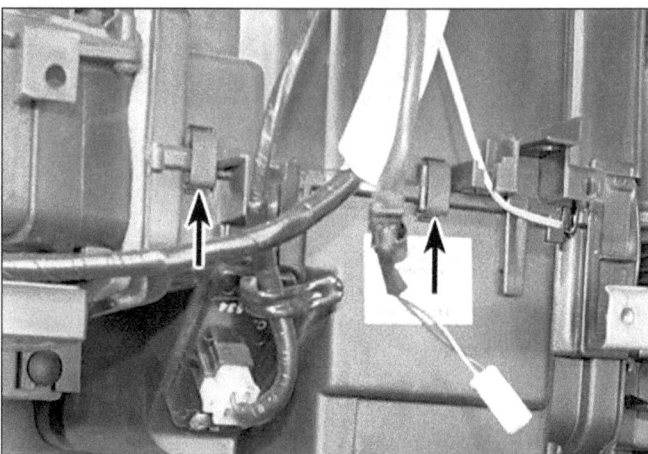

**17.10** Remove the retaining clips from around the perimeter of the evaporator case and separate the case halves (arrows)

structures from the dash panel.

7   Disconnect the electrical connectors from the evaporator unit.

8   Remove the evaporator unit upper mounting bolts and lower mounting nut **(see illustrations)**.

9   Carefully withdraw the evaporator unit from the vehicle.

10   Remove the evaporator case clips and separate the case halves **(see illustration)**.

11   Check the evaporator fins for blockage; if they are dirty clean them with compressed air - never use water for this purpose!

12   Check the fittings for cracks and signs of wear; renew parts as necessary.

13   Refitting is the reverse of the removal procedure. Be sure to renew all O-rings removed during disassembly with new O-rings and lubricate them with clean refrigerant oil.

14   If a new evaporator was refitted, add 10-ml of new refrigerant oil to the system - be sure to use the correct type of oil for R-134a.

15   Have the system evacuated, charged and leak tested by the shop that discharged it.

# Chapter 4
# Fuel and exhaust systems

## Contents

## Specifications

Fuel system operating pressure
  With vacuum hose connected ....... 270 kPa
  With vacuum hose disconnected ....... 330 to 350 kPa
Injector resistance ....... 13 to 19 ohms

### Torque specifications
| | Nm |
|---|---|
| Air inlet plenum-to-inlet manifold bolts | 15 to 20 |
| Throttle body-to-air inlet plenum bolts | 10 to 13 |
| Fuel rail bolts | 10 to 13 |
| Fuel hose-to-fuel rail bolt | 5 to 6 |
| Fuel pressure regulator bolts | 9 |
| Fuel pump flange nuts | 3 |

## 1 General information

The fuel system consists of a fuel tank, an electric fuel pump (located in the fuel tank), a fuel control relay, fuel injectors, an air cleaner assembly and a throttle body unit. The fuel injection systems are a Multi Point Fuel Injection (MPFI) system.

Multi Point Fuel Injection uses timed impulses to inject the fuel directly into the inlet port of each cylinder. The injectors are controlled by the Electronic Control Unit (ECU). The ECU monitors various engine parameters and delivers the exact amount of fuel required into the inlet ports. The throttle body serves only to control the amount of air passing into the system. Because each cylinder is equipped with its own injector, much better control of the fuel/air mixture ratio is possible.

### Fuel pump and lines

Fuel is circulated from the fuel tank to the fuel injection system, and back to the fuel tank, through a pair of metal lines running along the underside of the vehicle. An electric fuel pump is located inside the fuel tank.

The fuel pump will operate as long as the engine is cranking or running and the ECU is receiving ignition reference pulses from the electronic ignition system. If there are no reference pulses, the fuel pump will shut off after two or three seconds.

The fuel pressure regulator, located on the fuel rail, maintains a constant fuel pressure across the injectors. The regulator is connected to manifold vacuum, providing slight fuel pressure adjustments according to engine demand. The system is equipped with a fuel pressure solenoid that is directly controlled by the ECU. When inlet temperature is high (engine warmed-up), the ECU raises fuel pressure to prevent the generation of fuel vapor at very high temperatures.

### Exhaust system

The exhaust system includes an exhaust manifold fitted with an exhaust oxygen sensor, a catalytic converter, an exhaust pipe, and a muffler.

The catalytic converter is an emission control device added to the exhaust system to reduce pollutants. A single-bed converter is used in combination with a three-way (reduction) catalyst. Refer to Chapter 6 for more information regarding the catalytic converter.

## 2   Fuel pressure relief procedure

**Warning 1:** *Petrol is extremely flammable, so take extra precautions when you work on any part of the fuel system. Don't smoke or allow open flames or bare light bulbs near the work area, and don't work in a garage where a natural gas-type appliance (such as a water heater or clothes dryer) with a pilot light is present. If you spill any fuel on your skin, rinse it off immediately with soap and water. When you perform any kind of work on the fuel system, wear safety glasses and have a Class B type fire extinguisher on hand.*

**Warning 2:** *After the fuel pressure has been relieved, wrap shop towels around any fuel connection you'll be disconnecting. They'll absorb the residual fuel that may leak out, reducing the risk of fire and preventing contact with your skin.*

1    Before servicing any fuel system component, you must relieve the fuel pressure to minimise the risk of fire or personal injury.

2    Remove the fuel filler cap - this will relieve any pressure built up in the tank.

3    Disconnect the fuel pump power supply electrical connector at the fuel pump (see Section 7).

4    Start the engine and wait for it to stall, then turn off the ignition key.

5    The fuel system is now depressurised.

**Note:** *Place a rag around the fuel line before removing any hose clamp or fitting to prevent any residual fuel from spilling onto the engine.*

6    Reconnect the fuel pump connector. Do not turn the ignition key "ON" until the repairs are completed or the system will pressurise. As a security measure, disconnect the negative battery terminal immediately after removing the pressure from the system.

## 3   Fuel pump/fuel system pressure and component check

**Warning:** *Petrol is extremely flammable, so take extra precautions when you work on any part of the fuel system. Don't smoke or allow open flames or bare light bulbs near the work area, and don't work in a garage where a natural gas-type appliance (such as a water heater or clothes dryer) with a pilot light is present. If you spill any fuel on your skin, rinse it off immediately with soap and water. When you perform any kind of work on the fuel system, wear safety glasses and have a Class B type fire extinguisher on hand.*

**Caution:** *If the stereo in your vehicle is equipped with an anti-theft system, make sure you have the correct activation code before disconnecting the battery.*

**Note 1:** *To perform the fuel pressure test, you will need to obtain a fuel pressure gauge and adapter set (compatible with the fuel line fittings on your vehicle).*

**Note 2:** *The fuel pump will operate as long as the engine is cranking or running and the ECU is receiving ignition reference pulses*

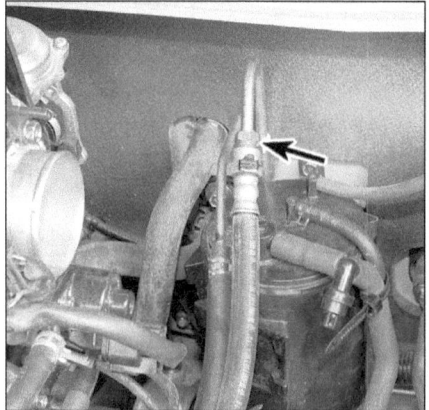

**3.8a  Disconnect the fuel inlet line (arrow) and fit a special tool T adapter**

*from the electronic ignition system. If there are no reference pulses, the fuel pump will shut off after two or three seconds.*

### Preliminary inspection

1    Should the fuel system fail to deliver the proper amount of fuel, or any fuel at all, inspect it as follows. Remove the fuel filler cap. Have an assistant attempt to start the engine while you listen at the fuel filler opening. You should hear a whirring sound as the engine is cranking (all models).

2    If you don't hear anything, fit a fused jumper wire from the positive (+) side of the battery to the fuel pump check terminal. The fuel pump check terminal (black/blue wire) in the engine check connector located on the firewall (TE-KE and TF-KF models only). Listen at the fuel filler opening again - if you now hear the whirring sound, the fuel injection control relay or its control circuit is faulty. If there still is no whirring sound, there is a problem in the fuel pump circuit from the diagnostic connector to the fuel pump, or a defective fuel pump.

3    Remove the fuel injection control relay, unplug it from its electrical connector and check for power to the relay at the connector. Check the control relay itself (refer to Steps 19 through 22 in this Section).

4    If there is no voltage to the fuel injection control relay, check the fusible links (see Chapter 12), the ignition switch and the wiring circuit for the fuel injection control relay. If the supply voltage reading is correct and the fuel pump only runs with the jumper wire in place, renew the fuel injection control relay with a new one.

5    If there is voltage present, check for battery voltage at the fuel pump electrical connector. If there is voltage present at the fuel pump connector and the ground circuit is good, refit the fuel pump.

### Operating pressure check
*Refer to illustrations 3.8a and 3.8b*

6    Relieve the fuel system pressure (see Section 2).

7    Detach the cable from the negative battery terminal.

**3.8b  Attach the pressure gauge hose to the end of the adapter and tighten fitting - the gauge should have a bleed line to allow the pressure and fuel to be released**

8    Disconnect the fuel inlet line and attach a fuel pressure gauge, using a special adapter which can be purchased from a tool dealer **(see illustrations)**. **Note:** *The factory specified tool kit is number E14M35.*

9    Attach the cable to the negative battery terminal, then start the engine.

10   Note the fuel pressure and compare it with the pressure listed in this Chapter's Specifications.

11   If the system fuel pressure is less than specified:

   a)  *Inspect the system for a fuel leak. Repair any leaks and recheck the fuel pressure.*
   b)  *If the fuel pressure is still low, renew the fuel filter (it may be clogged) and recheck the pressure.*
   c)  *If the pressure is still low, check the fuel pressure regulator. If the pressure regulator is good, refit the fuel pump.*

12   If the pressure is higher than specified:

   a)  *Check the fuel return line for an obstruction.*
   b)  *Check the fuel pressure regulator (see Section 16).*

13   Turn the ignition switch to Off, and observe the pressure on the gauge. If the pressure immediately begins to drop to zero:

   a)  *The fuel lines may be leaking.*
   b)  *The fuel pressure regulator may be allowing the fuel pressure to bleed through to the fuel return line (see Section 16).*
   c)  *A fuel injector (or injectors) may be leaking.*
   d)  *The fuel pump check valve may be stuck open.*

### Fuel pressure regulator check
**Note:** *This procedure assumes the fuel filter is in good condition.*

14   Perform Steps 6 through 10 above.

15   Disconnect the vacuum hose from the fuel pressure regulator (see Section 16) and verify that adequate vacuum is present. If there isn't vacuum present, check for a clogged hose or vacuum port. Plug the hose

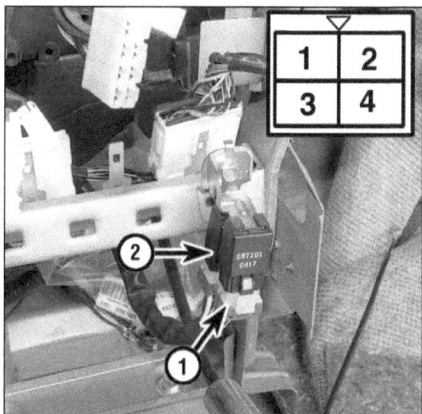

**3.19 Fuel injection control relay location and connector identification - (centre console removed for clarity)**

1   *Fuel pump relay*
2   *Engine control relay*

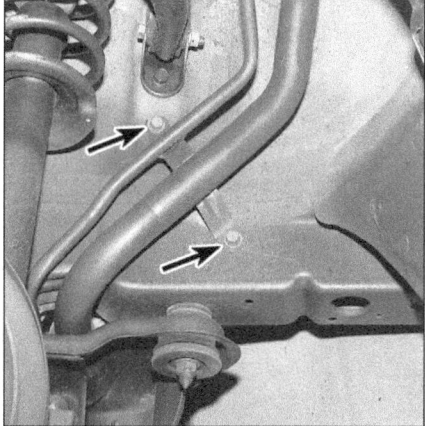

**5.5 Remove the fuel filler tube and vapor tube retaining bolts (arrows)**

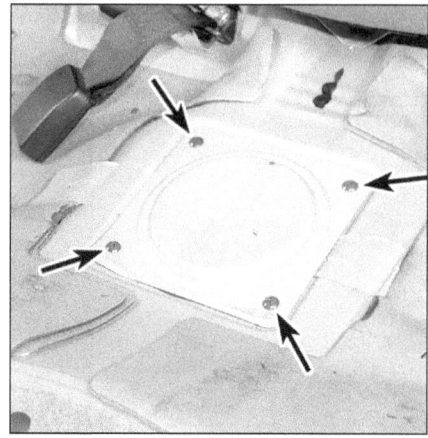

**5.6 Remove the fuel pump access panel screws (arrows)**

and observe the fuel pressure. The fuel pressure should increase approximately 50 kPa over the operating pressure with the engine idling and no vacuum applied to the regulator.

16   If the fuel pressure is low, pinch the fuel return line shut and watch the gauge. If the pressure doesn't rise, the fuel pump is defective or there is a restriction in the fuel feed line. If the pressure rises sharply, renew the pressure regulator.

17   If the fuel pressure is too high, turn the engine off. Disconnect the fuel return line and blow through it to check for a blockage. If there is no blockage, renew the fuel pressure regulator.

18   Check for the presence of raw fuel in the vacuum hose to the regulator. If there is any sign of fuel at the vacuum fitting, renew the fuel pressure regulator.

## *Fuel injection control relay check*

*Refer to illustration 3.19*

**Note:** *Failure in the fuel injection control relay will prevent power supply to the fuel pump, fuel injectors and ECU resulting in engine start failure.*

19   Locate and remove the fuel injection relay from its mounting **(see illustration)**.

20   Using fused jumper wires, apply battery voltage to terminals 2 and 4. Connect the positive terminal to terminal 4. There should be continuity as measured with an ohmmeter across terminals 1 and 3.

21   Without battery voltage applied, there should be continuity between terminals 2 and 4. **Note:** *If any of the above conditions are not met, check the battery, fusible links, ignition switch or related circuits.*

22   If the fuel injection control relay and related circuits are good and there is still no power to the fuel pump or injectors, the ECU may be defective - have the unit diagnosed by a dealership service department or other qualified repair specialist.

## 4   Fuel lines and fittings - repair and renewal

**Warning:** *Petrol is extremely flammable, so take extra precautions when you work on any part of the fuel system. Don't smoke or allow open flames or bare light bulbs near the work area, and don't work in a garage where a natural gas-type appliance (such as a water heater or clothes dryer) with a pilot light is present. If you spill any fuel on your skin, rinse it off immediately with soap and water. When you perform any kind of work on the fuel system, wear safety glasses and have a Class B type fire extinguisher on hand.*

### *Inspection*

1   Inspect the fuel lines and fittings for possible damage or deterioration whenever the vehicle is raised for service or you suspect a fault with the fuel system.

2   Check all hoses and pipes for cracks, kinks, deformation or obstructions.

3   Make sure all hose and pipe clips attach their associated hoses or pipes securely to the underside of the vehicle.

4   Verify all quick-disconnect ends attaching the plastic hoses are snug enough to assure a tight fit between the hoses and pipes.

### *Renewal*

5   If you must renew any damaged sections, use original equipment renewal hoses or pipes constructed from exactly the same material as the section you are renewing. Do not fit substitutes constructed from inferior or inappropriate material or you could cause a fuel leak or a fire.

6   Always, before detaching or disassembling any part of the fuel line system, note the routing of all hoses and pipes and the orientation of all clamps and clips to assure that renewal sections are refitted in exactly the same manner.

7   Before detaching any part of the fuel system, be sure to relieve the fuel tank pressure by removing the fuel filler cap.

## 5   Fuel tank - removal and refitting

**Warning:** *Petrol is extremely flammable, so take extra precautions when you work on any part of the fuel system. Don't smoke or allow open flames or bare light bulbs near the work area, and don't work in a garage where a natural gas-type appliance (such as a water heater or clothes dryer) with a pilot light is present. If you spill any fuel on your skin, rinse it off immediately with soap and water. When you perform any kind of work on the fuel system, wear safety glasses and have a Class B type fire extinguisher on hand.*

**Caution:** *If the stereo in your vehicle is equipped with an anti-theft system, make sure you have the correct activation code before disconnecting the battery.*

**Note:** *The following procedure is much easier if the tank is empty. Some tanks have a drain plug - if it doesn't, use a siphoning kit (available at most auto parts stores) and siphon the fuel into an approved fuel container. Don't start the siphoning action by mouth.*

1   Disconnect the cable from the negative terminal of the battery.

2   Remove the fuel tank filler cap.

3   Siphon the fuel into an approved petrol container. **Warning:** *Do not start the siphoning action by mouth, use a siphon kit available at most auto parts stores to start the siphoning action.*

4   Raise the rear of the vehicle and support it securely on jackstands.

### Sedan models

*Refer to illustrations 5.5, 5.6, 5.7 and 5.8*

5   Remove the fuel filler tube and return line **(see illustration)**. Be sure to plug the hoses to prevent leakage and contamination of the fuel system.

6   Remove the rear seat (see Chapter 11) and remove the fuel pump/sending unit access panel **(see illustration)**.

7   Disconnect the electrical connector to the fuel pump and fuel level sending unit **(see illustration)**. To disconnect the fuel line from the fuel tank fitting, squeeze the tabs together

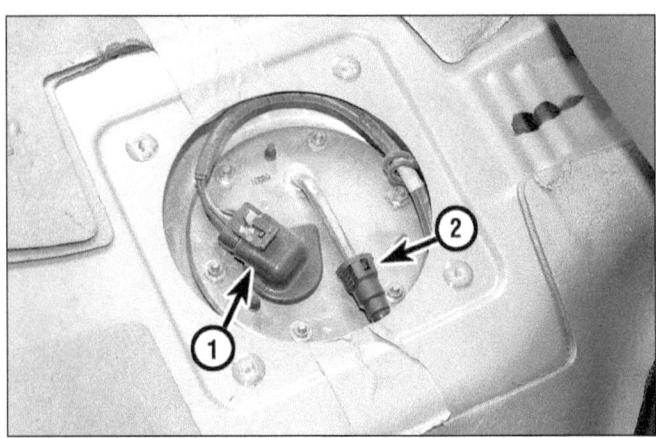

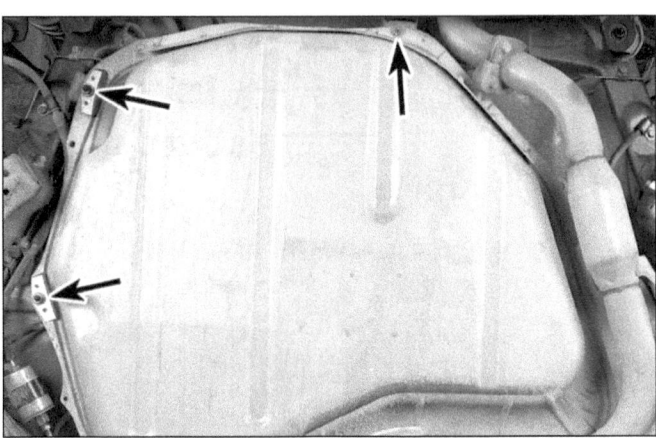

**5.7 Disconnect the fuel tank inlet line (2) and electrical connection (1) at the tank**

**5.8 Remove the fuel tank mounting bolts (arrows)- sedan**

and pull the line off the fitting. Remove the parking brake cable clamps. **Note:** *On sedan models it may be necessary to remove the exhaust flange bolts next to the tank and push the exhaust away from the tank to help with removal.*

8    Support the fuel tank with a floor jack. Position a piece of wood between the jack head and the tank to protect the tank and remove the tank mounting bolts **(see illustration)**.

9    Remove the tank from the vehicle.

10    Refitting is the reverse of removal.

### Station wagon models

*Refer to illustrations 5.11, 5.12 and 5.13*

11    Remove the fuel filler tube and return line **(see illustration)**. Be sure to plug the hoses to prevent leakage and contamination of the fuel system.

12    Disconnect the electrical connector to the fuel pump and fuel level sending unit **(see illustration)**. To disconnect the fuel line from the fuel tank fitting, push the line onto the fitting, squeeze the tabs together and pull the line off the fitting.

13    Support the fuel tank with a floor jack. Position a piece of wood between the jack head and the tank to protect the tank and

disconnect both fuel tank retaining straps **(see illustration)** and pivot them down until they are hanging out of the way.

14    Remove the tank from the vehicle.

15    Refitting is the reverse of removal.

---

### 6    Fuel tank - cleaning and repair

---

1    All repairs to the fuel tank or filler neck should be carried out by a professional who has experience in this critical and potentially dangerous work. Even after cleaning and flushing of the fuel system, explosive fumes can remain and ignite during repair of the tank.

2    If the fuel tank is removed from the vehicle, it shouldn't be placed in an area where sparks or open flames could ignite the fumes coming out of the tank. Be especially careful inside garages where a natural gas-type appliance is located, because the pilot light could cause an explosion.

---

### 7    Fuel pump - removal and refitting

---

*Refer to illustration 7.5*

**Warning:** *Petrol is extremely flammable, so*

*take extra precautions when you work on any part of the fuel system. Don't smoke or allow open flames or bare light bulbs near the work area, and don't work in a garage where a natural gas-type appliance (such as a water heater or clothes dryer) with a pilot light is present. If you spill any fuel on your skin, rinse it off immediately with soap and water. When you perform any kind of work on the fuel system, wear safety glasses and have a Class B type fire extinguisher on hand.*

**Caution:** *If the stereo in your vehicle is equipped with an anti-theft system, make sure you have the correct activation code before disconnecting the battery.*

1    Disconnect the cable from the negative battery terminal.

2    Siphon the fuel from the fuel tank into an approved petrol container. **Warning:** *Do not start the siphoning action by mouth, use a siphon kit available at most auto parts stores to start the siphoning action.*

3    On sedan models, remove the rear seat bottom (refer to Chapter 11). Remove the screws retaining the fuel pump access cover and remove the cover **(see illustration 5.6)**. On wagons, raise the rear of the vehicle and support it on jackstands. Make certain that there is clear access to the left front of the

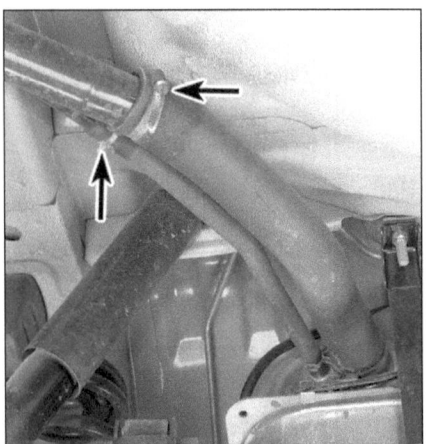

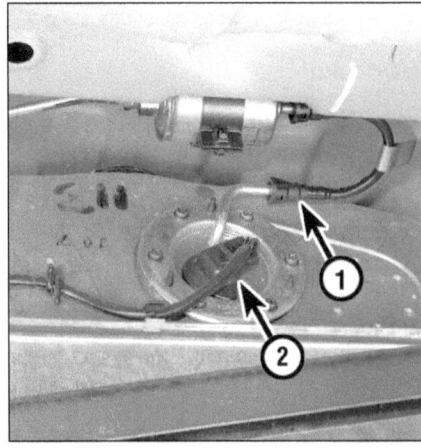

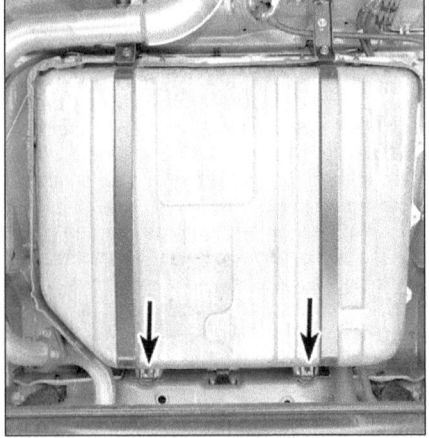

**5.11 Remove the fuel filler tube and vapor tube clamps (arrows)**

**5.12 Disconnect the fuel tank inlet line (1) and electrical connection (2) at the tank**

**5.13 Remove the fuel tank mounting strap nuts (arrows)**

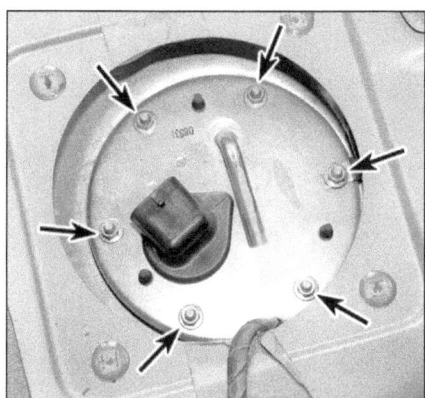

**7.5  Disconnect the fuel pump flange retaining nuts (arrows) and remove the fuel pump**

fuel tank.

4    Disconnect the fuel hoses and electrical connector from the fuel pump.

5    Remove the nuts around the perimeter of the fuel pump flange **(see illustration)**.

6    Withdraw the fuel pump from the fuel tank. Discard the gasket.

7    Clean the sealing area of the fuel tank and fit a new gasket on the fuel pump flange.

8    Inspect the fuel inlet sock filter (strainer) on the fuel pump suction tube for damage and contamination. Renew it if it's dirty or damaged.

9    Insert the fuel pump into the tank using a new gasket. Apply thread sealing compound or gasket sealant onto the flange screw threads and refit the nuts. Tighten the flange nuts to the torque listed in this Chapter's specifications.

10    Connect the fuel hose and electrical connector to the fuel pump.

11    The remainder of refitting is the reverse of removal.

## 8    Fuel level sending unit - check and renewal

*Refer to illustration 8.2*

**Warning:** *Petrol is extremely flammable, so*

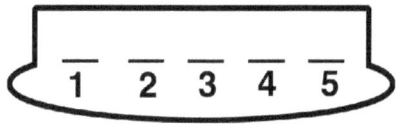

**8.2  Fuel level sending unit terminal identification**

*take extra precautions when you work on any part of the fuel system. Don't smoke or allow open flames or bare light bulbs near the work area, and don't work in a garage where a natural gas-type appliance (such as a water heater or clothes dryer) with a pilot light is present. If you spill any fuel on your skin, rinse it off immediately with soap and water. When you perform any kind of work on the fuel system, wear safety glasses and have a Class B type fire extinguisher on hand.*

**Caution:** *If the stereo in your vehicle is equipped with an anti-theft system, make sure you have the correct activation code before disconnecting the battery.*

1    Remove the fuel pump/sending unit from the fuel tank (see Section 7).

2    Using a ohmmeter, measure the resistance across terminals 2 and 3 of the connector **(see illustration)**.

3    Move the float to the very bottom, the resistance should be approximately 106 to 108 ohms with the float at the lower stop (tank empty). Now move the float to the upper stop (tank full) the resistance should decrease  smoothly to approximately 2.0 to 5.0 ohms. If the fuel level sending unit fails to operate as described, renew the unit.

### Renewal

4    Disconnect the cable from the negative battery terminal.

5    Siphon the fuel from the fuel tank into an approved petrol container. **Warning:** *Do not start the siphoning action by mouth, use a siphon kit available at most auto parts stores to start the siphoning action.*

6    On sedan models, remove the rear seat bottom (refer to Chapter 11). Remove the screws retaining the fuel pump access cover and remove the cover. On wagons, raise the rear of the vehicle and support it on jackstands. Make certain that there is clear access to the left front of the fuel tank.

7    Disconnect the fuel hoses and electrical connector from the fuel pump.

8    Remove the nuts around the perimeter of the fuel pump flange **(see illustration 7.5)**.

9    Withdraw the fuel pump from the fuel tank. Discard the gasket. l

10    Clean the sealing area of the fuel tank and fit a new gasket on the fuel pump.

11    Inspect the fuel inlet sock filter (strainer) on the fuel pump suction tube for damage and contamination. Renew it if it's dirty or damaged.

12    Insert the fuel pump into the tank using a new gasket. Apply thread sealing compound or gasket sealant onto the flange screw threads and refit the nuts. Tighten the flange screws to the torque listed in this Chapter's specifications.

13    Connect the fuel hose and from the airflow sensor.

14    The remainder of refitting is the reverse of removal.

## 9    Air cleaner assembly - removal and refitting

*Refer to illustrations 9.2, 9.4 and 9.5*

**Caution:** *If the stereo in your vehicle is equipped with an anti-theft system, make sure you have the correct activation code before disconnecting the battery.*

1    Detach the cable from the negative terminal of the battery.

2    Disconnect the inlet hose-to-throttle body clamp, electrical connector to the airflow sensor and air filter clips **(see illustration)**.

3    Remove the filter and assembly.

4    Remove the air intake duct **(see illustration)** retaining screws. Remove the intake air duct from the housing.

**9.2  Disconnect the inlet hose-to-throttle body clamp (1), electrical connector to the airflow sensor (2) and air filter clips (3)**

**9.4  Remove the air intake duct plastic mounting screws (arrows) and remove the intake duct**

**9.5  Remove the air cleaner front cover mounting bolts and nut (arrows) - nut not visible in photo**

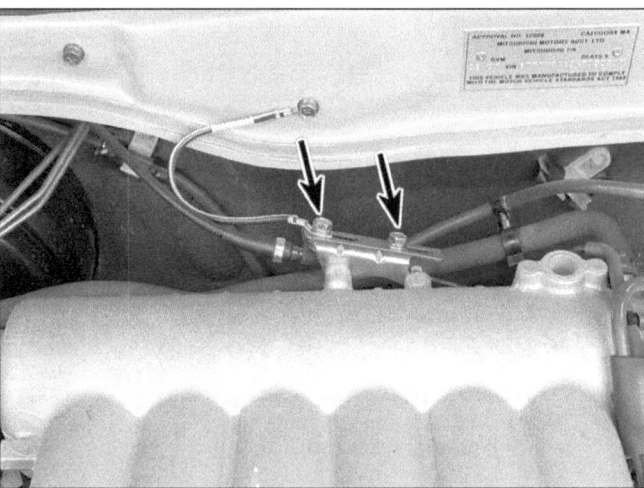

**10.2  Remove the two bolts retaining the cable adjusting bracket to the air inlet plenum**

5   Remove the mounting bolts and nut **(see illustration)** and lift the housing from the engine compartment.

6   Refitting is the reverse of removal.

## 10   Accelerator cable - removal, refitting and adjustment

### Removal

*Refer to illustration 10.2*

1   Detach the accelerator cable from the throttle lever.

2   Remove the bolts attaching the accelerator cable adjusting brackets to the inlet manifold plenum **(see illustration)**.

3   Working inside the driver's footwell compartment, remove the 2 nuts securing the accelerator cable to the firewall.

4   Remove the accelerator cable from the vehicle. Use care when pulling the cable through the firewall to avoid damaging the cable.

### Refitting

5   Refitting is the reverse of removal. Be sure the cable is routed correctly and operates freely without sticking or binding after refitting.

6   If necessary, on the engine compartment side of the firewall, apply sealant around the accelerator cable to prevent water from entering the driver's compartment.

## 11   Electronic Fuel Injection (EFI) system - general information

Electronic fuel injection provides optimum fuel/air mixture ratios at all stages of combustion and offers immediate throttle response characteristics. It also enables the engine to run at the leanest possible fuel/air mixture ratio, reducing exhaust fuel emissions.

These models are equipped with a Multi Port Fuel Injection (MPFI) system. The MPFI systems are controlled by an Electronic Control Unit (ECU) or computer located under the centre console (see Chapter 6). The ECU monitors engine performance and adjusts the air/fuel mixture according to the information it receives from the information sensors. See Chapter 6 for additional information and descriptions of the information sensors and the ECU control system.

An electric fuel pump located in the fuel tank pumps fuel to the fuel injection system through the fuel feed line and an in-line fuel filter. The fuel pump will operate as long as the engine is cranking or running and the ECU is receiving ignition reference pulses from the electronic ignition system. If there are no reference pulses, the fuel pump will shut off.

The throttle body has a throttle valve to control the amount of air delivered to the engine. The Throttle Position Sensor (TPS) and Idle Speed Control (ISC) motor are located on the throttle body.

The fuel rail is mounted on the top of the inlet manifold. It distributes fuel to the individual injectors. Fuel is delivered to the input end of the rail by the fuel feed line. At the other end of the fuel rail is the fuel pressure regulator, which keeps the pressure to the injectors at the required level. The excess fuel is bled off through the pressure regulator and is returned to the fuel tank via a separate line.

## 12   Fuel injection system - diagnosis

*Refer to illustrations 12.6, 12.7 and 12.8*

**Warning:** *Petrol is extremely flammable, so take extra precautions when you work on any part of the fuel system. Don't smoke or allow open flames or bare light bulbs near the work area, and don't work in a garage where a natural gas-type appliance (such as a water heater or clothes dryer) with a pilot light is present. If you spill any fuel on your skin, rinse it off immediately with soap and water. When you perform any kind of work on the fuel system, wear safety glasses and have a Class B type fire extinguisher on hand.*

**Note:** *The following procedure is based on the assumption that the fuel pump is working and the fuel pressure is adequate (see Section 3).*

1   Check all electrical connectors that are related to the system. Loose electrical connectors and poor grounds can cause many problems that resemble more serious malfunctions.

2   Check to see that the battery is fully charged, as the control unit and sensors depend on an accurate supply voltage in order to properly meter the fuel.

3   Check the air filter element - a dirty or partially blocked filter will severely impede performance and economy (see Chapter 1).

4   If a blown fuse is found, renew it and see if it blows again. If it does, search for a grounded wire in the harness to the fuel pump.

5   Check the air inlet duct to the inlet plenum for leaks, which will result in an excessively lean mixture. Also check the condition of the vacuum hoses connected to the inlet manifold.

6   Remove the air inlet duct from the throttle body and check for dirt, carbon or other residue build-up in the throttle body, particularly around the throttle plate. If it's dirty, clean it with aerosol carburettor cleaner and a shop towel **(see illustration)**.

7   With the engine running, place a stethoscope against each injector, one at a time, and listen for a clicking sound, indicating operation **(see illustration)**. If you don't have a stethoscope, place the tip of a screwdriver against the injector and press your ear against the handle.

8   If an injector isn't functioning (not clicking), purchase a special injector test light (sometimes called a "noid" light) and plug it into the injector electrical connector **(see illustration)**. Start the engine and make sure the noid light flashes. This will test for the

**12.6  Clean the throttle body with carburettor cleaner to remove sludge deposits**

**12.7  Use a stethoscope to determine if the injectors are working properly - they should make a steady clicking sound that rises and falls with engine speed changes**

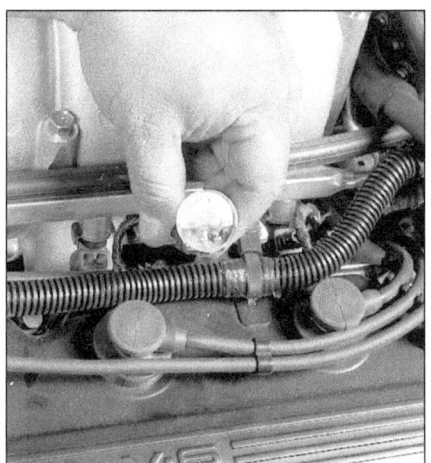

**12.8 Refit the "noid" light into the fuel injector harness and confirm that it blinks when the engine is running**

proper voltage signal to the injector. If the light doesn't flash, the ECU or the circuit is faulty.

9    With the engine turned Off and the fuel injector electrical connectors disconnected, measure the resistance of each injector. Compare your findings with the resistance values listed in this Chapter's Specifications. If the resistance of an injector is not as specified, renew it.

10    Check the fuel pressure, fuel injection control relay and the fuel pressure regulator (see Section 3).

11    All other checks to the system should be left to a dealer service department or other qualified repair shop, as there is a chance that the control unit may be damaged if the tests are not performed properly.

## 13    Throttle body - removal and refitting

*Refer to illustrations 13.3 and 13.6*

**Caution:** *If the stereo in your vehicle is equipped with an anti-theft system, make sure you have the correct activation code before disconnecting the battery.*

1    Disconnect the cable from the negative terminal of the battery.

2    Unplug all electrical connectors from the throttle body. Disconnect the heater hose and plug each open end.

3    Mark and disconnect any vacuum hoses connected to the throttle body **(see illustration)**.

4    Disconnect the accelerator cable from the throttle lever, then detach the cable housing from its bracket (see Section 10).

5    Detach the air inlet duct (see Section 9).

6    Remove the throttle body bolts and detach the throttle body **(see illustration)**. Clean off all traces of old gasket material.

7    Refit the throttle body and a new gasket and tighten the bolts to the torque listed in this Chapter's Specifications.

8    The refitting procedure is the reverse of removal.

## 14    Air inlet plenum - removal and refitting

**Caution:** *If the stereo in your vehicle is equipped with an anti-theft system, make sure you have the correct activation code before disconnecting the battery.*

**13.3  Remove all electrical connections, vacuum lines, water lines and hoses to the throttle body (arrows)**

**13.6  Remove the throttle body mounting bolts (arrows)**

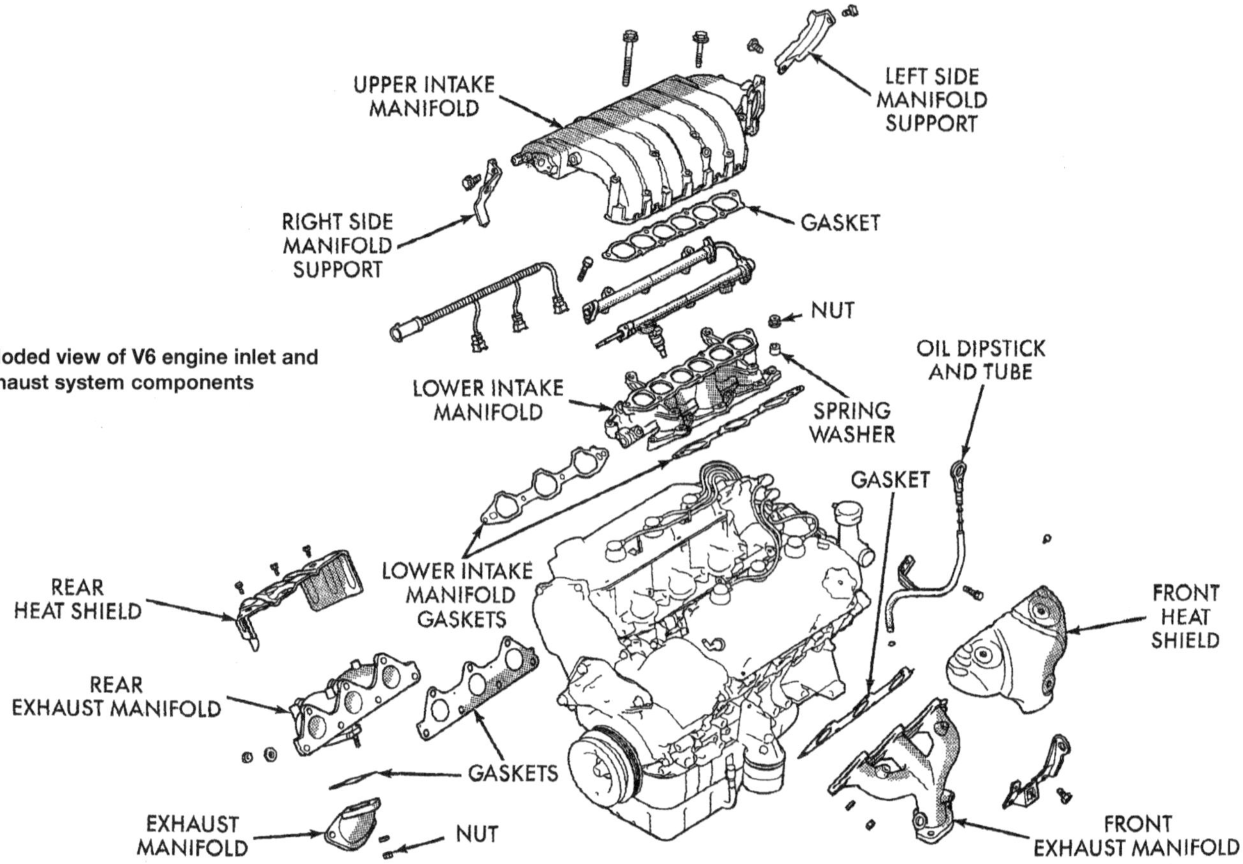

**14.5 Exploded view of V6 engine inlet and exhaust system components**

UPPER INTAKE MANIFOLD

LEFT SIDE MANIFOLD SUPPORT

RIGHT SIDE MANIFOLD SUPPORT

GASKET

NUT

LOWER INTAKE MANIFOLD

OIL DIPSTICK AND TUBE

SPRING WASHER

GASKET

REAR HEAT SHIELD

LOWER INTAKE MANIFOLD GASKETS

FRONT HEAT SHIELD

REAR EXHAUST MANIFOLD

GASKETS

EXHAUST MANIFOLD

NUT

FRONT EXHAUST MANIFOLD

## Removal

*Refer to illustrations 14.5, 14.6 and 14.7*

1    Disconnect the negative battery cable (see Chapter 5, Section 1).

2    Remove the air filter inlet duct from the throttle body (see Section 9).

3    Clearly label and disconnect all hoses, wires, brackets and emission lines which attach to the inlet.

4    Disconnect the accelerator cable and cruise control cable (if applicable) from the throttle body.

5    Remove the bolts securing the upper inlet plenum to the right and left side support brackets **(see illustration)**.

6    Remove the EGR tube **(see illustration)**.

7    Loosen the upper inlet plenum bolts 1/4 turn at a time until they can be removed by hand. Remove the upper inlet manifold from the engine **(see illustration)**. If it sticks, tap the plenum with a soft-face hammer or carefully prise it from the lower inlet plenum. **Caution:** *Do not prise between gasket sealing surfaces.*

8    To minimize the chance of gasket debris or other contamination from getting into the engine, place clean rags into the lower inlet manifold passages.

9    Remove all traces of gasket material from both the upper and lower inlet plenum by carefully scraping them using a suitable gasket scraper. **Caution:** *The inlet plenum components are made of aluminum and are easily nicked or gouged. Do not damage the gasket surfaces or a leak may result after the work is complete. Gasket removal solvents are available from auto parts stores and may prove helpful.*

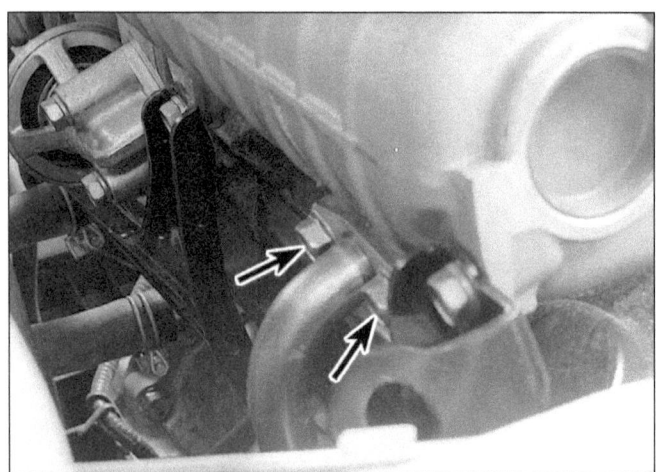

**14.6  From the rear of the upper inlet manifold remove the EGR mounting bolts (arrows)**

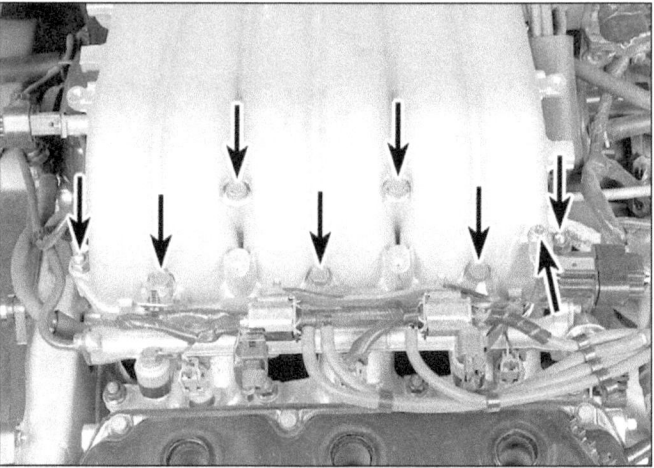

**14.7  Starting from the ends and working inward, remove the upper inlet plenum mounting bolts**

15.5  ISC motor terminal identification (arrow)

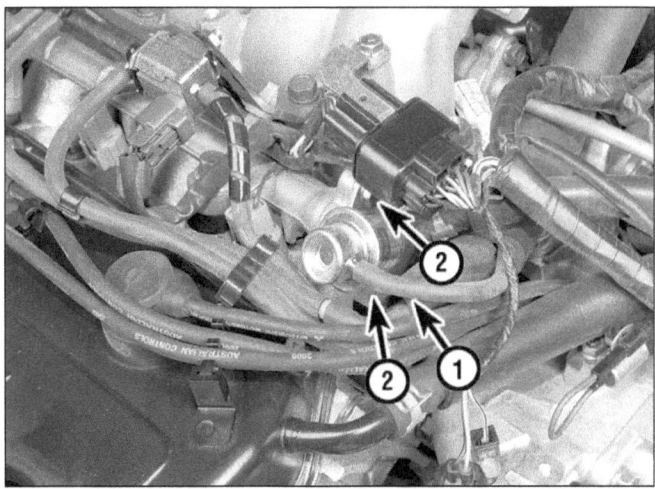

16.4  Remove the pressure regulator vacuum hose (1),
then the mounting bolts (2)

## Refitting

10   Remove the rags from the lower inlet plenum. Use a shop vacuum to remove any contamination that may be present.

11   Refit the upper inlet plenum, using a new gasket. Tighten the bolts in 3 stages, working from the centre out, to the torque listed in this Chapter's Specifications.

12   Refit the EGR tube using new gaskets. Tighten the bolts securely.

13   The remaining refitting steps are the reverse of removal.

## 15  Idle Speed Control (ISC) motor - general description, check and renewal

### General description

1   The ISC motor is mounted on the throttle body. It is a stepper type motor, connected to a pintle which extends or retracts into a by-pass air channel in the throttle body. The engine idle speed is controlled by alternating voltage and ground signals sent from the ECU. The ECU operates the motor in both directions to extend or retract the pintle, which in turn increases or decreases the amount of air by-passing the throttle plate - the more air by-passing the throttle plate, the higher the engine idle speed.

2   Incorporated within the ISC motor assembly is a fast idle air valve. The fast idle air valve is a wax-pellet device. Engine coolant is circulated around the wax-pellet, when the engine is cold, additional air is allowed the by-pass the throttle plate further increasing the cold idle speed. As the engine temperature increases, the wax-pellet valve closes the air passage.

### Check

*Refer to illustration 15.5*

3   A malfunction in the idle speed control system will cause an incorrect idle speed, a

rough idle, stalling and a starting problem. A constant high idle may indicate a problem with the fast idle air valve or a vacuum leak in the air inlet system.

4   Start the engine cold and observe the idle speed. The idle speed should decrease as the engine warms up. When the engine reaches operating temperature, turn on the air conditioning (if equipped), shift the transmission into drive (automatic) and turn the steering wheel to operate the power steering (if equipped). The engine idle speed should remain steady. If the idle drops or the engine stalls, a malfunction in the idle speed control system may exist.

5   To check the ISC motor, disconnect the electrical connector. Turn the ignition "ON" and check for power on the red wires of the harness connector corresponding to the ISC motor terminals 2 and 5 **(see illustration)** - turn the ignition Off. If power is not available, check the fuel injection control relay and related wiring (see Section 3). Using an ohmmeter, check for continuity between the ISC motor terminal 2 and terminals 1 and 3 and between terminal 5 and terminals 4 and 6. If the meter indicates an open circuit or high resistance, renew the ISC motor. Further checks of the control system, require specialised equipment and should be left to a dealer service department or other properly equipped repair facility.

### Renewal

6   Remove the air inlet duct from the throttle body.

7   Disconnect the electrical connector from the ISC motor.

8   Remove the ISC motor attaching screws and separate the assembly from the throttle body.

9   Refit the ISC motor assembly and tighten the screws securely.

10   Connect the electrical connectors to the ISC motor.

11   Start the engine and check for proper operation.

## 16  Fuel pressure regulator - removal and refitting

*Refer to illustration 16.4*

**Warning:** *Petrol is extremely flammable, so take extra precautions when you work on any part of the fuel system. Don't smoke or allow open flames or bare light bulbs near the work area, and don't work in a garage where a natural gas-type appliance (such as a water heater or clothes dryer) with a pilot light is present. If you spill any fuel on your skin, rinse it off immediately with soap and water. When you perform any kind of work on the fuel system, wear safety glasses and have a Class B type fire extinguisher on hand.*

**Caution:** *If the stereo in your vehicle is equipped with an anti-theft system, make sure you have the correct activation code before disconnecting the battery.*

1   Relieve the fuel system pressure (see Section 2).

2   Disconnect the cable from the negative terminal of the battery.

3   Detach the vacuum hose from the fuel pressure regulator.

4   Remove the bolts retaining the fuel pressure regulator to the fuel rail **(see illustration)**.

5   Fit new O-rings and lubricate them with a light coat of clean engine oil.

6   Refitting is the reverse of removal. Tighten the pressure regulator mounting screws/bolts securely.

## 17  Fuel rail and injectors - removal and refitting

**Warning:** *Petrol is extremely flammable, so take extra precautions when you work on any part of the fuel system. Don't smoke or allow open flames or bare light bulbs near the work area, and don't work in a garage where a natural gas-type appliance (such as a water*

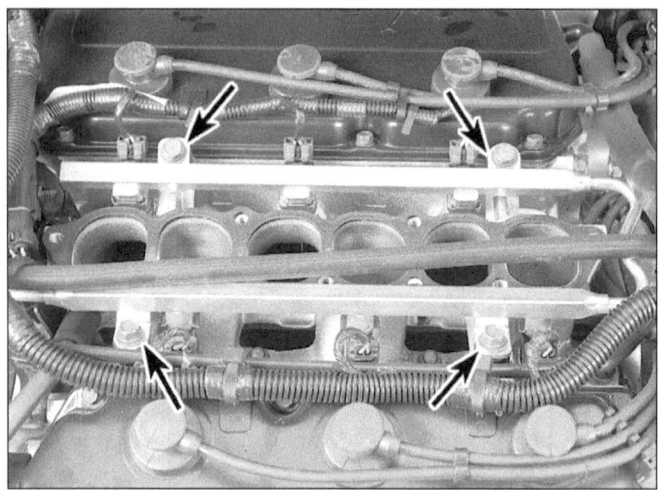

17.6  Fuel rail mounting bolts (arrows)

17.7  Removing the fuel rail and injectors

*heater or clothes dryer) with a pilot light is present. If you spill any fuel on your skin, rinse it off immediately with soap and water. When you perform any kind of work on the fuel system, wear safety glasses and have a Class B type fire extinguisher on hand.*

## Removal

*Refer to illustrations 17.6, 17.7, 17.8a and 17.8b*

1    Relieve the fuel system pressure (see Section 2). Disconnect the cable from the negative terminal of the battery.

2    Remove the inlet manifold/plenum support brace and, remove the inlet manifold plenum (see Section 14).

3    Disconnect the fuel return line from the fuel pressure regulator and the fuel feed line from the fuel rail assembly.

4    Detach the vacuum line from the pressure regulator.

5    Label and unplug the injector electrical connectors.

6    Remove the fuel rail retaining bolts **(see illustration)**.

7    Carefully remove the fuel rail with the injectors **(see illustration)**. **Caution:** *Use*

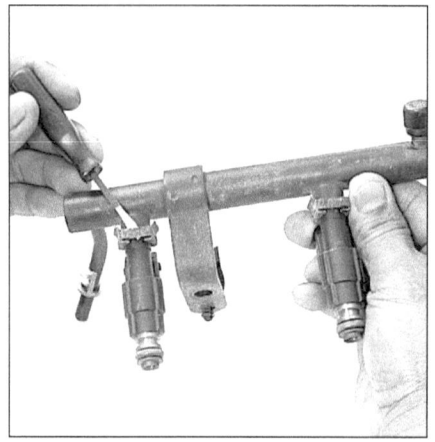

17.8a  Using a screwdriver or pliers, remove the clip retaining the fuel injector to the fuel rail

*care when handling the fuel rail assembly to avoid damaging the injectors.*

8    To remove a fuel injector, remove the retaining clip and carefully wiggle the end of the injector to separate it from the fuel rail **(see illustrations)**.

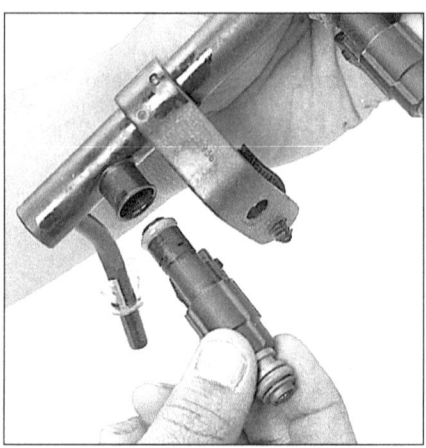

17.8b  Separate the fuel injector from the fuel rail

## Refitting

*Refer to illustrations 17.9 and 17.13*

9    Inspect the injector O-rings and seals. These should be renewed whenever the fuel rail is removed **(see illustration)**.

10    Fit the new O-rings on the injectors and

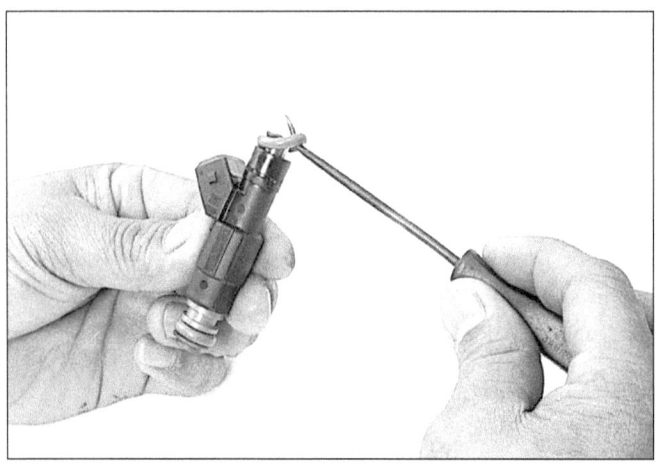

17.9  Be sure to renew the O-rings with new ones

17.13  These plastic spacers must be fitted between the fuel rail and lower inlet manifold

**18.1a  Check the exhaust system flexible pipe sections (arrows) for cracks, tears or damage**

**18.1b  The catalytic converter is supported by two hangers - make sure they are not damaged and the bolts are tight**

lubricate them with clean engine oil.

11   Refit the injectors on the fuel rail.

12   Secure the injectors with the retaining clips.

13   Refit the fuel rail into the inlet manifold **(see illustration)**. Carefully press the fuel rail/injector assembly into the injector bores until the injectors are completely seated. Refit the mounting bolts and tighten them to the torque listed in this Chapter's Specifications.

14   Connect the fuel feed line to the fuel rail. Use new washers on the banjo bolt or new O-rings of the fitting, as necessary.

15   Connect the fuel return line and vacuum hose to the fuel pressure regulator.

16   The remainder of refitting is the reverse of removal.

---

## 18   Exhaust system components - general information, removal and refitting

*Refer to illustrations 18.1a and 18.1b*

**Warning:** *Inspection and repair of exhaust system components should be done only after enough time has elapsed after driving the vehicle to allow the system components to cool completely. Also, when working under the vehicle, make sure it is securely supported on jackstands.*

1   The exhaust system consists of the exhaust manifold(s), the catalytic converter, the muffler, the tailpipe and all connecting pipes, brackets, hangers and clamps **(see illustrations)**. The exhaust system is attached to the body with mounting brackets and rubber hangers. If any of the parts are improperly refitted, excessive noise and vibration will be transmitted to the body.

2   Conduct regular inspections of the exhaust system to keep it safe and quiet. Look for any damaged or bent parts, open seams, holes, loose connections, excessive corrosion or other defects which could allow exhaust fumes to enter the vehicle. Deteriorated exhaust system components should not be repaired; they should be renewed with new parts.

3   If the exhaust system components are extremely corroded or rusted together, welding equipment will probably be required to remove them. The convenient way to accomplish this is to have a muffler repair shop remove the corroded sections with a cutting torch. If, however, you want to save money by doing it yourself (and you don't have a welding outfit with a cutting torch), simply cut off the old components with a hacksaw. If you have compressed air, special pneumatic cutting chisels can also be used. If you do decide to tackle the job at home, be sure to wear safety goggles to protect your eyes from metal chips and work gloves to protect your hands.

4   Here are some simple guidelines to follow when repairing the exhaust system:

a)   *Work from the back to the front when removing exhaust system components.*

b)   *Apply penetrating oil to the exhaust system component fasteners to make them easier to remove.*

c)   *Use new gaskets, hangers and clamps when refitting exhaust systems components.*

d)   *Apply anti-seize compound to the threads of all exhaust system fasteners during reassembly.*

e)   *Be sure to allow sufficient clearance between newly fitted parts and all points on the underbody to avoid overheating the floor pan and possibly damaging the interior carpet and insulation. Pay particularly close attention to the catalytic converter and heat shield.*

# Notes

# Chapter 5
# Engine electrical systems

## Contents

## Specifications

### Ignition system
Ignition coil resistance
| | |
|---|---|
| Primary resistance | 0.5 to 0.7 ohms |
| Secondary resistance | 9 to 13 K-ohms |

### Torque specifications
| | Nm |
|---|---|
| Starter mounting bolts | 31 |

## 1  General information

*Refer to illustration 1.1*

The engine electrical systems include all ignition, charging and starting components (see illustration). Because of their engine-related functions, these components are discussed separately from chassis electrical devices such as the lights, the instruments, etc. (which are included in Chapter 12).

Always observe the following precautions when working on the electrical systems:

a) *Be extremely careful when servicing engine electrical components. They are easily damaged if checked, connected or handled improperly.*

**1.1 Charging and ignition system components**

1  *Distributor*
2  *Battery (under cover)*
3  *Spark plug wires (front cylinder head)*
4  *Alternator*

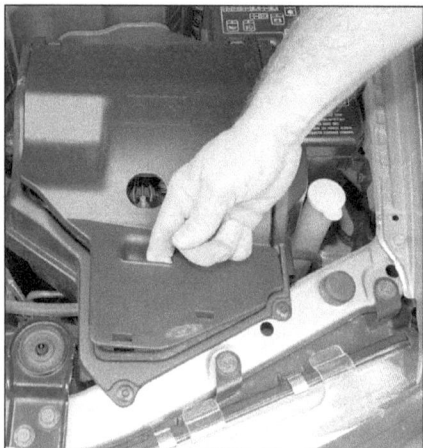

**3.1  Pull open the battery cover**

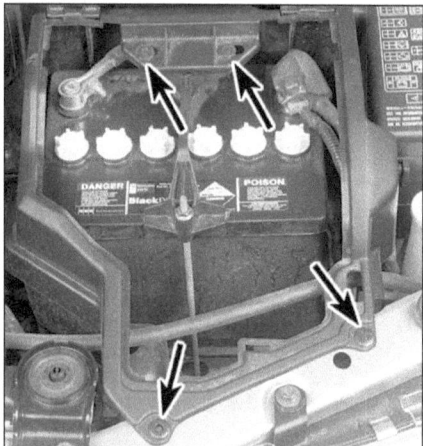

**3.2a  Remove the battery cover retaining clips . . .**

**3.2b  . . by pushing the center of the clip in just below the top of the clip, then pull the clip out**

b) *Never leave the ignition switch on for long periods of time with the engine off.*
c) *Don't disconnect the battery cables while the engine is running.*
d) *Maintain correct polarity when connecting a battery cable from another vehicle during jump starting.*
e) *Always disconnect the negative cable first and hook it up last or the battery may be shorted by the tool being used to loosen the cable clamps.*

It's also a good idea to review the safety-related information regarding the engine electrical systems located in the Safety first! Section near the front of this manual before beginning any operation included in this Chapter.

## 2    Battery - emergency jump starting

Refer to the Booster battery (jump) starting procedure at the front of this manual.

## 3    Battery - removal and refitting

*Refer to illustrations 3.1, 3.2a, 3.2b, 3.3 and 3.5*

**Caution 1:** *Always disconnect the negative cable first and hook it up last or the battery may be shorted by the tool being used to loosen the cable clamps.*
**Caution 2:** *If the stereo in your vehicle is equipped with an anti-theft system, make sure you have the correct activation code before disconnecting the battery.*

1    Open the battery cover **(see illustration).**
2    Remove the battery cover **(see illustrations).**
3    Disconnect the negative cable, then the positive cable from the battery terminals and remove the battery hold down clamp **(see illustration).**
4    Lift out the battery. Be careful - it's heavy.
5    While the battery is out, inspect the carrier (tray) for corrosion (see Chapter 1) and

renew if necessary **(see illustration).**
6    If you are renewing the battery, make sure that you get one that's identical, with the same dimensions, amperage rating, cold cranking rating, etc.
7    Refitting is the reverse of removal.

## 4    Battery cables - check and renewal

1    Periodically inspect the entire length of each battery cable for damage, cracked or burned insulation and corrosion. Poor battery cable connections can cause starting problems and decreased engine performance.
2    Check the cable-to-terminal connections at the ends of the cables for cracks, loose wire strands and corrosion. The presence of white, fluffy deposits under the insulation at the cable terminal connection is a sign that the cable is corroded and should be renewed. Check the terminals for distortion, missing mounting bolts and corrosion.

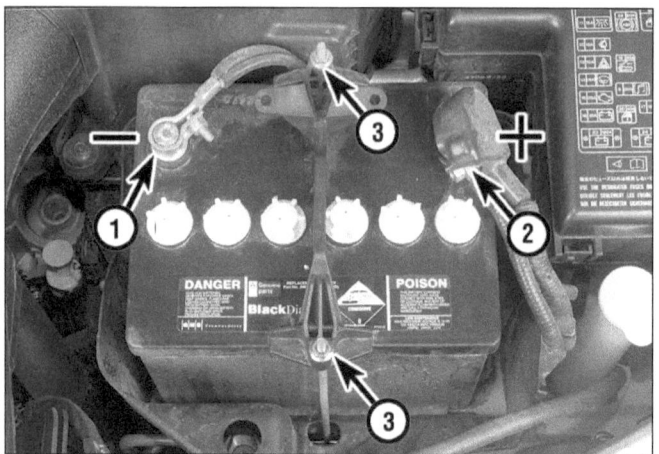

**3.3  To remove the battery . . .**

1    *Disconnect the cable from the negative terminal*
2    *Disconnect the cable for the positive terminal*
3    *Remove the nuts and detach the clamp*

**3.5  Remove the battery tray mounting bolts (arrow)**

6.2 To use a calibrated ignition tester (available at most auto parts stores), simply disconnect a spark plug wire, attach the wire to the tester and clip the tester to a good earth - if there is enough power to fire the plug, sparks will be clearly visible between the electrodes as the engine is cranked

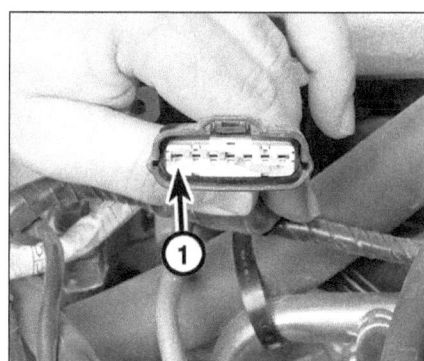

6.6 Check for battery voltage at terminal (1) of the distributor connector

3    When removing the cables, always disconnect the negative cable first and hook it up last or the battery may be shorted by the tool used to loosen the cable clamps. Even if only the positive cable is being renewed, be sure to disconnect the negative cable from the battery first (see Chapter 1 for further information regarding battery cable removal).

4    Disconnect the old cables from the battery, then trace each of them to their opposite ends and disconnect them from the starter solenoid and ground terminals. Note the routing of each cable to ensure correct refitting.

5    If you are renewing either one or both of the cables, take them with you when buying new cables. It is vitally important that you renew the cables with identical parts. Cables have characteristics that make them easy to identify: positive cables are usually red, larger in cross-section and have a larger diameter battery post clamp; earth cables are usually black, smaller in cross-section and have a slightly smaller diameter clamp for the negative post.

6    Clean the threads of the solenoid or earth connection with a wire brush to remove rust and corrosion. Apply a light coat of battery terminal corrosion inhibitor, or petroleum jelly, to the threads to prevent future corrosion.

7    Attach the cable to the solenoid or earth connection and tighten the mounting nut/bolt securely.

8    Before connecting a new cable to the battery, make sure that it reaches the battery post without having to be stretched.

9    Connect the positive cable first, followed by the negative cable.

## 5    Ignition system - general information

The ignition system includes the ignition switch, the battery, the coil, the primary (low voltage) and secondary (high voltage) wiring circuits, the distributor, crankshaft sensor and the spark plugs. The ignition timing is controlled by the Electronic Control Unit (ECU).

When working on the ignition system, take the following precautions:

a)    *Do not keep the ignition switch on for more than 10 seconds if the engine will not start.*

b)    *Always connect a tachometer in accordance with the manufacturer's instructions. Some tachometers may be incompatible with this ignition system. Consult a dealer service department before buying a tachometer for use with this vehicle.*

c)    *Never allow the primary terminals of the ignition coil to touch earth.*

d)    *Do not disconnect the battery when the engine is running.*

## 6    Ignition system - check

*Refer to illustrations 6.2 and 6.6*

**Warning:** *Because of the very high voltage generated by the ignition system, extreme care should be taken when this check is performed.*

1    If the engine turns over but won't start, disconnect the spark plug wire from any spark plug and attach it to a calibrated ignition tester (available at most auto parts stores).

2    Connect the clip on the tester to a bolt or metal bracket on the engine **(see illustration)**. If you're unable to obtain a calibrated ignition tester, remove the wire from one of the spark plugs and, using an insulated tool, hold the end of the wire about 5 mm from a good earth.

3    Crank the engine and watch the end of the tester or spark plug wire to see if bright blue, well-defined sparks occur. If you're not using a calibrated tester, have an assistant crank the engine for you. **Warning:** *Keep clear of drivebelts and other moving engine components that could injure you.*

4    If sparks occur, sufficient voltage is reaching the plug to fire it. Repeat the check at the remaining plug wires to verify the wires, distributor cap and rotor are good. However, the plugs themselves may be fouled, so remove them and check them as described in

Chapter 1.

5    If no sparks or intermittent sparks occur, remove the distributor cap and check the cap and rotor as described in Chapter 1. If moisture is present, dry out the cap and rotor, then refit the cap.

6    If there's still no spark, disconnect the wiring connector to the distributor. With the ignition switch in the ON position check for battery voltage at terminal #1 of the distributor connector **(see illustration)**. If no power is found check for cut or damaged wiring. If power is available, check the ignition coil (see Section 7).

7    If all the components are good and there's still no spark, there may be a problem with the ECU or related wiring, have the ECU diagnosed by a dealer service department or other qualified repair facility.

## 7    Ignition coil - check

*Refer to illustrations 7.2 and 7.3*

**Caution:** *If the stereo in your vehicle is equipped with an anti-theft system, make sure you have the correct activation code before disconnecting the battery.*

1    Disconnect the cable from the negative terminal of the battery.

2    Locate the distributor electrical connector **(see illustration)** and disconnect it.

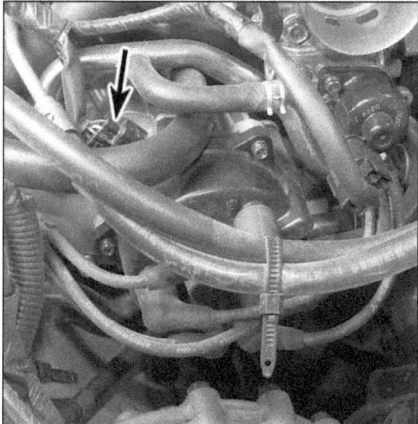

7.2 Disconnect the distributor electrical connector (arrow)

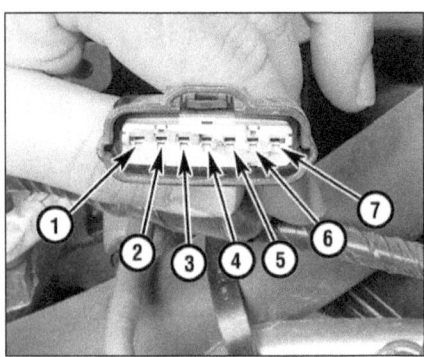

**7.3 Distributor connector terminal identification**

3    Using an ohmmeter, check the coil resistance as follows **(see illustration)**.

a) *Measure the resistance between terminals 1 and 2 of the distributor connector. Compare your reading with the primary coil resistance listed in this Chapter's Specifications.*

b) *Measure the resistance between terminal 1 or 2 of the distributor connector and the high tension terminal. Compare your reading with the secondary coil resistance listed in this Chapter's Specifications.*

4    If either of the above tests yield resistance values outside the specified resistance, renew the distributor (see Section 8).

5    If all the components are good and there's still no spark, there may be a problem with the ECU or related wiring, have the ECU diagnosed by a dealer service department or other qualified repair facility.

## 8    Distributor - removal and refitting

**Caution:** *If the stereo in your vehicle is equipped with an anti-theft system, make sure you have the correct activation code before disconnecting the battery.*

### Removal

*Refer to illustration 8.5*

1    Position the engine at TDC for number one cylinder (see Chapter 2).

2    Disconnect the cable from the negative battery terminal.

3    Remove the distributor cap and verify the rotor is pointing toward the number one spark plug wire terminal (locate the number one spark plug and trace the wire back to the terminal on the cap).

4    Disconnect electrical connector to the distributor.

5    Remove the distributor retaining nuts **(see illustration)**, then pull the distributor straight out to remove it.

### Refitting

6    Insert the distributor into the engine in exactly the same relationship to the block that it was in when removed.

7    To mesh the camshaft and distributor, it may be necessary to turn the rotor slightly until the distributor gear drops into the end of the camshaft.

8    Refit the distributor retaining nuts and tighten.

9    Reconnect the electrical lead.

10   Refit the distributor cap.

11   Reattach the spark plug wires to the plugs (if removed).

12   Connect the cable to the negative terminal of the battery.

13   Start the engine and check the ignition timing (see Chapter 1). Tighten the distributor retaining nuts securely.

## 9    Charging system - general information and precautions

The charging system includes the alternator with an external voltage regulator, the battery, the fusible links and wiring between all the components. The charging system supplies electrical power for the ignition system, the lighting system, the accessories, etc. The alternator is driven by a drivebelt at the front of the engine.

The purpose of the voltage regulator is to limit the alternator's voltage to a preset value. This prevents power surges, circuit overloads, etc., during peak voltage output.

The fusible link can be either a short length of insulated wire integral with the engine compartment wiring harness or a fuse-like device refitted in the underbonnet electrical panel. See Chapter 12 for additional information regarding fusible links.

The charging system doesn't ordinarily require periodic maintenance. However, the drivebelt, battery and wires and connections should be inspected at the intervals outlined in Chapter 1.

The dashboard warning light should come on when the ignition key is turned to Start, then go off immediately. If it remains on, there is a malfunction in the charging system.

Be very careful when making electrical circuit connections to a vehicle equipped with an alternator and note the following:

a) *When reconnecting wires to the alternator from the battery, be sure to note the polarity.*

b) *Before using arc welding equipment to repair any part of the vehicle, disconnect the wires from the alternator and the battery terminals.*

c) *Never start the engine with a battery charger connected.*

d) *Always disconnect both battery leads before using a battery charger.*

e) *The alternator is turned by an engine drivebelt which could cause serious injury if your hands, hair or clothes become entangled in it with the engine running.*

f) *Because the alternator is connected directly to the battery, it could arc or cause a fire if overloaded or shorted out.*

g) *Wrap a plastic bag over the alternator and secure it with rubber bands before steam cleaning the engine.*

## 10   Charging system - check

1    If a malfunction occurs in the charging circuit, don't automatically assume that the alternator is causing the problem. First check the following items:

a) *Check the drivebelt tension and condition (Chapter 1). Renew it if it's worn or deteriorated.*

b) *Make sure the alternator mounting and adjustment bolts are tight.*

c) *Inspect the alternator wiring harness and the connectors at the alternator. They must be in good condition and tight.*

d) *Check the fusible link(s). If burned, determine the cause, repair the circuit and renew the link (the vehicle won't start and/or the accessories won't work if the fusible link blows). Sometimes a fusible link may look good, but still be bad. If in doubt, remove it and check for continuity.*

e) *Start the engine and check the alternator for abnormal noises (a shrieking or squealing sound indicates a bad bearing).*

f) *Check the specific gravity of the battery electrolyte. If it's low, charge the battery (doesn't apply to maintenance free batteries).*

g) *Make sure the battery is fully charged (one bad cell in a battery can cause overcharging by the alternator).*

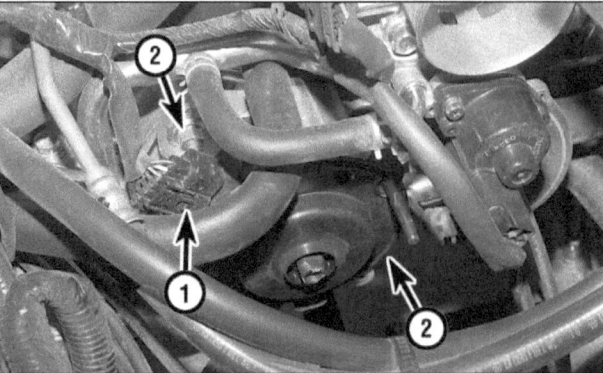

**8.5 Remove the distributor electrical connection (1), and then the mounting nuts (2)**

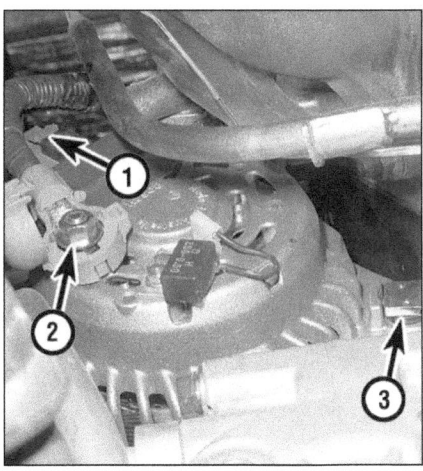

**11.2  Disconnect the electrical connector (1), and B+ terminal (2) from the alternator - (lower pivot bolt [3])**

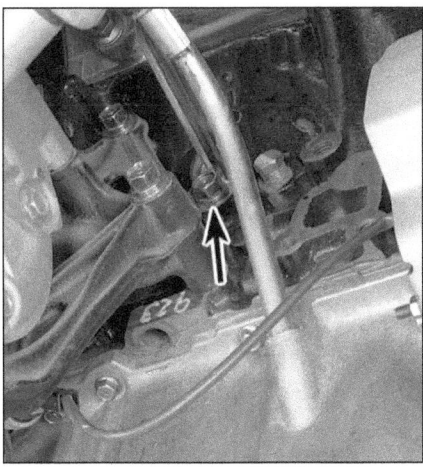

**11.4  Remove the oil dipstick tube mounting bolt (arrow) and remove the tube**

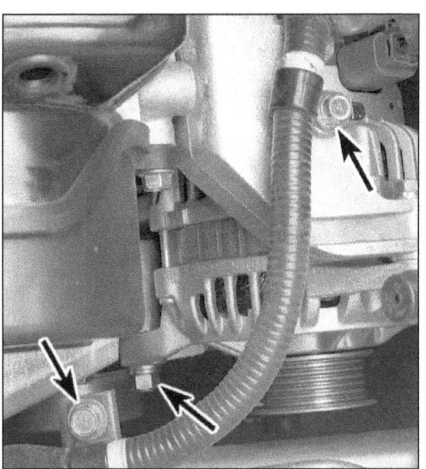

**11.5  Remove the alternator upper mounting bolt (arrow), harness bolts (arrows) and lower pivot bolt and nut (not shown)**

h) *Disconnect the battery cables (negative first, then positive). Inspect the battery posts and the cable clamps for corrosion. Clean them thoroughly if necessary (see Chapter 1). Reconnect the cable to the positive terminal.*

i) *With the key off, connect a test light between the negative battery post and the disconnected negative cable clamp.*

  1) *If the test light does not come on or shines dimly, reattach the clamp and proceed to the next step.*
  2) *If the test light shines brightly, there is a short (drain) in the electrical system of the vehicle. The short must be repaired before the charging system can be checked.*
  3) *Disconnect the alternator wiring harness.*
     a) *If the light goes out, the alternator is bad.*
     b) *If the light stays on, pull each fuse until the light goes out (this will tell you which component is shorted).*

2    Using a voltmeter, check the battery voltage with the engine off. If should be approximately 12-volts.

3    Start the engine and check the battery voltage again. It should now be approximately 13.5-to-15 volts.

4    Turn on the headlights. The voltage should drop, and then come back up, if the charging system is working properly.

5    If the voltage reading is more than the specified charging voltage, the voltage regulator is probably bad. If the voltage is less, the alternator diode(s), stator or rectifier may be bad or the voltage regulator may be malfunctioning. Renew the regulator assembly or the alternator with a new or rebuilt unit.

---

## 11  Alternator - removal, refitting and overhaul

---

**Caution:** *If the stereo in your vehicle is equipped with an anti-theft system, make sure you have the correct activation code before disconnecting the battery.*

### *Removal*

*Refer to illustrations 11.2, 11.4, 11.5, 11.6, 11.7 and 11.8*

1    Disconnect the cable from the negative battery terminal.

2    Disconnect the electrical connector from the alternator. Remove the nut from the B+ terminal and disconnect the B+ wire **(see illustration)**.

3    Loosen the alternator tensioner and remove the drivebelt (see Chapter 1).

4    Remove the oil dipstick and tube **(see illustration)**.

5    Remove the alternator mounting bolt and pivot nut and bolt **(see illustration)**.

6    Remove the two alternator mounting bracket bolts **(see illustration)** and remove the mounting bracket.

7    Remove the upper right side timing belt cover bolts **(see illustration) and remove the cover.**

8    While supporting the alternator, rotate the alternator so that the pulley is facing up **(see illustration)** and remove the alternator.

**11.6  Remove the alternator mounting bracket bolts (arrows) and remove the bracket**

**11.7  Remove the upper right timing belt cover bolts (arrows) and cover**

**11.8  Rotate the alternator up and towards the windscreen washer fluid bottle and pull the alternator out through the top**

**11.11  Remove the brush and regulator assembly mounting screws (arrows)**

**14.2  Remove the transaxle-to-starter upper bolt (arrow)**

## Overhaul

*Refer to illustration 11.11*

9    Alternators are not commonly overhauled due to the special tools and knowledge necessary for the job and the unavailability of certain renewal parts. Ordinarily, new or rebuilt alternators are purchased and fitted.

10   Always use new brushes or insure the old brushes are of acceptable length.

11   Remove the brush and regulator mounting screws **(see illustration)** and remove the assembly.

12   Fit the new brush and regulator assembly and tighten the screws securely.

13   Refitting is the reverse of removal. Refer to Chapter 1 and adjust the drivebelt tension.

## 12  Starting system - general information

The sole function of the starting system is to turn over the engine quickly enough to allow it to start.

The starting system consists of the battery, the starter motor, the starter solenoid and the wires connecting them. The solenoid is mounted directly on the starter motor.

The solenoid/starter motor assembly is refitted on the transaxle bellhousing.

When the ignition key is turned to the Start position, the starter solenoid is actuated through the starter control circuit. The starter solenoid then connects the battery to the starter. The battery supplies the electrical energy to the starter motor, which does the actual work of cranking the engine.

Always observe the following precautions when working on the starting system:

a)  *Excessive cranking of the starter motor can overheat it and cause serious damage. Never operate the starter motor for more than 15 seconds at a time without pausing to allow it to cool for at least two minutes.*

b)  *The starter is connected directly to the battery and could arc or cause a fire if mishandled, overloaded or shorted out.*

c)  *Always disconnect the cable from the negative terminal of the battery before working on the starting system.*

## 13  Starter motor and circuit - in-vehicle check

**Note:** *Before diagnosing starter problems, make sure the battery is fully charged.*

1    If the starter motor does not turn at all when the switch is operated, make sure that the shift lever is in Neutral or Park (automatic transaxle) or that the clutch pedal is depressed (manual transaxle).

2    Make sure that the battery is charged and that all cables, both at the battery and starter solenoid terminals, are clean and secure.

3    If the starter motor spins but the engine is not cranking, the overrunning clutch in the starter motor is slipping and the starter motor must be renewed.

4    If, when the switch is actuated, the starter motor does not operate at all but the solenoid clicks, then the problem lies with either the battery, the main solenoid contacts or the starter motor itself (or the engine is seized).

5    If the solenoid plunger cannot be heard when the switch is actuated, the battery is bad, the fusible link is burned (the circuit is open) or the solenoid itself is defective.

6    To check the solenoid, connect a jumper lead between the battery (+) and the ignition switch wire terminal (the small terminal) on the solenoid. If the starter motor now operates, the solenoid is OK and the problem is in the ignition switch, neutral start switch or the wiring.

7    If the starter motor still does not operate, remove the starter/solenoid assembly for disassembly, testing and repair.

8    If the starter motor cranks the engine at an abnormally slow speed, first make sure that the battery is charged and that all terminal connections are tight. If the engine is partially seized, or has the wrong viscosity oil in it, it will crank slowly.

9    Run the engine until normal operating temperature is reached. Disconnect the electrical connector from the distributor.

10   Connect a voltmeter positive lead to the positive battery post and connect the negative lead to the negative post.

11   Crank the engine and take the voltmeter readings as soon as a steady figure is indicated. Do not allow the starter motor to turn for more than 15 seconds at a time. A reading of 9 volts or more, with the starter motor turning at normal cranking speed, is normal. If the reading is 9 volts or more but the cranking speed is slow, the motor is faulty. If the reading is less than 9 volts and the cranking speed is slow, the solenoid contacts are probably burned, the starter motor is bad, the battery is discharged or there is a bad connection.

## 14  Starter motor - removal, refitting and overhaul

*Refer to illustrations 14.2, 14.3 and 14.4*

**Caution:** *If the stereo in your vehicle is equipped with an anti-theft system, make sure you have the correct activation code before disconnecting the battery.*

1    Disconnect the cable from the negative terminal of the battery.

2    Remove the transaxle-to-starter bolt **(see illustration)**.

3    Remove the starter heat shield mounting screws and nut **(see illustration)** and remove the shield.

4    Clearly label, then disconnect the wires from the terminals on the starter solenoid **(see illustration)** and remove the starter-to-transaxle bolt.

5    Refitting is the reverse of removal.

**14.3  Remove the starter heat shield mounting screws and nut (arrows)**

**14.4  Remove the electrical connections to the solenoid (1), and the lower starter-to-transaxle lower bolt (2)**

## Overhaul

*Refer to illustration 14.6*

**Note:** *Starter motor overhaul requires certain tools and techniques which can be out of the* scope for some home mechanics. Often, the fitting of a new or rebuilt starter is the preferred choice. For more information, see your local auto parts dealer.

6    If it is decided to dismantle the starter for overhaul, refer to the exploded view included in this section **(see illustrations)**.

7    Remove the through bolts and separate

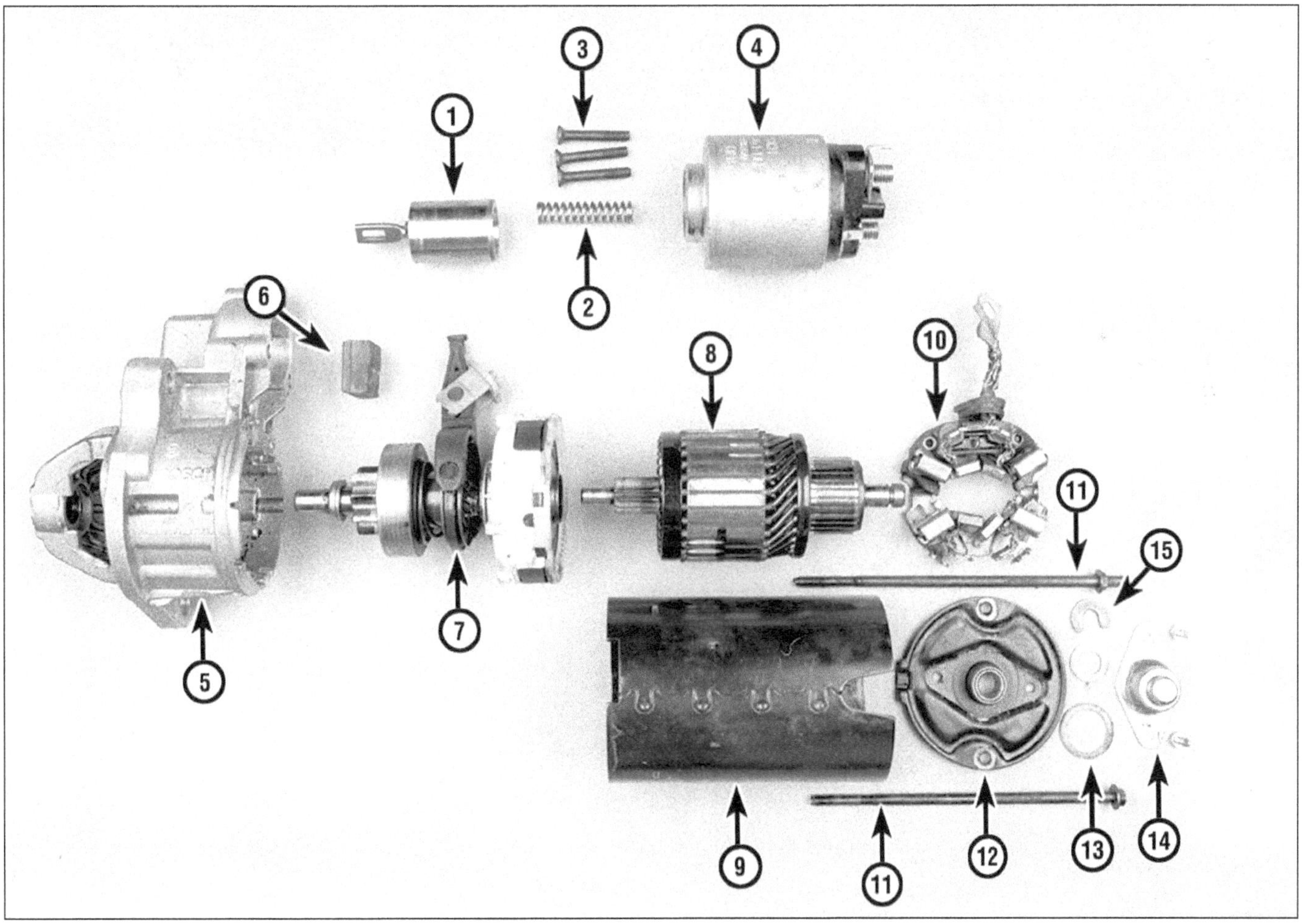

**14.6  Exploded view of a typical gear reduction starter motor**

| | | | | | | |
|---|---|---|---|---|---|---|
| 1 | Solenoid switch plunger | 6 | Rubber sealing block | 9 | Pole housing | 13 | Armature thrust washer |
| 2 | Spring | 7 | Drive assembly and fork | 10 | Field coil | 14 | Dust cover cap and |
| 3 | Solenoid screws | | lever and planetary drive | 11 | Through-bolts | | screws |
| 4 | Solenoid switch | 8 | Armature | 12 | Commutator end cover | 15 | Dust cap seal and circlip |
| 5 | Drive end housing | | | | | | |

**15.2  Remove the terminal nut**

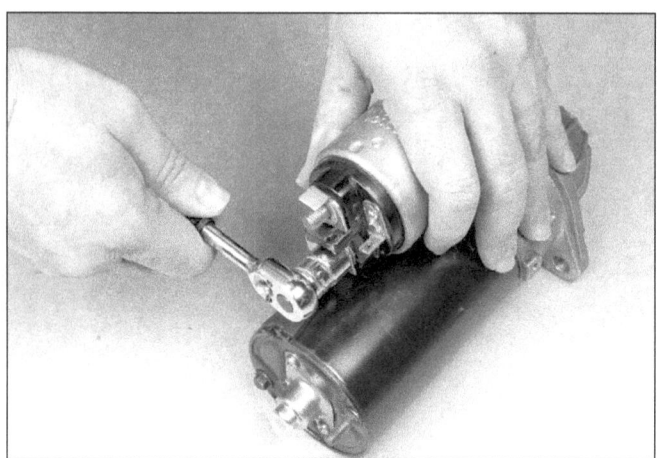

from the solenoid

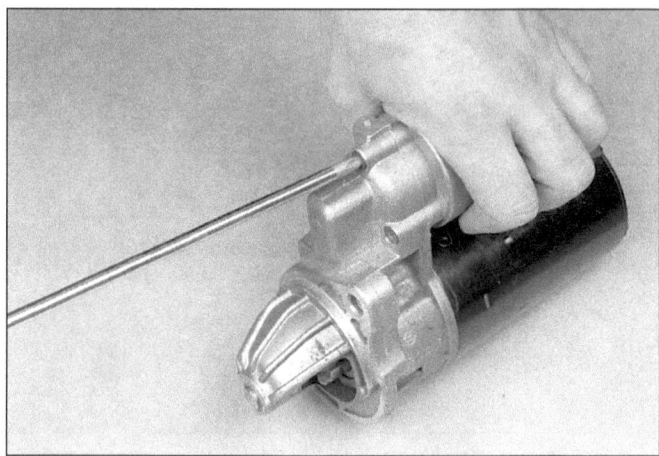
15.3a Remove the three mounting screws that retain the solenoid to the gear case

the starter housing.
8    Disassemble the remaining components.
9    Reassembly is the reverse of disassembly. Renew any worn bushes and fit new
brushes.

## 15   Starter solenoid - renewal

**Caution:** *If the stereo in your vehicle is
equipped with an anti-theft system, make
sure you have the correct activation code
before disconnecting the battery.*

### Removal
*Refer to illustrations 15.2, 15.3a and 15.3b*
1    Remove the starter motor assembly (see
Section 14).
2    Remove the nut from the solenoid "B+"
terminal and disconnect the electrical connection **(see illustration)**.
3    Unscrew and remove the solenoid
mounting screws and separate the solenoid
from the starter motor **(see illustrations)**.

### Refitting
4    Refitting is the reverse of removal.

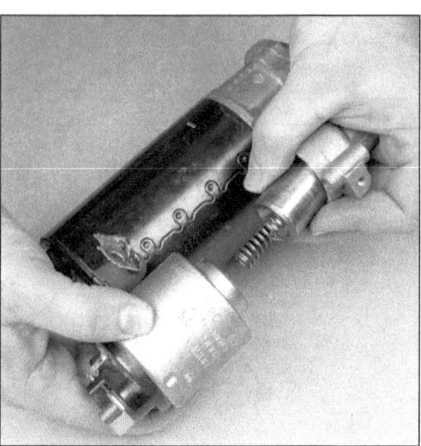
15.3b Remove the solenoid from the gear
case - note the positions of the plunger,
lever and return spring

# Chapter 6
# Emissions and engine control systems

## Contents

## Specifications

| | |
|---|---|
| Coolant temperature sensor sensor resistance | |
| At 20-degrees C............................................................... | 2.1 to 2.7 K-ohms |
| At 80-degrees C............................................................... | 0.26 to 0.36 K-ohms |
| Intake air temperature sensor resistance | |
| At 20-degrees C............................................................... | 2.3 to 3.0 K-ohms |
| At 80-degrees C............................................................... | 0.30 to 0.42 K-ohms |
| EGR control solenoid resistance at 20 degrees C ................................ | 36 to 44 ohms |
| Canister purge control solenoid resistance at 20-degrees C................. | 38 to 44 ohms |
| Oxygen sensor output voltage ....................................................... | 0.6 to 1.0 volts |

### Torque Specifications

| | Nm |
|---|---|
| Coolant temperature sensor................................................................. | 15 |
| Oxygen sensor ................................................................................. | 50 to 60 |
| Throttle position sensor bolts............................................................ | 1.5 to 2.5 |

## 1   General information

*Refer to illustration 1.1*

To minimise pollution of the atmosphere from incompletely burned and evaporating gases and to maintain good driveability and fuel economy, a number of emission control systems are used on these vehicles **(see illustration on following page)**. They include the:

*Electronic engine control system*
*Positive Crankcase Ventilation (PCV) system*
*Evaporative emission control system*
*Exhaust Gas Recirculation (EGR) system*
*Catalytic converter system*

The Sections in this Chapter include general descriptions, checking procedures within the scope of the home mechanic and component renewal procedures (when possible) for each of the systems listed above.

Before assuming an emissions control system is malfunctioning, check the fuel and ignition systems carefully (see Chapters 4 and 5). The diagnosis of some emission control devices requires specialised tools, equipment and training. If checking and servicing become too difficult or if a procedure is beyond the scope of your skills, consult your dealer service department or other repair shop.

This doesn't mean, however, that emission control systems are particularly difficult to maintain and repair. You can quickly and easily perform many checks and do most of the regular maintenance at home with common tune-up and hand tools. Note: The most frequent cause of emissions problems is simply a loose or broken electrical connector or vacuum hose, so always check the electrical connectors and vacuum hoses first.

Pay close attention to any special precautions outlined in this Chapter. It should be noted that the illustrations of the various systems may not exactly match the system refitted on your vehicle because of changes made by the manufacturer during production or from year-to-year.

The Vehicle Emissions Control Information (VECI) label and a vacuum hose diagram are located on the underside of the bonnet. These contain important emissions specifications and setting procedures, and a vacuum hose schematic with emissions components identified. When servicing the engine or emissions systems, the VECI label in your particular vehicle should always be checked for up-to-date information.

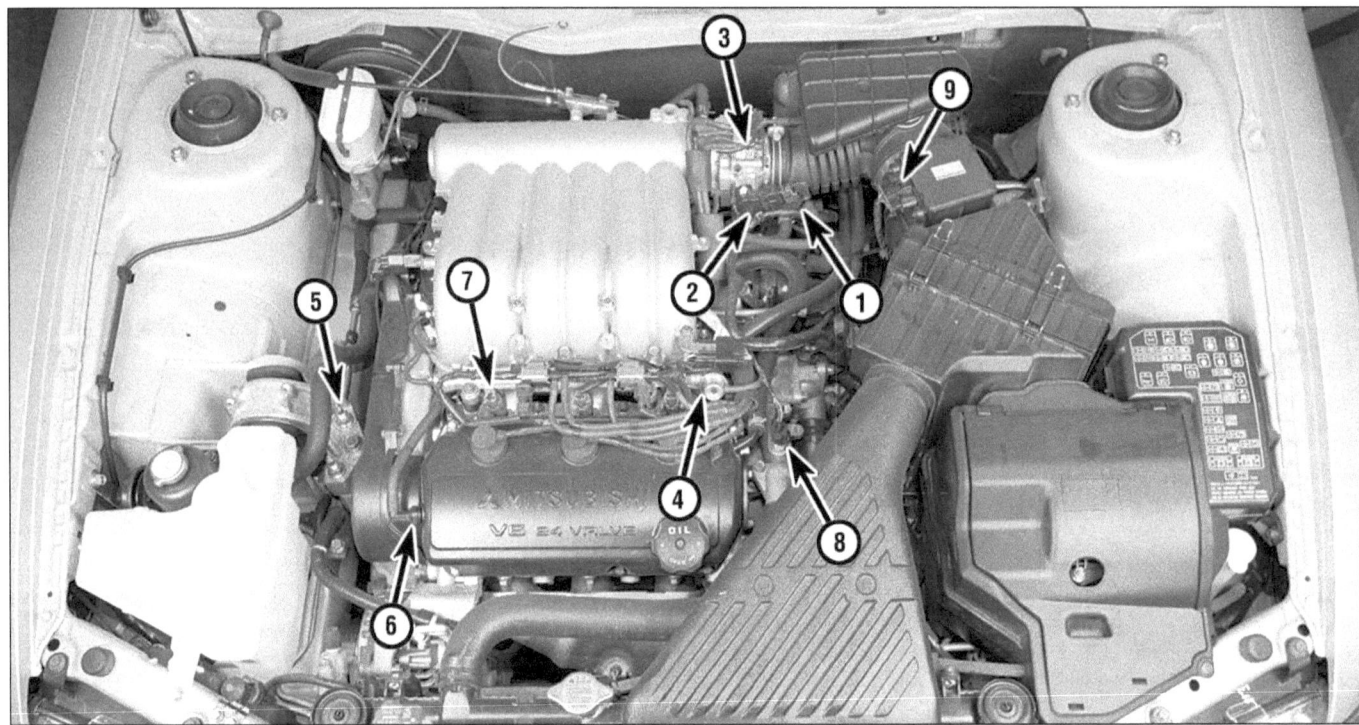

**1.1 Emission and engine control components**

1   Idle Speed Control (ISC) motor
    assembly
2   Throttle Position Sensor (TPS)
3   Throttle body
4   Fuel pressure regulator

5   Crankshaft position sensor (inside
    timing belt cover)
6   PCV valve
7   Fuel injector
8   Coolant temperature sensor

9   Airflow sensor assembly (including
    inlet air temperature sensor and
    barometric pressure sensor)

## 2   Electronic engine control system - general information

### General description

The electronic control system controls the Multi Port Fuel Injection system and some emissions control devices by means of a microcomputer known as the Electronic Control Unit (ECU).

The ECU receives signals from various sensors which monitor changing engine operating conditions such as intake air volume, intake air temperature, coolant temperature, engine rpm, acceleration/deceleration, exhaust oxygen content, etc. These signals are utilised by the ECU to determine the correct injection duration.

The system is analogous to the central nervous system in the human body: The sensors (nerve endings) constantly relay signals to the ECU (brain), which processes the data and, if necessary, sends out a command to change the operating parameters of the engine (body).

Here's a specific example of how one portion of this system operates: An oxygen sensor, located in the exhaust manifold, constantly monitors the oxygen content of the exhaust fuel. If the percentage of oxygen in the exhaust fuel is incorrect, an electrical signal is sent to the ECU. The ECU takes this information, processes it and then sends a command to the fuel injection system telling it to change the air/fuel mixture. This happens in a fraction of a second and it goes on continuously when the engine is running. The end result is an air/fuel mixture ratio which is constantly maintained at a predetermined ratio, regardless of driving conditions.

In the event of a sensor malfunction, a backup circuit will take over to provide driveability until the problem is identified and fixed.

### Precautions

a)  Always disconnect the power by either turning off the ignition switch or disconnecting the battery terminals before removing electrical connectors.
b)  When refitting a battery, be particularly careful to avoid reversing the positive and negative battery cables.
c)  Do not subject EFI, emissions related components or the ECU to severe impact during removal or refitting.
d)  Do not be careless during troubleshooting. Even slight terminal contact can invalidate a testing procedure and damage one of the numerous transistor circuits.
e)  Never attempt to work on the ECU or open the ECU cover. The ECU is protected by a government mandated extended warranty that will be nullified if you tamper with or damage the ECU.

f)  If you are inspecting electronic control system components during rainy weather, make sure that water does not enter any part. When washing the engine compartment, do not spray these parts or their electrical connectors with water.

## 3   Self-diagnosis system - general information and retrieving trouble codes

### General description

1   The ECU contains a built-in self-diagnosis system which detects and identifies malfunctions occurring in the network. When the ECU detects a problem, three things happen: the CHECK ENGINE light comes on, the trouble is identified and a diagnostic code is stored in the computer's memory. The ECU stores the failure code assigned to the specific problem area until the failure code is canceled.

2   The CHECK ENGINE warning light, which is located on the instrument panel, comes on when the ignition switch is turned to On and the engine is not running. When the engine is started, the warning light should go out. If the light remains on, the diagnosis system has detected a malfunction in the system.

### Retrieving a diagnostic trouble code

*Refer to illustrations 3.4 and 3.6*

3    To obtain an output of diagnostic codes, verify first that the battery voltage is above 11 volts, the throttle is fully closed, the transaxle is in Park or Neutral, the accessory switches are off and the engine is at normal operating temperature.

4    Locate the diagnostic test connector, below the dash near the centre of the steering wheel. Use a test lead to earth the upper left terminal (number 1) **(see illustration)**.

5    Turn the ignition switch to On, but don't start the engine.

6    Read the diagnostic trouble code as indicated by the number of flashes from the check engine light **(see illustration)**. If there are no codes present, the system will display a Code No. 0 as long as the earth lead is connected to the diagnostic connector. If the

**3.4 Diagnostic connector and terminal identification**

ECU or circuit is faulty, the light will remain on or not operate at all.

7    If there are any malfunctions in the sys-

| Malfunc-tion No. | Diagnosis item | Self-diagnosis output pattern and output code |
|---|---|---|
| 1 | Engine control unit | |
| 11 | Oxygen sensor | |
| 12 | Air flow sensor | |
| 13 | Intake air temperature sensor | |
| 14 | Throttle position sensor | |
| 21 | Engine coolant temperature sensor | |
| 22 | Crank angle sensor | |
| 23 | Top dead centre sensor | |

68756-6-7.6-HAYNES

**3.6 Diagnostic trouble code chart**

| Malfunc-tion No. | Diagnosis item | Self-diagnosis output pattern and output code |
|---|---|---|
| 24 | Vehicle speed sensor (reed switch) | |
| 25 | Barometric pressure sensor | |
| 31 | Knock sensor | |
| 36 | Ignition timing adjustment signal | |
| 41 | Injector | |
| 44 | Ignition coil and power transistor | |
| 54 | Immobiliser system | |
| 61 | Communication with A/T ECU system (auto transmission vehicles | |
| 62 | Intake air control valve position sensor | |
| 64 | Alternator FR terminal system | |
| 0 | Normal state | |

tem, their corresponding trouble codes are stored in computer memory and the light will flash the requisite code for the indicated trouble area. If there's more than one trouble code in the memory, they'll be displayed in numerical order (from lowest to highest) with a pause interval between each one. After the last code has been displayed, there will be another pause and then the sequence will begin all over again.

8    To ensure correct interpretation of the flashes, watch carefully for the interval between the end of one code and the beginning of the next (otherwise, you will become confused by the apparent number of flashes and misinterpret the display). Have a pencil and paper handy to write down the trouble code(s) as they are displayed.

## *Canceling a diagnostic code*

9    After the malfunctioning component has been repaired/renewed, the trouble code(s) stored in computer memory must be canceled. To accomplish this, simply disconnect the negative battery cable from the battery for at least 10 seconds with the ignition switch off. **Caution:** *If the audio system in your vehicle is equipped with an anti-theft system, make sure your have the correct activation code before disconnecting the battery.*

10    Cancellation by removing the cable from the battery negative terminal will effect other systems as well (memory to the radio and clock will be canceled).

11    If the diagnosis code is not canceled, it will be stored by the ECU and appear with any new codes in the event of future trouble. Allow the engine to idle for approximately ten minutes after connecting the battery.

12    Should it become necessary to work on engine components requiring removal of the battery terminal, first check to see if a diagnostic code has been recorded.

---

## 4    Information sensors

**Note:** *Refer to Chapters 4 and 5 for additional information on certain sensors and the ECU controlled devices that are not directly covered in this Section.*

## *Airflow sensor and barometric pressure sensor*

### General description

1    The airflow sensor is attached in the air cleaner housing. The airflow sensor measures the amount of air entering the engine. The ECU uses this information to control fuel delivery. A large volume of air indicates high power output, while a small volume of air indicates deceleration or idle. The airflow sensor is equipped with an intake air temperature sensor as well as a barometric pressure sensor as a single integral unit. Any malfunctions with the airflow sensor will be recorded as Code 12. A malfunction of the barometric sensor will set a Code 25.

**4.8  Location of the coolant temperature sensor (arrow)**

### Check

2    The airflow sensor must be tested by a repair facility with the proper electronic scan test equipment.

### Renewal

3    Disconnect the electrical connector from the sensor.

4    Loosen the clamps and remove the air intake duct from the sensor.

5    Detach the clamps and separate the cover from the air cleaner housing (see Chapter 4).

6    Remove the screws that retain the airflow sensor to the cover and remove the sensor.

7    Refitting is the reverse of removal.

## *Coolant temperature sensor*

*Refer to illustration 4.8*

### General description

8    The coolant temperature sensor is a thermistor (a resistor which varies the value of its resistance in accordance with temperature changes). The change in the resistance values will directly affect the voltage signal from the coolant temperature sensor. The ECU uses this signal to control fuel enrichment and timing when the engine is cold. As the engine warms-up and the coolant temperature INCREASES, the resistance value of the sensor will DECREASE. As the sensor temperature DECREASES, the resistance values will INCREASE. A failure in this sensor or circuit should set a Code 21. In most cases the appropriate solution to the problem will be either repair of the circuit or renewal of the sensor. The coolant temperature sensor is located in the thermostat housing **(see illustration)**.

### Check

9    Drain the cooling system (see Chapter 1).

10    Locate the sensor and depress the locking tabs on the connector and unplug the electrical connector, then carefully unscrew the sensor.

11    Suspend the sensor in a pan of water with the tip submerged. Connect an ohm-

meter to the sensor terminals. Heat the water while monitoring the water temperature with a cooking thermometer and note the resistance of the sensor as the water heats.

12    Compare your findings with the coolant temperature sensor resistance values found in this Chapter's Specifications. If the measured sensor resistance is not within specifications at the corresponding temperature, renew the sensor.

### Renewal

13    To remove the sensor, depress the locking tabs, unplug the electrical connector, then carefully unscrew the sensor.

14    Before fitting the new sensor, wrap the threads with Teflon sealing tape to prevent leakage and thread corrosion.

15    Refitting is the reverse of removal.

## *Crankshaft angle sensor*

### General description

16    The sensor is located at the front of the engine behind the timing belt cover. A problem with the crankshaft angle sensor will set a Code 22.

### Check

17    Due to the complexity of the system and special equipment required for diagnosis, diagnosis should be performed by a dealer service department or properly equipped repair facility.

### Renewal

18    Remove the timing belt cover (refer to Chapter 2A). Remove the crankshaft angle sensor from its position near the front of the crankshaft.

## *Inlet air temperature sensor*

*Refer to illustration 4.21*

### General description

19    The Inlet Air Temperature (IAT) sensor is incorporated in the airflow sensor assembly. Like the coolant temperature sensor, the IAT is a thermistor which changes resistance values according to the temperature of the air entering the engine. Low temperatures produce a high resistance value while high temperatures produce low resistance values. The ECU uses this signal in calculating the amount of fuel injected into the cylinders. A failure in this sensor or circuit should set a Code 13.

### Check and renewal

20    Remove the airflow sensor (see above).

21    Using an ohmmeter, probe terminals 5 and 6 of the sensor side of the electrical connector **(see illustration)**. Place a thermometer near the sensor. Heat the air temperature sensor with a heat gun or hair dryer and note the resistance of the sensor.

22    Compare your findings with the inlet air temperature sensor resistance values found in this Chapter's Specifications. If the measured sensor resistance is not within specifications at the corresponding temperature, renew the airflow sensor.

4.21 Airflow sensor connector details

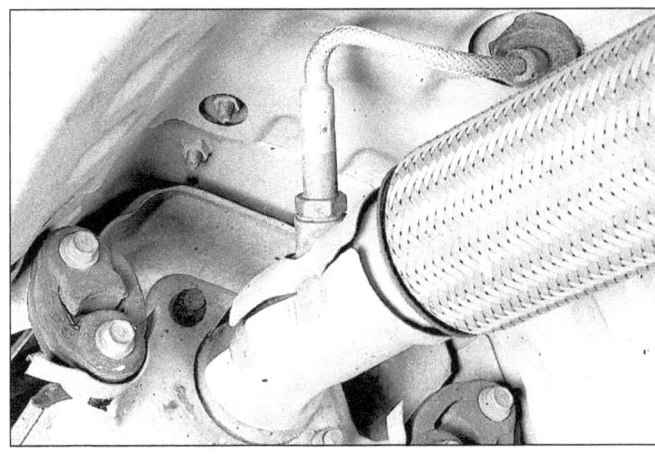

4.23 Location of the oxygen sensor

## Oxygen sensor

*Refer to illustrations 4.23 and 4.35*

### General description

23   The oxygen sensor, located in the exhaust manifold or exhaust pipe, monitors the oxygen content in the exhaust fuel stream **(see illustration)**. The oxygen content in the exhaust reacts with the oxygen sensor to produce a voltage output which varies from 0.1-volt (high oxygen, lean mixture) to 0.9-volts (low oxygen, rich mixture). The ECU constantly monitors this variable voltage output to determine the ratio of oxygen to fuel in the mixture. The ECU alters the air/fuel mixture ratio by controlling the pulse width (open time) of the fuel injectors. A mixture ratio of 14.7 parts air to 1 part fuel is the ideal mixture ratio for minimizing exhaust emissions, thus allowing the catalytic converter to operate at maximum efficiency. It is this ratio of 14.7 to 1 which the ECU and the oxygen sensor attempt to maintain under normal cruise conditions.

24   The oxygen sensor produces no voltage when it is below its normal operating temperature of about 300-degrees C. During this initial period before warm-up, the ECU operates in OPEN LOOP mode (controls fuel delivery in accordance with a programmed default value instead of feedback information from the oxygen sensor).

25   If the engine reaches normal operating temperature and/or has been running for two or more minutes, and if the oxygen sensor is producing a steady signal voltage below 0.45-volts at 1,500 rpm or greater, the ECU will set a Code 11. When there is a problem with the oxygen sensor or its circuit, the ECU operates in the open loop mode.

26   The proper operation of the oxygen sensor depends on four conditions:

a)   **Electrical** - *The low voltages generated by the sensor depend upon good, clean connections which should be checked whenever a malfunction of the sensor is suspected or indicated.*

b)   **Outside air supply** - *The sensor is designed to allow air circulation to the internal portion of the sensor. Whenever the sensor is removed and refitted or*

renewed, make sure the air passages are not restricted.

c)   **Proper operating temperature** - *The ECU will not react to the sensor signal until the sensor reaches approximately 300-degrees C. This factor must be taken into consideration when evaluating the performance of the sensor.*

d)   **Unleaded fuel** - *The use of unleaded fuel is essential for proper operation of the sensor. Make sure the fuel you are using is of this type.*

27   In addition to observing the above conditions, special care must be taken whenever the sensor is serviced.

a)   *The oxygen sensor has a permanently attached pigtail and electrical connector which should not be removed from the sensor. Damage or removal of the pigtail or electrical connector can adversely affect operation of the sensor.*

b)   *Grease, dirt and other contaminants should be kept away from the electrical connector and the louvered end of the sensor.*

c)   *Do not use cleaning solvents of any kind on the oxygen sensor.*

d)   *Do not drop or roughly handle the sensor.*

e)   *The silicone boot must be refitted in the correct position to prevent the boot from being melted and to allow the sensor to operate properly.*

### Check

28   Disconnect the wiring from the oxygen sensor. Use a multimeter to test the sensor as follows.

29   Verify that there is 7 to 40 ohms resistance between terminals 3 and 4. **Note:** *The oxygen sensor connector is numbered 1, 2, 3, 4, left to right.*

30   Warm the engine. Connect terminal 3 to the battery positive side with a fused jumper wire. Connect terminal 4 to the battery earth. Connect the multimeter to measure voltage between terminal 1 and 2.

31   When the engine is raced several times, the voltage should be between 0.6 and 1.0 volts.

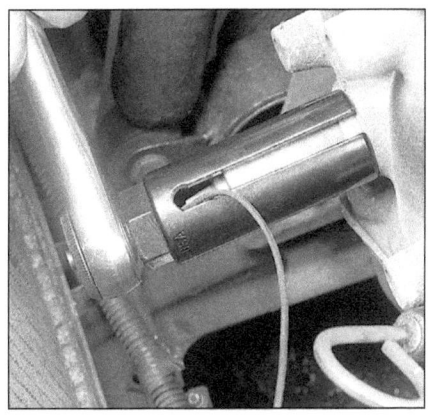

4.35 Special slotted sockets are available for removing the oxygen sensor

32   Fluctuation that appears slow (less than 7 or 8 times in 10 seconds) with little variation may also indicate a defective oxygen sensor. A steady reading, either high or low, may not necessarily indicate a defective oxygen sensor, but another problem in the fuel system causing the system to run lean or rich, such as a vacuum leak, defective fuel pressure regulator, plugged fuel filter, etc.

### Renewal

**Note:** *Because it is fitted in the exhaust manifold or pipe, which contracts when cool, the oxygen sensor may be very difficult to loosen when the engine is cold. Rather than risk damage to the sensor (assuming you are planning to reuse it in another manifold or pipe), start and run the engine for a minute or two, then shut it off. Be careful not to burn yourself during the following procedure.*

33   Disconnect the cable from the negative battery terminal.

34   Carefully disconnect the electrical connector from the sensor.

35   Unscrew the oxygen sensor from the exhaust pipe **(see illustration)**. **Caution:** *Excessive force may damage the threads.*

36   Anti-seize compound must be used on the threads of the sensor to facilitate future removal. The threads of new sensors will already be coated with this compound, but if

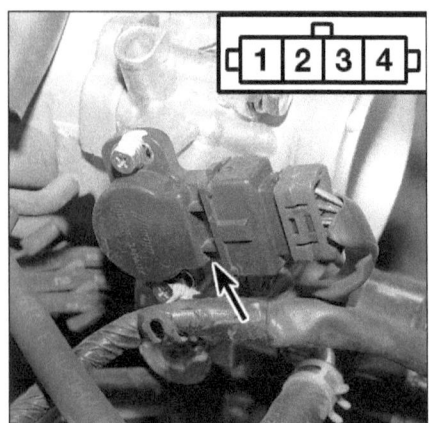

**4.41  TPS location and terminal identification**

**4.46  Remove the TPS mounting screws (arrows)**

**4.61  Accelerator pedal position sensor location and terminal identification**

an old sensor is removed and refitted, recoat the threads.

37   Refit the sensor and tighten it securely.

38   Reconnect the electrical connector of the pigtail lead to the main engine wiring harness.

39   Reconnect the cable to the negative battery terminal.

## Throttle position sensor
*Refer to illustrations 4.41 and 4.46*

### General description
40   The Throttle Position Sensor (TPS) is a variable resistor located on the end of the throttle shaft on the throttle body. By monitoring the output voltage from the TPS, the ECU can determine fuel delivery based on throttle valve angle (driver demand). A broken or loose TPS can cause intermittent bursts of fuel from the injector and an unstable idle because the ECU thinks the throttle is moving. A failure in the TPS or circuit will set a Code 14.

### Check
41   Backprobe terminal no. 2 and 4 (positive to terminal no. 2) **(see illustration)**. Turn the ignition ON (engine not running), with the throttle closed, the voltage should be 0.5 to 1.0 volt. Open the throttle by hand, the voltage should increase to 4.5 to 5.0 volts at full throttle.

42   If the voltage is not as specified, turn the ignition switch Off and disconnect the electrical connector to the sensor. Using an ohmmeter, measure the resistance between terminal no. 1 and 4 of the sensor. The resistance should read 3.5 to 6.5 K-ohms. If the TPS does not perform as indicated, renew it with a new one.

### Renewal
43   Disconnect the cable from the negative battery terminal.

44   Disconnect the electrical connector from the TPS.

45   Detach the wiring connector clamp from the connector.

46   Remove the retaining bolts and remove

the throttle position sensor from the throttle body **(see illustration)**.

47   Refitting is the reverse of removal. Adjust the throttle position sensor as follows:

a)  *With the electrical connector disconnected, connect an ohmmeter to terminal no. 3 and 4* **(see illustration 8.41)**. *Insert a 0.65 mm feeler gauge between the idle stop screw and the throttle lever.*

b)  *Loosen the TPS mounting screws and rotate the TPS counterclockwise. Verify continuity exists between terminal no. 3 and 4.*

c)  *Slowly rotate the TPS clockwise until the ohmmeter indicates an open circuit. Tighten the TPS mounting screws at this point. Remove the ohmmeter and feeler gauge. Connect the electrical connector to the TPS.*

## Vehicle speed sensor
### General description
48   The vehicle speed sensor is located in the transaxle. The speed sensor signal is used by the ECU to determine vehicle speed. A failure in the vehicle speed sensor or circuit may set a code 24.

### Check
49   Gain access the vehicle speed sensor wiring connector. Using a suitable probe (such as a straight pin), backprobe terminal numbers 2 and 3 of the connector. **Note:** *The connector is numbered 1, 2, 3 left to right.*

50   Connect a voltmeter to the pins (positive lead to terminal number 3).

51   Raise one front wheel and place a jack stand under the suspension. Leave the other front wheel on the ground.

52   Turn the ignition ON (engine NOT running) and have an assistant rotate the wheel that's off the ground while you watch the meter. The meter should fluctuate, indicating speed sensor operation.

53   If the meter doesn't fluctuate, remove the sensor and check the drive gear If the components are good renew the vehicle speed sensor.

### Renewal
54   Remove the air filter assembly (see Chapter 4).

55   Disconnect the electrical connector, remove the bolt and withdraw the sensor from the transaxle (see Chapter 7A).

## Top dead centre sensor
### General description
56   The top dead centre sensor is located in the distributor. The top dead centre sensor signal is used by the ECU to determine fuel injection synchronization. A malfunction with the top dead centre sensor will set a Code 23.

### Check
57   Due to the complexity of the system and special equipment required for diagnosis, diagnosis should be performed by a dealer service department or properly equipped repair facility.

### Renewal
58   The top dead centre sensor is an integral part of the distributor, if the top dead centre sensor requires renewal, renew the distributor (see Chapter 5).

## Accelerator pedal position sensor
### General description
59   The accelerator pedal position sensor (APS) is a variable resistor that works much like the throttle position sensor and is mounted on the end of the throttle shaft on the throttle body. The traction control system uses this signal to determine the position of the throttle.

### Check
60   Disconnect the APS sensor electrical connector.

61   Measure the resistance between terminals 1 and 4. The resistance should be 3.5–6.5 k/ohms.

62   Reconnect the sensor electrical connector and backprobe terminal 2 of the connector.

63   Have an assistant depress the accelerator pedal slowly and check as follows:

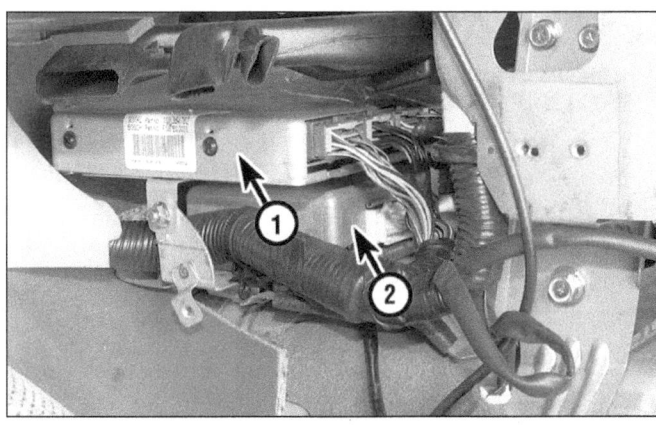

**5.2 Control unit location**

| | | |
|---|---|---|
| *1* | *Engine ECU* | *2* | *SRS-ECU* |

**6.2 Location of the charcoal canister (arrow)**

a) *Ensure that the voltage varies smoothly in relation to throttle movement.*
b) *Ensure that the voltage is between 0.3-1.0 volts when the throttle is fully closed.*
c) *Ensure that the voltage is approximately 4.5 volts when the throttle is fully opened.*

64 If the sensor does not perform as indicated, renew it with a new one.

### Renewal

65 Disconnect the cable from the negative battery terminal.
66 Disconnect the electrical connector from the APS sensor.
67 Detach the wiring harness clamp, sensor mounting screws and remove the sensor from the throttle body.
68 Refitting is the reverse of removal. Adjust the sensor as follows:

a) *Connect an ohmmeter between terminals 3 and 4 of the sensor electrical connector. Insert a 0.85 mm feeler gauge between the throttle lever and the free lever; no more than 3 mm.*
b) *Loosen the accelerator pedal position sensor mounting screws, and rotate the sensor body until the ohmmeter reading switches between indicating continuity and indicating open circuit.*
c) *Tighten the throttle pedal position sensor mounting screws at the point where the ohmmeter changes to open circuit, indicating the idle contacts are open.*

### 5 Electronic Control Unit (ECU) - removal and refitting

*Refer to illustration 5.2*
**Warning:** *The models covered by this manual are equipped with airbags. Always disable the Supplemental Restraint System before working in the vicinity of the impact sensors, steering column or instrument panel to avoid the possibility of accidental deployment of the airbag, which could cause personal injury (see Section 26).*

**Caution 1:** *To avoid electrostatic discharge damage to the ECU, handle the ECU only by its case. Do not touch the electrical terminals during removal or refitting. If available earth yourself to the vehicle with a anti-static earth strap, available at computer supply stores.*
**Caution 2:** *If the stereo in your vehicle is equipped with an anti-theft system, make sure you have the correct activation code before disconnecting the battery.*
1 Disconnect the cable from the negative battery terminal.
2 The engine ECU is located behind the centre of the dash immediately below the sound system **(see illustration)**.
3 Gain access to the ECU by removing the interfering dash components. Refer to Chapter 11 for additional information.
4 Carefully disconnect the electrical connectors from the ECU, remove the ECU retaining screws and slide the ECU down out of the bracket.
5 Refitting is the reverse of removal.

### 6 Evaporative Emission Control system

#### General description
*Refer to illustration 6.2*
1 The evaporative emission control system is designed to trap and store fuel that evaporates from the fuel tank or throttle body and inlet manifold that would normally enter the atmosphere in the form of hydrocarbon (HC) emissions.
2 The Evaporative Emission Control system consists of a charcoal-filled canister **(see illustration)**, the lines connecting the canister to the fuel tank and a purge control valve **(see illustration 7.7)**.
3 Fuel vapors are transferred from the fuel tank to a canister where they're stored when the engine isn't running. When the engine is running, the fuel vapors are purged from the canister by intake air flow and consumed in the normal combustion process.
4 The purge control valve is controlled by

the ECU. Depending upon the running conditions (coolant temperature, volume of airflow, intake air temperature and barometric pressure) and the pressure in the fuel tank, the ECU operates the purge control valve solenoid, allowing vacuum to purge the storage canister.

#### Check and renewal
*Refer to illustrations 6.11 and 6.12*
5 Rough idle, stalling and poor driveability can be caused by an inoperative purge control valve, a damaged canister, split or cracked hoses or hoses connected to the wrong fittings. Check the fuel filler cap for a damaged or deformed gasket (see Chapter 1).
6 Evidence of fuel loss or fuel odor can be caused by liquid fuel leaking from fuel lines, a cracked or damaged canister, an inoperative check valve, disconnected, misrouted, kinked, deteriorated or damaged vapor or control hoses.
7 Inspect each hose attached to the canister for kinks, leaks and cracks along its entire length. Repair or renew as necessary.
8 Inspect the canister. If it's cracked or damaged, renew it.

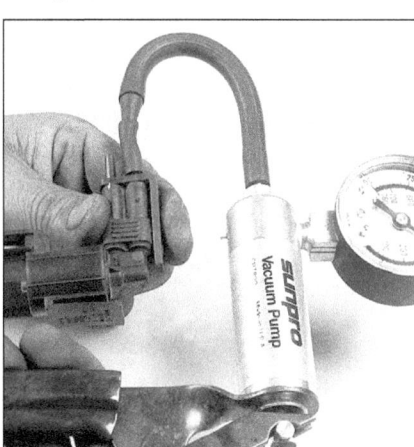

**6.11 Attach a vacuum pump to the lower port of the purge control valve and apply battery voltage to the solenoid and test the valve**

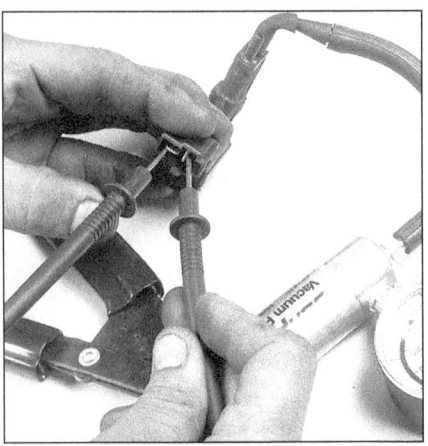

**6.12 Check the resistance of the purge control valve solenoid**

9    Look for fuel leaking from the bottom of the canister. If fuel is leaking, renew the canister and check the hoses and hose routing.

### Purge control valve

10   Disconnect the vacuum hoses from the purge solenoid valve and disconnect the electrical connector from the purge solenoid.
11   Connect a hand held vacuum pump to the lower port and using fused jumper wires, apply battery voltage to the solenoid **(see illustration)**. When the solenoid is energised, the vacuum should leak down. When no voltage is applied, the vacuum should hold steady.
12   If the valve does not operate as described, measure the resistance of the purge solenoid **(see illustration)**. It should be within the values listed in the Specifications in this Chapter.
13   If the test results are incorrect, renew the purge solenoid valve with a new part.

### Charcoal canister

14   Remove the vacuum hoses from the canister and remove the canister from the vehicle.
15   Plug the purge port and the throttle

body port. Verify that air flows through the tank port into filter.
16   Plug the tank port and the throttle body port. Verify that air flows through the purge port.
17   If the canister does not perform as described, renew it.

---

## 7   Exhaust Gas Recirculation (EGR) system

### General description

1    This system is used only on TH-KH and later models. To reduce oxides of nitrogen (NOx) emissions, some of the exhaust gases are recirculated through the EGR valve to the inlet manifold to lower combustion chamber temperatures. The EGR system consists of the EGR valve, vacuum regulator valve, and the EGR solenoid.

### Check and renewal

*Refer to illustration 7.3*

**EGR valve**

2    Remove the air cleaner. Start the engine, warm it up to operating temperature and allow it to idle.
3    Detach the green stripped vacuum hose from the EGR valve and attach a hand-held vacuum pump in its place **(see illustration)**. Disconnect and plug the hose to the vacuum regulator valve.
4    Apply vacuum of 220 mm-Hg or more to the EGR valve. Vacuum should remain steady and the engine should run poorly or stall. If the engine still idles smoothly, renew the EGR valve.

**Vacuum regulator valve**

5    Disconnect the vacuum hose with the white stripe from the regulator valve. Plug the disconnected hose.
6    Connect a vacuum gauge to the control valve. Start the engine and allow it to idle. The gauge should indicate approximately 170

mm-Hg. Renew the valve if the reading differs substantially.

**EGR solenoid**

7    Disconnect the vacuum hoses and the wiring from the EGR solenoid **(see illustration)**. Mark the locations of the hoses so they do not become interchanged.
8    Connect a vacuum pump to the port from which the green striped hose was removed. Apply vacuum to the solenoid.
9    Apply fused 12 volt power to the terminals of the solenoid. When vacuum is applied, there should be no vacuum leak. Vacuum should leak when power is removed.
10   Check the resistance between the terminals of the solenoid. Compare your reading to that in the Specifications in this Chapter.

---

## 8   Positive Crankcase Ventilation (PCV) system

### General description

1    The Positive Crankcase Ventilation (PCV) system reduces hydrocarbon emissions by scavenging crankcase vapors. It does this by circulating fresh air from the air cleaner through the crankcase, where it mixes with blow-by gases and is then rerouted through a PCV valve to the inlet manifold.
2    The main components of the PCV system are the PCV valve, a fresh air intake and the vacuum hoses connecting these components with the engine.
3    To maintain idle quality, the PCV valve restricts the flow when the inlet manifold vacuum is high. If abnormal operating conditions (such as piston ring problems) arise, the system is designed to allow excessive amounts of blow-by gases to flow back through the crankcase vent tube into the air cleaner to be consumed by normal combustion.

### Check and renewal

4    To check the valve, remove it from the valve cover with the hose attached (see

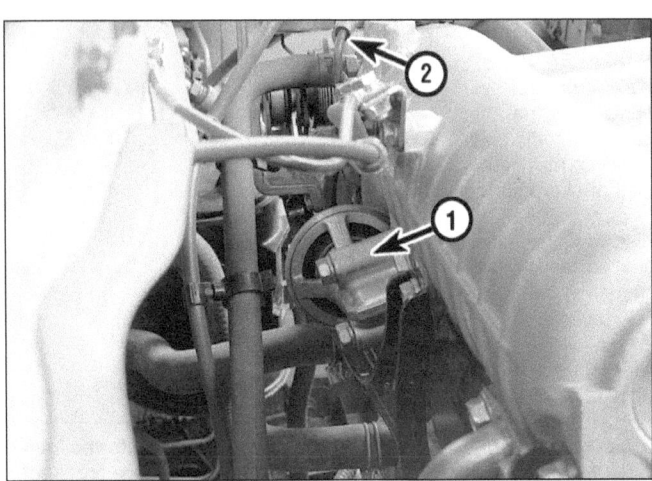

**7.3 Attach a hand-held vacuum pump to the EGR valve (1), green stripped vacuum line (2) to test its operation**

**7.7 Location of the EGR solenoid valve**

1    EGR solenoid valve
2    Purge control solenoid valve

Chapter 1). Start the engine and allow it to idle, then place your finger over the end of the valve. You should feel vacuum, and you should hear the plunger inside the valve move back and forth as you cover and uncover the valve with your finger.

5    Remove the valve and insert a thin rod into its bottom. The plunger should move, indicating that it is not clogged with deposits. If the valve does not move, try cleaning the valve with carburettor cleaner.

6    If the valve doesn't operate as described, renew it.

7    Check the hose for damage, wear and deterioration. Make sure it fits snugly on the fittings. If it doesn't, renew it with a new one. **Note:** *Don't use fuel line as a substitute - use only a molded vacuum hose intended for this purpose.*

## 9    Catalytic converter

### *General description*

1    To reduce hydrocarbon, carbon monoxide and oxides of nitrogen emissions, all vehicles covered by this manual (except those designed for leaded fuel) are equipped with a monolith type catalyst system which oxidises and reduces these chemicals, converting them into harmless nitrogen, carbon dioxide and water.

2    The catalytic converter is mounted in the exhaust system much like a muffler (see Chapter 4).

### *Check*

3    Periodically inspect the catalytic converter-to-exhaust pipe mating flanges and bolts. Make sure that there are no loose bolts and no leaks between the flanges.

4    Look for dents in or damage to the catalytic converter protector. If any part of the protector is damaged or dented enough to touch the converter, repair or renew it.

5    Inspect the heat insulator for damage. Make sure there is adequate clearance between the heat insulator and the catalytic converter.

### *Renewal*

6    To refit the catalytic converter, refer to Chapter 4.

# Notes

# Chapter 7 Part A
# Manual transaxle

Contents

## Specifications

### General

| | |
|---|---|
| Fluid type and capacity | See Chapter 1 |
| Transaxle type | |
|   6G72 and 6G74 engines | Mitsubishi F5M51 |

### Torque specifications

| | Nm |
|---|---|
| Backup light switch | 30 to 35 |
| Speedometer driven gear assembly bolt | 3.0 to 5.0 |
| Transaxle-to-engine bolts | 43 to 55 |
| Transaxle mount-to-body bolts | 40 to 50 |
| Transaxle mount bracket-to-transaxle bolts | 30 to 40 |
| Transaxle mount through-bolt | 73 to 87 |

## 1 General information

The vehicles covered by this manual are equipped with either a 5-speed manual or a 4-speed automatic transaxle. Information on the manual transaxle is included in this part of Chapter 7. Service procedures for the automatic transaxle are contained in Chapter 7, Part B.

Both the manual transaxle and the differential are housed in a compact, lightweight, two-piece aluminum alloy housing.

The procedures in this Chapter tell you how to refit and adjust those parts of the transaxle that can be serviced at home, as well as how to remove and refit the transaxle itself. Because of the complexity of the transaxle internals, the difficulty of obtaining renewal parts and the special tools needed to service those parts, we don't recommend repairing the transaxle at home.

## 2 Oil seal renewal

1 Oil leaks frequently occur at the driveaxle seals and at the speedometer drive-gear O-ring. Renewing these seals is relatively easy, since you don't have to remove the transaxle to get to them.

### Driveaxle seals

*Refer to illustrations 2.4 and 2.6*

2 The driveaxle seals are located in the sides of the transaxle, where the splined inner ends of the driveaxles mate with the differential side gears. If you suspect that one of these seals is leaking, raise the vehicle and support it securely on jackstands. If the seal is in fact leaking, you'll see lubricant running down the side of the transaxle below the seal.

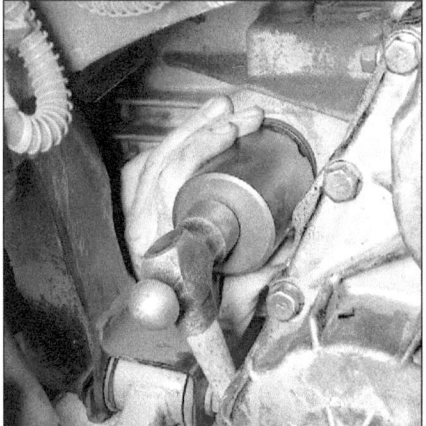

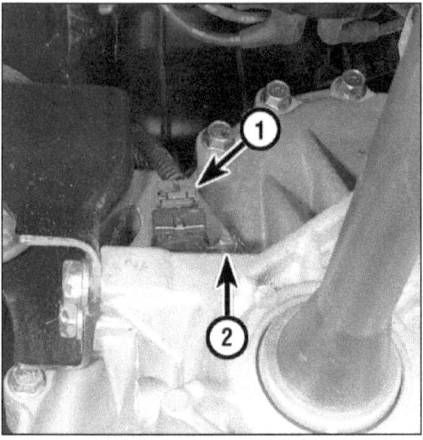

**2.4  Using a large screwdriver or lever, carefully prise the oil seal (arrow) out of the transaxle (if you can't remove the oil seal with a screwdriver or lever, you may need to obtain a special seal removal tool)**

**2.6  Using a large section of pipe or a large deep socket as a drift, drive the new seal squarely into the bore and make sure that it's completely seated; lubricate the lip of the new seal with multi-purpose grease**

**2.9  The speed sensor driven-gear assembly is located on the upper rear area of the transaxle, just behind the differential housing; to remove it, simply disconnect the speed sensor electrical connector (1) and remove the hold-down bolt (2) and pull the assembly straight up**

3    Remove the driveaxle (see Chapter 8).
4    Using a large screwdriver or lever, carefully prise the oil seal out of the transaxle **(see illustration)**.
5    If you can't remove the oil seal with a screwdriver or prise bar, you may need to obtain a special seal removal tool (available at most auto parts stores) to do the job.
6    Using a large section of pipe or a large deep socket as a drift, fit the new oil seal **(see illustration)**. Drive it into the bore squarely and make sure that it's completely seated. Lubricate the lip of the new seal with multi-purpose grease.

7    Refit the driveaxle (see Chapter 8). Be careful not to damage the lip of the new seal.

### Speed sensor O-ring
*Refer to illustration 2.9*
8    The speed sensor driven-gear housing is located on top of the differential housing, immediately above and behind the left driveaxle seal. If you suspect that the speed sensor O-ring is leaking, look for telltale streaks of lubricant on the sides of the housing below the driven-gear assembly.
9    Disconnect the electrical connector and

remove the mounting bolt **(see illustration)**.
10   If the seal or the O-ring is leaking, clean the area around the driven-gear assembly to prevent dirt from falling into the differential assembly, remove the driven-gear hold-down bolt and pull the driven-gear straight up and out of the differential.
11   If the O-ring is damaged, remove it from the sleeve, coat the new O-ring with clean engine oil or transmission lubricant, slide it onto the sleeve and into its groove, and refit the driven gear assembly.

---

**3    Select and shift cables - removal and refitting**

---

### Removal
*Refer to illustrations 3.2 and 3.5*
1    Remove the centre console assembly (see Chapter 11).
2    Remove the split pins from the select and/or shift cables at the shift lever **(see illustration)**.

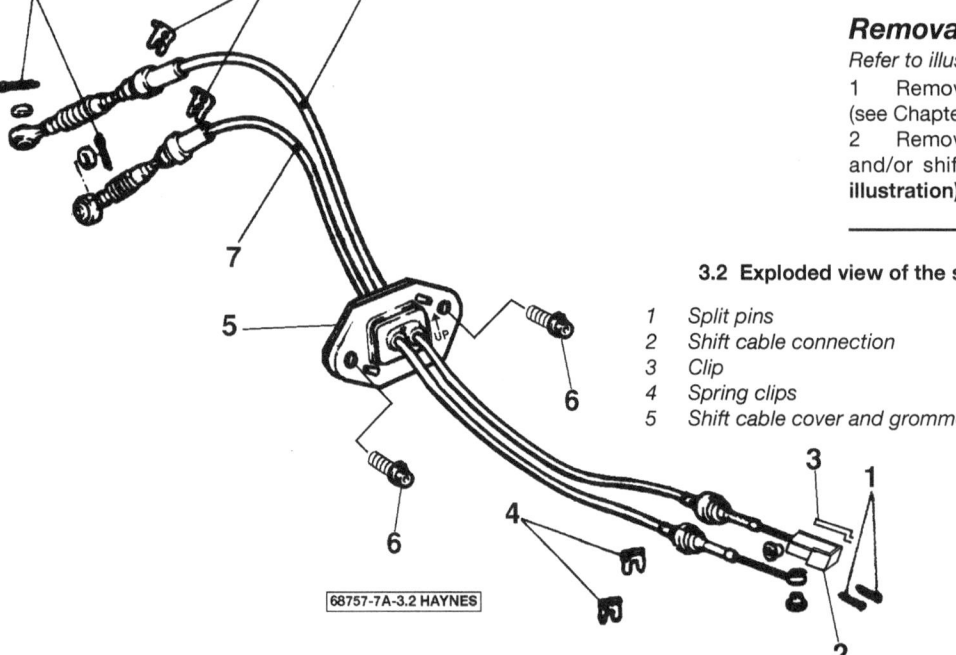

**3.2  Exploded view of the shift and select cables**

| | | | |
|---|---|---|---|
| 1 | Split pins | 6 | Cover bolts |
| 2 | Shift cable connection | 7 | Select cable |
| 3 | Clip | 8 | Shift cable |
| 4 | Spring clips | 9 | Spring clips |
| 5 | Shift cable cover and grommet | 10 | Split pins |

68757-7A-3.2 HAYNES

**3.5 Remove the cable cover and grommet mounting bolts (arrows) from the firewall and pull the cable grommet and cover through the firewall**

**6.2 To check the transaxle mount for wear, insert a prise bar between the mount and the transaxle bracket and try to prise it back and forth; the transaxle should not move excessively - if it does, renew the mount**

3    Prise out the cable retainer clips with a screwdriver.

4    Remove the cable grommet cover mounting bolts from the floorboard **(see illustration)**.

5    Remove the air cleaner housing (see Chapter 4).

6    At the transaxle, remove the split pins from the select and/or shift cables and prise off the cable retaining clips from the cable brackets with a screwdriver.

7    Prise the cable grommet and cover out of the firewall and pull the cables out through the firewall from the passenger compartment side.

8    Refitting is the reverse of removal. Be sure the cable grommet cover has the arrow pointing up.

---

### 4    Shift lever - removal and refitting

---

1    Remove the centre console assembly (see Chapter 11).

2    Disconnect the select and shift cables (see Section 3).

3    Unbolt the shift lever bracket bolts and remove the shift lever.

4    Refitting is the reverse of removal.

---

### 5    Backup light switch - check and renewal

---

## Check

1    The backup light switch is located on top of the transaxle, near the right front corner of the housing.

2    Turn the ignition key to the On position and move the shift lever to the Reverse position. The backup light switch should turn on the backup lights.

3    If it doesn't, check the 10A backup light fuse in the fuse box under the instrument

panel on the driver's side (see Chapter 12).

4    If the fuse is okay, verify that there's voltage available on the battery side of the switch (with the ignition turned to On, of course).

5    If there's no voltage on the battery side of the switch, check the wire between the fuse and the switch; if there is voltage, put the shift lever in Reverse and see if there's voltage on the earth side of the switch.

6    If there's no voltage on the earth side of the switch, renew the switch (see below); if there is voltage, note whether only one or both back-up light bulbs are out.

7    If only one bulb is out, renew it; if they're both out, it could be the bulbs but it's more likely that the wire between the switch and the bulbs has an open somewhere.

## Renewal

8    Unplug the electrical connector from the backup light switch.

9    Unscrew the switch.

10    Screw in the new switch and tighten it to the torque listed in this Chapter's Specifications.

11    Plug in the connector.

12    Check the operation of the backup lights to be sure the switch is working correctly.

---

### 6    Transaxle mount - check and renewal

---

*Refer to illustration 6.2*

1    Remove the air cleaner assembly.

2    Insert a large screwdriver or lever between the mount and the transaxle and prise up **(see illustration)**. The transaxle should not move excessively away from the mount. If it does, renew the mount.

3    To renew the mount, Raise the vehicle and support it securely on jackstands. Remove the left front wheel.

4    Support the transaxle with a jack

and remove the through bolt. Remove he mount retaining nuts (and bolts if equipped). Remove the mount. It may be necessary to raise the transaxle slightly to provide enough clearance to remove the mount.

5    Refitting is the reverse of removal.

---

### 7    Manual transaxle - removal and refitting

---

**Caution:** *If the stereo in your vehicle is equipped with an anti-theft system, make sure you have the correct activation code before disconnecting the battery.*

1    Disconnect the negative cable from the battery.

2    Remove the air cleaner assembly and the intake duct (see Chapter 4).

3    Disconnect the speed sensor electrical connection.

4    Disconnect the select and shift cables from the transaxle levers (see Section 3). Remove the bracket bolts and position the cables aside.

5    Unplug the electrical connector for the backup light switch (see Section 5) and disconnect the earth strap from the transaxle.

6    Remove the starter (see Chapter 5).

7    Remove the upper transaxle-to-engine bolts.

8    Loosen the front wheel lug nuts. Raise the vehicle and place it securely on jackstands. Remove the front wheels.

9    Remove the engine splash shield.

10    Disconnect the clutch release cylinder from the transaxle, but don't disconnect the clutch fluid line fitting from the release cylinder. Instead, disconnect the bracket that attaches the clutch fluid line to the transaxle and set the release cylinder, line, bracket and hose aside (if you disconnect the line either at the hose-to-line bracket or at the release cylinder, you'll have to bleed the clutch hydraulic system).

11   Drain the transaxle fluid (see Chapter 1).
12   Remove both driveaxle assemblies and the intermediate shaft (see Chapter 8).
13   Remove any exhaust components which will interfere with transaxle removal (see Chapter 4).
14   Remove any remaining chassis or suspension components which will interfere with transaxle removal.
15   Remove the flywheel inspection cover. Remove the access covers from the top and bottom of the bellhousing. Insert two screwdrivers (one through each access hole) and carefully pry the release bearing free of the clutch pressure plate.
16   Support the engine from above with a suitable support fixture, an engine hoist or place a jack and a block of wood under the sump to spread the load.
17   Support the transaxle with a transmission jack, if available, or with a floor jack. Safety chains will help steady the transaxle on the jack.
18   Remove the transaxle mount and bracket (see Section 6).
19   Remove the lower transaxle-to-engine bolts.
20   Make a final check that all wires and hoses have been disconnected from the transaxle, then move the transaxle and jack toward the side of the vehicle until the transaxle is clear of the engine. Make sure you keep the transaxle level as you do this.
21   Once the input shaft is clear, lower the transaxle and remove it from under the vehicle. **Caution:** *Do not depress the clutch pedal while the transaxle is removed from the vehicle.*
22   Inspect the clutch components (see

Chapter 8). In most cases, the clutch components should be renewed with new ones whenever the transaxle is removed.

## *Refitting*

23   Refit the clutch components if you removed them (see Chapter 8).
24   With the transaxle secured to the jack, raise it into position and carefully slide it forward, engaging the input shaft with the clutch splines. Do not use excessive force to refit the transaxle - if the input shaft doesn't slide into place, readjust the angle of the transaxle so it's level. You may also need to turn the input shaft so the splines are properly engaged with the clutch.
25   Refit the two lower engine-to-transaxle bolts and the lower transaxle to engine bolt and tighten them to the torque listed in this Chapter's Specifications.
26   Refit the transaxle mounting bracket (see Section 6) and tighten the bolts and nuts securely.
27   Refit the flywheel inspection cover and tighten the bolts securely.
28   Refit all drivetrain components that were removed (see Chapter 8).
29   Refit the under cover.
30   Refit any exhaust components you removed (see Chapter 4).
31   Refit the wheels and lug nuts. Lower the vehicle, and tighten the lug nuts to the torque listed in the Chapter 1 Specifications.
32   Refit the two upper transaxle-to-engine bolts and tighten them to the torque listed in this Chapter's Specifications.
33   Refit the starter (see Chapter 5).
34   Plug in the electrical connector for the

backup light switch (see Section 5) and reattach the earth wire to the transaxle.
35   Attach the clutch fluid hose bracket and the clutch release cylinder to the transaxle (see Chapter 8).
36   Attach the select and shift cable bracket and tighten the two bolts securely.
37   Connect the speed sensor electrical connector.
38   Refit the air cleaner assembly and the intake duct (see Chapter 4).
39   Refit the battery and attach the battery cables (see Chapter 5).
40   Fill the transaxle with lubricant (see Chapter 1).
41   Fill the clutch hydraulic system and bleed it (see Chapter 8).

---

## 8   Manual transaxle overhaul - general information

Overhauling a manual transaxle is difficult for the do-it-yourselfer. Not only must you disassemble and reassemble many small parts, but you must also measure numerous clearances and, if necessary, change them with select-fit shims, thrust washers and spacer collars.

If your transaxle reaches the end of its service life, you can save a great deal of money by removing and refitting it yourself, but you're better off leaving the overhaul to a transmission repair shop. Better yet, buy a rebuilt unit from a dealer parts department or an auto parts store. The cost in time and money to overhaul a transaxle yourself will almost surely exceed the cost of a rebuilt unit.

# Chapter 7 Part B
# Automatic transaxle

## Contents

## Specifications

### General

| | |
|---|---|
| Fluid type and capacity | See Chapter 1 |
| Transaxle model | |
| Transaxle model | |
| 6G72 engines | F4A51 4-speed transaxle |
| 6G74 engines | F4A51 4-speed or F5A51 5-speed transaxles |

### Torque specifications

| | Nm |
|---|---|
| Manual lever nut | 17 to 21 |
| Inhibitor switch mounting bolts | 10 to 12 |
| Transaxle-to-engine bolts | |
| Upper bolts | 74 |
| Lower bolts | 65 |
| Transaxle mounting bracket-to-transaxle bolts | 60 to 80 |
| Roll stopper bracket | 70 |
| Torque converter-to-driveplate bolts | 33 to 38 |
| Driveplate-to-crankshaft bolts | 74 |

## 1 General information

All vehicles covered in this manual come equipped with either a 5-speed manual transaxle, 4-speed or a 5-speed electronically controlled automatic transaxle. All information on the automatic transaxle is included in this Part of Chapter 7. Information for the manual transaxle can be found in Part A of this Chapter.

Due to the complexity of the automatic transaxles covered in this manual and to the specialised equipment necessary to perform most service operations, because of the electronic shift control of this automatic transaxle, this Chapter contains only those procedures related to general diagnosis, routine maintenance, adjustment and removal and refitting.

If the transaxle requires major repair work, it should be left to a dealer service department or an automotive or transmission repair shop. You can, however, remove and refit the transaxle yourself and save the expense, even if the repair work is done by a transmission shop.

## 2 Diagnosis - general

**Note:** *Automatic transaxle malfunctions may be caused by five general conditions: poor engine performance, improper adjustments, hydraulic malfunctions, mechanical malfunctions or malfunctions in the computer or its signal network. Diagnosis of these problems should always begin with a check of the easily repaired items: fluid level and condition (see Chapter 1) shift cable adjustment and shift lever refitting. Next, perform a road test* *to determine if the problem has been corrected or if more diagnosis is necessary. If the problem persists after the preliminary tests and corrections are completed, additional diagnosis should be done by a dealer service department or transmission repair shop. Refer to the* Troubleshooting *section at the front of this manual for information on symptoms of transaxle problems.*

### *Preliminary checks*

1    Drive the vehicle to warm the transaxle to normal operating temperature.

2    Check the fluid level as described in Chapter 1:

   *a) If the fluid level is unusually low, add enough fluid to bring the level within the designated area of the dipstick, then check for external leaks (see below).*

   *b) If the fluid level is abnormally high, drain off the excess, then check the drained fluid for contamination by coolant. The presence of engine coolant in the automatic transmission fluid indicates that a failure has occurred in the internal radiator walls that separate the coolant from the transmission fluid (see Chapter 3).*

   *c) If the fluid is foaming, drain it and refill the transaxle, then check for coolant in the fluid, or a high fluid level.*

3    Check the engine idle speed. **Note:** *If the engine is malfunctioning, do not proceed with the preliminary checks until it has been repaired and runs normally.*

4    Check and adjust the shift cable, if necessary (see Section 4).

5    Inspect the shift lever linkage under the console and the manual lever on the transaxle (see Section 3). Make sure that both are operating properly and smoothly.

### *Fluid leak diagnosis*

6    Most fluid leaks are easy to locate visually. Repair usually consists of renewing a seal or gasket. If a leak is difficult to find, the following procedure may help.

7    Identify the fluid. Make sure it's transmission fluid and not engine oil or brake fluid (automatic transmission fluid is a deep red colour).

8    Try to pinpoint the source of the leak. Drive the vehicle several kilometers, then park it over a large sheet of cardboard. After a minute or two, you should be able to locate the leak by determining the source of the fluid dripping onto the cardboard.

9    Make a careful visual inspection of the suspected component and the area immediately around it. Pay particular attention to gasket mating surfaces. A mirror is often helpful for finding leaks in areas that are hard to see.

10    If the leak still cannot be found, clean the suspected area thoroughly with a degreaser or solvent, then dry it.

11    Drive the vehicle for several kilometers at normal operating temperature and varying speeds. After driving the vehicle, visually inspect the suspected component again.

12    Once the leak has been located, the cause must be determined before it can be properly repaired. If a gasket is renewed but the sealing flange is bent, the new gasket will not stop the leak. The bent flange must be straightened.

13    Before attempting to repair a leak, check to make sure that the following conditions are corrected or they may cause another leak. **Note:** *Some of the following conditions cannot be fixed without highly specialised tools and expertise. Such problems must be referred to a transmission shop or a dealer service department.*

### Gasket leaks

14    Check the valve body cover and rear cover periodically. Make sure the bolts are tight, no bolts are missing, the gasket is in good condition and the cover is flat (dents in the cover may indicate damage to the valve body inside).

15    If the gasket(s) is leaking, the fluid level may be too high, the vent may be plugged, the cover bolts may be too tight, the pan sealing flange may be warped, the sealing surface of the transaxle housing may be damaged, the gasket may be damaged or the transaxle casting may be cracked or porous. If sealant instead of gasket material has been used to form a seal between the cover and the transaxle housing, it may be the wrong sealant.

### Seal leaks

16    If a transaxle seal is leaking, the fluid level or pressure may be too high, the vent may be plugged, the seal bore may be damaged, the seal itself may be damaged or improperly refitted, the surface of the shaft protruding through the seal may be damaged or a loose bearing may be causing excessive shaft movement.

17    Make sure the dipstick tube seal is in good condition and the tube is properly seated. Periodically check the area around the speedometer gear or sensor for leakage. If transmission fluid is evident, check the O-ring for damage.

### Case leaks

18    If the case itself appears to be leaking, the casting is porous and will have to be repaired or renewed.

19    Make sure the oil cooler hose fittings are tight and in good condition.

### Fluid comes out vent pipe or fill tube

20    If this condition occurs, the transaxle is overfilled, there is coolant in the fluid, the case is porous, the dipstick is incorrect, the vent is plugged or the drain-back holes are plugged.

### Electronic control system

21    This transaxle is equipped with a transaxle control unit (T-ECU), located inside of the car under the centre console. The control unit uses data from various sensors which monitor the engine and transaxle operations. The control unit changes or controls shift points through solenoids located in the valve body as the data from the sensors is received. The control unit is capable of generating trouble codes; in the event that this should occur, take the vehicle to a dealer service department or other qualified repair shop so a scanner can be used to retrieve the codes.

---

### 3    Shift lever - removal and refitting

*Refer to illustrations 3.2, 3.3 and 3.5*

1    Remove the centre console (see Chapter 11).

2    Remove the spring clip retaining the cable to the shift lever housing **(see illustration)**.

3    Remove the clevis pin holding the shift cable to the shift lever **(see illustration)**.

4    Disconnect the illumination lamp wiring harness connector and indicator panel wiring harness from the shift lever.

5    Remove the shift lever base mounting bolts **(see illustration)**. Remove the shift lever assembly.

6    Refitting is the reverse of removal.

**3.2 Prise the cable retaining spring clip from the housing (arrow)**

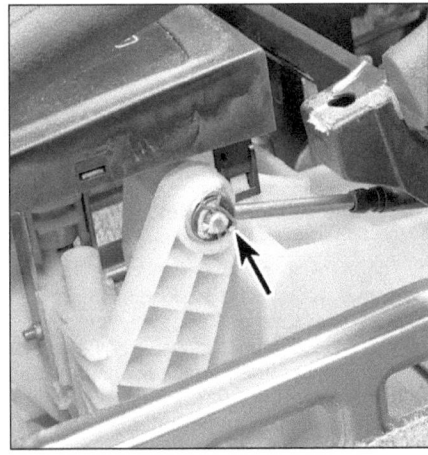

**3.3 Remove the clevis pin and disconnect the cable from the lever (arrow)**

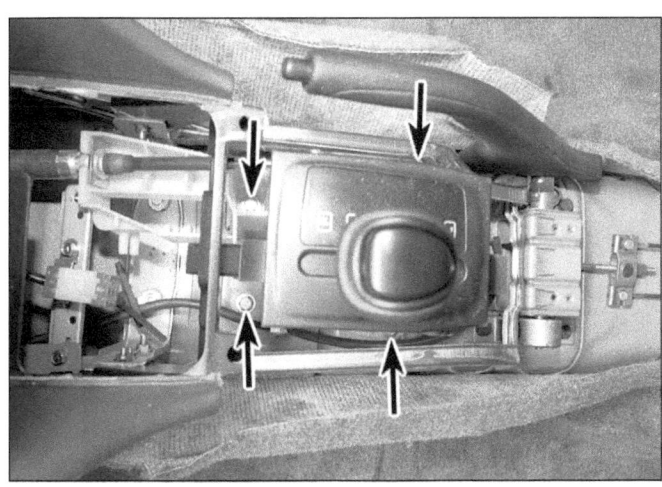

3.5  Shift lever assembly mounting bolts (arrows)

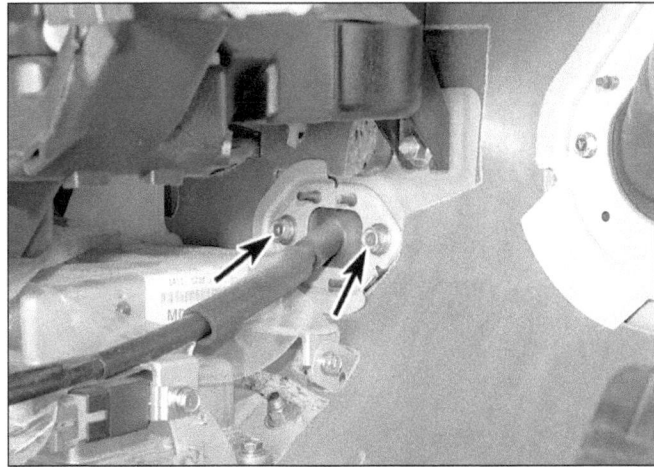

4.4  From inside the vehicle, remove the bolts attaching the cable grommet to the floorboard

## 4  Shift cable - renewal

*Refer to illustrations 4.4, 4.5 and 4.6*

1    Remove the centre console (see Chapter 11).

2    Detach the shift cable from the shift lever (see Section 3).

3    Raise the vehicle and support it securely on jackstands.

4    Remove the bolts attaching the cable grommet to the floorboard **(see illustration)**.

5    Remove the spring clip at the transmission **(see illustration)**.

6    Disconnect the forward end of the shift cable from the manual lever arm **(see illustration)**.

7    Place the shift lever and the transaxle manual lever in the Neutral position and attach the new shift cable.

8    To adjust the shift cable, refer to the inhibitor switch adjustment procedure in Section 5.

9    Refitting is otherwise the reverse of removal. Be sure to tighten the cable nuts securely.

## 5  Inhibitor switch - renewal and adjustment

### Renewal

*Refer to illustration 5.3*

1    Place the shift lever in the Neutral position.

2    Disconnect the shift cable from the manual lever (see Section 4). Disconnect the electrical connector from the inhibitor switch.

3    Remove the manual control lever, the inhibitor switch bolts and remove the switch **(see illustration)**.

4    Refitting is the reverse of removal. Be sure to adjust the switch when you're done (see below).

### Adjustment

*Refer to illustration 5.7*

5    With the shift cable disconnected from the manual lever, place the shift lever in the Neutral position.

6    Place the manual control lever in the Neutral position. This can be accomplished

4.5  Prise the cable retaining clip from the transmission bracket (arrow)

by rotating the manual lever clockwise to the Park position, then counterclockwise two detents to the Neutral position.

7    Loosen the body bolts and rotate the switch body so that the alignment hole in

4.6  Remove the clevis pin and disconnect the shift cable from the manual lever

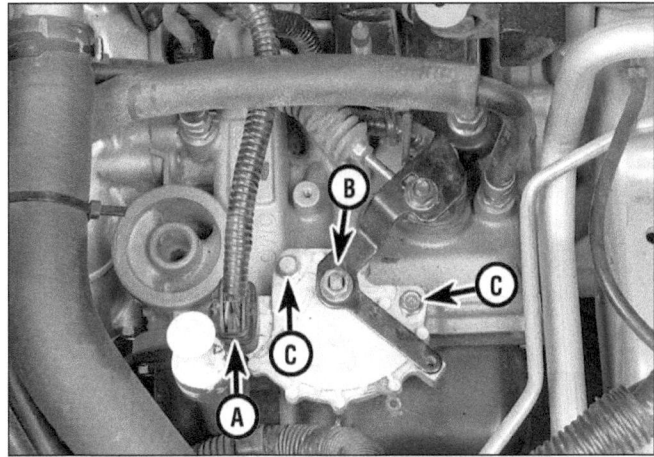

5.3  To remove the inhibitor switch, unplug the electrical connector (A), remove the manual control lever (B) and remove the two switch mounting bolts (C)

**5.7 To adjust the inhibitor switch, loosen the switch bolts (A), rotate the switch body so that the holes in the manual control lever and the switch body are aligned; insert a 6 mm drill bit to align the holes**

**6.8 Remove the upper transaxle-to-engine bolts (arrow) - one of four shown**

the manual control lever aligns with the hole in the switch body **(see illustration)**. Insert a 6 mm drill bit through the holes, rotating the switch body to engage the holes as necessary.

8    Tighten the switch body mounting bolts to the torque listed in this Chapter's Specifications. Remove the drill bit.

9    Verify that the shift lever is in the Neutral position.

10   Loosen the adjusting nut at the shift cable pivot, adjust the pivot so that it slides easily onto the manual lever. Tighten the adjusting nut securely and refit the clevis pin.

11   Move the shift lever through all the positions and verify the shift indicator aligns with the proper range. Verify that the starter operates ONLY in the Neutral and Park positions and that the backup lights operate in the Reverse position.

## 6    Automatic transaxle - removal and refitting

### Removal

*Refer to illustrations 6.8, 6.13, 6.19a and 6.19b*

1    Disconnect the cable from the negative battery terminal.

2    Remove the air cleaner assembly (see Chapter 4) and battery tray (see Chapter 5). Remove the coolant reservoir (see Chapter 3).

3    Clearly label, then unplug, all electrical connectors from the transaxle.

4    Disconnect the shift cable from the manual lever and remove the bracket (see Section 4).

5    Disconnect the speedometer connector

from the speedometer driven gear.

6    Loosen the hose clamps and disconnect the oil cooler hoses. Plug the hoses to prevent contamination and leaks.

7    Remove the starter motor (see Chapter 5).

8    Remove the upper transaxle-to-engine bolts **(see illustration)**.

9    Loosen the wheel lug nuts, raise the vehicle and support it securely on jackstands. Remove the wheels.

10   Remove the engine splash shield (if equipped).

11   Drain the differential and transaxle fluid (see Chapter 1).

12   Remove both driveaxle assemblies (see Chapter 8).

13   Remove the torque converter cover and mark the relationship of the torque converter to the driveplate so they can be refitted in the

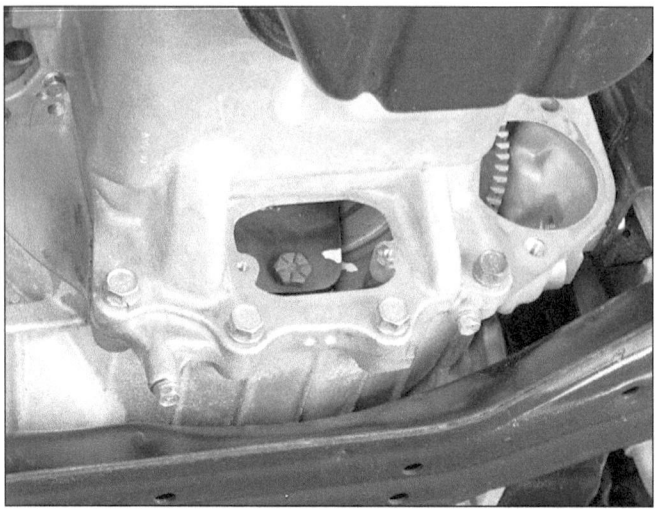

**6.13 Mark the relationship of the torque converter to the driveplate so they can be refitted in the same position**

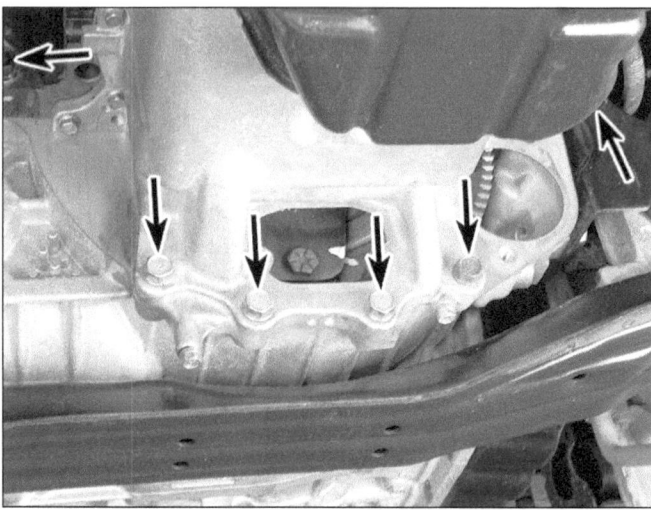

**6.19a Remove the six engine-to-transaxle bolts (arrows)**

same relative position **(see illustration)**.

14 Remove all four torque converter-to-driveplate bolts. Turn the crankshaft 120-degrees at a time for access to each bolt. After all four bolts are removed, push the torque converter into the bellhousing as far as you can and remove it with the transaxle.

15 Support the engine from above with a suitable support fixture, engine hoist or place a jack and a block of wood under the sump to spread the load.

16 Support the transaxle with a transmission jack (a special jack made for this purpose), if available, or with a floor jack. Safety chains will help steady the transaxle on the jack.

17 Raise the transaxle slightly and remove the transaxle mount through-bolt. Working in the right-side wheel well, prise the caps from the inner fender, remove the bolts and remove the transaxle mount/bracket (see Chapter 7A). Remove the mount bracket from the transaxle.

18 Remove any remaining chassis or suspension components which will interfere with transaxle removal. **Note:** *Place a block of wood between the strut spring and the inner body to keep it away while working.*

19 Remove the lower transaxle-to-engine bolts **(see illustrations)**.

20 Move the transaxle to the side to disengage it from the engine block dowel pins. Make sure the torque converter is detached from the driveplate. Secure the torque converter to the transaxle so that it will not fall out during removal. Lower the transaxle from the vehicle.

## Refitting

21 Make sure the torque converter hub is securely engaged in the pump prior to refitting. This can be confirmed by pushing on the torque converter and turning it (if it isn't seated completely, it will drop into place as

this is done).

22 With the transaxle secured to the jack, raise it into position. Be sure to keep it level so the torque converter does not slide forward.

23 Move the transaxle carefully into place until the dowel pins are engaged and the torque converter is engaged.

24 Turn the torque converter to align the bolt holes with the holes in the driveplate. The match marks on the torque converter and driveplate, made during step 13, must align.

25 Refit the lower transaxle-to-engine bolts and tighten them to the torque listed in this Chapter's Specifications.

26 Refit the transaxle mounting brackets, mount and through bolt. Tighten the bolts to the torque listed in this Chapters Specifications.

27 Remove the jacks supporting the transaxle and the engine.

28 Refit the torque converter-to-driveplate bolts and tighten them to the torque listed in this Chapter's Specifications. **Note:** *Once the weight the engine has been put back on all of the bolts tighten all of them to the torque listed in this Chapter's Specifications.* Refit the torque converter cover and tighten the bolts securely.

29 Refit all drivetrain components that were removed (see Chapter 8). Tighten all drivetrain components to the torque listed in the Chapter 8 Specifications.

30 Refit all suspension components that were removed. Tighten all suspension fasteners to the torque listed in the Chapter 10 Specifications.

31 Refit the engine splash shield (if equipped).

32 Refit the wheels, remove the jack stands and lower the vehicle.

33 Refit the upper transaxle-to-engine bolts and tighten them to the torque listed in this

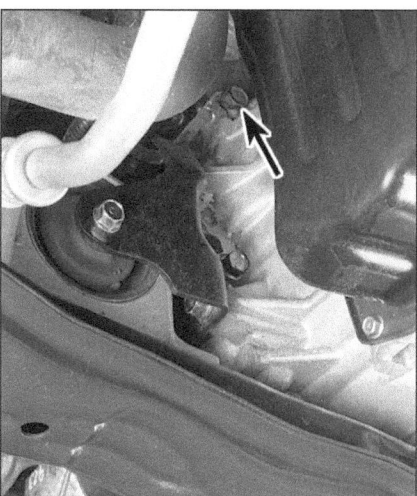

**6.19b Remove the two lower transaxle-to-engine bolts (arrow) - left side shown**

Chapter's Specifications.

34 Refit the starter motor (see Chapter 5).

35 Unplug the oil cooler hoses and reattach them to the transaxle. This is a good time to inspect and if necessary, renew the hoses. Use new hose clamps - once they've been removed, the original clamps can cause leaks.

36 Reconnect the speed sensor connector to the speed sensor driven gear housing.

37 Reconnect the shift cable to the manual lever (see Section 4). Adjust the inhibitor switch, if necessary (see Section 5).

38 Plug in all electrical connectors.

39 Refit the air cleaner assembly (see Chapter 4).

40 Attach the cable to the negative battery terminal.

41 Fill the differential and transaxle (see Chapter 1). Run the vehicle and check for fluid leaks.

# Notes

# Chapter 8
# Clutch and driveaxles

## Contents

## Specifications

### Clutch

| | |
|---|---|
| Fluid type | See Chapter 1 |
| Type | Single dry plate, diaphragm spring |
| Actuation | Hydraulic |
| Clutch pedal height | 168 to 173 mm |
| Clutch pedal freeplay | 6 to 13 mm |

### Driveaxle

| | |
|---|---|
| Standard inner boot length (measured between the centreline of each boot clamp) | 75 ± 3 mm |

### Torque specifications

| | Nm |
|---|---|
| Driveaxle/hub nut | 200 to 260 |
| Intermediate shaft bearing bracket-to-engine block bolts | 45 |
| Pressure plate-to-flywheel bolts | 15 to 21 |

## 1 General information

The information in this Chapter deals with the components that transmit power to the wheels, except for the transaxle, which are in Chapter 7. The components covered in this Chapter are grouped into two categories - clutch and driveaxles. You'll find general descriptions, inspection and overhaul procedures for these components in this Chapter.

**Warning:** *Since nearly all the procedures covered in this Chapter involve working under the vehicle, make sure it's securely supported on sturdy jackstands or on a hoist where the vehicle can be easily raised and lowered.*

## 2 Clutch - description and check

*Refer to illustration 2.1*

1    All vehicles with a manual transaxle use a single dry plate, diaphragm spring type clutch **(see illustration)**. The clutch disc has a splined hub which allows it to slide along the splines of the transaxle input shaft. The clutch and pressure plate are held in contact by spring force exerted by the diaphragm in the pressure plate.

2    The clutch release system is operated by hydraulic pressure. The hydraulic release system consists of the clutch pedal, a master cylinder and fluid reservoir, the hydraulic line, a slave cylinder which actuates the clutch release lever and the clutch release (or throwout) bearing.

3    When force is applied to the clutch pedal to release the clutch, hydraulic pressure is exerted against the outer end of the clutch release lever. As the lever pivots, the shaft fingers push against the release bearing. The bearing pushes against the fingers of the diaphragm spring of the pressure plate assembly, which in turn releases the clutch plate.

4    Terminology can be a problem regarding the clutch components because common names have in some cases changed from that used by the manufacturer. For example, the driven plate is also called the clutch plate or disc, the pressure plate assembly is sometimes referred to as the clutch cover, the clutch release bearing is sometimes called a throw-out bearing, and the release cylinder is sometimes called the operating or slave cylinder.

5    Other than renewing components that have obvious damage, some preliminary checks should be performed to diagnose a clutch system failure.

a) *The first check should be of the fluid level in the clutch master cylinder (see Chapter 1). If the fluid level is low, add fluid as necessary and inspect the hydraulic clutch system for leaks. If the master cylinder reservoir has run dry, bleed the system (see Section 8) and retest the clutch operation.*

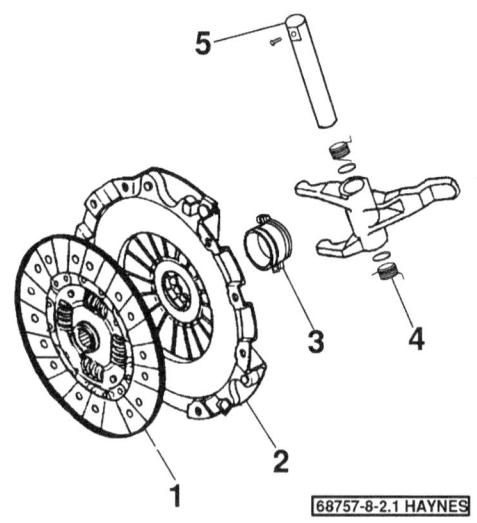

**2.1 An exploded view of the clutch assembly**

1    *Clutch disc*
2    *Pressure plate*
3    *Release bearing*
4    *Fork assembly*
5    *Pivot shaft*

68757-8-2.1 HAYNES

b) *To check "clutch spin down time," run the engine at normal idle speed with the transaxle in Neutral (clutch pedal up - engaged). Disengage the clutch (pedal down), wait several seconds and shift the transaxle into Reverse. No grinding noise should be heard. A grinding noise would most likely indicate a problem in the pressure plate or the clutch disc.*

c) *To check for complete clutch release, run the engine (with the parking brake applied to prevent movement) and hold the clutch pedal approximately 13 mm from the floor. Shift the transaxle between 1st gear and Reverse several times. If the shift is not smooth, component failure is indicated. Check the release cylinder pushrod travel. With the clutch pedal depressed completely the release cylinder pushrod should extend substantially. If it doesn't, check the fluid level in the clutch master cylinder.*

d) *Visually inspect the clutch pedal bush at the top of the clutch pedal to make sure there is no sticking or excessive wear.*

e) *Under the vehicle, check that the clutch release lever is solidly mounted on the ball stud.*

## 3 Clutch pedal height and freeplay - check and adjustment

1    Measure the clutch pedal height (the distance from the top of the clutch pedal to the floor). The distance should be as listed in this Chapter's Specifications.

2    If the pedal height is not correct, reach under the dash and loosen the locknut on the clutch pedal adjusting bolt until the bolt turns freely. Turn the adjusting bolt to achieve the specified pedal height.

3    Press down lightly on the clutch pedal and, with a small steel ruler, measure the distance that it moves freely before the clutch resistance is felt. The freeplay should be

within the limits listed in this Chapter's Specifications. If it isn't, it must be adjusted.

4    To adjust the freeplay, reach up under the dash, loosen the lock-nut and adjust the clutch pedal pushrod until the freeplay is correct, then tighten the locknut securely.

## 4 Clutch components - removal, inspection and refitting

**Warning:** *Dust produced by clutch wear and deposited on clutch components may contain asbestos, which is hazardous to your health. DO NOT blow it out with compressed air and DO NOT inhale it. DO NOT use petrol or petroleum based solvents to remove the dust. Brake system cleaner should be used to flush the dust into a drain pan. After the clutch components are wiped clean with a rag, dispose of the contaminated rags and cleaner in a labeled, covered container.*

### Removal

*Refer to illustration 4.6*

1    Access to the clutch components is normally accomplished by removing the transaxle, leaving the engine in the vehicle. If, of course, the engine is being removed for major overhaul, then the opportunity should always be taken to check the clutch for wear and renew worn components as necessary. However, the relatively low cost of the clutch components compared to the time and labor involved in gaining access to them warrants their renewal any time the engine or transaxle is removed, unless they are new or in near-perfect condition. The following procedures assume that the engine will stay in place.

2    Remove the release cylinder (see Section 7). Hang it out of the way with a piece of wire - it's not necessary to disconnect the hose.

3    Remove the transaxle from the vehicle (see Chapter 7A). **Note:** *Disconnect the bearing from the pressure plate before removing*

**4.6 If you're going to re-use the same pressure plate, mark the relationship of the pressure plate to the flywheel**

**4.10 Inspect the clutch disc for signs of excessive wear such as smeared friction material, chewed-up rivets, worn hub splines and distorted damper cushions or springs**

**4.12a Examine the pressure plate friction surface for score marks, cracks and evidence of overheating**

*the transaxle*. Support the engine while the transaxle is out. Preferably, an engine hoist should be used to support it from above. However, if a jack is used underneath the engine, make sure a piece of wood is used between the jack and sump to spread the load. **Caution:** *The pick-up for the oil pump is very close to the bottom of the sump. If the pan is bent or distorted in any way, engine oil starvation could occur.*

4    The release fork and release bearing can remain attached to the transaxle for the time being.

5    To support the clutch disc during removal, fit a clutch alignment tool through the clutch disc hub.

6    Carefully inspect the flywheel and pressure plate for indexing marks. The marks are usually an X, an O or a white letter. If they cannot be found, scribe marks yourself so the pressure plate and the flywheel will be in the same alignment during refitting **(see illustration)**.

7    Slowly loosen the pressure plate-to-flywheel bolts. Work in a diagonal pattern and loosen each bolt a little at a time until all spring pressure is relieved. Then hold the pressure plate securely and completely remove the bolts, followed by the pressure plate and clutch disc.

### Inspection

*Refer to illustrations 4.10, 4.12a and 4.12b*

8    Ordinarily, when a problem occurs in the clutch, it can be attributed to wear of the clutch driven plate assembly (clutch disc). However, all components should be inspected at this time.

9    Inspect the flywheel for cracks, heat checking, score marks and other damage. If the imperfections are slight, a machine shop can resurface it to make it flat and smooth. Refer to Chapter 2 for the flywheel removal procedure.

10    Inspect the lining on the clutch disc. There should be at least 1.5 mm of lining above the rivet heads. Check for loose rivets, distortion, cracks, broken springs and other obvious damage **(see illustration)**. As mentioned above, ordinarily the clutch disc is renewed as a matter of course, so if in doubt about the condition, renew it with a new one.

11    The release bearing should be renewed along with the clutch disc (see Section 5).

12    Check the machined surface and the diaphragm spring fingers of the pressure plate **(see illustrations)**. If the surface is grooved or otherwise damaged, renew the pressure plate assembly. Also check for obvi-

ous damage, distortion, cracking, etc. Light glazing can be removed with emery cloth or sandpaper. If a new pressure plate is indicated, new or factory rebuilt units are available.

### Refitting

13    Before refitting, carefully wipe the flywheel and pressure plate machined surfaces clean. It's important that no oil or grease is on these surfaces or the lining of the clutch disc. Handle these parts only with clean hands.

14    Position the clutch disc and pressure plate with the clutch held in place with an alignment tool. Make sure it's refitted properly (most renewal clutch plates will be marked "flywheel side" or something similar - if not marked, refit the clutch disc with the damper springs or cushion toward the transaxle).

15    Refit the pressure plate-to-flywheel bolts only finger tight, working around the pressure plate.

16    Centre the clutch disc by ensuring the alignment tool is through the splined hub and into the recess in the crankshaft. Wiggle the tool up, down or side-to-side as needed to bottom the tool. Tighten the pressure plate-to-flywheel bolts a little at a time, working in a criss-cross pattern to prevent distortion of the cover. After all of the bolts are snug, tighten

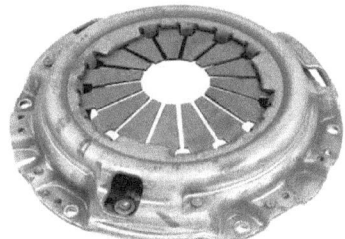

**NORMAL FINGER WEAR**

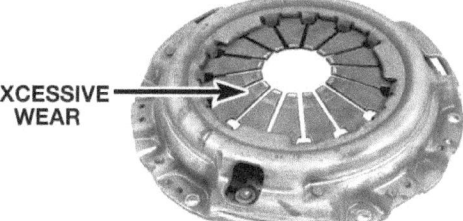

EXCESSIVE
WEAR

**EXCESSIVE FINGER WEAR**

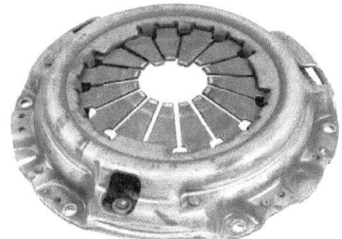

**BROKEN OR BENT FINGERS**

**4.12b  Renew the pressure plate if excessive wear is noted**

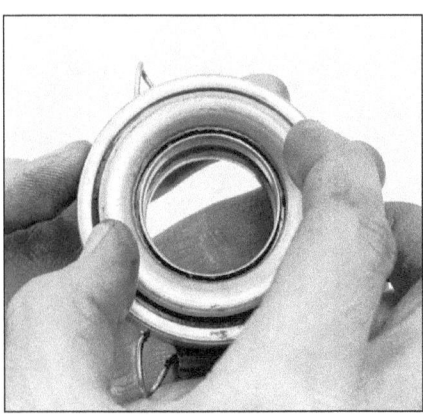

**5.4 To check the operation of the release bearing, hold it by the outer race and rotate the inner race while applying pressure - the bearing should turn smoothly - if it doesn't renew it**

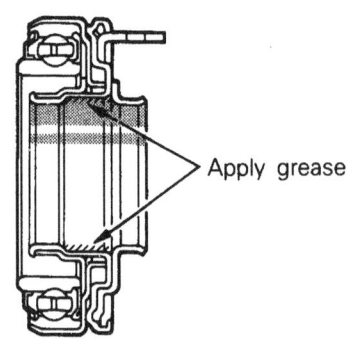

Apply grease

**5.5 Fill the groove of the release bearing with high-temperature grease in the indicated area; also apply a light coat of the same grease to the transaxle input shaft splines and bearing retainer sleeve**

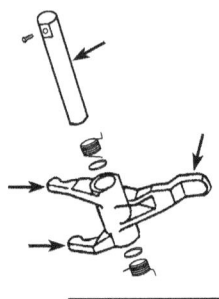

68757-8-5.6 HAYNES

**5.6 Using high-temperature grease, lubricate the release lever shaft, the contact surfaces of the lever tips that push against the release bearing and the release cylinder pushrod socket**

them to the torque listed in this Chapter's Specifications. Remove the alignment tool.

17   Using high-temperature grease, lubricate the inner groove of the release bearing (see Section 5). Also place grease on the release lever contact areas and the transaxle input shaft bearing retainer.

18   Refit the clutch release bearing (see Section 5).

19   Refit the transaxle, release cylinder and all components removed previously, tightening all fasteners to the proper torque specifications.

## 5   Clutch release bearing and lever - removal, inspection and refitting

**Warning:** *Dust produced by clutch wear and deposited on clutch components may contain asbestos, which is hazardous to your health. DO NOT blow it out with compressed air and DO NOT inhale it. DO NOT use petrol or petroleum-based solvents to remove the dust. Brake system cleaner should be used to flush it into a drain pan. After the clutch components are wiped clean with a rag, dispose of the contaminated rags and cleaner in a labeled, covered container.*

### Removal

1   Disconnect the negative cable from the battery.

2   Remove the transaxle (see Chapter 7A). **Note:** *Disconnect the bearing from the pressure plate before removing the transaxle.*

3   Remove the bearing. Unbolt the clutch release lever pivot shaft from the transaxle, then remove the return spring, sealing boot, packing and the fork.

### Inspection

*Refer to illustration 5.4*

4   Hold the bearing by the outer race and rotate the inner race while applying pres-

sure **(see illustration)**. If the bearing doesn't turn smoothly or if it's noisy, renew the bearing. Wipe the bearing with a clean rag and inspect it for damage, wear and cracks. Don't immerse the bearing in solvent - it's sealed for life and to do so would ruin it. Also check the release lever for cracks and bends.

### Refitting

*Refer to illustrations 5.5 and 5.6*

5   Fill the inner groove of the release bearing with high-temperature grease. Also apply a light coat of the same grease to the transaxle input shaft splines and the front bearing retainer **(see illustration)**.

6   Lubricate the release shaft, lever ends and release cylinder pushrod socket with high temperature grease **(see illustration)**.

7   Attach the release bearing to the release lever.

8   Slide the release bearing onto the transaxle input shaft front bearing retainer while passing the end of the release lever through the opening in the clutch housing. Assemble the fork and pivot assembly to the transaxle.

9   Apply a light coat of high-temperature grease to the face of the release bearing where it contacts the pressure plate diaphragm fingers.

10   The remainder of refitting is the reverse of the removal procedure.

## 6   Clutch master cylinder - removal, overhaul and refitting

**Caution:** *If the stereo in your vehicle is equipped with an anti-theft system, make sure you have the correct activation code before disconnecting the battery.*

**Note:** *Before beginning this procedure, contact local parts stores and dealer parts departments concerning the purchase of a rebuild kit or a new master cylinder. Availability and cost of the necessary parts may dictate whether the cylinder is rebuilt or renewed*

with a new one. If it's decided to rebuild the cylinder, inspect the bore as described in Step 9 before purchasing parts.

### Removal

*Refer to illustration 6.2*

1   Disconnect the negative cable from the battery.

2   Under the dashboard, remove the split pin and clevis pin and disconnect the pushrod clevis from the clutch pedal lever **(see illustration)**.

3   Disconnect the hydraulic line at the clutch master cylinder. If available, use a flare-nut spanner on the fitting to prevent the fitting from being rounded off. Have some rags handy to absorb any fluid lost as the line is removed. **Caution:** *Don't allow brake fluid to come into contact with paint, as it will damage the finish.*

4   Working in the engine compartment, remove the nuts which secure the master cylinder to the firewall. Loosen the clamp that secures the reservoir to the fire wall.

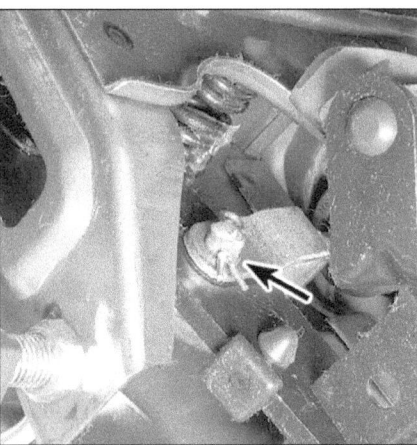

**6.2 To disconnect the clutch master cylinder pushrod from the clutch pedal, remove this retaining clip and clevis pin (arrow)**

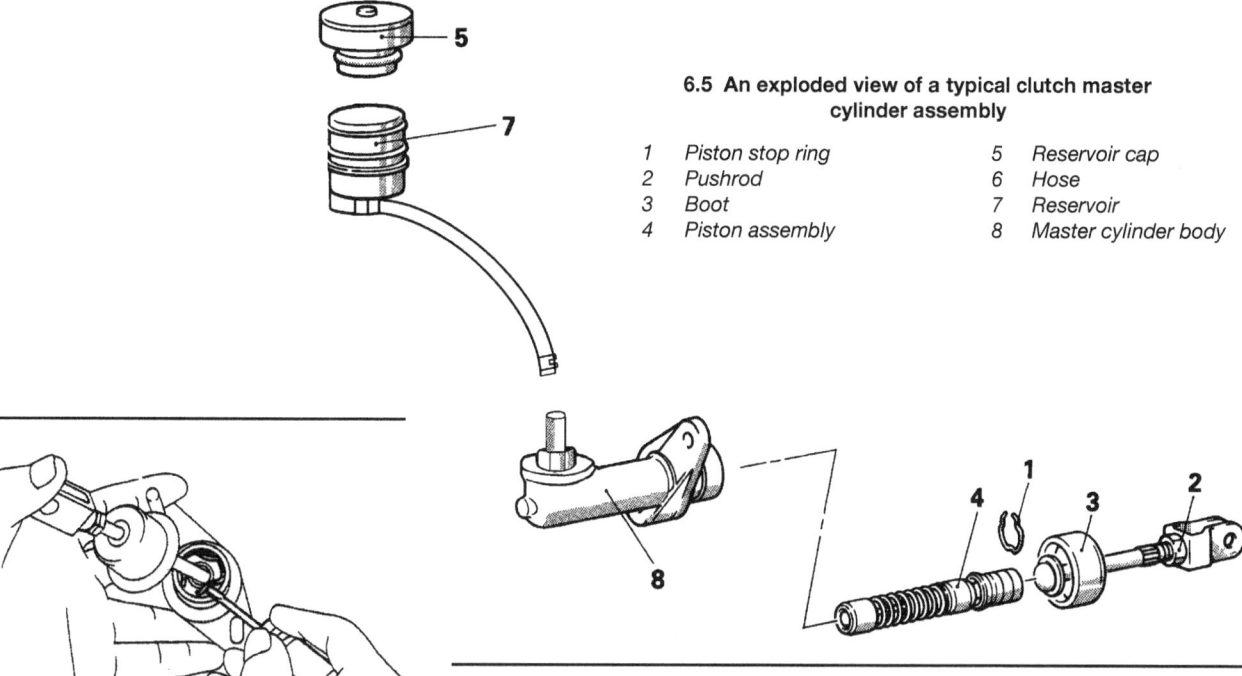

**6.5 An exploded view of a typical clutch master
cylinder assembly**

| | | | |
|---|---|---|---|
| 1 | Piston stop ring | 5 | Reservoir cap |
| 2 | Pushrod | 6 | Hose |
| 3 | Boot | 7 | Reservoir |
| 4 | Piston assembly | 8 | Master cylinder body |

**6.6 Pull back the dust cover on the
pushrod and prise the snap-ring
from its groove**

Disconnect the reservoir hose and separate
the reservoir from the body **(see illustration)**.
Remove the master cylinder, again being
careful not to spill any of the fluid.

## Overhaul

*Refer to illustrations 6.5, 6.6, 6.8 and 6.13*
**Caution:** *Do not attempt to disassemble the
piston/spring/seal assembly. If any part is
defective, you must renew the entire assembly; separate pieces aren't available.*

5    Remove the reservoir cap and drain all
fluid from the master cylinder.
6    Pull back the dust cover on the pushrod
and remove the snap-ring **(see illustration)**.
7    Remove the pushrod and boot from the
cylinder.
8    Tap the master cylinder on a block
of wood to eject the piston assembly from
inside the bore **(see illustration)**.
9    Inspect the bore of the master cylinder
for deep scratches, score marks and ridges.
The surface must be smooth to the touch. If
the bore isn't perfectly smooth, the master
cylinder must be renewed with a new or factory rebuilt unit.
10    If you're rebuilding the master cylinder,
use the new parts contained in the rebuild
kit and follow any specific instructions which
may have accompanied the rebuild kit. Wash
all parts to be re-used with brake cleaner,
denatured alcohol or clean brake fluid. DO
NOT use petroleum-based solvents.
11    Lubricate the bore of the cylinder and
the seals with plenty of fresh brake fluid.
12    Carefully guide the new piston assembly into the bore, being careful not to damage

the seals. Make sure the spring end is refitted
first, with the pushrod end of the piston closest to the opening.
13    Apply a liberal amount of silicone grease
to the contact surfaces between the pushrod
and the piston and between the pushrod and
the boot **(see illustration)**. Position the pushrod in the bore, compress the spring and fit a
new snap-ring.

## Refitting

14    Refit the fluid reservoir hose and tighten
the clamp.
15    Position the master cylinder on the firewall and refit the mounting nuts finger-tight
and reservoir in its clamp.
16    Connect the hydraulic line to the master
cylinder, moving the cylinder slightly as necessary to thread the fitting properly into the
bore. Don't cross-thread the fitting.
17    Tighten the mounting nuts, reservoir
clamp and the hydraulic line fitting securely.
18    Apply a light film of grease to the clevis
pin and washer, then connect the pushrod
to the clutch pedal lever with the clevis pin,
washer and a new split pin.

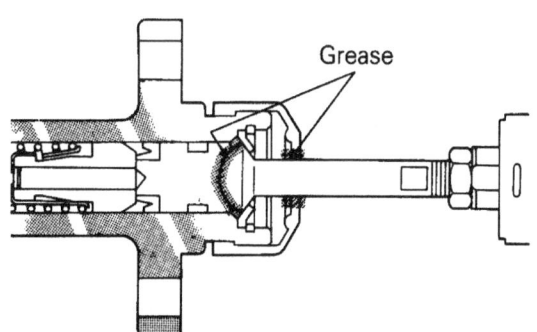

**6.13 Apply a liberal
amount of silicone grease
to the contact surfaces
between the pushrod and
the piston assembly, and
between the pushrod and
the boot as shown**

**6.8 To remove the piston assembly from
the clutch master cylinder, grasp the
cylinder with its open end facing down
and tap it against a block of wood**

19   Fill the clutch master cylinder reservoir with the brake fluid listed in the Chapter 1 Specifications and bleed the clutch system (see Section 8).

20   Check and, if necessary, adjust the clutch pedal height and freeplay (see Section 3). Connect the negative battery cable.

## 7   Clutch release cylinder - removal, overhaul and refitting

**Caution:** *If the stereo in your vehicle is equipped with an anti-theft system, make sure you have the correct activation code before disconnecting the battery.*

**Note:** *Before beginning this procedure, contact local parts stores and dealer parts departments concerning the purchase of a rebuild kit or a new release cylinder. Availability and cost of the necessary parts may dictate whether the cylinder is rebuilt or renewed with a new one. If it's decided to rebuild the cylinder, inspect the bore as described in Step 8 before purchasing parts.*

### Removal

1   Disconnect the negative cable from the battery.

2   Raise the vehicle and support it securely on jackstands.

3   Disconnect the hydraulic line fitting from the release cylinder. **Note:** *Use a line type spanner to prevent rounding the fitting edges.* Plug the open fitting to prevent fluid loss and contamination. Have a small can and rags handy, as some fluid will be spilled as the line is removed. Discard the sealing washers and be sure to use new ones upon fitting.

4   Remove the release cylinder mounting bolts.

5   Remove the release cylinder.

### Overhaul

*Refer to illustration 7.6*

6   Remove the pushrod and the boot **(see illustration)**.

7   Tap the cylinder on a block of wood to eject the piston and seal. Remove the spring from inside the cylinder. If the piston is stuck in the bore, you may have to use compressed air to pop it out. If you do so, wear goggles to protect your eyes and place a rag over the end of the release cylinder to prevent the piston from shooting out of the cylinder. Use only enough compressed air to ease the piston out of the bore.

8   Carefully inspect the bore of the cylinder. Check for deep scratches, score marks and ridges. The bore must be smooth to the touch. If any imperfections are found, the release cylinder must be renewed with a new one.

9   Using the new parts in the rebuild kit, assemble the components using plenty of fresh brake fluid for lubrication. Note the direction of the spring and the seal.

### Refitting

10   Refit the release cylinder on the clutch

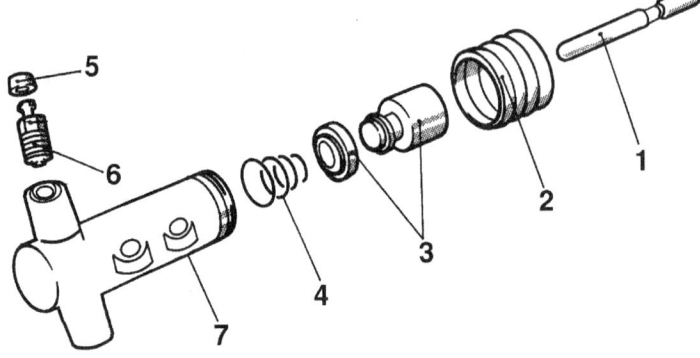

**7.6 An exploded view of the clutch release cylinder assembly**

| | | | | | |
|---|---|---|---|---|---|
| 1 | Pushrod | 4 | Conical spring | 6 | Bleeder plug |
| 2 | Boot | 5 | Cap | 7 | Release cylinder |
| 3 | Piston and cup | | | | |

housing. Make sure the pushrod is seated in the release fork pocket.

11   Using new sealing washers, connect the hydraulic line to the release cylinder. Tighten the banjo bolt securely.

12   Fill the clutch master cylinder with brake fluid (conforming to DOT 4 specifications).

13   Bleed the system (see Section 8).

14   Lower the vehicle and connect the negative battery cable.

## 8   Clutch hydraulic system - bleeding

1   The hydraulic system should be bled of all air whenever any part of the system has been removed or if the fluid level has been allowed to fall so low that air has been drawn into the master cylinder. The procedure is very similar to bleeding a brake system.

2   Fill the master cylinder with new brake fluid conforming to DOT 4 specifications. **Caution:** *Do not re-use any of the fluid coming from the system during the bleeding operation or use fluid which has been inside an open container for an extended period of time.*

3   Raise the vehicle and place it securely on jackstands to gain access to the release cylinder, which is located on the left side of the clutch housing.

4   Remove the dust cap which fits over the bleeder valve and push a length of plastic hose over the valve. Place the other end of the hose into a clear container partially filled with of brake fluid. The hose end must be submerged in the fluid.

5   Have an assistant depress the clutch pedal and hold it. Open the bleeder valve on the release cylinder, allowing fluid to flow through the hose. Close the bleeder valve when fluid stops flowing from the hose. Once closed, have your assistant release the pedal slowly.

6   Continue this process until all air is evacuated from the system, indicated by a full, solid stream of fluid being ejected from the

bleeder valve each time and no air bubbles in the hose or container. Keep a close watch on the fluid level inside the clutch master cylinder reservoir; if the level drops too low, air will be sucked back into the system and the process will have to be started all over again.

7   Refit the dust cap and lower the vehicle. Check carefully for proper operation before placing the vehicle in normal service.

## 9   Driveaxles - general information and inspection

1   Power is transmitted from the transaxle to the front wheels through a pair of driveaxles. The inner end of the left driveaxle is splined to the differential side gear. The inner end of the right driveaxle is splined to the intermediate shaft. The outer ends of the driveaxles are splined to the axle hubs and locked in place by a large nut.

2   The inner ends of the driveaxles are equipped with tripod type joints, which are capable of both angular and axial motion. The outer joints are a "Birfield" design, which consists of ball bearings running between an inner race and an outer cage. Driveaxle inner joints can be disassembled and cleaned in the event of a boot failure, but if any parts are damaged, the joints must be renewed as a unit (see Section 9).

3   The outer CV joint is not serviceable. DO NOT attempt to disassemble the outer joint. If necessary, renew the outer joint and shaft assembly or renew the entire driveaxle with a rebuilt unit.

4   The boots should be inspected periodically for damage and leaking lubricant. Torn CV joint boots must be renewed immediately or the joints can be damaged. Boot renewal involves removal of the driveaxle. **Note:** *Some auto parts stores carry "split" type renewal boots, which can be refitted without removing the driveaxle from the vehicle. This may seem like a convenient alternative, but the CV joint(s) should be disassembled and cleaned*

**10.4  Remove the split pin from the driveaxle/hub nut**

**10.5  To prevent the hub from turning when you're breaking loose the driveaxle/hub nut, wedge a lever between two of the wheel studs and allow the lever to rest against the ground or the floorpan of the vehicle**

*to ensure the joint is free from contaminants such as moisture and dirt which will accelerate CV joint wear.* The most common symptom of worn or damaged CV joints, besides lubricant leaks, is a clicking noise in turns, a clunk when accelerating after coasting and vibration at highway speeds. To check for wear in the CV joints and driveaxle shafts, grasp each axle (one at a time) and rotate it in both directions while holding the CV joint housings, feeling for play indicating worn splines or sloppy CV joints. Also check the driveaxle shafts for cracks, dents and distortion.

## 10  Driveaxles and intermediate shaft - removal and refitting

*Refer to illustrations 10.4, 10.5, 10.6, 10.9, 10.10 and 10.11*

**Caution:** *If the stereo in your vehicle is equipped with an anti-theft system, make sure you have the correct activation code before disconnecting the battery.*
1    Disconnect the cable from the negative terminal of the battery.
2    Set the parking brake.
3    Loosen the front wheel lug nuts, raise

the vehicle and support it securely on jack-stands. Remove the wheel.
4    Remove the split pin from the driveaxle/hub nut **(see illustration)**.
5    Remove the driveaxle/hub nut and washer. To prevent the hub from turning, wedge a lever between two of the wheel studs and allow the lever to rest against the ground or the floor pan of the vehicle **(see illustration)**.
6    To loosen the driveaxle from the hub splines, tap the end of the driveaxle with a soft-faced hammer or a hammer and a soft metal drift **(see illustration)**. If the driveaxle is stuck in the hub splines and won't move, it may be necessary to remove the brake disc and push it from the hub with a two-jaw puller (but only after the control arm is separated from the steering knuckle.
7    Place a drain pan underneath the transaxle to catch any lubricant that leaks out when the driveaxle is removed.
8    Separate the control arm from the steering knuckle and the tie-rod (see Chapter 10).
9    Pull out the steering knuckle and detach the driveaxle from the hub **(see illustration)**.
10    If you're removing the left driveaxle, carefully prise the inner CV joint out of the

**10.6  To loosen the driveaxle from the hub splines, tap the end of the driveaxle with a soft-faced hammer or a hammer and a soft metal drift punch; if the driveaxle is stuck in the hub splines and won't move, it may be necessary to remove the brake disc (see Chapter 9) and push it from the hub with a two-jaw puller**

transaxle **(see illustration)**. Remove the driveaxle, being careful not to overextend the inner CV joint.

**10.9  Pull out on the steering knuckle and detach the driveaxle from the hub**

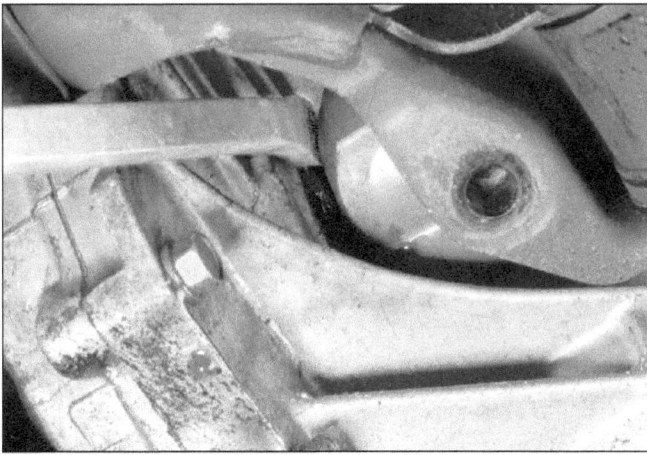

**10.10  If you're removing the right driveaxle, prise the inner CV joint out of the transaxle**

**10.11 The intermediate shaft bearing bracket is fastened to the engine block with three bolts (arrows) - two of three bolts shown**

**11.3  Lift the tabs on all the boot clamps with a screwdriver, then open the clamps**

**11.4  Use a brass bar and a hammer to remove the inner race from the driveaxle (be careful not to hit the cage)**

11    If you're removing the right driveaxle, remove the intermediate shaft bearing bracket-to-engine block bolts **(see illustration)**. Support the driveaxle and pull the intermediate shaft out of the transaxle. If it's stuck, tap on the bearing bracket with a plastic hammer. Check the intermediate shaft bearing for smooth operation. If it feels rough or sticky it should be renewed. Special tools are needed for disassembling the intermediate shaft/bearing bracket assembly. Take it to a dealer service department or an automotive machine shop to have the bearing renewed.

12    Refer to Chapter 7A for the driveaxle seal renewal procedure.

13    Refitting is the reverse of removal, with the following additional points:

a) *When refitting the splined inner end of the driveaxle, push the driveaxle sharply inward to seat the retaining ring on the splined end of the inner CV joint into the groove in the bore of the differential side gear.*

b) *If you're refitting the left driveaxle/intermediate shaft assembly, be sure to tighten the bearing bracket bolts to the*

torque listed in this Chapter's Specifications.

c) *Refit the hub nut washer with the concave side against the hub. Tighten the driveaxle/hub nut to the torque listed in this Chapter's Specifications, then fit a new split pin.*

d) *Refit the wheel and lug nuts, lower the vehicle and tighten the lug nuts to the torque listed in the Chapter 1 Specifications.*

e) *Check the transaxle lubricant and add, if necessary, to bring it to the proper level (see Chapter 1).*

## 11  Driveaxle boot renewal and CV joint inspection

**Note:** *If the driveaxle boots must be renewed, it is imperative that the CV joints be thoroughly cleaned and inspected. Complete rebuilt driveaxles are available on an exchange basis, which eliminates much time and work. Whichever route you choose to take, check on the cost and availability of parts before disassembling the vehicle.*

1    Remove the driveaxle (see Section 10).

### Outer CV joint
#### Removal
*Refer to illustrations 11.3, 11.4, 11.8a, 11.8b, 11.9, 11.10, 11.12a and 11.12b*

2    Mount the driveaxle in a vise with wood lined jaws (to prevent damage to the axleshaft). Check the CV joint for excessive play in the radial direction, which indicates worn parts. Check for smooth operation throughout the full range of motion for each CV joint. If a boot is torn, the recommended procedure is to remove the joint, clean the components and inspect for damage due to loss of lubrication and possible contamination by foreign matter.

3    Using a small screwdriver, prise up on the boot clamp retaining tabs to loosen them **(see illustration)**, then slide the clamps off.

4    Slide the boot back on the axleshaft. Carefully drive the outer CV joint off the axleshaft using a brass punch and a hammer **(see illustration)**. Strike on the inner race only - be careful not to damage the splines or the cage.

5    Remove the boot.

#### Check

6    Clean the CV joint thoroughly with sol-

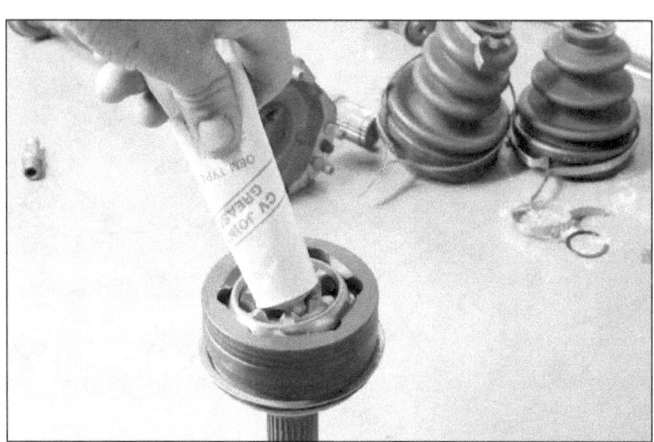

**11.8a  Apply the grease through the hole in the inner race . . .**

**11.8b  . . . then push the grease down into the joint with your finger or a dowel (this will have to be done a few times until the joint is completely packed)**

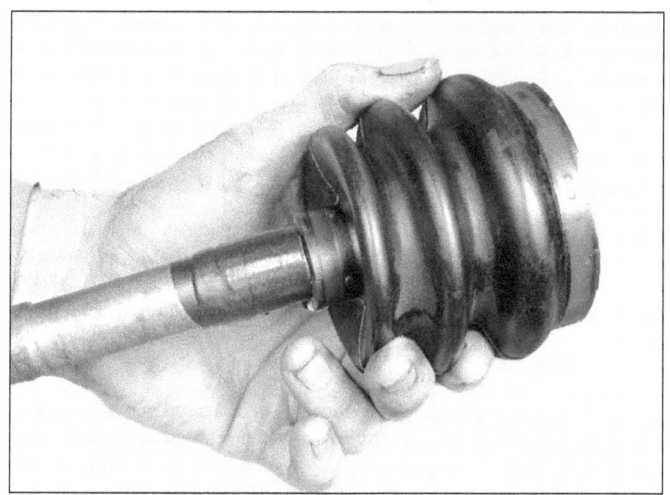

11.9 Wrap the axleshaft splines with tape to prevent damage to the boot

11.10 To refit the outer CV joint onto the axleshaft, place the axleshaft in a vise and tap the joint onto the shaft splines with a hammer and a brass punch

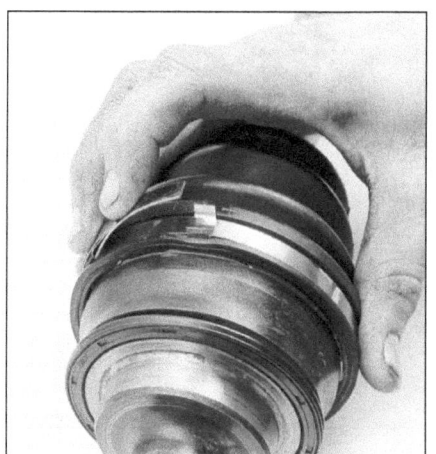

11.12a To fit the new boot clamps, bend the tang down . . .

11.12b . . . then bend the tabs over to hold it in place

11.15 Remove the snap-ring with a pair of snap-ring pliers

vent to remove all grease. Blow the solvent out of the joint with compressed air, if available (if not, rinse the joint out with brake system cleaner, which will dry and leave no residue). Check for cracks, pitting, scoring and other signs of wear. **Caution:** *Don't disassemble the joint.*

7    If there are any signs of damage or excessive wear, renew the outer CV joint as an assembly. There are no parts available separately, so it can't be overhauled.

### Refitting

8    Pack the CV joint with the CV joint grease included in the boot kit **(see illustrations)**. If grease was not included, obtain some CV joint grease - don't use any other type.

9    Slide the new small clamp and the new boot onto the axleshaft. It's a good idea to wrap the splined end of the axleshaft with tape to protect the boot from damage **(see illustration)**. Partially fill the boot with CV joint grease. Place the large boot clamp onto the axleshaft.

10    Fit a new retaining clip onto the end of the axleshaft. Refit the CV joint on the axleshaft and, using a brass hammer, drive the joint onto the shaft **(see illustration)**. Pull out on the CV joint to make sure the retaining clip has seated completely in it's groove in the CV joint inner race.

11    Wipe any excess grease from the boot groove on the outer race of the CV joint. Seat the small diameter end of the boot in the recessed area on the axleshaft. Push the other end of the boot onto the CV joint housing.

12    Insert a small screwdriver between the boot and the housing to equalise the pressure in the boot. Refit the boot clamps and tighten them **(see illustrations)**.

### Inner CV joint

*Refer to illustrations 11.15, 11.18, 11.20 and 11.21*

### Disassembly

13    After removing the boot clamps **(see illustration 11.3)**, pull the boot back from the

inner CV joint and separate the outer housing from the driveaxle. On some models it is necessary to first remove a retaining ring.

14    If you are working on the right driveaxle/ intermediate shaft assembly and you find it necessary to separate the CV joint housing from the intermediate shaft, take the assembly to an automotive machine shop, as a hydraulic press is required.

15    Remove the snap-ring from the end of the axleshaft **(see illustration)**, then slide the tripod joint and bootoff the shaft.

### Check

16    Clean all of the components with solvent to remove the grease. Check for cracks, pitting scoring and other signs of wear. Renew the entire joint if problems are found.

### Reassembly

17    Slide the clamps and boot onto the axleshaft. It's a good idea to wrap the axleshaft splines with tape to prevent damaging the boot **(see illustration 11.9)**.

18    Place the tripod joint on the shaft, mak-

**11.18  Refit the tripod with the recessed portion of the splines facing the axleshaft**

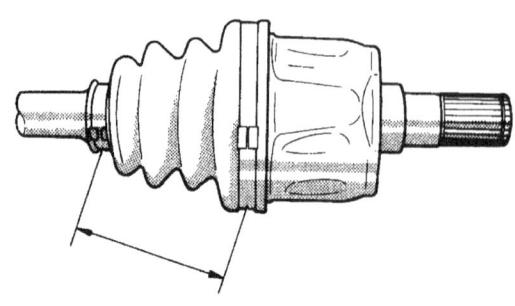

**11.20  Before tightening the boot clamps, adjust the driveaxle length as shown in accordance with the dimensions listed in this Chapter's Specifications (this dimension is critical for maintaining the correct pressure inside sliding CV joints)**

ing sure the chamfered side of the joint faces the centre of the shaft **(see illustration)**. Refit the snap-ring. Apply CV joint grease to the tripod assembly, the inside of the joint housing and the inside of the boot (use CV joint grease only).

19   Refit the joint housing and slide the boot onto the joint. Refit and tighten the small boot clamp **(see illustrations 11.12a and 11.12b)**.

20   Place the driveaxle assembly on a flat surface and pull the shaft out of the inner joint until the distance between the joints is as listed in this Chapter's Specifications. Set the large boot clamp into place and measure the length of the joint between the centrelines of the boot clamps **(see illustration)**.

21   Equalise the pressure in the boot **(see illustration)**, then tighten the outer boot clamp **(see illustrations 11.12a and 11.12b)**.

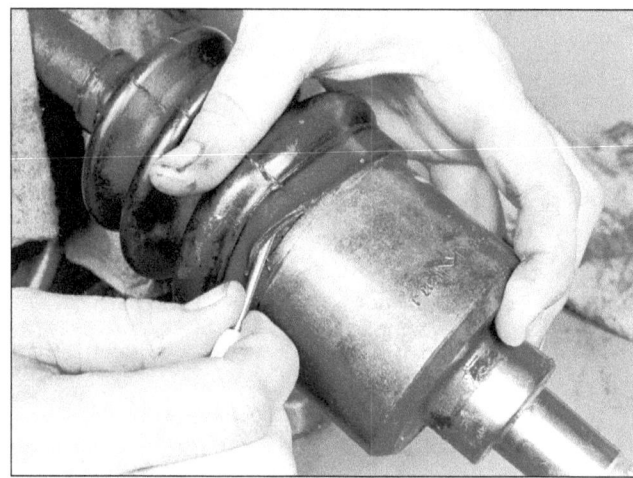

**11.21  Equalise the pressure inside the boot by inserting a small, dull screwdriver between the boot and the outer race**

# Chapter 9   Brakes

## Contents

## Specifications

### General

| | |
|---|---|
| Brake fluid type | See Chapter 1 |
| Brake pedal | |
| Height (between pedal and floorboard) | 168 to 173 mm |
| Freeplay (amount of pedal movement before resistance is met) | 3 to 8 mm |
| Brake light switch-to-brake pedal stopper | 0.5 to 1.0 mm |
| Minimum brake pad thickness | See Chapter 1 |
| Disc thickness limit (minimum)* | |
| Front | 22.4 mm |
| Rear | 8.4 mm |
| Disc runout limit (maximum) | |
| Front | 0.05 mm |
| Rear | 0.06 mm |

* Refer to the marks stamped on the disc (they supersede information printed here).

### Torque specifications

| | Nm |
|---|---|
| Front brake caliper | |
| Caliper mounting bracket bolts | 80 to 100 |
| Guide pin bolts | 30 to 34 |
| Rear brake caliper | |
| Caliper mounting bracket bolts | 50 to 60 |
| Guide pin bolts | 30 to 34 |
| Master cylinder-to-brake booster nuts | 10 to 20 |
| Power brake booster mounting nuts | 11 to 17 |
| Wheel lug nuts | See Chapter 1 |

**2.5 Using a large G-clamp, push the piston back into the caliper - note that one end of the clamp is on the back side of the caliper and the other end (screw end) is pressing on the outer brake pad**

**2.6a Before removing anything, spray the disc, caliper and brake pads with brake system cleaner to remove the dust produced by brake pad wear - DO NOT blow the dust off with compressed air!**

## 1 General information

The vehicles covered by this manual are equipped with hydraulically operated front and rear disc brake systems. All calipers are of a single-piston design. Both the front and rear brakes automatically compensate for disc and pad wear: As the pads wear down, the pistons gradually protrude farther from the calipers, but don't retract as far, automatically compensating for the thinner pads.

### Hydraulic system

The hydraulic system consists of two separate circuits that are diagonally split (one circuit operates the left front and right rear brakes, while the other circuit operates the right front and left rear brakes). The master cylinder has separate reservoirs for the two circuits, and, in the event of a leak or failure in one hydraulic circuit, the other circuit will remain operative. A dual proportioning valve, incorporated within the master cylinder, provides brake balance between the front and rear brakes. A brake warning light switch illuminates a light on the instrument panel if a loss of pressure is indicated in either circuit.

### Power brake booster

The power brake booster, which is mounted on the firewall, utilises engine manifold vacuum and atmospheric pressure to provide assistance to the hydraulically operated brakes.

### Parking brake

The parking brake mechanically operates a dedicated drum brake within the centre portion of each rear brake disc. It's activated by a hand lever mounted in the centre console. Adjustments can be made on the cable inside of the car while each shoe can be adjusted through the adjustment holes on the front of each rotor.

### Service

After completing any operation involving disassembly of any part of the brake system, always test drive the vehicle to check for proper braking performance before resuming normal driving. When testing the brakes, perform the tests on a clean, dry, flat surface. Conditions other than these can lead to inaccurate test results.

Test the brakes at various speeds with both light and heavy pedal pressure. The vehicle should stop evenly without pulling to one side or the other. Avoid locking the brakes, because this slides the tyres and diminishes braking efficiency and control of the vehicle.

Tyres, vehicle load and wheel alignment are factors which also affect braking performance.

### Precautions

There are some general cautions and warnings involving the brake system on this vehicle:

a) *Use only brake fluid conforming to DOT 4 specifications.*

b) *The brake pads and linings may contain asbestos fibres which are hazardous to your health if inhaled. Whenever you work on brake system components, clean all parts with brake system cleaner or denatured alcohol. Do not allow the fine dust to become airborne.*

c) *Safety should be paramount whenever any servicing of the brake components is performed. Do not use parts or fasteners which are not in perfect condition, and be sure that all clearances and torque specifications are adhered to. If you are at all unsure about a certain procedure, seek professional advice. Upon completion of any brake system work, test the brakes carefully in a controlled area before putting the vehicle into normal service.*

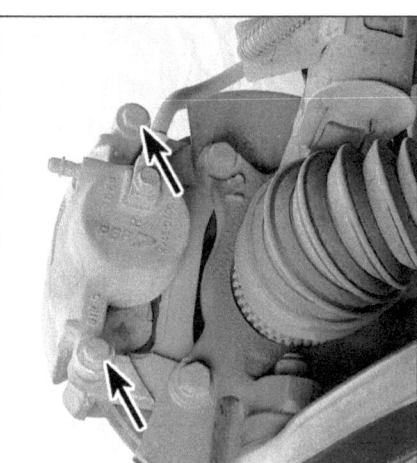

**2.6b Remove the caliper mounting bolts (arrows) and remove the caliper . .**

If a problem is suspected in the brake system, don't drive the vehicle until it's fixed.

## 2 Disc brake pads - renewal

**Warning:** *Disc brake pads must be renewed on both front or rear wheels at the same time - never renew the pads on only one wheel. Also, the dust created by the brake system may contain asbestos, which is harmful to your health. Never blow it out with compressed air and don't inhale any of it. An approved filtering mask should be worn when working on the brakes. Do not, under any circumstances, use petroleum-based solvents to clean brake parts. Use brake system cleaner only!*
**Note 1:** *2002 models use dual piston calipers.*
**Note 2:** *This procedure applies to front and rear disc brakes.*
1 Remove the cap from the brake fluid reservoir.
2 Loosen the wheel lug nuts, raise the

2.6c ... support it in this position with a piece of wire.

2.6d Remove the outer pad and shims

2.6e Remove the inner pad and shims

2.6f Remove the caliper guide pins and dust boots, and inspect them for tears, cracks or heavy wear; if damaged, renew them

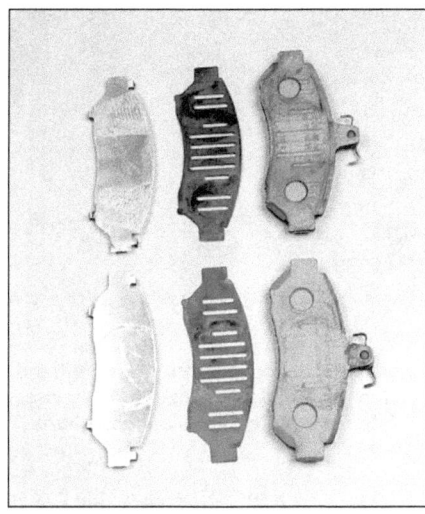

2.6g Typical shim arrangement, 2001 and earlier shown, later models similar

2.6h 2002 and later models use upper and lower anti-rattle clips (arrows)

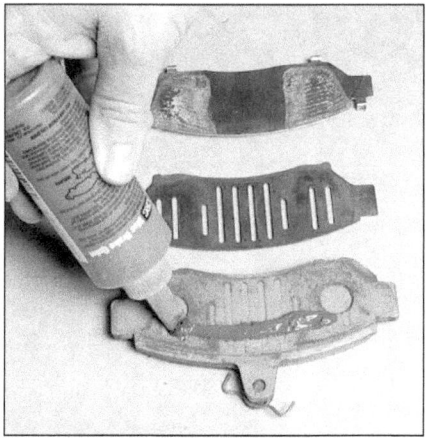

2.6i Apply anti-squeal compound (available at auto parts stores - follow label instructions) to the back of the brake pads, 2001 and earlier shown, 2002 similar

front or rear of the vehicle and support it securely on jackstands.

3    Remove the front or rear wheels. Work on one brake assembly at a time, using the assembled brake for reference if necessary.

4    Inspect the brake disc carefully as outlined in Section 4. If machining is necessary, follow the information in that Section to remove the disc, at which time the pads can be removed as well.

## Front Pads

*Refer to illustrations 2.5 and 2.6a to 2.6n*

5    Push the piston back into its bore to provide room for the new brake pads. A G-clamp can be used to accomplish this **(see illustration)**. As the piston(s) is depressed to the bottom of the caliper bore, the fluid in the master cylinder will rise. Make sure that it doesn't overflow. If necessary, siphon off some of the fluid.

6    Follow the accompanying photos, beginning with **illustration 2.6a**, for the

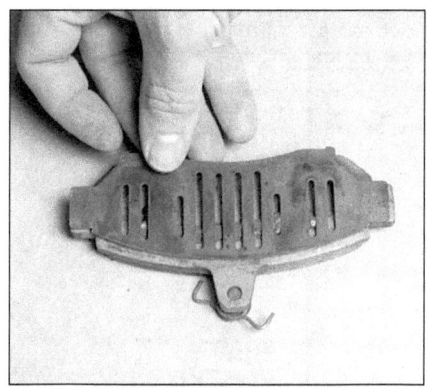

2.6j Refit the inner shim (rubber coated), 2001 and earlier shown, 2002 similar . .

actual pad renewal procedure. Be sure to stay in order and read the caption under each illustration. When you have completed the Steps described in the accompanying photos, proceed to Step 9.

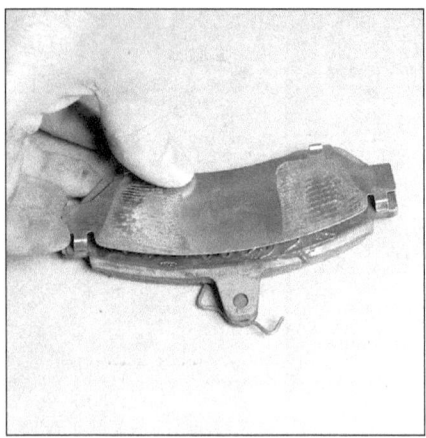

2.6k  then the outer shim (stainless), 2001 and earlier shown, 2002 similar

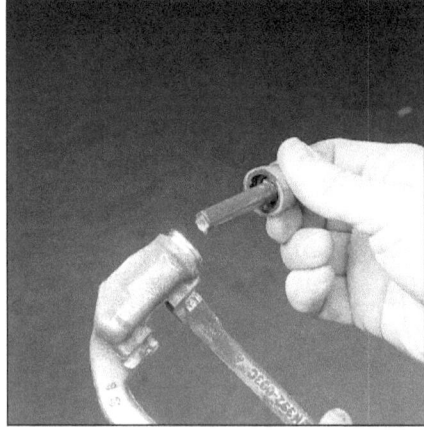

2.6l  Lubricate the guide pins with grease before refitting

2.6m  Fit the new inner pad . . .

2.6n  . . . and the new outer pad into the mounting bracket - make sure both pads are fully seated

2.6o  Refit the caliper into place, refit the lock bolts and tighten them to the torque listed in this Chapter's Specifications

2.7  Using a large G-clamp, push the piston back into the caliper - note that one end of the clamp is on the back side of the caliper and the other end (screw end) is pressing on the outer brake pad

## Rear Pads

*Refer to illustrations 2.7 and 2.8a to 2.8f*

7    Push the piston back into its bore to provide room for the new brake pads. A G-clamp can be used to accomplish this **(see illustration)**. As the piston is depressed

to the bottom of the caliper bore, the fluid in the master cylinder will rise. Make sure that it doesn't overflow. If necessary, siphon off some of the fluid.

8    Follow the accompanying photos, beginning with **illustration 2.8a**, for the

actual pad renewal procedure. Be sure to stay in order and read the caption under each illustration. When you have completed the Steps described in the accompanying photos, proceed to Step 9.

2.8a  Remove the lower caliper mounting bolt - its only necessary to remove the upper bolt if you're removing the caliper from the vehicle

2.8b  Swing the caliper up and secure it with a piece of wire

2.8c  Remove the outer pad and shims

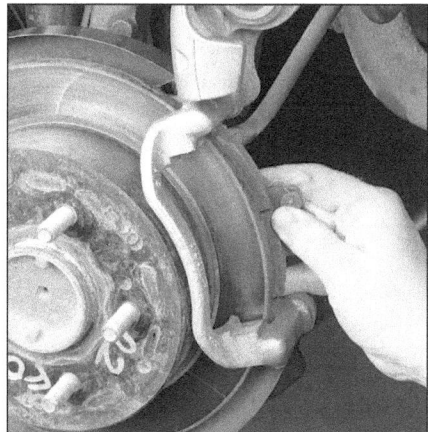

2.8d  Remove the inner pad and shims

2.8e  Fit the new inner pad . . .

2.8f  . . . and the new outer pad into the mounting bracket - make
sure both pads are fully seated

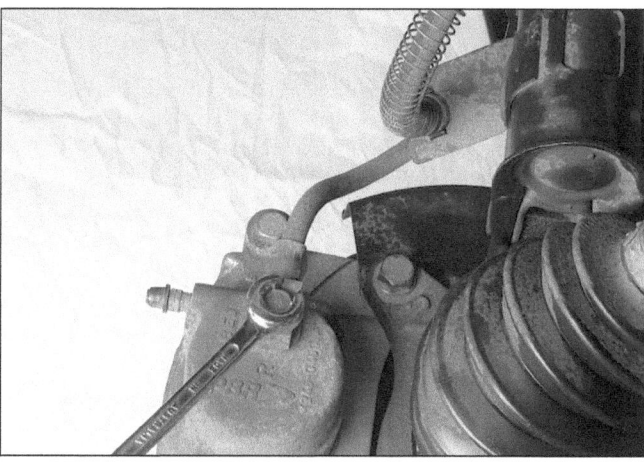

3.1  After the fitting at the other end of the hose has been
disconnected, unscrew the brake hose from the caliper (use a
flare-nut spanner to protect the fitting)

9    When refitting the caliper, be sure to tighten the guide pins to the torque listed in this Chapter's Specifications. After the job has been completed, firmly depress the brake pedal a few times to bring the pads into contact with the disc. Check the level of the brake fluid, adding some if necessary. Check the operation of the brakes carefully before placing the vehicle into normal service.

---

### 3    Caliper - removal, overhaul and refitting

---

**Warning:** *Dust created by the brake system may contain asbestos, which is harmful to your health. Never blow it out with compressed air and don't inhale any of it. An approved filtering mask should be worn when working on the brakes. Do not, under any circumstances, use petroleum-based solvents to clean brake parts. Use brake system cleaner only!*

**Note:** *If an overhaul is indicated (usually because of fluid leakage), explore all options before beginning the job. New and factory rebuilt calipers are available on an exchange*

basis, which makes this job quite easy. If it's decided to rebuild the calipers, make sure a rebuild kit is available before proceeding. Always rebuild the calipers in pairs - never rebuild just one of them.*

### Front
#### Removal
*Refer to illustrations 3.1 and 3.3*

1    Loosen the ABS sensor wire at the strut bracket **(see illustration 6.3)**. Unscrew the brake hose from the caliper **(see illustration)**. **Note:** *If you're removing the caliper to renew the brake pads or to remove the brake disc, go to Section 2 - it isn't necessary to disconnect the brake hose from the caliper unless you're completely removing the caliper from the vehicle.*

2    Plug the brake hose to keep contaminants out of the brake system and to prevent losing any more brake fluid than is necessary.

3    Remove both caliper guide pin locking bolts **(see illustration)** and slide the caliper off.

#### Refitting
4    Refit  the  caliper  by  reversing  the

removal procedure. Tighten the guide pins to the torque listed in this Chapter's Specifications.

5    Bleed the brake system (see Section 7). Make sure there are no leaks from the hose connections. Test the brakes carefully before returning the vehicle to normal service.

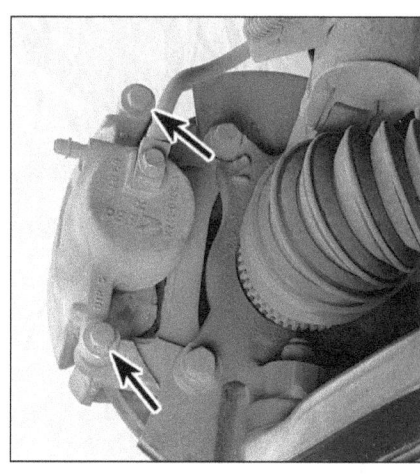

3.3  Front caliper mounting bolt
locations (arrows)

**3.6  Remove the brake hose banjo bolt using a flare-nut spanner to protect the fitting**

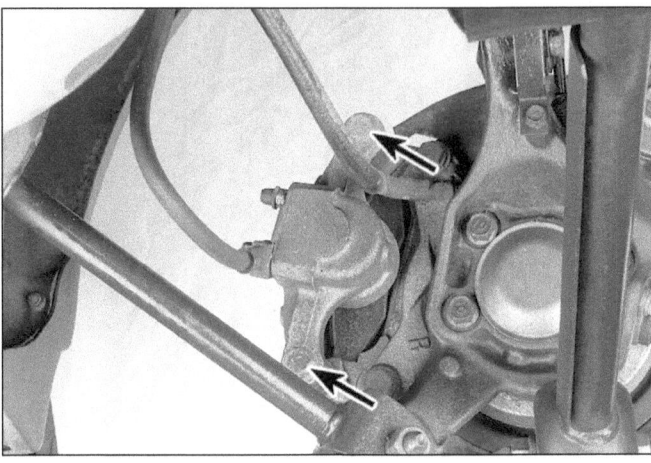

**3.8  Rear caliper mounting bolt locations (arrows)**

## *Rear*

### Removal

*Refer to illustrations 3.6 and 3.8*

6     Unscrew the brake hose from the caliper **(see illustration)**. **Note:** *If you're removing the caliper to renew the brake pads or to remove the brake disc, go to Section 2 - it isn't necessary to disconnect the brake hose from the caliper unless you're completely removing the caliper from the vehicle.*

7     Plug the brake hose to keep contaminants out of the brake system and to prevent losing any more brake fluid than is necessary.

8     Remove both caliper guide pin locking bolts **(see illustration)** and slide the caliper off.

### Refitting

9     Refit the caliper by reversing the removal procedure. Tighten the guide pins to the torque listed in this Chapter's Specifications. Bleed the brake system (see Section 7).

10     Bleed the brake system (see Section 7). Make sure there are no leaks from the hose connections. Test the brakes carefully before returning the vehicle to normal service.

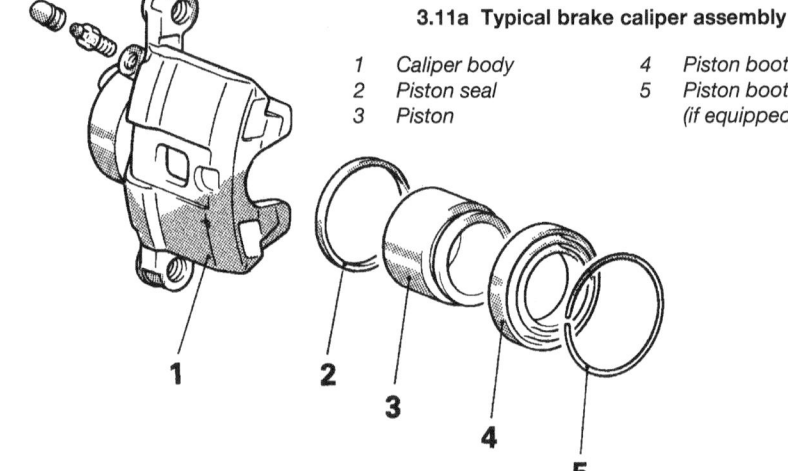

**3.11a  Typical brake caliper assembly**

| | |
|---|---|
| 1   Caliper body | 4   Piston boot |
| 2   Piston seal | 5   Piston boot retainer |
| 3   Piston | (if equipped) |

## *Overhaul*

*Refer to illustrations 3.11a, 3.11b, 3.12, 3.14, 3.18a, 3.18b, 3.18c and 3.18d*

11     Clean the caliper with brake cleaner. If you're working on a dual-piston caliper or a rear caliper on a model with ABS, remove the boot retaining ring(s) and the boot(s) **(see illustrations)**.

12     Place a wood block between the piston and caliper to prevent damage as it is

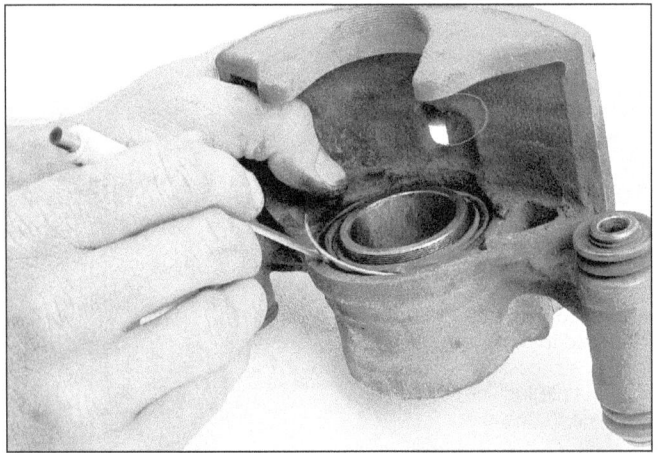

**3.11b  Remove the boot retaining ring with a small screwdriver - be extremely careful not to gouge or scratch the piston or the piston bore**

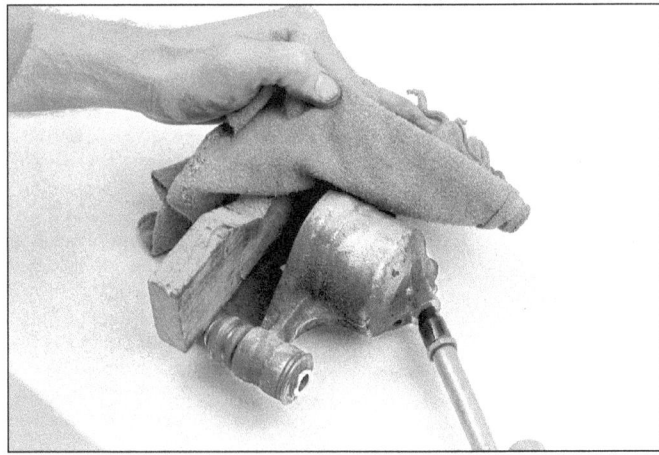

**3.12  With the caliper padded to catch the piston, use compressed air to force the piston out of its bore - make sure your fingers aren't between the piston and the caliper**

**3.14 Remove the piston seal from the caliper bore with a plastic or wood tool - a pencil will do the job (metal tools may damage the cylinder bore)**

**3.18a Fit the dust boot in the upper groove in the caliper bore, making sure it's completely seated**

removed. Apply compressed air to the brake fluid hose connection on the caliper body **(see illustration)**. Use only enough pressure to ease the piston out of its bore. **Warning:** *Be careful not to place your fingers between the piston and the caliper, as the piston may come out with some force. If necessary, remove the piston boot.*

13    Inspect the mating surfaces of the piston and caliper bore wall. If there is any scoring, rust, pitting or bright areas, renew the complete caliper unit with a new one. **Warning:** *Do not attempt to hone the caliper bore.*

14    If these components are in good condition, remove the piston seal from the caliper bore using a wooden or plastic tool **(see illustration)**. Metal tools may damage the cylinder bore.

15    Remove the guide pin dust boots from the caliper body.

16    Wash all the components with brake system cleaner.

17    If you're working on a caliper with a boot retaining ring, submerge the new piston seal(s) and the piston(s) in brake fluid and refit them into the caliper bore. Do not force the piston into the bore, but make sure that it is squarely in place, then apply firm force to bottom it in the bore. Fit the new piston dust boot and the retaining ring.

18    If you're working on a caliper without a boot retaining ring, lubricate the new piston seal with clean brake fluid and fit it in the lower groove in the caliper bore. Fit the flange of the new dust boot in the upper groove in the caliper bore, making sure it is completely seated **(see illustration)**. Lubricate the caliper piston with clean brake fluid. Insert the piston into the lip of the dust boot, using a turning motion to roll the lip over the piston **(see illustration)**. Push the piston to the bottom of the caliper bore, then seat the lip of the dust boot in the groove on the piston **(see illustration)**.

19    Lubricate the guide pins and sleeves with the special grease supplied with the rebuild kit. Fit the guide pin sleeve and the dust boots.

## Refitting

20    Refit the caliper by reversing the removal procedure. Tighten the guide pins to the torque listed in this Chapter's Specifications.

21    Bleed the brake system (see Section 7). Make sure there are no leaks from the hose connections. Test the brakes carefully before returning the vehicle to normal service.

---

**4    Brake disc - inspection, removal and refitting**

---

**Note:** *This procedure applies to both front and rear brake discs.*

## Inspection

*Refer to illustrations 4.3, 4.4a, 4.4b, 4.5a and 4.5b*

1    Loosen the wheel lug nuts, raise the vehicle and support it securely on jackstands. Release the parking brake.

2    Remove the brake caliper (see Section 3) but don't disconnect the brake hose from the caliper. After removing the caliper

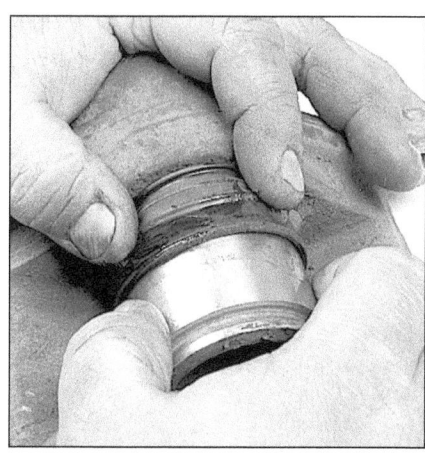

**3.18b Lubricate the piston and bore with clean brake fluid, insert the piston into the dust boot (not the bore) at an angle, then, using a rotating motion, work the piston completely into the dust boot . . .**

lock bolts, suspend the caliper out of the way with a piece of wire **(see illustration 2.6d)**. Fit two lug nuts on the front disc to retain it in place.

**3.18c . . . and push it straight into the caliper as far as possible by hand**

**3.18d Seat the lip of the dust boot in the groove on the caliper piston**

**4.3 The brake pads on this vehicle were obviously neglected - they wore down completely and cut deep grooves into the disc (wear this severe means the disc must be renewed)**

**4.4a Use a dial indicator to measure disc runout - if the reading exceeds the maximum allowable runout limit, the disc will have to be machined or renewed**

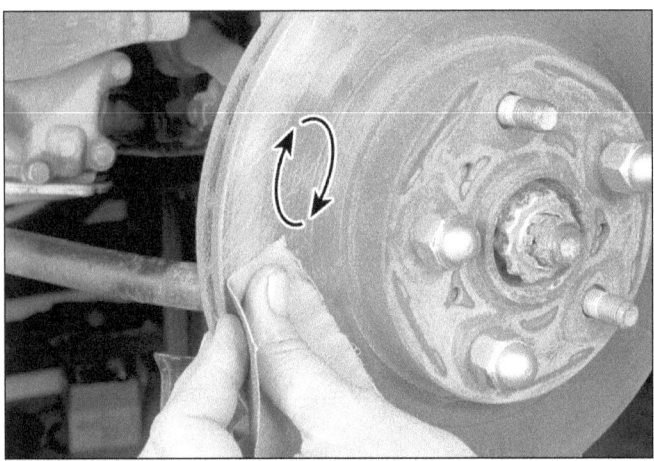

**4.4b Using a swirling motion, remove the glaze from the disc surface with sandpaper or emery cloth**

**4.5a The minimum wear dimension is cast into the back side of the disc (arrow)**

3    Visually inspect the disc surface for score marks and other damage. Light scratches and shallow grooves are normal

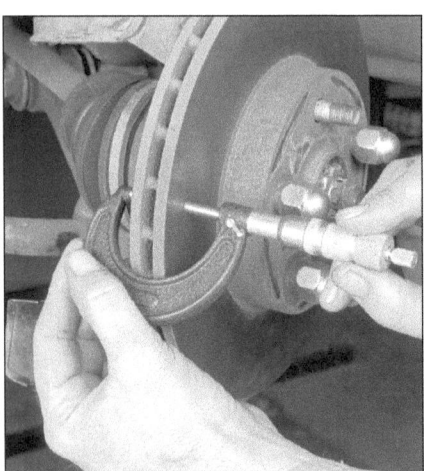

**4.5b Use a micrometer to measure disc thickness**

after use and may not always be detrimental to brake operation, but deep scoring requires disc removal and refinishing by an automotive machine shop. Be sure to check both sides of the disc **(see illustration)**. If pulsating has been noticed during application of the brakes, suspect disc runout.

4    To check disc runout, place a dial indicator at a point about 12 mm from the outer edge of the disc **(see illustration)**. Set the indicator to zero and rotate the disc. The indicator reading should not exceed the specified allowable runout limit. If it does, the disc should be refinished by an automotive machine shop. **Note:** *The discs should be resurfaced regardless of the dial indicator reading, as this will impart a smooth finish and ensure a perfectly flat surface, eliminating any brake pedal pulsation or other undesirable symptoms related to questionable discs. At the very least, if you elect not to have the discs resurfaced, remove the glaze from the surface with emery cloth using a swirling motion* **(see illustration)**.

5    It's absolutely critical that the disc not

be machined to a thickness under the specified minimum allowable disc refinish thickness. The minimum wear (or discard) thickness is cast into the inside of the disc **(see illustration)**. The disc thickness can be checked with a micrometer **(see illustration)**.

### Removal

*Refer to illustrations 4.7a, 4.7b and 4.8*

6    Remove the caliper. **Note:** *If you're removing the caliper to remove the brake disc, go to Section 3 - it isn't necessary to disconnect the brake hose from the caliper unless you're completely removing the caliper from the vehicle.*

7    Remove the caliper mounting bracket **(see illustrations)**.

8    Remove the lug nuts retaining the disc in place and remove the disc from the hub. If the disc is stuck to the hub and won't come off, thread the appropriate size bolts into the holes provided and tighten them. Alternate between the bolts, turning them 1/4-turn at a time, until the disc is free **(see illustration)**.

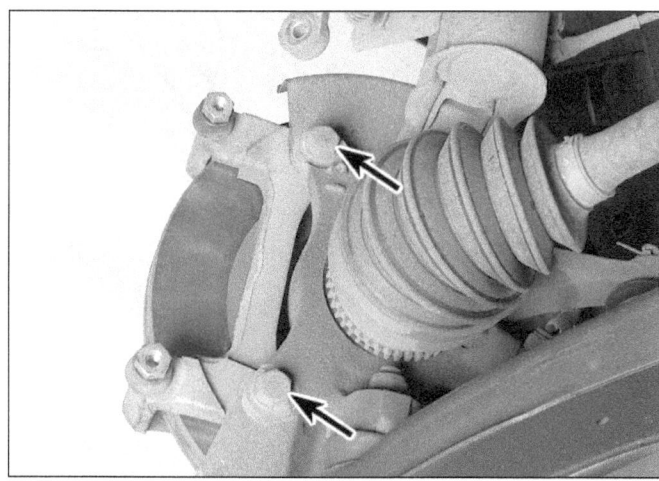

4.7a  Typical front caliper bracket mounting bolts (arrows)

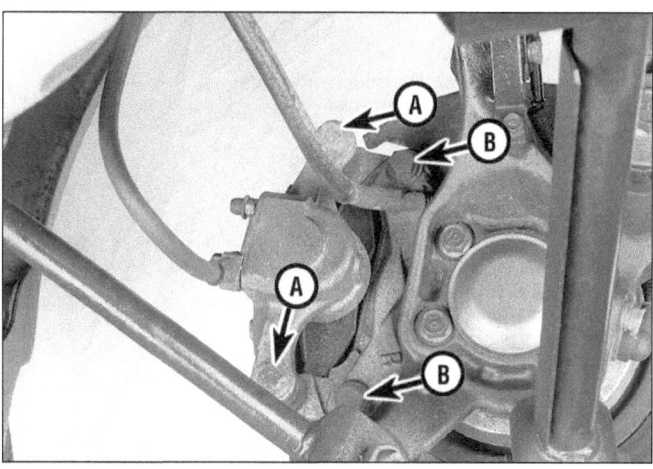

4.7b  Typical rear caliper bracket mounting bolts (arrows)

A    Caliper mounting bolts
B    Caliper bracket mounting bolts

4.8  To help free a stuck disc, thread bolts of the appropriate size into the holes provided in the disc. Alternate between the bolts, turning them a little at a time until the disc is free

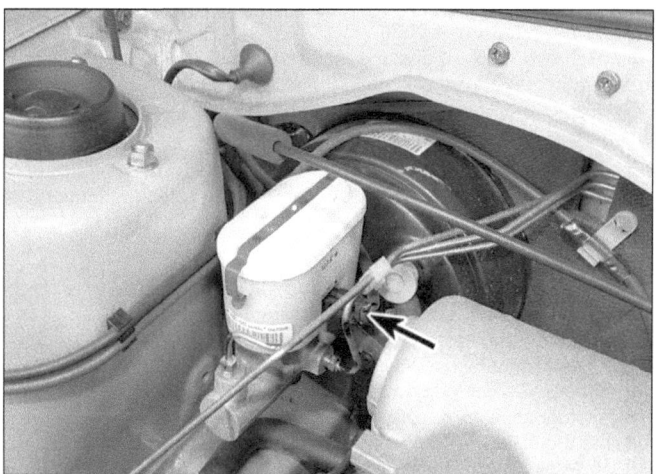

5.4  Disconnect the electrical connector

## Refitting

9    Place the disc in position over the threaded studs.

10   Refit the mounting bracket, tightening the bolts to the torque listed in this Chapter's Specifications.

11   Refit the caliper (see Section 3).

12   Refit the wheel, then lower the vehicle to the ground. Tighten the lug nuts to the torque listed in the Chapter 1 Specifications. Depress the brake pedal a few times to bring the brake pads into contact with the disc. Bleeding won't be necessary unless the brake hose was disconnected from the caliper. Check the operation of the brakes carefully before driving the vehicle.

## 5    Master cylinder - removal, overhaul and refitting

**Note:** *Before deciding to overhaul the master cylinder, check the availability and cost of a new or factory rebuilt unit and also the availability of a rebuild kit.*

## Removal

*Refer to illustrations 5.4 and 5.5*

1    The master cylinder is mounted to the power brake booster.

2    Remove as much fluid as possible from the reservoir with a syringe.

3    Place rags under the fittings and prepare caps or plastic bags to cover the ends of the lines once they're disconnected. **Caution:** *Brake fluid will damage paint. Cover all body parts and be careful not to spill fluid during this procedure.*

4    Disconnect the electrical connector from the brake warning switch **(see illustration)**.

5    Loosen the fittings that attach the brake lines to the master cylinder **(see illustration)**. To prevent rounding off the flats, use a flarenut spanner, which wraps around the fitting hex.

6    Pull the brake lines away from the master cylinder and plug the ends to prevent contamination.

7    Remove the two nuts attaching the master cylinder to the power booster and pull

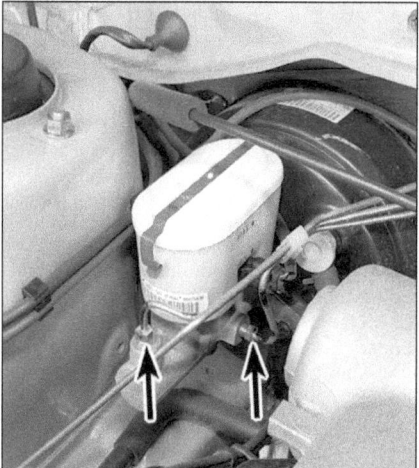

5.5  Completely loosen the brake line fittings (arrows) - use a flare nut spanner so you don't round off the fittings

the master cylinder off the studs. Again, be careful not to spill the fluid as this is done.

## Overhaul

*Refer to illustration 5.9*

8    Thoroughly clean the master cylinder body. Remove the reservoir cap, then discard any fluid remaining in the reservoir.

9    Remove the reservoir retaining bolt, separate the plastic reservoir from the aluminium body, and remove the grommet from each reservoir port **(see illustration)**.

10    Hold the cylinder body so the reservoir ports point down. Using a wooden dowel, push the primary piston into the cylinder until it bottoms in the main bore. The secondary piston stop pin should fall out of the secondary reservoir port; if it doesn't, remove it with needle-nose pliers.

11    Remove the primary piston assembly from the cylinder bore.

12    Tap the cylinder against a block of wood to expel the secondary piston and its spring from the main bore.

13    Taking care not to mar the piston surfaces, carefully prise the seal retainer from the primary piston.

14    Remove the seal and the recuperating guide from the primary piston.

15    Remove all remaining seals from both the primary and secondary pistons.

16    Clean the master cylinder body and components with brake system cleaner. **Warning:** *DO NOT use petroleum-based solvents to clean brake parts - use brake system cleaner only.*

17    Inspect the cylinder bore for corrosion and damage. If any corrosion or damage is found, renew the master cylinder body, as abrasives cannot be used on the bore. **Warning:** *Do not attempt to hone the cylinder bore!*

18    Before assembly, lubricate all parts with clean brake fluid.

19    Fit a new large O-ring onto the large end of the primary piston.

20    At the other end of the primary piston, fit a new recuperating guide onto the piston, then fit a new primary seal and new seal retainer. Use a small screwdriver to clip the retainer legs to the piston groove. Take care not to damage the piston or seal.

21    Be sure the small end of the secondary spring engages the end of the secondary piston.

22    Carefully insert the secondary piston assembly into the main bore of the cylinder. Be sure that the end with the secondary spring goes in first and that the larger slotted hole faces up towards the reservoir ports.

23    Use a wooden dowel to press the secondary piston to the bottom of the main bore, and then pin the piston in place by inserting the stop pin through the secondary reservoir port so the pin engages the large slotted hole in the piston. No more than 6 mm of the pin should protrude above the port.

24    Insert the primary piston into the main bore until the piston end is flush with the end of the bore. Be sure the primary piston properly engages the end of the secondary piston.

25    Compress the piston through several strokes to be sure the movement is smooth

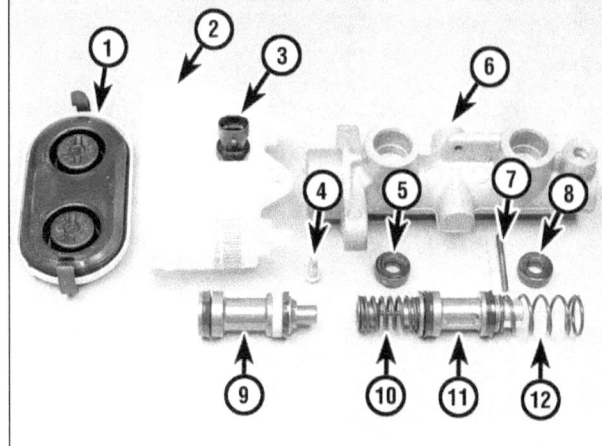

**5.9 Typical master cylinder exploded view**

1    *Reservoir cap and diaphragm*
2    *Reservoir*
3    *Brake fluid level switch*
4    *Reservoir bolt*
5    *Reservoir seal*
6    *Master cylinder body*
7    *Piston stopper pin*
8    *Reservoir seal*
9    *Primary piston*
10   *Primary piston spring*
11   *Secondary piston*
12   *Secondary piston spring*

and that the primary piston returns to the end of the bore.

26    Lubricate both ports and both grommets with clean brake fluid and refit each grommet so it's seated against the shoulder of its respective bore.

27    Set the reservoir in place in the ports. Press the reservoir down into the ports so its retaining bolt hole is aligned with the hole in the cylinder body. Secure the reservoir in place with the retaining bolt.

28    **Note:** *Whenever the master cylinder is removed, the complete hydraulic system must be bled. The time required to bleed the system can be reduced if the master cylinder is filled with fluid and bench bled (refer to Steps 29 through 32) before the master cylinder is refitted on the vehicle.*

29    Insert threaded plugs of the correct size into the cylinder outlet holes and fill the reservoirs with brake fluid. The master cylinder should be supported in such a manner that brake fluid will not spill during the bench bleeding procedure.

30    Loosen one plug at a time, starting with the secondary outlet port first, and push the piston assembly into the bore to force air from the master cylinder. To prevent air from being drawn back into the cylinder, the appropriate plug must be renewed before allowing the piston to return to its original position.

31    Stroke the piston three or four times for each outlet to ensure that all air has been expelled.

32    Since high pressure is not involved in the bench bleeding procedure, an alternative to the removal and renewal of the plugs with each stroke of the piston assembly is available. Before pushing in on the piston assembly, remove one of the plugs completely. Before releasing the piston, however, instead of renewing the plug, simply put your finger tightly over the hole to keep air from being drawn back into the master cylinder. Wait several seconds for the brake fluid to be drawn from the reservoir to the piston bore, then repeat the procedure. When you push down on the piston it will force your finger off the hole, allowing the air inside to

be expelled. When only brake fluid is being ejected from the hole, renew the plug and go on to the other port.

33    Refill the master cylinder reservoirs and refit the diaphragm and cap assembly.

## Refitting

34    Refit the master cylinder over the studs on the power brake booster and tighten the nuts only finger-tight at this time. Connect the reservoir hoses to the inlet fittings and refit the clamps.

35    Thread the brake line fittings into the master cylinder. Since the master cylinder is still a bit loose, it can be moved slightly so the fittings thread in easily. Don't strip the threads as the fittings are tightened.

36    Tighten the mounting nuts and the brake line fittings.

37    Fill the master cylinder reservoir with fluid, then bleed the master cylinder and the brake system (see Section 7). To bleed the master cylinder on the vehicle, have an assistant depress the brake pedal and hold it down. Loosen the fitting to allow air and fluid to escape. Tighten the fitting, then allow your assistant to return the pedal to its rest position. Repeat this procedure on both fittings until the fluid is free of air bubbles. Check the operation of the brake system carefully before driving the vehicle.

---

## 6    Brake hoses and lines - inspection and renewal.

---

## Inspection

1    About every six months, with the vehicle raised and supported securely on jackstands, the rubber hoses which connect the steel brake lines with the front and rear brake assemblies should be inspected for cracks, chafing of the outer cover, leaks, blisters and other damage. These are important and vulnerable parts of the brake system and inspection should be complete. A light and mirror will be helpful for a thorough check. If a hose exhibits any of the above conditions, renew it with a new one.

**6.3 To disconnect a brake hose from a metal line, locate the bracket on the strut where they're connected, hold the hose fitting with an open-end spanner and unscrew the brake line fitting from the hose with a flare-nut spanner to prevent rounding off the corners**

## Renewal

### Front brake hose

*Refer to illustrations 6.3 and 6.4*

2    Loosen the wheel lug nuts, raise the vehicle and support it securely on jackstands. Remove the wheel.

3    At the strut or frame bracket, hold the hose fitting with an open-end spanner and unscrew the brake line fitting from the hose **(see illustration)**. Use a flare-nut spanner to prevent rounding off the corners.

4    Remove the U-clip from the female fitting at the bracket with a pair of pliers, then pass the hose through the bracket **(see illustration)**.

5    Unscrew the hose from the caliper.

6    To refit the hose, thread the hose into the caliper and tighten it securely.

7    Insert the female end of the hose into the strut bracket and refit the U-clip. Make sure the hose isn't twisted.

8    Connect the brake line fitting, starting the threads by hand. Tighten the fitting securely.

9    Bleed the caliper (see Section 7).

10    Refit the wheel and lug nuts, lower the vehicle and tighten the lug nuts to the torque listed in the Chapter 1 Specifications.

### Rear brake hose

11    Perform Steps 2, 3 and 4, then repeat Steps 3 and 4 at the other end of the hose. Be sure to bleed the caliper (see Section 7).

### Metal brake lines

12    When renewing brake lines, be sure to use the correct parts. Don't use copper tubing for any brake system components. Purchase steel brake lines from a dealer or auto parts store.

13    Prefabricated brake line, with the tube ends already flared and fittings refitted, is available at auto parts stores and dealer parts departments. These lines are also bent to the proper shapes.

14    When fitting the new line, make sure it's securely supported in the brackets and has plenty of clearance between moving or hot components.

15    After refitting, check the master cylinder fluid level and add fluid as necessary. Bleed the brake system (see Section 7) and test the brakes carefully before driving the vehicle in traffic.

---

## 7    Brake hydraulic system - bleeding

*Refer to illustration 7.8*

**Warning:** *Wear eye protection when bleeding the brake system. If the fluid comes in contact with your eyes, immediately rinse them with water and seek medical attention.*

**Note:** *Bleeding the hydraulic system is neces-*

*sary to remove any air that manages to find its way into the system when it's been opened during removal and refitting of a hose, line, caliper or master cylinder.*

1    You'll probably have to bleed the system at all four brakes if air has entered it due to low fluid level, or if the brake lines have been disconnected at the master cylinder.

2    If a brake line was disconnected only at a wheel, then only that caliper or wheel cylinder must be bled.

3    If a brake line is disconnected at a fitting located between the master cylinder and any of the brakes, that part of the system served by the disconnected line must be bled.

4    Remove any residual vacuum from the brake power booster by applying the brake several times with the engine off.

5    Remove the master cylinder reservoir cover and fill the reservoir with brake fluid. Refit the cover. **Note:** *Check the fluid level often during the bleeding operation and add fluid as necessary to prevent the fluid level from falling low enough to allow air bubbles into the master cylinder.*

6    Have an assistant on hand, as well as a supply of new brake fluid, a clear plastic container partially filled with clean brake fluid, a length of plastic, rubber or vinyl tubing to fit over the bleeder valve and a spanner to open and close the bleeder valve. **Note:** *If you're working on a model equipped with ABS, start the engine and allow it to idle throughout the procedure. Make sure the wheels are securely blocked.*

7    Beginning at the left rear wheel, loosen the bleeder valve slightly, then tighten it to a point where it's snug but can still be loosened quickly and easily.

8    Place one end of the tubing over the bleeder valve and submerge the other end in brake fluid in the container **(see illustration)**.

9    Have the assistant pump the brakes slowly a few times to get pressure in the system, then hold the pedal down firmly.

10    While the pedal is held down, open the bleeder valve just enough to allow a flow of

**6.4 Remove the U-clip from the female fitting at the bracket with pliers, then pass the hose through the bracket**

**7.8 When bleeding the brakes, connect a hose to the bleed screw at the caliper and submerge the end in brake fluid - air will be seen as bubbles in the tube and container (all air must be expelled before moving to the next wheel)**

fluid to leave the valve. Watch for air bubbles to exit the submerged end of the tube. When the fluid flow slows after a couple of seconds, close the valve and have your assistant release the pedal.

11   Repeat Steps 9 and 10 until no more air is seen leaving the tube, then tighten the bleeder valve and proceed to the right front wheel, the right rear wheel and the left front wheel, in that order, and perform the same procedure. Be sure to check the fluid in the master cylinder reservoir frequently.

12   Never use old brake fluid. It contains moisture which can boil, rendering the brakes useless.

13   Refill the master cylinder with fluid at the end of the operation.

14   Check the operation of the brakes. The pedal should feel solid when depressed, with no sponginess. If necessary, repeat the entire process. *Warning: Do not operate the vehicle if you're in doubt about the effectiveness of the brake system.*

---

**8   Power brake booster - check, removal and refitting**

## *Operating check*

1   Depress the pedal and start the engine. If the pedal goes down slightly, operation is normal.

2   Depress the brake pedal several times with the engine running and make sure there's no change in the pedal reserve distance.

## *Airtightness check*

3   Start the engine and turn it off after one or two minutes. Depress the brake pedal slowly several times. If the pedal depresses farther the first time but gradually rises after the second or third time, the booster is airtight.

4   Depress the brake pedal while the engine is running, then stop the engine with

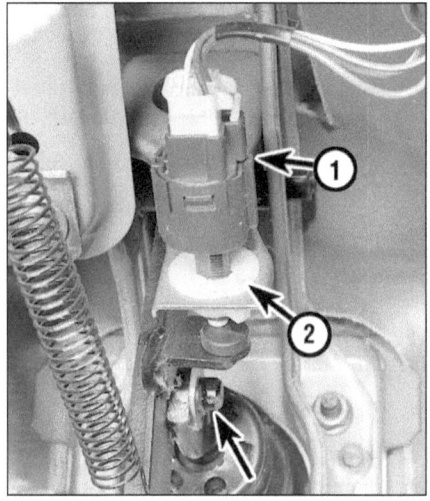

**8.7   To disconnect the brake booster pushrod from the brake pedal, remove the split pin (arrow), pull out the clevis pin and detach the clevis from the brake pedal; to renew the brake light switch, unplug the electrical connector (1) from the switch and unscrew the switch from the pedal bracket (2)**

the pedal depressed. If there's no change in the pedal reserve travel after holding the pedal for 30 seconds, the booster is airtight.

## *Removal*

*Refer to illustrations 8.7 and 8.11*

5   Power brake booster units shouldn't be disassembled. They require special tools not normally found in most automotive repair stations or shops. They're fairly complex and, because of their critical relationship to brake performance, should be renewed with a new or rebuilt one.

6   To remove the booster, first remove the brake master cylinder (see Section 5).

7   Remove the right side under-dash panel. Locate the pushrod clevis connecting the booster to the brake pedal **(see illustration)**. It's accessible from inside the vehicle,

under the dash on the driver's side.

8   Remove the clevis pin retaining clip with pliers.

9   Slide the pushrod off the clevis pin.

10   Disconnect the hose leading from the engine to the booster. Be careful not to damage the hose when removing it from the booster fitting.

11   Remove the four nuts and washers holding the brake booster to the firewall **(see illustration)**.

12   Slide the booster straight out from the firewall until the studs clear the holes.

## *Refitting*

13   Fitting procedures are basically the reverse of removal. Tighten the booster mounting nuts to the torque listed in this Chapter's Specifications.

14   After the final fitting of the master cylinder and brake hoses and lines, the brake pedal height and freeplay must be adjusted and the system must be bled. See the appropriate Sections of this Chapter for the procedures.

---

**9   Parking brake - adjustment**

*Refer to illustrations 9.3, 9.5 and 9.6*

1   The parking brake lever, when properly adjusted, should travel three to five clicks when a moderate pulling force is applied. If it travels less than four clicks, there's a chance the parking brake might not be releasing completely and might be dragging. If the lever can be pulled up more than eight clicks, the parking brake may not hold adequately on an incline, allowing the car to roll.

2   To gain access to the parking brake cable adjuster, remove the centre console (see Chapter 11).

3   Loosen the adjusting nut **(see illustration)** to allow a little slack in the cables.

4   Raise the rear of the vehicle and support it securely with jackstands. Remove both rear wheels.

5   Prise the adjustment hole cover out

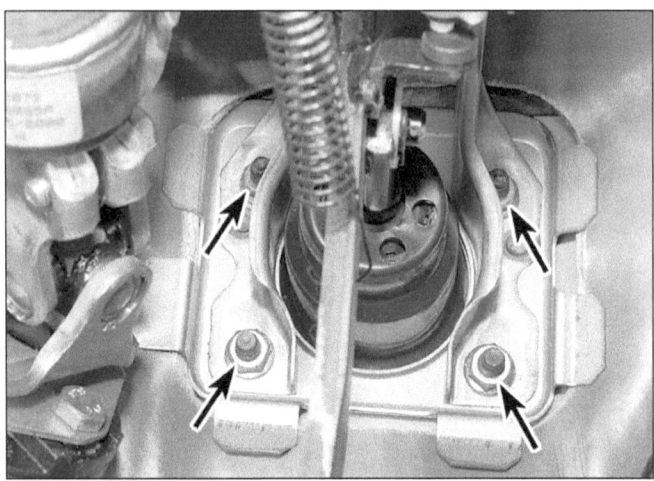

**8.11   Remove the four nuts (arrows) and washers holding the brake booster to the firewall**

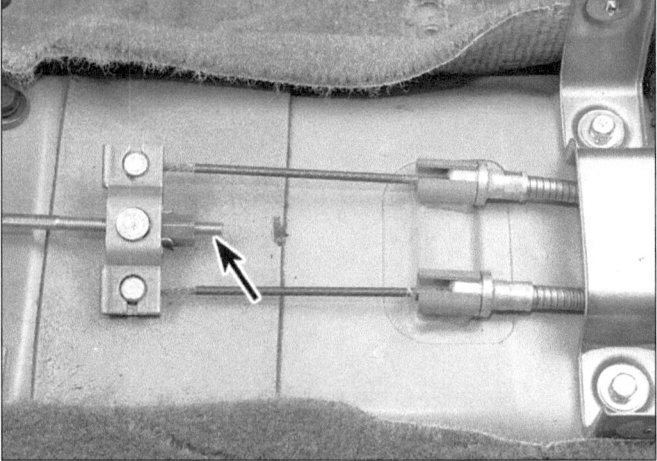

**9.3   The parking brake is adjusted by tightening this nut (arrow) at the parking brake equaliser**

**9.5  Prise the rubber plug from the disc**

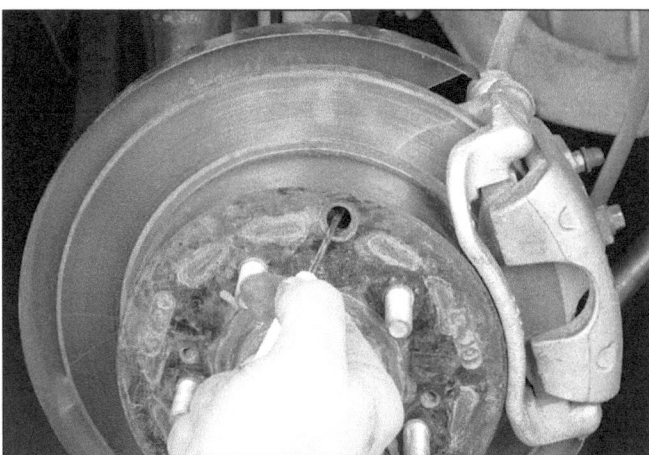

**9.6  Use a small screwdriver to adjust the starwheel**

using a small screwdriver **(see illustration)**

6    Insert a small screwdriver into the access hole in each disc and adjust the star wheels so that the discs cannot be moved. Back off the adjustment 5 clicks so that the discs rotate freely **(see illustration)**.

7    Tighten the hand brake cable adjuster until all the slack is removed.

8    If necessary, repeat the hand lever adjustment to attain 3 to 5 clicks movement with a firm lever operation.

9    Refit the wheel, then lower the vehicle to the ground. Tighten the lug nuts to the torque listed in the Chapter 1 Specifications.

10    Refit the console.

## 10  Parking brake lever and cables - renewal

### Parking brake lever

1    Remove the centre console (see Chapter 11).

2    With the lever in the down (off) position, remove the adjusting nut from the equaliser (see Section 9) and detach the cables from the equaliser **(see illustration 9.3)**.

3    Disconnect the parking brake warning light switch and remove the parking brake lever mounting bolts. Remove the assembly from the vehicle.

4    Refitting is the reverse of the removal procedure. Apply a light coat of grease to the portion of the cable end that contacts the equaliser. Adjust the parking brake (see Section 9).

### Parking brake cables

*Refer to illustrations 10.9 and 10.10*

5    Remove the centre console and the rear seat cushion (see Chapter 11).

6    Remove the adjusting nut (see Section 9) and disconnect the cables from the equaliser.

7    Pull back the carpet and remove the cable clamp from inside the vehicle.

8    Raise the vehicle and support it securely on jackstands. Remove the rear wheel.

9    Remove the upper caliper bracket mounting bolt and remove the bolt from the cable attaching strap **(see illustration)**.

10    Disconnect the cable eyelet from the parking brake lever **(see illustration)**.

11    Remove the cable clamps from the body and rear suspension members.

12    Pull the cable through the body opening

from inside the vehicle.

13    Refit the cable, connecting the eyelets to the brake. Refit the cable clamps, but leave the bolts loose at this time.

14    Tighten the front and rear cable clamps from underneath the vehicle, apply the parking brake then tighten the centre clamp. With the parking brake still applied, tighten the clamp inside the vehicle.

15    Apply a bead of RTV sealant around the grommets and fit the grommets to the body.

16    Refit the wheel, then lower the vehicle to the ground. Tighten the lug nuts to the torque listed in the Chapter 1 Specifications.

17    Adjust the parking brake (see Section 9).

18    The remainder of refitting is the reverse of removal.

## 11  Parking brake shoe - inspection and renewal

*Refer to illustrations 11.3, 11.4, 11.5 and 11.7*

**Warning 1:** *Dust created by the brake system may contain asbestos, which is hazardous to your health. Never blow it out with compressed air and don't inhale any of it. An approved filtering mask should be worn*

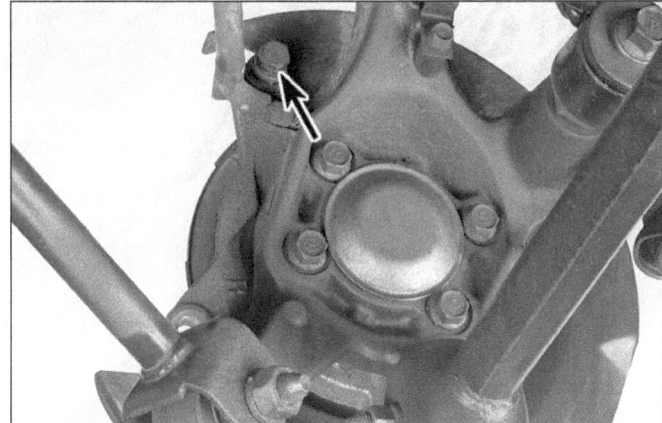

**10.9  Remove the upper caliper bracket mounting bolt and cable attaching strap (arrow) - (sedan shown wagon similar)**

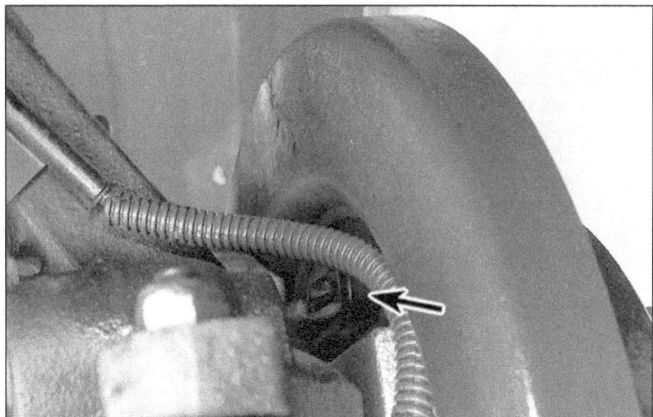

**10.10  Remove the cable eyelet (arrow) from the lever by pulling away from the cable and over the lever - (sedan shown wagon similar)**

**11.3  Before removing anything, spray the parking brake shoe with brake system cleaner to remove the dust produced by brake shoe wear - DO NOT blow the dust off with compressed air! - (sedan shown wagon similar)**

**11.4  Loosen the star adjuster wheel to allow the shoe to be removed easily - (sedan shown wagon similar)**

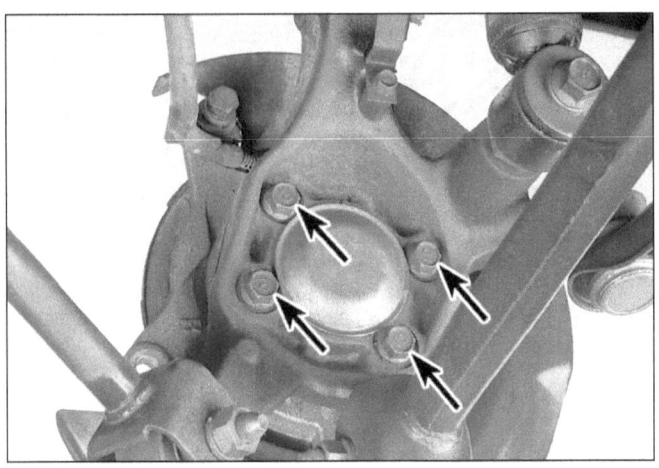

**11.5  Remove the hub mounting bolts and remove the hub assembly - (sedan shown wagon similar)**

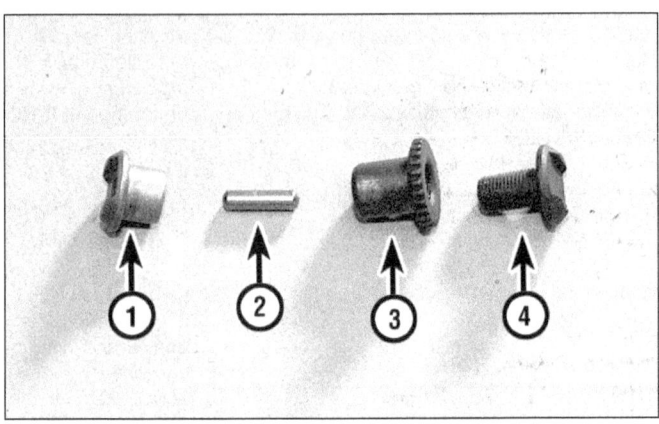

**11.7  Exploded view of the brake shoe adjuster**

| | | | |
|---|---|---|---|
| 1 | Tappet | 3 | Starwheel |
| 2 | Pushrod | 4 | Adjuster tappet |

when working on the brakes. Do not, under any circumstances, use petroleum-based solvents to clean brake parts. Use brake system cleaner only!

**Warning 2:** Parking brake shoes must be renewed on both wheels at the same time - never renew the shoes on only one wheel.

1    Remove the brake disc (see Section 4).

2    Inspect the thickness of the lining material on the shoes. If the lining has worn down to 1 mm or less, the shoe must be renewed.

3    Wash off the brake parts with brake system cleaner **(see illustration)**.

4    Loosen the star adjuster to allow the shoe to come off freely **(see illustration)**.

5    Remove the four hub mounting bolts and remove the hub assembly for improved access to the parking brake shoes **(see illustration)** (see Chapter 10).

6    Slide the shoe off. **Note:** On station wagon models slide the shoe off from the top (upwards) and on sedan models slide the shoe off from the bottom (downwards).

7    Clean and inspect the adjuster assembly **(see illustration)**.

8    Apply a thin coat of high-temperature brake grease to the shoe contact areas of the backing plate.

9    Fit the new shoes by reversing the removal procedure.

10    Refit the brake disc. Temporarily thread three of the wheel lug nuts onto the studs to hold the disc in place.

11    Remove the hole plug from the brake disc. Adjust the parking brake shoe clearance by turning the adjuster star wheel **(see illustration 9.6)** with a brake adjusting tool or screwdriver until the shoes contact the disc and the disc can't be turned. Back-off the adjuster 5 clicks or until the disc can turn without the parking brake shoes dragging, then refit the hole plug.

12    Refit the caliper mounting bracket and brake caliper. Be sure to tighten the bolts to the torque listed in this Chapter's Specifications.

13    Refit the wheel and tighten the lug nuts to the torque specified in Chapter 1.

14    Adjust the parking brake lever if necessary (see Section 9).

## 12  Brake light switch - removal, refitting and adjustment

### Removal and refitting

1    The brake light switch is located on a bracket at the top of the brake pedal **(see illustration 8.7)**.

2    Disconnect the negative battery cable from the battery.

3    Disconnect the wiring harness connector from the brake light switch.

4    Loosen the locknut and unscrew the switch from the pedal bracket.

5    Refitting is the reverse of removal.

### Adjustment

6    Loosen the locknut, adjust the switch so the brake pedal has 3 to 8 mm of freeplay at the pedal pad. Tighten the locknut.

7    Connect the wiring harness connector to the switch. Connect the negative cable to the battery. Make sure the brake lights are functioning properly.

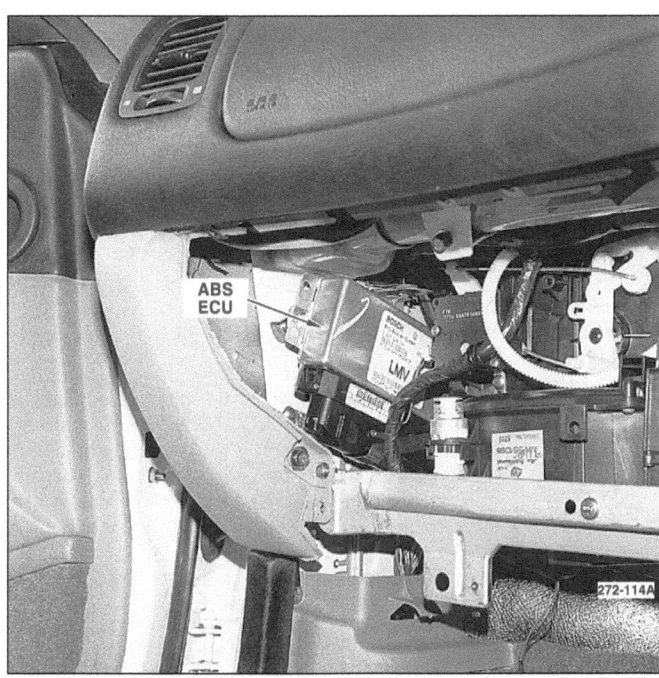

**13.2a ABS ECU viewed with the glove compartment removed**

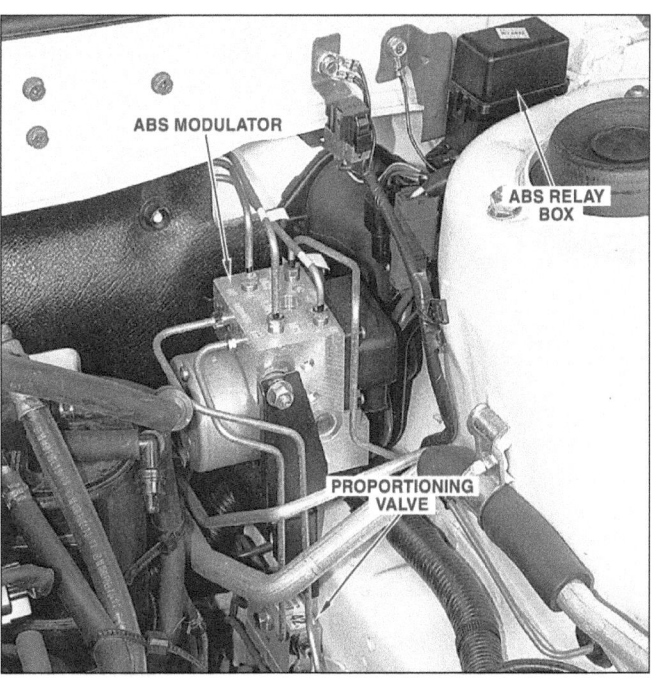

**13.2b The ABS modulator is located in front of the firewall on the passenger side of the engine compartment**

## 13  Antilock Brake System (ABS) and Traction/Slip Control (TCL)

*Refer to illustrations 13.2a and 13.2b*

### Description

1    The Anti-lock Brake System (ABS) and Traction/slip control (TCL) are designed to help maintain vehicle steerability, directional stability and optimum deceleration under severe braking or maneuvering conditions and on most road surfaces. The ABS system is primarily designed to prevent wheel lockup during heavy or panic braking situations. It works by monitoring the rotational speed of each wheel and controlling the brake line pressure to each wheel when engaged. Data provided by the ABS wheel speed sensors is shared with the Traction/slip control (TCL). The traction/slip control is a very sophis-

ticated system, which helps with traction control, over/under-steering and acceleration control under all driving conditions with the use of ABS-ECU, TCL-ECU, A/T-ECU, accelerator pedal position sensor (APS) and the steering wheel sensor. Overall, these systems aid in vehicle control and handling.

2    The antilock braking system (ABS) consists of a modulator located in front of the firewall in the left hand side of the engine compartment, an electronic control unit (ECU) located behind the instrument cluster, sensors mounted to the front steering knuckles, sensors mounted to the rear carrier brackets and pulse rings mounted to the drive shafts and to the inside of the rear hub assemblies **(see illustrations)**.

3    The slots in the pulse ring generate pulses in the wheel sensor which are transmitted to the ECU which then calculates wheel speed and deceleration rates.

4    The ECU signals the modulator assembly to increase or decrease hydraulic pressure to each wheel individually, to maintain minimum wheel rotation without locking.

5    Illumination of the dashboard warning lamp longer than 3 seconds after the engine is started, indicates a problem within the ABS system. Below are a several minor checks that can assist in tracing some of the more common faults within the ABS system. If these checks fail to find the fault, refer the vehicle to an authorised dealer or brake specialist with the equipment and knowledge needed to diagnose and repair the ABS system.

### ABS System checks

*Refer to illustrations 13.8, 13.9a and 13.9b*

6    Raise the front and rear of the vehicle and support on chassis stands. Refer to General Information (chapter 1) for the position of

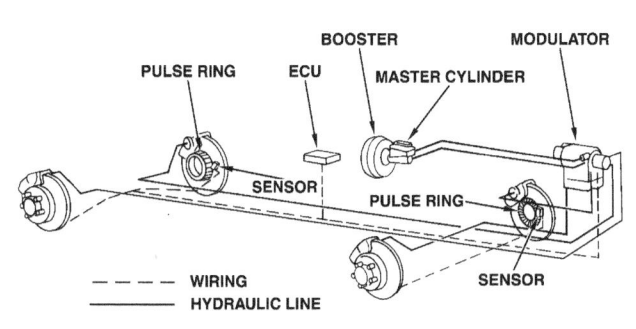

**13.8 Typical ABS components**

**13.9a Front ABS sensor and pulse ring**

**13.9b  Rear ABS sensor, Sedan
model shown**

the jacking and support points.

7    Check the front and rear wheel bearings, ensuring that there is no excessive free-play or wear. Refer to the relevant Axle and Suspension chapter, if necessary.

8    Inspect the front and rear ABS wheel sensors and front pulse rings for any signs of damage or being loose. Tighten or renew the ABS wheel sensors where necessary, or renew the drive shaft or the rear hub assembly **(see illustration)**. **Note:** *The wheel sen-*

*sors and pulse rings can be damaged from objects picked up by the wheels. Shake each sensor to ensure it is not loose or cracked.*

9    Disconnect the wiring connectors from each wheel sensor. Check that the terminals are not corroded or backed out of the rear of the connector. Using an ohmmeter, check that the resistance between the sensor terminals is 1.4 – 1.8 k/ohms. Repair any damaged terminals or renew the wheel sensors where necessary **(see illustration)**.

10    Working in the engine compartment, check that the ABS modulator wiring connector is making good contact and the terminals are free of corrosion. Repair where necessary.

11    If no fault can be found, it is recommended that the vehicle be referred to an authorised dealer or brake specialist with the specialised equipment to isolate the fault.

### *Renew wheel sensors*

12    Remove the relevant wheel/s from the vehicle.

13    Disconnect the wiring connector and manoeuvre the sensor wiring from any brackets.

14    Remove the bolt retaining the sensor to the steering knuckle, on the front brakes, or the rear axle/rear axle carrier on the rear

brakes, and remove the sensor from the vehicle.

15    Installation is a reversal of the removal procedure with attention to the following points:

16    Check that the pulse ring is not damaged or distorted prior to installing the wheel sensor.

17    Ensure that the wiring connector is not corroded or damaged and that is making good electrical contact.

### *Renew pulse rings*

#### Rear Pulse Ring

The rear ABS wheel sensor pulse ring can be renewed separately and is pressed onto the rear hub assembly. If damaged the pulse ring can be renewed using a bearing separator and a press. Care must be taken when pressing the new pulse ring on to ensure that it is square. Refer to the Rear Axle and Suspension (chapter 14) for the correct procedure to remove and install the rear hub.

#### Front Pulse Ring

At the time of publication the front pulse ring was only available as part of the drive shaft assembly and if damaged, must be renewed as a complete unit. Consult your parts supplier prior to purchase.

# Chapter 10
# Suspension and steering systems

*Contents*

## Specifications

### Torque specifications

Nm

**Front suspension**

Strut

| | |
|---|---|
| Upper mounting nuts | 39 to 49 |
| Damper rod-to-insulator nut | 60 to 70 |
| Strut-to-steering knuckle bolts/nuts | 95 to 105 |
| Stabiliser bar bracket bolts | 34 to 44 |
| Balljoint-to-steering knuckle nut | 60 to 72 |

Control arm

  U-bracket-to-body bolts/nuts

| | |
|---|---|
| Long bolt | 80 to 100 |
| Short bolt | 70 to 90 |
| Nuts | 35 to 47 |
| Pivot bolt nuts | 98 to 118 |

### Rear suspension

Sedan

  Shock absorber/spring assembly

| | |
|---|---|
| Upper spring retainer mounting nuts | 40 to 50 |
| Shock-to-rear axle bolt | 80 to 100 |
| Piston rod nut | 20 to 25 |
| Lateral rod-to-axle bolt | 100 to 120 |
| Lateral rod-to-body bolts | 80 to 100 |
| Rear axle trailing arm pivot bolts | 80 to 100 |

## Torque specifications (continued)

Nm

### Rear suspension (continued)

Station wagon

    Shock absorber mounting bolts

        Upper................................................................................. 40 to 50

        Lower................................................................................. 60 to 80

    Lower control arm mounting bolts.................................................. 220 to 240

    Upper control arm mounting bolts.................................................. 220 to 240

    Lateral rod-to-axle bolt ............................................................... 140 to 160

    Lateral rod-to-body bolt............................................................... 80 to 100

### Steering system

Steering wheel nut

    Without airbag............................................................................ 34 to 44

    With airbag................................................................................. 39 to 49

Steering gear mounting bracket bolts..................................................... 60 to 80

Intermediate shaft pinch bolt................................................................. 15 to 20

Tie-rod-to-steering knuckle nut.............................................................. 24 to 34

Power steering pressure line fitting nut.................................................. 40 to 50

Wheel lug nuts..................................................................................... See Chapter 1

## 1 General information

*Refer to illustrations 1.1, 1.2 and 1.3*

The front suspension is a MacPherson strut design. The upper end of each strut is attached to the vehicle body. The lower end of the strut is connected to the upper end of the steering knuckle. The steering knuckle is attached to a balljoint in the outer end of the control arm. A stabiliser bar is attached to both control arms to minimise body roll during cornering **(see illustration)**.

The rear suspension on sedan models utilises a shock absorber/coil spring assembly **(see illustration)**. The upper end of each

shock is attached to the vehicle body. The lower end of the shock is attached to the rear axle assembly. The rear axle assembly is located by a lateral rod and training arms; the trailing arms are welded to the rear axle assembly.

On station wagon models, the rear suspension consists of coil springs mounted between the body and the lower control arms. Upper control arms are positioned between the axle and the frame. Shock absorbers are mounted to the rear axle and the vehicle body. Lateral motion of the rear axle is controlled by a lateral rod **(see illustration)**.

The rack-and-pinion steering gear is

located below and behind the engine/transaxle assembly on the crossmember and actuates the tie-rods, which are attached to the steering knuckles. The steering column is designed to collapse in the event of an accident.

Frequently, when working on the suspension or steering system components, you may come across fasteners which seem impossible to loosen. These fasteners on the underside of the vehicle are continually subjected to water, road grime, mud, etc., and can become rusted or "seized," making them extremely difficult to remove. In order to unscrew these stubborn fasteners without damaging them (or other components),

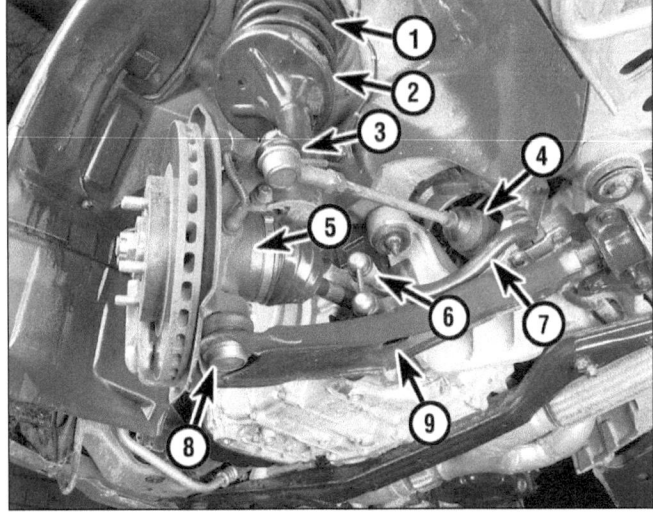

**1.1 Front suspension components (view from rear of vehicle)**

| | | | |
|---|---|---|---|
| 1 | Coil spring | 6 | Stabiliser bar link |
| 2 | Strut assembly | 7 | Stabiliser bar |
| 3 | Tie rod Stabiliser bar | 8 | Lower ball joint |
| 4 | Steering gear | 9 | Lower arm |
| 5 | Steering knuckle | | |

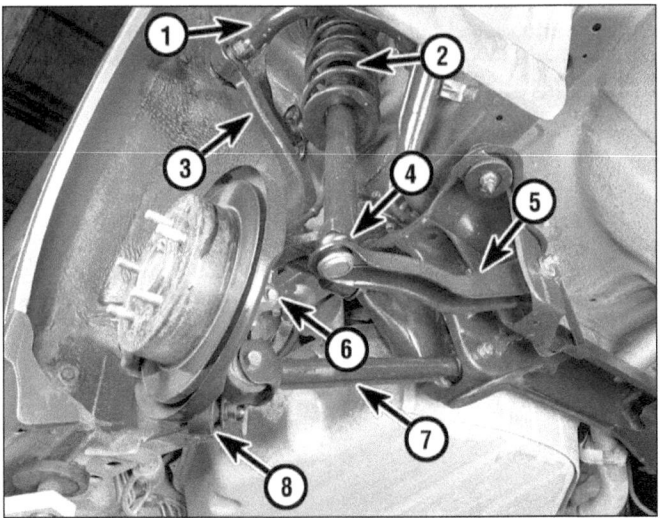

**1.2 Rear suspension components (sedan) (view from rear of vehicle)**

| | | | |
|---|---|---|---|
| 1 | Upper control arm | 5 | Toe control arm |
| 2 | Shock absorber and coil | 6 | Hub assembly |
| | spring | 7 | Lower control arm |
| 3 | Knuckle | 8 | Trailing arm |
| 4 | Ball joint | | |

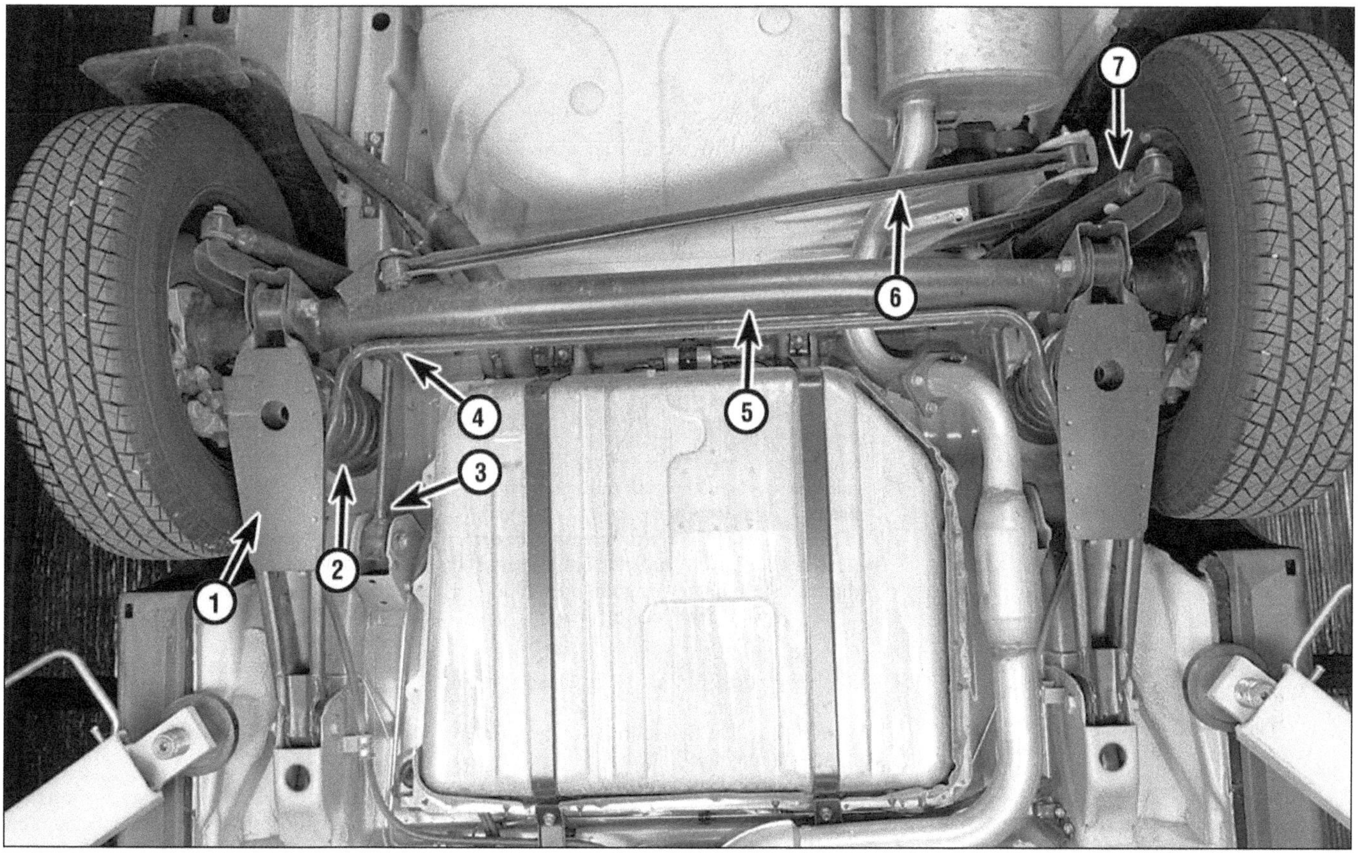

**1.3 Wagon rear suspension components**

| | | | | | | | |
|---|---|---|---|---|---|---|---|
| 1 | Lower control arm | 3 | Upper trailing arm | 5 | Axle assembly | 7 | Shock absorber |
| 2 | Spring | 4 | Stabilizer bar | 6 | Lateral rod | | |

be sure to use lots of penetrating oil and allow it to soak in for a while. Using a wire brush to clean exposed threads will also ease removal of the nut or bolt and prevent damage to the threads. Sometimes a sharp blow with a hammer and punch will break the bond between a nut and bolt threads, but care must be taken to prevent the punch from slipping off the fastener and ruining the threads. Heating the stuck fastener and surrounding area with a torch sometimes helps too, but isn't recommended because of the obvious dangers associated with fire. Long

breaker bars and extensions increase leverage, but never use an extension pipe on a ratchet - the ratcheting mechanism could be damaged. Sometimes tightening the nut or bolt first will help to break it loose. Fasteners that require drastic measures to remove should always be renewed with new ones.

Since most of the procedures dealt with in this Chapter involve jacking up the vehicle and working underneath it, a good pair of jackstands will be needed. A hydraulic floor jack is the preferred type of jack to lift the vehicle, and it can also be used to support

certain components during various operations. **Warning:** *Never, under any circumstances, rely on a jack to support the vehicle while working on it. Whenever any of the suspension or steering fasteners are loosened or removed they must be inspected and, if necessary, renewed with new ones of the same part number or of original equipment quality and design. Torque specifications must be followed for proper reassembly and component retention. Never attempt to heat or straighten any suspension or steering components. Instead, renew any bent or damaged part with a new one.*

---

**2   Front stabiliser bar and bushes - removal and refitting**

---

### Removal

*Refer to illustrations 2.3, 2.4 and 2.5*

1   Raise the front of the vehicle and support it securely on jackstands. Apply the parking brake and block the rear wheels to keep the vehicle from rolling off the stands.

2   Remove the front exhaust pipe (see Chapter 4).

3   Remove the front roll stopper through-bolt (see Chapter 2A). Remove the centre member **(see illustration)**.

**2.3 Remove the bolts retaining the centre member underneath the engine/transaxle assembly (arrows)**

**2.4 Remove the upper and lower nuts (arrows) to detach the stabiliser bar from the control arm**

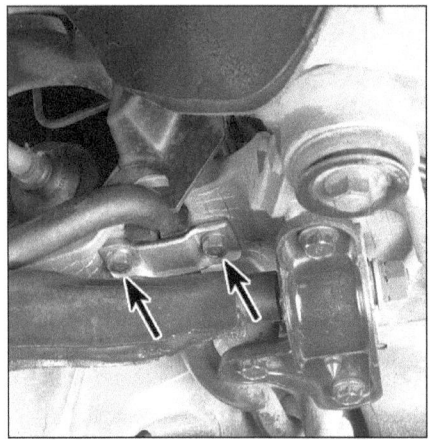

**2.5 Remove the stabiliser bar bracket bolts (arrows) from each stabiliser bar bracket and detach the stabiliser bar and the brackets from the crossmember; before refitting the stabiliser bar, inspect the rubber bushes and renew them if they're cracked or torn**

**3.2 Detach ABS electrical wire from the strut (arrow)**

4    Detach the stabiliser bar links from the control arms **(see illustration)**.
5    Detach both stabiliser bar brackets from the crossmember **(see illustration)**.
6    Remove the stabiliser bar.
7    While the stabiliser bar is off the vehicle, slide the bracket bushes off and inspect them. If they're cracked, worn or deteriorated, renew them.
8    Clean the bush area of the stabiliser bar with a stiff wire brush to remove any rust or dirt.

### Refitting

9    Lubricate the inside and outside of the new bushes with silicone grease to simplify reassembly. **Caution:** *Don't use petroleum or mineral-based lubricants or brake fluid - they will lead to deterioration of the bushes.*
10    Refitting is the reverse of removal.

---

3    **Front strut assembly - removal, inspection and refitting**

---

### Removal

*Refer to illustrations 3.2, 3.3 and 3.5*
1    Loosen the wheel lug nuts, raise the

vehicle and support it securely on jackstands. Remove the wheel.
2    Unbolt the ABS sensor wire from the strut **(see illustration)**.
3    Remove the strut-to-knuckle nuts and knock the bolts out with a hammer and punch **(see illustration)**. **Note:** *Paint alignment marks on the knuckle and strut body to help on refitting.*
4    Separate the strut from the steering knuckle. Be careful not to overextend the inner CV joint. **Caution:** *Don't allow the steering knuckle and hub assembly to swing outward.*
5    Remove the dust cover from the upper mount. Support the strut and spring assembly with one hand and remove the strut upper mounting nuts **(see illustration)**. Remove the assembly out from the fenderwell.

### Inspection

6    Check the strut body for leaking fluid, dents, cracks and other obvious damage which would warrant repair or renewal.

7    Check the coil spring for chips or cracks in the spring coating (this will cause premature spring failure due to corrosion). Inspect the spring seat for cuts, hardness and general deterioration.
8    If any undesirable conditions exist, proceed to the strut disassembly procedure (see Section 4).

### Refitting

9    Guide the strut assembly up into the fenderwell and refit the mounting nuts. This is most easily accomplished with the help of an assistant, as the strut is quite heavy and awkward.
10    Slide the steering knuckle into the strut flange and insert the two bolts. Refit the nuts and tighten them to the torque listed in this Chapter's Specifications.
11    Refit the brake caliper (see Chapter 9) and attach the brake hose bracket to the strut.
12    Refit the wheel and lug nuts, then lower the vehicle and tighten the lug nuts to the torque listed in the Chapter 1 Specifications.
13    Tighten the upper mounting nuts to the torque listed in this Chapter's Specifications.
14    Drive the vehicle to an alignment shop to have the front end alignment checked, and if necessary, adjusted.

**3.3 Remove the strut-to-steering knuckle bolts and nuts (arrows)**

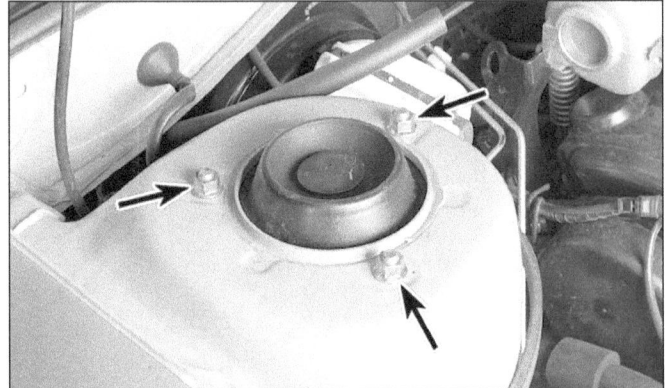

**3.5 Support the strut and spring assembly with one hand (or have an assistant hold it for you) and remove the strut-to-spring tower nuts (arrows)**

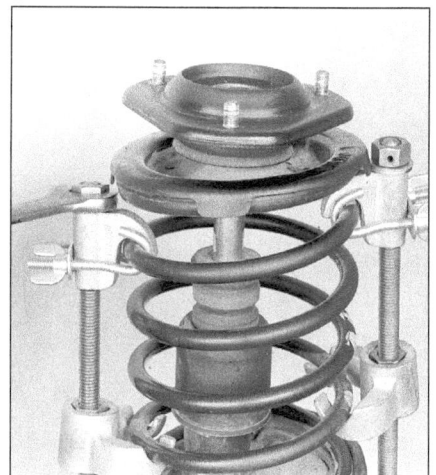

**4.3 Fit the spring compressor in accordance with the tool manufacturer's instructions and compress the spring until all pressure is relieved from the upper spring seat (you can verify the spring is loose by wiggling it)**

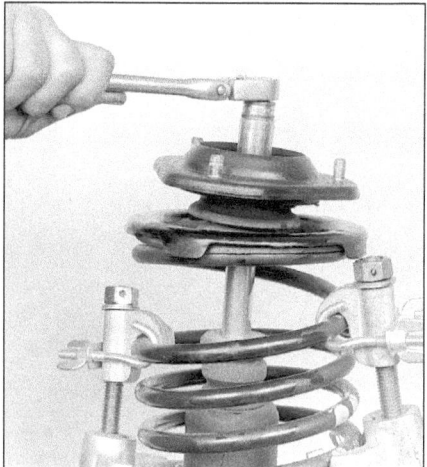

**4.4 Remove the damper shaft nut**

**4.5 Lift the strut insulator off the shaft**

## 4  Strut/spring assembly - renewal

1   If the struts or coil springs exhibit the telltale signs of wear (leaking fluid, loss of damping capability, chipped, sagging or cracked coil springs) explore all options before beginning any work. The strut/shock absorber assemblies are not serviceable and must be renewed if a problem develops. However, strut assemblies complete with springs may be available on an exchange basis, which eliminates much time and work. Whichever route you choose to take, check on the cost and availability of parts before disassembling your vehicle. **Warning:** *Disassembling a strut assembly is a potentially dangerous undertaking and utmost attention must be directed to the job, or serious injury may result. Use only a high quality spring*

*compressor and carefully follow the manufacturer's instructions furnished with the tool. After removing the coil spring from the strut assembly, set it aside in a safe, isolated area.*

### Disassembly

*Refer to illustrations 4.3, 4.4, 4.5, 4.6 and 4.7*

2   Remove the strut and spring assembly following the procedure described in the previous Section. Mount the strut assembly in a vise. Line the vise jaws with wood or rags to prevent damage to the unit and don't tighten the vise excessively.

3   Following the tool manufacturer's instructions, refit the spring compressor (which can be obtained at most auto parts stores or equipment yards on a daily rental basis) on the spring and compress it sufficiently to relieve all pressure from the strut insulator **(see illustration)**. This can be verified by wiggling the spring.

4   Loosen the damper shaft nut with a socket **(see illustration)**.

5   Remove the nut and the strut insulator **(see illustration)**. Inspect the bearing in the

insulator for smooth operation. If it doesn't turn smoothly, renew the insulator. Inspect the rubber portion of the insulator for cracking and general deterioration. If there is any separation of the rubber, renew it.

6   Lift the upper spring seat and upper pad from the damper shaft **(see illustration)**. Check the spring seat for cracking and hardness, renewing it if necessary.

7   Carefully lift the compressed spring from the assembly **(see illustration)** and set it in a safe place. **Warning:** *Never place your head near the end of the spring!*

8   Slide the rubber bumper and dust cover off the damper shaft.

### Reassembly

*Refer to illustrations 4.10 and 4.11*

9   If the lower insulator is being renewed, set it into position with the dropped portion seated in the lowest part of the seat. Extend the damper rod to its full length and refit the rubber bumper and dust cover.

10   Carefully place the coil spring onto the lower insulator, with the end of the spring

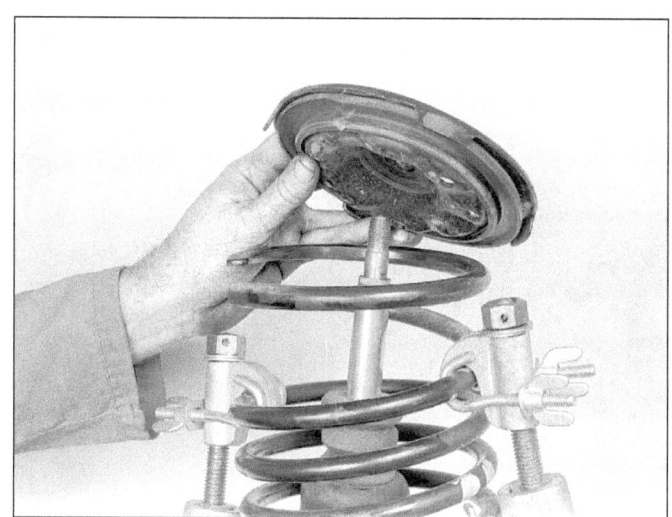

**4.6 Remove the upper spring seat and the upper pad from the damper shaft**

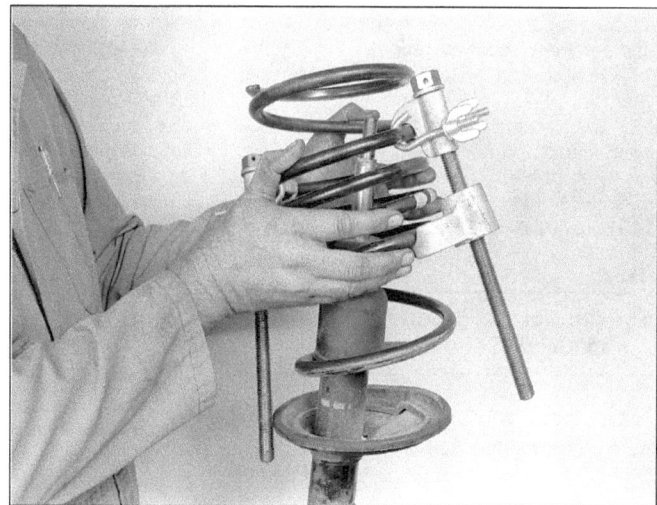

**4.7 Remove the compressed spring from the strut assembly - keep the ends of the spring pointed away from your body**

4.10  When refitting the spring, make sure
the end fits into the recessed portion of
the lower seat

4.11  The flat on the damper shaft (arrow)
must match up with the flat in the upper
spring seat

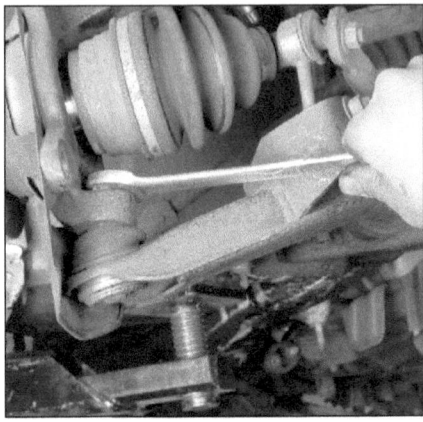

5.3a  Remove the nut from the balljoint
stud, give the knuckle a few firm hits with
a large ball peen hammer in the vicinity
of the ball stud . . .

5.3b  . . . then use a prisebar to separate the control arm from the
steering knuckle

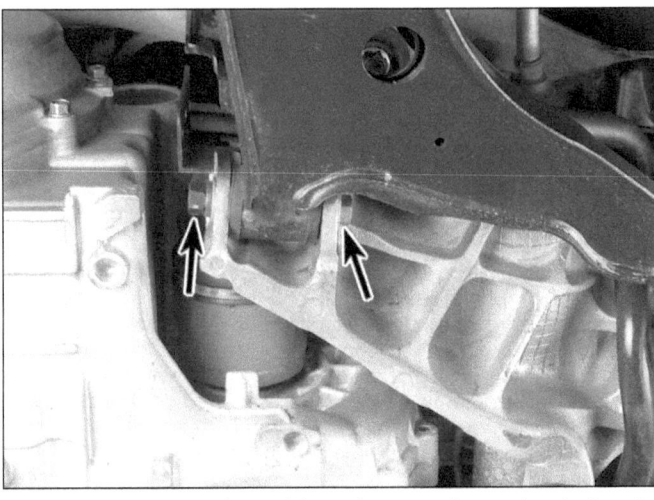

5.4  Remove the nut (arrow) from the control arm pivot bolt and
pull out the bolt (arrow)

resting in the lowest part of the insulator **(see
illustration)**.
11  Refit the upper pad and upper spring
seat, making sure that the flats in the hole
in the seat match up with the flats on the
damper shaft **(see illustration)**.
12  Refit the strut insulator onto the damper
shaft.
13  Refit the nut and tighten it to the torque
listed in this Chapter's Specifications.
14  Refit the strut/shock absorber and coil
spring assembly following the procedure outlined previously (see Section 3).

---

### 5   Control arm (front) - removal, inspection and refitting

#### Removal

*Refer to illustrations 5.3a, 5.3b, 5.4 and 5.5*
1  Loosen the wheel lug nuts on the side
to be disassembled, raise the front of the
vehicle, support it securely on jackstands and
remove the wheel.

2  Disconnect the stabiliser bar from the
control arm (see Section 2).
3  Remove the nut from the balljoint stud
**(see illustration)**. Using a large ball peen
hammer (and wearing goggles to protect
your eyes), rap the steering knuckle in the
vicinity of the balljoint stud to break the stud
loose from the knuckle. Use a prisebar to
disconnect the control arm from the steering
knuckle **(see illustration)**.
4  Remove the nut and washer from the
control arm pivot bolt **(see illustration)**. Pull
out the pivot bolt.
5  Remove the three bolts from the clamp
for the rear control arm bush **(see illustration)**.
6  Remove the control arm.

#### Inspection

7  Check the control arm for distortion and
the bushes for wear. If the arm is bent or any
of the bushes are cracked, torn or worn out,
renew the control arm. These parts are not
renewable and you can't straighten a bent
control arm. Check the balljoint (see Section 6). If a balljoint is worn out, renew the

control arm; it's not recommended to renew
the balljoint.

#### Refitting

8  Refitting is the reverse of removal. Do

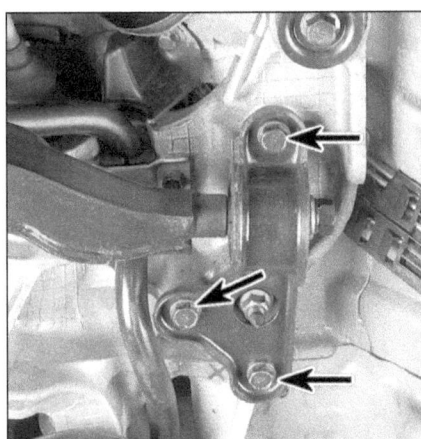

5.5  Remove the three bolts (arrows) from
the clamp for the rear control arm bush
and remove the control arm

6.2  If there is any play apparent in the balljoint when prising on the control arm, the control arm must be renewed

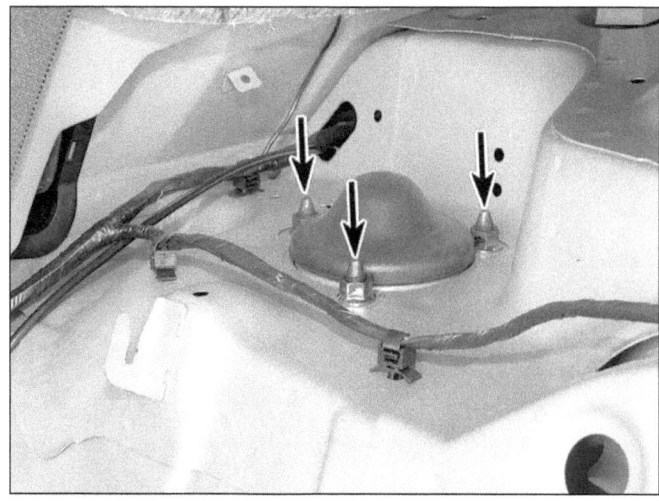

9.3  Remove the shock absorber/spring assembly upper mounting nuts (arrows)

NOT reuse self-locking nuts - renew them. Temporarily tighten all fasteners securely.

9    Refit the wheel and lug nuts, lower the vehicle and tighten all the fasteners to the torque listed in this Chapter's specifications. Tighten the lug nuts to the torque listed in Chapter 1 Specifications.

10    Have the front wheel alignment checked, and if necessary, adjusted after this job has been performed.

## 6    Balljoints - check and renewal

*Refer to illustration 6.2*

1    Raise the vehicle and support it securely on jackstands.

2    Place a large block of wood under the tyre, block the wheel with chocks and lower the jack until there's about half a load on the coil spring. Now move the control arm up and down with a prisebar **(see illustration)** and verify that there's no freeplay in the balljoint. If there is, renew the control arm (see Section 5); due to the wear factors involved between the balljoint and control arm, it's not recommended to renew the balljoint.

3    Remove the chocks, the block of wood and the jackstands and lower the vehicle.

## 7    Steering knuckle and hub assembly - removal and refitting

**Warning:** *Dust created by the brake system may contain asbestos, which is harmful to your health. Never blow it out with compressed air and don't inhale any of it. Do not, under any circumstances, use petroleum-based solvents to clean brake parts. Use brake system cleaner only.*

## *Removal*

1    Loosen the wheel lug nuts, raise the vehicle and support it securely on jackstands.

Remove the wheel.

2    Remove the brake caliper and support it with a piece of wire as described in Chapter 9. Remove the caliper mounting bracket, separate the brake disc from the hub, then loosen the driveaxle/hub nut (see Chapter 8).

3    Loosen, but do not remove the strut-to-steering knuckle bolts **(see illustration 3.3)**.

4    Separate the tie-rod end from the steering knuckle arm (see Section 19).

5    Remove the balljoint-to-steering knuckle nut and separate the control arm from the steering knuckle **(see illustrations 5.3a and 5.3b)**.

6    Push the driveaxle from the hub as described in Chapter 8. Support the end of the driveaxle with a piece of wire.

7    Remove the bolts and carefully separate the steering knuckle from the strut and lower arm.

## *Refitting*

8    Guide the knuckle and hub assembly into position, inserting the driveaxle into the hub.

9    Push the knuckle into the strut flange and refit the bolts and nuts, but don't tighten them yet.

10    Connect the balljoint to the control arm and refit the bolt and nuts (don't tighten them yet).

11    Attach the tie-rod end to the steering knuckle arm (see Section 19). Tighten the strut bolt nuts, the balljoint-to-control arm bolt and nuts and the tie-rod end nut to the torque values listed in this Chapter's Specifications.

12    Place the brake disc on the hub and refit the caliper as outlined in Chapter 9.

13    Refit the driveaxle/hub nut washer with the concave side against the hub. Refit the driveaxle/hub nut and tighten it to the torque listed in the Chapter 8 Specifications.

14    Refit the wheel and lug nuts.

15    Lower the vehicle and tighten the lug nuts to the torque listed in the Chapter 1 Specifications.

## 8    Hub and bearing assembly - renewal

## *Front*

Due to the special tools and expertise required to press the hub and bearing from the steering knuckle, this job should be left to a professional mechanic or machine shop. However, the steering knuckle and hub may be removed and the assembly taken to a dealer service department or other repair shop where the press work can be performed. See Section 7 for the steering knuckle and hub removal procedure.

## *Rear*

Due to the special tools and expertise required to press the bearings from the hub, this job should be left to a professional mechanic or machine shop. However the hub may be removed and the assembly taken to a dealer service department or other repair shop where the press work can be performed. See Chapter 9, Section 11.

## 9    Rear shock absorber/spring assembly (sedan models) - removal, shock absorber renewal and refitting

## *Removal*

*Refer to illustrations 9.3 and 9.4*

1    Loosen the wheel lug nuts, raise the vehicle and support it securely on jackstands. Remove the wheel.

2    Support the knuckle with a floor jack. Raise the jack just enough to support the weight.

3    Working inside the car, remove the rear seat and package tray. Remove the cap and remove the shock/spring assembly retaining nuts **(see illustration)**.

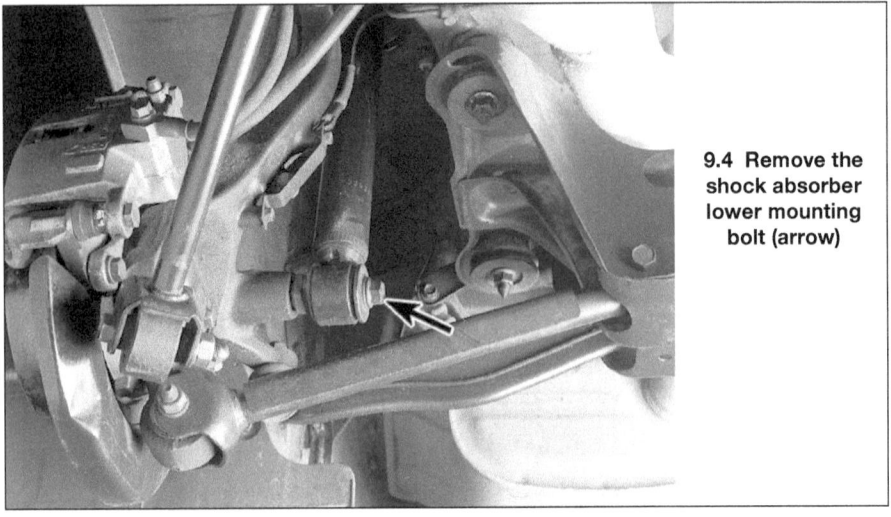

**9.4 Remove the shock absorber lower mounting bolt (arrow)**

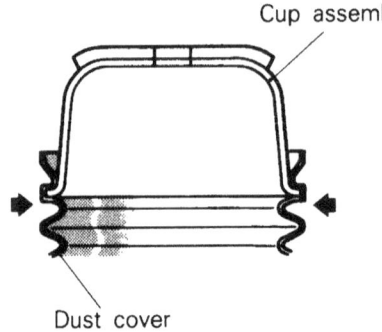

**9.7 Make sure the dust cover and cup assembly fit together like this**

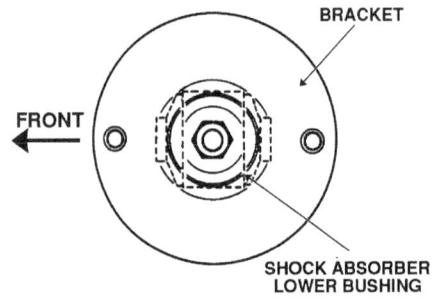

**9.8 Before tightening the damper shaft nut, make sure the bracket and lower bush are aligned like this**

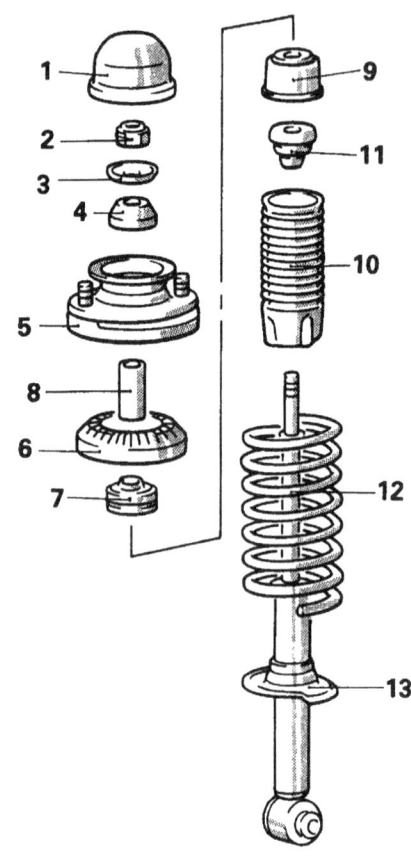

**9.5 An exploded view of a typical rear shock absorber**

| 1 | Cap | 8 | Collar |
|---|---|---|---|
| 2 | Damper shaft nut | 9 | Cup assembly |
| 3 | Washer | 10 | Dust cover |
| 4 | Upper bush | 11 | Bump stop |
| 5 | Bracket assembly | 12 | Coil spring |
| 6 | Spring pad | 13 | Shock absorber assembly |
| 7 | Lower bush | | |

4    Remove the shock absorber lower mounting bolt and remove the shock **(see illustration)**.

### Inspection

*Refer to illustrations 9.5, 9.7 and 9.8*

5    Follow the inspection procedures described in Section 3. If the shock absorber assembly must be disassembled for renewal of the shock or the coil spring, refer to Section 4 and the **accompanying illustration)**.
6    When reassembling the shock, make sure the lower end of the coil spring is correctly seated **(see illustration 4.10)** and the upper end is seated in the spring pad groove.
7    Make sure the dust cover and cup assembly fit together as shown **(see illustration)**.
8    Before tightening the damper shaft nut, make sure the bracket and lower bush are aligned as shown **(see illustration)**.

### Refitting

9    Maneuver the shock absorber assembly up into the fenderwell and insert the mounting studs through the holes in the body. Refit the nuts, but don't tighten them yet.
10   Push the lower end of the shock into its bracket on the knuckle, refit the bolt and nut,

and tighten them to the torque listed in this Chapter's Specifications.
11   Refit the wheel and lug nuts, lower the vehicle and tighten the lug nuts to the torque listed in the Chapter 1 Specifications.
12   Tighten the three upper mounting nuts to the torque listed in this Chapter's Specifications. Refit the cap and trim panel.

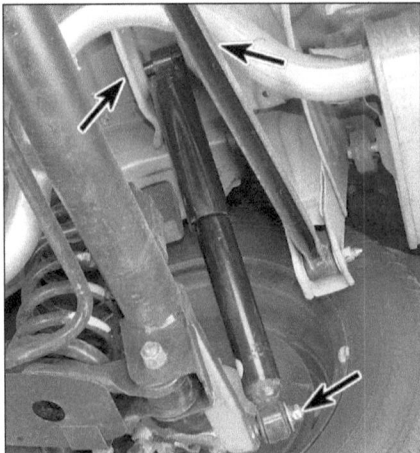

**10.4 Rear shock absorber mounting details - station wagon**

### 10   Rear shock absorber (station wagon models) - removal and refitting

*Refer to illustration 10.4*

1    Loosen the wheel lug nuts, raise the vehicle and support it securely on jackstands placed under the rear axle (not under the frame). Remove the wheels.
2    Remove the upper shock absorber mounting nut, lock washer and flat washer.
3    Remove the lower shock absorber mounting nut, lock washer and flat washer.
4    Remove the shock absorber from the lower stud by pulling toward the rear of the vehicle **(see illustration)**.
5    Refitting is the reverse of removal. Be sure to tighten the nuts to the torque listed in this Chapter's Specifications.

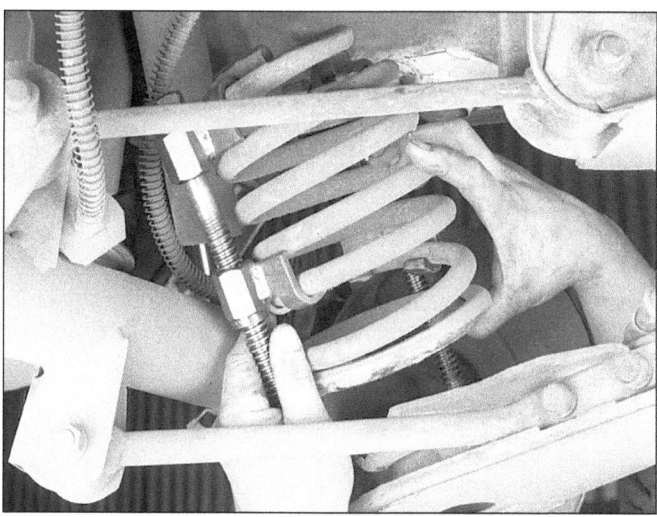

**11.4  Lower the axle and remove the rear coil spring**

**11.5  Remove the nuts and bolts from each end of the control arm and detach the control arm from the vehicle**

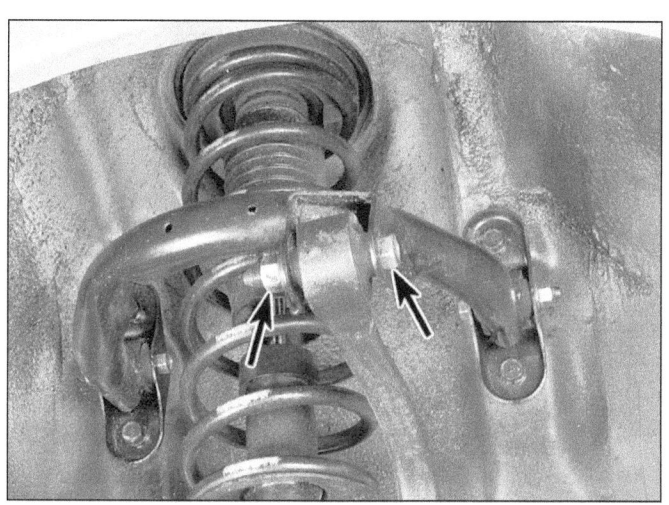

**12.2  Remove the nut and bolt (arrow) securing the upper control arm to the knuckle**

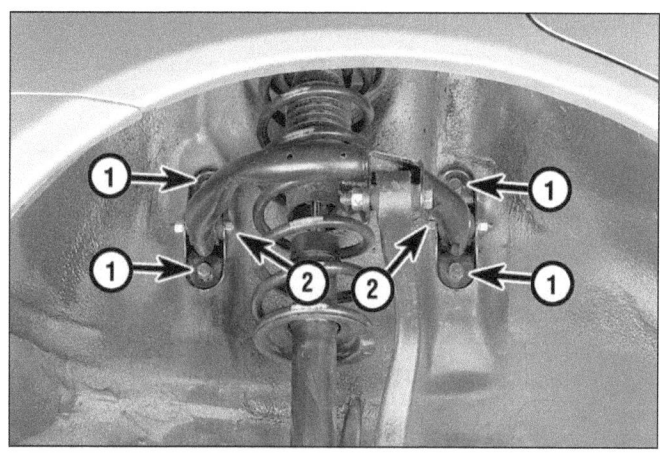

**12.3  Remove the bolts securing the upper control arm to the body (arrows)**

1    Upper control arm-to-body mounting bolts
2    Upper control arm-to-bracket mounting bolts

## 11    Rear coil spring and lower control arm (station wagon models) - removal and refitting

*Refer to illustrations 11.4 and 11.5*

1    Loosen the wheel lug nuts, raise the vehicle and support it securely on jackstands placed under the frame (not under the rear axle). Remove the wheels.
2    Place a jack under the axle beam as close to the control arm as possible. Raise the axle slightly to support the weight.
3    Remove the lower shock absorber retaining nut and washers and slide the shock absorber off the stud.
4    Lower the jack, to the point where the coil spring can be removed, and maneuver the coil spring out **(see illustration)**.
5    Raise the axle slightly with the jack and remove the lower control arm mounting bolts **(see illustration)**. Remove the lower control arm.
6    Refitting is the reverse of removal. Do NOT reuse self-locking nuts - renew them.

Temporarily tighten all fasteners securely.
7    Refit the wheel and lug nuts, lower the vehicle and tighten all the fasteners to the torque listed in this Chapter's specifications. Tighten the lug nuts to the torque listed in Chapter 1 Specifications.

## 12    Rear upper control arm - removal and refitting

1    Loosen the wheel lug nuts, raise the vehicle and support it securely on jackstands placed under the frame (not under the rear axle). Remove the wheels.

### Sedan models

*Refer to illustrations 12.2 and 12.3*

2    Remove the upper control arm to knuckle nut and bolt **(see illustration)**.
3    Remove the upper control arm bracket bolts **(see illustration)**.
4    Remove the upper control arm from the vehicle.
5    Check the condition of the bushes and

pivot bolts for signs of wear or damage.
6    Refitting is the reverse of removal. Do NOT reuse self-locking nuts - renew them. Temporarily tighten all fasteners securely.
7    Refit the wheel and lug nuts, lower the vehicle and tighten all the fasteners to the torque listed in this Chapter's specifications. Tighten the lug nuts to the torque listed in Chapter 1 Specifications.

### Station wagon models

*Refer to illustration 12.10*

8    Lift the axle with the jack until the axle is approximately to its normal riding position.
9    Remove the bolts, nuts and washers retaining the upper control arm.
10    Remove the upper control arm from the vehicle **(see illustration)**.
11    Check the condition of the bushes and pivot bolts for signs of wear or damage.
12    Refitting is the reverse of removal. Do NOT reuse self-locking nuts - renew them. Temporarily tighten all fasteners securely.
13    Refit the wheel and lug nuts, lower the vehicle and tighten all the fasteners to the torque listed in this Chapter's specifications.

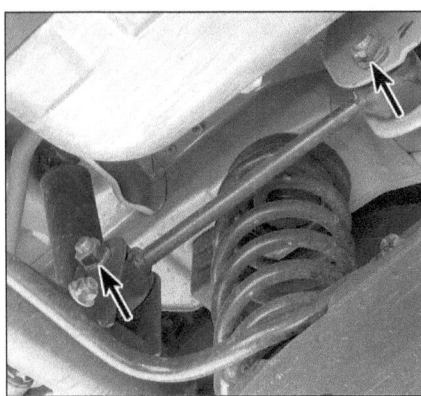

**12.10  Remove the bolts securing the upper control arm to the body and axle (arrows)**

Tighten the lug nuts to the torque listed in Chapter 1 Specifications.

## 13  Lateral rod (station wagon models) - removal and refitting

*Refer to illustrations 13.3 and 13.4*

1    Loosen the wheel lug nuts, raise the vehicle and support it securely on jackstands placed under the frame (not under the rear axle assembly). Remove the wheels.
2    Place a floor jack underneath the cen-tre of the rear axle assembly. Make sure the jack doesn't contact the lateral rod. Raise the jack just enough to support the axle assembly.
3    Remove the nut, washer and bolt that attach the upper end of the lateral rod to the body **(see illustration)**.
4    Remove the nut, washer and bolt that attach the lower end of the lateral rod to the rear axle assembly **(see illustration)**, and remove the lateral rod.
5    Inspect the bushes in each lateral rod "eye" for cracks and deterioration. If either bush is worn, renew it.
6    Refitting is the reverse of removal. Make sure you refit the bolts with the heads facing forward. Do NOT reuse self-locking nuts - renew them. Temporarily tighten all fasteners securely.
7    Refit the wheel and lug nuts, lower the vehicle and tighten all the fasteners to the torque listed in this Chapter's specifications. Tighten the lug nuts to the torque listed in Chapter 1 Specifications.

## 14  Rear lower control arm (sedan models) - removal and refitting

*Refer to illustration 14.3*

1    Loosen the wheel lug nuts, raise the vehicle and support it securely on jackstands placed under the frame (not under the rear axle). Remove the wheels.
2    Using the jack, raise the knuckle slightly to support the weight.
3    Remove the lower control arm mounting nuts **(see illustration)**.
4    Inspect the bushes in each control arm "eye" for cracks and deterioration. If either bush is worn, renew it.
5    Refitting is the reverse of removal. Make sure you refit the bolts with the heads facing forward. Do NOT reuse self-locking nuts - renew them. Temporarily tighten all fasteners securely.
6    Refit the wheel and lug nuts, lower the vehicle and tighten all the fasteners to the torque listed in this Chapter's specifications. Tighten the lug nuts to the torque listed in Chapter 1 Specifications.

## 15  Rear trailing arm (sedan models) - removal and refitting

*Refer to illustrations 15.3 and 15.4*

1    Loosen the wheel lug nuts, raise the vehicle and support it securely on jackstands placed under the frame (not under the rear axle). Remove the wheels.
2    Using the jack, raise the knuckle slightly to support the weight.
3    Remove the trailing arm bolt cover from

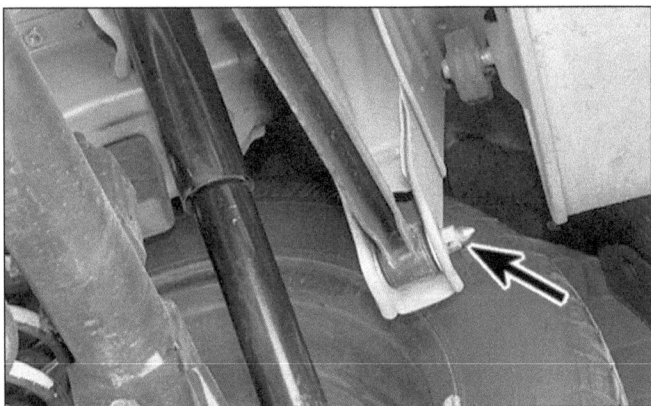

**13.3  Remove the nut, washer and bolt (arrow) that attach the upper end of the lateral rod to the body**

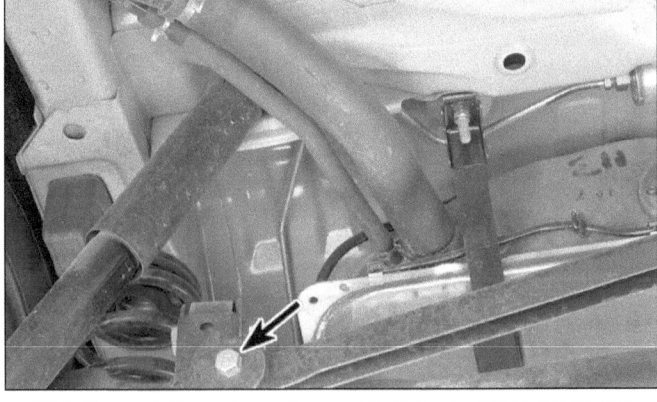

**13.4  Remove the nut, washer and bolt (arrow) that attach the lower end of the lateral rod to the rear axle assembly**

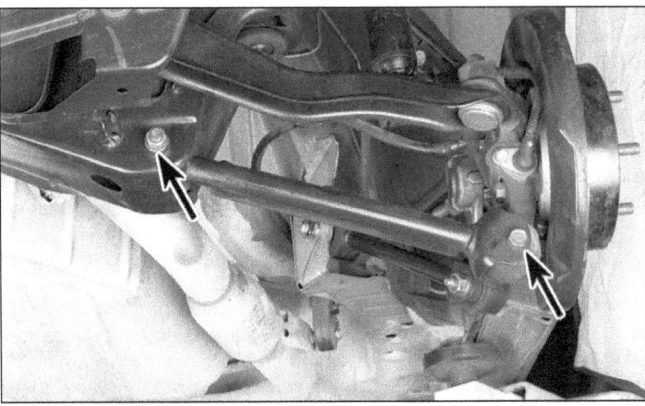

**14. 3  Remove the lower control arm mounting nuts and bolts (arrows)**

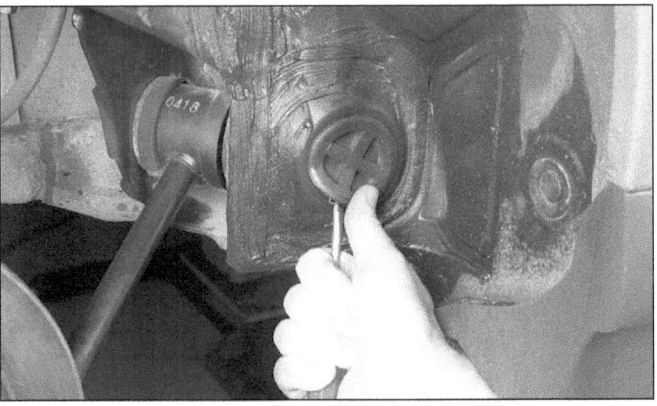

**15.3  Using a screwdriver, prise the trailing arm access plug out**

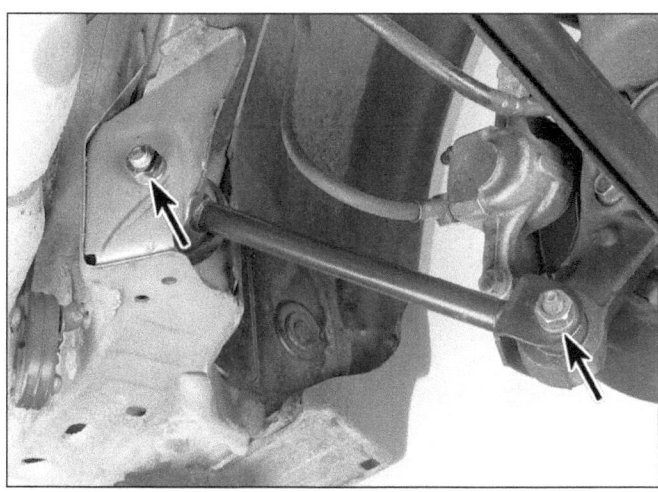

**15.4  Remove the trailing arm mounting nuts and bolts (arrows)**

**16.9  To disconnect the rear axle assembly from the vehicle, remove crossmember mounting bolts (arrows, right side shown, left side similar)**

inside of the fenderwell **(see illustration)**.
4    Remove the trailing arm mounting nuts **(see illustration)**.
5    Inspect the bushes in each trailing arm "eye" for cracks and deterioration. If either bush is worn, renew it.
6    Refitting is the reverse of removal. Make sure you refit the bolts with the heads facing forward. Do NOT reuse self-locking nuts - renew them. Temporarily tighten all fasteners securely.
7    Refit the wheel and lug nuts, lower the vehicle and tighten all the fasteners to the torque listed in this Chapter's specifications. Tighten the lug nuts to the torque listed in Chapter 1 Specifications.

### 16  Rear suspension assembly - removal and refitting

1    Raise the vehicle and support it securely on jackstands.

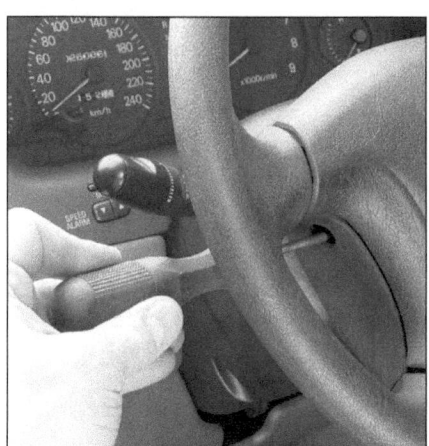

**18.2a  Remove the Torx screws and detach the airbag module from the steering wheel**

## Sedan models

*Refer to illustration 16.9*
2    Remove the interfering section of exhaust pipe (see Chapter 4).
3    Remove the shock absorber/coil spring upper mounting nuts (see Section 9).
4    Remove the brake calipers and discs (see Chapter 9).
5    Disconnect the parking brake cables.
6    Disconnect the speed sensor wiring.
7    Remove the upper control arm-to-body mounting bolts **(see illustration 12.3)**.
8    Disconnect the front of each trailing arm.
9    Place a trolley jack to support the centre of the crossmember. Remove the crossmember mounting bolts **(see illustration)** and carefully lower the entire assembly to the floor with the aid of an assistant.

## Station wagon models

10    Place a trolley jack underneath the centre of the rear axle assembly. Raise the jack just enough to support the axle assembly.
**Note:** *If two trolley jacks are available, place one at each end of the axle beam.*
11    Disconnect the lower ends of both shock absorbers (see Section 10).
12    Lower the axle and remove the coil springs (see Section 11). Unbolt the lateral rod from the axle (see Section 13).
13    Remove the pivot bolts securing the upper and lower control arms to the axle.
14    With an assistant helping to balance the axle assembly, carefully lower the axle.

## All models

15    Refitting is the reverse of removal. Make sure you tighten all fasteners to the torque listed in this Chapter's Specifications. Do not tighten the bolts completely until the weight of the vehicle is on the floor and its normal ride height has been achieved.
**Note:** *Raise the axle to normal ride height before tightening the fasteners.*

### 17  Steering system - general information

All models are equipped with rack-and-pinion steering. The steering gear is bolted to the crossmember and operates the steering arms via tie-rods. The inner ends of the tie-rods are protected by rubber boots which should be inspected periodically for secure attachment, tears and leaking lubricant.

The power assist system consists of a belt-driven pump and associated lines and hoses. The fluid level in the power steering pump reservoir should be checked periodically (see Chapter 1).

The steering wheel operates the steering shaft, which actuates the steering gear through universal joints. Looseness in the steering can be caused by wear in the steering shaft universal joints, the steering gear, the tie-rod ends and loose retaining bolts.

### 18  Steering wheel - removal and refitting

**Warning:** *The models covered by this manual may be equipped with a Supplemental Restraint system (SRS), more commonly known as airbags. Always disconnect the negative battery cable, then the positive battery cable and wait two minutes before working in the vicinity of impact sensors or steering column to avoid the possibility of accidental deployment of the airbag, which could cause personal injury (see Chapter 12). Do not use electrical test equipment on any of the airbag system wiring or tamper with them in any way.*
**Caution:** *If the stereo in your vehicle is equipped with an anti-theft system, make sure you have the correct activation code before disconnecting the battery.*

18.3  Remove the steering wheel retaining nut, then mark the relationship of the steering shaft to the hub to simplify refitting and ensure proper steering wheel alignment

18.4  Use a puller to disconnect the steering wheel from the shaft

## Removal

*Refer to illustrations 18.2a, 18.2b, 18.3 and 18.4*

1    Position the steering wheel so the front wheels are pointing straight ahead. Turn the ignition switch to the Lock position and remove the key. Disconnect the cable from the negative terminal of the battery. If the vehicle is equipped with an airbag, wait at least 60 seconds before continuing. Also, wrap tape around the battery terminal to prevent the possibility of the battery cable contacting it.
2    On models with an airbag, remove the screws and detach the airbag module **(see illustrations)**. On models without an airbag, remove the horn pad.
3    Remove the steering wheel retaining nut. Mark the relationship of the steering shaft to the hub (if marks don't already exist or don't line up) to simplify refitting and ensure steer-

ing wheel alignment **(see illustration)**.
4    Use a puller to disconnect the steering wheel from the shaft **(see illustration)**. Do NOT hammer on the shaft in an attempt to remove the steering wheel.

## Refitting

5    On models equipped with airbags, make sure the NEUTRAL mark on the airbag clockspring is aligned with the corresponding arrow **(see illustration)** and tape the clockspring to prevent it from accidentally being moved or damaged.
6    To refit the wheel, align the mark on the steering wheel hub with the mark on the shaft and slip the wheel onto the shaft. Refit the nut and tighten the nut to the torque listed in this Chapter's Specifications.
7    Refit the horn pad or airbag module.
8    Connect the negative battery cable.

## 19  Tie-rod ends - removal and refitting

## Removal

*Refer to illustrations 19.2a, 19.2b and 19.4*

1    Loosen the wheel lug nuts. Raise the front of the vehicle, support it securely on jackstands, block the rear wheels and set the parking brake. Remove the front wheel.
2    Hold the tie-rod with a pair of locking pliers or spanner and loosen the jam nut enough to mark the position of the tie-rod end in relation to the threads **(see illustrations)**.
3    Remove the split pin and loosen the nut on the tie-rod end stud.
4    Disconnect the tie-rod from the steering knuckle arm with a puller **(see illustration)**. Remove the nut and separate the tie-rod end.
5    Unscrew the tie-rod end from the tie-rod.

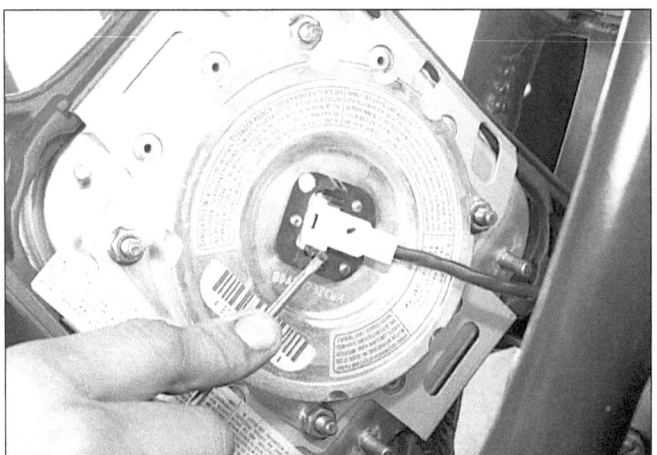

18.2b  On models equipped with an airbag, detach the electrical connector from the airbag module, then place the module in an isolated area (carry the airbag module with the trim side facing away from your body, and store the module with the trim side facing up)

18.5  Before refitting the steering wheel, make sure the clockspring has not rotated and the mating marks (arrow) are aligned

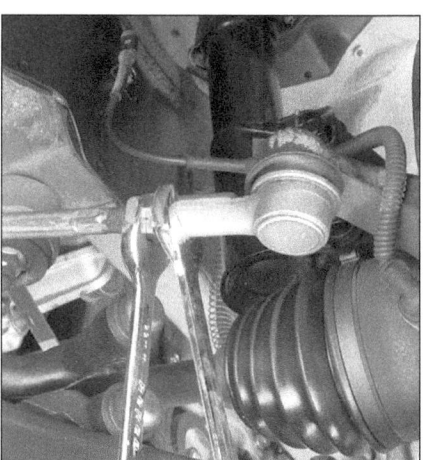

**19.2a  Loosen the tie-rod end jam nut . . .**

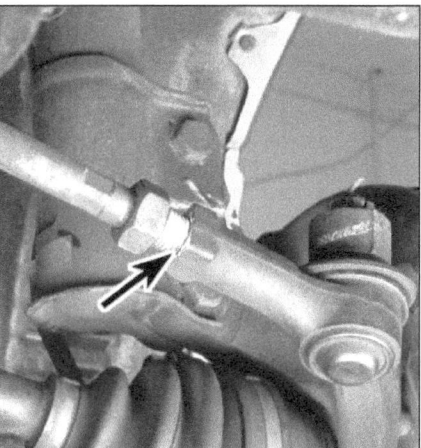

**19.2b  . . . and mark the relationship of the tie-rod end to the tie-rod (arrow)**

**19.4  A tie-rod end separator is being used here to detach the tie-rod end from the steering knuckle - if you don't have one of these tools, a two-jaw puller may work**

## Refitting

6    Thread the tie-rod end on to the marked position and insert the tie-rod stud into the steering knuckle arm. Tighten the jam nut securely.

7    Refit the castle nut on the stud and tighten it to the torque listed in this Chapter's Specifications. Fit a new split pin.

8    Refit the wheel and lug nuts. Lower the vehicle and tighten the lug nuts to the torque listed in the Chapter 1 Specifications.

9    Have the alignment checked by a dealer service department or an alignment shop.

## 20   Steering gear boots - renewal

1    Loosen the lug nuts, raise the vehicle and support it securely on jackstands. Remove the wheel.

2    Remove the tie-rod end and jam nut (see Section 19).

3    Remove the steering gear boot clamps and slide the boot off.

4    Before fitting the new boot, wrap the threads and serrations on the end of the steering rod with a layer of tape so the small end of the new boot isn't damaged.

5    Slide the new boot into position on the steering gear until it seats in the grooves, then fit new clamps.

6    Remove the tape and fit the tie-rod end (see Section 19).

7    Refit the wheel and lug nuts. Lower the vehicle and tighten the lug nuts to the torque listed in the Chapter 1 Specifications.

8    Have the alignment checked by a dealer service department or an alignment shop.

## 21   Steering gear - removal and refitting

**Warning:** *If the model being worked on is equipped with an airbag, make sure the steering shaft is not turned while the steering gear is removed (the airbag clockspring could be damaged). To prevent the shaft from turn-*

*ing, turn the ignition key to the lock position before beginning work, or run the seat belt through the steering wheel and clip the seat belt into place.*

## Removal

*Refer to illustrations 21.2 and 21.7*

1    Park the vehicle with the wheels pointing straight ahead. Loosen the front wheel lug nuts, raise the front of the vehicle and support it securely on jackstands. Apply the parking brake and remove the wheels.

2    Mark the relationship of the lower universal joint to the steering gear input shaft. Remove the lower intermediate shaft pinch bolt **(see illustration)**.

3    If equipped with power steering, place a drain pan under the steering gear. Detach the power steering pressure and return lines and cap the ends to prevent excessive fluid loss and contamination.

4    Separate the tie-rod ends from the

**21.2  Remove the lower intermediate shaft pinch bolt (arrow)**

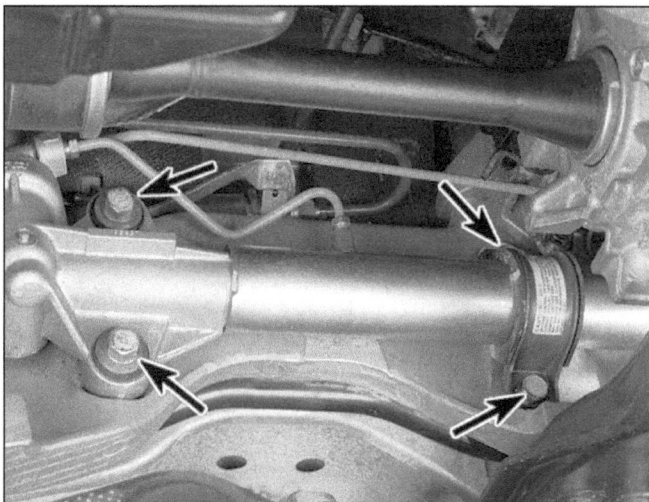

**21.7  To detach the steering gear from the crossmember, support the steering gear and remove the steering gear bracket-to-crossmember mounting bolts (arrows)**

steering knuckle arms (see Section 19).

5    Remove the front roll stopper mounting bolt. If equipped with a manual transaxle, remove the vibration damper. Remove the crossmember-to-centre member brace. Remove the centre member (see Section 2).

6    Disconnect the exhaust pipe from the exhaust manifold and lower the exhaust pipe.

7    Support the steering gear and remove the steering gear bracket-to-crossmember mounting bolts **(see illustration)**. Separate the intermediate shaft from the steering gear input shaft, move the steering gear unit to the right as far as it will go, then lower the left end down and pull it out to the left.

8    Check the steering gear mounting grommets for excessive wear or deterioration, replacing them if necessary.

## *Refitting*

**Caution:** *Make sure the steering gear is centred before refitting it.*

9    Raise the steering gear into position and connect the U-joint, aligning the marks.

10    Refit the mounting brackets and bolts and tighten them to the torque listed in this Chapter's Specifications.

11    Connect the tie-rod ends to the steering knuckle arms (see Section 19).

12    Refit the U-joint pinch bolt and tighten it to the torque listed in this Chapter's Specifications.

13    Connect the power steering pressure and return hoses to the steering gear.

14    The remainder of refitting is the reverse of removal.

15    Lower the vehicle. If equipped with power steering, fill the power steering pump reservoir with power steering fluid and bleed the steering system (see Section 23).

## 22    Power steering pump - removal and refitting

*Refer to illustration 22.4*

## *Removal*

1    Disconnect the cable from the negative battery terminal.

2    Using a large syringe or suction gun, remove as much fluid from the power steering fluid reservoir as possible. Place a drain pan under the vehicle to catch any fluid that spills out when the hoses are disconnected.

3    Loosen the alternator pivot and adjuster bolt and remove the drivebelt. Disconnect the pressure switch wiring from the pump.

4    Loosen the clamp and disconnect the fluid return hose from the power steering pump. Loosen the pressure line-to-pump fitting and separate the pressure line from the pump **(see illustration)**.

5    Remove the mounting bolts and remove the pump from the vehicle.

## *Refitting*

6    To refit the pump, reverse the removal procedure. Adjust the drivebelt tension following the procedure described in Chapter 1.

7    Fill the power steering pump reservoir with power steering fluid and bleed the system (see Section 23).

## 23    Power steering system - bleeding

1    Following any operation in which the power steering fluid lines have been disconnected, the power steering system must be bled to remove all air and obtain proper steering performance.

2    With the front wheels in the straight ahead position, check the power steering fluid level and, if low, add fluid until it reaches the Cold mark on the dipstick.

3    Start the engine and allow it to run at fast idle. Recheck the fluid level and add more if necessary to reach the Cold mark on the dipstick.

4    Bleed the system by turning the wheels from side to side, without hitting the stops. This will work the air out of the system. Keep the reservoir full of fluid as this is done.

5    When the air is worked out of the system, return the wheels to the straight ahead position and leave the vehicle running for several more minutes before shutting it off.

6    Road test the vehicle to be sure the steering system is functioning normally and

noise free.

7    Recheck the fluid level to be sure it is up to the Hot mark on the dipstick while the engine is at normal operating temperature. Add fluid if necessary (see Chapter 1).

## 24    Wheels and tyres - general information

*Refer to illustration 24.1*

1    Vehicles covered by this manual are equipped with metric-sized fiberglass or steel belted radial tyres **(see illustration)**. Use of other size or type of tyres may affect the ride and handling of the vehicle. Don't mix different types of tyres, such as radials and bias belted, on the same vehicle as handling may be seriously affected. It's recommended that tyres be renewed in pairs on the same axle, but if only one tyre is being renewed, be sure it's the same size, structure and tread design as the other.

2    Because tyre pressure has a substantial effect on handling and wear, the pressure on all tyres should be checked at least once a month or before any extended trips (see Chapter 1).

3    Wheels must be renewed if they are bent, dented, leak air, have elongated bolt holes, are heavily rusted, out of vertical symmetry or if the lug nuts won't stay tight. Wheel repairs that use welding or peening are not recommended.

4    Tyre and wheel balance is important in the overall handling, braking and performance of the vehicle. Unbalanced wheels can adversely affect handling and ride characteristics as well as tyre life. Whenever a tyre is refitted on a wheel, the tyre and wheel should be balanced by a shop with the proper equipment.

## 25    Wheel alignment - general information

*Refer to illustration 25.1*

1    A wheel alignment refers to the adjustments made to the wheels so they are in proper angular relationship to the suspension and the ground. Wheels that are out of proper alignment not only affect vehicle control, but also increase tyre wear. The front end should be measured for camber, caster and toe-in **(see illustration)**; toe-in can be adjusted by turning the tie-rods in or out but camber and caster are pre-set at the factory and cannot be adjusted. If camber and caster aren't within the specified dimensions, suspension parts are bent or worn and must be renewed. The rear should be measured for camber and toe-in, but neither is adjustable. It's set at the factory. If it is not within the standard dimensions, suspension parts are bent or worn and must be renewed.

Getting the proper wheel alignment is a very exacting process, one in which com-

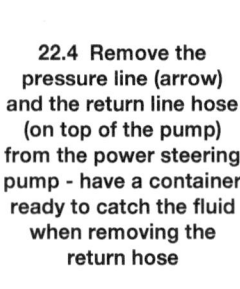

**22.4 Remove the pressure line (arrow) and the return line hose (on top of the pump) from the power steering pump - have a container ready to catch the fluid when removing the return hose**

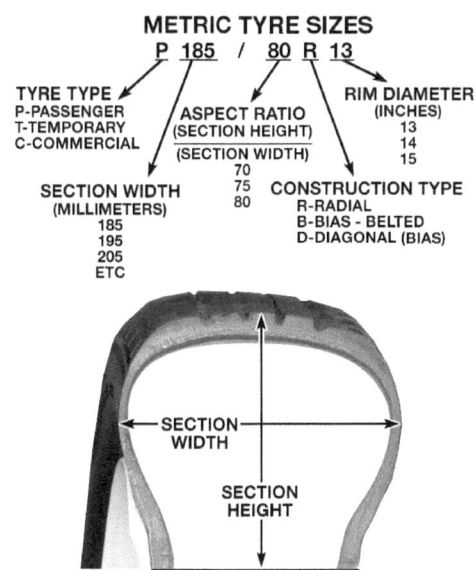

METRIC TYRE SIZES

P 185 / 80 R 13

TYRE TYPE
P-PASSENGER
T-TEMPORARY
C-COMMERCIAL

ASPECT RATIO
(SECTION HEIGHT)
(SECTION WIDTH)
70
75
80

RIM DIAMETER
(INCHES)
13
14
15

SECTION WIDTH
(MILLIMETERS)
185
195
205
ETC

CONSTRUCTION TYPE
R-RADIAL
B-BIAS - BELTED
D-DIAGONAL (BIAS)

SECTION
WIDTH

SECTION
HEIGHT

24.1  Metric tyre size code details

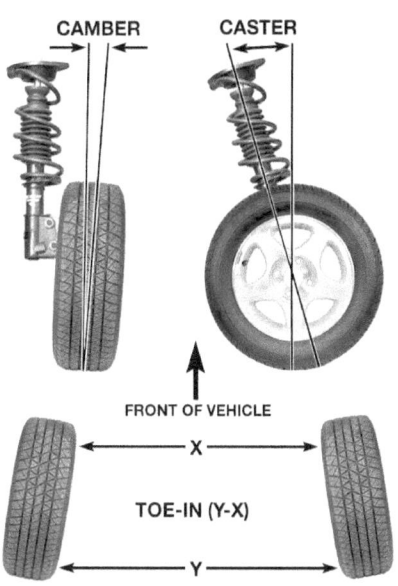

CAMBER          CASTER

FRONT OF VEHICLE

X

TOE-IN (Y-X)

Y

25.1  Front wheel alignment details

plicated and expensive machines are necessary to perform the job properly. Because of this, you should have a technician with the proper equipment perform these tasks. We will, however, use this space to give you a basic idea of what is involved with a wheel alignment so you can better understand the process and deal intelligently with the shop that does the work.

Toe-in is the turning in of the wheels. The purpose of a toe specification is to ensure parallel rolling of the wheels. In a vehicle with zero toe-in, the distance between the front edges of the wheels will be the same as the distance between the rear edges of the wheels. The actual amount of toe-in is normally only a fraction of an mm. On the front end, toe-in is controlled by the tie-rod end position on the tie-rod. Incorrect toe-in will cause the tyres to wear improperly by making them scrub against the road surface.

Camber is the tilting of the wheels from vertical when viewed from one end of the vehicle. When the wheels tilt out at the top, the camber is said to be positive (+). When the wheels tilt in at the top the camber is negative (-). The amount of tilt is measured in degrees from vertical and this measurement is called the camber angle. This angle affects the amount of tyre tread which contacts the road and compensates for changes in the suspension geometry when the vehicle is cornering or traveling over an undulating surface.

Caster is the tilting of the front steering axis from the vertical. A tilt toward the rear is positive caster and a tilt toward the front is negative caster.

# Notes

# Chapter 11   Body

**Contents**

## 1   General information

These models feature a "unibody" lay-out, using a floor pan with front and rear frame side rails which support the body components, front and rear suspension systems and other mechanical components.

Certain components are particularly vulnerable to accident damage and can be unbolted and repaired or renewed. Among these parts are the body mouldings, bum-pers, bonnet and luggage compartment lids and all glass.

Only general body maintenance prac-tices and body panel repair procedures within the scope of the do-it-yourselfer are included in this Chapter.

## 2   Body - maintenance

1   The condition of your vehicle's body is very important, because the resale value depends a great deal on it. It's much more difficult to repair a neglected or damaged body than it is to repair mechanical com-ponents. The hidden areas of the body, such as the wheel wells, the frame and the engine compartment, are equally important, although they don't require as frequent atten-tion as the rest of the body.

2   Once a year, or every 20,000 kilometres, it's a good idea to have the underside of the body steam cleaned. All traces of dirt and oil will be removed and the area can then be

These photos illustrate a method of repairing simple dents. They are intended to supplement *Body repair - minor damage* in this Chapter and should not be used as the sole instructions for body repair on these vehicles.

1  If you can't access the backside of the body panel to hammer out the dent, pull it out with a slide-hammer-type dent puller. In the deepest portion of the dent or along the crease line, drill or punch hole(s) at least one inch apart . . .

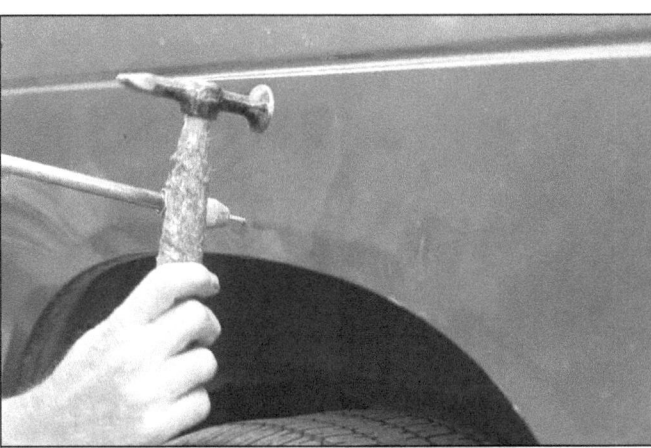

2  . . . then screw the slide-hammer into the hole and operate it. Tap with a hammer near the edge of the dent to help 'pop' the metal back to its original shape. When you're finished, the dent area should be close to its original contour and about 3 mm below the surface of the surrounding metal

3  Using coarse-grit sandpaper, remove the paint down to the bare metal. Hand sanding works fine, but the disc sander shown here makes the job faster. Use finer (about 320-grit) sandpaper to feather-edge the paint at least one inch around the dent area

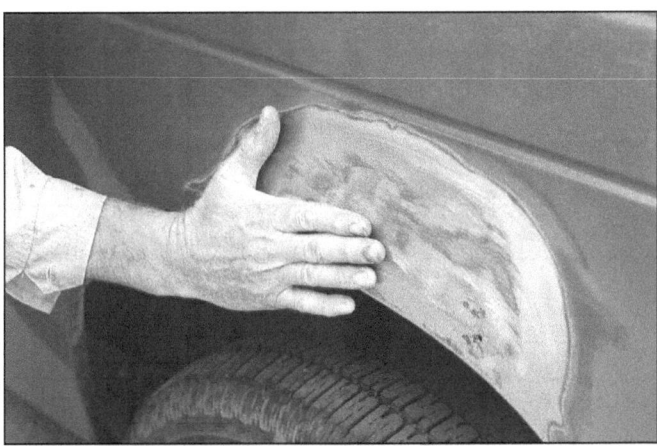

4  When the paint is removed, touch will probably be more helpful than sight for telling if the metal is straight. Hammer down the high spots or raise the low spots as necessary. Clean the repair area with wax/silicone remover

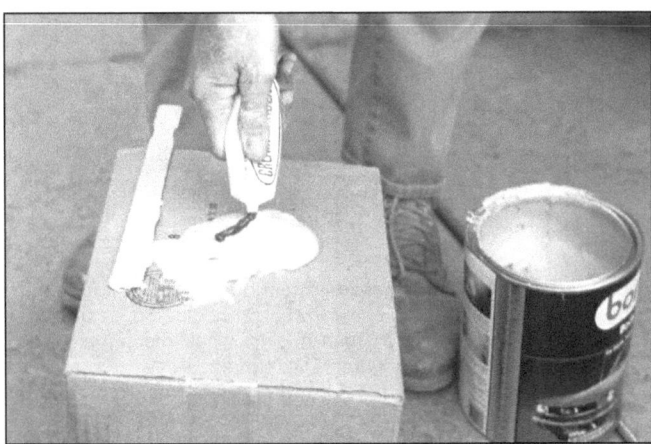

5  Following label instructions, mix up a batch of plastic filler and hardener. The ratio of filler to hardener is critical, and, if you mix it incorrectly, it will either not cure properly or cure too quickly (you won't have time to file and sand it into shape)

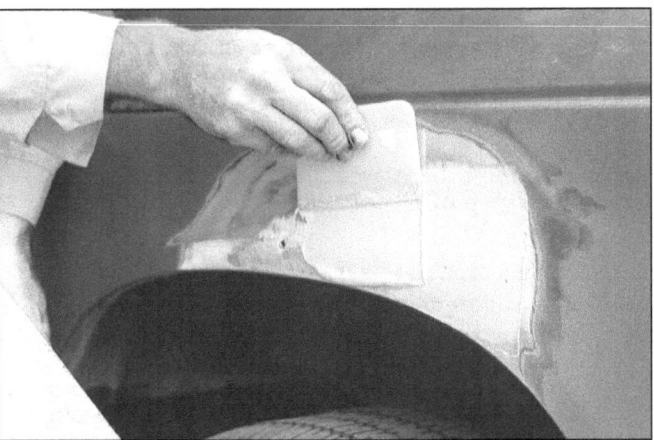

6  Working quickly so the filler doesn't harden, use a plastic applicator to press the body filler firmly into the metal, assuring it bonds completely. Work the filler until it matches the original contour and is slightly above the surrounding metal

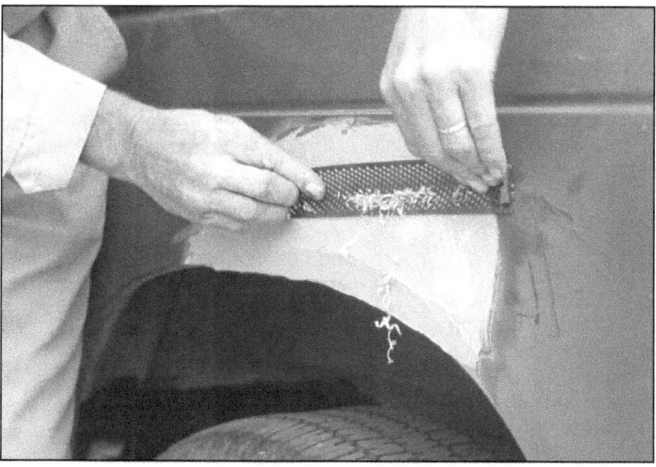

7 Let the filler harden until you can just dent it with your fingernail. Use a body file or Surform tool (shown here) to rough-shape the filler

8 Use coarse-grit sandpaper and a sanding board or block to work the filler down until it's smooth and even. Work down to finer grits of sandpaper - always using a board or block - ending up with 360 or 400 grit

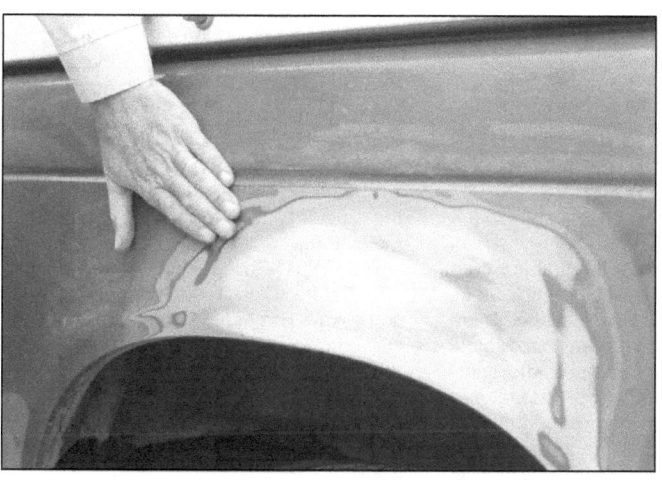

9 You shouldn't be able to feel any ridge at the transition from the filler to the bare metal or from the bare metal to the old paint. As soon as the repair is flat and uniform, remove the dust and mask off the adjacent panels or trim pieces

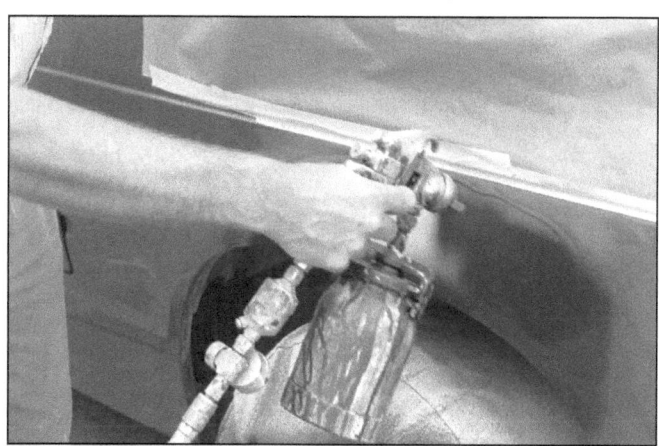

10 Apply several layers of primer to the area. Don't spray the primer on too heavy, so it sags or runs, and make sure each coat is dry before you spray on the next one. A professional-type spray gun is being used here, but aerosol spray primer is available inexpensively from auto parts stores

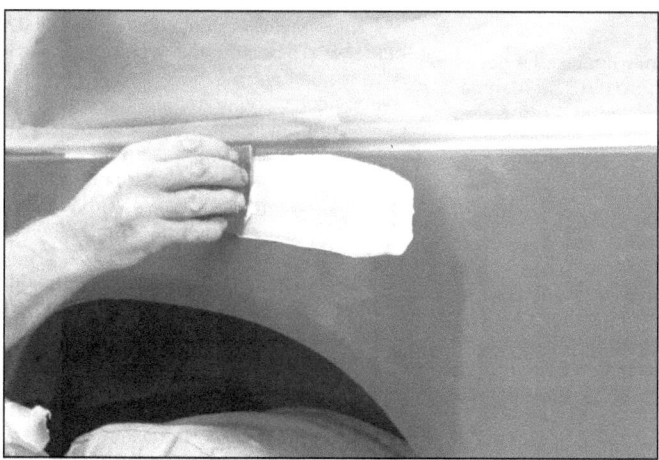

11 The primer will help reveal imperfections or scratches. Fill these with glazing compound. Follow the label instructions and sand it with 360 or 400-grit sandpaper until it's smooth. Repeat the glazing, sanding and respraying until the primer reveals a perfectly smooth surface

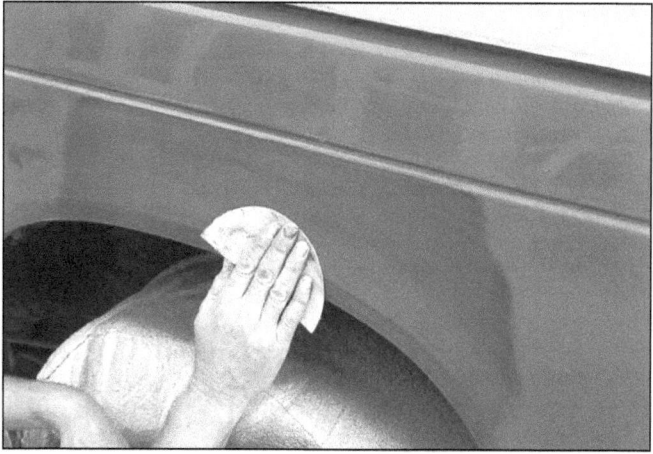

12 Finish sand the primer with very fine sandpaper (400 or 600-grit) to remove the primer overspray. Clean the area with water and allow it to dry. Use a tack rag to remove any dust, then apply the finish coat. Don't attempt to rub out or wax the repair area until the paint has dried completely (at least two weeks)

inspected carefully for rust, damaged brake lines, frayed electrical wires, damaged cables and other problems. The front suspension components should be greased after completion of this job.

3   At the same time, clean the engine and the engine compartment with a steam cleaner or water soluble degreaser.

4   The wheel wells should be given close attention, since undercoating can peel away and stones and dirt thrown up by the tyres can cause the paint to chip and flake, allowing rust to set in. If rust is found, clean down to the bare metal and apply an anti-rust paint.

5   The body should be washed about once a week. Wet the vehicle thoroughly to soften the dirt, then wash it down with a soft sponge and plenty of clean soapy water. If the surplus dirt is not washed off very carefully, it can wear down the paint.

6   Spots of tar or asphalt thrown up from the road should be removed with a cloth soaked in solvent.

7   Once every six months, wax the body and chrome trim. If a chrome cleaner is used to remove rust from any of the vehicle's plated parts, remember that the cleaner also removes part of the chrome, so use it sparingly.

## 3   Vinyl trim - maintenance

Don't clean vinyl trim with detergents, caustic soap or petroleum-based cleaners. Plain soap and water works just fine, with a soft brush to clean dirt that may be ingrained. Wash the vinyl as frequently as the rest of the vehicle.

After cleaning, application of a high quality rubber and vinyl protectant will help prevent oxidation and cracks. The protectant can also be applied to weather-stripping, vacuum lines and rubber hoses, which often fail as a result of chemical degradation, and to the tyres.

## 4   Upholstery and carpets - maintenance

Every three months remove the carpets or mats and clean the interior of the vehicle (more frequently if necessary). Vacuum the upholstery and carpets to remove loose dirt and dust.

## 5   Body repair - minor damage

*See photo sequence*

### *Repair of minor scratches*

1   If the scratch is superficial and does not penetrate to the metal of the body, repair is very simple. Lightly rub the scratched area with a fine rubbing compound to remove

loose paint and built-up wax. Rinse the area with clean water.

2   Apply touch-up paint to the scratch, using a small brush. Continue to apply thin layers of paint until the surface of the paint in the scratch is level with the surrounding paint. Allow the new paint at least two weeks to harden, then blend it into the surrounding paint by rubbing with a very fine rubbing compound. Finally, apply a coat of wax to the scratch area.

3   If the scratch has penetrated the paint and exposed the metal of the body, causing the metal to rust, a different repair technique is required. Remove all loose rust from the bottom of the scratch with a pocket knife, then apply rust inhibiting paint to prevent the formation of rust in the future. Using a rubber or nylon applicator, coat the scratched area with glaze-type filler. If required, the filler can be mixed with thinner to provide a very thin paste, which is ideal for filling narrow scratches. Before the glaze filler in the scratch hardens, wrap a piece of smooth cotton cloth around the tip of a finger. Dip the cloth in thinner and then quickly wipe it along the surface of the scratch. This will ensure that the surface of the filler is slightly hollow. The scratch can now be painted over as described earlier in this Section.

### *Repair of dents*

4   When repairing dents, the first job is to pull the dent out until the affected area is as close as possible to its original shape. There is no point in trying to restore the original shape completely as the metal in the damaged area will have stretched on impact and cannot be restored to its original contours. It is better to bring the level of the dent up to a point which is about 3 mm below the level of the surrounding metal. In cases where the dent is very shallow, it is not worth trying to pull it out at all.

5   If the back side of the dent is accessible, it can be hammered out gently from behind using a soft-face hammer. While doing this, hold a block of wood firmly against the opposite side of the metal to absorb the hammer blows and prevent the metal from being stretched.

6   If the dent is in a section of the body which has double layers, or some other factor makes it inaccessible from behind, a different technique is required. Drill several small holes through the metal inside the damaged area, particularly in the deeper sections. Screw long, self-tapping screws into the holes just enough for them to get a good grip in the metal. Now the dent can be pulled out by pulling on the protruding heads of the screws with locking pliers.

7   The next stage of repair is the removal of paint from the damaged area and from 25 mm or so of the surrounding metal. This is done with a wire brush or sanding disk in a drill motor, although it can be done just as effectively by hand with sandpaper. To complete the preparation for filling, score the

surface of the bare metal with a screwdriver or the tang of a file, or drill small holes in the affected area. This will provide a good grip for the filler material. To complete the repair, see the subsection on filling and painting later in this Section.

### *Repair of rust holes or gashes*

8   Remove all paint from the affected area and from 25 mm or so of the surrounding metal using a sanding disk or wire brush mounted in a drill motor. If these are not available, a few sheets of sandpaper will do the job just as effectively.

9   With the paint removed, you will be able to determine the severity of the corrosion and decide whether to renew the whole panel, if possible, or repair the affected area. New body panels are not as expensive as you may think and it is often quicker to fit a new panel than to repair large areas of rust.

10   Remove all trim pieces from the affected area except those which will act as a guide to the original shape of the damaged body, such as headlight shells, etc. Using metal snips or a hacksaw blade, remove all loose metal and any other metal that is badly affected by rust. Hammer the edges of the hole inward to create a slight depression for the filler material.

11   Wire brush the affected area to remove the powdery rust from the surface of the metal. If the back of the rusted area is accessible, treat it with rust inhibiting paint.

12   Before filling is done, block the hole in some way. This can be done with sheet metal riveted or screwed into place, or by stuffing the hole with wire mesh.

13   Once the hole is blocked off, the affected area can be filled and painted. See the following subsection on filling and painting.

### *Filling and painting*

14   Many types of body fillers are available, but generally speaking, body repair kits which contain filler paste and a tube of resin hardener are best for this type of repair work. A wide, flexible plastic or nylon applicator will be necessary for imparting a smooth and contoured finish to the surface of the filler material. Mix up a small amount of filler on a clean piece of wood or cardboard (use the hardener sparingly). Follow the manufacturer's instructions on the package, otherwise the filler will set incorrectly.

15   Using the applicator, apply the filler paste to the prepared area. Draw the applicator across the surface of the filler to achieve the desired contour and to level the filler surface. As soon as a contour that approximates the original one is achieved, stop working the paste. If you continue, the paste will begin to stick to the applicator. Continue to add thin layers of paste at 20-minute intervals until the level of the filler is just above the surrounding metal.

16   Once the filler has hardened, the excess can be removed with a body file. From then on, progressively finer grades of sandpa-

per should be used, starting with a 180-grit paper and finishing with 600-grit wet-or-dry paper. Always wrap the sandpaper around a flat rubber or wooden block, otherwise the surface of the filler will not be completely flat. During the sanding of the filler surface, the wet-or-dry paper should be periodically rinsed in water. This will ensure that a very smooth finish is produced in the final stage.

17   At this point, the repair area should be surrounded by a ring of bare metal, which in turn should be encircled by the finely feathered edge of good paint. Rinse the repair area with clean water until all of the dust produced by the sanding operation is gone.

18   Spray the entire area with a light coat of primer. This will reveal any imperfections in the surface of the filler. Repair the imperfections with fresh filler paste or glaze filler and once more smooth the surface with sandpaper. Repeat this spray-and-repair procedure until you are satisfied that the surface of the filler and the feathered edge of the paint are perfect. Rinse the area with clean water and allow it to dry completely.

19   The repair area is now ready for painting. Spray painting must be carried out in a warm, dry, windless and dust free atmosphere. These conditions can be created if you have access to a large indoor work area, but if you are forced to work in the open, you will have to pick the day very carefully. If you are working indoors, dousing the floor in the work area with water will help settle the dust which would otherwise be in the air. If the repair area is confined to one body panel, mask off the surrounding panels. This will help minimise the effects of a slight mismatch in paint colour. Trim pieces such as chrome strips, door handles, etc., will also need to be masked off or removed. Use masking tape and several thickness of newspaper for the masking operations.

20   Before spraying, shake the paint can thoroughly, then spray a test area until the spray painting technique is mastered. Cover the repair area with a thick coat of primer. The thickness should be built up using several thin layers of primer rather than one thick one. Using 600-grit wet-or-dry sandpaper, rub down the surface of the primer until it is very smooth. While doing this, the work area should be thoroughly rinsed with water and the wet-or-dry sandpaper periodically rinsed as well. Allow the primer to dry before spraying additional coats.

21   Spray on the top coat, again building up the thickness by using several thin layers of paint. Begin spraying in the centre of the repair area and then, using a circular motion, work out until the whole repair area and about 50 mm of the surrounding original paint is covered. Remove all masking material 10 to 15 minutes after spraying on the final coat of paint. Allow the new paint at least two weeks to harden, then use a very fine rubbing compound to blend the edges of the new paint into the existing paint. Finally, apply a coat of wax.

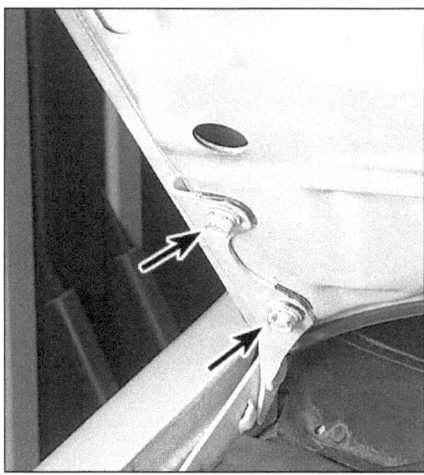

**9.2  Mark around the entire hinge plate before removing the bonnet - loosen the bolts (arrows) and move the bonnet to adjust its position**

## 6   Body repair - major damage

1   Major damage must be repaired by an auto body shop specifically equipped to perform unibody repairs. These shops have the specialised equipment required to do the job properly.

2   If the damage is extensive, the body must be checked for proper alignment or the vehicle's handling characteristics may be adversely affected and other components may wear at an accelerated rate.

3   Due to the fact that all of the major body components (bonnet, fenders, etc.) are separate and renewable units, any seriously damaged components should be renewed rather than repaired. Sometimes the components can be found in a wrecking yard that specialises in used vehicle components, often at considerable savings over the cost of new parts.

## 7   Hinges and locks - maintenance

Once every 4800 kilometers, or every three months, the hinges and latch assemblies on the doors, bonnet and luggage compartment should be given a few drops of light oil or lock lubricant. The door latch strikers should also be lubricated with a thin coat of grease to reduce wear and ensure free movement. Lubricate the door and luggage compartment locks with spray-on graphite lubricant.

## 8   Windscreen and fixed glass - renewal

Renewal of the windscreen and fixed glass requires the use of special fast-setting adhesive/caulk materials and some specialised tools. It is recommended that these

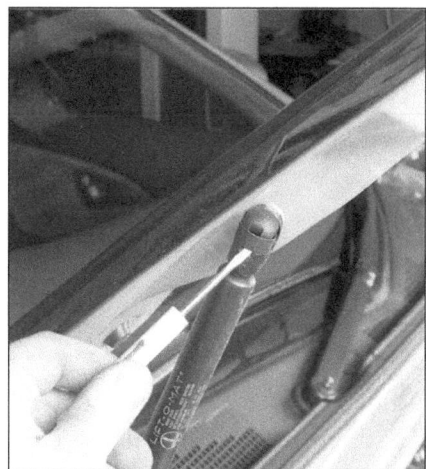

**9.3  Prise the retaining clips from the bonnet support struts**

operations be left to a dealer or a shop specializing in glass work.

## 9   Bonnet - removal, refitting and adjustment

*Refer to illustrations 9.2, 9.3, 9.10 and 9.11*
**Caution:** *Never attempt to incinerate, puncture or repair the support rods; they are gas-charged with high pressure gas in order to maintain the bonnet open.*
**Note:** *The bonnet is heavy and somewhat awkward to remove and refit - at least two people should perform this procedure.*

### *Removal and refitting*

1   Use blankets or pads to cover the cowl area of the body and fenders. This will protect the body and paint as the bonnet is lifted free.

2   Use a scribe or a permanent marker to make alignment marks around the hinge plate to ensure proper alignment upon refitting **(see illustration)**.

3   Disconnect the washer hoses. Use a screwdriver to prise off the bonnet support gas struts **(see illustration)**.

4   Have an assistant support the weight of the bonnet. Remove the hinge-to-bonnet screws or bolts.

5   Lift off the bonnet.

6   Refitting is the reverse of removal.

### *Adjustment*

7   Front-and-rear and side-to-side adjustment of the bonnet is made by moving the hinge plate slot after loosening the bolts or nuts **(see illustration 9.2)**.

8   Mark a line around the entire hinge plate so you can judge the amount of movement **(see illustration 9.2)**.

9   Loosen the bolts and move the bonnet into correct alignment. Move the bonnet only a little at a time. Tighten the hinge bolts and carefully lower the bonnet to check the position.

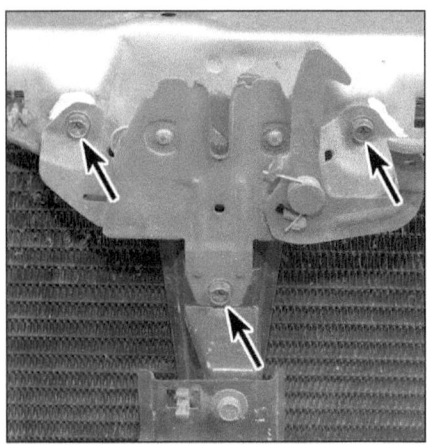

**9.10  To adjust the bonnet latch, mark lines around the bonnet latch mounting bolts (arrows), loosen the bolts, position the latch where required and retighten the bolts**

10   If necessary after refitting, the entire bonnet latch assembly can be adjusted up-and-down as well as side-to-side on the fire-wall (front hinged bonnet) or radiator brace (rear hinged bonnet) so the bonnet closes securely, with the bonnet flush with the fenders. To perform this adjustment, mark around the bonnet latch mounting screws to provide

**10.5  Remove the two screws retaining the bonnet release cable handle**

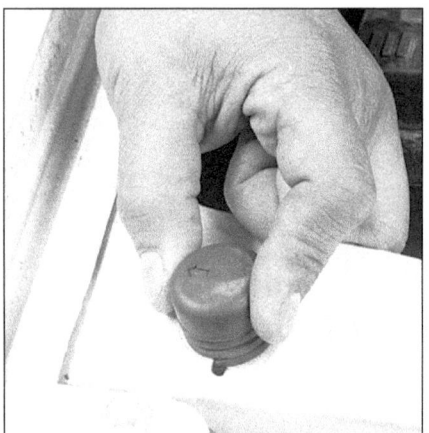

**9.11  Adjust the bonnet flush with the fenders using the bonnet bumpers (arrow)**

a reference point, then loosen them and repo-sition the latch assembly, as necessary **(see illustration)**. Following adjustment, retighten the mounting bolts. On some models the bonnet can be further adjusted up-and-down by screwing the bonnet latch hook assembly in or out.
11   Finally, adjust the bonnet bumpers so that the bonnet, when closed, is flush with the fenders **(see illustration)**.
12   The bonnet latch assembly, as well as the hinges, should be periodically lubricated with white lithium base grease to prevent sticking or jamming.

---

**10   Bonnet latch and release cable - removal and refitting**

---

*Refer to illustrations 10.4 and 10.5*

### Latch

1     Remove the radiator grille (refer to Sec-tion 11).
2     Remove the bolts, disconnect the cable and remove the latch.
3     Refitting is the reverse of removal. Adjust the bonnet latch as described in Sec-tion 9).

**10.4  Disconnect the bonnet release cable from the latch**

### Cable

4     Disconnect the bonnet release cable from the bonnet latch after removing the splash shield **(see illustration)**.
5     Remove the right-side kick panel and remove the bolts retaining the bonnet release cable handle **(see illustration)**.
6     Disconnect the cable from the retain-ing clips and pull the cable into the interior. Attach a section of stiff wire to aid in pulling the new cable through the body.
7     Refitting is the reverse of removal.

---

**11   Radiator grille - removal and refitting**

---

### TE/TF/TH/TJ and KE/KF/KH/ KJ models
*Refer to illustrations 11.1 and 11.2*
1     Remove the plastic splash shield attach-ing screws **(see illustration)** and remove the shield.
2     Open the bonnet and using a flat-bladed screwdriver, press in on the centre tab of the grille retaining clips while gently pulling out on the grille **(see illustration)**.

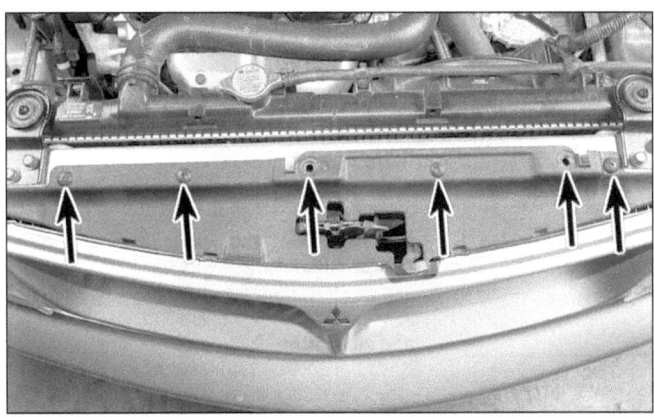

**11.1  Remove the splash shield retaining screws (arrows) and remove the shield**

**11.2  Using a flat-bladed screwdriver, press the radiator grille retaining clips in**

12.1 Remove the lower splash shield mounting screws (arrows)

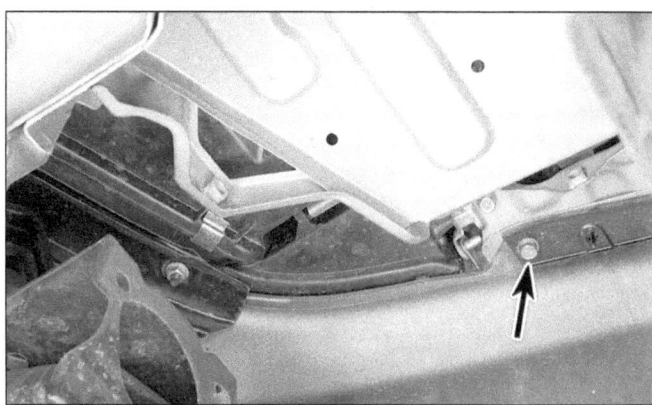

12.3 Remove the front bumper cover bracket retaining screws (arrow) from underneath (right side shown)

12.4 Typical bumper mounting bolts (arrows)

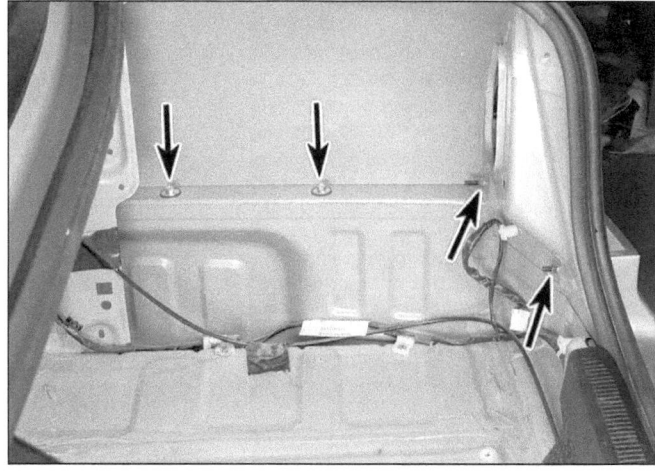

12.8 Remove the bumper cover-to-body attaching nuts and bolts (arrows)

3    After releasing all the clips, remove the radiator grille.
4    Align the grille retainers with the clips and very carefully push the grille in until all the clips lock into place.
5    Verify that the grille is secured properly at all points.

### TL/TW and KL/KW models

6    Open the bonnet and remove the retaining screws from the top of the grille.
7    Carefully pull the grille forward to disengage the four clips at the bottom of the grille and remove the grille.
8    Refitting is the reverse of removal.

## 12   Bumpers - removal and refitting

### Front bumper

*Refer to illustrations 12.1, 12.3 and 12.4*

1    Remove the grille (see Section 11). Remove the lower splash shield and panel **(see illustration)**.
2    Remove the front fog/turn signal lamp assemblies from the bumper (see Chapter 12).
3    Remove the bumper cover-to-body bolts from underneath **(see illustration)**.

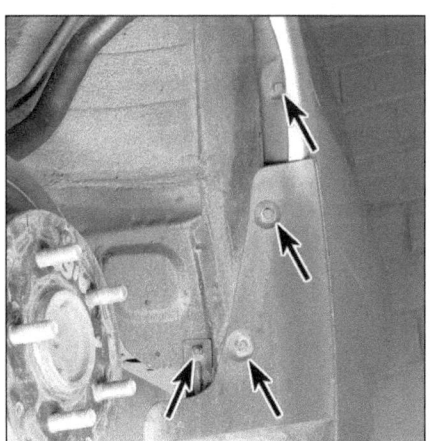

12.9a Remove the splash shield-to-bumper cover mounting bolts (arrows) - sedan models

4    Support the bumper's weight with a jack or jackstand, or have an assistant support the bumper. Remove the upper retaining bolts located at the corner of each headlight then the lower retaining bolts and detach the bumper **(see illustration)**.
5    Refitting is the reverse of removal. Tighten the retaining bolts securely.

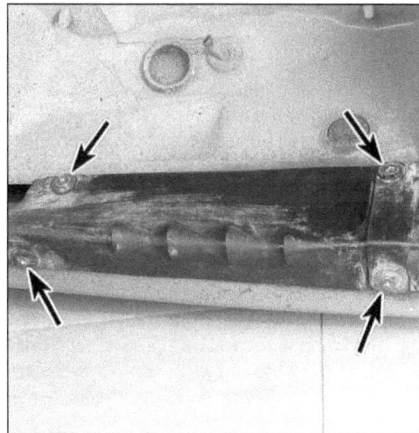

12.9b Remove the splash shield-to-bumper cover mounting screws (arrows) - wagon models

6    Refit the bumper cover and any other components which were removed.

### Rear bumper

*Refer to illustrations 12.8, 12.9a, 12.9b and 12.11*

7    Remove the right-side, left-side and rear trim from inside the luggage compartment.

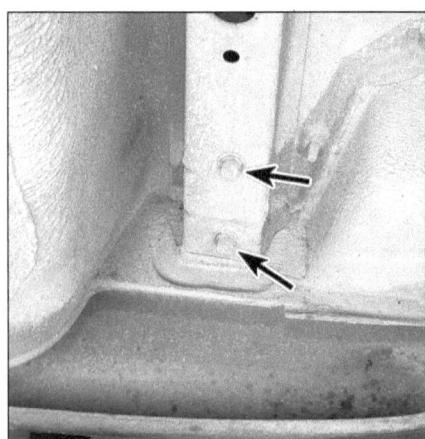

**12.11 Remove the rear bumper mounting bolts (arrows) - right side shown**

8    Remove the bumper cover attaching nuts and bolts **(see illustration)**.
9    Remove the lower splash shield-to-bumper cover bolts **(see illustrations)** and remove the shields.
10   Support the bumper's weight with a jack or jackstand, or have an assistant support the bumper.
11   Remove the mounting nuts **(see illustration)** and remove the bumper from the vehicle. **Note:** *Remove the muffler hangers to gain access to the right side bolts.*
12   Refitting is the reverse of removal. Tighten the retaining bolts securely.

## 13   Luggage compartment lid - removal, refitting and adjustment

*Refer to illustrations 13.3 and 13.7*
1    Open the luggage compartment lid and cover the edges of the luggage compartment with pads or cloths to protect the painted surfaces when the lid is removed.
2    Disconnect any cable or electrical connectors which are attached to the luggage compartment lid and would interfere with removal.
3    Scribe or paint alignment marks around the hinge plates **(see illustration)**.
4    While an assistant supports the lid, remove the lid-to-hinge bolts on both sides and lift off the lid **(see illustration 13.3)**.
5    Refitting is the reverse of removal. **Note:** *When refitting the luggage compartment lid, align the hinge plate with the marks made during removal.*
6    After refitting, close the lid and check that it is in proper alignment with the surrounding panels. Front and rear and side-to-side adjustments of the lid are controlled by the position of the lid-to-hinge bolts in their slots. To adjust, loosen the lid-to-hinge bolts, reposition the lid and retighten the bolts.
7    The height of the lid in relation to the surrounding body panels when closed can be adjusted by loosening the striker bolts, repositioning the striker and tightening the bolts **(see illustration)**. Some models also are equipped with rubber bumpers which can

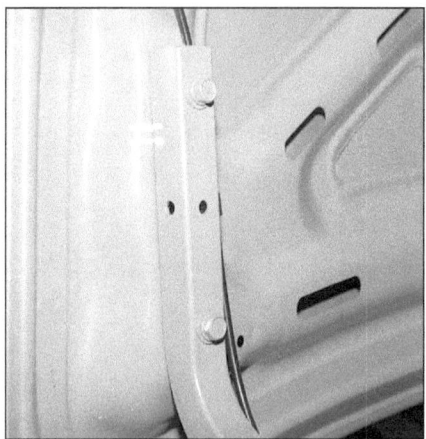

**13.3 Scribe or paint around the hinge plates so you can re-fit the luggage compartment lid to its proper location - unscrew or loosen the lid-to-hinge bolts to remove or adjust the luggage compartment lid**

be screwed in or out for a final adjustment of the luggage compartment lid so that it is even with the surrounding body.

## 14   Luggage compartment lid latch and release cable - removal and refitting

*Refer to illustrations 14.1 and 14.3*

### *Luggage compartment lid latch*
1    Open the luggage compartment lid latch trim cover **(see illustration)**. Scribe a line around the luggage compartment latch as a reference point for refitting.
2    Disconnect the luggage compartment latch release cable, if equipped.
3    Remove the two bolts retaining the luggage compartment latch **(see illustration)**.
4    Refitting is the reverse of removal.
5    Adjust the latch striker (see Section 13).

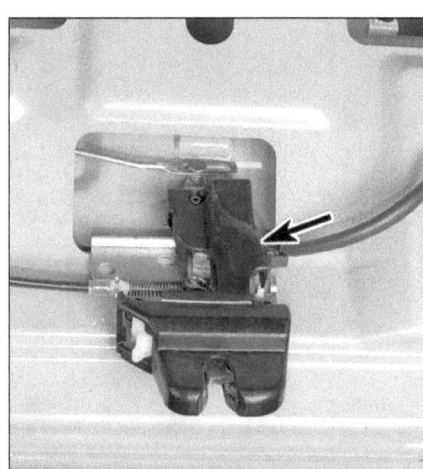

**14.1 Remove the latch cover (arrow)**

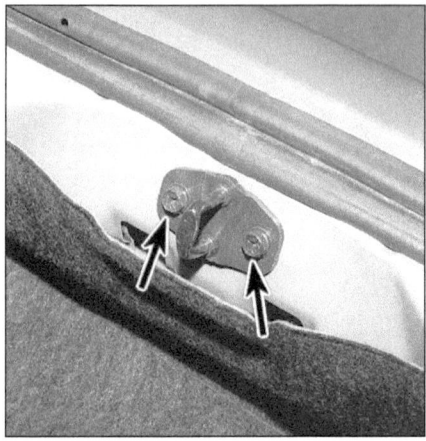

**13.7 After loosening the bolts (arrows), you can move the striker to adjust the luggage compartment lid position**

### *Release cable*
6    Remove the scuff plates from the right front and right rear doors.
7    Remove the rear seat (see Section 31).
8    From inside the luggage compartment, remove the right-side and rear trim panels.
9    Disconnect the cable from the release handle.
10   Disconnect the retaining clips from the luggage compartment lid and remove the cable.
11   Refitting is the reverse of removal.

## 15   Liftgate (station wagon models) - removal, refitting and adjustment

*Refer to illustration 15.4*
1    Open the liftgate and cover the upper body area around the opening with pads or cloths to protect the painted surfaces when the liftgate is removed.
2    Disconnect any cables, hoses or electrical connectors which would interfere with removal of the liftgate. Detach the headliner for access to the tailgate hinge retaining nuts.

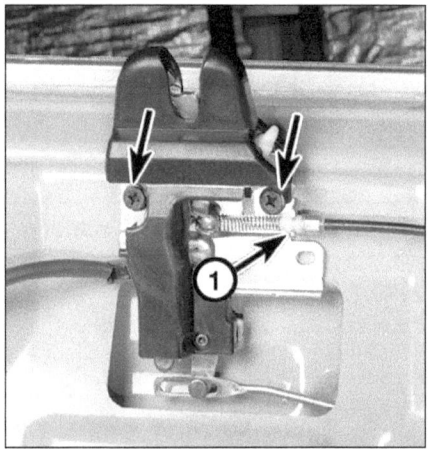

**14.3 Remove the release cable end (1) and retaining bolts (arrows) then remove the latch**

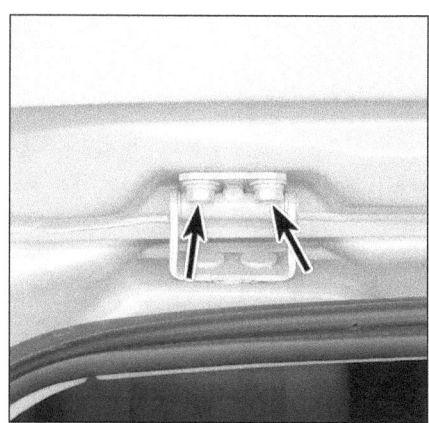

**15.4  After marking the hinge location, remove the bolts (arrows)**

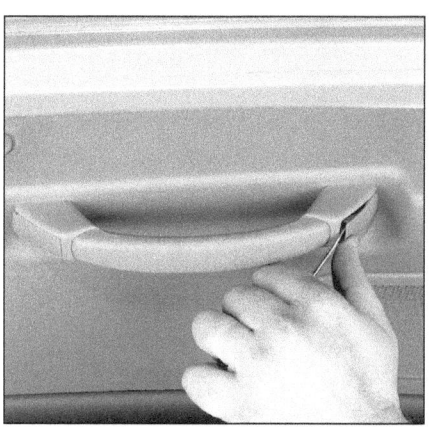

**16.2  Using a flat-bladed screwdriver, prise the screw cover caps from the handle**

**16.3  Remove the handle mounting screws (arrows) and remove the handle**

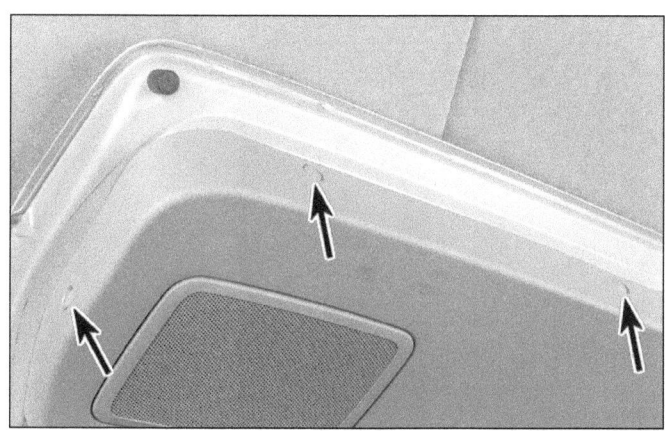

**16.4  Remove the trim cover plastic retainers (arrows) - left side shown**

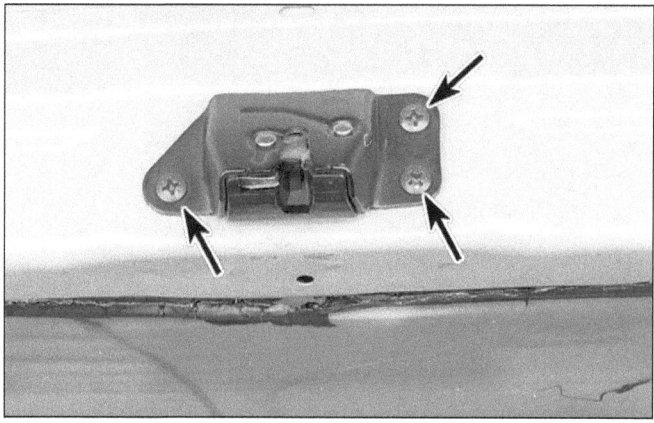

**16.7  Remove the liftgate latch retaining screws**

3    While an assistant supports the liftgate, disconnect the support struts (see Section 17).
4    Remove the hinge nuts and detach the liftgate from the vehicle **(see illustration)**.
5    Refitting is the reverse of removal.
6    After refitting, close the liftgate and check that the door is in proper alignment with the surrounding panels. Adjustments to the liftgate are made by moving the position of the hinge bolts in their slots. To adjust, loosen the hinge bolts and reposition the hinge either side-to-side or front-to-rear the desired amount and retighten the bolts **(see illustration 15.4)**.
7    The engagement of the liftgate can be adjusted by loosening the latch striker bolts, repositioning the latch striker and tightening the bolts.

## 16  Liftgate latch and lock cylinder (station wagon models) - removal and refitting

*Refer to illustrations 16.2, 16.3, 16.4 and 16.7*
1    Open the liftgate and maintain the liftgate securely open.
2    From inside the liftgate, remove the liftgate handle screw caps **(see illustration)**.

3    Remove the handle mounting screws **(see illustration)** and remove the handle.
4    Remove the trim panel retaining clips **(see illustration)** and remove the trim panel from the liftgate. Be very careful not to damage the paint surface.
5    Carefully remove the plastic sealing sheet around the liftgate and place it on a flat clean surface. Mark around the latch for future reference.
6    Disconnect any cables, rods or wiring connectors that may be connected to the liftgate latch.
7    Remove the bolts retaining the liftgate latch and remove it **(see illustration)**.
8    Remove the control rod clip, and separate the rod from the lock.
9    Remove the lock cylinder retaining clip and remove the lock, be careful not the damage the paint surface.
10    Refitting is the reverse of removal.

## 17  Support rods - removal, refitting and adjustment

*Refer to illustration 17.2*
**Caution:** *Never attempt to incinerate, puncture or repair the support rods; they are gas-*

*charged with high pressure gas in order to maintain the liftgate open.*
1    Open the liftgate and maintain the liftgate securely open.
2    From inside the liftgate, use a small screwdriver to prise out the retaining clip and separate the support rod from the ball-stud **(see illustration)**.
3    Disconnect the upper end of the support

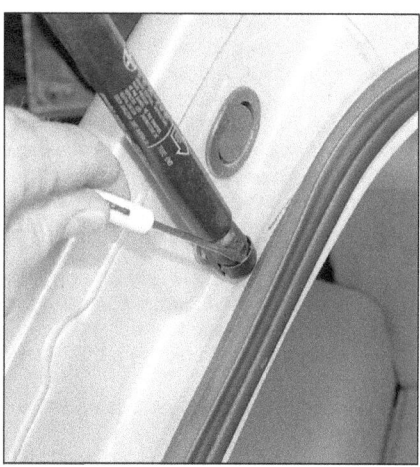

**17.2  From inside the liftgate, prise out the support rod retaining clip**

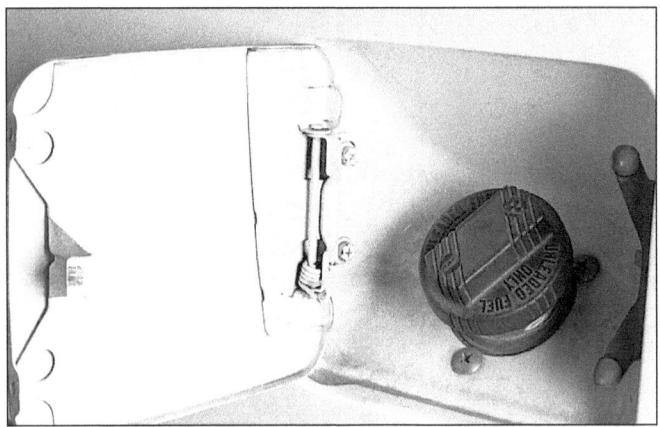

18.2 With the filler door open remove the two bolts and remove the door

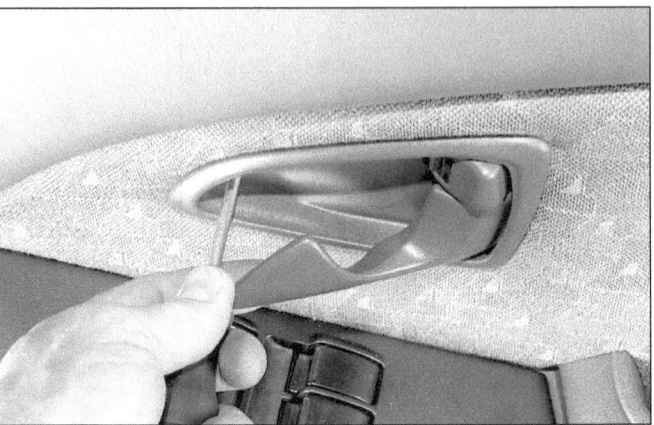

20.2a Remove the door handle cover

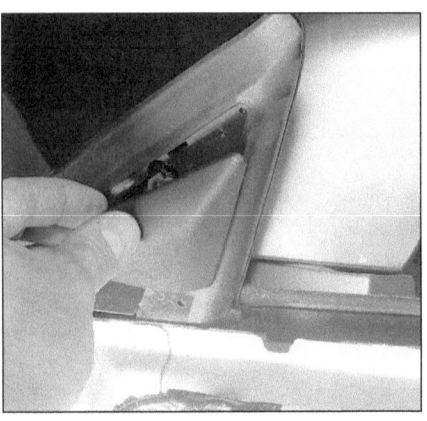

20.2b Remove the inner delta or tweeter trim cover

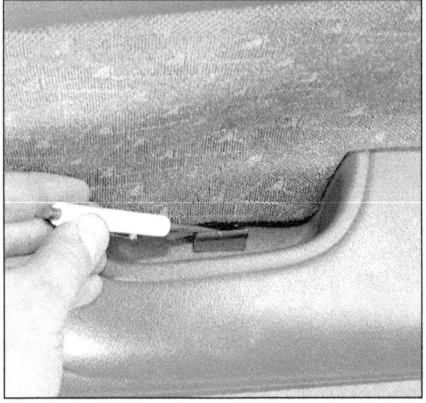

20.3 Prise off the cap for access to the screw beneath it

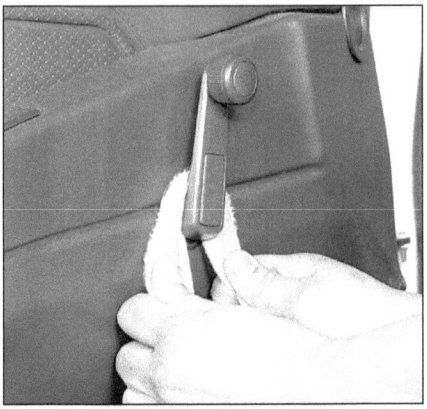

20.4a Work a cloth back and forth behind the window handle until the clip is dislodged

rod from the liftgate **(see illustration 17.2)**.
4    Refit one support rod at a time.
5    Refitting is the reverse of removal.

---

## 18 Fuel filler door - removal and refitting

*Refer to illustration 18.2*

### Fuel filler door
1    Open the fuel tank filler neck door.
2    With the filler door open remove the two bolts and remove the door **(see illustration)**.
**Note:** *Some vehicles are equipped with an electric fuel filler door release. On these models, there is an emergency door release cable located in the rear luggage compartment.*
3    To remove the release cable on vehicles so equipped, remove the scuff plates from the right front and right rear doors.
4    Remove the rear seat (see Section 31).
5    From inside the luggage compartment, remove the left-side and rear trim panels.
6    Disconnect the cable from the release handle.
7    Disconnect the release cable from the filler door latch.
8    Remove the clips that retain the cable to body and remove the cable.
9    Refitting is the reverse of removal.

---

## 19 Front fender - removal and refitting

1    Lever off the side signal light assemblies using a screwdriver while protecting the paint with a cloth (see Chapter 12). Remove the front side air dam.
2    Remove the inner splash shield.
3    Remove the screws and detach the splash shield and extension.
4    Remove the bolts and detach the fender.
5    Prior to refitting, apply body sealant to the contact surfaces of the fender and body. Refitting is the reverse of removal.

---

## 20 Door trim panel - removal and refitting

*Refer to illustrations 20.2a, 20.2b, 20.3, 20.4a, 20.4b, 20.5, 20.6, 20.7a, 20.7b and 20.7c*
**Caution:** *If the stereo in your vehicle is equipped with an anti-theft system, make sure you have the correct activation code before disconnecting the battery.*
1    If equipped with power windows, disconnect the negative cable from the battery.
2    Remove the inner door handle cover **(see illustration)**. Remove the inner delta or

tweeter cover at the upper front of the front door **(see illustration)**.
3    Remove the cap and the screw beneath it at the armrest **(see illustration)**.
4    On manual window vehicles, remove the window regulator handle **(see illustrations)**.
5    Remove the screw located in the vent supply duct **(see illustration)**.
6    Starting from the bottom of the panel carefully pull the trim panel away from the

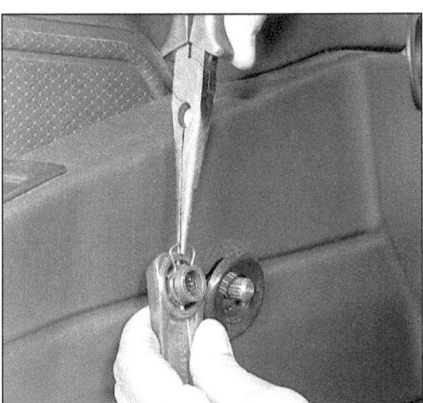

20.4b Snap the clip back into the groove - the window crank is now ready to be refitted by pushing it on the shaft

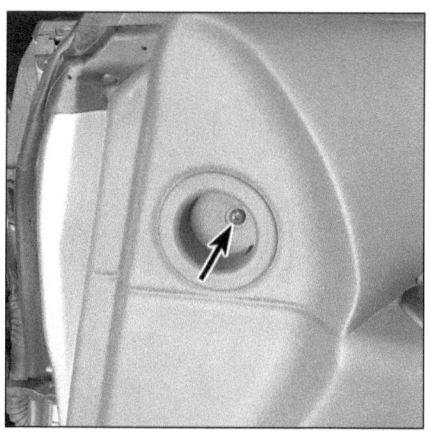

**20.5 Remove the door panel retaining screw hidden in the air vent seal**

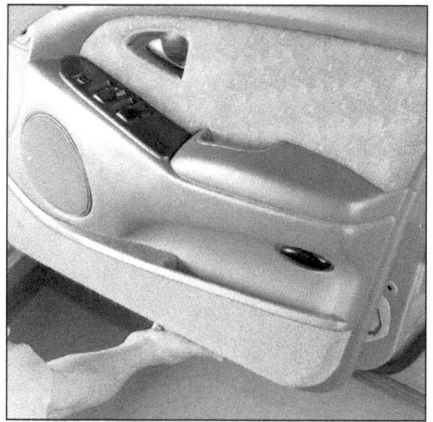

**20.6 Carefully separate the door panel from the door**

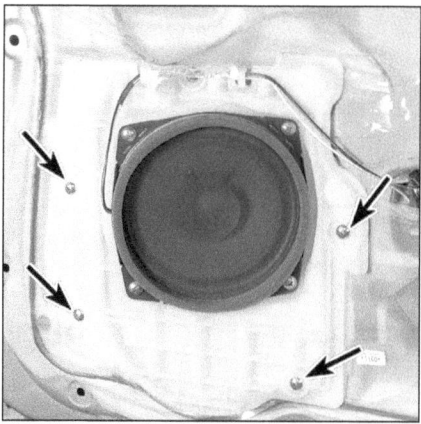

**20.7a Remove the speaker cover mounting screws (arrows)**

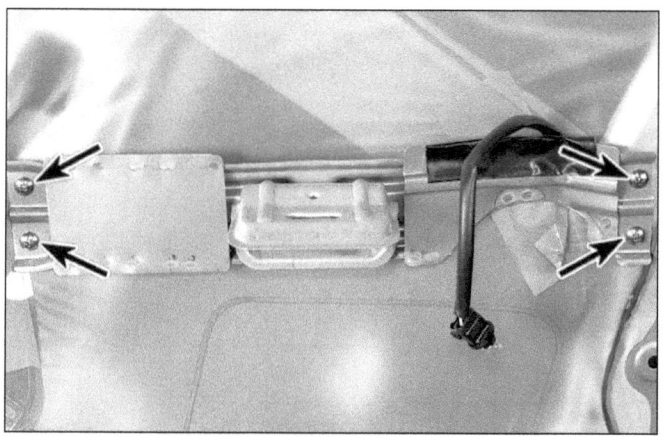

**20.7b Remove the armrest bracket (arrows)**

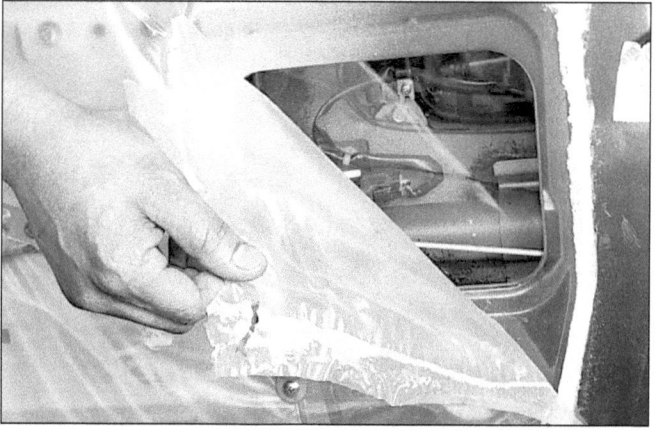

**20.7c Be very careful when pulling the watershield off - don't tear or distort it**

door **(see illustration)**. Disconnect any electrical wiring and then lift the panel up and free.

7    For access to the inner door, remove the door handle (see Section 21), speaker cover, armrest bracket and peel back the plastic watershield, taking care not to tear it **(see illustrations)**. To refit, place the watershield in position and press it in place.

8    Prior to refitting of the door panel, make sure to refit any clips in the panel which may have come out during the removal procedure and remain in the door itself.

9    Plug in any electrical connectors and place the panel in position in the door. Press the door panel into place until the clips are seated and refit any retaining screws and armrest/door pulls. Refit the manual regulator window crank if so equipped.

---

### 21    Door latch, lock cylinder and handles - removal and refitting

1    Remove the door trim panel and plastic watershield (Section 20).

2    Temporarily refit the window crank handle or switch and raise the door window glass to the up position.

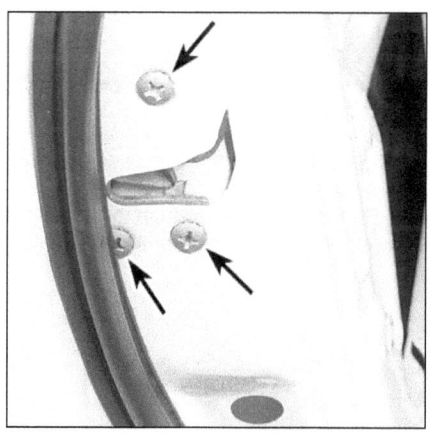

**21.5 Remove the latch screws from the end of the door (arrows)**

### *Door latch*

*Refer to illustration 21.5*

3    Remove the inside handle. Disconnect the wiring harness. Use pliers to slide the retaining clip off and remove the lock cylinder from the door.

4    Reach in through the door service hole and disconnect the door safety rod and the door inside handle rod from the latch.

5    Remove the three door latch retaining

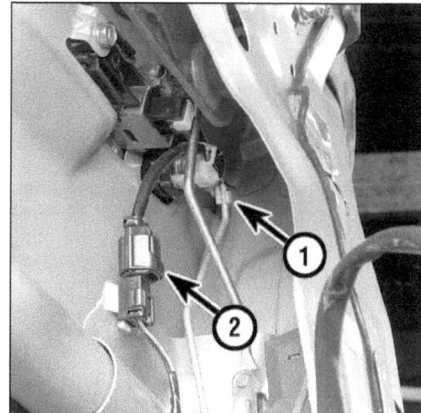

**21.7 Disconnect the lock cylinder rod (1) and electrical connector (2) from the lock cylinder**

screws from the end of the door **(see illustration)**. Remove the door latch.

6    Refitting is the reverse of removal.

### *Lock cylinder*

*Refer to illustration 21.7*

7    Disconnect the lock cylinder rod, electrical connector from the lock cylinder **(see illustration)** and remove the retaining screw

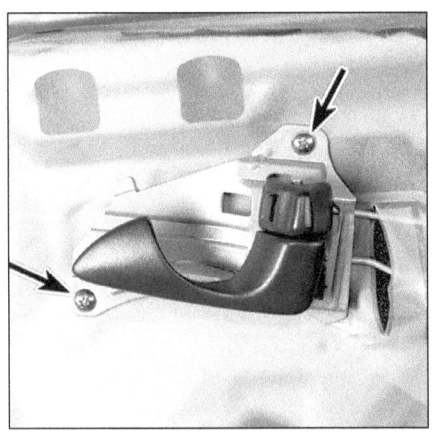

**21.9a  Remove the handle retaining screws (arrows). . .**

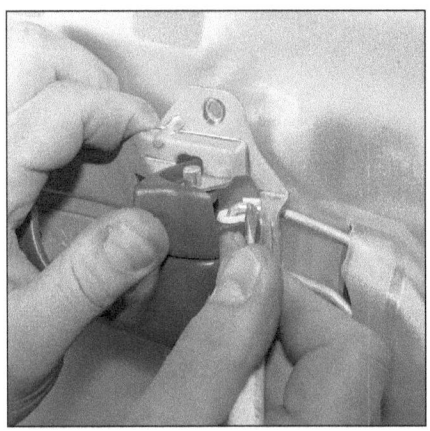

**21.9b  and remove the latch rod retaining clip using a small screwdriver**

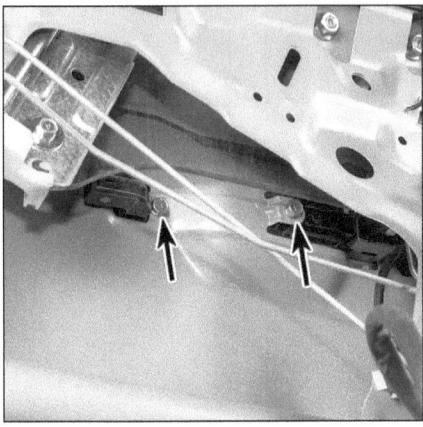

**21.13  Remove the outside handle retaining screws through the access hole in the door frame**

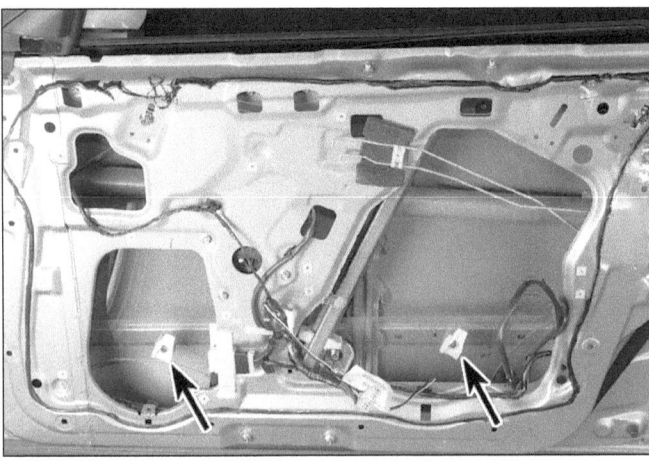

**22.2  Remove the wedge stops from the glass (arrows)**

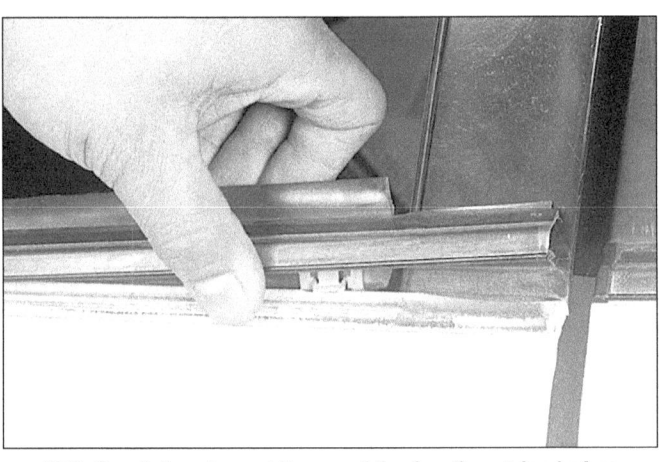

**22.3  Carefully prise out the moulding/sealing strips before removing the glass**

and lock cylinder.

8    Refitting is the reverse of removal.

### Inside handle

*Refer to illustrations 21.9a and 21.9b*

9    Remove the retaining screws **(see illustration)**. Detach the control rod **(see illustration)**.

10    Rotate the handle away and detach it from the door.

11    Refitting is the reverse of removal.

### Outside handle

*Refer to illustration 21.13*

12    Disconnect the control rod from the handle.

13    Remove the screws from inside the door and detach the handle from the door **(see illustration)**.

14    Refitting is the reverse of removal.

---

### 22   Door window glass - removal and refitting

*Refer to illustrations 22.2, 22.3 and 22.4*

1    Remove the door trim panel and plastic

watershield (see Section 20).

2    Lower the window glass and remove the wedge stops **(see illustration)**.

3    Carefully prise off the door glass moulding/sealing strip from the top of the door **(see illustration)**.

4    Raise the window enough to access the glass-to-channel retaining bolts and remove

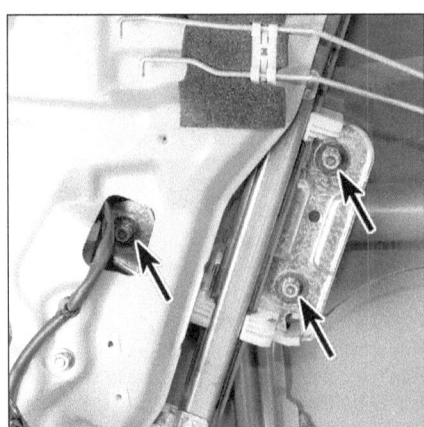

**22.4  Raise the window just enough to access the glass retaining bolts through the hole in the door frame**

the bolts **(see illustration)**.

5    Remove the window glass by tilting the front edge of the glass down and then sliding the glass up and out of the door.

6    Refitting is the reverse of removal. If the glass is to be removed from the glass run, make sure to measure from the rear edge of the glass to the run bolt hole so the new glass can be refitted in the same position.

7    If it is necessary to adjust the glass position, loosen the mounting screws, move the glass to the desired position, then tighten the screws.

---

### 23   Door window glass regulator - removal and refitting

*Refer to illustrations 23.4a and 23.4b*

1    Remove the door trim panel and plastic watershield (Section 20).

2    Raise the window enough to access the glass-to-channel retaining bolts and remove the bolts (see Section 22).

3    Lift the door glass up and secure it to the door frame with tape or wedge a rubber block between the glass and door frame. **Caution:** *Make sure the door glass is properly*

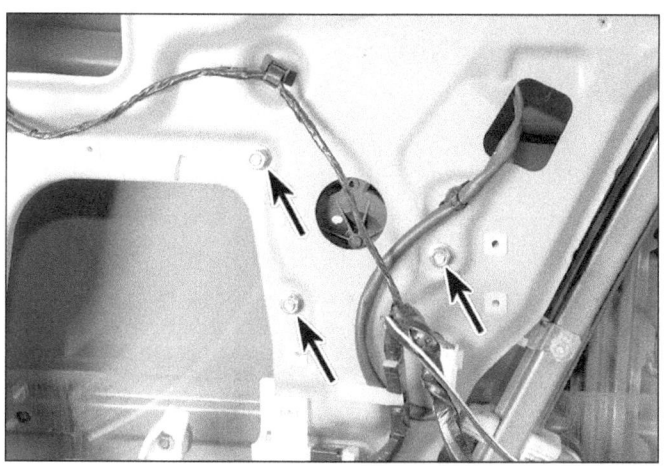

**23.4a  Remove the power window motor mounting nuts - (power window shown manual similar)**

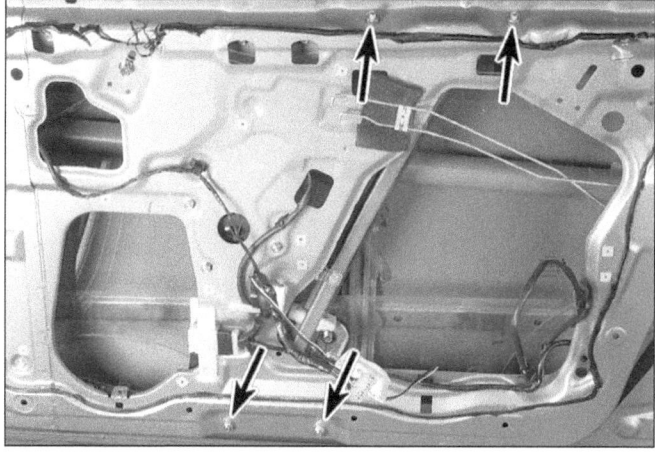

**23.4b  Remove the window regulator-to-door nuts (arrows)**

**24.2  Remove the outside mirror mounting bolts (arrows) and remove the mirror**

**25.3a  Support the door securely and remove the door check-to-body bolt (arrow)**

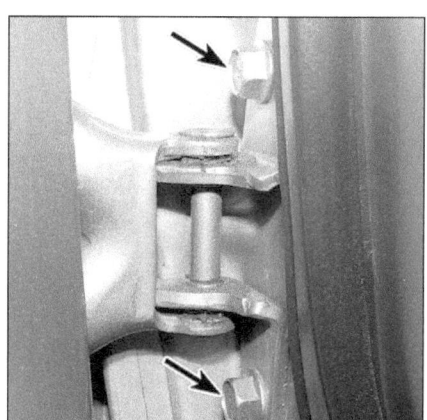

**25.3b Remove the upper and lower hinge-to-door bolts (arrows)**

secured or remove it completely.

4  Remove the bolts retaining the regulator to the door **(see illustrations)**.

5  Slide the regulator spindle down out of the pressed groove and pull the regulator assembly back and out through the access hole.

6  Refitting is the reverse of removal. Lubricate all of the sliding parts with grease.

## 24  Outside rear view mirrors - removal and refitting

*Refer to illustration 24.2*

**Caution:** *If the stereo in your vehicle is equipped with an anti-theft system, make sure you have the correct activation code before disconnecting the battery.*

1  If equipped with power mirrors, disconnect the cable from the negative battery terminal.

2  Rotate the mirror body to expose the mounting bolts **(see illustration)**.

3  Remove the retaining screws, lift off the mirror and unplug the electrical connector (if equipped).

4  Refitting is the reverse of removal.

## 25  Door - removal, refitting and adjustment

*Refer to illustrations 25.3a, 25.3b and 25.4*

1  If equipped with power windows or door locks, remove the door trim panel. Disconnect any electrical connectors and push them through the door opening so they won't interfere with door removal.

2  Place a jack or stand under the door or have an assistant on hand to support it when the hinges are removed. **Note:** *If a jack or stand is being used, place a rag between it and the door to protect the door's painted surfaces.*

3  Disconnect the door check **(see illustration)**. Remove the hinge-to-door bolts **(see illustration)** and carefully lift off the door. Refitting is the reverse of removal.

4  Following refitting of the door, check that it is in proper alignment and adjust it, if necessary, as follows:

a)  *Up-and-down and forward-and-backward adjustments are made by loosening the hinge-to-body bolts and moving the door, as necessary.*

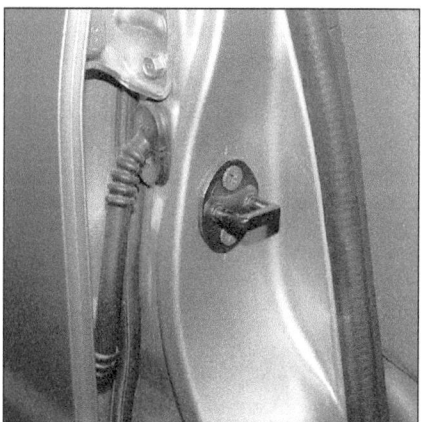

**25.4  Adjust the door lock striker by loosening the screws and tapping the striker in the desired direction with a plastic mallet**

b)  *The door lock striker can also be adjusted both up-and-down and sideways to provide a positive engagement with the locking mechanism. This is done by loosening the retaining screws and moving the striker, as necessary* **(see illustration)**.

26.3 Remove the two bezel screws

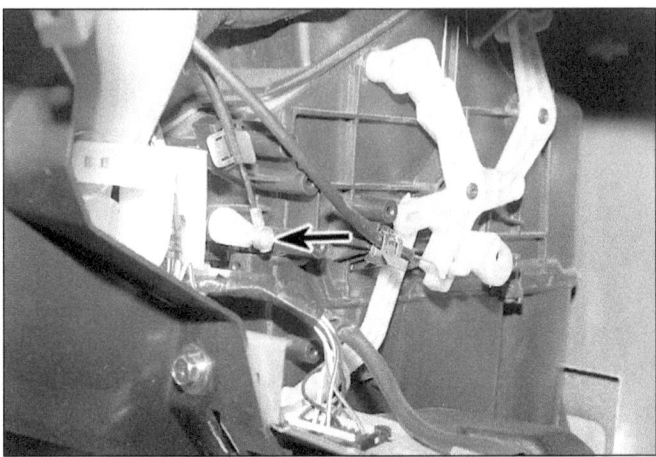

27.3a Disconnect the centre air out let cable from the lever (arrow) under the drivers side dash . . .

27.3b .. then carefully prise the centre air outlet from the dash

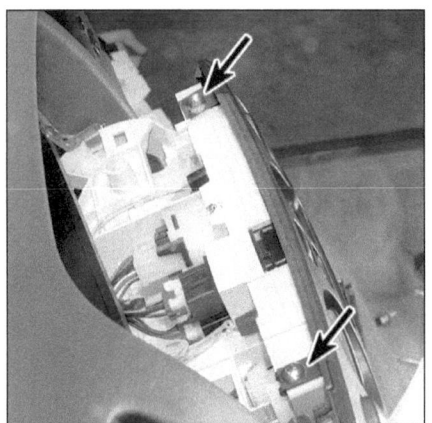

27.4a Remove the temperature control assembly to trim panel retaining screws (arrows)

27.4b. . . and carefully pull the panel out to release the retaining clips

## 26   Instrument cluster bezel - removal and refitting

*Refer to illustration 26.3*

**Warning:** *Some models covered by this manual are equipped with airbags. Always disable the Supplemental Restraint System before working in the vicinity of the impact sensors, steering column or instrument panel to avoid the possibility of accidental deployment of the airbag, which could cause personal injury* (see Chapter 12).

**Caution:** *If the stereo in your vehicle is equipped with an anti-theft system, make sure you have the correct activation code before disconnecting the battery.*

1   Disconnect the cable from the negative battery terminal.

2   Remove the lower dash trim panels (see Section 27).

3   Remove the instrument cluster bezel retaining screws **(see illustration)**.

4   Grasp the bezel securely and pull it straight back to detach it and remove the electrical connection to the dimmer.

5   Refitting is the reverse of removal.

## 27   Dashboard trim panels - removal and refitting

**Warning:** *Some models covered by this manual are equipped with airbags. Always disable the Supplemental Restraint System before working in the vicinity of the impact sensors, steering column or instrument panel to avoid the possibility of accidental deployment of the airbag, which could cause personal injury* (see Chapter 12).

**Caution:** *If the stereo in your vehicle is equipped with an anti-theft system, make sure you have the correct activation code before disconnecting the battery.*

1   Disconnect the cable from the negative battery terminal.

### *Centre trim panel*

*Refer to illustrations 27.3a, 27.3b, 27.4a and 27.4b*

2   Pull the ashtray out and remove the drivers-side lower trim panel **(see illustration 27.6)**

3   Remove the centre air outlet assembly **(see illustrations)**.

4   Remove the two temperature control head-to-trim panel retaining screws and remove the panel **(see illustrations)**.

5   Pull the panel out, disconnect the wiring harness connectors and remove the panel.

### *Drivers-side lower trim panel*

*Refer to illustration 27.6*

6   Prise out the right side screw cover for access, then remove the screws **(see illustration)**.

7   Detach the trim panel, lower it from the instrument panel and disconnect the bonnet release cable.

8   Refitting is the reverse of removal.

### *Glove box*

*Refer to illustrations 27.9, 27.10, 27.12a and 27.12b*

**Warning:** *Do not disconnect the harness without disabling the airbag system* (see Chapter 12).

9   Remove the undercover panel under the glove box **(see illustration)**.

10   Remove the glovebox hinge retaining screws **(see illustration)**.

11   Open the glovebox, press the two rub-

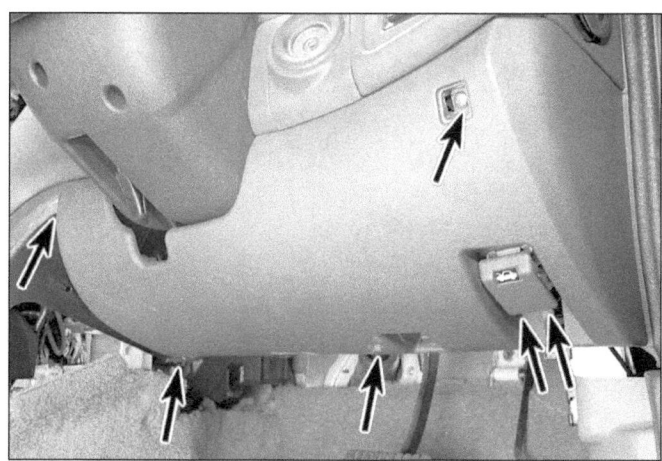

**27.6 Prise off the small screw access cover and remove the retaining screws (arrows)**

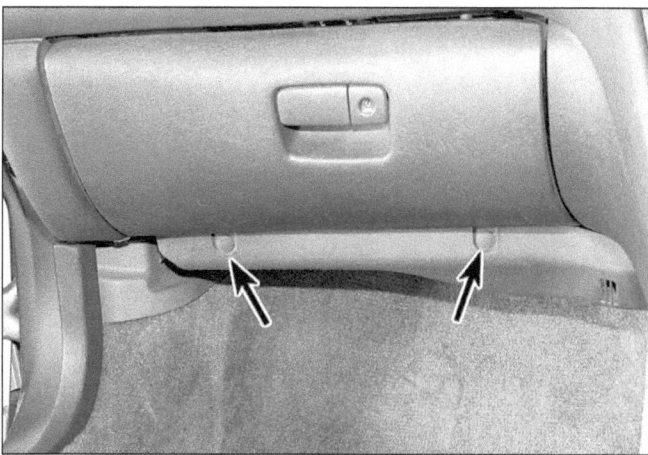

**27.9 Remove the undercover panel plastic retaining clips (arrows)**

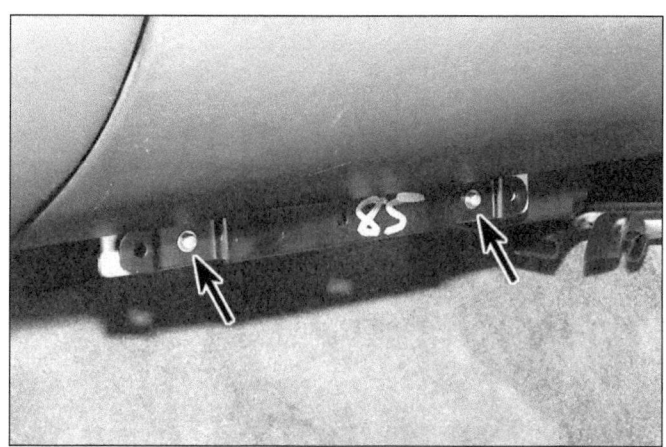

**27.10 Remove glove box hinge two retaining screws (arrows)**

**27.12a Remove the glove box outer case retaining screws (arrows)**

ber stoppers in and lower the glove box from the instrument panel.

12   Remove the glove box outer casing mounting screws **(see illustration)**, disconnect the boot release connector and lower the case. If equipped with a passenger side airbag, unclip the airbag harness from the case **(see illustration)**.

## 28   Steering column covers - removal and refitting

*Refer to illustration 28.3*

**Warning:** *Some models covered by this manual are equipped with airbags. Always disable the Supplemental Restraint System before working in the vicinity of the impact sensors, steering column or instrument panel to avoid the possibility of accidental deployment of the airbag, which could cause personal injury* (see Chapter 12).

1   Remove the driver's-side lower panel (see Section 27).
2   Remove the steering wheel, if necessary (see Chapter 10).

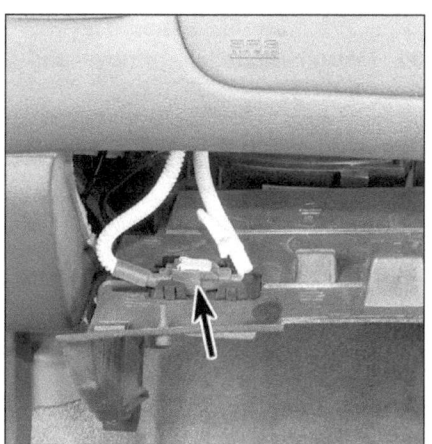

**27.12b Unclip the passenger side airbag harness from the case (arrow)**

3   Remove the column cover screws **(see illustration)**.
4   Rotate the upper cover up and off, disconnect the wiring connectors and remove the lower cover.
5   Refitting is the reverse of removal procedure.

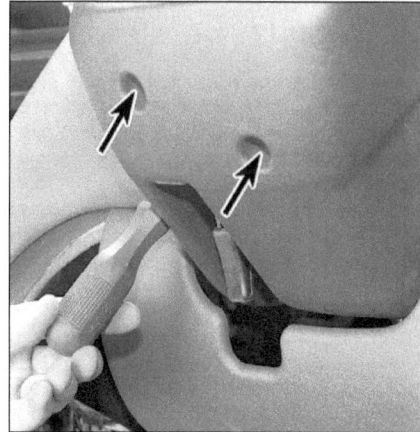

**28.3 Remove the screws retaining the upper and lower steering column covers**

## 29   Centre floor console - removal and refitting

*Refer to illustrations 29.2, 29.3, 29.4 and 29.5*
**Warning:** *Some models covered by this manual are equipped with airbags. Always disable*

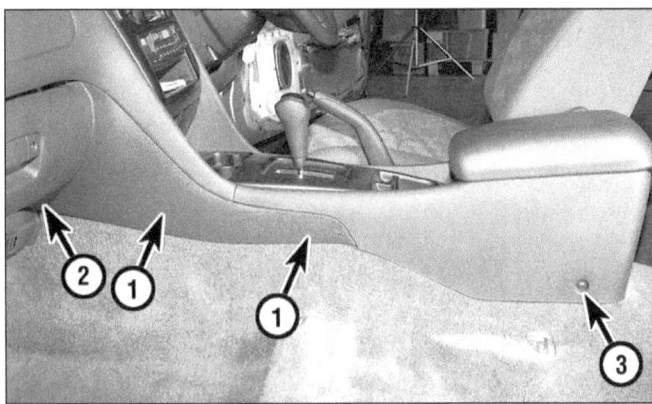

**29.2 Remove side trim and lower console box exterior screws (arrows) - Left side shown**

*1　Side trim panel (hidden) plastic clips*
*2　Side trim front retaining screw*
*3　Console box retaining screw*

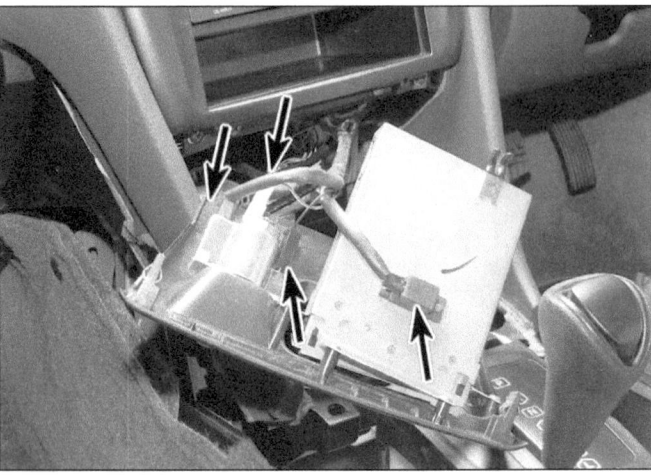

**29.3 Disconnect the electrical connectors (arrows) and remove the ashtray**

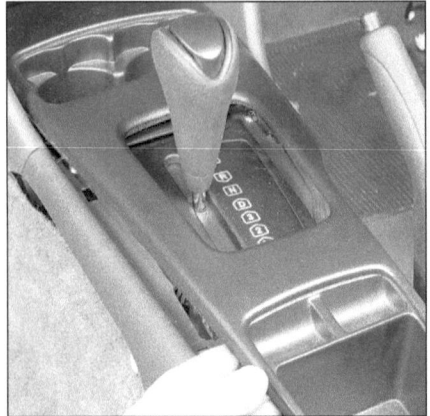

**29.4 Carefully remove the centre console trim panel from the rear side**

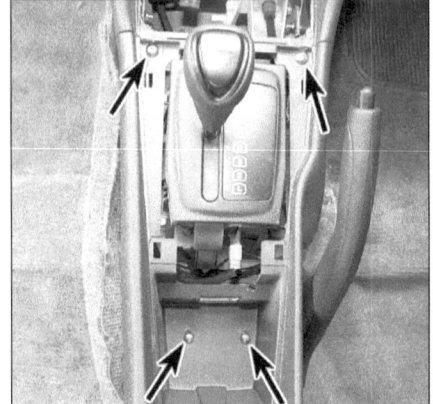

**29.5 Remove the lower console box retaining screws (arrows)**

**30.5 Remove the key cylinder trim retaining screws (arrows) and remove the support foam and trim**

the Supplemental Restraint System before working in the vicinity of the impact sensors, steering column or instrument panel to avoid the possibility of accidental deployment of the airbag, which could cause personal injury (see Chapter 12).
**Caution:** *If the stereo in your vehicle is equipped with an anti-theft system, make sure you have the correct activation code before disconnecting the battery.*
1　Disconnect the cable from the negative battery terminal.
2　Remove the console side covers and floor console box side retaining screws **(see illustration)**. **Note:** *The side covers are also retained with (hidden) plastic clips.*
3　Pull the ashtray out and remove electrical connections **(see illustration)**. On Verada models, prise out the cup holder and coin holder.
4　Carefully prise the top trim panel off **(see illustration)**.
5　Remove the screws from the lower console box retaining screws **(see illustration)**. Lift the console upwards.
6　Refitting is the reverse of removal.

## 30　Instrument panel - removal and refitting

*Refer to illustrations 30.5, 30.8, 30.10, 30.12a, 30.12b, 30.14 and 30.16*
**Warning:** *Some models covered by this manual are equipped with airbags. Always disable the Supplemental Restraint System before working in the vicinity of the impact sensors, steering column or instrument panel to avoid the possibility of accidental deployment of the airbag, which could cause personal injury (see Chapter 12).*
**Caution:** *If the stereo in your vehicle is equipped with an anti-theft system, make sure you have the correct activation code before disconnecting the battery.*
1　Disconnect the cable from the negative battery terminal.
2　Remove the steering wheel (see Chapter 10).
3　Remove the instrument cluster bezel (see Section 26), the dashboard trim panels (see Section 27), the steering column covers (see Section 28) and the centre console (see Section 29).

4　Remove the instrument cluster (see Chapter 12).
5　Remove the key cylinder panel **(see illustration)**.
6　Prise out the centre air outlet. Prise out the ashtray.
7　Remove the radio and air conditioning control panel assembly (refer to Section 27).
8　Remove the centre message display **(see illustration)** and disconnect the electri-

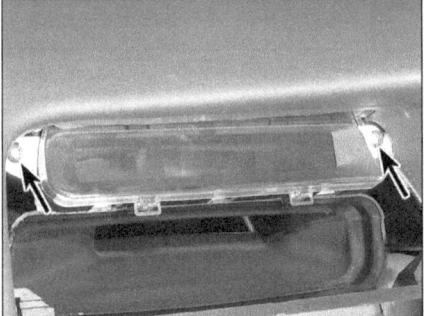

**30.8 Remove the centre display retaining screws, (arrows) and carefully pull the display from the dash**

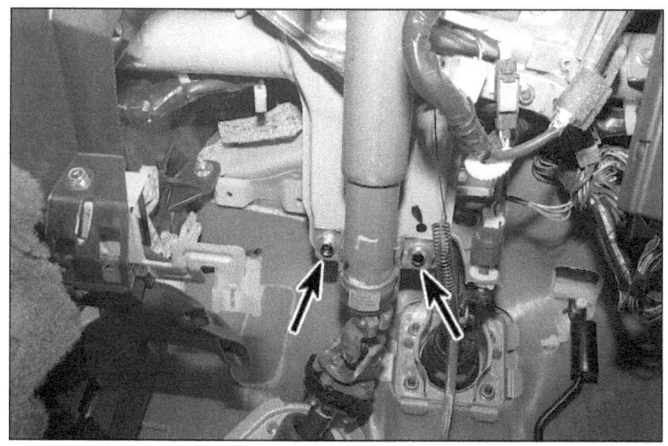

30.10 Remove the steering column mounting bolts (arrows) and lower the column - support the column do not allow the column to hang by the electrical connections

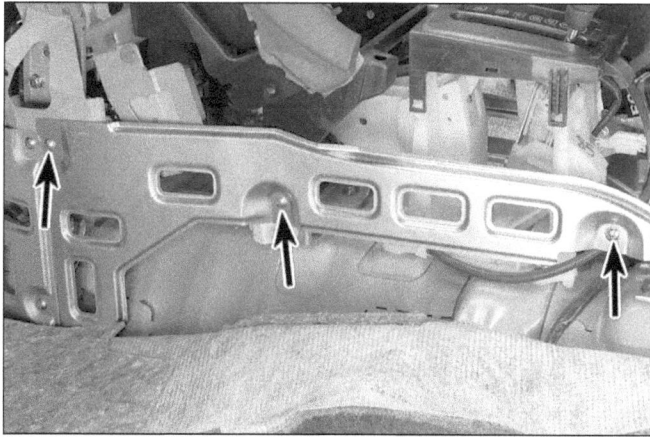

30.12a Remove the centre console rear side panel mounting screws (arrows) (left side shown)

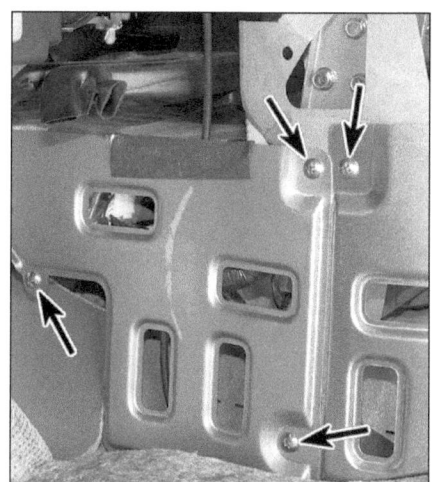

30.12b Remove the centre console front side panel mounting screws (arrows)

30.14 Remove the instrument panel retaining bolts (arrows)

cal connections.

9    Remove the cover under the glove box. Remove the glove box latch striker and the glove box case.

10    Remove the steering column mounting bolts and lower the steering column **(see illustration)**.

11    Remove the passenger side airbag unit (see Chapter 12).

12    Remove the centre console side panels

and remove the two instrument panel bolts behind the side panels **(see illustrations)**.

13    Remove the both door weather stripping and interior pillar trim pieces.

14    Remove the instrument panel retaining nuts and bolts **(see illustration)**.

15    Pull the instrument panel out slightly, disconnect the wiring harness connectors and remove the panel from the vehicle.

16    If you're removing the instrument panel for access to the heater core, remove the centre support brace assembly **(see illustration)**.

17    Refitting is the reverse of removal.

## 31    Seats - removal and refitting

### *Front seat*

*Refer to illustrations 31.1 and 31.2*

1    Remove the mounting nut/seat track

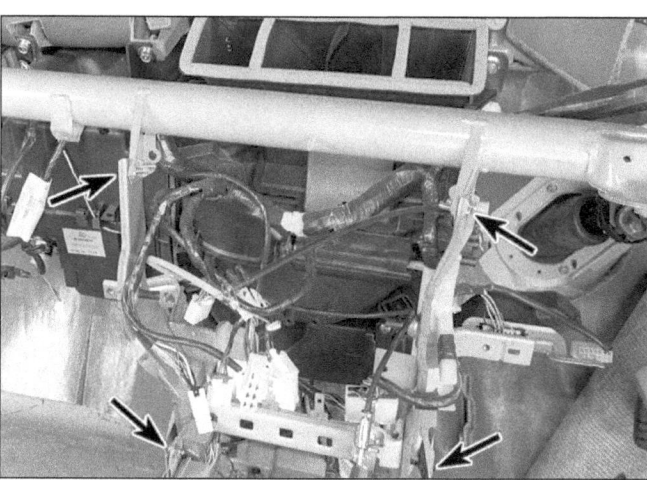

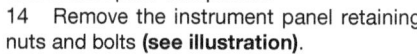

30.16  If necessary, remove the four bolts retaining the centre brace assembly and remove the brace

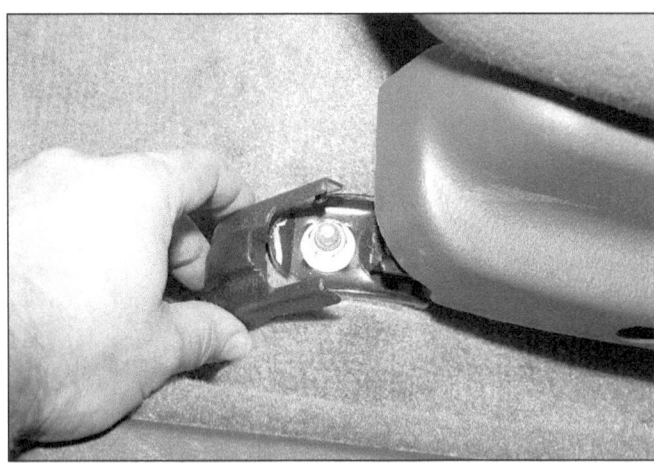

**31.1  Prise the seat track covers from track - (1of 4 shown) and remove the front seat mounting nuts**

**31.2  Remove the covers to access the (arrows) bolts retaining the rear of the front seat tracks to the floor**

covers from each side **(see illustration)**.
2    Remove the retaining nuts **(see illustration)**, unplug any electrical connectors and lift the seat from the vehicle.
3    Refitting is the reverse of removal.

## Rear seat

*Refer to illustrations 31.4 and 31.5*

### Sedan

4    Pull the seat cushion release lever out **(see illustration)**, lift the front of the seat cushion up and remove the cushion from the vehicle.
5    Remove the seat back retaining bolts **(see illustration)**.
6    Lift the seat back up to disengage the seat back from the upper retaining hooks and remove the seat back from the vehicle.

### Station Wagon

7    Pull the seat cushion release levers out **(see illustration 31.4)**, lift the front of the seat cushion up and remove the cushion from the vehicle.
8    Remove the seat back mounting bolts, detach the seat belts and lift the seat back assembly out of the vehicle.
9    Refitting is the reverse of removal.

## 32  Seat belt check

1    Check the seat belts, buckles, latch plates and guide loops for any obvious damage or signs of wear.
2    Check that the seat belt reminder light comes on when the key is turned to the On or Start positions. A chime should also sound.
3    The seat belts are designed to lock up during a sudden stop or impact, yet allow free movement during normal driving. Check that the retractors return the belt against your chest while driving and rewind the belt fully when the buckle is unlatched.
4    If any of the above checks reveal problems with the seat belt system, renew parts as necessary.

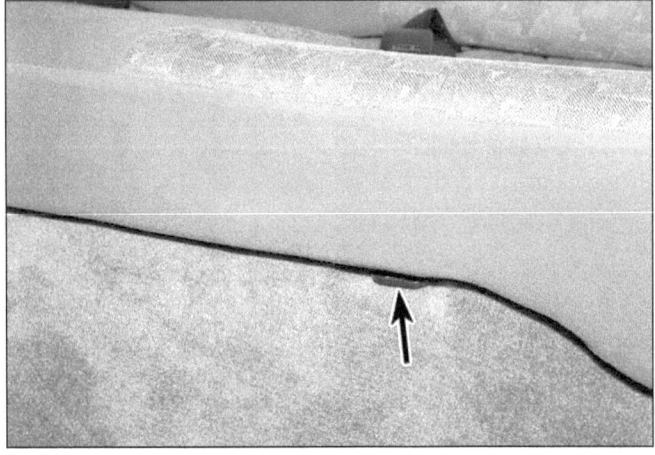

**31.4  Pull out on the rear seat cushion release (arrow) - 1 of 2 shown**

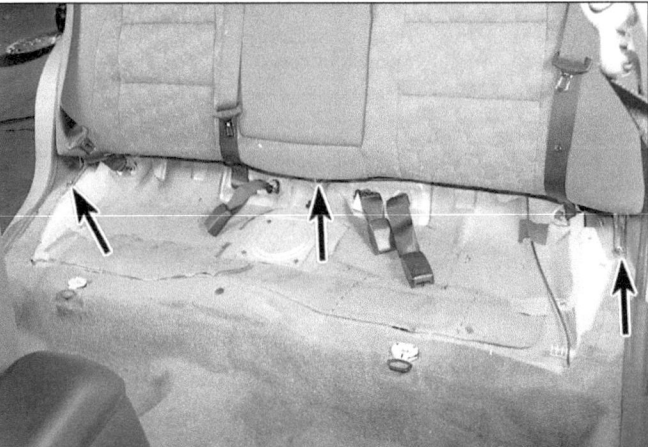

**31.5  Remove the seat back retaining bolts (arrows)**

# Chapter 12
# Chassis electrical system

## Contents

## 1  General information

The electrical system is a 12-volt, negative earth type. Power for the lights and all electrical accessories is supplied by a lead/acid-type battery which is charged by the alternator.

This Chapter covers repair and service procedures for the various electrical components not associated with the engine. Information on the battery, alternator, distributor and starter motor can be found in Chapter 5.

It should be noted that when portions of the electrical system are serviced, the cable should be disconnected from the negative battery terminal to prevent electrical shorts and/or fires.

## 2  Electrical troubleshooting - general information

A typical electrical circuit consists of an electrical component, any switches, relays, motors, fuses, fusible links or circuit breakers related to that component and the wiring and electrical connectors that link the component to both the battery and the chassis. To help

you pinpoint an electrical circuit problem, wiring diagrams are included at the end of this book.

Before tackling any troublesome electrical circuit, first study the appropriate wiring diagrams to get a complete understanding of what makes up that individual circuit. Trouble spots, for instance, can often be narrowed down by noting if other components related to the circuit are operating properly. If several components or circuits fail at one time, chances are the problem is in a fuse or earth connection, because several circuits are often routed through the same fuse and earth connections.

Electrical problems usually stem from simple causes, such as loose or corroded connections, a blown fuse, a melted fusible link or a bad relay. Visually inspect the condition of all fuses, wires and connections in a problem circuit before troubleshooting it.

If testing instruments are going to be utilised, use the diagrams to plan ahead of time where you will make the necessary connections in order to accurately pinpoint the trouble spot.

The basic tools needed for electrical troubleshooting include a circuit tester or voltmeter (a 12-volt bulb with a set of test

leads can also be used), a continuity tester, which includes a bulb, battery and set of test leads, and a jumper wire, preferably with a circuit breaker incorporated, which can be used to bypass electrical components. Before attempting to locate a problem with test instruments, use the wiring diagram(s) to decide where to make the connections.

### Voltage checks

Voltage checks should be performed if a circuit is not functioning properly. Connect one lead of a circuit tester to either the negative battery terminal or a known good earth. Connect the other lead to a electrical connector in the circuit being tested, preferably nearest to the battery or fuse. If the bulb of the tester lights, voltage is present, which means that the part of the circuit between the electrical connector and the battery is problem free. Continue checking the rest of the circuit in the same fashion. When you reach a point at which no voltage is present, the problem lies between that point and the last test point with voltage. Most of the time the problem can be traced to a loose connection. **Note:** *Keep in mind that some circuits receive voltage only when the ignition key is in the Accessory or Run position.*

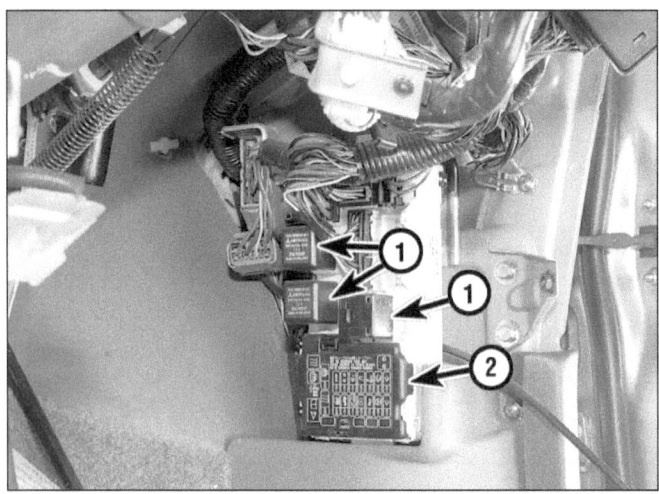

**3.1a  The main fuse box is located below the instrument panel, to the right of the steering column**

*1   Relays                    2   Fuses*

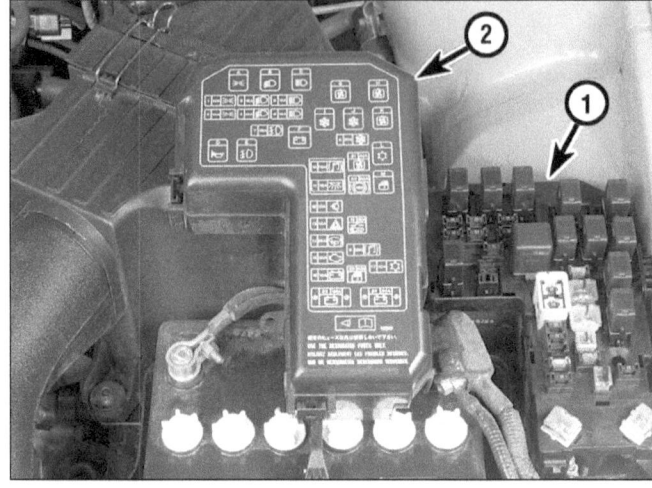

**3.1b  The engine compartment fuse box is located near the battery**

*1   Fuse box                    2   Fuse box cover*

## Finding a short

One method of finding shorts in a circuit is to remove the fuse and connect a test light or voltmeter in its place to the fuse terminals. There should be no voltage present in the circuit. Move the wiring harness from side to side while watching the test light. If the bulb goes on, there is a short to earth somewhere in that area, probably where the insulation has rubbed through. The same test can be performed on each component in the circuit, even a switch.

## Earth check

Perform a earth test to check whether a component is properly earthed. Disconnect the battery and connect one lead of a self-powered test light, known as a continuity tester, to a known good earth. Connect the other lead to the wire or earth connection being tested. If the bulb goes on, the earth is good. If the bulb does not go on, the earth is not good.

## Continuity check

A continuity check is done to determine if there are any breaks in a circuit - if it is passing electricity properly. With the circuit off (no power in the circuit), a self-powered continuity tester can be used to check the circuit. Connect the test leads to both ends of the circuit (or to the "power" end and a good earth), and if the test light comes on the circuit is passing current properly. If the light doesn't come on, there is a break somewhere in the circuit. The same procedure can be used to test a switch, by connecting the continuity tester to the power in and power out sides of the switch. With the switch turned On, the test light should come on.

## Finding an open circuit

When diagnosing for possible open circuits, it is often difficult to locate them by sight because oxidation or terminal misalign-

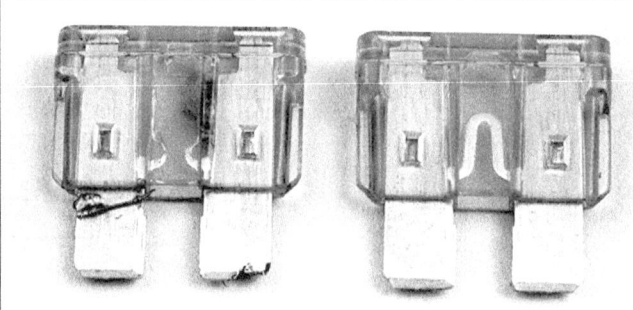

**3.3 The fuses used in these models can be checked visually to determine if they are blown**

ment are hidden by the electrical connectors. Merely wiggling an electrical connector on a sensor or in the wiring harness may correct the open circuit condition. Remember this when an open circuit is indicated when troubleshooting a circuit. Intermittent problems may also be caused by oxidised or loose connections.

Electrical troubleshooting is simple if you keep in mind that all electrical circuits are basically electricity running from the battery, through the wires, switches, relays, fuses and fusible links to each electrical component (light bulb, motor, etc.) and to earth, from which it is passed back to the battery.

## 3   Fuses - general information

*Refer to illustrations 3.1a, 3.1b and 3.3*

The electrical circuits of the vehicle are protected by a combination of fuses and fusible links. The fuse blocks are located below the instrument panel to the right of the steering column under a cover, and in the engine compartment near the battery **(see illustrations)**.

Each of the fuses is designed to protect a specific circuit, and the various circuits are identified on the fuse panel cover.

Miniaturised fuses are employed in the

fuse block. These compact fuses, with blade terminal design, allow fingertip removal and renewal. If an electrical component fails, always check the fuse first. A blown fuse is easily identified through the clear plastic body. Visually inspect the element for evidence of damage **(see illustration)**. If a continuity check is called for, the blade terminal tips are exposed in the fuse body.

Be sure to renew blown fuses with the correct type. Fuses of different ratings are physically interchangeable, but only fuses of the proper rating should be used. Renewing a fuse with one of a higher or lower value than specified is not recommended. Each electrical circuit needs a specific amount of protection. The amperage value of each fuse is moulded into the fuse body.

If the renewal fuse immediately fails, don't renew it again until the cause of the problem is isolated and corrected. In most cases, this will be a short circuit in the wiring caused by a broken or deteriorated wire.

## 4   Fusible links - general information

*Refer to illustration 4.1*

Power to all circuits in the vehicle, except the starter motor, is supplied through

**4.1  Fusible links are located at the bottom of the engine compartment fuse box (arrows)**

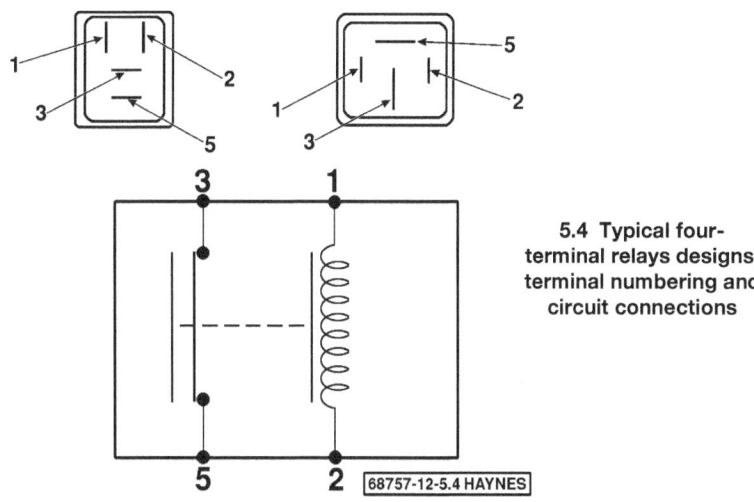

**5.4  Typical four-terminal relays designs, terminal numbering and circuit connections**

68757-12-5.4 HAYNES

the main fusible link. The main fusible link is located in the underbonnet relay/fuse box near the battery **(see illustration)**. The main fusible link is designed to burn-out in the event of a direct short in the vehicle wiring system. If a complete power failure is indicated, remove the main fusible link and check it for continuity with an ohmmeter. After repairing the wiring system, renew the main fusible link with one designed for this vehicle.

Some circuits are protected by secondary fusible links. The secondary links are used in circuits which are not ordinarily fused, such as the head lamps and ignition circuits. The secondary fusible links on these models are located in the underbonnet relay/fuse box. They are similar to fuses in that they can be visually checked to determine if they are melted or check for continuity with an ohmmeter.

To renew a secondary fusible link, first disconnect the negative cable from the battery. Unplug the burned-out link and renew it with a new one (available from your dealer or auto parts store). Always determine the cause for the overload which melted the fusible link before fitting a new one.

---

**5   Relays - general information and testing**

---

## General information

1   Several electrical circuits and accessories in the vehicle, such as the lighting system, horn and air conditioning system use relays to transmit the electrical signal to the component. Relays use a low-current circuit (the control circuit) to open and close a high-current circuit (the power circuit). If the relay is defective, that component will not operate properly. The various relays are mounted in several locations throughout the vehicle, although many key relays are located in the engine compartment relay/fuse block **(see**

**illustration 3.1b)**. Other relays are located in the interior relay block **(see illustration 3.1a)**. If a faulty relay is suspected, it can be removed and tested using the procedure below or by a dealer service department or a repair shop. Defective relays must be renewed as a unit.

## Testing

*Refer to illustration 5.4*

2   It's best to refer to the wiring diagram for the circuit to determine the proper hook-ups for the relay you're testing. However, if you're not able to determine the correct hook-up from the wiring diagrams, you may be able to determine the test hook-ups from the information that follows.

3   On most relays with four or six terminals, two of the terminals are the relay's control circuit (they connect to the relay coil which, when energised, closes the large contacts to complete the circuit). The other terminals are the power circuit (they are connected together within the relay when the control-circuit coil is energised).

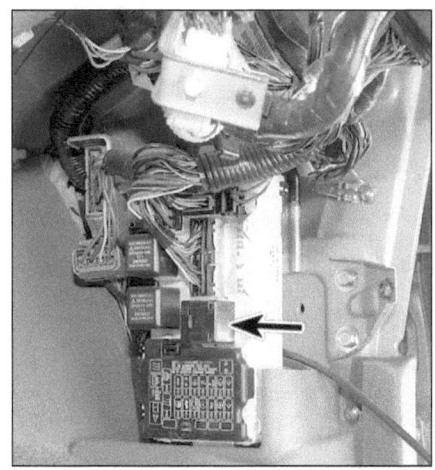

**6.1  The turn signal/hazard flasher unit is located in the interior relay block above the fuse box**

4   Most relays are marked as an aid to help you determine which terminals are the control circuit and which are the power circuit **(see illustration)**.

5   Connect a fused jumper wire between one of the two control circuit terminals and the positive battery terminal. Connect another jumper wire between the other control circuit terminal and earth. When the connections are made, the relay should click. On some relays, polarity may be critical, so, if the relay doesn't click, try swapping the jumper wires on the control circuit terminals.

7   With the jumper wires connected, check for continuity between the power circuit terminals. Now, there should be continuity.

8   If the relay fails any of the above tests, renew it.

---

**6   Turn signal/hazard flasher - check and renewal**

---

*Refer to illustration 6.1*

**Warning:** *Some models covered by this manual are equipped with airbags. Always disconnect the negative battery cable, then the positive cable and wait two minutes before working in the vicinity of the impact sensors, steering column or instrument panel to avoid the possibility of accidental deployment of the airbag, which could cause personal injury* (see Section 25).

1   The turn signal/hazard flasher, a square module located in the interior relay block **(see illustration)**, flashes the turn signals and hazard flashers.

2   When the flasher unit is functioning properly, an audible click can be heard during its operation. If the turn signals fail on one side or the other and the flasher unit does not make its characteristic clicking sound, a faulty turn signal bulb is indicated.

3   If both turn signals fail to blink, the problem may be due to a blown fuse, a faulty flasher unit, a broken switch or a loose or open connection. If a quick check of the fuse

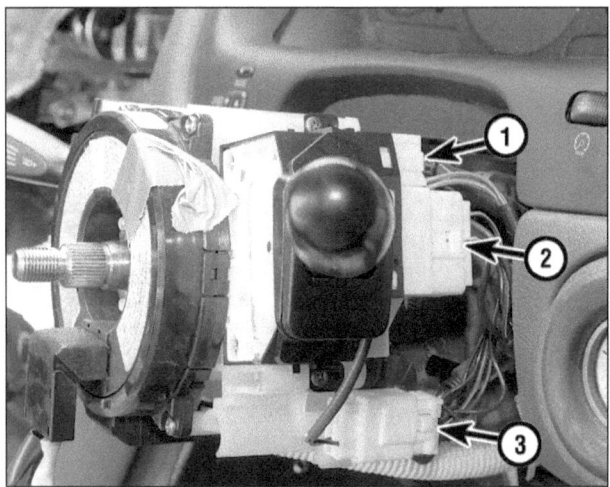

**7.4a  Typical combination switch connector identification (right side)**

1   Connector 1 (Turn signal)
2   Connector 2 (Light switch)
3   Connector 3 (Dimmer switch)

**7.4c  Typical wiper/washer switch connector location (arrow)**

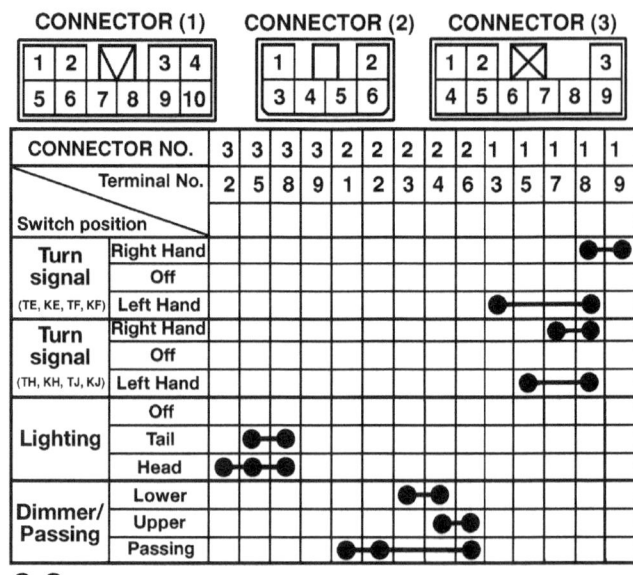

| CONNECTOR NO. | | 3 | 3 | 3 | 3 | 2 | 2 | 2 | 2 | 2 | 1 | 1 | 1 | 1 | 1 |
|---|---|---|---|---|---|---|---|---|---|---|---|---|---|---|---|
| Terminal No. | | 2 | 5 | 8 | 9 | 1 | 2 | 3 | 4 | 6 | 3 | 5 | 7 | 8 | 9 |
| **Switch position** | | | | | | | | | | | | | | | |
| **Turn signal** (TE, KE, TF, KF) | Right Hand | | | | | | | | | | | | | ● | ● |
| | Off | | | | | | | | | | | | | | |
| | Left Hand | | | | | | | | | | | ● | | ● | |
| **Turn signal** (TH, KH, TJ, KJ) | Right Hand | | | | | | | | | | | | ● | ● | |
| | Off | | | | | | | | | | | | | | |
| | Left Hand | | | | | | | | | | | ● | | ● | |
| **Lighting** | Off | | | | | | | | | | | | | | |
| | Tail | | ● | ● | | | | | | | | | | | |
| | Head | ● | ● | ● | | | | | | | | | | | |
| **Dimmer/ Passing** | Lower | | | | | | | | ● | ● | | | | | |
| | Upper | | | | | | | | ● | ● | | | | | |
| | Passing | | | | | ● | ● | | | | | | | | |

●—● indicates that there is continuity between terminals. [68756-12-7.4b HAYNES]

**7.4b  Turn signal, headlight and dimmer switch terminal guide and continuity table**

| | | | | | |
|---|---|---|---|---|---|
| 1 | 2 | ⊠ | 3 | 4 | 5 |
| 6 | 7 | 8 | 9 | 10 | 11 | 12 |

| Switch position | | 8 | 9 | 10 | 11 | 12 |
|---|---|---|---|---|---|---|
| **Wiper switch** | OFF | | | ● | ● | |
| | INT | | | ● | ● | |
| | LO | ● | | ● | | |
| | HI | ● | | | ● | |
| **WASHER SWITCH** | ON | ● | | | | ● |

●—● indicates that there is continuity between terminals. [68757-12-7.4d HAYNES]

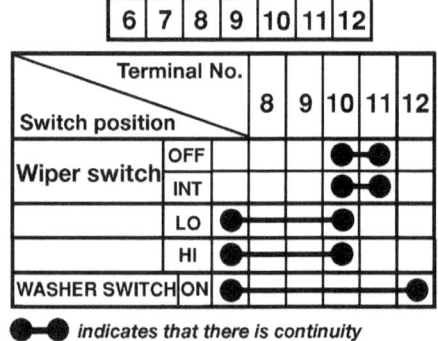

**7.4d  Windscreen wiper/washer switch terminal guide and continuity table**

---

box indicates that the turn signal fuse has blown, check the wiring for a short before fitting a new fuse.

4   To renew the flasher, remove it from the relay block by pulling it straight out.

5   Make sure the renewal unit is identical to the original. Compare the old one to the new one before fitting it.

6   Refitting is the reverse of removal.

---

## 7   Combination switch - check and renewal

**Warning:** *The models covered by this manual are equipped with airbags. Always disable the Supplemental Restraint System before working in the vicinity of the impact sensors, steering column or instrument panel to avoid the possibility of accidental deployment of the airbag, which could cause personal injury (see Section 25).*

**Caution:** *If the stereo in your vehicle is equipped with an anti-theft system, make sure you have the correct activation code before disconnecting the battery.*

### Check

*Refer to illustrations 7.4a, 7.4b, 7.4c and 7.4d*

1   Disconnect the cable from the negative battery terminal.

2   Remove the steering column covers (see Chapter 11).

3   Follow the wiring harness up to the combination switch and wiring harness connectors. Disconnect the wiring harness connectors from the combination switch.

4   Using the accompanying chart, check the various switches for continuity on the indicated terminals with the switch in the indicated position **(see illustrations)**.

5   If the switch fails to indicate continuity in any one position, renew the combination switch assembly.

### Renewal

*Refer to illustrations 7.9 and 7.10*

6   Disconnect the negative cable at the battery.

7   Place the front wheels in the straight-ahead position, lock the steering column and remove the key. Remove the airbag module and the steering wheel (see Chapter 10). **Warning:** *Handle the airbag module carefully and store it with the trim side facing UP in a safe location.*

8   Remove the steering column covers (see Chapter 11).

9   Make sure to align the marks the airbag clockspring and secure the spring by taping it. Remove the clockspring mounting screws **(see illustration)**. Carefully lift the clock spring off and allow it to hang by the wiring harness. **Warning:** *Handle the airbag system components very carefully. DO NOT rotate the clock spring off the neutral marks during the removal and refitting procedure. Damage to the airbag system components could lead*

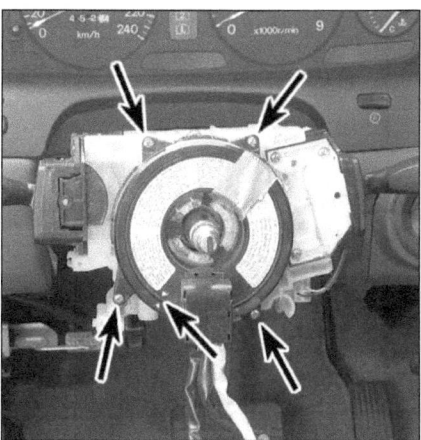

**7.9 Air bag clock spring retaining screws (arrows) - note the alignment of the NEUTRAL marks (arrow)**

**7.10 Combination switch retaining screws (arrows)**

| CONNECTOR (1) | | | CONNECTOR (2) | | | |
|---|---|---|---|---|---|---|
| 1 | 2 | 3 | 1 | | | |
| 4 | 5 | 6 | 2 | 3 | 4 | 5 |

| CONNECTOR NO. | | 1 | 1 | 1 | 1 | 1 | 1 | 2 | | | | |
|---|---|---|---|---|---|---|---|---|---|---|---|---|
| Key | Terminal No. | Ignition switch | | | | | | Key reminder switch | | | | |
| Position | | 1 | 2 | 3 | 4 | 5 | 6 | 1 | 2 | 3 | 4 | 5 |
| Lock | Removed | | | | | | | | ●─── | ── | ──● | |
| ACC | | ●── | ── | ── | ──● | | | | | | | |
| ON | Inserted | ●─●── | | ──●── | ── | ──● | | | | | | |
| Start | | ●─●── | | | | ──● | | | | | | |

**8.4 Ignition switch terminal guide and continuity table**

●━━● indicates that there is continuity between terminals. `68757-12-8.4 HAYNES`

to an airbag system failure and serious personal injury.

10   Remove the combination switch retaining screws **(see illustration)**.

11   Release the wiring retainer clamps, if equipped, disconnect the connector and slide the switch off the column.

12   Refitting is the reverse of removal.

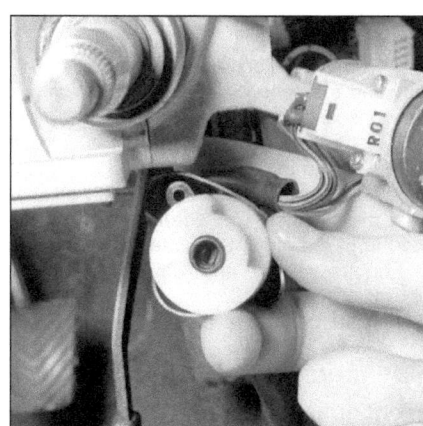

**8.9 Be sure to align the slot in the ignition switch with the lock cylinder tab when refitting the switch**

## 8   Ignition switch and key lock cylinder - check and renewal

**Warning:** *The models covered by this manual are equipped with airbags. Always disable the Supplemental Restraint System before working in the vicinity of the impact sensors, steering column or instrument panel to avoid the possibility of accidental deployment of the airbag, which could cause personal injury* (see Section 25).

**Caution:** *If the stereo in your vehicle is equipped with an anti-theft system, make sure you have the correct activation code before disconnecting the battery.*

### *Ignition switch*

#### Check

*Refer to illustration 8.4*

1   Disconnect the cable from the negative battery terminal.

2   Remove the steering column covers (see Chapter 11).

3   Disconnect the wiring harness connector from the ignition switch.

4   Using the accompanying chart, check the switch for continuity on the indicated terminals with the switch in each of the indi-

cated positions **(see illustration)**.

5   If the switch fails to indicate continuity in any one position, renew the ignition switch.

#### Renewal

*Refer to illustration 8.9*

6   Disconnect the cable from the negative terminal of the battery.

7   Remove the steering column covers (see Chapter 11).

8   Disconnect the electrical connector, remove the screw, then detach the switch from the housing.

9   Refitting is the reverse of removal, but be sure to align the slot in the ignition switch with the tab on the lock cylinder **(see illustration)**.

### *Ignition lock cylinder*

*Refer to illustration 8.13*

10   Disconnect the cable from the negative terminal of the battery.

11   Remove the steering wheel (see Chapter 10).

12   Remove the steering column covers (see Chapter 11).

13   With the key in the ACC position, insert a pin in the hole in the casting, pull the lock cylinder straight out and remove it from the steering column **(see illustration)**.

14   Refitting is the reverse of removal.

## 9   Rear window defogger switch - renewal

**Warning:** *The models covered by this manual are equipped with airbags. Always disable the Supplemental Restraint System before working in the vicinity of the impact sensors, steering column or instrument panel to avoid the possibility of accidental deployment of the airbag, which could cause personal injury* (see Section 25).

**Caution:** *If the stereo in your vehicle is equipped with an anti-theft system, make sure you have the correct activation code before disconnecting the battery.*

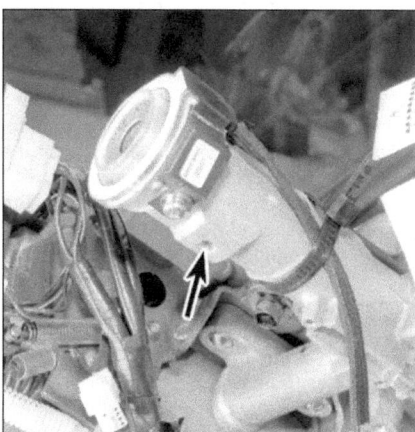

**8.13 Turn the key to the ACC position and depress the retaining pin (arrow) while at the same time pulling out on the lock cylinder**

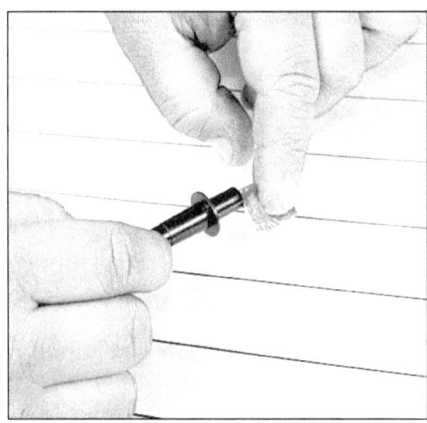

**10.5  When measuring the voltage at the rear window defogger grid, wrap a piece of aluminum foil around the positive probe of the voltmeter and press the foil against the heating element with your finger**

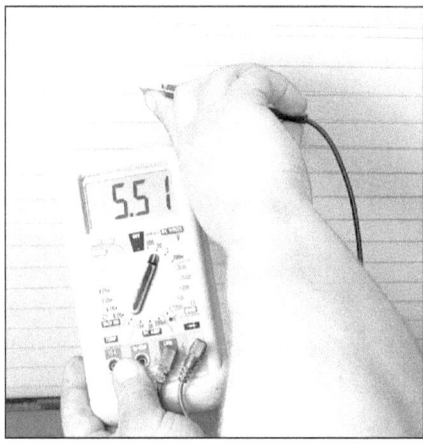

**10.6  To determine if a heating element is broken, check the voltage at the centre of each element - if the voltage is 6-volts, the element is unbroken**

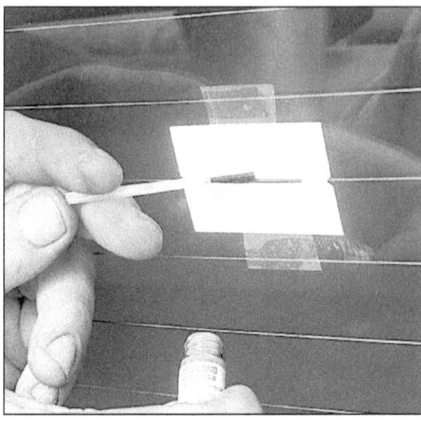

**10.13  To use a defogger repair kit, apply masking tape to the inside of the window at the damaged area, then brush on the special conductive coating**

1    Disconnect the cable from the negative battery terminal.
2    Remove the heater and air conditioning control panel bezel (see Chapter 11).
3    Disconnect the wiring harness connector to the defogger switch.
4    Prise the retaining tabs in and remove the switch from the panel.
5    Refitting is the reverse of removal.

## 10   Rear window defogger - check and repair

### Check

*Refer to illustrations 10.5 and 10.6*

1    The rear window defogger consists of a number of horizontal elements baked onto the glass surface.
2    Small breaks in the element can be repaired without removing the rear window.
3    Turn the ignition switch and defogger system switches On.
4    Using a voltmeter, place the positive probe against the battery feed terminal and the negative probe against the negative (earth) bus bar. The positive terminal is located on the drivers side and the negative terminal is located on the passengers side. If battery voltage is not indicated, check the fuse, defogger switch and related wiring.
5    When measuring voltage during the next two tests, wind a piece of aluminum foil around the tip of the voltmeter positive probe and press the foil against the heating elements with your finger **(see illustration)**.
6    Place the negative lead against the negative (earth) bus bar. Check the voltage at the centre of each heating element **(see illustration)**. If the voltage is 6-volts, the element is okay (there is no break). If the voltage is 10-volts or more, the element is broken somewhere between the mid-point and earth. If the voltage is zero volts the element is broken between the mid-point and the positive side.

7    To find the break, slide the probe toward the appropriate side. The point where the voltmeter indicates either zero or several volts is the point at which the heating element is broken. **Note:** *If the heating element is not broken, the voltmeter will indicate 12-volts at the positive side and gradually decrease to 0-volts as you slide the positive probe toward the earth side.*

### Repair

*Refer to illustration 10.13*

8    Repair the break in the element using a repair kit specifically recommended for this purpose, such as ACME conductive adhesive/solder No. 3201 (or equivalent). Included in this kit is plastic conductive epoxy.
9    Prior to repairing a break, turn off the system and allow it to cool off for a couple of hours.
10   Lightly buff the element area with fine steel wool, then clean it thoroughly with isopropyl alcohol.
11   Use masking tape to mask off the area being repaired.
12   Thoroughly mix the epoxy thoroughly, following the instructions provided with the repair kit.
13   Apply the epoxy material to the slit in the masking tape, overlapping the undamaged area about 20-mm on either end **(see illustration)**.
14   Allow the repair to cure for 24 hours before removing the tape and using the system.

## 11   Radio and speakers - removal and refitting

**Warning:** *The models covered by this manual are equipped with airbags. Always disable the Supplemental Restraint System before working in the vicinity of the impact sensors, steering column or instrument panel to avoid the possibility of accidental deployment of*

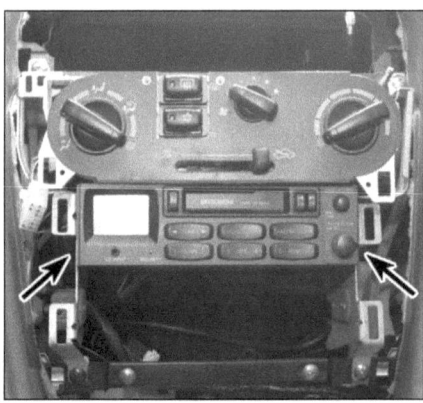

**11.3  Radio mounting screws (arrows)**

*the airbag, which could cause personal injury* (see Section 25).
**Caution:** *If the stereo in your vehicle is equipped with an anti-theft system, make sure you have the correct activation code before disconnecting the battery.*
1    Disconnect the cable from the negative terminal of the battery.

### Radio

*Refer to illustration 11.3*

2    Remove the centre air vent and the ashtray and the center trim panel. Also remove the console (refer to Chapter 11).
3    Remove the bracket and the audio unit **(see illustration)**.
4    Pull the radio out far enough to disconnect the electrical connectors and the aerial lead from the radio. Separate the radio from the centre console and remove it from the vehicle.
5    Refitting is the reverse of removal.

### Speakers

#### Front speakers

*Refer to illustration 11.7*

6    Carefully prise off the speaker grille.
7    Remove the speaker retaining screws, pull the speaker up, disconnect the electri-

**11.7  Remove the mounting screws (arrows), pull the speaker out and disconnect the electrical connector**

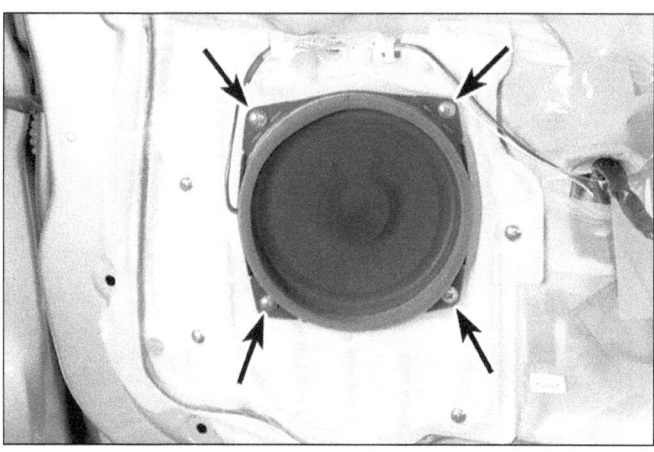

**11.10  Remove the door speaker mounting screws (arrows)**

**11.13  Remove the speaker cover mounting nuts and remove the cover from inside - sedan**

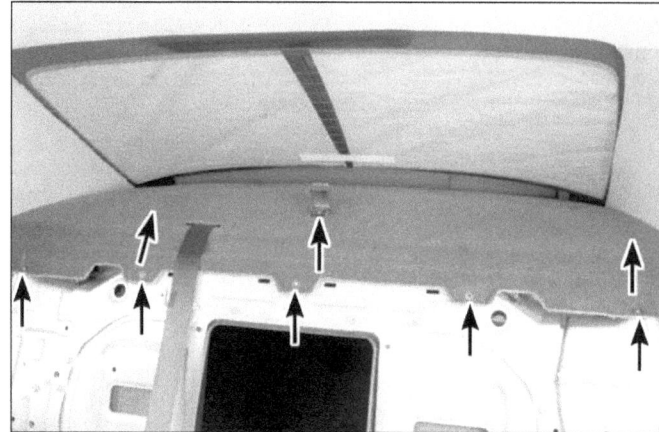

**11.14  Remove the parcel shelf carpet retaining clips and screws (arrows) - sedan**

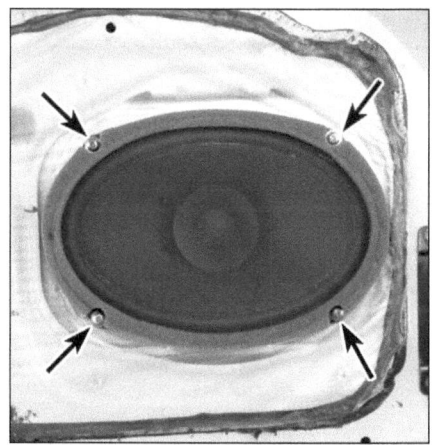

**11.18  Speaker mounting screws (arrows) - wagon**

cal connector and remove the speaker **(see illustration)**.

8    Refitting is the reverse of removal.

### Door mounted speakers

*Refer to illustration 11.10*

9    Remove the door trim panel (see Chapter 11).

10    Remove the speaker mounting screws **(see illustration)**, pull the speaker out and disconnect the electrical connector.

11    Refitting is the reverse of removal.

### Rear parcel shelf mounted speakers (sedan models)

*Refer to illustrations 11.13 and 11.14*

12    Remove the rear seat (see Chapter 11).

13    From inside of the boot remove the speaker grill cover nuts **(see illustration)** and disconnect the electrical connector.

14    Remove the speaker covers and remove the parcel shelf panel **(see illustration)**.

15    Remove the speaker mounting screws **(see illustration 11.18)**, pull the speaker out.

16    Refitting is the reverse of removal.

### Tailgate mounted speakers (wagon models)

*Refer to illustration 11.18*

17    Remove the tailgate trim panel (see Chapter 11).

18    Remove the speaker mounting screws **(see illustration)**, pull the speaker out and disconnect the electrical connector.

19    Refitting is the reverse of removal.

**12.2  Using angled pliers turn the ring anticlockwise to remove it (arrow)**

### 12   Radio aerial - removal and refitting

### *Manual aerial*

*Refer to illustration 12.2*

1    From inside the boot prise off the plastic carpet retaining clips and fold the carpet back. **Note:** *On wagon models remove the lower panel side trim panel screws, panel and scuff plate.*

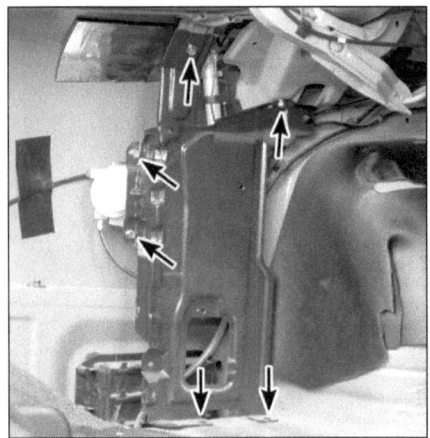

**12.9  Remove the aerial motor bracket retaining screws (arrows)**

**13.3  Remove the rubber cover, detach the spring retainer and pull the bulb straight out of the housing**

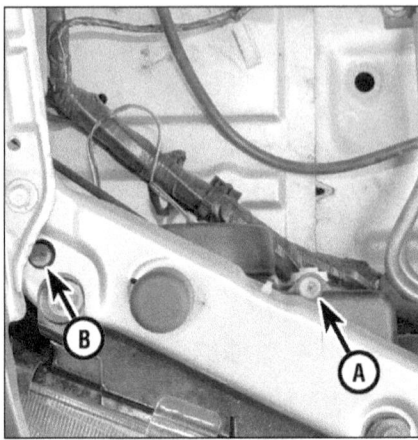

**14.1  Headlight adjusting screw location**

*A   High beam adjusting screw*
*B   Low beam adjusting screw*

2    Using angled pliers remove the aerial base ring nut **(see illustration)**. Lift off the aerial base.
3    Disconnect the lower aerial bracket from inside the rear luggage compartment.
4    Slide the aerial mast from the assembly.
5    Disconnect the aerial cable and the drain tube, then remove the aerial body.
6    Refitting is the reverse of removal.

### Power aerial

*Refer to illustration 12.9*
7    From inside the boot prise off the plastic carpet retaining clips and fold the carpet back. **Note:** *On wagon models remove the lower panel side trim panel screws, panel and scuff plate.*
8    Using angled pliers remove the aerial base ring nut **(see illustration 12.2)**. Lift off the aerial base.
9    Disconnect the aerial bracket **(see illustration)** from inside the rear luggage compartment.
10    Remove the aerial tube upper mast and lower motor nuts.
11    Disconnect the aerial cable and the drain tube, then remove the aerial body.
12    Refitting is the reverse of removal.

### Mast renewal

13    Remove the ring nut **(see illustration 12.2)**.
14    Turn the ignition key to the ACC position and turn the radio on as the aerial comes up continue pulling on the mast this will allow the rack cable to be released from the motor. Remove the mast and cable assembly.
15    Fit the new mast rack cable with the teeth on the cable pointing to the boot then rotate the cable so that the teeth point to the rear of the vehicle. This will mesh the cable with the aerial motor gear if the cable can be pulled out easily it hasn't meshed with the gear properly.
16    Once the cable has been properly meshed, turn the radio off and allow the cable and mast to be freely pulled into the aerial assembly.
17    Refit the ring nut securely.

## 13  Headlight bulb - renewal

*Refer to illustration 13.3*
**Warning:** *Halogen gas filled bulbs are under pressure and may shatter if the surface is scratched or if the bulb is dropped. Wear eye protection and handle the bulbs carefully, grasping only the base whenever possible. Do not touch the surface of the bulb with your fingers because the oil from your skin could cause the bulb to overheat and fail prematurely. If you do touch the bulb surface, clean it with isopropyl alcohol.*
**Caution:** *If the stereo in your vehicle is equipped with an anti-theft system, make sure you have the correct activation code before disconnecting the battery.*
1    Disconnect the cable from the negative terminal of the battery.

2    Disconnect the electrical connector from the headlight bulb.
3    Remove the dust cover and release the retaining clip **(see illustration)**.
4    Withdraw the bulb assembly from the housing.
5    Refitting is the reverse of removal.

## 14  Headlights - adjustment

*Refer to illustrations 14.1 and 14.6*
1    The adjusting screws control the up-and-down and side-to-side movement of the headlight housing. The adjusting screws are located on the back-side of the housing **(see illustration)**.
2    There are several methods of adjusting the headlights. The simplest method

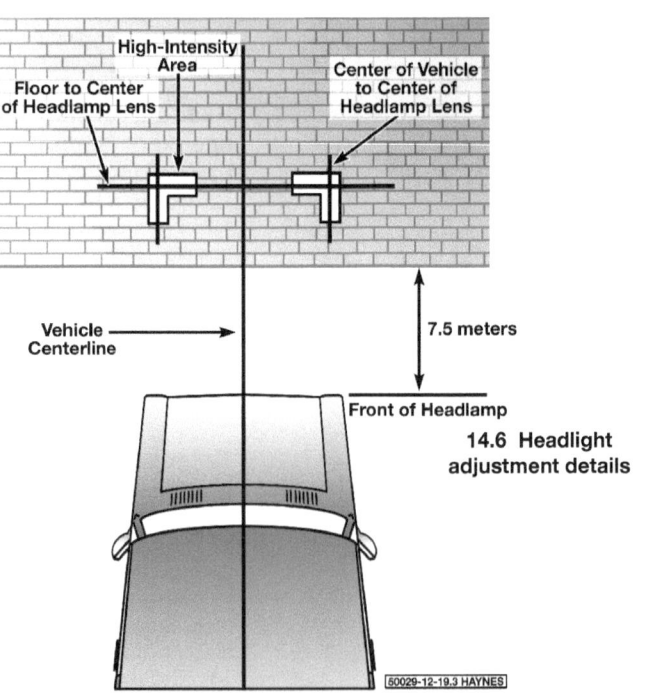

**14.6  Headlight adjustment details**

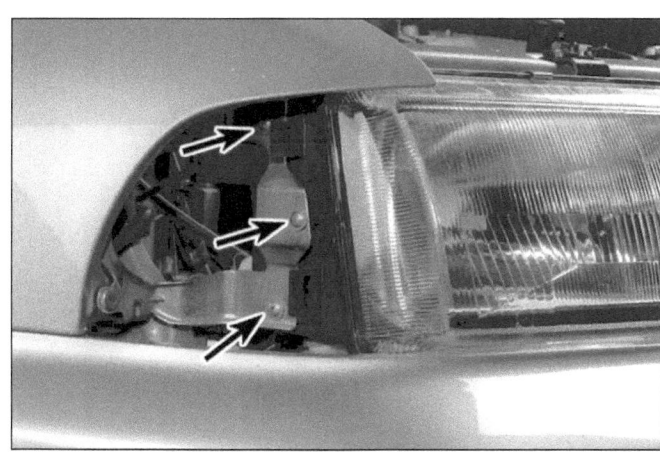

**15.5a Remove the headlight housing retaining screws from the front support (arrows) . . .**

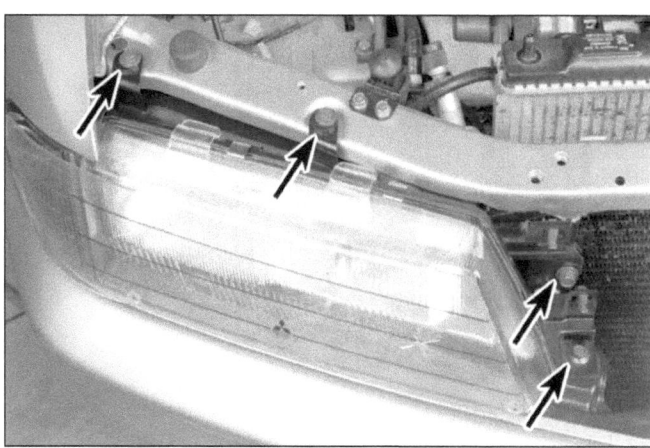

**15.5b . . . and front mounting bolts (arrows)**

requires masking tape, a blank wall and a level floor.

3    Position masking tape vertically on the wall in reference to the vehicle centreline and the centrelines of both headlights.

4    Position a horizontal tape line in reference to the centreline of all the headlights. **Note:** *It may be easier to position the tape on the wall with the vehicle parked only a few centimeters away from the wall.*

5    Adjustment should be made with the vehicle parked 7.5-meters from the wall, sitting level, the fuel tank half-full and no unusually heavy load in the vehicle.

6    Starting with the low beam adjustment, position the high-intensity zone so it's five centimeters below the horizontal line and five centimeters to the side of the headlight vertical line **(see illustration)**, away from oncoming traffic. Turn the adjustment screws until the desired level has been achieved.

7    With the high beams on, the high intensity zone should be vertically centred with the exact centre just below the horizontal line. **Note:** *It may not be possible to position the headlight aim exactly for both high and low beams. If a compromise must be made, keep in mind that the low beams are the most used and have the greatest effect on driver safety.*

8    Have the headlights adjusted by a dealer service department or other repair shop at the earliest opportunity.

### 15    Headlight housing - removal and refitting

**Caution:** *If the stereo in your vehicle is equipped with an anti-theft system, make sure you have the correct activation code before disconnecting the battery.*

*Refer to illustrations 15.5a and 15.5b*

1    Disconnect the cable from the negative terminal of the battery.

2    Disconnect the electrical connectors from the headlight bulbs.

3    Remove the side marker light assembly (see Section 16).

4    Remove the radiator grille (see Chapter 11).

**Note:** *On TL/TW and KL/KW models, remove the top bumper screws so that the bumper can be pulled down to aid headlamp removal.*

5    Remove the screws retaining the headlight housing and withdraw the housing **(see illustrations)**.

6    Refitting is the reverse of removal. Adjust the headlight aim (see Section 14).

### 16    Bulb renewal

#### *Front turn signal*

*Refer to illustration 16.1*

1    Pull the retaining spring **(see illustration)**, located on the inner fender, and withdraw the light assembly.

2    Rotate the bulb socket counterclockwise, withdraw the socket from the lens and remove the bulb.

#### *Side turn signal*

*Refer to illustrations 16.3 and 16.5*

3    Using a flat blade screwdriver, place a cloth between the screwdriver and paint pushing the marker back **(see illustration)** towards the door then prise out to release the plastic lock.

**Note:** *On TL/TW and KL/KW models, carefully prise the rear edge of the side turn signal housing out, where the housing meets the inner wheel opening.*

4    Remove the marker from the fender.

5    Grasp the bulb **(see illustration)**, press in, rotate it anticlockwise and remove the bulb from the socket.

**16.1 Pull the turn signal marker clip (arrow) and slide the lamp out to the front of the vehicle**

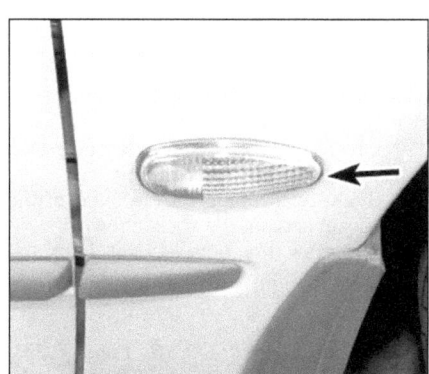

**16.3 Push the side turn signal lamp towards the rear (arrow) then prise the lamp out**

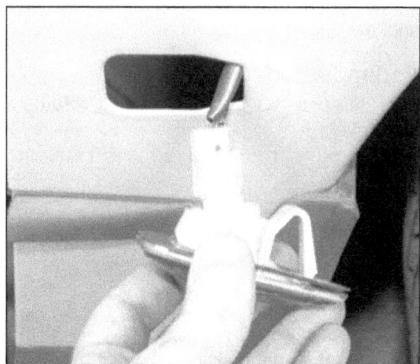

**16.5 Hold the lamp and turn the socket anticlockwise to release the socket**

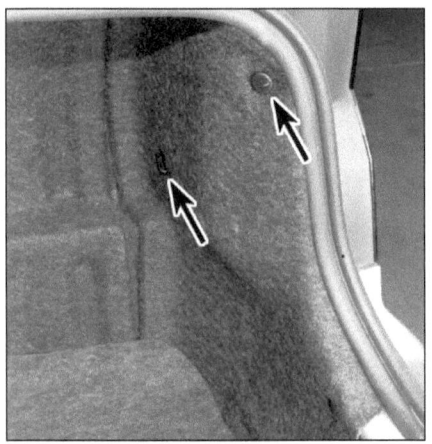

**16.6 To access the rear tail light assembly on a sedan models remove the carpet retaining clips (arrows) - sedan**

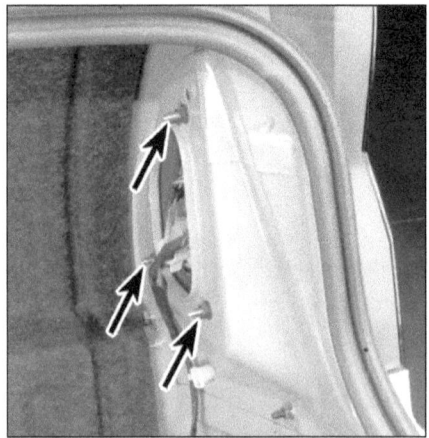

**16.7 Remove the lamp mounting nuts (arrows) - sedan**

**16.12 Remove the lamp assembly mounting screws (arrows) and pull the lamp assembly out**

**16.15 Remove the number plate light mounting screws (arrows)**

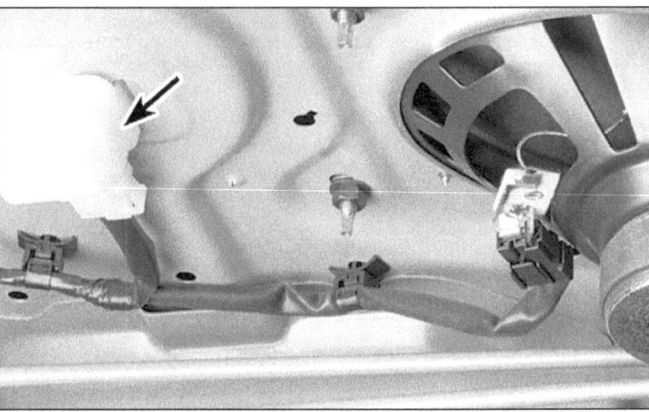

**16.17 The high stop lamp is located in the boot between the speakers (arrow)**

## Rear combination lamps

### Sedan (Magna)

*Refer to illustrations 16.6 and 16.7*

6    Remove the carpet cover retainers from inside the luggage compartment **(see illustration)** and fold the carpet down.

7    Remove the combination lamp mounting nuts **(see illustration)** and remove the lamp.

8    Grasp the bulb, press in, rotate it anticlockwise and remove the bulb from the socket.

### Sedan (Verada)

9    Remove the boot lid plastic retainers and covers.

10   Remove the bulb socket retaining screws.

11   Grasp the bulb, press in, rotate it anticlockwise and remove the bulb from the socket.

### Station wagon

*Refer to illustration 16.12*

12   Remove the lamp retaining screws **(see illustration)** and pull the lamp out from the body.

13   Grasp the socket, rotate it anticlockwise

and withdraw it from the housing.

14   Grasp the bulb, press in, rotate it anticlockwise and remove the bulb from the socket.

## Number plate lamp

*Refer to illustration 16.15*

15   Remove the screws retaining the light assembly to the boot lid.

16   Remove the socket from the housing and remove the bulb.

## High-mounted brake lamp

### Sedan

*Refer to illustration 16.17*

17   Locate the brake light under the parcel shelf in the boot **(see illustration)**.

18   Squeeze the tabs on the ends of the bulb socket and pull the socket down.

19   Withdraw the bulb socket from the housing and remove the bulb.

### Wagon

*Refer to illustrations 16.20, 16.21 and 16.22*

20   With the tailgate open remove the brake light screw covers **(see illustration)**.

21   Remove the light cover mounting screws **(see illustration)** and carefully prise

**16.20 Use a small screwdriver to prise off the high mounted brake light screw cover - wagon**

the cover off.

22   Grasp the socket, rotate it anticlockwise and withdraw it from the housing **(see illustration)**.

23   Withdraw the bulb from the socket and remove the bulb.

## Interior lamps

*Refer to illustration 16.24*

24   Carefully prise the lens from the light

**16.21 Remove the light cover mounting screws (arrows)**

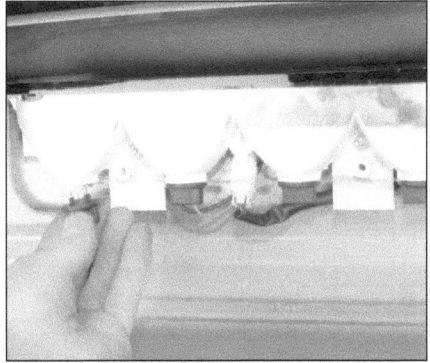

**16.22 Rotate the sockets anticlockwise to remove the sockets then pull the bulbs from the sockets**

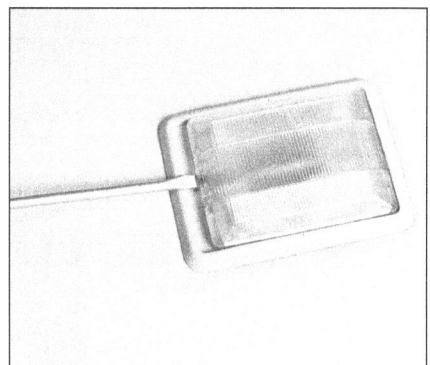

**16.24 Use a small screwdriver to prise off the lens from the interior light assembly**

assembly **(see illustration)**.
25    Withdraw the bulb from the socket.

## Instrument panel lamps

*Refer to illustration 16.27*
26    Remove the instrument cluster (see Section 18).
27    Rotate the bulb holder anticlockwise and withdraw it from the instrument cluster **(see illustration)**.
28    Withdraw the bulb from the bulb holder.

---

### 17    Windscreen wiper motor - renewal

---

**Caution:** *If the stereo in your vehicle is equipped with an anti-theft system, make sure you have the correct activation code before disconnecting the battery.*
1    Disconnect the cable from the negative terminal of the battery.

## Windscreen wiper motor

2    Remove the wiper arm mounting nuts and remove the arms.
3    Remove the plastic front deck garnish (one on each side).
4    Unbolt the wiper motor and linkage.
5    Disconnect the electrical connector.
6    Pull the motor out and lift the motor from the engine compartment.
7    Refitting is the reverse of removal.

## Rear window wiper motor (station wagon models)

*Refer to illustration 17.11*
8    Remove the liftgate inner trim panel (see Chapter 11).
9    Lift up the cap, remove the nut and remove the rear wiper arm.
10    Remove the wiper shaft nut and washers, taking care to keep them in order.
11    Open the liftgate and disconnect the electrical connector, then remove the bolts and detach the wiper motor **(see illustration)**.
12    Refitting is the reverse of removal.

---

### 18    Instrument cluster - removal and refitting

---

*Refer to illustration 18.3*
**Warning:** *The models covered by this manual are equipped with airbags. Always disable the Supplemental Restraint System before working in the vicinity of the impact sensors, steering column or instrument panel to avoid the possibility of accidental deployment of the airbag, which could cause personal injury (see Section 25).*
**Caution:** *If the stereo in your vehicle is equipped with an anti-theft system, make sure you have the correct activation code*

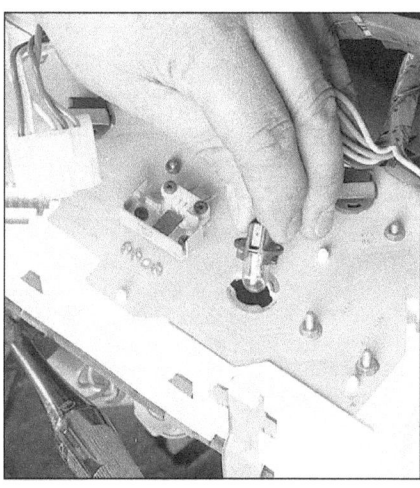

**16.27 Instrument cluster bulbs can be renewed after the cluster is removed**

*before disconnecting the battery.*
1    Disconnect the cable from the negative battery terminal.
2    Remove the instrument cluster trim panel (see Chapter 11).
3    Remove the four retaining screws, grasp the cluster securely and pull it straight out to detach it from the electrical connectors **(see illustration)**.
4    Refitting is the reverse of the removal procedure.

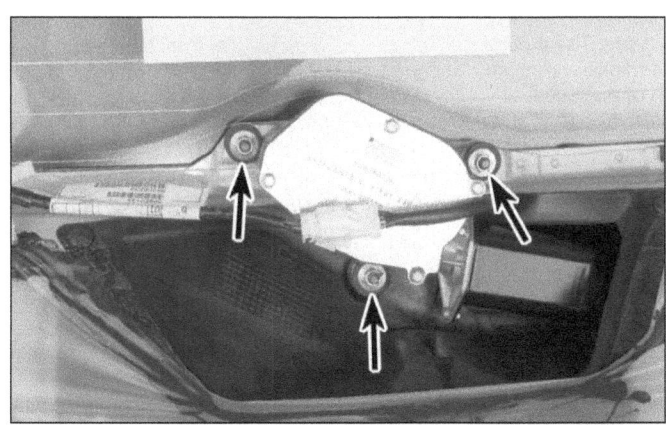

**17.11 Rear wiper motor mounting nuts (arrows)**

**18.3 The instrument cluster is secured by four screws (arrows)**

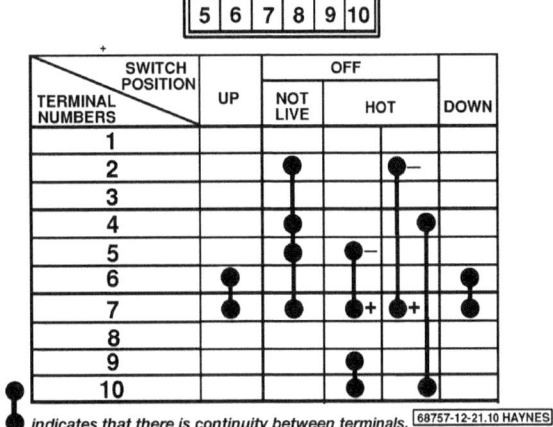

CONNECTOR NO.

| 1 | 2 | | 3 | 4 |
|---|---|---|---|---|
| 5 | 6 | 7 | 8 | 9 | 10 |

| TERMINAL NUMBERS | SWITCH POSITION | UP | OFF | | | DOWN |
|---|---|---|---|---|---|---|
| | | | NOT LIVE | HOT | | |
| 1 | | | | | | |
| 2 | | | ● | ●– | | |
| 3 | | | | | | |
| 4 | | | ● | ● | | |
| 5 | | | | ●– | | |
| 6 | | ● | | | | ● |
| 7 | | ● | ● | ●+ | ●+ | ● |
| 8 | | | | | | |
| 9 | | | | ● | | |
| 10 | | | | ● | ● | |

● indicates that there is continuity between terminals. 68757-12-21.10 HAYNES

**21.10 Power window switch terminal guide and continuity table**

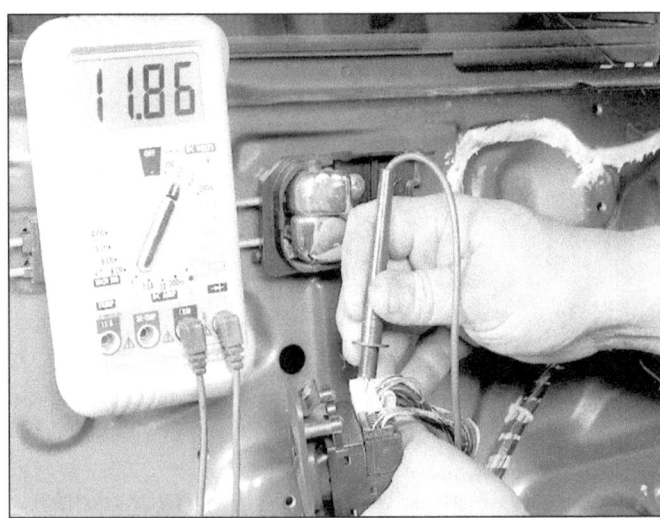

11.86

**21.12 If no voltage is present at the motor with the switch depressed, check for voltage at the switch**

---

### 19  Horn - check and renewal

#### Check

1    If one of the horns sounds but not the other, that horn is probably faulty.
2    If neither horn sounds, check the horn fuse located in the underbonnet relay/fuse box **(see illustration 3.1b)**.
3    If the fuse is good and the horns do not sound, disconnect the electrical connector at each horn and using a test light, check for battery voltage at the terminal as the horn pad is pressed. If power is available, refit the horn.
4    If no power is indicated at the horn, remove the steering wheel (see Chapter 10) and check the horn pad and contacts.

#### Renewal

5    Working from underneath the left side bumper cover (next to the windscreen washer fluid reservoir), disconnect the electrical connector from the horn, remove the mounting nut and remove the horn from the bracket.
6    Refitting is the reverse of the removal procedure.

---

### 20  Cruise control system - description and check

The cruise control system maintains vehicle speed by means of an electronically controlled module located behind the A/C and radio trim facia and a control switch in the engine compartment, which is connected to the throttle linkage by a cable. The system consists of the electronic module, throttle actuator unit, vacuum pump, brake light switch, control switches and associated wiring.

Because of the complexity of the cruise control system and the special tools and techniques required for diagnosis and repair,

this should be left to a dealer or properly equipped shop. However, it is possible for the home mechanic to make simple checks of the wiring and connections for minor faults which can be easily repaired. These include:

a)  *Inspecting the cruise control actuating switches and wiring for broken wires or loose connections.*
b)  *Checking the cruise control fuse.*
c)  *Checking the accelerator cable for proper operation and adjustment (see Chapter 4).*

---

### 21  Power window system - description and check

*Refer to illustrations 21.10 and 21.12*

1    The power window system operates electric motors, mounted in the doors, which lower and raise the windows. The system consists of the control switches, a relay, the motors, regulators, glass mechanisms and associated wiring.
2    The power windows can be lowered and raised from the master control switch by the driver or by remote switches located at the individual windows. Each window has a separate motor which is reversible. The position of the control switch determines the polarity and therefore the direction of operation.
3    The circuit is protected by a fuse and a circuit breaker. Each motor is also equipped with an internal circuit breaker, this prevents one stuck window from disabling the whole system.
4    The power window system will only operate when the ignition switch is ON. In addition, many models have a window lock-out switch at the master control switch which, when activated, disables the switches at the rear windows and, sometimes, the switch at the passenger's window also. Always check these items before troubleshooting a window problem.

5    These procedures are general in nature, so if you can't find the problem using them, take the vehicle to a dealer service department or other properly equipped repair facility.
6    If the power windows won't operate, always check the fuse and circuit breaker first. Next, check the power window system relay, located in the underbonnet relay/fuse box (see Section 5).
7    If only the rear windows are inoperative, or if the windows only operate from the master control switch, check the rear window lockout switch for continuity in the unlocked position. Renew it if it doesn't have continuity.
8    Check the wiring between the switches and fuse panel for continuity. Repair the wiring, if necessary.
9    If only one window is inoperative from the master control switch, try the other control switch at the window. **Note:** *This doesn't apply to the drivers door window.*
10    If the same window works from one switch, but not the other, check the switch for continuity **(see illustration)**.
11    If the switch tests OK, check for a short or open in the circuit between the affected switch and the window motor.
12    If one window is inoperative from both switches, remove the trim panel from the affected door and check for voltage at the switch **(see illustration)** the motor while the switch is operated.
13    If voltage is reaching the motor, disconnect the glass from the regulator (see Chapter 11). Move the window up and down by hand while checking for binding and damage. Also check for binding and damage to the regulator. If the regulator is not damaged and the window moves up and down smoothly, renew the motor. If there's binding or damage, lubricate, repair or renew parts, as necessary.
14    If voltage isn't reaching the motor, check the wiring in the circuit for continuity between the switches and motors. You'll need to con-

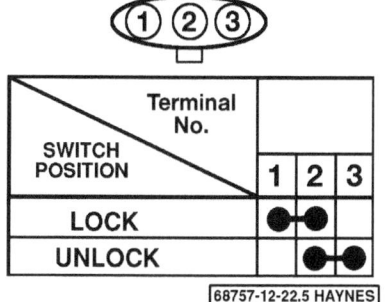

**CONNECTOR**

| SWITCH POSITION \ Terminal No. | 1 | 2 | 3 |
|---|---|---|---|
| LOCK | ●━● | | |
| UNLOCK | | ●━● | |

68757-12-22.5 HAYNES

**22.5 Door lock key switch terminal guide and continuity table**

sult the wiring diagram for the vehicle. Check that the relay is earthed properly and receiving voltage.

15 Test the windows after you are done to confirm proper repairs.

## 22 Power door lock system - description and check

*Refer to illustrations 22.5 and 22.9*

1 The power door lock system operates the door lock actuators mounted in each door. The system consists of the switches, a relay, actuators, a control unit and associated wiring. Diagnosis can usually be limited to simple checks of the wiring connections and actuators for minor faults, which can be easily repaired. Since this system uses an electronic control unit in-depth diagnosis should be left to a dealership service department or other qualified repair facility. The door lock control unit is located behind the instrument panel, to the far right side.

2 Power door lock systems are operated by bi-directional solenoids located in the doors. The lock switches have two operating positions: Lock and Unlock. When activated,

the switch sends a earth signal to the door lock control unit to lock or unlock the doors. Depending on which way the switch is activated, the control unit reverses polarity to the solenoids, allowing the two sides of the circuit to be used alternately as the feed (positive) and earth side.

3 Some vehicles may have an anti-theft alarm system incorporated into the power locks. If you are unable to locate the trouble using the following general Steps, consult your a dealer service department.

4 Always check the circuit protection first. Some vehicles use a combination of circuit breakers and fuses. Next, check the power door lock system relay (see Section 5), located attached to the inner fender in the right front corner of the engine compartment.

5 Operate the door lock key cylinder switches in both directions (Lock and Unlock) with the engine off. Listen for the click of the solenoids operating **(see illustration)**.

6 Test the switches for continuity. Renew the switch if there's not continuity in both switch positions.

7 Check the wiring between the switches, control unit and solenoids for continuity. Repair the wiring if there's no continuity.

8 Check for a bad earth at the switches or the control unit.

9 If all but one lock solenoids operate, remove the trim panel from the affected door (see Chapter 11) and check for voltage at the solenoid while the lock switch is operated **(see illustration)**. One of the wires should have voltage in the Lock position; the other should have voltage in the Unlock position.

10 If the inoperative solenoid is receiving voltage, renew the solenoid.

11 If the inoperative solenoid isn't receiving voltage, check for an open or short in the wire between the lock solenoid and the control unit. **Note:** *It's common for wires to break in the portion of the harness between the body and door (opening and closing the door fatigues and eventually breaks the wires).*

## 23 Electric side view mirrors - description and check

*Refer to illustration 23.6*

1 Most electric rear view mirrors use two motors to move the glass; one for up and down adjustments and one for left-right adjustments.

2 The control switch has a selector portion which sends voltage to the left or right side mirror. With the ignition ON but the engine OFF, roll down the windows and operate the mirror control switch through all functions (left-right and up-down) for both the left and right side mirrors.

3 Listen carefully for the sound of the electric motors running in the mirrors.

4 If the motors can be heard but the mirror glass doesn't move, there's probably a problem with the drive mechanism inside the mirror.

5 If the mirrors don't operate and no sound comes from the mirrors, check the fuse.

6 If the fuse is OK, remove the mirror control switch **(see illustration)** from its mounting without disconnecting the wires attached to it. Turn the ignition ON and check for voltage at the switch. There should be voltage at one terminal. If there's no voltage at the switch, check for an open or short in the circuit between the fuse panel and the switch.

7 If there's voltage at the switch, disconnect it. Check the switch for continuity in all its operating positions. If the switch does not have continuity, renew it.

8 Reconnect the switch. Locate the wire going from the switch to earth. Leaving the switch connected, connect a jumper wire between this wire and earth. If the mirror works normally with this wire in place, repair the faulty earth connection.

9 If the mirror still doesn't work, remove the mirror and check the wires at the mirror for voltage. Check with ignition ON and the mirror selector switch on the appropriate side. Operate the mirror switch in all its posi-

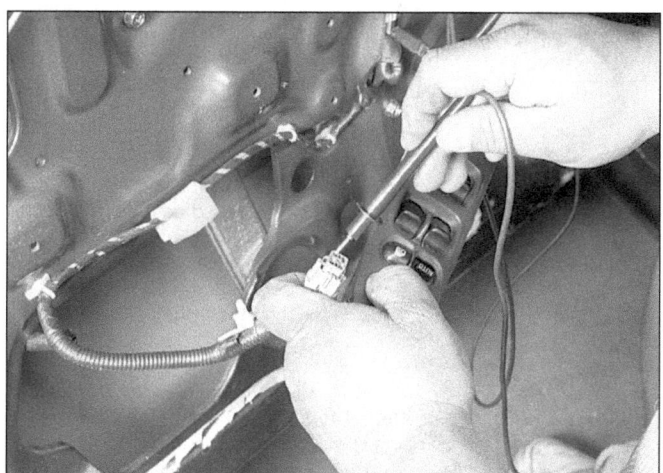

**22.9 Check for voltage at the door lock actuator while the lock switch is operated**

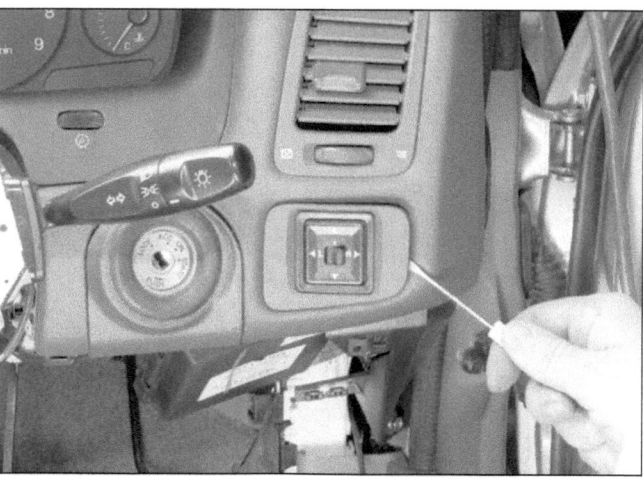

**23.6 Remove the mirror remote switch from the dash by carefully prising on the switch using a small screwdriver**

tions. There should be voltage at one of the switch-to-mirror wires in each switch position (except the neutral "off" position).

10   If there's not voltage in each switch position, check the circuit between the mirror and control switch for opens and shorts.

11   If there's voltage, remove the mirror and test it off the vehicle with jumper wires. Renew the mirror if it fails this test.

## 24  Power seats - description and check

1   Power seats allow you to adjust the position of the seat with little effort. These models feature a six-way seat that goes forward and backward.

2   The are powered by three reversible motors mounted in one housing that are controlled by switches on the side of the seat. Each switch changes the direction of seat travel by reversing polarity to the drive motor.

3   Diagnosis is a simple matter, using the following procedures.

4   Look under the seat for any object which may be preventing the seat from moving.

5   If the seat won't work at all, check the fuse or circuit breaker.

6   With the engine off to reduce the noise level, operate the seat controls in all directions and listen for sound coming from the seat motors.

7   If the seat won't work at all, check the fuse or circuit breaker. **Note:** *The ignition must be ON for the power seats to work.*

8   If the motor runs or clicks but the seat doesn't move, check the seat drive mechanism for wear or damage and correct as necessary.

9   If the motor doesn't work or make noise, check for voltage at the motor while an assistant operates the switch.

10   If the motor is getting voltage but doesn't run, test it off the vehicle with jumper wires. If it still doesn't work, renew it.

11   If the motor isn't getting voltage, check for voltage at the switch. If there's no voltage at the switch, check the wiring between the fuse panel and the switch. If there's voltage

at the switch, check the switch for continuity in all its operating positions. Renew the switch if there's no continuity.

12   If the switch is OK, check for a short or open in the wiring between the switch motor. If there's a relay between the switch and motor, check that its earthed properly and there's voltage to the relay. Also check that there's voltage going from the relay to the motor when the switch is operated. If there's not, and the relay is earthed properly, renew the relay.

13   Test the completed repairs.

## 25  Supplemental Restraint System (SRS) - general information

### *Description*

*Refer to illustration 25.2*

1   The models covered by this manual are equipped with a Supplemental Restraint System (SRS), more commonly known as an airbag. This system is designed to protect the driver and passenger from serious injury in the event of a head-on or frontal collision.

2   The SRS system consists of an SRS airbag control unit (SRS-ECU) - which contains a safing G sensor, analog G sensor, self diagnosis circuit and aback-up power circuit - located under the centre console **(see illustration)**. A clockspring - located behind the steering wheel, a warning light - located in the instrument cluster, an air bag assembly/module in the centre of the steering wheel and a second air bag assembly/module for the front seat passenger, located in the dashboard right above the glove box.

### *Operation*

3   For the air bag(s) to deploy, the safing G and analog G sensors must be activated. When this condition occurs, the circuit to the airbag inflator is closed and the airbag inflates. If the battery is destroyed by the impact, or its too low to power the inflator, a back-up power unit inside SRS-ECU unit provides the power.

### *Self-diagnosis system*

4   A self diagnosis circuit in the SRS-ECU unit displays a light when the ignition switch is turned to the ON position. If the system is operating normally, the light will out after about six seconds. If the light doesn't come on, or doesn't go out after six seconds, or if it comes on while driving the vehicle, there's a malfunction in the SRS system. Have it inspected and repaired as soon as possible. Do not attempt to trouble shoot or service the SRS system yourself. Even a small mistake could cause the SRS system to malfunction when you need it.

### *Servicing components near the SRS system*

5   Nevertheless, there are times when you need to remove the steering wheel, radio or service other components on or near the dashboard. At these times, you'll be working around components and wiring harnesses for the SRS system. The SRS wiring harnesses are easy to identify: They're all bright yellow. Do not unplug the connectors for these wires. And do not use electrical test equipment on yellow wires; it could cause the airbag(s) to deploy. **ALWAYS DISABLE THE SRS SYSTEM BEFORE WORKING NEAR THE SRS SYSTEM COMPONENTS OR RELATED WIRING.**

### *Precautions*

**Warning:** *Failure to follow these precautions could result in accidental deployment of the airbag and personal injury.*

6   Whenever working in the vicinity of the steering wheel, steering column or any of the other SRS system components, the system must be disarmed. To disarm the system:

 a) *Point the wheels straight ahead and turn the key to the Lock position.*

 b) *Disconnect the cable from the negative battery terminal.*

 c) *Wait at least two minutes for the back-up power supply to be depleted.*

7   Whenever handling an airbag module, always keep the airbag opening pointed away from your body. Never place the airbag module on a bench of other surface with the airbag opening facing the surface. Always place the airbag module in a safe location with the airbag opening facing up.

8   Never measure the resistance of any SRS component. An ohmmeter has a built-in battery supply that could accidentally deploy the airbag.

9   Never use electrical welding equipment on a vehicle equipped with an airbag without first disconnecting the yellow airbag connector, located under the steering column near the combination switch connector.

10   Never dispose of a live airbag module. Return it to your dealer for safe deployment, using special equipment, and disposal.

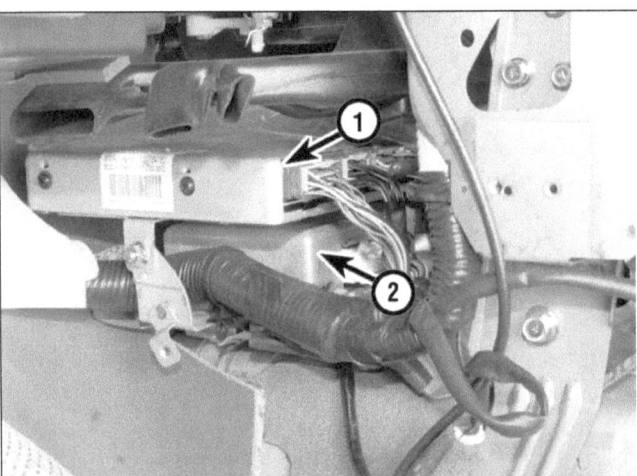

**25.2  Control unit location**

*1   Engine ECU*
*2   SRS-ECU*

### *Disabling the SRS system*

**Warning:** *Any time you are working in the*

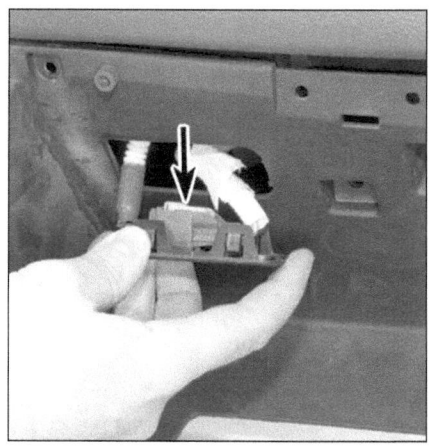

**25.13 Pull the two-pin harness holder into the glove box (arrow)**

**25.22 Passenger side airbag module retaining bolts (arrows)**

*vicinity of airbag wiring or components, DIS-ABLE THE SRS SYSTEM.*

11   Disconnect the battery negative cable, then disconnect the positive cable and wait three minutes. **Caution:** *If the stereo in your vehicle is equipped with an anti-theft system, make sure you have the correct activation code before disconnecting the battery.*

### Drivers side airbag

12   Remove the air bag module and horn pad mounting screws and unplug the two-pin connector between the module and steering wheel (see Chapter 10).

### Passengers side airbag

*Refer to illustration 25.13*

13   Pull the airbag harness connector through to the glove box **(see illustration)**.

14   Unplug the yellow two-pin connector between the passenger side airbag and the main harness **(see illustration 25.13)**.

### *Enabling the system*

15   After you've disabled the airbag and performed the necessary service, reconnect

the two-pin airbag connector into the main harness. Refit the airbag module to the steering wheel or the glove box.

16   Reattach the positive battery cable first and then the negative cable.

### *Removal and refitting*

**Warning:** *Any time you are working in the vicinity of airbag wiring or components, DIS-ABLE THE SRS SYSTEM.*

17   Disconnect the battery negative cable, then disconnect the positive cable and wait three minutes. **Caution:** *If the stereo in your vehicle is equipped with an anti-theft system, make sure you have the correct activation code before disconnecting the battery.*

### Drivers side airbag

18   Refer to Chapter 10 for removal and refitting of the driver's side airbag and clock spring.

### Passengers side airbag

*Refer to illustration 25.22*

19   Disconnect the cable from the negative battery terminal.

20   Lower the glove box (see Chapter 11).

21   Unplug the yellow two-pin connector

between the passenger side airbag and the main harness **(see illustration 13)**.

22   Remove the airbag module **(see illustration)** mounting bolts and remove the module from the dash.

23   Refitting is reverse of removal.

---

### 26   Wiring diagrams - general information

Since it isn't possible to include a complete wiring diagram for every model covered by this manual, the following diagrams are those that are typical and most commonly needed.

Prior to troubleshooting any circuits, check the fuse and circuit breakers (if equipped) to make sure they are in good condition. Make sure the battery is properly charged and has clean, tight cable connections (see Chapter 1).

When checking the wiring system, make sure that all electrical connectors are clean, with no broken or loose pins. When disconnecting an electrical connector, do not pull on the wires, only on the connector housings themselves.

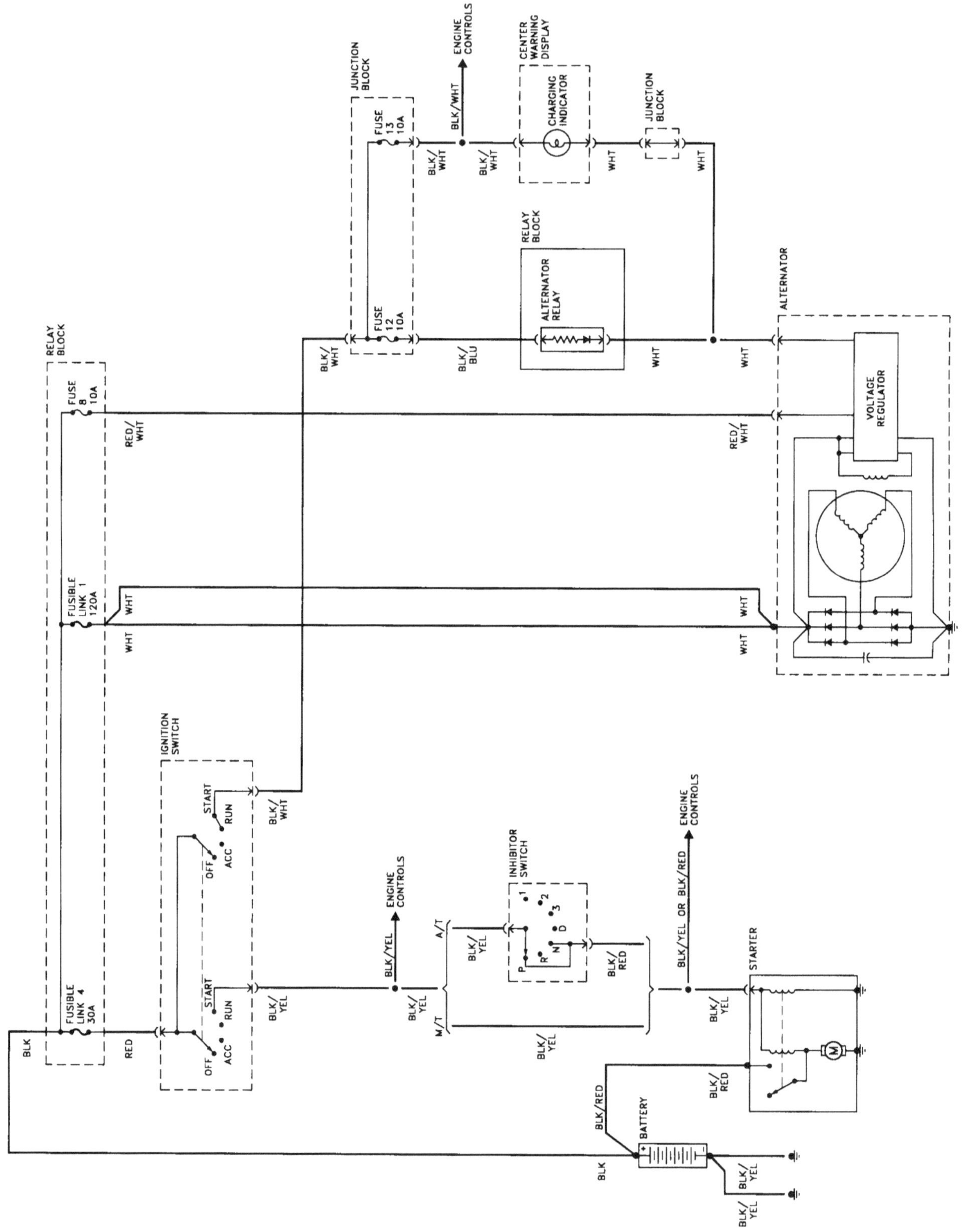

Typical starting/charging circuit diagram

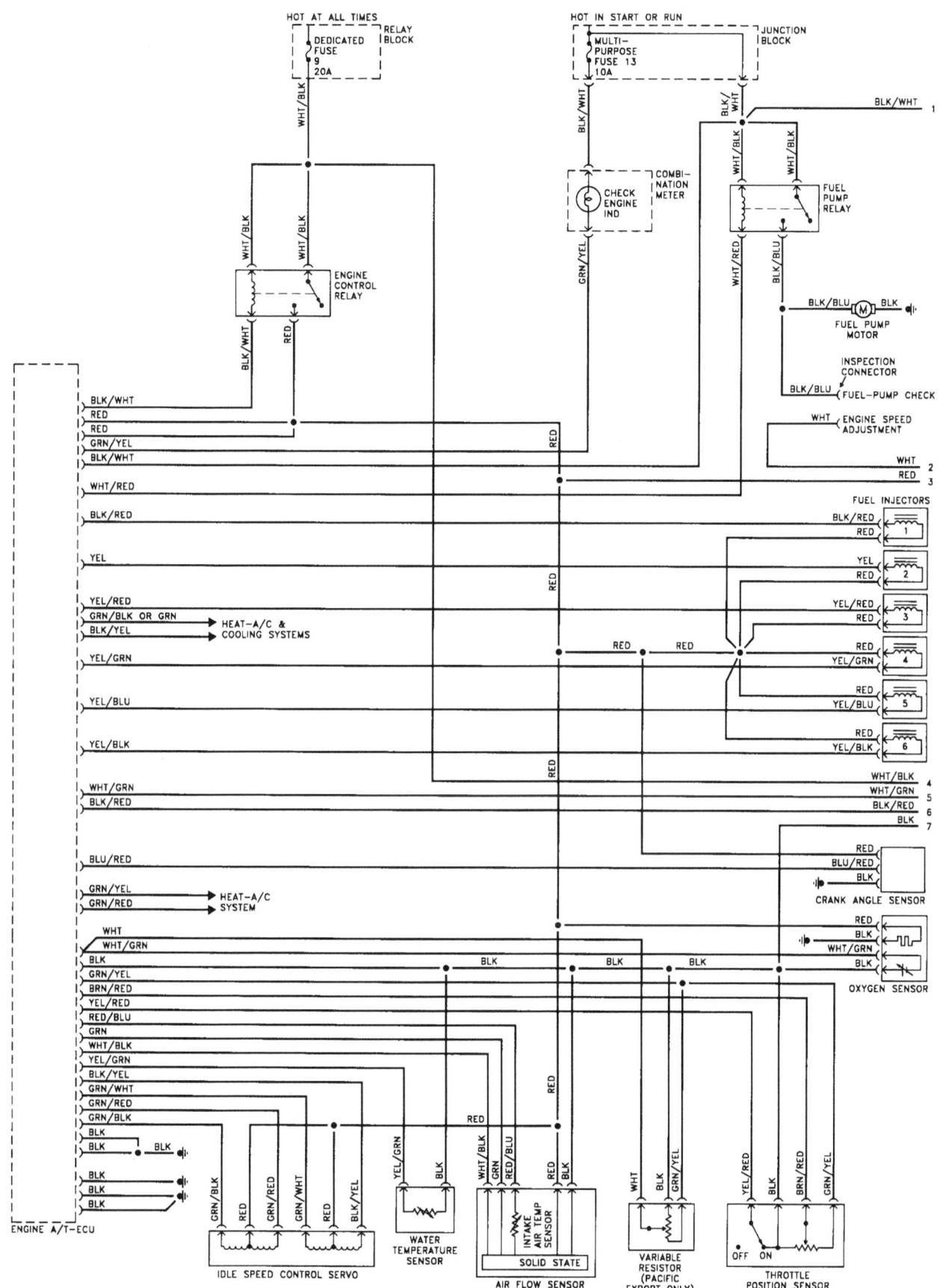

**Typical engine control circuit diagram (automatic transmission) (1 of 3)**

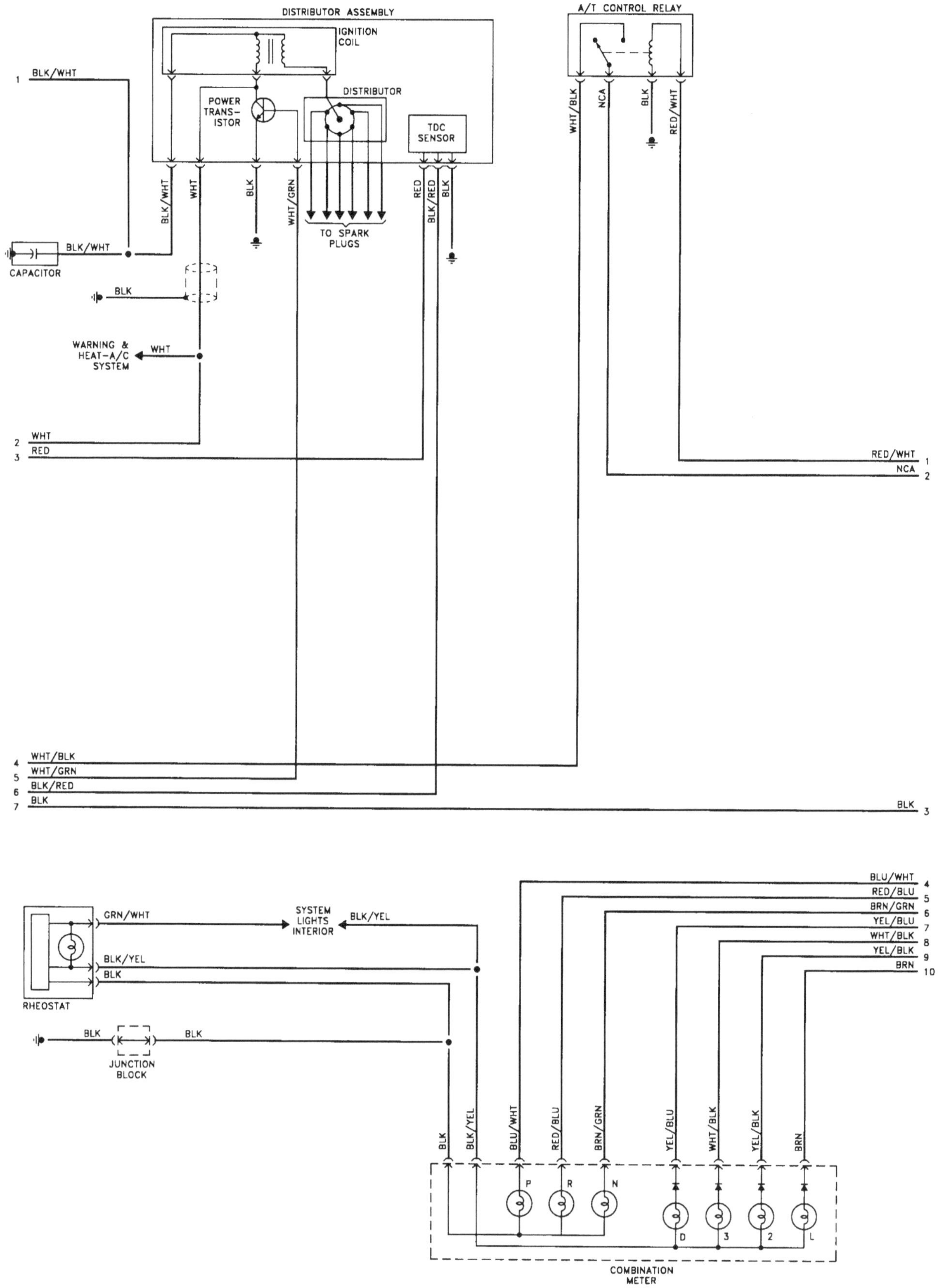

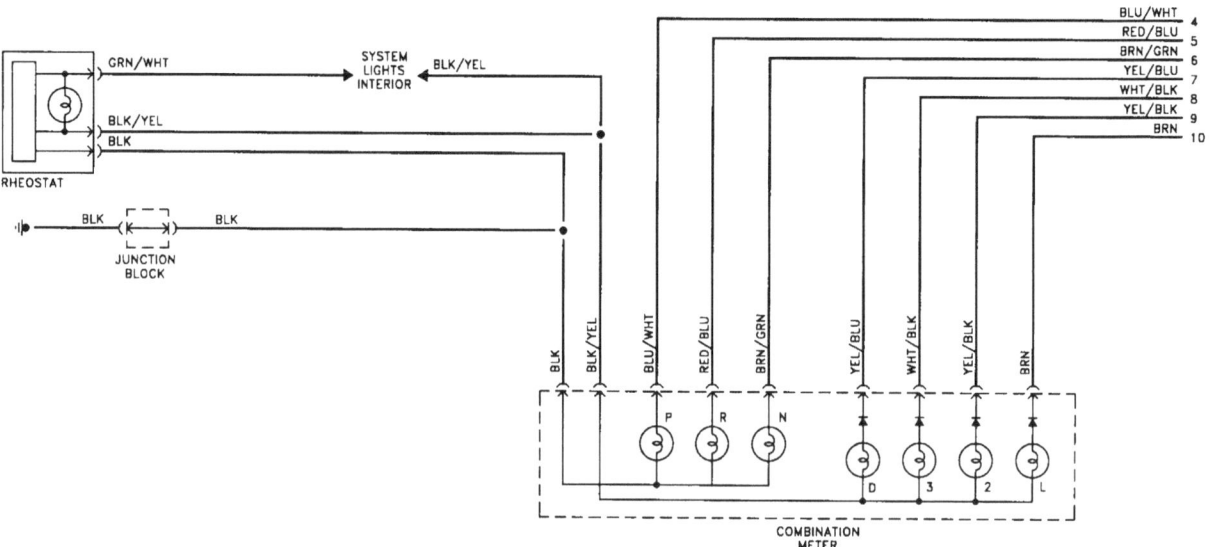

**Typical engine control circuit diagram (automatic transmission) (2 of 3)**

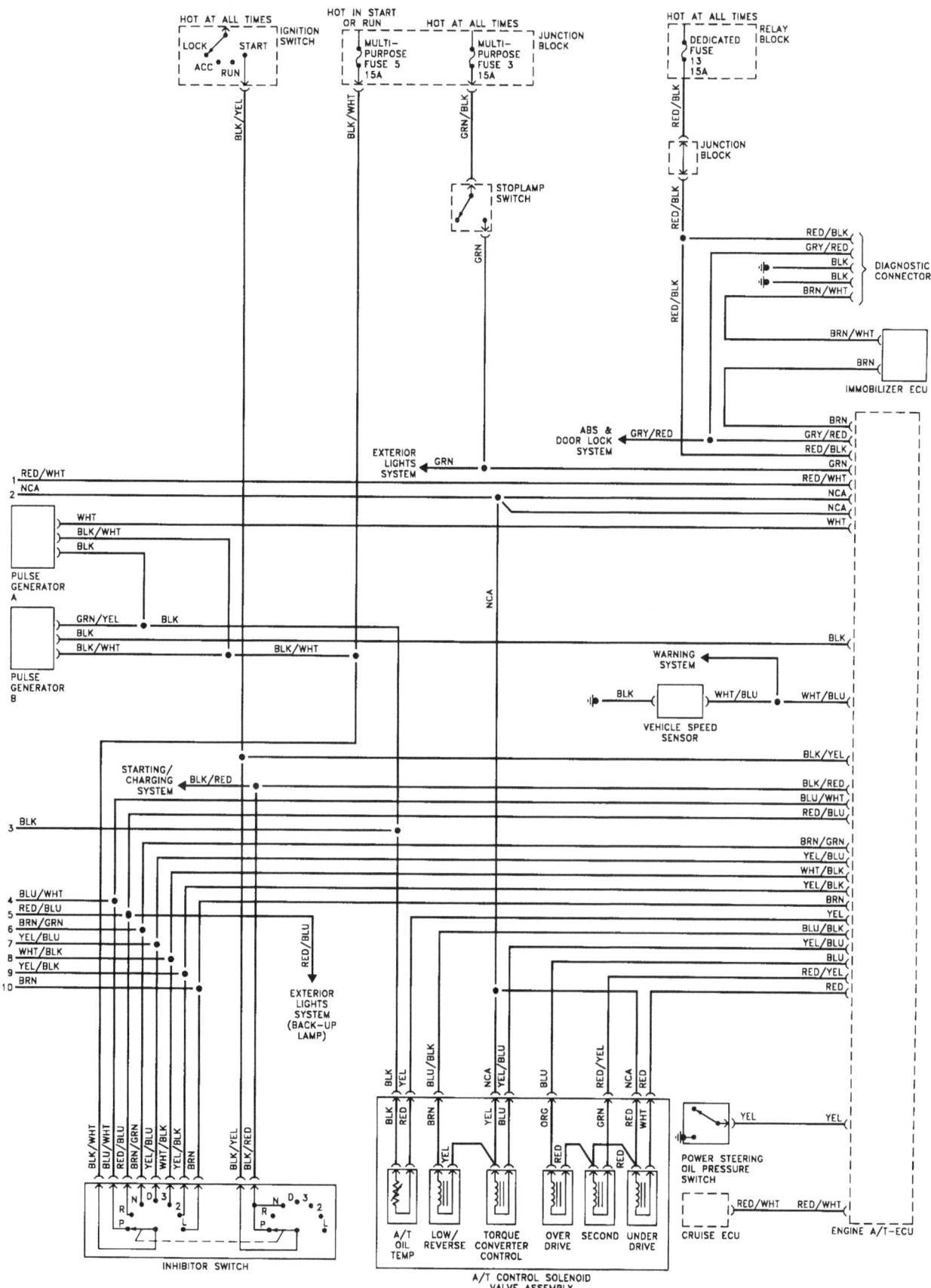

**Typical engine control circuit diagram (automatic transmission) (3 of 3)**

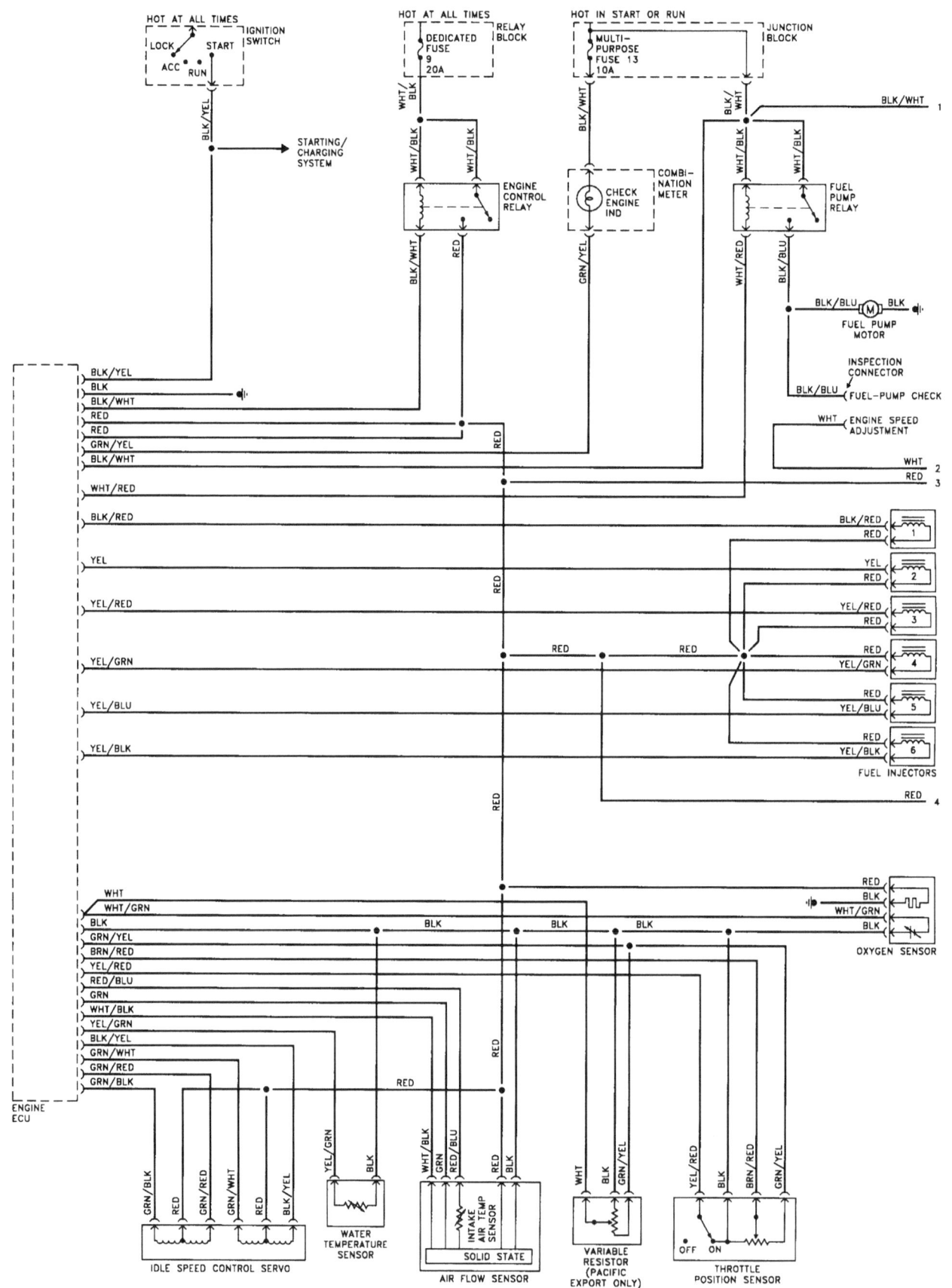

**Typical engine control circuit diagram (manual transmission) (1 of 2)**

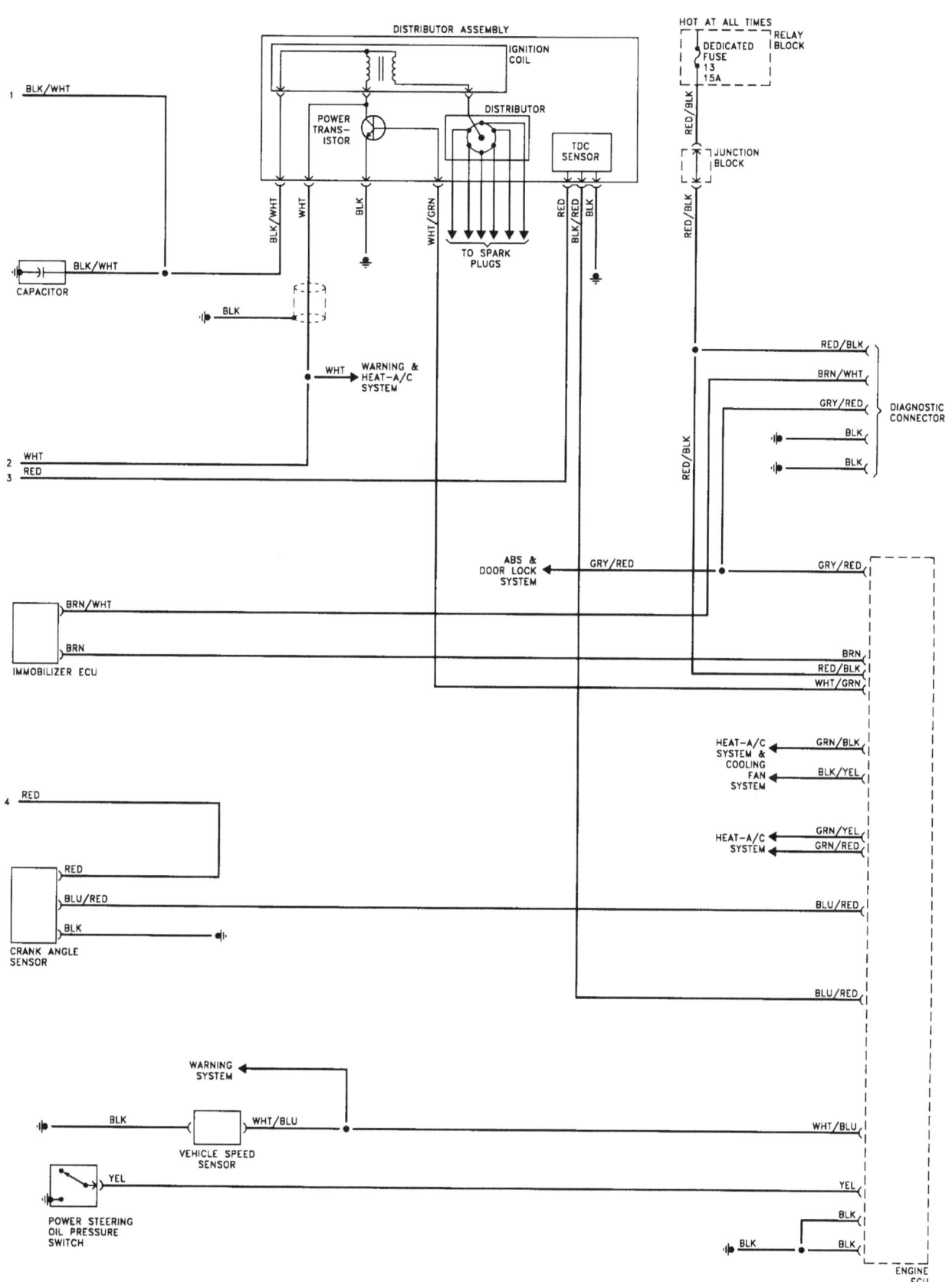

**Typical engine control circuit diagram (manual transmission)  (2 of 2)**

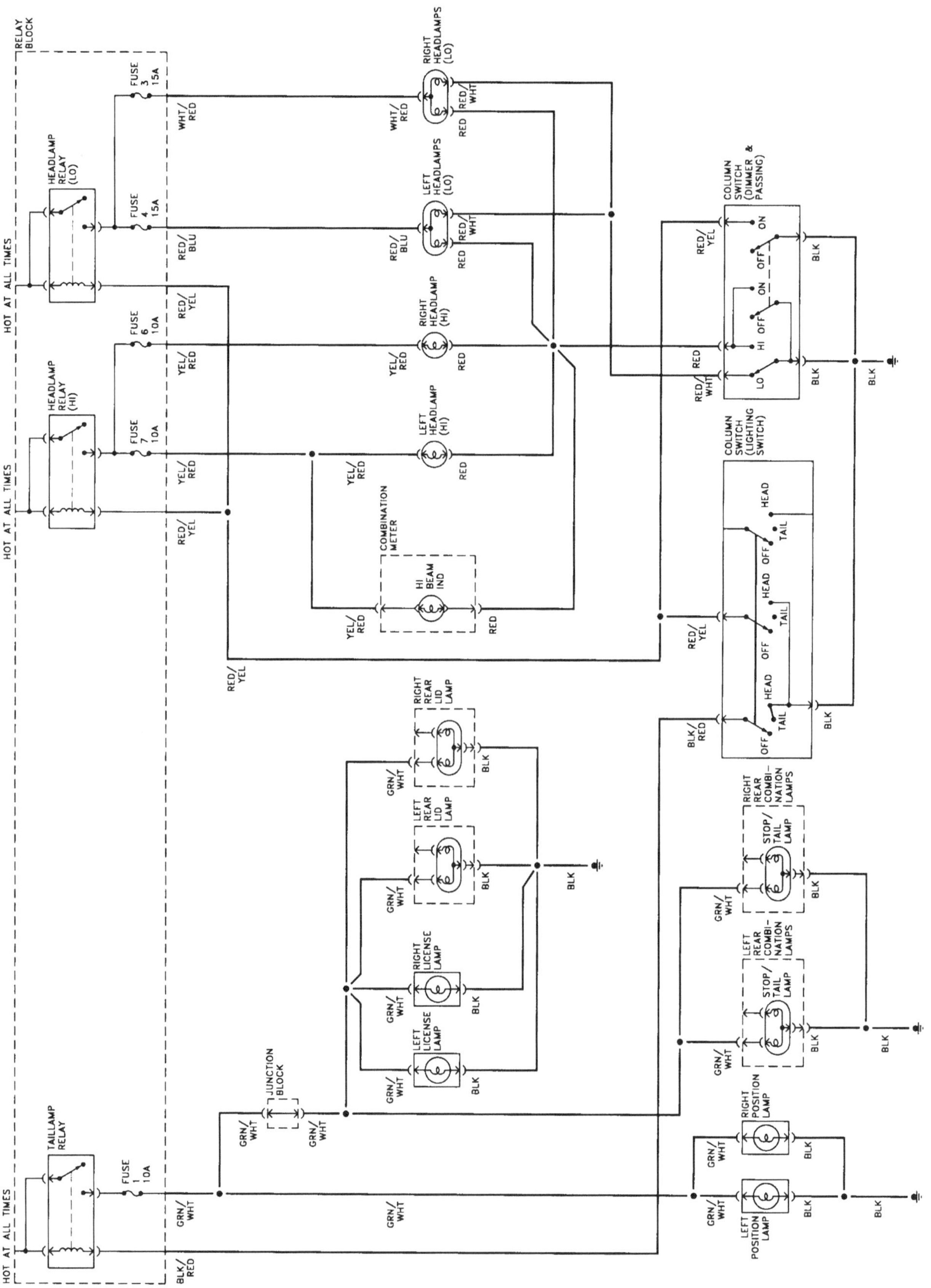

Typical exterior light circuit diagram (1 of 2)

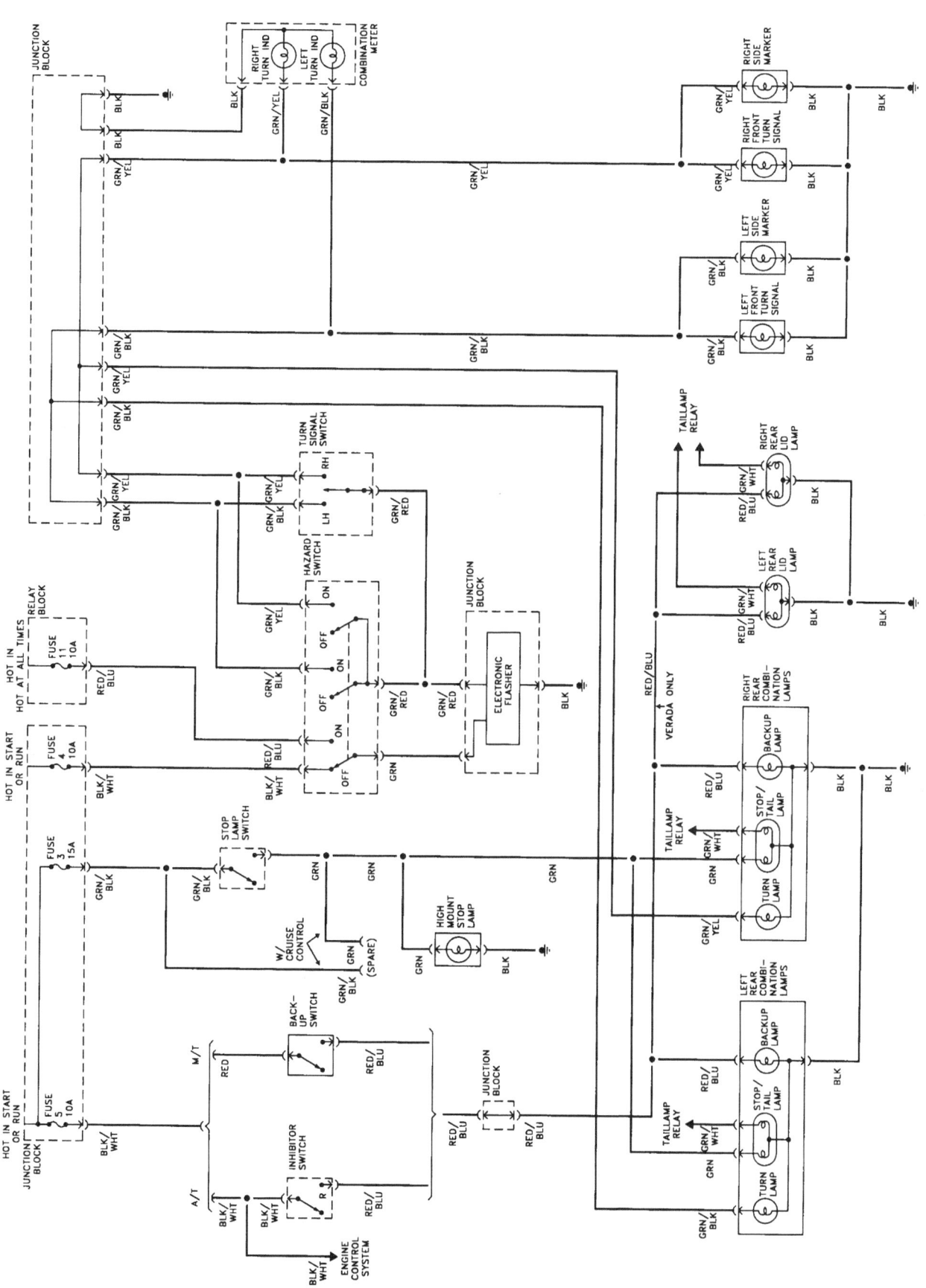

Typical exterior light circuit diagram (2 of 2)

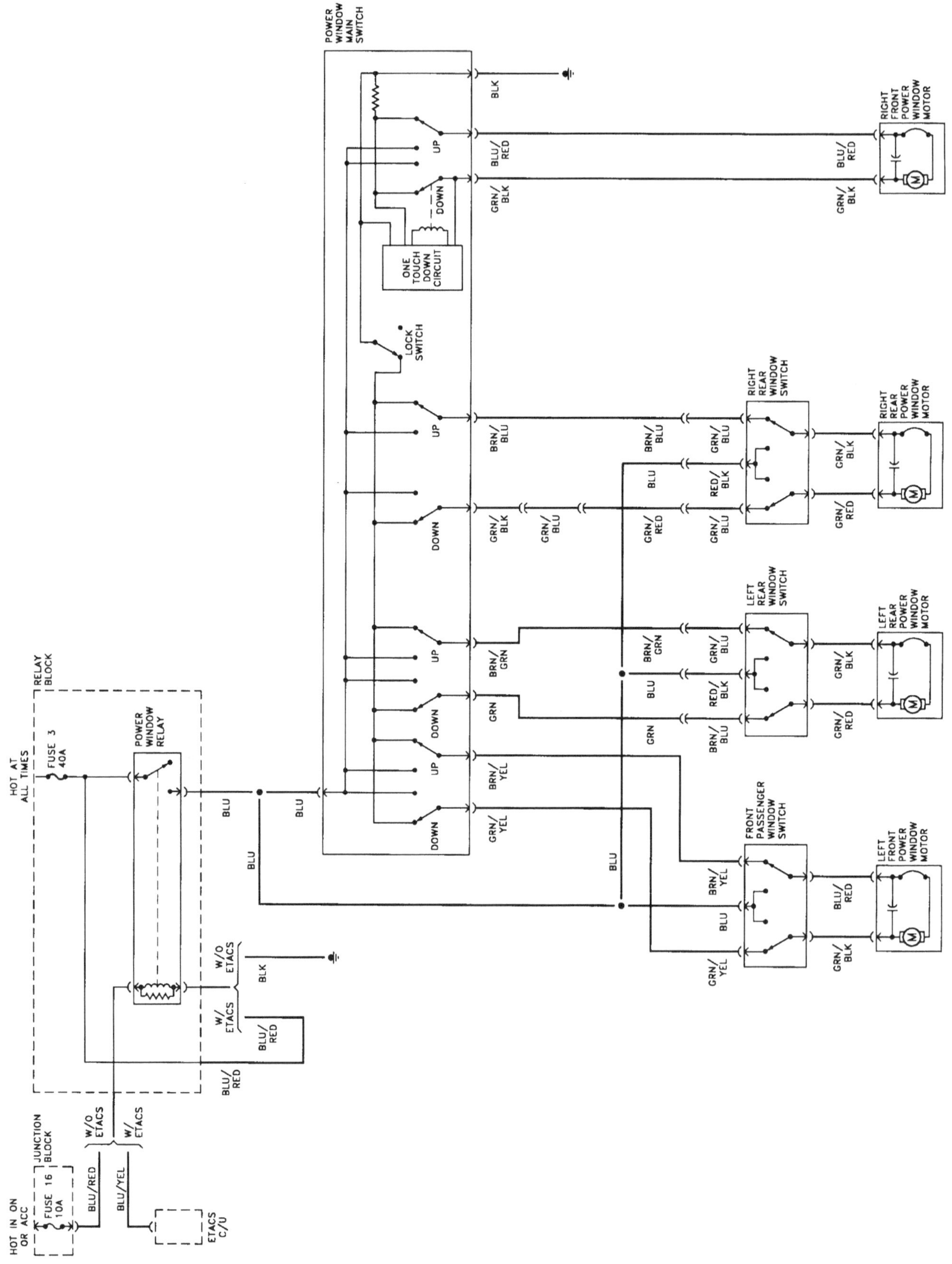

**Typical power window circuit diagram**

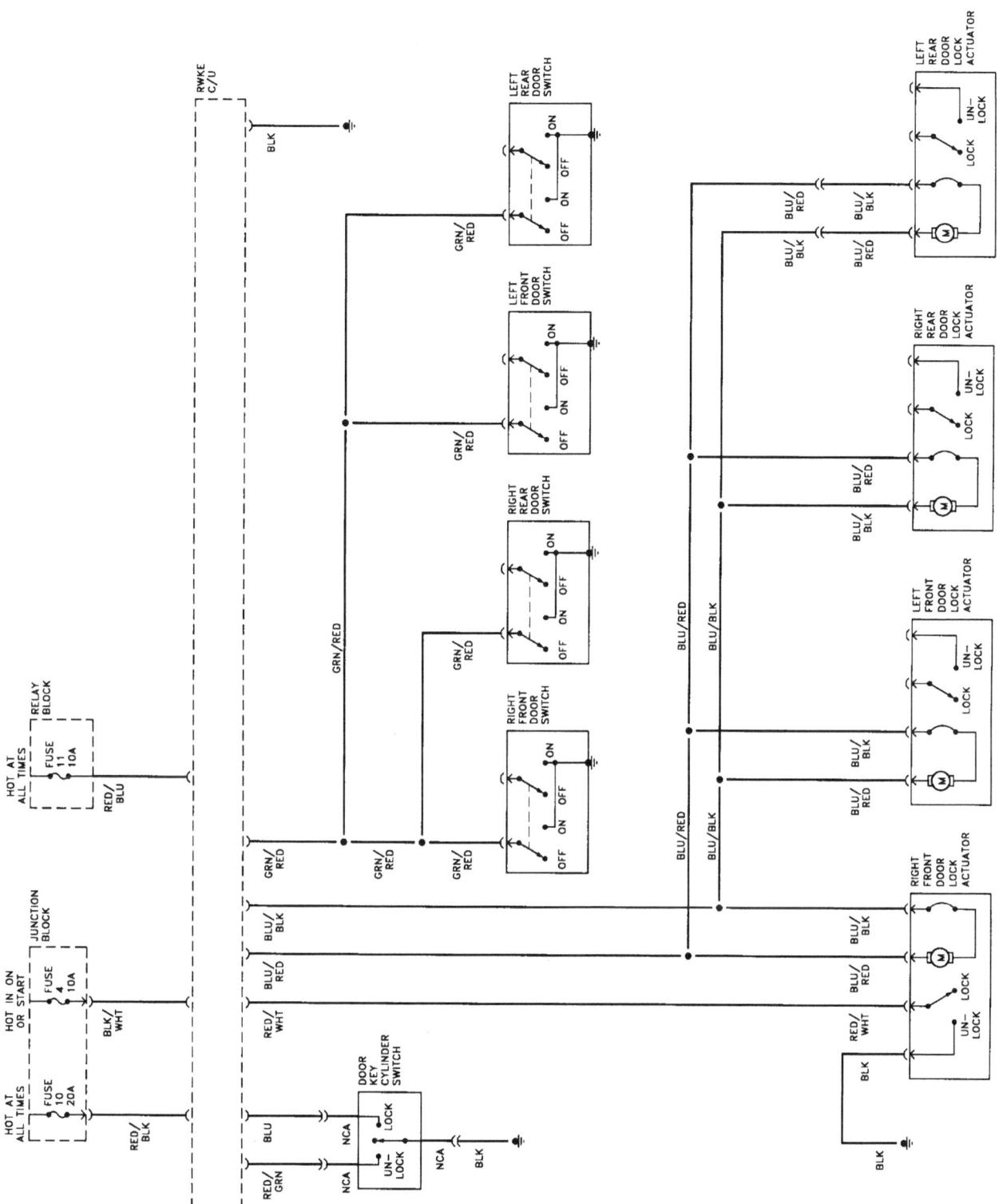

Typical power door lock circuit diagram

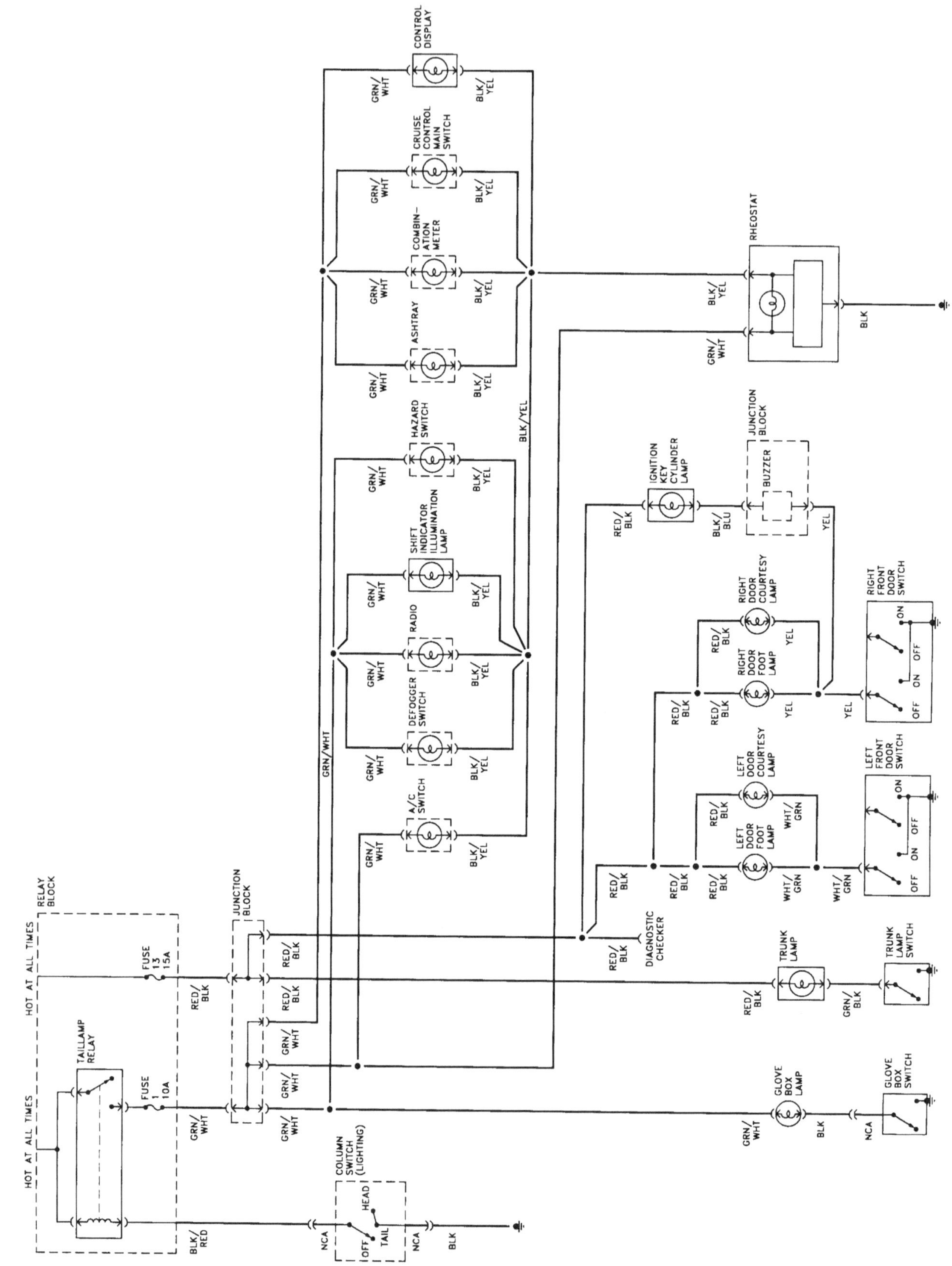

**Typical interior lights circuit diagram**

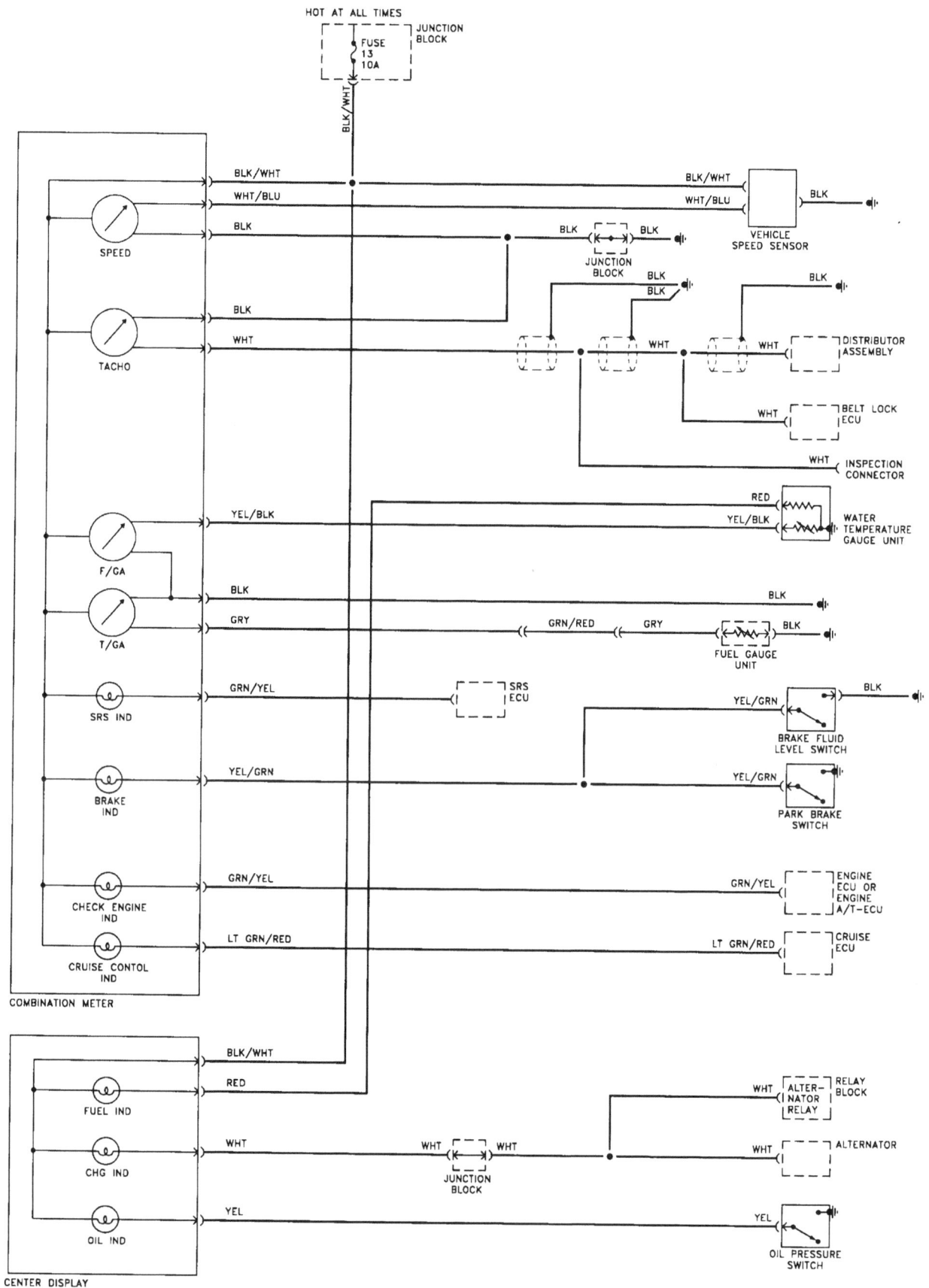

**Typical gauges and warning light system circuit diagram**

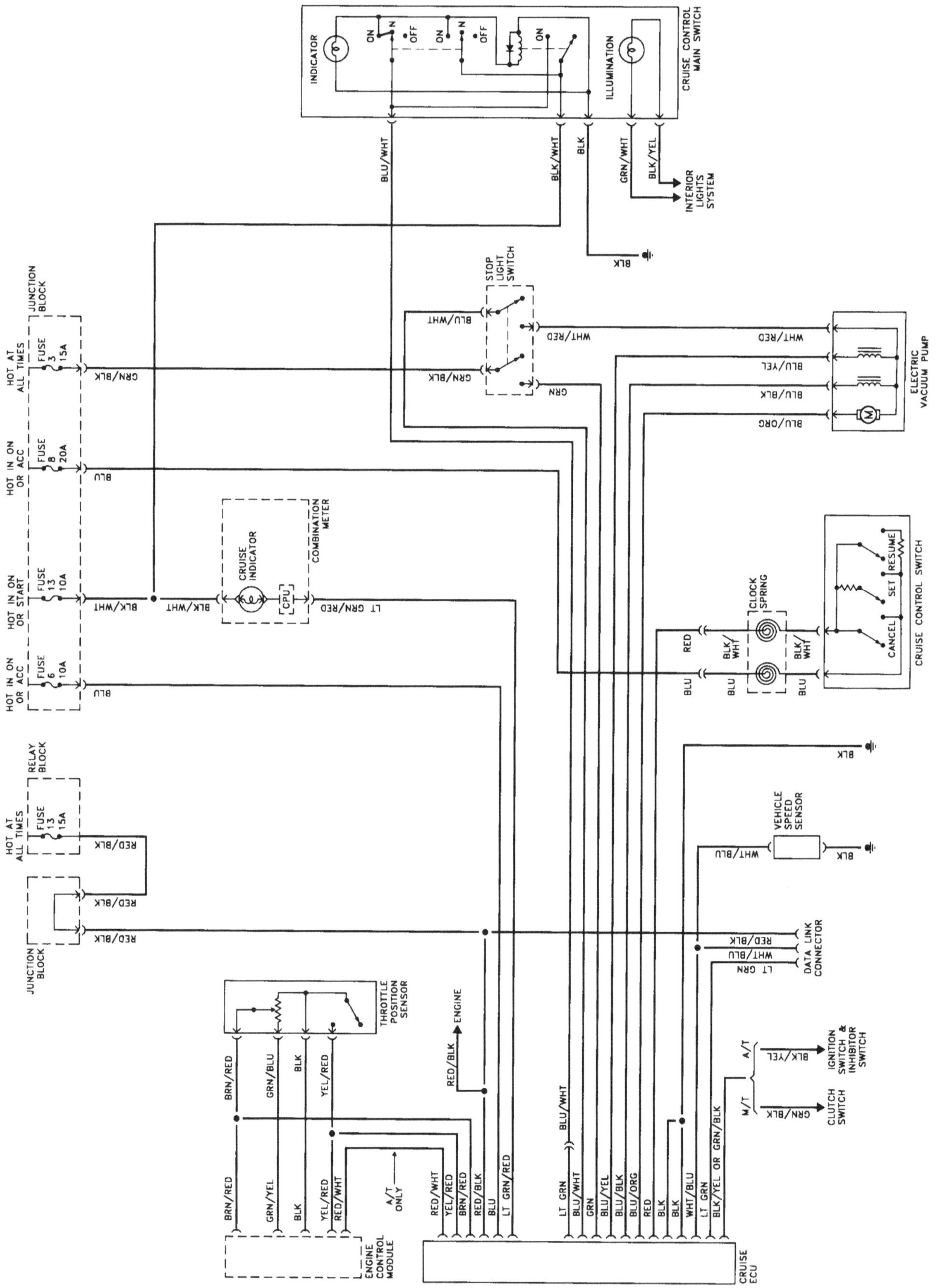

Typical cruise control circuit diagram

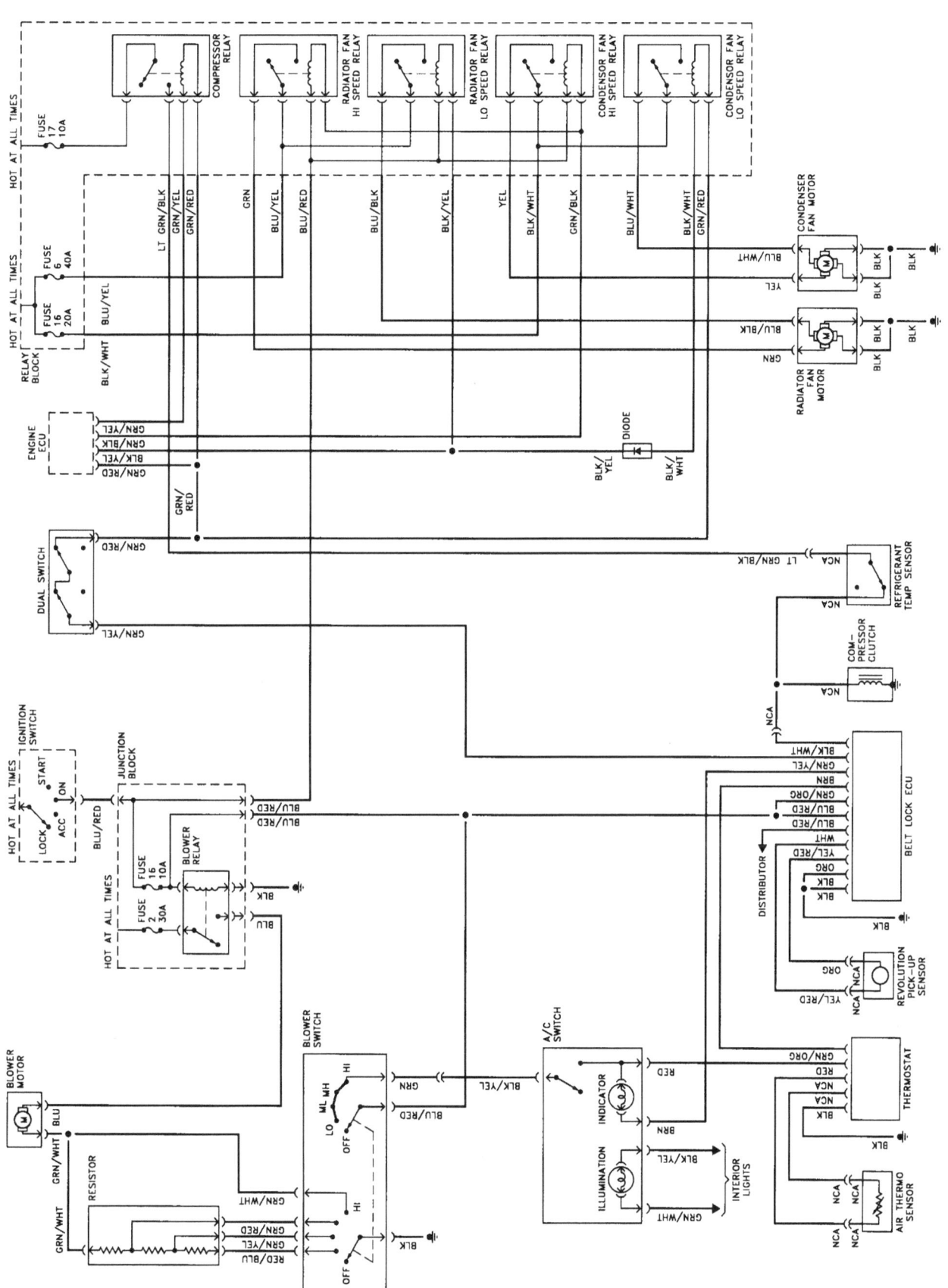

Typical heating and air conditioning system circuit diagram (includes engine cooling fans)

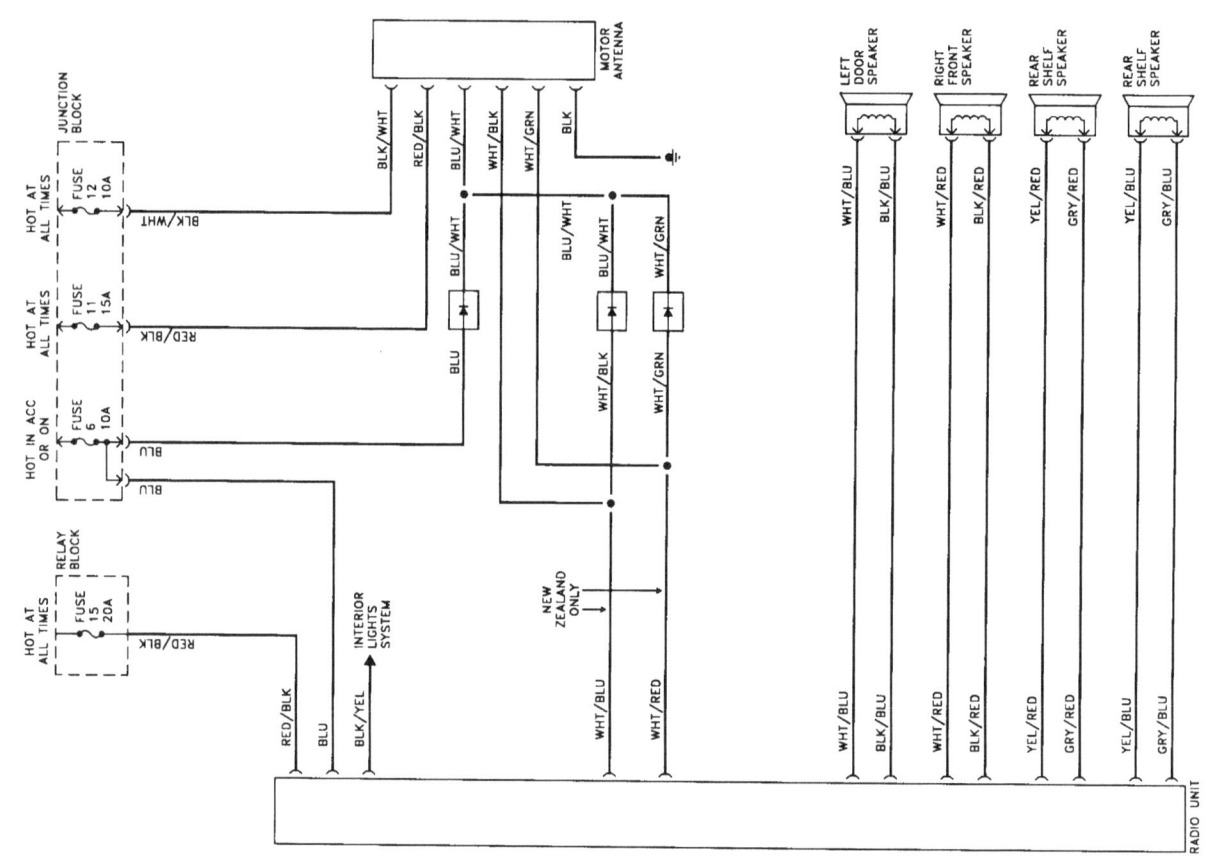

Typical radio circuit diagram

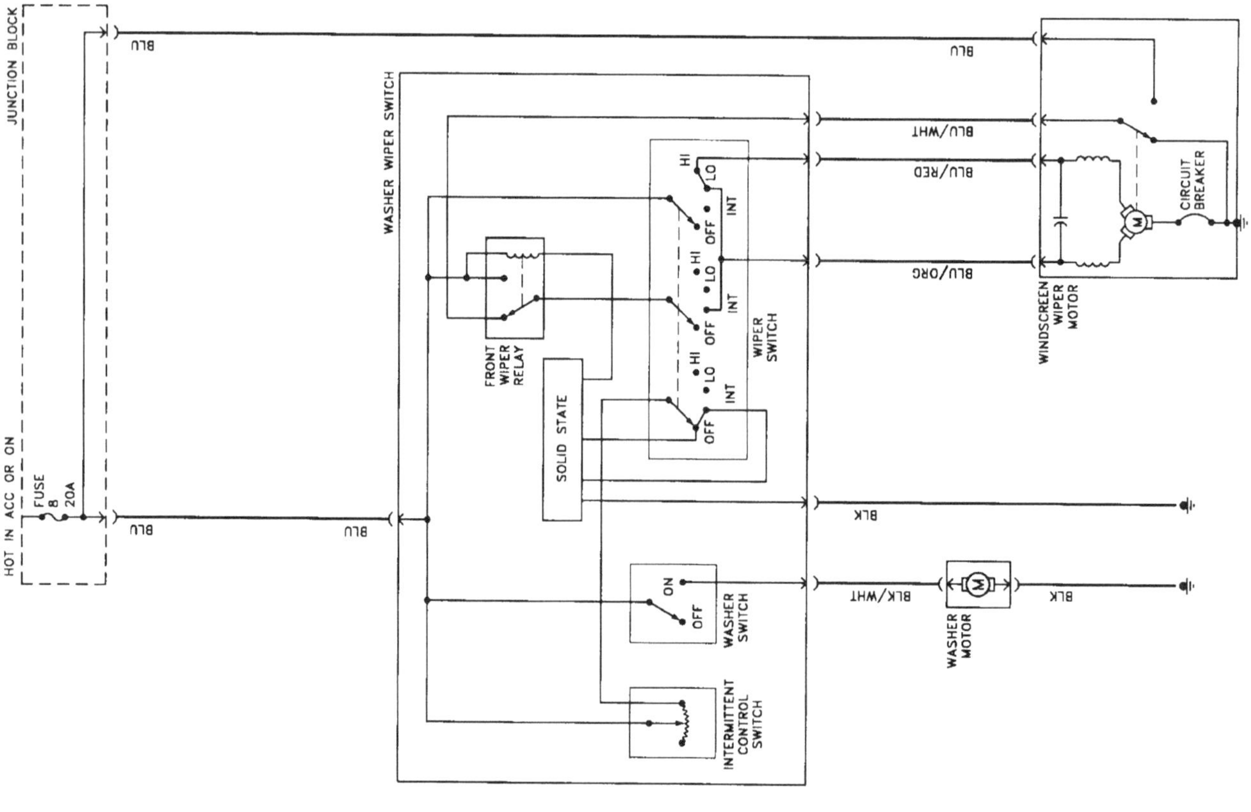

Typical wiper/washer circuit diagram

# Index

Zeitfracht Medien GmbH
Ferdinand-Jühlke-Straße 7
99095 Erfurt, Deutschland
produktsicherheit@kolibri360.de